COMPANION TO

Contemporary Musical Thought

Volume 1

EDITED BY

John Paynter

Tim Howell

Richard Orton

Peter Seymour

LONDON AND NEW YORK

First published in 1992
by Routledge
11 New Fetter Lane, London E C 4P 4E E

Simultaneously published in the U S A and Canada
by Routledge
a division of Routledge, Chapman and Hall, Inc.
29 West 35th Street, New York, N Y 10001

Filmset in $10\frac{1}{2}/12\frac{1}{2}$ Ehrhardt Monophoto
by Selwood Systems, Midsomer Norton
Printed and bound in Great Britain by Butler & Tanner Ltd,
Frome and London

∞ Printed on paper manufactured in accordance with the proposed
A N S I / N I S O Z 39.48-199X and A N S I Z 39.48-1984

British Library Cataloguing in Publication Data
A catalogue record for this book is available from the British Library

Library of Congress Cataloging-in-Publication Data
A catalog record for this book is available on request

ISBN 0–415–03092–7 (set)
ISBN 0–415–07224–7 (Vol. 1)
ISBN 0–415–07225–5 (Vol. 2)

CONTENTS

VOLUME 1

CONTENTS

VOLUME 2

CONTENTS

NOTES ON CONTRIBUTORS

ISTVAN ANHALT (born 1919, Budapest) was educated at the Royal Hungarian Academy of Music and the Conservatoire National de Musique de Paris. His composition teachers were Zoltán Kodály and Nadia Boulanger. He received instruction in conducting from Louis Fourestier and in piano from Soulima Stravinsky. In 1949 he went to Canada on a fellowship awarded by the Lady Davis Foundation, and at the same time was appointed to the Faculty of Music at McGill University, Montreal. In 1964, after several years of experimentation and compositional work at various electronic music laboratories in Canada and the United States, he installed an electronic music studio at McGill and was appointed director. He took up the Slee professorship at the New York State University, Buffalo, in 1969. From 1971 to 1981 he was head of the music department at Queen's University, Kingston, Ontario.

FRANCIS BAINES studied composition and double bass at the Royal College of Music, London, where he subsequently became a professor. With his wife, June, he founded the Jaye Consort of Viols, playing on instruments by the celebrated seventeenth-century maker Henry Jaye. The consort also play medieval instruments, including the hurdy gurdy and ancient bagpipes.

IRMGARD BONTINCK is a musicologist and sociologist, and Professor of Music Sociology and Head of the Institute of Music Sociology at the Hochschule for Music and the Performing Arts in Vienna. She is also currently Director of the International Institute for Audio-visual Communication and Cultural Development (Mediacult) in Vienna. She has been Secretary General of the Austrian National Committee of the International Music Council of UNESCO and a member of the Austrian Commission for UNESCO, and she is also on the Board of Directors of the International Society for Music Education. Her publications include many books and articles concerned with the sociology of music, the evaluation of cultural policies, and the influence of the mass media on young people's musical behaviour.

WALTER BRANCHI (born 1941, Rome) is a composer and rose-grower. He is currently professor of Electronic Music Composition at the G. Rossini Conservatory in Pesaro, where he founded the Laboratorio Elettronico per la Musica Sperimentale. He was formerly at the S. Cecilia Conservatory in Rome. He is a collaborator with the UNESCO Italian Commission for Music and Technology.

With Guido Baggiani he founded the musical association Musica Verticale. He is the inventor and co-founder of Musica Complessita (Music and Computer between Science and Knowledge).

Walter Branchi has spent several periods of time composing and teaching in American and Canadian Universities; as Fulbright Fellow at Princeton University, Visiting Composer at Stanford University (CCRMA) and Composer-in-Residence at Simon Fraser University.

Each of his compositions is part of a larger work, *Intero*, which will be realized throughout his life.

YEHEZKEL BRAUN is a composer and Professor Emeritus at Tel Aviv University, where he has been teaching music theory since 1966. Among his compositions are songs, *a capella* and accompanied choral pieces, symphonic music, concertos and chamber music. In addition he has composed music for the theatre, for ballet, and some 150 arrangements of traditional Jewish songs. Among his recent compositions are *King David's Lyre*, for children's choir and orchestra, commissioned by the Israel Philharmonic Orchestra, and a concerto for harp and orchestra. His main academic interests are Jewish sacred music and Gregorian Chant, and the modal affinities between them, on which subjects he has lectured widely in Israel, Europe and the United States.

JOHN BRYAN is senior lecturer in music at the University College of Ripon and York St John, York, England, and a member of several leading British Renaissance ensembles. As a director of the Landini Consort he has performed and made radio broadcasts in most European countries, Canada and the United States, and has made records with the Consort of Musicke, Rose Consort of Viols, and Musica Antiqua of London. He is a tutor on a number of international summer schools for Renaissance music, and an artistic director of the York Early Music Festival.

JOEL CHADABE composes for an interactive computer music system and performs with it throughout the world in concerts with Jan Williams, percussionist, and other musicians. A native of New York City, Chadabe's music is recorded on Opus One, CP2, Folkways, and Lovely Music labels. He has received fellowships and grants from the Ford Foundation, Rockefeller Foundation, New York Foundation for the Arts, and National Endowment for the Arts. His articles on aspects of electronic and computer music have appeared in many magazines and journals, among them *Perspectives of New Music, Electronic Music Review, Melos, Musique en Jeu,* and *Computer Music Journal.* He presently teaches electronic music at State University of New York at Albany and at Bennington College, and he is president of Intelligent Music, a research and development company.

ERIC F. CLARKE (born 1955) studied neurobiology and music at Sussex University, and took a master's degree there in analysis and aesthetics. His Ph.D. research on expression in piano performance was carried out at Exeter University in its psychology department. He joined the music department at City University, London, in 1981, and since 1990 has been Director of Postgraduate Studies and Reader in Music, teaching courses in the psychology of music, improvisation, music analysis, and Viennese Modernism. His research has concentrated on expression and timing in musical performance. He is an associate editor of the journal *Psychology of Music,* and is a member of the improvising string quartet The Lapis String Quartet.

ROGERS COVEY-CRUMP began his singing career as a boy chorister in the choir of New College, Oxford. He developed an absorbing interest in the organ and harpsichord and their concomitant tuning systems. Initial contact with David Munrow's Early Music Consort of London led, eventually, to membership of Andrew Parrott's Taverner Consort, Christopher Page's Gothic Voices, and the Hilliard Ensemble. His interest in tuning has become, in the eyes of his colleagues and friends, something of an obsession. In preparing the article for the *Companion,* he acknowledges his indebtedness to Easley Blackwood, Ross Duffin, Patricia Carpenter, Christopher Page, Andrew Parrott, Elizabeth Randell, Wayne Slawson, and to his wife Janet.

HUGH DAVIES (born 1943) is a composer, performer, inventor of new musical instruments and musicologist. He was Director, from 1968 to 1986, and Consultant Researcher, until 1991, at the Electronic Music

Studio, Goldsmiths' College, University of London. He is also Consultant to the Music Department, Gemeentemuseum, in The Hague, The Netherlands. His compositions for traditional instruments, his own invented amplified instruments, live electronics and tape have been performed and/or broadcast in twenty-three countries, with several issued on commercial recordings; his instruments and sound sculptures (more than 130 invented) have been exhibited in nine countries. He is the compiler of the *International Electronic Music Catalog* (MIT Press, 1968) and contributed 305 articles to *The New Grove Dictionary of Musical Instruments*.

GRAHAM DIXON is a senior producer with responsibilities for Early Music at BBC Radio 3. He studied at the Universities of London and Durham. Although his original field of doctoral research was music and liturgy in seventeenth-century Rome, his interests now extend as far as Handel. He is the author of numerous articles on Baroque music, and his monograph on Carissimi is published by Oxford University Press. He is musicological adviser to the York Early Music Festival, and serves as the musicologist on the faculty of the British School at Rome.

DUNCAN DRUCE (born 1939, Nantwich, Cheshire) is known as a violinist and viola-player, and as a composer. As a member of the Pierrot Players and the Fires of London he worked closely with Harrison Birtwistle and Peter Maxwell Davies, but he has also been playing the Baroque and Classical stringed instruments for over twenty years, and has performed with many of the well-known specialist groups. Since 1978 he has taught at Bretton Hall College, West Yorkshire. Recent compositions include *Venkatamakhi's Dream*, for clarinet and string quartet; *We were like them that dream*, for mixed chorus; a string quintet; and a completion of the Mozart Requiem.

JONATHAN DUNSBY (born 1953) is Professor of Music and Head of Department at the University of Reading, having previously been Lecturer at King's College London, and Associate Professor at the University of Southern California, Los Angeles. Trained as a pianist by Fanny Waterman, he won prizes in various international competitions, and pursued graduate and post-doctoral research with Alexander Goehr, Edward Cone and Leonard Stein. He is co-author of *Music Analysis in Theory and Practice* (Faber, 1988), and Founding Editor of the periodical *Music Analysis*, which first appeared in 1981. He has recently completed a monograph on Schoenberg's *Pierrot Lunaire* for Cambridge University Press.

JAMES FULKERSON (born 1945, Streator, Illinois) received his musical training at the University of Illinois and Illinois Wesleyan University. His major compositional studies have been with Salvatore Martirano, Kenneth Gaburo, Ben Johnston and Herbert Brün. His principal trombone studies have been with Carmine Caruso and John Silber.

He has been resident composer-performer at the Center for the Creative and Performing Arts in Buffalo (New York), and composer-in-residence with the New York State CAPS programme, the DAAD (Berlin), the Victorian College of the Arts (Melbourne, Australia) and Dartington College of the Arts (Totnes, England). He has taught composition at Dartington College of the Arts and at the University of Nottingham, where he was also Director of the Computer and Electronic Music Studios.

He has composed for various media, including experimental film and dance, collaborating with the choreographers Mary Fulkerson, Richard Alston, Jaap Flier and Rosemary Butcher. A further collaboration with Rosemary Butcher and the architect John Lyall resulted in a work for Glasgow's 1990 celebrations as European City of Culture.

Fulkerson's music has been performed throughout the world, is recorded on Folkways, Irida, and Move Records, and is published by Edition Modern (Munich) and Seesaw Music (New York).

JOSCELYN GODWIN (born 1945) was educated at Magdalene College, Cambridge, and holds a Ph.D. in musicology from Cornell University. He has written *Harmonies of Heaven and Earth: The Spiritual Dimension of Music from Antiquity to the Avant-Garde* (Thames & Hudson, 1988) and several books on the Western esoteric tradition, and edited the sourcebooks *Music, Mysticism and Magic* (Routledge, 1986, and Penguin, 1990) and *Harmony of the Spheres* (Inner Traditions International, 1992). He is Professor of Music at Colgate University, Hamilton, New York State.

CRAIG HARRIS is active as a composer, researcher and consultant in computer music. His current research concerns the modelling of next generation computer music instruments and the tools for incorporating technology into several aspects of musical activity. His compositions include works for traditional instruments as well as those which incorporate new technology in both concert and multi–media contexts.

Harris completed his Ph.D. and M.Mus. in Composition at the Eastman School of Music, University of Rochester, New York, and received a B.Mus. in Composition at the University of Toronto. At Eastman he was involved in the development of the Computer Music Studio, and continues to assist in this developing facility. He has held faculty positions at the University of Michigan School of Music and at the Eastman School of Music. He is president of the International Computer Music Association.

ELLEN T. HARRIS, Associate Provost for the Arts and Professor of Music at the Massachusetts Institute of Technology, is the author of *Handel and the Pastoral Tradition* (Oxford University Press, 1980) and *Henry Purcell's 'Dido and Aeneas'* (Oxford University Press, 1987). She has also edited a thirteen–volume critical facsimile edition of Handel's opera librettos (Garland, 1989). Her articles and reviews concerning Handel, Baroque opera, Purcell, vocal performance practice, and music based on Shake-spearean texts have appeared in numerous publications, including *Journal of the American Musicological Society, Händel Jahrbuch, Göttinger-Händel-Beiträge, American Choral Review, The Musical Quarterly, Notes,* and *The New York Times*. She has received research fellowships from the Columbia Council for Research in the Humanities, the American Council of Learned Societies, and the National Endowment for the Humanities. Professor Harris is past President of the American Handel Society.

LOU HARRISON (born 1917, Portland, Oregon) studied music with Cooper, Cowell, Schoenberg and Thomson. He has been a clerk, journalist and writer, florist, forestry fire fighter, animal nurse and, for about a third of a century, teacher. He is Professor Emeritus, San José State University, holds an Honorary Doctorate of Fine Arts, Mills College, and is a member of the American Academy and Institute of Arts and Letters.

JONATHAN HARVEY (born 1939) was a choirboy at St Michael's College, Tenbury, England, in his early youth. There he encountered a vast repertoire of early church music. Later he played cello in the National Youth Orchestra and won a major scholarship to Cambridge. During that period, on Benjamin Britten's advice, he studied composition with Erwin Stein and Hans Keller. He gained a Ph.D. at Glasgow University, combining this with work in the BBC Scottish Symphony Orchestra. A lectureship at Southampton University followed, and later a move to

xvi

Sussex University where he is now Professor. Meanwhile there had been visits to Darmstadt and Princeton and a book on Stockhausen. From the 1980s on he worked frequently at IRCAM in Paris, producing three works and giving many lectures. His works now number over a hundred and have been given in nearly all countries with Western music facilities.

HANNS-WERNER HEISTER (born 1946, Plochingen/Neckar, Germany) received his university education in Music, German Studies and Linguistics in Tübingen, Frankfurt and Berlin. Since 1970 he has held various teaching posts at the Academy of Music and Performing Arts of Berlin (musical sociology); at the University of Hamburg (aesthetic theory of musical theatre); and at the Academy of Arts in Berlin (commodity aesthetics and mass-culture). Since 1971 he has been working as a freelance musicologist and music critic.

His research is concerned principally with the relationship of musical aesthetics to musical sociology; semiotics and music as language; forms and functions of music culture (institutions, media, behaviour); new music; and the theory and history of opera.

PETER HOLMAN has taught in universities and conservatories in Britain and the United States, and is currently Senior Associate Lecturer at the Colchester Institute, Colchester, England. He has contributed papers on English seventeenth-century music and the early history of stringed instruments to many learned journals and conferences. His book *Four and Twenty Fiddlers: The Violin at the English Court 1540–1690* is published by Oxford University Press. As a performer he has been director of the Parley of Instruments since 1979, broadcasting and recording frequently with that and other groups. In 1985 he became musical director of the newly-formed Opera Restor'd, and has toured extensively in Britain with productions of English eighteenth-century operas.

TIM HOWELL has been a lecturer in the Department of Music at the University of York, England, since October, 1986. After graduating from Southampton University, he studied with Arnold Whittall for the M.Mus. in Theory and Analysis at King's College, London, while working on the *New Grove Dictionary of Music and Musicians*. His doctoral research, on the symphonies and tone-poems of Jean Sibelius, was completed at Southampton University under the supervision of Eric Graebner and Peter Evans and the thesis has recently been published by Garland Press. A contributor to *Music Analysis* and *Music and Letters*, he is currently writing an analytical book on the music of Sibelius.

DAVID KERSHAW (born 1947, Manchester) read music at King's College, Cambridge, and following post-graduate research into film-music at the University of York, England, was appointed Lecturer in 1971. He is a composer of concert and film music (e.g. his experiment in absolute animated film, *Opus I*, 1983, Arts Council of Great Britain). He was awarded the Guinness Prize for composition in 1980, and a Churchill Travelling Fellowship in 1987 to visit film-music archives in the USA. He is founder-director of the Film Music Resource Centre based in the Music Department, University of York.

PETER LE HURAY is formerly a University Lecturer in Music and President (Vice-Master) of St Catharine's College, Cambridge. He is the author of *Music and the Reformation in England* (Cambridge University Press, 1978), and co-author with James Day of *Music and Aesthetics in the late-eighteenth and early-nineteenth centuries* (Cambridge University Press, 1981). Among his editions are *The Anthems of Thomas Weelkes* (*Musica Britannica*, Stainer & Bell, 1966: jointly with Walter Collins and David Brown), *The Motets and Anthems of Matthew Locke* (*Musica Britannica*, Stainer & Bell, 1976), a *Treasury of English Church Music* (Cambridge University Press, 1982), and music in the Oxford University Press *Tudor Church Music* series. He has been on the editorial boards of the *New Grove* and *Early English Church Music*, and he has been president of the *Incorporated Association of Organists*. He has given many recitals and talks for the BBC, his latest recording being of J.S. Bach's Trio Sonatas for organ.

EDWIN LONDON, composer/conductor, has, since 1980, been Music Director of the Cleveland Chamber Symphony, an award-winning ensemble dedicated to the performance of new music in effective conjunction with lesser-known masterworks of the past. He also serves as Professor in the Music Department of the Cleveland State University, and Director of the Center for Experimental Music. Among his most recent compositions are *Two A'Marvell's for Words*, *In Heinrich's Shoes*, the documentary opera, *Death of Lincoln*, and *A Hero of our Time*.

PETER MANNING (born 1948, London) studied music at Durham University, completing a Ph.D. on electronic and computer music in 1977. In 1973 he joined the staff at Durham, directing research into computer music applications, and in 1989 was appointed Senior Lecturer in Music. In 1987, with Alan Purvis, he established Durham Music Technology, an interdisciplinary engineering/music research group which has been specifically concerned with developing high-speed parallel architecture for computer music. He is the author of *Electronic and Computer Music* (Oxford University Press, 1985), and has written many articles on music technology, including entries for *The New Oxford Companion to Music* and *Grove Dictionary of Musical Instruments*.

WILFRID MELLERS (born 1914, Leamington, England) was educated at Cambridge, where he read English and music. His principal composition teachers, however, were members of the Oxford faculty, Edmund Rubbra and Egon Wellesz. He taught in the universities of Cambridge and Birmingham; between 1960 and 1963 he was Andrew Mellon Professor of Music in the University of Pittsburgh. In 1964 he became founding Head of Department and Professor in the then new University of York, England, a position he occupied until his retirement in 1981. In 1990 he became Visiting Andrew Mellon Professor at Tulane University, New Orleans. He has also taught at the Guildhall School of Music, London.

His reputation was established with his book *François Couperin and the French Classical Tradition* (1950; revised edition, Faber, 1987). He has written *Bach and the Dance of God* (Faber, 1980); *Beethoven and the Voice of God* (Faber, 1983); a comprehensive study of American music (including jazz) entitled *Music in a New Found Land* (1964; revised edition Faber, 1988). He has published *Harmonious Meeting* (Dobson, 1965), a study of the relationship between English music and poetry; and smaller books on the Beatles, Bob Dylan, and women jazz and pop singers. His most recent books are *The Masks of Orpheus: Seven Stages in the Story of European Music* (Manchester University Press, 1987), *Vaughan Williams and the Vision of Albion* (Barrie & Jenkins, 1989; reprinted Pimlico, 1991), *Le Jardin Retrouvé: In Memoriam Federico Mompou, 1893–1987* (Fairfax Press, 1989) and *Percy Grainger* (Oxford University Press, 1992).

The eclectic nature of his interests is revealed in his own music, which includes works in most media, though with a bias towards those with literary or theatrical associations. Over the last twenty years he has been especially interested in music that overrides barriers between categories – art, folk, jazz, pop.

RICHARD MOORE completed his studies in music composition, theory and performance at Carnegie-Mellon University, Pittsburgh, and the

University of Illinois, after which he worked for twelve years at the AT&T Bell Laboratories. There he helped design and implement the MUSIC V program (the first generally-distributed computer music, software) and GROOVE (the first real-time computer music system), both of which he used to create works of computer music, including several experimental film scores. Dissatisfied with the musical qualities of analogue sound synthesis, he resolved to learn how to make digital musical instruments, eventually earning a Ph.D. in computer engineering at Stanford University. There, as part of his doctoral work in computer music, he designed and built the FRMbox – one of the first operational real-time digital music synthesizers. Since 1979, Moore has been Professor of Music at the University of California, San Diego, where he directs the Computer Audio Research Laboratory (CARL) and the UCSD Center for Music Experiment and Related Research (CME). He has written extensively on computer music and related topics, including a text and reference book entitled *Elements of Computer Music* (Prentice-Hall, 1989).

KLAUS L NEUMANN (born 1933, Innsbruck) studied musicology in Hamburg and Kiel. His thesis concerned the distribution of a certain type of folk melody (*Oktavmelodik*) around the world. He worked for Deutsches Rundfunkarchiv in Frankfurt 1964–71, and has been with Radio Cologne since 1971, first as head of their Sound Archives, then, since 1976, as head of their Early Music Department.

RICHARD ORTON (born 1940, Derby, England) won, in 1961, a tenor Choral Scholarship to St John's College, Cambridge, and took his BA and B.Mus. degrees there. In 1967, after research into contemporary musical notation, he was appointed Lecturer in Music at the University of York, England, and established its Electronic Music Studio, a pioneering venture in the field. He founded the live electronic performance group *Gentle Fire*, has fulfilled composer's residencies in Australia (Adelaide) and the United States (Illinois and Cleveland, Ohio), and has established undergraduate and postgraduate courses in Music Technology at the University of York. He is a founder-director of the *Composers' Desktop Project*, which has made available to composers a broad range of composition and analytical software within a comprehensive computer sound synthesis and manipulation environment. His over fifty compositions include the hour-long electroacoustic *Timescape*, composed for the 1984 York Festival, *Icarus*, a work for solo violin and tape, and a *Guitar Concerto*.

JOHN PAYNTER is a teacher and a composer. Throughout his career, in primary and secondary schools, in colleges of education and universities, he has promoted composition as the basis of musical education. His books and other writings on this subject have been translated into many languages, and he has travelled extensively, lecturing and organizing courses for teachers in many countries. From 1973 to 1983 he directed a national project for the British Schools Council: *Music in the Secondary School Curriculum*, which produced reports, video programmes and documentary films of classroom music activities, established regional music education centres, and had an important influence upon the subsequent development of music education in Britain.

John Paynter's compositions include orchestral and choral works, two string quartets, a large-scale piano sonata, and a number of works for young performers; among them *Galaxies for Orchestra and Audience*, commissioned by the BBC and first performed at a Robert Mayer Concert in 1978, bringing together the BBC Symphony Orchestra and the entire audience of young people in the Royal Festival Hall, London. Similar compositions include *Contrasts* and *Variations*, commissioned by the Apollo Trust.

The music-drama *The Voyage of St Brendan*, a large-scale community music project involving a wide age range of young singers and instrumentalists with adult professionals, was given its first performance in Norwich Cathedral in 1979.

John Paynter is Head of the Department of Music at the University of York, England. He was appointed OBE in the Queen's Birthday Honours 1985.

BRUCE PENNYCOOK (born 1949, Toronto) completed a B.Mus. and M.Mus. in theory and composition at the University of Toronto under John Weinzweig and Gustave Ciarnaga, and after working as a freelance studio musician studied for the Doctorate of Musical Arts with John Chowning at Stanford University. From 1978 to 1987 he held a cross-appointment in the School of Music and the Department of Computing and Information Science at Queen's University, Kingston, Ontario, and he is now an associate professor of music at McGill University, Montreal. He has published numerous articles on computer applications in music and digital audio technologies and his works are performed frequently in Canada, the United States and Europe.

GEORGE PRATT is Professor and Head of the Department of Music at Huddersfield Polytechnic, England. While writing a textbook, *The Dynamics of Harmony: Principles and Practice* (Open University Press, 1986), he was alerted to the inadequacy of conventional aural training, and subsequently established the unit for Research into Applied Musical Perception (RAMP) in 1985. This generated a course for first-year undergraduates, written up in *Aural Awareness: Principles and Practice* (Open University Press, 1990).

By a happy accident of timing, some of this in turn influenced the thinking of the National Curriculum Music Working Group on which George Pratt served from 1990 to 1991.

Future plans for the RAMP unit include the development of 'distance learning' material and of more specialized aural courses aimed at the distinctive needs of composers, performers and historical analysts, reflecting the main areas of specialization in the degree courses at Huddersfield.

THOMAS A. REGELSKI is presently Distinguished Teaching Professor of Music in the School of Music, State University of New York College at Fredonia, where he teaches graduate and undergraduate courses in music education and choral conducting. He holds a Masters Degree in Choral Music from Teachers College, Columbia University, and a Ph.D. in Comparative Arts from Ohio University. He has published two major textbooks concerning music education, a monograph involving arts education and brain research, and numerous articles in such journals as the *Music Educator's Journal, British Journal of Music Education, Canadian Music Educator, Japanese Journal of Music Education, International Brain Dominance Review* and the *Journal of Humanistic Psychology.*

LORENTZ REITAN (born 1946) is a Norwegian musicologist and writer. He has degrees in musicology from the University of Oslo and in linguistics and mass communication from the University of Bergen. From 1976 to 1989 he was Professor at the Bergen College of Education. From 1989 he has been artistic and managing director of the Bergen International Festival. He has also been active as a performer (flute) and as the conductor of chamber orchestras. He founded the Bergen branch of Ny Musikk (the Norwegian section of the ISCM), and has worked as a music consultant and producer for NRK-TV (Norwegian Broadcasting Corporation, Television).

JEAN-CLAUDE RISSET (born 1938, Le Puy, France) studied piano and composition with André Jolivet, and science at the Ecole Normale Supérieure, Paris.

He worked with Max Mathews at Bell Laboratories to develop the musical resources of computer sound synthesis (imitation of real synthesis, pitch paradoxes, synthesis of new timbres and sonic development processes). He published a catalogue of computer synthesized sounds (1969), and set up computer sound systems at Orsay (1970–1), at Marseille-Luminy (1974), and at IRCAM, where Pierre Boulez invited him to head the Computer Department (1975–79), and was Professor at the Faculté de Luminy, Université d'Aix-Marseille (1975–85). He is presently Directeur de Recherche at the Centre National de Recherche Scientifique, working on computer music in Marseille. He has received scientific awards (prize of French Acousticians, 1967; silver medal of CNRS, 1988) and musical awards (UFAM piano prize, 1963; Dartmouth International Electronic Music Competition 1970, for *Mutations 1*, entirely synthesized by computer; first prize for Digital Music at Bourges, 1980; Grand Prix SACEM de la promotion de la musique symphonique, 1981; Golden NICA, Ars Electronica 1987; Grand Prix National de la Musique, 1990).

CURTIS ROADS studied composition at the California Institute of the Arts and the University of California, San Diego. He was the editor of *Computer Music Journal* (MIT Press) 1978–89 and is currently associate editor. He was a researcher in computer music at MIT from 1980 to 1987. He has taught electronic music composition at IRCAM, Oberlin Conservatory, Harvard University and the University of Naples, and has performed and lectured throughout North America, Europe, and Asia. Recently he consulted on the design of a new centre for computer music at the Kunitachi College of Music in Tokyo. He is the author and editor of several books on computer music, including a textbook, *Computer Music Tutorial* (MIT Press, 1993). His compositions are available on compact disc from the MIT Media Laboratory/Sony Corporation and Wergo Schallplatten.

ANTHONY ROOLEY has established an international reputation in several fields: as a lute-player discovering the forgotten masterpieces of the Renaissance; as the Director of the Consort of Musicke (which he founded in 1969), an ensemble dedicated to the research and performance of the vast repertoire of music for voices and instruments from the sixteenth and seventeenth centuries; and as a producer of music-theatre from that time, combining music, gesture, drama and dance. In all this activity he has received critical acclaim and is regarded as a pioneer. Despite his enthusiasm for the performing arts of the Renaissance and their authentic revival today, his first interest is in the ideas, concepts and philosophy of the period, and he has dedicated his energies to the modern dissemination of these, through lectures, performances, articles, and his book *Performance: Revealing the Orpheus Within* (Element Books, 1990).

MURRAY SCHAFER is a Canadian composer, author, educator and environmentalist. He has written all forms of music (including large-scale works for music theatre). He is the author of several books, of which the most important musically are *The Tuning of the World* (1976), a text for soundscape theory, and *The Thinking Ear* (1986), a work stressing creativity in music education; both are available from Arcana Editions, Indian River, Ontario.

PETER SEYMOUR studied at the University of York, England, researching into the performance of Baroque music. He is director of the Yorkshire Baroque Soloists and of the Yorkshire Bach Choir, and regularly performs and records in many European countries as conductor or keyboard player. He is also artistic adviser to the York Early Music Festival and Lecturer in Music and Organist at the University of York.

JOHN SHEPHERD is a Professor of Music and Sociology at Carleton University, Ottawa, where he is also Director of the School for Studies in Art and Culture. In addition to many articles in the fields of the sociology and aesthetics of music, popular music studies, the sociology of music education, and theory and method in musicology, he is the co-author of *Whose Music? A Sociology of Musical Languages* (Latimer, 1977), author of *Tin Pan Alley* (Routledge, 1982), *La Musica come sapere sociale* (Unicopli/Ricordi, 1988) and *Music as Social Text* (Polity Press, 1991), editor of *Alternative Musicologies* (Toronto University Press, 1990 – a special issue of the *Canadian University Music Review*), and co-editor of *The Music Industry in a Changing World* (Routledge, 1991 – a special issue of *Cultural Studies*). Shepherd is currently completing a book with Peter Wicke entitled *The Sound of Music: Meaning and Power in Culture*, which is to be published by Polity Press in 1993. From 1983 until 1987 Shepherd was General Secretary of the International Association for the Study of Popular Music.

ROBERT SHERLAW JOHNSON (born 1932, Sunderland, England) has degrees from the University of Durham and diplomas from the Royal Academy of Music, where he studied piano and composition. In 1957 he won the Charles W. Black Award and studied piano in Paris with Jacques Février and composition with Nadia Boulanger, and attended Messiaen's classes at the Conservatoire. He has served as Lecturer in music at Leeds and York Universities, subsequently being appointed Fellow of Worcester College and University Lecturer, University of Oxford, in 1970. In 1971 he was awarded the degree of D.Mus. at Leeds University and in 1984 was elected to a Fellowship of the Royal Academy of Music. In 1990 he was awarded the degree of D.Mus. at Oxford University.

In 1975 he published a comprehensive survey of the music of Olivier Messiaen (Dent and California University Press), and has contributed a chapter on 'The European Tradition' to *How Music Works* (ed. Keith Spence, Macmillan, 1981), and a chapter on Messiaen and Boulez to *A Heritage of Music*, Vol. 4 (ed. Michael Raeburn and Alan Kendall, Oxford University Press, 1989).

As a pianist he has specialized in the performance of the music of the twentieth century and of Liszt, a selection of whose early and late works he has recorded on compact disk. He has composed a large number of works of many different genres including three piano sonatas, works with electronic tape, chamber works, song cycles and an opera: *The Lambton Worm*. Recent works include a piano concerto, a clarinet concerto, a sextet (*Encounters*, commissioned by the Allegri String Quartet) and *Sinfonietta Concertante* for the Aquarius Ensemble.

JOHN A. SLOBODA is Professor of Psychology and Dean of Social Sciences at the University of Keele. His books include *The Musical Mind: The Cognitive Psychology of Music* (Oxford University Press, 1985), and *Generative Processes in Music: The Psychology of Performance, Improvisation, and Composition* (Oxford University Press, 1988). He is Associate Editor of the journal *Psychology of Music* and a consulting editor for *Music Perception*. He is principal conductor of the Keele Bach Choir.

DENIS SMALLEY is a senior lecturer in music at the University of East Anglia, Norwich, where he is Director of the Recording and Electroacoustic Music Studio. He has an international reputation as a composer specializing in electroacoustic and computer music and has won many prizes for his works, including the Prix Ars Electronica in 1988. His research work centres on aesthetic questions relating to the electroacoustic musical medium and includes a seminal chapter entitled 'Spectro-morphology and Structuring Processes' in *The Language of Electro-acoustic Music* (ed. S. Emmerson, Macmillan, 1986).

NEIL SORRELL is a senior lecturer in music at the University of York, England, specializing in Asian music. His doctoral thesis was on Indian music, and he is the author (with his teacher, the great sarangi player, Pandit Ram Narayan) of a book on the subject. In 1980 he co-founded the English Gamelan Orchestra, the first group of British musicians dedicated to the study, composition, and performance of music for the Javanese Gamelan, and in 1981 he organized the manufacture of Gamelan Sekar Petak, the first complete Javanese Gamelan in a British teaching institution. His publications include *Indian Music in Performance: A Practical Introduction* (Manchester University Press, 1980) and *A Guide to the Gamelan* (Faber & Faber, 1990).

JOHN STEVENS studied classics and English at Magdalene College, Cambridge. After war service with the Royal Navy he returned to Cambridge where he became successively Bye-Fellow, Research Fellow, Fellow and Tutor of Magdalene and Director of Studies in English; from 1953 he was Lecturer in the English Faculty. In 1974 he was appointed to an *ad hominem* Readership in English and Musical History, and in 1978 elected to the Professorship of Medieval and Renaissance English. He was President (Vice-Master) of Magdalene College from 1983 until his retirement in 1988. His publications include *Music and Poetry in the Early Tudor Court* (Cambridge University Press, 1979); *Words and Music in the Middle Ages: Song, Narrative, Dance and Drama, 1050–1350* (Cambridge University Press, 1986); three volumes of *Musica Britannica* (*Medieval Carols*, *Music at the Court of Henry VIII* and *Early Tudor Songs and Carols*, Stainer & Bell, 1970, 1973, 1975); articles on 'Carol', 'Troubadours and Trouvères' and 'Medieval Drama' in the *New Grove* (Macmillan, 1980). He is a Fellow of the British Academy, and in the Queen's Birthday Honours of 1980 was appointed CBE for services to musicology.

KEITH SWANWICK is Professor of Music Education at the University of London Institute of Education. After graduating from the Royal Academy of Music, he trained as a teacher and taught in comprehensive and grammar schools.

In his first book he explored the educational implications of jazz and pop traditions (*Popular Music and the Teacher*, Pergamon, 1968). He was appointed in 1976 to the London Chair of Music Education. His book *A Basis for Music Education* (NFER-Nelson, 1979) was a systematic attempt to develop a conceptual framework for music in the curriculum. These ideas were developed further in *Discovering Music* (with Dorothy Taylor, Batsford, 1982). His most recent book is *Music, Mind, and Education* (Routledge, 1988; published in Spanish, Ediciones Morata, 1991).

Professor Swanwick has directed two research projects funded by the EC; one a study of music-teacher education in Europe, the other developing intercultural music resources for teachers of young children.

Since 1984 he has, with John Paynter, been co-editor of the *British Journal of Music Education*, published by Cambridge University Press. In 1991 he was elected Chair of the UK Council for Music Education and Training.

BARRY TRUAX is an associate professor in both the Department of Communication and the School for the Contemporary Arts at Simon Fraser University, Burnaby, British Columbia, where he teaches courses in acoustic communication and electroacoustic music. He has worked with the World Soundscape Project, editing its *Handbook for Acoustic Ecology*, and has published a book, *Acoustic Communication* (Ablex, 1984), dealing with all aspects of sound and technology. As a composer, Truax is best known for his work with the PODX computer music system, which he has used for tape solo works and those which combine tape with live performance. A recent selection of these pieces may be heard on his recording *Sequence of Earlier Heaven* on the Cambridge Street Records label and the Compact Discs *Digital Soundscapes* and *Pacific Rim*.

PHILIP WILBY (born 1949, Pontefract, England) was educated at Keble College, Oxford. He attributes the awakening of his interest in composition to Herbert Howells, whose extra-curricular composition classes he attended while a violinist in the National Youth Orchestra of Great Britain. A serious commitment to composition developed during the years at Oxford and, having gained his B.Mus. in composition in 1971, he continued to write music even while working as a professional violinist (first at Covent Garden and later with the City of Birmingham Symphony Orchestra). He moved to Yorkshire in 1972 and is currently Principal Lecturer in Composition at the University of Leeds.

Among his wide-ranging output is a considerable body of wind music, and since 1985 this interest has led to an annual residency at the California State University, Fresno. His church music is widely performed, and he has built a continuing relationship with the choir of St Paul's Cathedral, London, who have recently commissioned a work from him. His orchestral piece *The Wings of Morning* was commissioned to celebrate the twenty-first anniversary of the orchestra of St John's Smith Square, London, in 1988. His Symphony No. 2, commissioned by the BBC Philharmonic Orchestra, will be given its premiere in 1993. As well as concert music he has written educational pieces and incidental music for television, and his growing body of music for brass band has led him to be chosen as the composer for the 1991/92 National and Open Brass Band Championships. At Leeds, his research has led to a series of reconstructions of Mozart fragments, and in 1985 these were the subject of a television documentary featuring the Amadeus String Quartet, and were included in the Philips *Complete Mozart* CD Collection.

PETER WILLIAMS is Arts and Sciences Distinguished Professor of Music at Duke University, North Carolina, and Visiting Director of the Russell Collection of Harpsichords in the University of Edinburgh, where until recently he held a Personal Chair in Music (Performance Practice). He moved to Edinburgh from Cambridge, where he had been a Music Scholar of St John's College and where his doctoral research on Handel led to an interest in old instruments, and to the writing of a fundamentally new history of the organ, *The European Organ* (Batsford, 1966).

In 1970 he produced a two-volume work *Figured Bass Accompaniment*, in 1980 *A New History of the Organ from the Greeks to the Present Day*, and in 1980–4 a monumental three-volume study *The Organ Music of J. S. Bach* (Cambridge University Press). All these books have become standard works in several editions. A further major enterprise of his is the journal *The Organ Yearbook*, now at its twenty-second number.

His playing is limited to specialized repertories, chiefly the music of J. S. Bach and of the English school; in each year he performs several tours of the United States and Europe and has played at the Festivals of Halle, Camden, Rovereto, Linz, Pistoia, Edinburgh, Aldeburgh, Barcelona, and London's South Bank, either as organist or harpsichordist. Work-in-progress includes the complete harpsichord works of Handel (Wiener Urtext) and the general editorship of the projected New Oxford Bach Organ Works series.

CHRISTOPHER WINTLE (born 1945) lectures in music at King's College, London, and specializes in musical analysis. He was educated at St Catherine's College, Oxford and Southampton University, and has held lecturing posts at the Universities of Southampton, Reading and London (Goldsmiths' College and King's). In 1974 he was a Visiting Fellow at Princeton University. He is on the editorial boards of *Music Analysis* and the *Cambridge Opera Journal*, and has written analytical studies of music ranging from Corelli to Babbitt. He has also written for the English National Opera's *Opera Handbooks*, and published on Wagner in *Reading Opera* (ed. Parker and Groos, Princeton University Press, 1988).

TREVOR WISHART (born 1946) is a composer living and working in the North of England. He has performed and lectured on his work throughout Europe and in Australia, Cuba, Japan and the United States. He has received commissions from the Massachusetts State Council for the Arts, IRCAM and the BBC, and prizes at the Bourges International Electro-Acoustic Music Festival, the Gaudeamus Composers Competition and the Linz Ars Electronica Festival.

His works include *Red Bird, a political prisoner's dream* (Prizewinner at Bourges, 1978), *Tuba Mirum* (1979, music-theatre for prepared tuba, electrically-operated audio-visual mutes, tape and actors) and the *Vox* cycle (1980–8), a series of vocal works for four performers using new vocal techniques, electronics and computer technology, first performed in full at the 1988 season of BBC Promenade Concerts and now available on compact disc from Virgin Classics.

He is also well known for his experimental environmental and participatory multimedia projects of the 1970s, and for his contributions to music education. His book of musical games *Sounds Fun* has recently been translated into Japanese.

In 1985 he published *On Sonic Art* (available from 83 Heslington Road, York YO1 5AX), which explores the new world of aesthetic possibilities opened up by computer technology. He was a founder member of the Composers' Desktop Project and (1990) Chairperson of Sonic Arts Network UK. He is currently Special Professor of Music at the University of Nottingham.

ALISON WRAY completed her doctorate in linguistics at the University of York, England, early in 1988, and moved immediately into the Department of Music there with a Leverhulme Research Fellowship, investigating aspects of pronunciation in singing. Her concern is the acquisition by singers of accurate pronunciation in foreign languages, and the restoration of 'authentic' pronunciation in vocal music of earlier centuries. She also sustains a successful singing career in her own right. She is now a full-time lecturer in linguistics at the University Colleges of Ripon and York St John, York.

PREFACE

The origin of this book was an invitation, in 1987, from the publishers to staff of the Department of Music in the University of York, to explore the possibilities for a wide-ranging musical compendium. In the event it became a very considerable undertaking – as anyone who has ever tried to put together a 'symposium' publication will appreciate. There are peculiar difficulties in trying to create a coherent book largely by correspondence, and with a large number of authors spread out across the world. Above all, it cannot be done quickly; and in this case, certainly, it would not have been possible without the sustained commitment of a great many people.

We must thank first the contributing authors, all of whom have exercised admirable patience while the collection of articles was being assembled. We also gratefully acknowledge the work of the translators: Rebecca Leftwich (for the article by Hanns-Werner Heister), Graham Dixon (for the articles by Irmgard Bontinck and Klaus Neumann), and Michela Mollia and Barry Truax (for 'Verso-l'uno' by Walter Branchi).

Special thanks are due to Professor Emeritus Wilfrid Mellers for agreeing to introduce the book with his essay 'Music, the modern world and the burden of history', and to colleagues in the Department of Music of the University of York for their encouragement. We also thank members of the Routledge editorial staff for their professional advice at various stages of this project.

Finally, it is our pleasure to record deep gratitude to one person without whose forbearance, skill and dedication our purpose would not have been accomplished. Jane Allen, nominally 'secretary to the editors', has played a central and crucial role: maintaining the links between editors, publishers and more than fifty authors; transferring material to and from authors' disks generated in a variety of word-processing systems; rekeying and collating articles at every stage of a long and complicated editorial process; organizing translations; keeping a tally of illustrations and musical examples; and coping with many changes and updates of the text, ultimately bringing the whole production together and – as though all that were not enough – transporting the disks and four large boxes of printout from York to London!

JOHN PAYNTER
TIM HOWELL
RICHARD ORTON
PETER SEYMOUR

INTRODUCTION
John Paynter, Chair of the Editorial Committee

By and large our educational systems are geared to 'subjects'. Even in the primary school, where we expect class teachers to maintain a wholeness in the way children learn, some things – such as 'reading' and 'number' – acquire such substantially agreed methodologies that they take on a degree of independence – separate 'wholenesses' of their own. Later, in secondary and tertiary education, although we may try to cultivate cross-curricular reference wherever possible, there is still the assumption that the subject emphasis should prevail: so we study Mathematics, Physics, Geography, History, Music, and so on. Similar groupings of knowledge and ideas occur everywhere in our social and intellectual lives, as a result of which we collect and collate experience, identifying each area with a label, not unlike an academic subject title: Politics, Finance, Religion, Health, the Media, Sport, Gardening.

All these labels, whether or not they represent conventional areas of academic study, imply the existence of accepted bodies of knowledge: facts, suppositions, and interpretations. Over the centuries, new facts are discovered, ideas are generated, and views change. In consequence, the practitioners in each area develop three important ways of knowing about their 'subject': the pragmatic ('This is what I do' or 'This is how it works for me'), the historically speculative (what people have thought about these things in the past), and the current speculative (what people think about them now). The extent to which the viewpoints merge or are combined varies from individual to individual, and within that we find further variation: for example, speculation may be of a very general nature or it may be closely focused.

A cross-section of the pragmatic and the speculative in a particular area of human experience at a given point can provide a useful sample of the then current techniques, theories and opinions. Less tangible, though no less significant, is the characteristic attitude of mind that is revealed, the milieu in which scholarship and practice are thriving at that time. Sampling 'thought' in this way may not give access to the minutiae of every major topic within the body of knowledge represented by a subject label in the way that the standard reference works and major dictionaries set out to do, but it can tell us quite a lot – perhaps, rather better than a dictionary can – about the subject's place in the grand scheme of things, and, above all, why the ideas matter. It does this both through what is written and through the way in which the writers convey their commitment to ideas.

This is the field in which the *Companion to Contemporary Musical Thought* is operating. Naturally, we hope that the range of topics and the extensive index will make it a useful reference resource, but the book is not, and was never intended to be, encyclopedic. From the start our principal aim has been to enable readers to experience something of the attitudes of mind current in musical scholarship and practice in the late 1980s and early 1990s, and thereby to feel that they are part of the debate. We asked ourselves the question: what is it that those who, at this time, are most closely involved with it think music is about? And to get the answer we invited musicologists, music historians, sociologists and educationists, composers, performers, producers, analysts and critics from a variety of backgrounds in a number of different countries to contribute articles on topics of their own choice, topics that were, therefore, of the utmost importance to the writers themselves. The only constraint was that each article should develop its argument within the framework of one of the four general headings under which the contents of the *Companion* would be organized.

Obviously there are numerous ways in which a subject can be explored and its multifaceted features categorized. No doubt a different editorial committee would have set about the task in a different way and come up with a different scheme; we make no apologies or special claims for our solution. The plan has been to provide four easily recognizable gateways into the world of music. There could, of course, have been many more, but we hope that those we have chosen will be acceptable starting points for a wide readership – students, academics, professional musicians, teachers, and also 'general' music-lovers: in short, all those people who are looking for something more than dates and musical facts, and seek a wider understanding of what scholars, composers and performers today think about music, of the topics and projects that excite them, and of the new directions that they are exploring.

Music is primarily an expression of what people feel. Even today, in some parts of the world it is such an essential part of the social fabric that there is no word that specifically identifies 'music'. In every human society music is functional (in the sense of serving religious, political and recreational ends), but it may also be entertaining (in its own right or as a support for other forms of entertainment), and revelatory – in the manner of all the arts in their attempts to engage with something beyond the mundane.

People and Music is therefore the first of our four entrance points, leading into an area that is broadly concerned with musical culture: sociological, historical, psychological. In their various ways the writers here confront the question 'Why music?' Some answer it as objectively as possible by focusing on particular examples of the public manifestation of music, or of musicianship, musical usage and influence. Others respond subjectively – for example, the essays by Walter Branchi, Lou Harrison and Ed London, the latter a witty 'verbal music' which as much embodies its topic as explains it. Yet again, others are set somewhere between these two positions. Our overall title, *A Companion to Contemporary Musical Thought*, indicates a certain roundness of sensibility in which more conventional 'scholarly' approaches to the subject are balanced with poetic and philosophical, but no less intensely musical, contributions. Nowhere is this more clearly necessary than in this wide-ranging opening section of the book.

Music is only possible because we live in an acoustic environment; that is to say, we are able to hear sounds and react to them. Part II, *The Technology of Music*, is concerned with the use of instruments to produce and control musical sounds, and in particular with the most recent developments in electroacoustic and 'computer' music. That is hardly surprising at this point in the twentieth century. Most of the writers who have contributed to this section are themselves composers working with these resources. The invention of digital sound synthesis and its extension into more and more refined techniques of sampling and transformation has had far-reaching effects upon much of the music that comes to us daily via radio and television. In those circumstances we may not always pay much attention to what we are hearing, partly because synthesizers are quite often used to imitate familar instrumental sounds, and also because the more obviously 'electronic' music has come to be widely accepted as an adjunct of, for instance, science-fiction drama – or indeed of anything that is odd, or unfamiliar, or 'weird'. Unfortunately, that very acceptance creates an even more formidable barrier to wider understanding, first because it is hard for listeners to hear such music without the direct association of 'space-age' images, and second because, to produce the desired effect of symbolizing something strange, the music itself must remain strange. Yet to enjoy music as music a degree of familiarity is essential, not so much that we can no longer find something fresh and unexpected in it, but at least enough to generate a sympathetic attitude towards the idiom. Only then can we begin to take pleasure in the sound qualities and forms. For those already involved with 'music technology' this section of the book will present a fascinating variety of viewpoints from some eminent practitioners. At the same time we hope that other readers will find here accessible explanations of what it is that interests and excites composers working with the new technology, and will thereby be encouraged to listen to more of this music.

The writers in Part III, *The Structure of Music*, are concerned with various ways of examining the 'art objects' themselves: the pieces of music we experience by listening to them or performing them. Like every other art object, the form of a piece of music is largely dictated by the qualities of the ideas it embodies. 'Understanding' a piece of music is a matter of being able to appreciate how the composer's imagination has developed those ideas, and carried the developments forward in time, to create a structure which affords pleasure in particular features (melodies, rhythmic patterns, combinations of different instruments or voices, and so on) as well as aesthetic satisfaction in its overall completeness; its form fulfilling the expectations raised in our minds by the first hearing of the principal ideas. Investigating how this understanding comes about is a complex process involving analysts, critics, psychologists, historians and, of course, composers.

In Part IV, we draw upon the thinking of those who are directly, or very closely, involved in the business of presenting music, making it happen in the present. This is an area where attitudes have changed importantly in recent years. Broadly speaking, in the early and middle decades of this century the predominant view on performance was that musicians should acquire a 'good' technique that would serve them equally well whatever the music they played. The symphony orchestra had settled to a standard (large) size and was regarded as a satisfactory medium for virtually any orchestral music – from the suites of Bach to Mozart and Beethoven symphonies, Brahms and Tchaikowsky concertos, Mahler, Elgar and beyond. All this music was made to sound more or less the same; that is, it was given a very similar quality of sound. By the same token, arrangers did not hesitate to produce for this style of orchestra versions of works designed for very different circumstances: for example, preludes and fugues that Bach had composed for the organ. A very similar attitude prevailed in the field of chamber music.

New music sometimes demanded a different approach, but then the audience for new music was generally a small and dedicated one. There were also – from the earliest years of the twentieth century – those who sought to restore the authentic sound of music from the sixteenth, seventeenth and eighteenth centuries, but, once again, their performances did not reach a large public, and in many quarters they were regarded as harmless eccentrics.

In the 1960s attitudes began to change. A new wave of 'Early Music' performers appeared, soon to be supported by professional scholarship of an order that previously had not been so widely available. The point of focus was now the musical text, as it comes down to us from the composer, and what that has to tell us about the appropriate performance practice for the music's realization. Since the late 1980s, 'historically informed' presentation has been increasing in popularity, greatly assisted by recordings and by the establishment of specialist orchestras. Specialist departments have also been set up in broadcasting, as, for example, at Westdeutscher Rundfunk, Cologne, under the direction of Klaus Neumann, one of the contributors to this section of the *Companion*.

The impetus of the most recent Early Music studies can also be seen to be driving a much wider review of performance practice. By now it is generally accepted that the idea of a 'standard' technique that would enable a musician to cope with all music is inadequate; different historical periods require not only different instruments but also radically different performing skills. Moreover, the music of our own time, as much as any other, presents such a variety of technical demands that few musicians are able to deal adequately with all styles. The writers in this section – distinguished performers and scholars – lead us through a very useful range of the thinking which underpins these new approaches to presentation in old and new music alike.

There is a maxim that says, if you want to read a book that will give you the essence of a subject, read a big one. A potted digest will provide signposts but it cannot show you the really important characteristics of the landscape. The dictionary is even less able to do so because it is designed to deliver detailed information at specific points of reference. This *Companion* is so organized that, if you want to get a general but significant impression of the current landscape of musical thought, you can do so by reading the four parts, one after another, exploring the subject from cultural, technological, structural and interpretational viewpoints. But it can also be dipped into. The four areas are not mutually exclusive, and they can be taken in any order (as, indeed, can any of the articles). There are overlaps, offering alternative views of the same topic or different approaches to the same question. Above all, you will find opinions (not always in agreement with one another) to stimulate further thought about music now.

The contributors to this volume include some of the foremost scholars and practical musicians of our time, chosen for the importance of their views. Among them is Dr Peter le Huray, until recently President of St Catharine's College in the University of Cambridge. In his article in the first section of this book he suggests that, notwithstanding the hazards, to review music in larger cultural frames can be worthwhile if only to identify areas of disagreement that need further debate, and from which new musical understanding may emerge. That, it seems to me, succinctly sums up the *Companion*'s objectives and justifies its 'symposium' format.

1

Music,
the Modern World,
and the Burden of History

WILFRID MELLERS

We cannot escape it: we live in a music-producing world; 'musical' sounds assail our ears at most hours of the day and night. So much so that we seldom reflect on what these sounds mean in relation to our lives, or even notice many of them.

What music have we heard, and what music has washed over us, over the past day, week, month? By way of records, radio and tape we've probably encountered fragments of European 'art' music covering a time-span of seven or eight centuries, from medieval and early Renaissance music to Stravinsky and Stockhausen. We'll have heard more of some periods of music, especially the eighteenth and nineteenth centuries, than of others, and we'll have accepted some indubitably 'great' composers as still a vital part of our experience, whereas lesser figures will have seemed peripheral, even meaningless. Even so, merely within the confines of European art music, an extraordinary diversity of aural experience will have come our way. To this we must add, in our increasingly global village, transient awareness of the musics of non-Western cultures, both those which remain intrinsically alien to us and those that come to us directly by way of Afro-American jazz and the various folk and tribal pop musics spawned from that central oral–aural culture. So the musics we hear cover a bewildering range of time and space. They embrace, too, a multiplicity of sonorous resources, from single voice or drum to mammoth symphony orchestra and electrophonic tape. They even include music which, corrupted to *Muzak*, is meant to be *not listened to* since its purpose, designed to lower sales resistance in supermarkets, allay panic in airports and the like, is always extra-musical and sometimes anti-human.

How can we make sense of such crazy multifariousness? Only by beginning at the beginning and asking: what is music, and what is it for? The most fundamental answers to these fundamental questions are likely to be given by the most fundamental peoples: by so-called savages and by our children who are of their nature small savages. From them we may learn of the primacy of the human voice and body, since these are the instruments with which (nearly) everyone is endowed by nature, and sound is, apparently, considered by most primitive peoples to be the *fons et origo* of life. The reason why primitive peoples believe that it is the *voice* of God that stirs creation within the void may be implicit in the cry of the new-born babe who, separated from its mother as it struggles into an alien world, yells for mammalian security. The baby's cry, according to Geza Roheim, is 'the only form of permitted crying which gains sympathetic attention and earns symbolic gratifications'; and many authorities from Darwin onwards have pointed out that in this respect the utterance of the human infant resembles that of the beasts. Both speak a language pre-existent to consciousness, which consciousness must and does efface. None the less, we can never totally forget this language, which links us holistically and holily to Nature; or if we do so, it is to our peril. The seventeenth-century theologian and mystic, Jacob Boehme, regretted that in his day (and we are his heirs) 'no people understands any more the sensual language, and the birds in the air and the beasts in the forests do understand it according to their species. Therefore man may reflect what he has been robbed of, and what he is to recover in the Second Birth, for in the sensual language all spirits speak with each other.'

We may still observe, among primitive peoples, the origins of music in the cries of infants, the yells of created Nature. Eskimo children, for instance, take empty tubs used by their parents for storing whale oil and blow into them rhythmically, creating a (fairly) ordered interplay of pitches and metrical patterns. While these breathing exercises are practised by children as a giggly game, the procedure is also, for adult Eskimos, of deep ritual significance. All the time God is pouring out life into animate nature; what would happen if, one day, he had no puff left? Humbly, the Eskimos recognize their part in the ultimate mystery, which is being itself: each rhythmically stylized exhalation is a cry, a sigh, that pays back to God the tribute of the breath of life. Similarly the African Bushmen who live in the

2

Kalahari deserts create a weird music by emulating the sounds of birds and beasts. In becoming, through sound and movement, their totemic creatures, they employ disguise and illusion as a propitiatory act, conquering fear of the unknown in making a gesture of reverence to the creatures on whom they rely for subsistence. Likewise the Australian Aborigines, in the silent emptiness of the Outback, use magical, pre-articulate syllables to invoke the natural phenomena – the sun, moon, cloud and water – on which their minimal existence depends. The magic vocables, yelled against the 'everlasting' drone of the didgeridoo (itself a part of Nature in being a hollowed-out tree), and ballasted by the clicking of the rhythm-sticks, dramatize the basic fact of their lives: the beating of the pulse, the thudding of the heart. Through song and dance they would remain whole, hale and holy as part of the cosmos; and much the same is true when, at a more sophisticated level, song and dance become an act of affirmation rather than of propitiation.

For the South Plains Amerindians the half-domesticated horse is not a wild, unknowable creature they fear but one they depend on: so they may perform dance-songs that fulfil its and their phallic dominance, an expression of joy and pride in their ability, within their patriarchal community, to control Nature. Beginning on a high, strained note, their horse-chants are 'tumbling strains' that topple down with an effect of uncontrolled libido, reinforced by the rattles' furiously pounding beat. Though the cry has become aggressive, its relationship to the baby's yell is unmistakable; and it is interesting that, although the chants have words, they are not articulate but magical – a 'music of the vowels'.

To all these musics the notion of history – a sequence of events existing in chronological time – is irrelevant, for they celebrate an eternal present which, releasing us from linearity, conceives of time as circular: in Orazio Paz's words, 'not succession and transition, but rather the perpetual sound of a fixed present in which all times, past and future, are contained'. This is true not only of rudimentary societies but also of more culturally complex African groups, for whom music is a present activity for the instigation of work and play, for the praise or dispraise of the famous, and for the celebration of the fundamental rites of passage – birth, copulation and death. Music is an ambience that affirms life; and one can say as much, if in more sophisticated terms, of the great oriental cultures of India, China and Japan. Technically, all these musics are in essence monodic and rhythmic, stemming from voice and body, the fundamentals of song and dance. They are *incarnate* in melody and metre – even when the 'function' of music has become a metaphysical sublimation of the physicality we start from. It is

3

significant that many non–Western cultures have no term to denote art. The 'work' of art occurs only when we accept the burden of consciousness unequivocally. This necessitates the acknowledgement of past, present and future as differentiated, and therefore demands that we submit to the passing of time and eventually to the inescapable fact of death. This is an achievement that first flowered with the Greeks, but became peculiarly identified with Christianity: a religion which, more than any other, attempted to confront mortality and guilt, associating both with an event presumed to exist in historical time – the Crucifixion of Christ. This equation between guilt and time is a peculiarly European phenomenon, and one which has radically transformed our notions of art as communication.

Musically, medieval Christians followed their oriental forebears in seeking through their art time's transcendence, whether in the form of liturgical plainchant or in the secular forms of troubadour song which worshipped an Eternal, and humanly unattainable, Beloved. But when, in the fourteenth century, the European Renaissance gradually ousted medieval theocracy in favour of a stumbling search for self-responsibility, the timeless tin-tinnabulations of religious and ecclesiastical *cloches* were slowly superseded by time-measuring, secular and civic *clocks*; and the way was open to Locke's statement that 'duration is one common measure of all existence whatsoever'.

The acceptance of linear time as an absolute made possible the develop-ment of ratiocinative logic. Being conscious of being conscious enabled humans to evolve a language of communication; and this in turn made feasible the scientific exploration of nature. When once we know that we know, we wish to know how; and the modern tag, 'knowing how things tick', provides the link between intellectual enquiry and clock, pendulum and temporal progression. Though there is no such overtly revolutionary development in the visual arts, the discovery, or rather the enthusiastic investigation, of perspective is a parallel phenomenon, which made possible literal (photographic) representation. Primitive people – and perhaps 'religious' people in a wider sense – draw, paint and sculpt to effect practical ends by magical means: whereas modern people make visual artefacts in order to 'freeze' a moment existing in historical time.

Music cannot, except in a very crude way, imitate reality in the way a painting can; nor can it convey intellectual concepts as language can. Perhaps it is not surprising, therefore, that throughout the centuries European music has preserved closer ties with the old magical notions of art than have literature and painting; and that only in Europe has music made any attempt to embrace and to transcend humanity's most crucial development in

4

consciousness. As we might expect, the growth of music from ritual into art is manifest in a technical development – harmonic perspective – which is peculiar to the West. Significantly, it emerged at about the same time as visual perspective. We have noted that the timeless quality of primitive song and dance and of religious cantillation is inseparable from their purely melodic and rhythmic nature. A corporeal beat, endlessly repeated, destroys time even as it measures it, while a melodic-rhythmic pattern, insidiously reiterated, effaces the identity it would seem to establish; if we participate in this so-called 'primitive' music, we are unaware of beginning, middle and end and enter a timeless state of *identification* with the world we live in. Complementarily, a purely melodic line such as characterizes oriental chant – and the more elemental types of folk-song – will tend to be independent of metrical stress, moving freely in additive rather than divisive rhythms; and this asymmetry may be encouraged by the association of the vocal line with the rhythms of the spoken word. Moreover, this flexibility is unaffected by the fact that chants may sometimes be sung at different pitches simultaneously; indeed Peter Crossley-Holland has reported that Tibetan monks, chanting at what seems to be a multiplicity of pitches, are unaware that they are not uttering the same note! Most *ad hoc* polyphony and homophony in primitive folk and sophisticated oriental music is more accurately termed heterophony: in other words, the same line is sung by everyone with slight variations of pitch and rhythm, at first probably unconsciously, later with intent. Certainly these musics are not harmonic in our Western sense. Harmonic consciousness occurred only when simultaneously sounding tones created an *awareness* of duality, wherein two or more tones bore to one another different vibration ratios. The 'forms' of music may then become gradations of tension and relaxation existing in time; and it is significant that we may almost 'date' a moment when the implications of harmony were recognized as such.

In one of his last compositions – a four-voiced 'Ave Regina Coelorum' which he asked to have sung at his death-bed – Guillaume Dufay, canon-composer of fifteenth-century Rheims, incorporated an appeal to God to have mercy on his dying Dufay. This unmedieval intrusion of the personal (we may compare the portraits of the artist and/or donor that find their way into Renaissance paintings) provokes, too, a 'modern' harmonic technique. Up to this point the four-voiced music has absorbed its consonant triadic sensuousness into the continuous flow of melody. With the words *'miserere tui labentis Dufay'*, however, the liquid major triad sonorities are abruptly contradicted by a minor third; and the dramatic effect of this is inseparable from the fact that it implies opposition, and therefore dualism rather than monism. Because it is a shock, we are conscious of *when it happens*; momentarily, the music no longer carries us outside Time but makes us aware of history: the sands of time are running out.

One might almost encapsulate the story (history) of European music in terms of its three main phases of compositional technique. The first, **mono**phony, enshrines the *monos* of the One God in its single voice, which moves mainly by step and in rhythms untrammelled by the metrical beat of the earth; unsurprisingly such music is associated with the theocratically orientated 'circular' concepts of the Middle Ages. With the great watershed of the Renaissance, covering a period of two to three hundred years, the basic formulation of music becomes **poly**phony: 'many' voices, each in itself unfolding on principles analogous to those of medieval monophony, now cohere to create harmonic congruence. The device of the suspension, whereby a dissonant tone suspended on the 'strong' beat is resolved on the 'weak', is impossible except in reference to chronometric time. The suspended dissonance, stimulating complex vibrations, excites and hurts to varying degrees; thus the acceptance of time involves not only an awareness of beginnings, middles and ends, but also the consciousness of passion and of pain. This became more pressing the more human material existence seemed not so much a step towards eternity as a good in itself. Whereas monody is basically a religious act hingeing on the relationship of men and women to God, European polyphony involves their relationship both to their Creator and to their fellow creatures. William Byrd, the greatest composer of Shakespeare's day, spoke of the divine and the civic musics, the former exemplified in his masses and motets, the latter in his instrumental dance music. But the 'divine' and 'civic' techniques are mutually enriching; one could not exist without the other for, as we saw, polyphony is impossible without a temporal beat, however subtly disguised.

The third stage we call **homo**phony: here homogeneous men and women combine to create order – socially, politically and artistically. In musical terms, whereas polyphony aims at coexistent independence and mutuality is considered 'horizontally', homophony imposes order 'vertically', from the top down, on the contradictions of simultaneously sounding tones. Such a development was abetted by the flowering of aristocratic autocracy – the apotheosis of the Renaissance belief in man as potential arbiter of his destiny. Unsurprisingly, its supreme expression occurs in the fusion of all the arts that came to be called opera, which evolved during the early years of the seventeenth century. Opera, being a stylized imitation of human action, a play in music, implies that human actions are, by virtue of their humanity, worth imitating. The human order begins (homo-phonically) to efface the

6

divine; and the process is at once a triumph of human courage and a tragedy of human frailty; as Sir John Davies put it, in 1596, 'Man is a proud, and yet a wretched, Thing.'

In 1607 Monteverdi produced the earliest opera that has remained part of the standard repertory, and which has in a sense never been superseded. Significantly, it was based on a then fashionable myth: the legend of Orpheus, a man who aspired to godhead, controlling Nature, challenging even death itself. Technically, Monteverdi employed in his opera many elements from Europe's past, including 'religious' monody and religious-social polyphony. Increasingly, however, the core of his music becomes recitative: wherein the solo voice – an individualized man or woman – assumes primacy over the continuo instruments, which create the 'continuum' within which specific human creatures exist. *Identification* between the self and the world is no longer the aim; on the contrary, the solo voice seeks to define its *identity* as a godlike hero or heroine: an identity which the harmony usually supports.

This development is evident in one of the decisive moments in the history of music. As the Messenger recounts the story of Eurydice's death, the continuo chords shift abruptly from an E major triad (a key later to become a synonym for paradise) to a G minor triad (a key later to be associated with tragic conflict and often with death itself). This startling event affects us as a moment in chronological time, or history: *then* this happened, and nothing could ever be the same.

In the latter part of the seventeenth and the first half of the eighteenth century, European man did what he could to allay his fear and to succour belief in his absolutism. At a social and political level this is most conspicuous in the France of Louis XIV, where society was codified to the most meticulous detail, from the King down to rural peasants. In France, and then at the courts of the more dispersed, but no less materially powerful, princelings of Italy, salvation was sought, musically, through human-made tonal and rhythmic order. The fortuity and licence of seventeenth-century techniques crystallized into a schematic diatonic tonality, based, with what was believed to be scientific logic, on the cycle of fifths; and into symmetrically proportioned rhythms which were as 'architecturally' balanced as were the proportions of classical buildings, of which the prototype was no longer the church, but the theatre or opera-house. Music invokes 'Glory to Man in the Highest' by way of the 'closed' forms of binary dance (which, as originally danced by the nobility, was a representation of a human-made paradise on earth), and of the ternary *da capo* aria (which, admitting to human duality in its central section, evades its implications by a recap-

7

itulation of the first section, so that the form is non-evolutionary). Even Handelian fugal polyphony is designed to *fit into* the pre-ordained social-harmonic togetherness; and the fact that Bach, with his archaistic Lutheran German background, is the greatest polyphonist and contrapuntist in the history of music is the exception that proves the rule.

But the Classical Baroque's celebration of Man in the Highest always involved what we would call a wish-fulfilment, which could not long survive as 'civilization' became broader and more amorphous. Though Handel's noble perorations may sound sublimely assured, even at times complacent, his greatness lies in the fact that his human leaders, aspiring to godhead, prove to be tragically fallible. As society was slowly democratized, a blind acceptance of authority imposed from 'above' was no longer tenable. On the way to rational Enlightenment, people recognized that even the god-king grew old and died. Democratic individuals had to seek a more reasonable authority: this they could find only by looking within themselves, by putting their own houses in order before they could assume responsibility for each other. This is what the next great phase in European music – that of sonata – is about; and it was centred in Austria, and in particular Vienna, because the city was a crucial melting-pot of the nations from which democracy would emerge. Whereas Classical Baroque forms are basically if not exclusively 'closed' and monistic, the forms of classical sonata are 'open' and dualistic. Music seeks identity *through* conflict: as is spelt out in the themes of Mozart's simultaneously comic and tragic (and therefore dualistic) operas, which turn on tension between an inherited aristocratic order and the new world of democratic men and women – such as barbers and ladies' maids. These dualities are incarnate in the music's compromise between the old closed conventions of binary dance and ternary aria and the new, dynamic, open principle of sonata.

Ultimately, an individual's discovery of his or her identity is an inner psychological process, however manifest it may be in the world outside. This is clear in Beethoven's self-contained instrumental forms. In his symphonies and still more his sonatas and quartets, form becomes a search for the undivided whole within the psyche. No longer – not even in his solitary opera, which is a public dramatization of a private inner conflict – is form imposed in accordance with the values of Church or State, or even with an abstract concept like musical tradition; it is rather a morphological process of discovery, wherein predictability is increasingly undermined by surprise. And if in his symphonies Beethoven still sees his music as having a public function in that the discovery of (his) identity is relevant to the fulfilment of a democratic ideal in society, rendered apprehensible by being

8

played to relatively large numbers of people in relatively large halls, it is also true that throughout Beethoven's life the relationship between the public and the private dimensions grew increasingly complex. His deafness, indeed, was at once a physiological fact and a psychological allegory; at least from the Op. 59 quartets onwards, Beethoven's inner life, as manifest in his linear techniques, is no longer a Faustian pilgrimage towards a specific end. Increasingly his music deals in human *potential*, adumbrating *alternative futures*. In this he remains the most progressively 'modern' composer we have.

Up to this point, then, one may say that music began as magic, a dynamo that supplies practical living with the energy that drives it. 'Primitive' people live in their music while it lasts, and are unconcerned with personal communication. This magic overlaps into the religious affirmations of the great Oriental cultures and of medieval Christendom, wherein music's function is to transcend the material self. With the European Renaissance, temporality and ego jointly prosper, until sixteenth-century polyphony achieves an equilibrium between the civic and the divine. The dance-dominated structures of the seventeenth and eighteenth centuries assert self-responsible control; duality between public and private life widens, until music comes to have two distinct functions, one of which whiles away empty time, while the other – supremely in the later music of Beethoven – seeks to conquer time and heal breaches, rediscovering an identity between self and not-self.

Beethoven dealt with inner tensions through the abstraction of instrumental forms. Wagner, who regarded himself, to a degree justifiably, as Beethoven's successor, was an opera composer, though his opera is no longer an imitation of human action in a social context, but a projection of his inner life into archetypal terms. The ultimate triumph of European ego-consciousness lies in the fact that the Wagnerian opera house at Bayreuth, erected through the agency of a young, mad king, is a temple wherein the worshippers congregate to celebrate the self in a total art form made possible only by the superhuman (godly?) might of industrial capitalism, the ultimate material apotheosis of Renaissance ideology.

Paradoxically, what Wagner's last operas reveal is the *twilight* of Europe's egomaniac gods. He borrowed the Tristan theme from the theocratic Middle Ages, when the old Europe was dying. Tristan's name means *triste*; born out of death, he suffers the wound of duality, and dies into life, ending the egoistic cycle of humanism. So at the apex of European 'consciousness' Wagner does what those Eskimo children were doing in handing back to God the tribute of breath. His passion-laden chromatic harmony carries the

9

burden of our hundreds of years of purgatorial aspiration, suffering and guilt, and returns them to unconscious nirvana. Technically, Wagner thus reverses the process that had occurred in the late sixteenth and early seventeenth centuries. Then, the intrusion of chromatic notes into vocally modal, plainsong-like lines had weakened the freely fugal principles of polyphony; and the destructive force of harmonic shock and metrical surprise (as manifest in the recitative of Orfeo's Messenger) had to be counteracted by new, dance-founded principles of musical-social order. Now, in *Tristan* and the closely related *Parsifal*, Wagner's chromaticism effects a weakening, if not the demise, of those principles of tonal and metrical order. From horizontalized chromatic chords Wagner evolves what he called an 'endless Melos': a quasi-religious quasi-polyphony that identifies reality with a transcendent mystical act. The return to nirvana is initiated in the Prelude to Act III, when the ripe swell of harmonic tensions evaporates into rootless whole-tone progressions, or rather non-progressions; and Tristan is awakened from near-paralysis (which we would call a nervous breakdown) by the *monody* of a primitive Shepherd's pipe. This rural incantation is a monophonically 'horizontalized' version of the interlaced perfect and imperfect fourths and fifths (traditionally musical synonyms for God and Devil) which, in the very first bars of the opera, had made Tristan's anguish incarnate.

Tristan's disintegrative chromaticism and the Shepherd's reintegrative monody (which sounds simultaneously occidental and oriental) release us from the self and from the trammels of Europe's harmonic consciousness. Self-deification, however courageous, cannot but imply a fragmentation of socially attested values, for few can believe sufficiently in the self to sustain the chaos it unlooses. This is why *Tristan* is often called the beginning of modern music; and we have only to look at the major composers of our century to recognize our divisiveness. Half a century ago the central figures – Debussy, Stravinsky, Bartók, Schoenberg and Hindemith – were already established. All still seem considerable forces, though Hindemith is no longer a mover and shaker: almost certainly because he alone of those major talents denied the experience of *Tristan*. Admittedly his start was in German romanticism of a Brahmsian and Schumanesque tinge; but his philosophy of music became a deliberate attempt to salvage classical traditions, especially as manifest in the motor rhythm and continuous line of Bach: an attempt unlikely to satisfy without the religious-social faith that made Bach possible.

Schoenberg still maintains his seminal position, though he was wrong in claiming that he had settled the destiny of European music for the foreseeable future, and his music has made little inroad into the normal repertory.

Yet his centrality is attested by the fact that his music stems from two prime sources: late Wagner and late Beethoven. The string sextet that made him famous might be considered as an appendix to *Tristan*, for it is a one-movement instrumental opera with a title, *Transfigured Night*, that exactly defines *Tristan*'s theme. Wordless, it tells a story parallel to Tristan's arche-typal myth: love is consummated, guilt absolved, in a 'transfigured' night of unconscious ecstasy wherein love and death become one. The sextet's chromaticism and 'endless melos' are *Tristan* in so ripe a stage of dis-integration that they lead Schoenberg into his 'free' atonal phase, wherein the tonal and formal props of eighteenth- and nineteenth-century tradition are no longer operative. Not surprisingly, the works of this period are either very short, being sensory moments sufficient unto themselves; or, if long, are supportive of a literary-theatrical text, as in *Erwartung*, which has more or less the same theme as *Verklärte Nacht*, though its descent into the night of unconsciousness is murkier, its implications more obscure.

But Schoenberg, rooted in Austrian tradition, could not be content to find a be-all and end-all in the sensory moment, however transcendent; and in seeking renewal he was an heir to Beethoven, whose 'morphological' processes suggested possibilities of linear organization wherein Schoenberg found the germ of his (fully chromatic) serialism. In his Hebraic-Christian opera *Moses and Aaron* he confronts Beethoven's lifelong search for the undivided whole, with the crucial difference that he did not find it. Though the serial row may be 'God's will', Schoenberg left his opera unfinished, breaking off at the phrase 'O Word that I lack'.

Of the major composers of our century Hindemith and Schoenberg are closest to what had become the mainstream European tradition. Bartók now seems an equally great composer, but more peripheral in that he owed much to his agrarian environment in Hungary. He discovered himself in rediscovering folk traditions that in themselves counteracted 'Western' intellectual values, and suggested musical techniques that, in modality, rhythm and sonority, were alternatives to Teutonic harmony and homo-phony. He once said that he hoped to effect liaison between the three European masters he most admired – Bach, Beethoven, and Debussy. Seen or heard through a pristine folk orality, Bach's fugal unities and continuing rhythms merge into primitive ostinato techniques, while Beethoven's sonata-style handling of tonal and metrical contradiction acquires, in con-junction with primitively orgiastic rhythms, an explosively re-creative force. The catalyst is Debussy, whose sensory 'moments' are used by Bartók to evoke – in the magical *night*-musics – pre-conscious states of being still accessible to those living in, or in contact with, agrarian societies. One also

11

finds this sensual speech in Bartók's Moravian contemporary Janáček, who sometimes created creature-musics as immediate as those of the Bushmen in the African forests, and who always envisaged human social life in the context of Nature. He now seems a figure of perhaps even greater physical and imaginative potency than Bartók.

Bartók's 'catalyst', Debussy, was French. Outside Austrian tradition, he was the more readily able to exploit the subversive implications of *Tristan*. His purely melodic *Syrinx* for solo flute reinstates music as magic, echoing the monodic piping of Tristan's Shepherd: basically pentatonic in contour, but filigreed with oriental arabesques and with microtonal distortions of pitch. More usually, Debussy's music stems from *Tristan*esque and *Parsifal*-like harmonic 'moments', while carrying subversion beyond Wagner. For whereas Wagner still yearned, however abortively, for the resolution of harmonic tension, Debussy accepts the higher chromatic – especially the 'rootless' whole-tone – chords as ends in themselves. Harmony may be deprived of antecedence and consequence, so that we live in the sensory moment. Since Debussy said that 'Nature' had more to offer him than 'civilization', it is not surprising that the Javanese music he heard at the Paris Exhibition proved a spiritual revelation rather than an exotic excitation. Instead of 'projecting' the ego, he would live, like the Edenic Javanese, in an eternal continuum of sound. A 'retreat from the West' is patent not only in the monodic-pentatonic *Syrinx* and in the often gamelan-like whole-tone non-progressions of his piano pieces, but even in the textures of his large-scale symphonic works, including *La Mer*, which is the closest he came to dialectical symphonic argument.

Debussy's revocation of pagan gods in *Syrinx* was composed in 1913, on the eve of the First World War that may have been the beginning of the end of the West. In the same year Stravinsky was gestating his *Rite of Spring* – a sacrificial murder and fertility rite presented as a ballet for highly sophisticated people, by no less sophisticated dancers and choreographers, with a mammoth symphony orchestra made possible, like Wagner's orchestra, only by the resources of industrial technocracy. If Stravinsky is the supreme representative of modern divisiveness it is because he more than anyone – with the possible exception of Picasso – confronts our cataclysmic fragmentation, our divorce of Apollo from Dionysus, of head from body. In the neo-primitive phase that sprang from his youth in Old Russia, he tempers fairy-tale irreality, deriving from Wagner and Skriabin by way of Rimsky-Korsakov, with a resurgence of pagan primitivism at once affirmative and destructive. *The Rite of Spring* and *Les Noces* use modern orchestral forces in a mainly percussive manner; they are ritual games of let's-pretend carried through with such electrifying intensity that they seemed literal threats to a war-racked world.

Deracinated from his native Russia by Revolution as well as war, Stravinsky produced in Swiss exile *The Soldier's Tale*. This theatre piece, explicitly about exile, effected a wry perversion of the progressive Faust legend, reassembling fragments of Russia's and Europe's past, along with America's future in a jazzily cubist aural geometry. This initiated Stravinsky's second creative life, when he'd settled in Paris after the war: for in his so-called neo-classical period he attempts to salvage shattered Europe, even in the heart of the Waste Land. A line from Eliot's seminal poem of 1921 – 'These fragments have I shored against our ruins' – is a precise description of what Stravinsky does in correlating snippets of Europe's past from Lully, Bach, Pergolesi, Mozart, Clementi and others. In the greatest works of this period, notably *Oedipus Rex* and *A Symphony of Psalms*, Dionysus and Apollo are creatively mated, as are the sophistications of Europe with the primitive energy of Old Russia.

Stravinsky's interpretation of the story of Oedipus inverts post-Renaissance man's attempt at self-deification, a process continued when, as a consequence of a Second World War, he experienced a second deracination. Significantly, he inaugurated his American phase with a ballet (1947) dealing directly with the Orpheus story. Monteverdi and his successors in the Western world had taken the legend as a tribute to human, nearly superhuman, courage; Stravinsky reinstates the catastrophic conclusion of the Greek original, wherein Orpheus is punished for his patriarchal pride, being dismembered by the maenads or Terrible Mothers. The religious motif, here negatively covert, becomes overt in most of the creations of Stravinsky's American years, in which, beginning with the *Cantata* of 1952, he adopts a highly personal form of serialism related more to the medievally affiliated Webern than to Schoenberg himself. Throughout his long life Stravinsky had searched for icons: first in primitive ritual, then in European time-and-space travelling, finally in this 'pre-ordained' quasi-medieval serialism, which proffers a Law beyond time and space. How far this amounts to a faith, how far it is a wish-fulfilment, remains an open question. Unsurprisingly, the works of the octogenerian Stravinsky do not have the electrifying physical and metaphysical charge of the greatest creations of his middle years. None the less they are testaments that speak hopefully on our behalf.

If Stravinsky is the most representative composer of the Old World in the last ditch, his contemporary Charles Ives occupies a no less crucial position in relation to his New World and to its – and our – future. Stravinsky was a traveller both geographically and artistically: a conservative cosmopolitan, backed by acceptance of, if not entire faith in, his Russian, Greek and Roman churches, even while recording Europe's disintegration. Ives, Stravinsky's polar opposite yet complement, never left the States, accepting their chaos as well as their burgeoning promise. From one point of view he was a high romantic composer, whose great *Concord* piano sonata may be regarded as a not unworthy successor to Beethoven's *Hammerklavier*. Yet even in the *Concord* Sonata Ives is a democratic composer not merely in translating late Beethoven's transcendentalism into New England terms, but also in a more general sense: for he found his materials in the world around him, with few if any distinctions between the artistic and the demotic. His music consisted of sounds made and heard by people in a multiplicity of social contexts. If these sounds include art music, especially that of the 'manly' classical composers like Beethoven, they also embrace hymns and marches, the ragtime and jazz of bars and shanty-town caffs. It was basic to Ives's American pragmatism that, despite his technical skill, acute ear and exceptional intelligence, he deliberately remained an amateur. He was a most uncommon Common Man who, while making a fortune in the insurance business he genuinely believed to be for the betterment of humanity, discovered and defined through his music a morality and a faith. That, in accord with his pragmatism, was at once real and transcendental: so his Fourth Symphony, his most adventurous piece, mingles inwardly psychological dialectic with a gallimaufry of hymns, marches, rags and boogie. Such a creative hurly-burly, reflecting the American small-town and city, inevitably finds expression in half-formalized notations – at the opposite extreme to Stravinsky's finicky precision.

Here and elsewhere Ives's democratic techniques embrace not only 'musical' sounds but also random acoustic phenomena (bands passing one another on the march, music heard over water, and so on); parody, game-playing and problem-solving; partial and total recall of past experience; the mechanics and semantics of improvisation both within and without formal composition. Many years later such notions were to be explored by the American and European avant-garde. And while Ives's prophetic qualities are not what makes him a great composer, they testify to his crucial significance as a composer 'between' worlds. Maybe only in the next century will the full implications of his achievement be clear.

Ives's empirical music is always unpredictable yet always unsurprising, since it accepts *what is*: as do the subversive Europeans, notably Debussy and Stravinsky, and as did the French-American iconoclast Edgard Varèse who, trained as a mathematical engineer, made a music constructed partly on primitively ritualistic principles and partly on architectural and scientific principles such as rock and crystal formation. (Today, he has a successor in the Greek Iannis Xenakis, likewise trained as mathematician and engineer.) But Debussy, Stravinsky, Varèse and probably Xenakis still belong in part to the traditions of 'art' music, which Ives, in his telescoping of past, present and future, in part overrode. Emerson's fabled riposte to the theosophical lady who announced that she accepted the Universe ('Madame, you'd better.') is applicable to Ives in both its splendour and its irony. And in this respect Ives has a social and philosophical counterpart in another composer of a New World, albeit that of South rather than North America.

The Brazilian Heitor Villa-Lobos is not, by the standards of a Bach or Beethoven or for that matter an Ives, a great composer; he is however an extraordinary phenomenon, who encourages reflection on the relation between the artist and the community in a pluralistic, hopefully democratic world like ours. His documentary significance is inherent in the very nature of Latin America, which is neither a new world nor an old. As background in his native land Villa-Lobos had an immensely ancient if moribund Indian civilization and a still tenuously extant Indian peasant culture. In the foreground he found survivals of Spanish–Portuguese and other European conquests and explorations, an African Negroid culture precipitated from the slave trade, and a rapidly encroaching, streamlined mechanistic culture exuding from the United States. So Villa-Lobos's fecund imagination teemed with images of the Brazilian jungle, of the lost Indian cities, of Spanish and Portuguese colonial architecture, of voodooistic African rites, and of the American skyscraper and roadhouse. The musical synonyms for these cultural cross-currents included Indian peasant musics, Negro song and dance, frail vestiges of Hispanic ecclesiastical polyphony harking back to missionary days, Spanish and Portuguese rural folk music, European and American urban pop musics deriving from the eighteenth to the twentieth centuries. All these cultural layers coexist, hardly integrated with one another, in contrast to the fusion of primitive and civilized elements in the music of Europeans like Bartók and Janáček or even, with more self-conscious sophistication, in Stravinsky.

It is obvious that in his jungle-like appetite for life in the raw Villa-Lobos has something in common with Ives. Both were avid for the demotic multifariousness of their environment; but whereas Ives, the greater and more central composer, sought a new world materially and spiritually, Villa-Lobos combined a Latin exuberance with a Latin passivity. Accepting the chaos of the contemporary scene, he seems to have been almost entirely unself-critical. This is why his music impresses most when it is most fortuitous. But if this is a limitation to Villa-Lobos's status as an artist, it is the source of his strength as a phenomenon. Though he picked up much of value to him during his belated student days in Paris – metaphorphosing Debussyan and Ravellian dream-music into the Latin American *recherche du temps perdu* known as *saudades* – it doesn't follow that his most technically expert works are his most convincing. Certainly the wellsprings of his creativity had little to do with Europe's civilized artifices, but stemmed direct from his early environment. Brazilian folk and street musicians relished the Latin American jam session known as *choros*, at which any number of players, equipped with guitar, mandolin, flute, ophicleide, trumpet, trombone and a miscellany of indigenous percussion instruments, roamed the night bars and cafés, improvising a collage of fragmented folk and pop songs, with reminiscences of polite parlour musics thrown in for good measure. Since such was Villa-Lobos's musical initiation in childhood and adolescence it is not surprising that his many *choros*-styled works, scored for anything from a single guitar to an immense symphony orchestra, are composed music of which the notations are slapdash. In many cases a definitive score neither exists nor would be appropriate, since Villa-Lobos rejoices in maximum prolixity of detail swept on a tide of maximum rhythmic momentum.

While Villa-Lobos's wildest works – such as the breath-taking *Rudepoema* for piano, the corybantic *Nonet* and, in smaller vein, the *Suite* for voice and violin, all written in the early 1920s – are his best, it didn't worry him, as it would worry us Europeans, that he poured out a stream of literally countless works – he lost track around the thousand mark – working on the principle of hit or, more often, miss. Nor did he clearly differentiate between pieces that came out wildly *sui generis*, like those revocations of jungloid violence mentioned above, and those that found themselves cast in some conventionally academic-romantic mould, like the guitar concerto, or were spawned into the pop-pap of the Rio parlour, saloon or cocktail lounge. All was grist to the mill because Villa-Lobos was little concerned about the 'work of art', vividly responsive to the musical needs of his community. This remains true though he was not, in fact, a savage but a man of unusual charisma, playing a potent part in the metamorphosis of 'primitive' Brazil into a modern civilization, allied to her North American counterpart. In this knowledge or awareness he devised his series of works called *Bachianas Brasileiras*, which sought for synthesis between Bach's counterpoint and motor-rhythms and the metrical and sonorous excitations of his Brazilian heritage. Most of these more artful works date from the 1930s rather than from his vintage years in the 1920s; improbably, they demonstrate that there are affinities between some of Bach's inherited compositional principles and

16

those Villa-Lobos arrived at by topical and local trial and error. The fairly well-known first *Bachianas Brasileiras* for eight cellos achieves a Bachian fusion of sustained line with harmonic and textural density. The opulence, not being a faith attested or received, lacks Bach's tense serenity, but it has more of Bach's spirit than have Hindemith's conscious imitations. In the slow movement – a *modinha* or sentimental urban pop song derived from a nineteenth-century Portuguese tradition – nostalgia becomes a positive virtue. Listening to it, one understands how Brasilia, the miraculous New City, could arise from the jungle, while one also senses in the music's haunting melancholy how that New World may obliterate the very heart of the old.

This fusion of worlds and of genres is most strikingly manifest in the best known of the *Bachianas*, the fifth: which incorporates a wordless vocalise that has acquired the status of a pop number, graduating to the televisual commercials. The tune is marvellous, magical, and memorable; and this brings us to the reasons why the Villa-Lobos 'phenomenon' bears on our situation in the Western world, where barriers between art, folk, jazz and pop are also being broken down. It is pertinent to note that many of Villa-Lobos's 'wildest' works, such as the brilliantly written piano suites *Prole do Bebê* of 1921–3, are concerned with childhood, whether recapturing his own, or evoking an indigenous Eden rampant with birds and beasts that squawk and yowl more startlingly than those portrayed by Messiaen forty or more years later, and almost as naturalistically as those emulated by the Kalahari Bushmen. For Villa-Lobos, however artful in technique, is not so much a traditional 'art' composer as a composer of fiesta; and in this context we may note that one of today's most talented pop musicians, the Brazilian singer–pianist–composer Tania Maria, makes a jazzy pop in many ways comparable with Villa-Lobos's quasi-art music. Her songs, too, draw on memories of childhood and live in timeless moments of fiesta, embracing forest, village, and the cocktail lounges and discos of Rio. The samba-style polymetres and the harmonic and figurative luxuriance of her piano vividly recall Villa-Lobos's pianism, though it is improbable that Tania was 'influenced' by him except to the degree that no educated Rio woman of her generation could have escaped the impact of his work on Brazilian music education in schools and colleges.

If Villa-Lobos is a phenomenon of greater import than the intrinsic value of his compositions, the reason is that he has sundered barriers between 'works' of art and oral intuition in a manner made possible only by the transitional nature of the society he lived in. In North America, with its sturdy white Puritan heritage, there was a dichotomy, rather than fusion,

17

of values, though from the tense interplay of cultures sprang forces that have shaped the modern world. For music is not, whatever our Western attitudes may have tried to make of it, an object 'out there' to be bought and sold; it is a means – for Africans (whether in their native environment as referred to at the beginning of this essay, or in their alien white land) probably the main means – whereby people explore actual and potential relationships to one another. In the conditions of indigence and oppression in which New World blacks were obliged to live, music became a technique for survival; and although all music must, in the deepest sense and to some degree, be this, Afro-American music is indubitably the ultimate instance of art's therapeutic efficacy. The story is painful but triumphant, as African work-and-play songs and dances merge into Afro-American gospel music and blues, and so through the multifaceted strands of urban jazz to the no less various and contrarious warp and woof of industrialized rock and tribal pop – assimilating *en route* white literacy in the forms of march, hymn and hill-billy.

Why did the music of an alienated, oppressed, often persecuted black minority make so potent an impression on the entire industrialized world? That the violence of the impact was in part a consequence of fear is patent; negative emotions of moral outrage were a trigger response to the presumed threat of black virility, not merely in the sexual sense. But this cannot be the whole story; more significant, because deeper, is a positive response – a half-conscious recognition that black orality may be more conducive to happiness and health than the aesthetic traditions which Europe had pain-fully evolved over many centuries, only to end up, musically, with a consumer society wherein concert-hall and symphony orchestra, mas-terminded by producer, composer and conductor on principles exactly analogous to a factory, offered to individual members of the audience or congregation little or no active participation in the event. Compared with a jazz session, or even a pop festival, our concert schedule is often an audible museum, in which the music (and still more opera) presented is that of a not too distant, cosily familiar past: a self-regarding hermeticism that may be interpretated, in narrowly political terms, as an ossification contrived by a threatened if not wilfully malign Establishment.

Confusedly, the anger and violence of black people – understandable in the context of their place in industrial society – elicited a response in white people because it dimly echoed their own half-conscious awareness that humanity today is, in D.H. Lawrence's phrase, 'like an uprooted tree'. At the same time white people admired, even envied, the corporeal affirmation of life in the present moment that they perceived in black people. They could be moved by instinctive creativity, though they were themselves seldom expert at it – until in the second half of the century the newly created phenomenon of the relatively affluent young metamorphosed it into their own neo-tribal music of simultaneous protest and celebration. It is relevant to note that black jazz singing and instrumental playing often emulate the 'music of the vowels', the language of birds, beasts and insects, inherent in Jacob Boehme's 'sensual speech' mentioned at the beginning of this essay, and again in reference to Bartók and Villa-Lobos; and that this activity is more self-consciously imitated by tribal pop groups, many of whom sport animalistic names from Beatles and Monkees to Boomtown Rats. Moreover, such fundamental returns *ab ovo* now dominate some so-called avant-garde musics, in the guise of minimal or process music. Philosophically, this harks back almost half a century to the early works of the philosopher–sociologist–composer John Cage, who still makes pieces encouraging us to become part of the 'continuum' of our aural environment. The notorious 'silent' piece, *4'33"*, is the ultimate example of this, since in listening to the non-silence that occurs when the pianist fails to play the piano, we make our own music out of the noises of the world-as-it-is. Process composers *per se* are more equivocal, for they aim to re-create the eternal present of the sound continuum of (past) primitive societies by way of drones, ostinati and patterned reiterations. In the case of Steve Reich this concept stemmed from first-hand experience of African, Balinese and other exotic musics, translated into the mechanism of industrial society. Other minimalists, notably Philip Glass, make a music more cannily contrived, which has achieved a popularity no less than that of tribal rock, and for the same reason. It engulfs consciousness, and in a sense can be said to celebrate death at the expense of life. Minimalism and tribal pop need not, but often do, become phenomena not readily distinguishable from muzak or 'wallpaper' music.

The paradox at the heart of these musics lies in the fact that although they instigate rituals to alleviate the strains and stresses of industrial life, they must call on advanced technology in order to do so. One might say the same of Stockhausen who, at least since *Stimmung* of 1968, has become a self-styled guru to our sick age, a musician–scientist–priest who has revealed that modern science and ancient magic are not the opposite poles that rational enlightenment had supposed them to be. With or without electronic assistance, *Stimmung* releases us from chronometric time not merely by reinstating mythological time but also by giving musical meaning to modern theories of space–time and relativity, of cosmological and astrological time, and to those biological and astronomical clocks we now know to function, independent of chronometers, within the human subconscious and apparently within the senses of animals, birds, insects, even plants. Ironically, Stockhausen's abnegation of many Western values finds manifestation in almost Wagnerian delusions of grandeur! Given the ambiguity of the human condition at this stage in our troubled history, one can hardly 'blame' him for this. It is none the less a relief that a composer such as Arvo Pärt may still reinvoke 'spirit' with innocence and authenticity. If he is not 'adequate' to the complexities of the modern world, who could be, and is this even a desirable ideal?

Certainly, although the importance of the rediscovery of oral–aural traditions in our head-obsessed world cannot easily be exaggerated, we need sometimes to pause for thought. It is true that we have produced a world of scientific know-how which, cognizant of means but not ends, of price but not value, may literally blow us up. None the less, Western 'consciousness of being conscious' has also produced Shakespeare and Beethoven; and this does bring into human experience a dimension that no oral culture has known or can know. One may make the distinction in these terms: oral musics deal in human *solidarity*, without which we cannot survive; but a Western composer, making a 'work' of art as distinct from the momentary fiesta of *homo ludens*, deals, or at least may deal, in human *solitariness* – the ultimate condition, as King Lear discovered, of an unaccommodated being. Lear – like Beethoven – is the supreme instance; and perhaps I may, in conclusion, be permitted a personal gloss to explain what I mean.

Some years ago I was privileged to introduce, at a summer school, a series of recitals in which that unassumingly great Beethovenian, Bernard Roberts, played the complete cycle of Beethoven's piano sonatas in chronological sequence. At the end I found myself murmuring – not for the first time, and echoing the late Hans Keller – 'Beethoven is the greatest man who ever lived'. Such a notion is totally irrelevant to an oral–aural society wherein art is fiesta, and is perhaps not very pertinent to the mechanized version of such a community we are producing through the electronic media. Yet is it altogether nonsensical? True, Beethoven, like every artist, was moulded by the forces that made his age, and in one obvious sense the meaning of the *Eroica* Symphony then is not the same as its meaning now. Yet in another and more fundamental sense, the meaning is the same, since Beethoven's cycles of death and birth are perennial and, in our pseudo-scientific parlance, archetypal. Many people among today's vast audience for the *Eroica* listen to it because it is familiar; more *go on* listening to it because it never can be familiar since it is, in Ezra Pound's phrase, 'news that *stays* news'.

So while it is possible, even probable, that there will be 'civilized' communities to which Shakespeare and Beethoven will be irrelevant, I cannot think that the Western world, having created a Shakespeare and Beethoven, can passively acquiesce in their obliteration. Because of the awareness of the 'pain of consciousness' which they represent, any oral culture we might have could never be the same as that of the Africans, whatever one might learn from them about human happiness. If black jazz is essential therapy so, in a sublimer and psychologically more universal sense, is Beethoven's music, about which Beethoven himself remarked in reference to his *Missa Solemnis*, that 'he who truly understands this music will be freed thereby from all the miseries of the world.' Begging the implications of that adverb 'truly', this is not a meaningless statement; it may even be, in terms of the human psyche, truly true. In this context I recall some words of Sibelius: 'I do believe in civilization. Look at the great nations of Europe and what they have endured. No savage could have withstood so much.' And if one retorts that such a remark is self-defensive and that the moment-celebrating Africans and Balinese were better off without such self-inflicted agony, one has also to admit that Shakespeare and Beethoven, supreme representatives of 'Europe', have something worth defending.

It would seem that our future, if we have one, has no choice but to evolve by way of the kind of compromise detected in the life-work of men such as Ives and Villa-Lobos, even though they may not be the 'greatest' composers our frightful century can offer. Revealingly, we may find such a composer within the world of commerce itself, for Broadway and Tin Pan Alley produced in George Gershwin a genius whose major piece, *Porgy and Bess*, deals with precisely the dichotomy we've been discussing: the tension between art and commerce in a black world and a white; between heart and head, Dionysus and Apollo. From this apparent contradiction Gershwin creates not just a good musical, but a great opera. The terms have become interchangeable, for genius, like God, has many mansions. Stockhausen's *Stimmung* ends, or rather ceases, with a return to God of the gift of breath, exactly analogous to that of those Eskimo children. Gershwin's opera ends with his crippled black hero setting out in his rickety go-cart, to travel from the Deep South to distant industrial New York, seeking his Eternal Beloved who will almost certainly have been destroyed by Sportin Life (a *light* mulatto) and his Happy Dust – which is also the American Dream. The parable is exact: industrial technocracy is being reborn in the interests of humanity. How wonderful that, half a century ago, Gershwin created this music that makes us want to go on living, however hopeless the odds.

21

PART I

People and Music

EDITED BY
John Paynter

2

Music and People:
The Import of Structure and Form

JOHN PAYNTER

The story of music is the story of the human race. In every part of the world there is a tradition of music-making stretching back so far that its origins are unlikely ever to be discovered. All this musical activity relates in some way to the everyday lives of people.

Social change and technical developments have influenced the use of music and have altered attitudes towards it and towards those who create it, but nothing has diminished the rate of its production; if anything, that has surely increased. Today, in almost every part of life, we have come to expect music or we are at least obliged to tolerate it.

Yet the easier it is to have access to faithfully reproduced music, and the more that people draw upon those resources, the greater would seem to be the emphasis upon extra-musical interest. Perhaps it has something to do with receiving so much from loudspeakers; distinctive qualities begin to merge, and attention needs something else to focus upon. We have the paradox of people wanting music for non-musical reasons. It would also appear that the very unpopularity of certain kinds of music may, on occasion, be a greater attraction for some of its adherents than the music itself. Music is a serious business but just how seriously do we take it?

At first glance we might conclude that, whatever need there is for music in the modern world, it does not have the significance it had in former times; the more music we have, the less we value it, the less it means anything of real importance to us. However, we should be wary of seeing changes of use as being inevitably for the worse. Over the centuries the

25

variety of music's functions has increased, and it would be unwise to try to identify any one as more important than another. For example, if we consider, on the one hand, direct participation in music, at some time in the past, as an integral part of social or religious ritual, preparation for battle or the celebration of victory, and, on the other hand, the apparently detached position of a listener today, in the concert hall or alone with hi-fi loudspeakers or headphones, who can say which represents the deeper musical involvement? If the use of music seems largely to have shifted from people making it themselves for specific social, religious or political reasons to an apparently less committed receiving of the music-making of others, primarily as entertainment, that does not alter the fact that, all other associations apart, it is still music that people want. What is at the heart of that experience? What makes music matter so much?

Essentially, to engage with the felt rather than measured durations of music is to appropriate what Langer (1953: 109) calls 'virtual time'. This has little to do with the surface details of musical style: it includes anything that behaves as music, 'popular' and 'serious'; and it applies as much to the shortest piece, the most unsophisticated little song, as it does to elaborate symphonies, operas, Indian classical music or African drum ensembles that may last for several hours. It is what happens to the sounds and the musical ideas that matters. The smallest modifications of amplitude or emphasis, all nuances and inflexions, combine to 'describe' the structure that creates the whole piece. Some pieces of music are long, some are short, but each is complete in itself, an indivisible whole. Further performances may vary the details to a greater or lesser extent, but every performance will recreate the essential wholeness. The length may be determined by other events – ritual or drama, for instance; and then again, pieces of music will normally relate to the prevailing expectations (different in different parts of the world or at different periods in history) of how long such an experience should last – and, in consequence, what is likely to be acceptable and what may be deemed either inadequate or tedious. Irrespective of the culture of period or place, the essence of musical experience is the perception of music's duration: how it is made to go on in time and – most significantly – how it is made to stop.

This is not to suggest that more obvious elements of music – melodies, rhythmic patterns, timbres, associated words, gestures, and so on – are unimportant. On the contrary, these are the qualities for immediate delight; they engage our attention, we are moved by them, receive their message, and often remember them with deep and lasting pleasure. In some respects they are the most important features because their characteristics are the content which determines the form. In isolation, however, they have less significance. The ultimate musical power is released only through the careful elaboration, extension and development of these elements to make a form which completes itself within a duration which performers and listeners perceive as appropriate to the nature of the ideas. It is this model of time which gives true musical satisfaction.

Obviously, when anyone listens to music or performs it, any such notion of a 'model' will probably be far below the surface, and may never be articulated, even in a lifetime of musical experience. But this is no more surprising than that, in those for whom, say, watching football has become a way of life, the excitement and enjoyment of a match is most likely to be driven be deep-seated and intense feelings of comradeship, loyalty, and a sense of completeness in the final overcoming, all of which may be glimpsed but will probably remain undefined.

The things that excite the deepest passions, the worries and fears that confront humanity in its late twentieth-century global village, are not very different from those that aroused similar feelings in our remote ancestors. Two in particular are as insoluble – and possibly as frightening – as ever: fathomless space and unstoppable time, which together remind us of our inability to create a perfection that will remain.

The arts mediate between us and our environment, most particularly in relation to those fundamental constraints. The depiction of events in space offers aesthetic pleasure in the art object itself, but is also very clearly an attempt to come to terms with the idea of space, in some degree to 'fix' space in an accessible (and, by implication, satisfying – or even comforting) frame. Similarly, architecture delights us with its forms but is in essence a way of controlling space. Pyramids in ancient Egypt and bronze age burial barrows were constructed as complete 'worlds', and the great European cathedrals were (in Patrick Nuttgens's words) intended to be 'like nothing on earth', their forms helping the medieval mind to cope with the endlessness of heavenly space. The towering steel and glass of our modern commercial and public buildings may, at first sight, tell us more about earthly than heavenly power, but here too we find the age-old defiance of space, spectacularly enclosing the unfathomable within dazzling atriums that seem to emulate the mind-boggling grasp of space we experience in the cathedrals of Chartres, York and Cologne.

The parallel with music is obvious. Unencompassable space is troubling enough, and puzzling; but time reminds us of mortality. Music can delight and amuse us, can give us simple tune-humming, foot-tapping pleasure or move us deeply with melody and harmony. But the experience of music lifts us out of ourselves, not merely in sensuous enjoyment of the surface features but principally by the way the music starts, goes on and stops. The felt duration encapsulates time in an idealized state, holding up the process of decay.

This is evident in the long history of work songs. Singers are by no means unable to recognize and articulate the deeper currents symbolized by the structures of these songs – as Bruce Jackson's interviews with the inmates of Texas prisons have revealed:

> When a man get to singing, he doesn't get time to think about the problems or the work.
>
> I can do a whole lot more work workin' by time than I can workin' loose. ... When I sing, picking cotton, before I know anything I be three blocks ahead.
>
> The day wouldn't seem so hard. Even if we did have to stay here so long, we would soon forget about it and time just pass on by like that. That's one way of doin' time.
>
> (Texas prisoners quoted in Jackson 1972)

Work songs enable the singers to triumph over hard or even harsh conditions by 'possessing' time. Mark Booth suggests that buying records also makes time graspable:

> It is of the nature of song in general to stand still. Song turns away from linear process and gives participation in a standing pattern. A recorded song is a grasped chance for the owner–listener to seem to escape from time, or to escape from seeming to be bound to linear time.
>
> (Booth 1981: 193)

Booth also unravels the mechanics of this 'standing pattern' in a penetrating study of the old folk-ballad 'The Bitter Withy', following similar analyses of traditional songs by David Buchan, 'who argues that such patterns are actually the essence of oral narrative verse' (Booth, 1981: 65).

Ballads are words and music to be performed, not just text to be read. Even so, some of their time-structuring devices can be uncovered through study of the words, and the continuing appeal of these forms is demonstrated in songs orally preserved well into the twentieth century. Maud Karpeles prints the ballad 'On Board the Gallee' as it was sung by Mr J.T. Fitzpatrick at Marystown, Placentia Bay, Newfoundland on 13 July 1930:

28

In London there dwelt a fair damsel,
Most beautiful damsel was she,
She was courted by men of great honour,
But none like her lovely Jimmie.

When her father he first came to hear it,
And an angry old man was he,
Saying: Daughter, I'm told you're engaged
To a man that's below your degree.

Don't believe no such stories, dear father,
Don't believe no such stories on me,
For if ever I am inclined to get married,
It will be a man that's above my degree.

Her father he flew in a passion,
Like a man quite distracted did run.
It was into her room quite conveniently,
And brought out a well-loved gun.

Two choices, two choices, dear daughter,
Two choices I'll give unto thee,
Saying: which would you rather I'd shoot him
Or send him on board the Gallee.

I thank you, dear honourable father,
For those choices you gave unto me;
I would rather see Jimmie a-sailing
Than his innocent blood spilled for me.

My father he wants me to marry
A man that is very old,
But I would not lie in his bed, Jimmie,
No, not for a fortune of gold.

But Jimmie and I will be married,
And our friends all invited will be;
There'll be young men to wait upon Jimmie
And fair maids to wait upon me.

(Karpeles 1971: 218)

As in Booth's analysis of 'The Bitter Withy', 'On Board the Gallee' reveals a 'rigorous symmetrical pattern of boxes within boxes'; these are the markers that, in performance, stake out the territory of the time model.

The song pivots on the two central stanzas depicting the father's violent quarrel with his daughter. There can be no doubting that this is a crucial turning point. Here, his rage and the taking up of his gun are matched at

29

once by the ultimatum which includes the threat to shoot Jimmie. On either side of this vivid portrayal of the father's passion are two balancing stanzas in which the daughter quietly attempts to reason with him. The colloquy of the four stanzas has an immediacy which makes a dramatic contrast with the four outer stanzas. The pivotal action is thus framed by something between a detached 'history' ('In London there dwelt a fair damsel') and a possibly hopeless dream of what might be or might have been ('But Jimmie and I will be married'). The time-encapsulating strength of the pattern is constantly reinforced, both by the emphatic progression of the repeated 'she/he/me/thee' rhymes, with subtle recessions created by the unexpected shifts to 'run/gun' and 'old/gold', and by the resonance of phrases and ideas: the beautiful damsel (stanza 1) matched by the fair maids (stanza 8); men of great honour who court her at the start having their equivalence in young men who wait upon Jimmie at the end, and so on.

The time patterns of the oral tradition are prominent; easily identified, assimilated and understood in performance, they are complex but not complicated. The sophisticated structures of composed songs, on the other hand, as of all composed music – and indeed, all contrived art forms – are the product of the heightened consciousness, questioning, analysing and objectifying which have been the characteristics of education since the early seventeenth century. In these *works* (the term is not without significance) the techniques for controlling the medium, balancing unity and variety, tension and relaxation, departure and return, are likely to be complicated by an overlay of allusion, with the expectation that the educated mind will, through further study, tease out added subtleties of meaning.

Graham Parry, in his study of the culture of the Stuart court, gives us a picture of what was considered necessary at that time for an educated appreciation of the arts – an attitude which has had a profound effect on people's approach to works of art ever since. The *Entertainment* devised by Ben Jonson, Thomas Dekker and the architect Stephen Harrison for King James's triumphal entry into London in March 1604

> mingled delight with instruction, and although given before a vast popular audience, it was essentially courtly in its spirit, elegant, learned and allusive. The arches were so dense with meaning ... that it is not surprising that Dekker and Johnson and Harrison each published a detailed report of his own devising so that they could be studied and deciphered at leisure.
>
> (Parry 1981: 20, 3)

Complexities of this nature become the principal features of style. They

30

seem to emphasize what may be known *about* a work of art; they impress us by their intellectual challenge, and there is a kind of worldly wisdom that pleases, perhaps because it seems to be more worthy of attention than the uncomplicated but mysterious structural markers of the oral tradition.

The idealized condition had also been prominent in the paintings of the early Middle Ages. The artists depicted the world as it might be, from a heavenly viewpoint outside time and space, and without the dynamic the human eye would perceive. The introduction of perspective brought painting down to earth, capturing points in time and momentarily freezing figures and landscapes which we know are unquestionably mobile and always changing. Making a feature of everyday reality did not hinder the power of painting to grapple with the dilemma of space, but it did throw new emphasis upon aesthetic delight and artistic technique for its own sake. In the same way, European music, moving away from plainsong's imitation of timelessness, became earthbound, confronting and defying time's depressing characteristic. But the peculiar strength of monody has been sustained in the classical musics of India, Indonesia and the Far East; directly comparable with the highly complex rhythmic music of Africa, which articulates time but simultaneously loses itself in a seemingly timeless web.

Nevertheless, in one way or another the aesthetic of Western music has permeated most areas of the world; and, as with the visual arts, the close focus upon technique, action and allusion has generated, and continues to generate, a specialized body of 'writing about' music – from the ephemeral argot commentaries of the pop writers to the complex studies of musicologists and analysts.

Musicology is a relatively young science. It grew out of musical criticism, which in the first instance consisted largely of the writings of composers about their own and others' works, occasionally speculating on the nature of music itself. That was manifestly different from the writings of theorists who were attempting to draw together the threads of contemporary compositional and performance practice.

Allied to the output of musicology is the growing literature of music education and the psychology and sociology of music. Writing about music education, at least, has its pre-twentieth-century antecedents; although its latest manifestations and its links with psychology and sociology are very clearly products of our contemporary musical thought. Indeed, the composer Henri Pousseur has suggested (1985) that it was specifically the musical developments of the post-1945 avant-garde in Europe that made possible the opening up of new ideas about music in education in the 1960s.

Writing about music has increased during the twentieth century. We practice the art of music and theorize about it, as others have done before us, but in addition we are now much concerned with speculation; in particular about past theories and past attitudes to music, musicians and performance practice, about the music of other cultures, and about the forces that motivate our own varied contemporary musical scene. In other words, there is a widespread desire to supplement musical action with information.

This interest in analysis, comment and explanation is not confined to scholars; in somewhat different styles it is just as evident in pop magazines and concert programme notes. Music's public seems to need words, but some, perhaps, feel that music in our time is overwhelmed by verbiage. Morton Feldman certainly did – and was uncharacteristically vocal about it! His worry was that many of the young composers he encountered could not apparently write a note until they had verbally reasoned out a thorough explanation for everything that would happen in the music; 'Why', he asked, 'could they not simply allow the sounds to take their own directions?' By the same token, concert audiences often seem to rely more upon their eyes than their ears, and the reputations of performers are just as likely to be sustained by the hyperbole of the record sleeve notes as by their playing.

'Where is the knowledge we have lost in information?',[1] wrote T.S. Eliot in the first of his *Choruses from 'The Rock'*. Perhaps we should be cautious about the increasing literary industry that surrounds music today. On the other hand, fast and accurate dissemination of information is another important characteristic of our time and, on the positive side, the technology making that possible has also brought about an expansion of scholarly investigation and popular understanding.

The benefits of serious musical inquiry, speculation and comment are considerable and cannot be in doubt. Yet music persists – simple, complex, clever, entertaining, uplifting – not because we research, reason and write about it, nor because it is so easily available from radio, television, discs and cassettes, nor even because it carries powerful messages by association with texts or visual and dramatic forms, but because people continue to find in its forms a sense of rightness and a glimpse of perfection which resonates – just as the rhymes and chiastic forms of the folk-ballads did – with the strongest aspirations of humanity.

NOTE

1   The author and publishers would like to thank Faber & Faber Ltd for permission to reproduce line 16 from Chorus I of 'Choruses from "The Rock"', from *Collected Poems* by T. S. Eliot.

REFERENCES

BOOTH, M.W. (1981) *The Experience of Songs*, New Haven, Conn.: Yale University Press.

JACKSON, B. (1972) *Wake Up Dead Man: Afro-American Worksongs from Texas Prisons*, Cambridge, Mass.: Harvard University Press.

KARPELES, M. (1971) *Folk Songs from Newfoundland*, London: Faber & Faber.

LANGER, S.K. (1953) *Feeling and Form*, London: Routledge & Kegan Paul.

PARRY, G. (1981) *The Golden Age Restor'd: The Culture of the Stuart Court, 1603–42*, Manchester: Manchester University Press.

POUSSEUR, H. (1985) *Modern Music, Educational Music and Musical Education*, Strasbourg: Council of Europe.

3

Music, Non–music
and the Soundscape

R. MURRAY SCHAFER

In order to understand the term 'non-music' as I shall be using it here, it will first be necessary to define music. I do not want to enter on an elaborate philosophical discussion so I will make it brief. In the traditional Western sense music is an abstract entertainment for the pleasure of the ears alone. The word abstract is emphatic. Listeners are not encouraged to associate music with functions or purposes beyond the aesthetic enjoyment it provides. Functional music is relegated to a lower order and music that is made to serve political, mercantile or even religious purposes is always under critical suspicion. Religious music sometime escapes censure because so many Western composers wrote so much of it, but the conservatories and concert halls where it is taught and performed have been careful to minimize whatever religious messages it may sustain and emphasize its intrinsic beauty.

That this interpretation of music is unusual among world cultures is by now quite well known. Elsewhere music is effortlessly associated with dance, with physical tasks, with social festivities and celebrations of all kinds. In those cultures there are many musics, each associated with special activities.

In many cultures the word 'music' does not exist at all. In Africa, for example, there is no term corresponding to music in Tiv, Yoruba, Igbo, Efik, Birom, Hausa, the assorted Jarawa dialects, Idoma and Egoon, and many other languages have qualifying terms which only partly touch our concept of music (Keil 1979: 27). The same is true in other parts of the world: the Inuit have no generic term for music, nor can it be found in most North-American Indian languages. Much of the soundmaking in these cultures might better be described as tone magic. There is a special kind of music for healing, another for bringing rain, another to ensure a successful hunt or to defeat one's enemies, etc. Even though they may all use voices and instruments, for the people in these cultures the different kinds of music have completely separate identities and must never be confused. We recall also that the ancient Greeks originally employed the word *mousike* for a whole range of spiritual and intellectual activities before it gradually took on the more restricted meaning we have inherited. Our concept of music is a special one, nourished in the crucible of European civilization, from which it went out (along with Europeans) to many other parts of the world. What makes it special is its abstraction from daily life, its exclusivity. Music has become an activity which requires silence for its proper presentation – containers of silence called music rooms. It exhibits the signs of a cult or a religion, and to those outside who have not been initiated into its rituals it must appear strange and abnormal.

The origin of this concept of music owes much to the transition from outdoor to indoor living. It is always the contexts of culture which generate the shapes of its artefacts, and the thick walls of European architecture have been a shaping force behind the development of European music from Gregorian chant to serialism. In fact it would be possible to write the entire history of European music in terms of walls, showing not only how the varying resonances of its performance spaces have affected its harmonies, tempi and timbres, but also to show how its social character evolved once it was set apart from everyday life.

With indoor living, two things developed antonymously: the high art of music and noise pollution – for noises were the sounds that were kept outside. After art music had moved indoors, street music became an object of particular scorn. Hogarth's celebrated print, *The Enraged Musician*, shows the conflict in full view. A professional musician indoors clamps his hands over his ears in agony while outside his workroom a multitude of sonorous activities are in progress: a baby is screaming, a man is sharpening knives on a grindstone, children are playing with ratchets and drums, several hawkers are selling wares assisted by bells and horns and one shabbily-dressed beggar has targeted the musician's window for an oboe serenade. A study of noise abatement legislation between the sixteenth and nineteenth centuries shows how increasing amounts of it were directed against street criers and street music. An extremist position was reached in Weimar with the passage of a by-law in the nineteenth century forbidding the making of music unless conducted behind closed doors. Agitation elsewhere was

35

angling in the same direction, for instance in Michael Bass's proposed bill in 1864 to rid London of street music – a proposal which won the support of Dickens, Carlyle, Tennyson, Charles Babbage and two hundred 'leading composers and professors of music in the metropolis'. The street had now become the home of non-music, where it mixed with other kinds of sound-swill and sewage. From now on chamber music and street noise would develop obversely: the more intricate the one became, the cruder the other seemed.

The further back we go in European history, the less the antagonism. In Brueghel's painting *The Battle Between Carnival and Lent* (1559) the town square is filled with over a hundred people, many of whom are making sounds or playing instruments, yet no one is protesting at the noise. The plurality of the activities produces a dialectic in which no single sound dominates or is likely to dominate. Nothing is heard uninterruptedly: every sound is transpierced by its neighbours in a rich polyphony. Still, a careful inspection of the painting reveals that the square also contains its quiet zones where lovers may court or a baby may sleep in its cradle.

The difference between Brueghel and Hogarth is not merely temperamental: it is indicative of a sharpening distinction between music and the soundscape – a distinction which was given precision by the rapid spread of plate glass in the latter part of the seventeenth century.[1] Hogarth's print contains glass windows; Brueghel's painting does not. Brueghel's people have come to the open windows to listen; Hogarth's musician has come to the window to shut it.

The sonic environment is a plenum, for the world is always full of sounds. They come from far and near, high and low: they are discrete and continuous, loud and soft, natural, human and technological. They enter and depart in processions as events pass us or we pass them. This is why the music of the streets has no beginning or end but is all middle. Something is already in progress before our arrival and it succeeds our departure. Distant listening, like distant seeing, becomes less pronounced in the city, but up until the twentieth century the country was always at hand and every listener knew how sounds could be 'sweetened by distance'. Often music seemed to arise as an accompaniment to the *paysage sonore*, as when tool noise inspired the singer or bird song the flutist. For years I have tried to draw musicologists' attention to the fact that most of the world's music exists in counterpoise to the soundscape. This is easiest to appreciate in environments studied by ethnomusicologists but seems less evident when music moves indoors. At that point music inspires music and context is surrendered to style. Still, the great revolutions in music history have always been and always will be changes in context rather than style.

Often concert music evokes certain allusions to the more populous environment beyond the music room as a kind of nostalgia. Hunting horns or spinning wheels or locomotives find representation here. In fact the music room often assumes a kind of virtual space which is broader than its enclosure, as when soft sounds seem to fall away to the acoustic horizon or a loud sound seems to push right into the body. The frequency range of the music is another unconscious imitation of the external soundscape. Mozart's music is made up of mid- and high-frequency sounds as was his world, whereas the heavy infrasound of the modern city is reproduced in the guitars of the modern rock group.

Composers have often been explicit about inspiration they have drawn from the soundscape. A couple of examples will suffice; for example Wagner describes how an alphorn invaded *Tristan*:[2]

> This act promises famously; I drew profit for it even from my Riga excursion. At four in the morning we were roused by the Boots with an Alphorn – I jumped up and saw it was raining and returned to bed to try to sleep; but the droll call went droning round my head and out of it arises a very lusty melody which the herdsman now blows to signal Isolde's ship, making a surprising merry and naïve effect.

Similarly, George Gershwin recalls how *Rhapsody in Blue* was inspired by a train journey:[3]

> It was on the train, with its steely rhythms, its rattlety-bang that is so often stimulating to a composer (I frequently hear music in the very heart of noise), that I suddenly heard – even saw on paper – the complete construction of the *Rhapsody* from beginning to end. ... I heard it as a sort of musical kaleidoscope of America – of our vast melting-pot, of our incomparable national pep, our blues, our metropolitan madness. By the time I reached Boston, I had the definite plot of the piece, as distinguished from its actual substance.

Europeans will probably be unfamiliar with the jazz rhythms produced by the short-section unwelded tracks of the American railroad (European rails are welded in long lenghts) nor will they know how the three-tone triadic steam whistle could be warped by echoes and doppler shifts to suggest blue notes. But Walt Whitman sensed these variants when, in a poem called 'To a locomotive' he penned the line of shifting ee's:

> Thy trill of shrieks by rocks and hills returned.

But we are getting off the subject.

When we turned our backs on the external soundscape, we also began to modify our listening habits. The soundscape is a plenum. The music room is a vacuum. Music fills it. Without music in it, it is scarcely a room at all: chairs, a stage, music stands and a podium, these are its scant furnishings. But further observation reveals that there is a method in this arrangement. All the chairs face the stage and all the sounds will come from here. This will be the exclusive focus of attention during the concert. No longer are we at the centre of the soundscape with sounds reaching us from all directions; now they reach us from one direction only and to appreciate them we must point our ears, just as we point our eyes when we read. In this quiet space the composer will be able to fashion much more intricate structures than were possible outdoors. The music has a definite beginning and ending. The audience will arrive before the beginning and remain until after the ending, sitting in rows facing the performers. They have voluntarily surrendered the use of their bodies and their feet and have restricted the use of their hands and voices to express their appreciation at the end of the music. In order not to distract from the listening process, the performers also move as inconspicuously as possible and their faces are neutral and expressionless. Definitely the concert promises psychic rather than somatic satisfaction, and the composer uses the audience's concentration to arrange his material in a vast architecture of principal and secondary themes, transitions, harmonic centres, modulations, instrumental interplay and dynamic shading – an ideal soundscape of the imagination, elegant, controlled, dissonance-disciplined and invigorating. The economist, Jacques Attali, claims to find the clue to the political economy of nineteenth-century Europe in the concert of the eighteenth century, dutifully listened to by the bourgeoisie and faithfully transmuted into a harmonious industrial order in which commodities flowed out to fill the world just as tones had filled the music hall (Attali 1977: 93ff.). Sometimes I have thought the traditional sonata form is a model for a colonial empire: first theme (loud) – the mother nation: second theme (softer) – the supine colony; then follow the rhetorical and occasionally pugilistic exchanges of the development section, the *rapprochement* of mother and colony in the recapitulation (both now in the home key), and the coda – consolidation of the empire. The classical music of Europe during the era of colonial expansion was a music of departures and arrivals: exciting openings and exultant conclusions. There is always a relationship between the social aspirations of a society and the art it produces and when music moves into new contexts and takes on new forms, something is profoundly astir.

A few years ago the Viennese music sociologist Kurt Blaukopf began a series of studies in what he called the 'non-musical use of music'. He sensed an atrophy in the concentration habits of Western listeners as a result of the technical changes brought about by the new media. We all realize the extent to which music is losing its focus. It strikes us at odd times and in odd places. Often two or more pieces of music can be heard in a single environment and many other sounds as well. Sometimes while shopping we hear the music of one establishment superposed over that of another, like an overprinted photograph. Sometimes I have walked in shopping malls late at night and have overheard music playing to no one. And I have been violently assaulted by music on a lawn or beach and have exploded with animal venom. Sometimes I have imagined a plane crash in which the only survivor will be the recorded music.

It is as if, by some antinomian absurdity, the Western notion of music seems to be exploding in our faces, breaking out all around us, haemorrhaging into new environments: railway stations, book stores, hotel corridors, subway tunnels. We sense a social malaise in this profanation of art. We are especially annoyed to discover that the music in public places is not our favourite and probably is nobody's favourite. It is too late to simply call this non-music or to adopt the position of the International Music Council of UNESCO, which passed a resolution in 1969 denouncing 'the intolerable infringement of individual freedom and the right of everyone to silence by the abusive use, in private and public places, of recorded or broadcast music' and asking UNESCO to inform 'the authorities everywhere' to take 'measures to put an end to this abuse'.

It hasn't worked. It would be more to the point today to try to understand why. The power centres in society are shifting and multiplying, so that the authority once accorded to the concert as the modal point for musical stimulation has withered. European concert music gradually refined itself into states where even its most devoted listeners were reluctant to follow it (I mean ISCM festivals and the like); but even in its healthiest state it had given rise to a kind of aural hypertrophy in which the ear was not only isolated from the other senses but was even isolated from its more normal habits of functioning.

In *The Tuning of the World* (Schafer 1976) I predicted that by the end of the century music and the soundscape would draw together. I was speaking of the Western world. In other parts of the world they have never been completely separated, and thus for a solution to the dilemma confronting us today we might study the relationship between them as it once existed in the West and still exists in other parts of the world today. A recent trip to Japan gave me an opportunity to do this. There I learned how music (or sound for sound's sake) functioned in traditional Japanese life. The Japanese word for music, *ongaku*, simply means the enjoyment of sounds; it is an inclusive rather than exclusive concept. Thus the Tea Master may make music with his kettle.

> The kettle sings well, for pieces of iron are so arranged in the bottom as to produce a peculiar melody in which one may hear the echoes of a cataract muffled by clouds, of a distant sea breaking among the rocks, a rainstorm sweeping through a bamboo forest, or of the soughing of pines on some faraway hill.
>
> (Kakuzo 1956: 63)

It is just such a kettle that Kawabata describes in his novel, *Snow Country*:

> He could make out two pine breezes . . . a near one and a far one. Just beyond the far breeze he heard faintly the tinkling of a bell. He put his ear to the kettle and listened. Far away, where the bell tinkled on, he suddenly saw Komako's feet, tripping in time with the bell.
>
> (Kawabata 1957: 155)

The synaesthesia suggested by aural illusions is never despised by the Japanese; on the contrary, it is cultivated. In the game known as *Ko wo kiku*, 'listening to the incense', each scent is inhaled ceremoniously and then passed to the ear, as if somehow the resolving power of one sense was not enough to extract complete meaning, the experience being further complicated by the allusive name given each incense, intended to recall some scene or passage from a romance or legend.

From an active group of soundscape researchers I learned how Japanese gardeners traditionally cultivated the many variations which water produces, not only in their placement of rocks in the beds of streams to modulate the sound, but also in their use of decorative bamboo irrigation pumps which tip when filled with water and drop back against stones producing pleasant hollow pitches. One researcher, Ya Wakao, had devoted himself to the study of water harps (Figure 3.1) – resonating jars, buried under rock basins where the hands were washed before entering the tea house. The jars, which served no purpose, were set so that the spilled water which dropped into them would produce a melodic cascade of hollow pitches from below. The water harps are found only in the oldest gardens; the tradition seems to have been abandoned about two hundred years ago, but the soundscape group hopes to revive it.

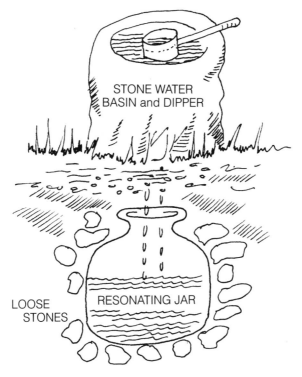

Figure 3.1 A Japanese water harp

These are examples of a consciousness that allows the beauty of sound to expand and permeate the whole of life. It would be futile to debate whether such things are music; I would call them examples of soundscape design.

Wondering what made this consciousness possible, I came to the conclusion that the traditional Japanese paper house had a good deal to do with it. One can still see such houses in Kyoto and throughout the Japanese countryside, houses with large sliding doors, carefully covered with rice paper. When slid back they open to beautiful enclosed gardens, the light and sounds of which reach in to fill the rudimentary and seemingly famished spaces of the house. Of course, in modern Japan (in Tokyo) such houses are seldom seen. They have been replaced by buildings of glass and concrete smudged with Muzak, for isolation from the natural environment requires cosmetics.

It seems necessary to point out that the rice-paper window is different from the glazed window. Glass resists nature; rice-paper invites its penetration. Glazing is a European treatment of wall openings – the result of primary visual consciousness; rice-paper suggests aural awareness.

We are just beginning to draw together the material necessary for a study of sense perception. We know that different cultures listen differently – the predilection for sound combinations in different musics hints at this. One of the significant characteristics of all sense perceptions is focusing. In visual perception this can be realized in comparing oriental and occidental art. The Western painter organizes events into an interconnected proportional alignment from viewer to horizon, called perspective. To appreciate such a painting one focuses on the vanishing point; one adopts a point of view, and there is only one point of view to be adopted. The oriental artist lets the pictorial elements float in their own spaces, seemingly scattered, but balanced in a wide distributive interdependence of shapes and vacancies. One must scan the picture to relate the elements, a practice which encourages peripheral vision. A related habit is the out-of-focus visualizing practised in Zen meditation.

It is also possible that the ear indulges equally in these contradictory habits; or rather that certain ears are trained to listen to sounds peripherally – that is, equally from all directions – while others are trained to place sounds in series which are proportionate to one another, the strong to the weak, the desired to the undesired.

In the external soundscape the ear is always wavering between choices. It soaks up information from all directions. Any sound may attract our attention if it moves close to us, or even remaining distant it may impart vital information. We are always at the centre of the soundscape, listening out in all directions simultaneously. We know that in Indian music one does not concentrate on the melodies but rather on the drone in order to hear the melodies and embellishments as though through a veil. One has the impression that in traditional Japanese music, while the drone is absent, a similar process is encouraged. This is not a music of resonance; it percusses on dry instruments. Its events are often layered so that several kinds of material may be presented simultaneously and independently, as is the case with Noh dramas. There seems to be no particular hierarchy in such music, no domination, no focus.

When we move indoors, this wavering of attention diminishes or ceases altogether. Just as a room is decorated with fixed furnishings, the sounds in such a room also begin to assume fixed positions. In the case of music, a point is sought where it will sound best. We accord it superiority over other sounds by turning to face it and by protecting it with closed doors and soundproof walls.

It is the absence of walls and doors that allows the Japanese, like many other peoples around the world, to imagine music which may impart beauty to the environment without being self-centred or wishing to dominate the entire soundscape. The sound sculptures of Akinoti Matsumoto are typical of this unstrained attitude. A kind of *bricolage*, they are created out of simple materials which might be found in any hardware shop. One of these (Figure 3.2) consists of nothing more than a length of plastic fishing line with a hook at one end to attach to the ceiling and a weight at the bottom to hold it taut. Down it slither a large number of small aluminium tubes of varying lengths, drilled at one end and passed through the line. As they descend they shake, touching their neighbours to produce a delicate tintinnabulation.

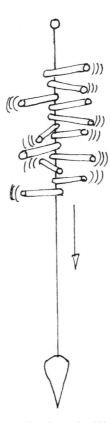

Figure 3.2   A sound sculpture by Akinoti Matsumoto

43

Another instrument consists of a series of thin metal bars, slowly raised by a small electric motor to fall back in turn on a series of strings tuned to different frequencies. The tempo of the falling bars is very slow so that one is reminded more of the single flowers in vases one often finds in the corners of Japanese homes, or of isolated calligraphy scrolls on walls, than anything approaching a musical instrument.

The sound environments of Hiroshi Yoshimura have similar intentions, as his description of Sound Process Design illustrates:

> What we are attempting to do, speaking generally, can be called sound design. This includes the adjustment and regulation of sound proper to an environment, along with the composition of music for environments. Possibly for a given environment just one sound would be sufficient. Sound design doesn't mean simply decorating with sounds. The creating of non-sound – in other words silence – would, if possible, be wonderful in a design.
>
> There is no question that our age, in which we are inundated with sound, is unprecedented in history. We need to develop a more caring attitude towards sounds. Presently the amount of sound and music in the environment have clearly exceeded man's capacity to assimilate them, and the audio ecosystem is beginning to fall apart. Background music, which is supposed to create atmosphere, is far too excessive. In our present condition we find that within certain areas and spaces aspects of visual design are well attended to, but sound design is completely ignored. It is necessary to treat sound and music with the same respect that we show for architecture, interior design, food, or the air we breathe.
>
> 'Wave Motion' was begun as an environment music series. This music could be said to be an 'object' or a kind of sound scenery to be listened to casually (peripherally). Not being music which excites the listener into another world, it should drift like smoke and become part of the environment surrounding the listener's activity.... This is not music of self-expression, not a 'completed work of art', rather it is music which changes the character and meaning of space, things and people by overlapping and shifting.
>
> (Yoshimura 1982)

Yoshimura's music exists for spaces. I have heard it in galleries, where it leads nowhere but affects the space it inhabits, changing it in subtly perceptible ways. It is mostly synthesizer music, and this assists its purpose, for the synthesizer is an apparatus of all modern cultures and therefore belonging to none. Most of the background music we know is attached to known instruments and these instruments, as well as playing styles, connect it with specific periods and places: the guitar is Spanish, the accordion is Bohemian, etc. One could listen to the Muzak system in any international hotel or airport and be doused almost exclusively with American tunes played on vintage European instruments. This is how cultural hegemonies are secured, by subliminal advertising.

There is something to be said for the use of innocuous soundmakers in acoustic design and there is something to be said for indigenous instruments to establish unique character. When a sound object is known and loved it functions more as a sensory anchor, assuring us that we are at home even when other features of the environment are alien or intimidating.

Soundscape designers should know these things. They belong to no camp; they understand the requirements of the situation, adding to one and subtracting from another. They also know the value of silence. Through their work, music, non-music and silence are woven together artistically and therapeutically to bring about a new consciousness where art and life touch, merge and are lost in one another.

NOTES

1 A method of casting invented in 1688 by Louis Lucas de Nehan made possible for the first time the production of large plates of glass of uniform thickness at reasonable prices.
2 Letter to Minna, quoted in *The Musical Quarterly* 31 (4), October 1945, p. 411.
3 Quote from the Everest Record sleeve of *Rhapsody in Blue*, William Steinberg conducting the Pittsburgh Symphony Orchestra.

REFERENCES

ATTALI, J. (1977) *Bruits: essai sur l'économie politique de la musique*, Paris: Presses Universitaires de France; published in English as *Noise: The Political Economy of Music*, Manchester: Manchester University Press.
KAKUZO, O. (1956) *The Book of Tea*, Rutland, Vt., and Tokyo: Charles E. Tuttle, 1971.
KAWABATA, Y. (1957) *Snow Country*, Rutland, Vt., and Tokyo: Charles E. Tuttle, 1983.
KEIL, C. (1979) *Tiv Song*, Chicago: University of Chicago Press.
SCHAFER, R.M. (1976) *The Tuning of the World*, New York: Alfred A. Knopf.
YOSHIMURA, H. (1982) *Sound Process Design*, Tokyo: Shibuya-Ku.

4

Music in Concert
and Music in the Background:
Two Poles of Musical Realization

HANNS-WERNER HEISTER

INTRODUCTION: CATEGORIES

The range of ways in which music can be realized has gradually become wider and more differentiated, at least in principle; although, in the process, opportunities have also been lost. There appears to have been some polarization in one or two areas, thereby moving away from the previous position in terms of internal structure and emphasis.

The enormous increase in the consumption of music, as well as its social and cultural relevance, is particularly remarkable and contrasts with an apparently universal indifference to music. This contrast, much more than a simple paradox, is explained by the representational polarity of 'music in the background' and 'music in concert'.

'Music in the background' and 'music in concert' must be understood not as material and substantial but as structural and processual categories. Therefore, the terms 'background music' and 'concert music' serve merely as formal abbreviations. In this sense concert music such as *Eine kleine Nachtmusik* or *Das Largo*, initially opera music, can be used as background music, even though there are varying degrees of accentuation in substance and subject. The reverse would also be true, although less typical, given that background music, genuinely and specifically written as such, is an exception. The decisive factor here is the structural context, the type or mode of realization.

46

'Realization' has a threefold meaning. First, productive realization is the materialization of music as an aesthetic event. By this we mean the translation of what is intended, composed and written into a sound pattern; in other words, the aggregate of musical production–reproduction, presentation and interpretation. Second, receptive realization involves the materialization of the sense and meaning of the musical object through the mediation of the 'activities' (*Tätigkeiten*) of comprehension and perception. Without this conversion of what is heard into what is perceived, the musical process (cf. Heister 1984: 598 ff., for definition) would be incomplete. Third, realization in economic terms is the materialization of 'music making' as an accepted part of material society; in a historically commercial environment, that means the conversion of music, as a service and as a product, into money.

Realization, as a general category, therefore, encompasses a series of specifically musical as well as not specifically musical 'activities' (see Stroh 1984 for definition) through which the musical process reaches its end. The ultimate aim of the process, however, is not reached until the overlapping subjective and objective purposes, along with the respective functions of the musical process (as a product of what is intended, the motive and the actual outcome) have been achieved. As such, within the concept of music in the background, 'music in the workplace' – i.e. in the functional environment of industry – can be seen by management as a means of increasing productivity while at the same time being a source of enjoyment for the workers. Alternatively, in purely psychological and physiological terms, 'music in the workplace' could be perceived as noise and therefore as a reason for decline in productivity.

CONTRASTS AND PERSPECTIVES

Concert music and background music are at first sight opposites. A concert is essentially a social gathering where people come together for the sake of the music (at least according to the social norm). Music is (re)produced live (i.e. by people) as a form of art or higher art, which at its ultimate is regarded as 'absolute' music.

Music as a background and in the background, on the other hand, has no specific social place. Rather than being the focal point for a gathering, background music is reproduced, diffused and casually 'taken over' by technological gadgets, and serves as a 'sound-tapestry' or 'sound-back-drop'. This industrially fabricated non-music can be labelled Muzak.

'Music in concert' and 'music in the background', therefore, represent genuine and characteristic polarities, adumbrating ideological polarities within the so-called middle-class music culture, which has become internationally and predominantly widespread as a part of industrial society and imperialism. Expressed in material and substantial terms, the following spheres stand in opposition to one another: 'serious' and 'entertainment' music; 'classical' and 'pop' music; art music and trivial music. From a functional or relational point of view, what we are witnessing here are extreme versions of the relationship between 'performance' music and 'social' music (Besseler 1925: 46), of – analogous yet conceived of in a different way – the relationship between 'autonomous' music as 'higher', and 'functional' music as 'lower' (Dahlhaus 1967: 17). However, these should not be treated as direct counterparts or corresponding identities, but as analogous dichotomies, parallel to each other through definition (cf. Braun and Kühn 1972: 622 ff.; Heister 1980: 536). In the following pages we shall explore, historically and systematically, the polarity of these two means of realization.

In its historical evolution the concert was the concrete 'annulment' of all other forms of musical culture and realization. As such, it became the common and – after the 1848 watershed – the characteristic, definitive and leading form of musical realization. This is true despite its complementary relationship to opera in the musical division of labour, which often dominated public musical awareness. The double limitation (of dealing with the upper-class music culture as well as its predominantly ideological reactions) must also be taken into account here. Technical developments in sound reproduction relieved the concert of its annulling role, but did so in the form of a mass culture; at least, after the epochal events of 1917/1918.

Conversely, the functional and adaptational capacities of music in the background form the abstract negation of the 'concert'; its technical prerequisite is the spread of the technological reproduction of music. Universally 'background music' has spread in leaps and bounds, especially from the United States, since the 1960s.

Historically and systematically 'music in concert' and 'music in the background' are similar in character to the two sides of what is known in Gestalt psychology as the '*Kippbild*': the one form of realization is the mirror image of the other. A number of points arise. Thus the eradication of the visual element of the 'hidden orchestra', in the concert hall reforms of 1900, represents a deliberate aesthetic arrangement, rooted in the ideology of 'absolute' music and of the 'purely musical'. This was a climax in a long

48

historical process. However, in the case of the quarter-of-a-century-old technical reproduction on Edison-phonograph or Berliner-gramophone, the eradication is simply a self-made necessity, the starting point of a very different development. On the other hand, both forms of realization (background music and concert music) converge, despite genetic and structural differences and differences in the actual quality of the music. This can be illustrated in both; for example, by the invisibility of the musical process and related trends below the surface, the closely connected lines of deconcentration and a sort of 'stream of consciousness' and indifference. There are other surprising and disguised parallels. Such relationships must be discovered, as in the puzzle-picture shown in Figure 4.1.

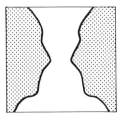

Figure 4.1   Kippbild: two faces in profile, or is it a goblet?

REAL AESTHETIC DIFFERENCES AND APPARENT INTEGRATION OF ART AND LIFE

The widening of its functional, local and temporal boundaries are both essential to, and characteristic of, the concert as an artistic event within everyday life. It becomes distant and different from generation of income, reproductive activity, social spheres of production and circulation, and everyday consumption. Both in and as concert, music builds the type of 'world of its own' (Moritz 1785) that is described by the middle-class version of artistic autonomy as the separate other world, as the 'realm of freedom' as opposed to the 'realm of necessity' (Schiller 1795). This difference is the prerequisite for the unfolding of aesthetic musical qualities and values of music as a higher, 'autonomous' form of art, which had not previously been experienced.

Eduard Hanslick (1869) characterizes the concert as the place of autonomous musical realization (see Heister 1983: 42). In the introduction to his work *The History of the Concert in Vienna*, he writes that

> The concert which, with the exception of theatre, church, and ball music, encompasses and represents all forms of musical production, can rightly claim to be of the richest artistic content. ... As such the concert [is] the main arena of music as a special form of art, the concert hall being the only place where the art of sound appears in this manner self-sufficient and self-justified. Anywhere else, music appears only in connection with other art forms or as part of a separate entity or purpose.
>
> (Hanslick 1869: IX)

The price of obtaining such new worth, which includes the possibility of qualitative development of the 'richest artistic content', is high: the loss of direct references to social reality and practice. This applies particularly to both function and effect, but also to the content, i.e. the music itself. Within this structural and historical framework, the relationship between 'concert music' and society operates within the field of reproduction and compensation of the given social circumstances.

Under the alienating circumstances of middle-class society, true self-realization, hindered as a real concept, can only be aspired to if it is limited by such a loss. In other words, if it becomes imaginary-real. In the realization of autonomous music, i.e. music that has been freed from simply practical use or other specific purposes, the public can and should see itself as an imaginary-real community of free, equal and brotherly or sisterly people. This, applied to practical activity outside the musical arena, can also be of social consequence (for detail see Heister 1983).

Even the realization of the 'richest artistic content' is only one possibility which suits the tendencies, the idea or ideal of the concert; reality and practice often deviate considerably from this. W. Salmen (1988) takes this into consideration in his definition:

> The concert ... is the most complete form of profound music, mediated on a stage involving distance from the audience, in which autonomous and other forms of music, determined by function or purpose, can be heard.
>
> (Salmen 1988: 7)

(cf. Schwab 1980). He draws attention critically to social limitations such as educational privilege. That privilege, he argues, not only prevents appropriate musical self-realization in the concert but also fails to meet the ideals of freedom, equality and fraternity:

As harmonious setting and 'friendly interplay' ... between the performers and the audience, the concert was and is more realistically an establishment furnished with social consequences. This, despite the Schillerian appeal in Beethoven's IX symphony, 'all people be brothers'. ...The intended harmonization is prevented not least by the difference in material and intellectual requirements of a concert performance

(ibid.)

Also, many accompanying circumstances of the concert institution contradict its idea, yet belong to the substance:

The concert hall, more so than the 'drawing-room', the place of worship or the public place, meant that music could be played for its own sake. This, however, did not mean that an instrumentarium had been established that was completely free of purpose. ...The diversity of concert forms more or less openly revealed the complex material connections with competition, conditions of trade, cost–benefit relationships, with unartistic aims, representational intentions, functions for charity or homage, considerations of prestige and political implications. Even the display of apparent wealth, ritualized good conduct and grateful remuneration for performance were neither able nor intended to disguise these connections.

(ibid.)

Such pragmatic deviations from the emphatic norm are based upon the fact that the constitutive, essential difference between concert and practice excludes or annuls the 'unartistic', or in fact makes it relative. In this way the higher aesthetic–political requirement, which is tied to the realization of autonomous music, is distorted. So 'silent listening [became] an obligatory behavioural model'. Real as this model was, it engendered the concert situation of 'listening away, and intensively listening to, at the same time' (Braun 1970: 223)

ASSEMBLAGE AND DISPERSION

What is lacking in background music from the beginning is precisely the aesthetic distance, and thereby also the pathos of autonomy with the emphatic functional designation of (imaginary-real) 'self-realization'.

Background music is more a part of everyday life, thus satisfying Erik Satie's somewhat limited, yet noteworthy and memorable, vision of a *musique d'ameublement*. As such, concert music and background music are dia-

51

metrically opposed. Not bound to a (specific/special) time, background music can be found *anywhere at any time* (and is thereby connected to the technical 'reproducibility' of music). The uniqueness of concert performance and the very character of musical realization are entirely destroyed, as is the performance character of so-called 'opus music' (a term not without contemptuous undertones). 'Fragmentation' (see Blaukopf 1968 for definition) appears in the place of the 'self-sufficient whole' (Moritz 1785). If the concert audience has a tendency to glorify and worship music to the point of a secular 'art religion', so the consumers of background music tend towards indifference. They are less comforted by an aesthetic and apparent unravelling of their circumstances and social conditions (see Haug 1972). But more, their behaviour is tamed by the artificial 'acoustic bell' (Liedtke 1988), the masking gauge (*Maskierungspegel*), which drowns out material-physical noise and oppositional thought, and is thereby ideologically effective.

Music can be in the 'background' in potentially any social environment, public or private: in the home, in production work, office and waiting rooms, supermarkets and 'superlearning', hotels and restaurants, in nature and so on. Background music, whether in the case of buying and selling or dealing out labour, empty or leisure times, brings a new, synthetic form of communication into situations where interpersonal communication is either not desired or is unnecessary. The issue is predominantly one of manipulative interests (see Fehling 1976). Such interests are tied to social needs that are, once adapted, put into practice until they seem to the subject to be (second) nature. Once the surrogate has thus been established, socially and physically, as normal, or indeed normative and natural, it is able to graft genuinely communicative, yet less musical, requirements and fixations onto other forms of music.

Background music appears mainly in two forms. The first is self-determined, individual and spontaneous. This used to be the portable radio; nowadays, however, it is the more civilized 'Walkman' (Braun and Kühn (1972: 624) refer to 'chosen background music'). The second form is the imposed background music manifested either as coincidental, objective or subjective relatively diffused background, or as not individually but communally selected and packaged background (ibid.). This is produced and marketed purposively by specialized industries. It is here that background music, free of charge to the recipients or victims, becomes a commodity for mainly commercial users. The fact that these two – or, in reality, three – forms of background music overlap is a specific problem. The difference between being determined from the outside, being self-made, and being alienated and apparently self-made, is blurred. At any rate, when the respective self-made musics are encountered in public they amount to a somewhat 'coincidental' background, proving that the most liberal harmonious impression of the formula 'private vices, public benefits' (Mandeville) is an illusion.

Music, defined as background, is not self-justified and independent. On the contrary, it works as 'part of the whole' – that is, of the respective situation or atmosphere – and serves 'other ends'; for instance, relaxation or distraction of a non-musical kind. The term 'other ends', however, presupposes a notion of function and purpose for such music, which is itself tied to autonomous ideology. Not wanting to overdo the trivial thesis that all music has some sort of 'function', we should nevertheless be aware of the difference between that music which is autonomous and independent by having its own purpose and that which is not a purpose in itself.

Background music, on the contrary, is merely an invisible and, whenever possible, unobtrusive medium. The public gathering of the concert aspires to external and internal selection and concentration, be it for short-term latent collective education or for musical reception. But those who hear background music are a dispersed crowd. Thus, instead of listening *to* the music, the constitutive mode of reception here is to listen *away* from the music.

THE RETREAT OF THE MIMESIS: AUTONOMOUS, FUNCTION AND FUNCTIONAL MUSIC

The concert, manifesting itself virtually as a 'natural form', is a historically evolved cultural entity whose tradition can be traced to the Renaissance (see Salmen 1988). At the same time, it contains long-term, overlapping, and almost universal 'logical' structures, in which its specifically aesthetic potential as the distinctive characteristic of musical realization is manifestly concentrated and brought together. This characteristic is often only partially and latently present in other forms of realization. Analogies exist with background music.

Music's potential for realization as a pleasurable or annoying additive is actualized, purely and independently, in background music. In Hegelian terms, therefore, the potential becomes reality. Probably the most closely related form of music is aristocratic–feudal *Tafelmusik*. Even in this case, it is surely the exception – and the expression of pronounced arrogance (still a part of luxury consumption) – to marginalize music for the sake of a high-class game of cards, as it is described with indignation by Louis Spohr in the well-known account in his autobiography (Spohr 1954). In normal circumstances the relative rarity and expensiveness of music is enough to command the minimum of attention.

Attention is further weakened in that background music is in theory costless. It is an optional extra and, with the aid of musical appliances, 'home-made'. As it is not in this sense a commodity, the financial incentive – the psychological stimulus for listening – is lost (see Heister 1974).

Background music is therefore a new level and quality of musical realization. It is made possible (and, as a result, also necessary as compensation for 'technology' and 'industrial society') only by the technical reproduction of music, along with its widespread distribution and application. The fact that background music is perceived with indifference, is decidedly coincidental or is taken in unconsciously is a condition for its realization. Here too, however, there is a difference between 'functional' music and that which is 'privately' self-chosen, the latter requiring minimal activity (also of a practical kind – e.g. switching on the apparatus) and attention.

Apart from the 'modern' or 'topical' repertoire, background music today differs from comparable types of music and realization in that the very function of being in the background is substantially different from 'service', 'everyday' and conventional 'utility' music. It has little or nothing to do with rumours to the contrary, spread mainly by the producers of background music and their 'knowledgeable' suppliers, who seek to make a historical connection between this 'worthless' music and traditional 'function' music. On the contrary, function music depends on clear and often 'signalistic' realization and effect, be it for work or dance music, march music or *Turmmusik*. If we are looking for historical connections, then music in advertising – with its enticing and baiting function, along with its cor-responding manner, which contrasts with background music – is a case in point. But (background) music, which should not disturb or be consciously perceived, is connected to this only abstractly, in that it is music, which is a 'part of the whole' (Hanslick): 'Part of a process, reaching beyond the music, part of a liturgic event or festivity, a procession or a dance' (Dahlhaus 1973: 845).

In concrete terms, the difference between background music and function music is greater and more important. Certain events, such as initiation or religio-ritual ceremonies, required music – especially for magical pres-entation – in order to be effective. Functionally, such music would be connected or genetically tied to its respective usage. A perfect example of this is 'work music' and the 'working song', as opposed to 'music in the workplace'. Only with the former is 'the rhythm of work' a part of the music (Braun and Kühn 1972: 623 ff.). Braun and Kühn have defined the difference with precision. They write that '"Function music" is "dependent" on (and motivated by) certain social events, whereas "functional music" must have particular effects.'

The criteria used for establishing the difference is the mimesis: that is, the reflective relationship between the respective context, social form and realizational circumstances and the aesthetic manner of the function music itself. Such a relationship is fundamentally lacking in background music. Because of this, all proceedings, functions, acts and situations in which background music is applied, or is even possible, can proceed as normal (or, in principle, even better) without this music. Instead, modern means are employed to create an atmosphere of a perfect world – the comfortable versus the prosaic. But it remains a false impression, stupefying and pacifying – a 'mask' of alienation.

THE PURELY MUSICAL

It is now paradoxical that, in historical and musico-sociological terms, background music too can be genetically and structurally autonomous. Like concert music, it is the result of the secular defunctionalization of music, that is, of its emancipation from its particular aims and usages. This process, for which the concert was the crucial historical event and the medium for carrying it out, is amplified by technical reproduction. So the behaviour of the listeners is reduced to simple receptivity. With a high degree of flexibility, it is also modelled on the possibilities of the concert situation and not on other situations, such as the relationship between dance music and dance. As a consequence, music in the background, whether as good or as bad as that in concert, is 'pure' music.

Background music can work as a special form of art (although not specifically as art), in that nothing is as operative, easy to use, ubiquitous or universally interchangeable as music. What background music and concert music have in common is that the music is not connected with other arts. Nevertheless, in this respect, comparisons between the two are legitimate and useful. As the visual element is reduced or indeed eliminated, we are confined to, and forced to concentrate on, the acoustic element, that is, the 'purely musical' (as is the norm in the concert). This is essential to the very constitution of background music. The physical setting, however, which in the case of the concert is the result of historical and ideological development, is, in background music, a technical prerequisite. It is also a prerequisite for its realization: the visual, which exists as a part of the whole, would create too much attention if combined with the musical. This is why music is so suited to be in the background.

Background music is fundamentally a relational-functional entity rather than a substantive one. To return to the terminology of Gestalt psychology, what is 'foreground' and what is 'background' can change, depending on the situation, context, type and direction of attention. In order to explain this we must look at anthropological and sensuous characteristics. The ear need not be as 'active' as the movable eye. The ear is already open whereas the eye can be opened and closed and used without head movement and thereby has a greater span.

Such factors were obviously taken into consideration in the development of film music. Here (at least in conventional understanding and use) the music should remain almost unnoticeable, although not quite as much as in the case of real background music (see Adorno and Eisler 1969, amongst others).

Hanslick refers to the openness of the ear, converting physiology of sense-organs into ontology of art. He writes,

> A painting, a church or a drama cannot be casually apprehended. An aria can. As such it can serve as an accessory, as no other art can. The best of compositions can be played as *Tafelmusik*, and thereby make the pheasant easier to digest. Music is the most importunate, but also the most indulgent form of art. One is forced to hear the wretched barrel-organ parading in front of the house. Even a Mendelssohnian symphony, however, does not have to be listened to.
>
> (Hanslick 1854: 73)

Furthermore, through the partly functional and complementary use of lyrics – also an acoustic medium – music has a particular affinity with the sphere of the emotive-affective and, additionally, the vegetative. This is why it is so suitable as an expression and as a means of communicative 'conviviality' (see Knepler 1977, 1988, amongst others). This 'sensuous' factor is especially exploited for the extensive, diffuse and scattered awareness of the background as well as its concentrated effect.

Hanslick was strong in his criticism of such effect. 'The essence of music,' he wrote, 'the sound and movement, is what awakes the emotions of so many friends of music' (Hanslick 1854: 70). He goes on (unaware of overemphasizing) to stress the significance of music for such 'enthusiasts': 'a fine cigar, a special delicacy or a warm bath has the same effect, subconsciously, as a symphony' (ibid. 72).

Since then, through technical progress of a commercial kind, it has become possible to realize a symphony even as a warm bath. The following is taken from a report entitled 'A sprinkler for the conscience' discussing the radio exhibition in West Berlin (during European Music Year, 1985):

> One exhibitor has made music into a 'physical experience'. His exhibit shows an armchair with foot-rests, in which one can 'bathe' in music. Sound is transmitted through a built-in chassis, bass sounds in the back and foot areas, middle and high pitch in the head rest.
>
> (*Neue Musik-Zeitung*, no. 5, October/November 1985, p. 36)

ABSOLUTE MUSIC AND MUZAK: ON THE LOGIC OF THE LOSS OF REALITY

Music can easily be used as a generalized effective and enticing phenomenon, not because it is the art furthest from reality or most abstract, as current musical awareness would suggest, but because it was defunctionalized, despecified and made all the more interchangeable through the development of middle-class music based on a commercial economy. The leading form of musical realization removes the genetic and substantial mimetic references to reality in music.

A reason for the removal of reality is that middle-class society is unwilling to look at itself, despite the opportunities that exist to do so, at least in art. Instead a 'false reality' (of the artistic kind) is required, with which the society can identify, without recognizing itself therein – a particular privilege of the upper-class and its ideology. This 'false reality', especially in the broad aesthetic sense (see Haug 1972), is further needed to disguise the full and fundamental reality and to distract from it. In view of these purposes and despite the contrasts in quality and material substance, background music and concert music are surprisingly comparable, both in terms of function and in terms of their treatment and expression of reality.

The main trend of the concert – which has its opposite in programme music – has been to remove the 'cognitive' from the core of musical realization. It is transferred to other parts of the concert such as the written announcement or the programme booklet, which are themselves connected to texts for oratory performances or to opera libretti. The 'cognitive', therefore, is not entirely lost.

Rather, the dialectic of the affective and the rational, of the emotional and the cognitive, are formalized in actual and especially receptive realization. Both dimensions of this dialectic are structurally (temporally) and functionally apart. This is especially so if, in accordance only with higher cultural norms, musical reception is essentially and exclusively about the formal, material and spiritual; that is, the abstractly cognitive. What remains of the content are isolated, dull and unidentified biogenic moments (see Knepler 1977 for definition) of 'atmosphere', charm and feeling. These are presented as natural, which – prototypical of Hanslick – stands in opposition to the spiritual in a dichotomous and polarizing way.

The evolution of the paradigm of absolute and instrumental music, here, is as much a prerequisite as a consequence. It is perhaps even the case that programme music, or more specifically the emergence of programme music, represents a half-hearted negation of absolute instrumental music, which itself is simply presumed to be valid. This is so, because the instrumental medium as such is taken for granted and only subsequently given substantive content.

Background music is now also absolute music, in the negative-private sense of emancipation from the mimesis. Users of background music, professional or non-professional, including those who are 'self-immersed' (*Selbstberieseler*), shy away from all that is conscious or rational or which is a reflection on music and beyond (which could actually encourage oppositional thought).

A characteristic of packaged background music is the elimination of vocal music in favour of pure instrumental music, recognized by Hanslick as instrinsic. 'The singing of unfamiliar text', he writes 'is unsuitable, as there is then a tendency to listen more closely in order to understand the words. If so, the worker is unintentionally distracted from the work' (from a Philips advertisement, cited in Fehling 1976: 28). By the same token, the attention of the workers could equally be directed intentionally to the music, along with whatever it might be referring to. To avoid this, various dimensions, at least in commercial background music, are adapted to make the lyrics imperceptible. These include choice itself, levelling volume and limiting the range of frequency.

Self-made background music is different, if only because entertainment music, as a result of its historical development, is essentially vocal music. A matter for further investigation in this respect would be whether or not instrumental dance music of the disco type has assumed a qualitatively and quantatively greater role than before, not least through the widening of the background function. Even in the case of vocal music, the use of key words in the text surely serves to create and strengthen the atmosphere and mood of the hit in an abstract and distracting way. Thus connections with a more reflective realization are blurred or lost entirely – more so, given that the means of realization are thereby dispersed.

In this sense, music in the background and music in concert are opposites. In the concert the cognitive remains at least as a part of the context. The cognitive is maintained as a norm through the structural requirements and because of the 'structural' and 'humanizing' functions of the concert. Its form is also different from that of adapted music (as in background). Both a reason for and a result of this use of the cognitive is that the normal reaction – that is, attention, at least in abstract terms – should be maintained. The direction of this attention is secondary, but the music must be the central point of interest.

In the case of background music, on the other hand, *in*attention is required, both for the realization and effect. 'Functional music from Muzak avoids anything that could distract. It never interferes with the listener's awareness and does not disturb.' 'Muzak does not have listeners, the music is not heard, but perceived' ('Muzak' – prospectus, approx. 1972).

This is different in the case of 'self-immersion' (*Selbstberieselung*). Here, a higher degree of potential attention can be expected, at least as a starting point. The Walkman, a special case, mediates both poles of realization. Even for the musically active person, music through a Walkman can turn reality and the outside world into a haze of visually, haptically and olfactorily perceived background. However, the dominant form of realization does operate in a way such that the recipients listen to the music virtually unconsciously and perceive the music as an optional extra. For the receptive victims – that is, the involuntary 'by-listeners' – on the other hand, the effect of such background music is as usual, and tends to be a disturbance.

Absolute music and Musak have in common the fading of reality, either through music or in the music itself; the lack of an intensive musical assessment of the world in the ideology of 'absolute' music, and the absence of any specific content in adaptation, perception and effect.

In addition, the specific dramaturgic-formal musical *valeurs* are lost in background music. Both the emotive and cognitive 'realistic' content and the very spirit of music tend to evaporate from music which has been reduced to 'spiritually capable' (*geistfähiges*) material (see Hanslick 1854). What remains of the content are moods, sounds and empty forms – as opposed to 'sounding moved forms' (*tönend bewegte*). In this case, the music has musically unspecific functions and has the same effect as the warm bath, which Hanslick refers to in his mocking description of aesthetic values that are oriented towards content and that have been narrowed down to 'feeling'.

In all types of convergence of effect and function, the difference in repertoire is considerable. The absence of language, terms and consciousness, which in concert music is due to its (secondary) ideological formation and is largely reconcilable, is constitutive in background music. In background music a universal repertoire of average music exists, which may be well known or anonymous. Neither works nor titles are given and there is little to experience or to learn (cf. Braun and Kühn 1972; Fehling 1976).

In the circumstances, it is both cynical and naïve for Glenn Gould in a post-modern fashion to somehow hope that

> In the meantime the listener, through this ingenious glossary [background music], is the recipient of a direct and associative experience of the post-Renaissance vocabulary. Not even the most imaginative of courses in musical understanding could offer this.
>
> (Gould 1986: 179)

Gould overestimates the diversity of musical language (the repertoire is indeed monchrome and simplistic). He also underestimates the limiting realizational requirements and the conscious, rational moments of musical experience themselves, along with the terminologically cognitive dimensions of musical understanding. And the imagination – satiated with reality – which at least can be freed in absolute music, has long since disappeared from Muzak. The issue here is not the art of music but the art of manipulation; in other words, the expropriation of the senses and the sense, the aesthetic veiling of the world and ultimately beauty, rather than the adaptation of the aesthetic and the aesthetic adaptation of the world.

MUSIC AS ART AND MUSIC AS ADDICTION

In a historical perspective, background music becomes somewhat ambivalent. In the first place, the music loses its artistic character. Of such 'entertainment' or 'trivial' music, Dahlhaus writes,

There is no colloquial language of a musical kind. Thus, the pop-song and twelve-tone composition are categorized under the same heading as those creations which stand apart from and above everyday reality. It would be more truthful to use the term music in plural form, although even here one hesitates.

(Dahlhaus and Eggebrecht 1985: 11)

Under the trade name Muzak, prefabricated background music is declared non-music, but still as 'musical'. As mentioned earlier, background music is indeed used specifically as non-art; especially on a physiological and basic psychological level; that is, in the biogenic musical dimension.

It is not without good reason that background music has been suggested for animals and plants in order, for example, to increase milk production or stimulate the growth of cereals. This is a clear example of how – anthropomorphically and almost magically – concepts from the commercial world are carried over to nature or the 'biological world' (see Liedtke (1988: 103–15) for a description of examples). De la Motte (1972: 302) apologetically accounts for the failure of 'scientifically' measurable results. He argues that the industrialists (i.e. the commercial users of background music) have been 'exploited' or taken advantage of. Although this image of the betrayer betrayed may occasionally and not unreasonably appear, it is not dissimilar to advertising or indeed to 'commodity aesthetics' in general (Haug 1972). Although it may be of no use to the individual firm – whether in production, sales or distribution – it may benefit the (general and economically determined) social order of people themselves, their sensuousness and sensibility.

In actual fact, there is a widespread addiction to music, which is more common the younger the afflicted. This addiction hardly affects the quality of the workforce or turnover. If anything, it is lucrative and promotional. However, it is certainly and latently destructive in the case of individuals and their collective-communicative relationships.

This addiction to music is not made less destructive by the fact that music (as opposed to drugs) is generally considered to be harmless and a form of art. Moreover, as a pleasurable and addictive substance, music is certainly the cheapest. As such, Hanslick's irony is virtually outdone. He considered that

The new age has brought a magnificent discovery. It offers much more than the art of music to those who seek its emotional sensation without intellectual participation – sulphuric ether. This magical narcotic produces a highly pleasurable and expanding intoxication, which moves in a heavenly way through the whole body – without underplaying the value of wine, which is also not without musical effects.

(Hanslick 1854: 72)

The environmental psychologist, Mehrabian, sees music as a universal means of stimulation and influence for any time and any place:

> At an informal gathering, for example, the complexity, modernity and intensity of the music can be used to balance the level of animation of the guests. As the guests warm to each other, the music can be lowered in volume. If the level of the guests' activity and animation remains low, however, the volume can be increased and more lively pieces can be introduced.

(Mehrabian 1978: 82)

Libraries, schools and even bedrooms are not to be spared such unnoticeable regulation and standardization. In these cases, Mehrabian commends the connection between self-manipulation and masturbation (solo or duet, etc.), that is, between music and pornography: 'A bedroom should have a source of music and possibly coloured lights. Certain motels now offer rooms with televisions or video recorders that are connected to an in-house system and on which pornographic feature films can be viewed' (Mehrabian 1978: 87). With such 'music connected to other arts', however, we are moving away from the 'pure', instrumental music.

In background music, the addictive mechanism can clearly be seen in the pure as well as the impure forms, and is tied to a genuine need which is communicatively mediated. (Stroh, on numerous occasions, asks whether there is any need for pure music at all.) But this need, which can only be sketched here, is put to use purposefully and turned into the 'solipsistic'; that is, the 'illusionary communicative'. Because the need is only partially or supposedly satisfied in this way, a vacuum appears, which requires repeated filling. The regularity of the established concert, by the way, points in the same direction. However, with the concert, the phenomena of distance, isolation and the limitation of time all work against the addiction mechanism, towards which the realization of background music works, whether deliberately or not.

The targeted commercial application of music in the background may now seem inhumane, because, even with people (music or Muzak deals with people more than with animals or plants), the 'purely' musical affects especially the '*physis*', or the '*vegetativum*' respectively. The positively or negatively disturbing effect is relatively independent of the will and the consciousness of the participants. Crudely but effectively, background music

62

can be either stimulating and animating or calming and sedating. The increase in output, which is what matters in industrial terms, is therefore deceptive. Rather than an increase in labour productivity, which presupposes a real improvement in machinery or indeed the organization of work, the effect of the music is at most an increase in work intensity: more work per unit is done. Accordingly, the workers' exhaustion is greater and, at best, perceived less.

The use of musical therapeutics, which can only be mentioned in passing here, shows analogies, especially with 'music in the work place'. With music therapy there is an internal tendency to polarize music 'in concert' or music 'as background' as art or non-art.

The use of the music as art can be traced back to shamanistic practices and performances, which have been reformed by Platonism, Chinese universalism, Christianity (see Möller 1971 amongst others) and various 'new therapies'. These new therapies take on and attempt to apply more or less direct analogies to receptive music therapy and to the causal effectual relationships obtaining between music and the psyche: that is, between music and the person. Without giving up the normative and norm-creating requirement associated with art, the surrendering of the constitutive aesthetic distance does contradict it. Moreover, apart from the therapeutic values of actually making music, e.g. playing a musical instrument, music serves as a mood maker, as preparation, as background and as an appendage to the therapeutic process.

Often the use of music as therapy serves the same placebo purpose as music in the workplace. The use of music in the background follows the basic rule of palliative medicine and cynical 'healing' – the principle of Roman politics: *ut aliquid fieri videatur*. When the use of the physical encroaches on the spiritual in this way, what is produced is imaginary and illusionary. The music conveys to the worker or other listener the sense that something good is being done for him or her. This is even more pronounced because the 'need for music' is as widespread as a 'need for substitution'.

In the final analysis, background music is effective as music – not only physiologically but at least as much psychologically – and, because it is music, as 'art'. Elements of music as a 'colloquial language' and as 'second nature' are to be found in the unconscious or subconscious. As such, the activation and effect of these elements does not necessarily require conscious participation or reflection. 'Music in the workplace' occurs in this dimension. Productivity is promoted less directly through magically rhythmic 'programmes' contrary to human nature (with its fatigue-curve), than indirectly through the Hawthorne-effect (placebo) and through a diffuse improvement of the mood – that is, the working atmosphere and the zest for work (see Hoffmann 1972, Heister 1973, Fehling 1976, Liedtke 1988 amongst others).

The use of music, therefore, despite decades of saturation, is still considered to be a luxury. As mentioned earlier, this is the after-effect – a cultural lag – of historical traditions and occupation, which has meant that music was not always readily available. Only as art can music be addictive.

In this way, we can (almost) all now enjoy music from all over the world, or, as is more generally the case, 'worldwide' music – at the press of a button and in private. And still the presence of music is partly a reflection of what is known as the 'other world', particularly in German-speaking romanticism; the sensuous-transcendental, the realm of freedom. This is so, even if this realm is generally condescending and nearly always recreational. We can also enjoy the fact that music is offered as an optional extra, a free good, by the salesperson, employer, publican or otherwise. The concept of humanization of the workplace by means of (background) music is an illusion in the same way that the acoustic masking of the environment is an aesthetic improvement, a reconciliation, of the discrepancy between art and life.

MUSIC BY CHOICE AND IMPOSED MUSIC

Enjoyment of background music is not entirely universal. From the point of view of the concert and higher culture, background music is nothing more than entertainment and diversion, and a miserable pastime. It also represents the alienation of music and education. It is non-culture.

In actual fact, those people who are not lovers of this type of music are adversely affected and disturbed by it – much more so than they would be by concert and other similar forms of music. In concert, music access is limited, at least through an entrance fee, but also by the principle of free choice. First, no one is forced to go. Second, the person who decides to go knows what to expect from the programme or advertisement. The element of disturbance (here mostly through new music) is, therefore, relative and limited. Every deviation from the programme is, in principle, irritating. This is because the recipient may feel threatened by the unaccustomed and unfamiliar. Deviation in the detail may be particularly irritating if the musical phenomena are in the area of the aleatory or the 'happening'.

In 'packaged' background music the manifest programme of the concert serves as a hidden 'programmer'. The 'human objects' are reached unnoticeably through differentiation in the types of programme, depending on function and planned time structure. Even if the programming is largely claimed to be 'scientific', the theory and the intention behind it remain only ideological. Background music succeeds without being noticed and without the possibility of resistance.

In background music, the single programme and the repertoire are modelled on primary forms and on the polarity of the functions of stimulation or sedation. The prerequisite and result of this, even in individual and spontaneous use of background music, is the aforementioned average or 'worldwide' music. Interestingly, the freedom of choice in the case of the concert, which means that the audience has continually to be attracted, leads to similar phenomena. As a form of commodity, operating within the laws of a free market (which is itself relative), a polarization in the concert repertoire tends to occur. On the one hand there are the 'good old' standard productions, and on the other hand there are constantly new interpreters or interpretations (often only made-up as new for market purposes) (see Heister 1983: 474–8). The standard production of background music is of a different aesthetic level and type, and is the result of different motives. It is the 'worldwide' repertoire, with its famous titles, which can be adapted according to fashion and trend.

The notion of free choice is so important to the concert that the insinuation of a German fascist and president of the Reichsmusikkammer, Peter Raabe, is almost absurd, and certainly contradicts the specific principle of the concert: that of public and voluntary access. He writes 'There is surely no "duty" to go to a concert. The person who goes to a concert for such a reason is better advised to stay outside' (Raabe 1936: 12). The realization of background music is not a duty. It is a compulsion, historically more total and totalitarian than National Socialism could ever have imagined.

Given that the imposition of background music can be explained by the generally unpleasant circumstances of life, it is surprising that it is only recognized as an imposition by a small but growing proportion of the population. These people also see in it the undefinable 'terror' that operates through 'pleasant' means and is represented by background music. The universal realization of background music and its general social 'acceptance' are the expression and instrument of self-manipulation and voluntary subjection, which represent an ideal of domination.

It is possible, in fact probable, that such 'ideological' behaviour and awareness will not last long. In the meantime, however, the addiction will become more common. Hopes for change, therefore, are unlikely to be raised by internal developments within music culture alone. Wider changes are necessary for a more hopeful outlook.

At all events, the fans (as they usually are, without always knowing it) of background music will also be harmed, in terms of their communicative social behaviour and their aesthetic musical awareness. Admittedly, so-called objective data from empirical investigations have come to light, which might be interpreted – as in the old saying – 'Everything goes better with music'. This is so for all kinds of work. Monotonous and boring work, in its technical and psychological content, characteristically lacks reflection. This is a prerequisite for such work, which, in accordance with its socio-cultural status, is not self-determined. It is most certain, however, that even if things are subjectively perceived to be 'better with music', the objective and general deconcentration, nervousness and exhaustion from the work, whose subjects are influenced or 'self-immersed' by silent agreement or self-manipulation, is increased.

After all, when considered subjectively, background music is a form of noise, independent of the will and awareness of the participants. Just how questionable the use of music as 'humanization of the workplace' really is, is depicted by the discussions as to whether or not music should be used as a 'masking gauge' in firms with noise levels at or above what is generally considered to be harmful.

It is true that the stimulus threshold between sound and disturbance varies. Even the desire for background music is subjective and independent of circumstance. Objectively, however, background music does increase the level of noise in the environment (see Schafer 1985, among others). At least in public places, there is no direct protection against noise. The disturbance and harm inflicted by the music is all the more noticeable because the receptive realization is involuntary. In general, one cannot avoid a medical check-up for instance, or travelling by aeroplane. One may, however, avoid going to a concert and one may certainly want to avoid background music.

If it is used symbolically, socially and acoustically to whitewash or drown out reality, it serves as an imposed or self-elected 'masking gauge' of disturbance; it is like making perfume from stench.

Because, with the loss of reality, background music is somewhat sem-antic – at least in the abstract form of sounds, mood and general aesthetic structure – and despite the dominant dispersion and semi-consciousness of its reception, it can be an obtrusive and persistent noise. In this sense it is the same as already scented stench.

A more realistic processing of modern, industrial-technical 'soundscape' (Schafer 1985) is illustrated, on the one hand, by the schools which followed Varèse, Mossolow and *musique concrète* and on the other hand, by compositional-musical education of awareness, along the lines of Cage. Both directions, especially in their acoustics, refer consciously and reflectively to reality. They portray reality mimetically and take a position on it through distance. Background music, however, disassociates itself from soundscape through its aesthetic form, whereas its realization is only an unconscious and dissociated part of soundscape.

A third and particularly urgent alternative to the obtrusive stench and its perfume is the preservation and expansion of places and times of at least relative silence. In this day and age, a 'human right to calm' must be demanded. An initiative in 1985 of leading European broadcasting managers (whose media make a strong contribution to musical pollution) was to proclaim that 'Every person has the right to choose what type of music and sounds he or she wishes to hear, as long as it is not an imposition to others' (see Heister and Wolff 1986: 39). An ecological decision, which reflects liberal views against illiberal musical imposition.

MUSICAL ALIENATION AND SELF-DETERMINATION

In the concert, the split between art and life, which admittedly were never clearly united, reaches an extreme in the context of the musical process and its historical development. In this sense, it would be acceptable for music to be integrated or reintegrated into life. The desire to do so, it must be said, is often the expression of a nostalgia towards the 'natural' orders of medieval society, the ancient Greek 'harmony' of the city-state, or 'undividedness'; or at least their imaginary models. Such retrospective, restorative and imaginary 'non-alienation' is virtually impossible – and inhumane – today. There is so much technically unavoidable noise on the one hand, and so much exposure to music on the other, that it is also quite unnecessary to increase the amount of musical realization for this purpose.

Music in the background, as an imaginary or real opposite to concert music, is therefore only an element of the function of abstract distraction, intoxication and manipulation which is so vital to a system of domination. Chosen, self-made and individually consumed music does not have to be directly antisocial or harmful to others. From the point of view of personal development of self-realization, however, such music is superfluous in all cases; whether it is played through relatively quiet speakers or through a louder Walkman.

In these circumstances another polarization appears, which can only be discussed briefly here. In somewhat anachronistic terminology it can be described as 'house music' or 'music at home'. This includes live music outside the home; in a jazz cellar, 'rock garage' or political demonstration. It also includes conscious and active receptive musical realization and musically oriented social activities, such as dance or disco. In both cases, general and specific musical and communicative activities are sufficiently bound to one another. Background music, furthermore, is the banal and infernal distortion and caricature of a reconciliation of art and life.

Given that absolute music and Muzak are *Kippbilder*, then the loss of worldliness, sensuality and sensuousness in concert music – as opposed to background music – is both compensated and balanced, all the more so because the loss of reality is a phenomenon of musical ideology. The fetish of absolute music can herewith be derived from the social environment and circumstances of the concert. Its mediation, too, has historically widespread and far-reaching consequences. The reasons for this, which lie in the reality of commercial society, are more significant than those of middle-class ideology.

This reality is characterized by alienation and the fact that real, individual or collective self-realization and self-determination about social conditions are impossible. By alienation – used here in the relative, historically specific sense – we mean 'reversal', which stems from the fetishism of commodities. That is, the self-made appears as made by others, and social relationships between subjects appear as relationships between objects. (Other forms of alienation, which are more politically generated, are still present even in actually existing socialism.)

Here, the need for self-determination – even if satisfied falsely by background music, through dispersion, distraction and the mediation of the sense – finds a starting point. The person who plays a part in determining his or her own social circumstances, does not need distraction. Real self-determination means that imaginary self-determination, or determination from the outside through music is superfluous. Such marginalization of 'pre-history' (to use a Marxist term) is surely a 'music of the future'.

For the time being, we should concentrate as much as possible on preserving and developing the better rather than the worse. To protect the environment (cultural and natural) from a musical point of view, noise should be reduced. Noise protection should be considered in numerous respects, from the planning of space or traffic to measures against imposed music. In addition, the realization of the concert must be preserved as an area of calm, concentration and important music. The 'masking gauge', the aesthetic-semantic noise, that is, the perfumed stench of background music, however, will one day return to where it belongs: the dustbin of cultural and musical history.

BIBLIOGRAPHY

ADORNO, T.W. and EISLER, H. (1969) *Komposition für den Film*, Munich: Rogner & Bernhard.

BESSELER, H. (1925) 'Grundfragen des muskalischen Hörens', *Jahrbuch Peters 1925*, pp. 35–52.

BLAUKOPF, K. (1968) *Werktreue und Bearbeitung. Zur Soziologie der Integrität des musikalischen Kunstwerks*, Musik und Gesellschaft, vol. 3, Karlsruhe: Braun.

BRAUN, W. (1970) 'Oper und Konzert – Gegensatz und Ergänzung', *Kongressbericht Bonn 1970*, Bärenreiter, Kassel 1972, pp. 220–35.

BRAUN, W., and KÜHN, H. (1972) 'Musik im Hintergrund. Zur Erkenntnis eines umstrittenen Phänomens', *Neue Zeitschrift für Musik*, 133, 11: 619–27.

DAHLHAUS, C. (1967) 'Trivialmusik und ästhetisches Urteil', in *Studien zur Trivialmusik des 19. Jahrhunderts*, Studien zur Musik geschichte des 19. Jahrhunderts, vol. 8, Regensburg: Bosse.

——(1973) 'Zur Problematik der musikalischen Gattungen im 19. Jahrhundert', in W. Arlt *et al.* (eds) *Gattungen der Musik in Einzeldarstellungen: Gedenkschrift Leo Schrade*, Berne and Munich: Francke Verlag, pp. 840–95.

DAHLHAUS, C. and EGGEBRECHT, H.H. (1985) *Was ist Musik?* Wilhelmshaven: Heinrichhofen's.

FEHLING, R. (1976) *Manipulation durch Musik. Das Beispiel 'Funktionelle Musik'*, Munich: Werner Raith.

GOULD, G. (1986) 'Die Zukunftsaussichten der Tonaufzeichnung', in Fischer, M., Holland, D., and Rzehulka, B. *Gehörgänge. Zur Ästhetik musikalischen Aufführung und ihrer technischen Reproduktion*, München: P. Kirchheim, pp. 151–82 (translated from 'The prospects of recording', *High Fidelity*, April 1966).

HANSLICK, E. (1854) *Vom Musikalisch-Schönen. Ein Beitrag zur Revision der Ästhetik der Tonkunst*, Leipzig (Reprint Wissenschaftliche Buchgemeinschaft, Darmstadt 1965).

HAUG, W.F. (1972) *Kritik der Warenästhetik*, Frankfurt a.M.: Suhrkamp.

HEISTER, H.-W. (1973) 'Zwischen Ästhetisierung und Profit. Musik am Arbeitsplatz in Fabrik, Kaufhaus und Büro', WDR III 7.2.1973.

——(1974) 'Die Musikbox. Studie zu Ökonomie, Sozialpsychologie und Ästhetik eines musikalischen Massenmediums', in *Segmente der Unterhaltungsindustrie*, Frankfurt a.M.: Suhrkamp, pp. 11–65.

——(1980) 'Zum Verhältnis von Funktionalität und Eigenständigkeit unter logisch-historischen Gesichtspunkten', *Kongressbericht Berlin (West) 1974*, Kassel: Bärenreiter, pp. 11–65.

——(1983) *Das Konzert. Theorie einer Kulturform*, 2 vols., Wilhelmshaven: Heinrichhofen's.

——(1984) *'Musik als Ausdruck und Konstruktion'*, *Kindler-Enzyklopädie der Mensch*, vol. 6, Munich: Kindler, pp. 597–619.

HEISTER, H.-W. and WOLFF, J. (1986) 'Musikkultur in der Bundesrepublik Deutschland. III. Teil: Musik als Service', *Neue Zeitschrift für Musik*, vol. 147, no. 7/8, pp. 34–9.

HOFFMANN, C. (1972) *Musik im Produktionprozess*, Wissenschaftl. Arbeit zur Zulassung zum Staatsexamen Musikpädagogik, Ms., Berlin (West).

KNEPLER, G. (1977) *Geschichte als Weg zum Musikverständnis, Zur Theorie, Methode und Geschichte der Musikgeschichtsschreibung*, Leipzig: Reclam.

——(1988) 'Die Rolle des Ästhetischen bei der Menschwerdung. Überlegungen zu einem vernachlässigten Problem', *Weimarer Beiträge* vol. 33, no. 3, pp. 365–400.

LIEDTKE, R. (1988) *Die Vertreibung der Stille. Wie uns das Leben unter der akustischen Glocke um unsere Sinne bringt*, Munich Deutscher Taschenbuch Verlag.

MEHRABIAN, A. (1978) *Räume des Alltags oder wie die Umwelt unser Verhalten bestimmt*, Frankfurt a.M. and New York: Campus (translated from *Public Places and Private Spaces: The Psychology of Work, Play, and Living Environment*, 1976).

MÖLLER, H.-J. (1971) *Musik gegen Wahnsinn. Geschichte und Gegenwart musiktherapeutischer Vorstellungen*, Stuttgart: J. Fink.

MORITZ, K.P. (1785) 'Über den Begriff des in sich selbst Vollendeten', in *Werke in 2 Bänden*, Berlin and Weimar: Aufbau 1973, pp. 203–10.

MOTTE, H. DE LA (1972) 'Musik in der Industrie', *Neue Zeitschrift für Musik*, vol. 133, no. 6, p. 302.

RAABE, P. (1936) 'Adolf Hitlers Kulturwille und das Konzertwesen', *Kulturwille im deutschen Musikleben. Kulturpolitische Reden und Aufsätze*, vol. 2, Regensburg: Gustav Bosse.

SALMEN, W. (1988) *Das Konzert. Eine Kulturgeschichte*, Munich: C.H. Beck.

SCHAFER, R.M. (1985) *Il paesaggio sonoro*, Milano Unicopli/Ricordi (1st edn.: *The Tuning of the World*, 1977).

SCHILLER, F. (1795) 'Über die ästhetische Erziehung des Menschen, in einer Reihe von Briefen', in *Schillers Werke*, ed. L. Bellerman *et al.*, Vol. 7, pp. 251–392, Leipzig: Bibliographisches Institut o.J. (*c*.1930).

SCHWAB, H.W. (1980) *Konzert. öffentliche Musikdarbietung vp, 17. bis 19. Jahrhundert*, vol. IV, Lfg.2, *Musikgeschichte in Bildern*, Leipzig: VEB Deutscher Verlag für Musik, 2nd edn (1st 1971).

SPOHR, L. (1954) *Selbstbiographie*, 2 vols., ed. E. Schmitz, Kassel and Basel: Bärenreiter.

STROH, W.M. (1984) *Leben ja: zur Psychologie musikalischer Tätigkeit. Musik in Kellern, auf Plätzen und vor Natodraht*, Stuttgart: Bertold Marohl.

5

Public Performance and the Concert as Categories of Musical Action

IRMGARD BONTINCK

> The public concert – a product of the last century, which arose partly from the development of art itself, and partly from the expansion of social interaction – is of great importance in two respects: one specifically musical and the other related to cultural history.
>
> (Hanslick 1869–70: IX)

The concept of the 'concert' is so familiar nowadays, that we have readily accepted it as a category of musical activity, at least since 1869 when Eduard Hanslick published his book, *Geschichte des Concertwesens in wien*. Certainly as far as the German-speaking world is concerned, he was the first writer to deal systematically with the phenomenon of public musical performance, and to describe more closely the crucial changes which contributed to the development of the modern concert. What does the public performance of music now mean in terms of a category of musical action?

MUSIC-MAKING AS SOCIAL ACTION

Because music is humanly organised sound, there ought to be a relationship between patterns of human organisation and the patterns of sound produced as a result of human interaction ... The sounds may be the object, but man is the subject; and the key to understanding music is in the relationship existing between subject and object

(Blacking 1974: 26)

This relationship is based on the occurrence of the communal music action of those who take part in the process of realizing a piece of music in sound. The musical activity connected with the work to be performed is the starting-point for the construction of a network of social relationships. For a long time, whenever musical practice was under consideration, there was a tendency to undervalue the communication aspects of musical action, and its social consequences for the development of musical structures. It is only recent neuro-psychological research which has stressed the importance of these extra-musical factors in clarifying the complex relationships between man and music:

For music, dismissed as perception of the 'musical art', is far more than simply an acoustic structure. Music is more concerned with behaviour, and consequently with the people who create it. This also means that musical communication – just like direct speech – is not confined to the auditory channel of the senses, but rather communicates on several levels.

(Reinecke 1980: 100)

In the course of a musical event the musical work reaches the listener through the intermediary activity of the performers; this process of communication can vary according to the social function and social environment of the music. In the following paragraphs, an attempt will be made to demonstrate variations in the interaction between social function, social change, and musical events. The development of the idea that music in society only really exists through being performed before a larger group of people in company may serve as a key to this essay on changes in musical behaviour and musical practice.[1]

THE ORIGIN OF THE COMPULSION TO REALIZE IN SOUND

The ephemeral character of music has meant that for a long time it was regarded as a genre subordinate in our Western cultural practice to the other arts. This concept was clearly expressed in Leonardo da Vinci's *Trattato della pittura*, written at the end of the fifteenth century, in which he ranked painting in relation to music as follows:

> For one must call music the sister and inferior of painting. Music may not be called other than the sister of painting, since it is the subject of hearing, the sense next in importance to seeing. ... But painting excels and rules over music because it does not die immediately after its creation, as 'unfortunate music' does [original: 'la sventurata musica']
>
> (da Vinci 1890: 19)

A musical work is present primarily through its realization in sound within society. For this it needs to be reproduced by those in the community who play music.

If in this context one regards the musical action as a process of communication between the composer, the intermediary (interpreter in the broadest sense) and the listener, then this process, up to the time of Leonardo da Vinci, appears as a rather closed circle. The composer was as a rule also the performer of his music; the mostly small, intimate circle of participants, known to the composer, were naturally familiar with the music, because they were unified in a communal musical experience with which the social occasion for music-making was connected. On this level of musical practice, music did not yet exist as an esteemed work of art in the later (or present-day) sense, and the event of the performance was not yet considered a musical activity in its own right. The American music-sociologist John H. Mueller characterized this situation:

> In former times music-in-performance was essentially contemporary music. Such a situation is reduced to its lowest terms in nonliterate society, where all known music is performed at appropriate times, and is of such elementary and unspecialised character that nearly every man is a potential musical executant.
>
> (Mueller 1951: 9–10)

With the development of musical notation the next great step forward was taken, and music which had existed previously just as sound could be captured in a form which enabled it to survive 'unperformed'. In practice, for as long as the music maintained its direct relationship with society as *music connected with an occasion*, and for as long as it was not possible to accomplish quick dissemination of the written original on a large scale, the activities of composing on paper and musical performance remained in the hands of the composer. 'Even as late as two centuries ago, music was usually composed to order, or was written with good prospects for production, usually by, or under the direction of, the composer himself' (Mueller 1951: 10).

Composition and performance were not separate spheres of musical action, in the sense that performance would have been called into question on principle. Far more crucial was the criterion of use; the appropriateness for a particular occasion. The meaning and purpose of music were in the final analysis understood according to social function. Until the late eighteenth century nearly all musical activity had its social obligation, its social function. The earlier method of composition distinguished three categories or styles in this connection: church music, theatre music and chamber music. Composers were not yet writing autonomous works which required public performance, but music for particular occasions and events. A commission, whether from a nobleman, the church, or the town magistrates, was in itself a guarantee of performance: to amuse court society, to enhance the solemnity of a church service, or to underline the splendour of a public festival. Generally the composer would have known the occasion, even the actual room, as well as the people who would take part in the performance both actively or passively. The composer's responsibilities included the provision and the performance of music which corresponded to those social circumstances.

One of the most important factors in the gradual separation of the composer's activities from this closed circle of communication was the steadily increasing precision of musical notation. Thus, little by little, notation became an essential part of the musical action, alongside the actual music-making. With this achievement, which enabled the work to be free from its direct social function, a new stage in musical practice began.

The composer's activity now assumes the character of a social action in respect of the anticipated behaviour of those who will perform the composition. The composer puts forward a written model, which must be followed in producing the sound-event. The work, as a precisely defined written model, demands an interpretation, namely the activity of music-makers who find within the work the rules for the production of a sound-event. This 'need to interpret' (Heister 1983: 406) has, as an important prerequisite, the exact written 'blueprint' of the musical work; and divorcing the invention of music from its performance increasingly promotes the idea of public performance as the real objective and principal aim of musical communication. This new orientation changes the social motivation of musical action and intensifies the importance of the field of interpretation.

According to Carl Dahlhaus, the fundamental effort at the turn of the nineteenth century was devoted to making music public; that is, 'to bring music, freed from specific purpose, before the public, to which any music secretly aspires, even when standing aloof from the world' (Dahlhaus 1973: 887).

What, then, are the social conditions that have contributed to musical works becoming emancipated from particular social occasions and the musical prerequisites they demanded, letting the public performance become the primary or even the *only* form of musical communication? Such notions of performance as the 'second nature of the musical work', strengthened composers' convictions that what they produced were unique works of art, not primarily for immediate use but for posterity.

THE ORIGINS OF THE MUSICAL PUBLIC

Towards the end of the eighteenth century various political, economic, technical and social factors contributed to the development of the idea of public performance. Principally through social and political changes, a new class of listeners came into being: the so-called 'bourgeois' society. As the eighteenth century had progressed, opposition to feudal, absolutist rule had grown in European countries, at various times and with differing social preconditions. Liberalism, a system of ideas about a social order that was worthy of humankind, had steadily been promulgated, having developed at the end of the seventeenth century and during the eighteenth century under the political and social conditions of Absolutism and Feudalism, and fostered by the values defined by the Enlightenment and natural law. In England a period of democratization began with technological, political and economic upheavals, '. . . no other given part of legislative right can be exercised without regard to the general opinion of those who are to be governed', wrote Edmund Burke in a letter (Habermas 1981: 117). And in France, the political and social revolution initiated an 'Era of European Revolution', during which the basis of a new social order was laid. This led to a strengthening of self-assurance and the recognition of the social standing of the bourgeois class. For artistic practice, these changes in society spelt the end of a feudal art based on commissions for an intimate circle of consumers.

But this liberal, democratizing development was also supported by a new movement of the spirit. The ideas of the Enlightenment led not only to a new absolutist form of government (enlightened Absolutism) in Prussia and Austria, moderated to conform to new idealistic developments, but also to the first cultural-policy maxims. In these two countries in particular, the educational and cultural ideal implicit in these ideas was fully established in various measures. These decrees, particularly those of Josef II in Austria, aimed at making art, which had previously been reserved for a privileged upper class, accessible to a wider public. These innovations in educational and cultural policy had a great influence, even on the social status of musical art within society. During the Enlightenment, the pursuit of the cultural ideal brought with it ideas about absolute artistic values, as well as ideas about the importance of involvement with art for the development of character and the social progress of society. This early type of demo-cratization in connection with art and culture made it necessary for the arts to come out into the public realm.

At this time there were technical aspects which also contributed sig-nificantly to the expansion of musical communication. Continuous improve-ment in the reproduction of musical originals (e.g. in music-printing, engraving, and lithography) towards the end of the eighteenth century enabled musical creations to have an existence independent of their actual performance. Written music could now be reproduced easily and distributed in bulk. Dissemination and availability on a grand scale enlarged the circle of those participating in musical performance and enabled further per-formances, independent of the composer's activity, in both time and place. In this way, not only the separation of creative and 'post-creative' (performing) musicians is complete, but also a musical work, detached from its creator, can be presented to an anonymous and virtually unlimited audience.

The attainment of this large, anonymous circle completed the step into the 'Öffentlichkeit' (a German term, which had not previously existed, meaning 'public-ness'), since the awareness of a 'public' also came about at this time in the train of the social changes mentioned above. It is in this sense that Habermas (1981) describes 'Öffentlichkeit' as an organizational principle of political and literary communication and judgement in the classic bourgeois society – the educated, thinking public linked together by clubs, salons, newspapers, books and the theatre. In the context of public opinion, and particularly in the field of politics, this idea had developed earlier in England and France than in German-speaking countries, where it became part of the consciousness only at the beginning of the nineteenth century. It was closely connected with working in partnership, critical reasoning, and the expansion of commerce, but it had appeared before the turn of the century in the form of the older adjective, 'öffentlich' ('public').

Its application in contemporary writings already shows, among other things, changes in the value accorded to musical performance; 'the so common, often public use of music', writes Friedrich Rochlitz in 1799, belongs to the striking changes in the practice of music which brought new problems for its reception.

Now too, for the first time, the 'Publikum' (audience, public) is mentioned. The term is used collectively for the participants at performances or public events to which entry could be gained by means of an entrance ticket. In the German-speaking countries the term 'Publikum' came into vogue at the turn of the nineteenth century. Until then one had referred to 'Lesewelt' (reading world). In England, on the other hand, the term 'public' appeared as early as the middle of the seventeenth century in place of general terms such as 'world' or 'mankind'. In the course of the eighteenth century the term 'publicity' emerged, taken from the French 'publicité'. Thus, anything submitted to the judgement of the public, namely 'opinion publique' or 'public opinion', wins publicity as a result. In parallel with the considerable progress in the development of 'public-ness', and a public in the sphere of political democracy, public music-making and general availability of musical performances came about earlier in England than in Central Europe. In the sphere of social, musical action, it was in fact the growth of the public concert which made possible the education of a musical public. The shift within the process of musical communication may be more easily demonstrated by the concert-going public than by the new public of readers and spectators, since it does not result from a regrouping of a previous audience, the musical public having been actually created by means of it. One of the earliest mentions of such a new audience is found in the writings of Johann Adam Hiller, who not only addresses the 'public' but also – rather disparagingly – refers to them as 'the rabble' (Hiller 1781: 196). Even this manner of expression indicates clearly the changed position of the composer with respect to his audience, and is, moreover, a sign of his uncertainty about the reception of his works.

CHANGES IN THE MUSICAL COMMUNICATION PROCESS THROUGH PUBLIC PERFORMANCE

'With the expression "musical performance" one ultimately associates also the concept of a concert. The term "musical performance" is used when several large and small works are presented by a number of musicians in a particular sequence' (Schilling 1835: 322). The idea of a public performance of music now approaches more and more the recital format of a concert. The sign of what constitutes the public nature of the concert is its availability to everyone on payment of an entrance charge. Thus the relationship of those who take part in the process of musical realization changes in significant ways, as does also, ultimately, the character of the music presented in this form.

The concert now became primarily a musical presentation or event for a public coming together to enjoy music for its own sake, and whose affiliation to other purposes became looser and looser. Gradually, the word 'concert' developed as an all-embracing term for the location of the performance, social occasion, and musical practice in the course of the interpretation of an autonomous musical work of art. Now the composer seldom has the opportunity of being present in person at such a public performance, of being closely connected with those listeners who will be present, or of exerting influence on the selection or the interpretation of his or her works. The listeners become an anonymous public, that scarcely any longer influences the music being presented, since the programme' of a concert is decided and publicized beforehand.

Because of the composer's progressive detachment from direct communication with the recipients of his or her musical message, the activity of those responsible for the performance of the work assumes ever greater importance. The field of interpretation – namely the musical action in the course of realization in sound – assumes a sort of intermediary position between composer, work and listener; and consequently takes on a central position in the musical communication process. The more the work can exist independently of its creator, the more the composition (with its written performance instructions) becomes a general frame of categories for the process of interpretation as well as reception.

With the development of the mature concert form in the context of 'public music-making', the relationships and functions of the factors involved in the realization of a musical work have shifted. Supply and demand now form a functioning mechanism, which scarcely anyone within the system can avoid. Printing, performance, dissemination, and reception by the public form the basis for the existence of a musical work. The fact that access to public musical performance is in principle open to anyone on payment lends it the character of a commodity, and in two respects. Besides the possibility of purchasing musical works in their printed form, it is possible, by buying an entrance-ticket, to be in a position to demand a 'service' in the form of the performance – that is to say, the interpretation. Thus the dissemination of music took on several aspects, not least a democratic one and a business one:

> The 'breaking up' of music in various directions also meant a dissemination on a vast scale: it gained ground not only in wider groups of the population, but also in extensive areas of human action ranging from creative activity to economic use.
>
> (Antonicek 1979: 216)

This 'breaking up' of music meant not only the creation of a market for musical works, but also for the services associated with it; namely the activity of those concerned with its public presentation (performing musicians, music publishers, concert impresarios, instrument makers, etc.). 'The music-making business has resulted in the formation of a music entrepreneurship' (Pinthus 1977: 142). Thus Gerhard Pinthus described these consequences.

It took barely a century to progress from the first notions of public performance in the middle of the eighteenth century to its complete realization in the public concert. By the middle of the nineteenth century, people were already conscious of the changes in musical behaviour brought about by the public concert. One of the first to recognize the mature concert form as a new category of the musical communication process was Eduard Hanslick. He analysed the features of the historical development of notions of performance from their beginnings in the court concert, through the social activities of amateur musical associations and early musicians' organizations, to the development of concerts as a particular art form. Hanslick, who was a pioneer of musico-sociological thinking in this area of musical practice, summed up the development of the new art of the concert as follows:

> To the same degree that the concert became organised and formed a large public, it forfeited its former link with sociability and family life; instead it has become much more important for the purely artistic presentation of music.
>
> (Hanslick 1869–70: IX)

NOTE

1 The present author has edited a comprehensive collection of writings on the subject of 'Youth and Music'; it deals with the question of the origins of new musical attitudes and their effect on musical practice: I. Bontinck (ed.) *New Patterns of Musical Behaviour of the Young Generation in Industrial Societies*, Vienna, Universal Edition, 1974.

REFERENCES

ANTONICEK, T. (1979) 'Biedermeierzeit und Vormärz', in R. Flotzinger and G. Gruber (eds) *Musikgeschichte Österreichs*, Vol. 2 (of 2 vols), Graz, Vienna, Cologne: Verlag Styria.

BLACKING, J. (1974) *How Musical is Man?*, Seattle and London: University of Washington Press.

DA VINCI, LEONARDO (1890) *Trattato della pittura*, preface by Marco Tabarrini, Rome: Unione Cooperativa Editrice.

DAHLHAUS, C. (1973) 'Zur Problematik der musikalischen Gattungen im 19. Jahrhundert', in W. Arlt *et al.* (eds) *Gattungen der Musik in Einzeldarstellungen. Gedenkschrift Leo Schrade*, Bern and Munich: Francke Verlag, pp. 840–95.

HABERMAS, J. (1981) *Strukturwandel der Öffentlichkeit*, Darmstadt: H. Luchterhand Verlag.

HANSLICK, E. (1869–70) *Geschichte des Concertwesens in Wien*, Vol. 1 (of 2 vols), Vienna: Wilhelm Braumüller, repr. 1979 Hildesheim and New York: Georg Olms Verlag.

HEISTER, H.-W. (1983) *Das Konzert, Theorie einer Kulturform*, Vol. 2 (of 2 vols), Wilhelmshaven: Heinrichshofen's Verlag.

HILLER, J.A. (1781) *Ueber die Musik und deren Wirkungen*, Leipzig: Friedrich Gotthold Jacobaer und Sohn.

MUELLER, J.H. (1951) *The American Symphony Orchestra*, Bloomington: Indiana University Press.

PINTHUS, G. (1977) *Das Konzertleben in Deutschland*, Sammlung musikwissenschaftlicher Abhandlungen, VIII, Baden-Baden: Verlag Valentin Koerner.

REINECKE, H.-P. (1980) 'Musik im Original und als technische Reproduktion', *Jahrbuch der Stiftung Preussischer Kulturbesitz*, XVI.

ROCHLITZ, F. (1799) 'Die Verschiedenheit der Urtheile über Werke der Tonkunst', *Allgemeine musikalische Zeitung*, No. 32, col. 497.

SCHILLING, G. (ed.) (1835) *Enzyklopädie der gesammten musikalischen Wissenschaften oder Universal-Lexikon der Tonkunst*, Vol. 1 (of 6 vols and supplement), Stuttgart: Verlag von Franz Heinrich Köhler.

6

What Makes Music Musical?

KEITH SWANWICK

The shaking air rattled Lord Edward's membrana tympani; the interlocked malleus, incus and strirrup bones were set in motion so as to agitate the membrane of the oval window and raise an infinitesimal storm in the fluid of the labyrinth. The hairy endings of the auditory nerve shuddered like weeds in a rough sea; a vast number of obscure miracles were performed in the brain, and Lord Edward ecstatically whispered 'Bach!' He smiled with pleasure, his eyes lit up.

(Aldous Huxley, *Point Counter Point*)

SOUND AND MUSIC

What are these 'obscure miracles' that transform Lord Edward from a set of vibrating tissues to a person responding positively to Bach? The answer is surely important for musicians, if they are to be sensitive both to their art and their audience, and for teachers of music who need to know something of how people can respond to music. The nature of musical response and the corresponding cultural environment is the theme of this article.

It is not my intention to review the literature on the psychology of music, a service which has already been performed by others, notably Shuter-Dyson and Gabriel (1968), Davies (1978), Deutsch (1982), Sloboda (1985) and Hargreaves (1986). Workers in psychology have sometimes appeared to forget that the central problem is to explain 'the structure and content of musical experience' (Sloboda 1986). Generally, psychological work in music has appeared to neglect this central problem and has been without a cohesive and unifying theory. From the perspective of the special area of child-development, David Hargreaves complains that there are virtually 'no coherent psychological theories of the specific developmental processes underlying children's musical perception, cognition or performance' (Hargreaves 1986: 3).

Early investigations began from a very simplistic, almost mechanistic view of human engagement with music. The most obvious way to investigate the effects of music seemed to many to be to try to find a corre-spondence between the physics of sound and its direct effect on human physiology. The shortcomings of this methodology are as obvious to us as they were to Aldous Huxley as he describes what is happening to Lord Edward. The 'obscure miracles' are not illuminated. A great deal depends on the state of health of the auditor, on the environment, on the degree of alertness or fatigue of the subject, on the degree to which the music used is familiar, and on the previous musical experience of the subjects. Generally speaking, music does tend to increase rates of pulse and respiration, though not always (Lundin 1953: 134). However, the physiological responses of musicians are likely to be less predictable than those of subjects picked up 'off the street', a finding which has proved something of a nuisance to investigators (Hunter 1970). Other early studies, while not relying on physiological measures, show a concentration on musically unstructured and fairly characterless sound material. Myers and Valentine carried out experiments with single tones and bichords, work modelled to some extent on that of Bullough who investigated single colours (Myers and Valentine 1914; Bullough 1906). Valentine tried to find out if subjects would agree on descriptions of the emotional effect of single intervals (Valentine 1962). They did not; this is hardly surprising, since isolated sound material of this kind tends to be what each individual chooses to make of it. For example, the minor third in one experiment was described as 'sad' or 'plaintive' by eleven people, as against twenty-six who thought that the major third had that character. Bits of musical material heard out of context are notoriously ambiguous. Within certain conventions of Western tonality, a minor third can be heard as the upper half of an incomplete major triad and a major third as part of a minor chord. Even at this impoverished level of musical experience, music-makers and music takers bring with them their own sets of expectations.

Since the 1940s, the field of the psychology of music has been littered with 'ability' tests and their evaluation. Some researchers attempt to include an 'appreciation' component, for example, Wing (1948); but many confine themselves to the safer ground of testing the identification of pitch changes or the ability to count the number of notes in chords or to discriminate between different timbres, sometimes asking for the comparison of melodic or rhythmic fragments on the basis of 'same' or 'different' (see for instance Seashore 1938; Lundin 1949; Bentley 1966).

These limited forms of investigation into musical response somehow miss the whole point of what music is really about, all richness is lost. Just as increase in pulse rate or respiration by themselves tell us little about the perceptual and affective worlds of the subjects, so correct or incorrect identification of pitch changes or the number of notes in a chord only begins to scratch the surface of how people construe music and respond to it. The listening agenda is just not the same.

MUSIC AND PLAY

In order to circumnavigate the dangerous waters of atomistic psychological investigation, while at the same time avoiding becoming bogged down in a vast literature, I shall propose that the essence of musical activity, indeed, of all significant cultural achievement, is rooted in the activity of play. From this beginning it is possible to approach the problem of what constitutes musical experience in a more comprehensive manner. To put the essential theory briefly; play in very early childhood is characterized especially by the pleasure of *mastery*, what Piaget calls 'a feeling of virtuosity or power' (Piaget 1951: 87–9). Think of the pleasure babies get from throwing a toy out of a pram over and over again, just enjoying the experience of physical control; or of the two-year-old who has just managed to climb steps, trekking up and down repeatedly for the sheer sense of achievement.

Play soon becomes *imaginative* in emphasis and 'subjects things to the child's activity, without rules or limitations'. This, according to Piaget, is pure assimilation, 'thought polarised by preoccupation with individual satisfaction', where children seem actually to think that their 'make-believe' world really exists. At one time, I was accompanied on walks not only by three children but also by a horse, which, though completely invisible, was something of a nuisance, causing us to open gates rather than climb stiles and making us wait while it was fed. This enigmatic animal was a fairly constant companion for several months, a vividly imagined being. Pretending to *have* a horse is very different from pretending to be one. That would be an instance of the third major element of play, also evident from the first year of life. Piaget calls it *imitation*, and regards it as the opposite of imaginative play. When imitating, the child accommodates him- or herself to the impression of external objects, people and events, taking over some of their characteristics, becoming like them to some extent; pretending to be an animal or whatever. In imaginative play, the world around us is transformed to our standards: in imitation, *we* are transformed. Each of these play dynamics – mastery, imitation and imaginative play – can be seen at work in music in fundamental ways, and I would contend that musical experience is the poorer if they are not in equilibrium.

MUSICAL MATERIALS AND MASTERY

The impulse towards *mastery*, towards 'virtuosity and power', obviously evolves into musical activities. The handling of voices and instruments; the development of ensemble skills; where appropriate, the use of notations; delight in the virtuosity of others: these are all elements of mastery. There is surely a developmental continuum from the pleasure experienced by a baby who has just learned to repeat a vocal sound or to shake a rattle repeatedly, to the achievement of a sitar player technically exploiting the potential of a particular raga.

Initially, mastery presupposed a focus on the materials of music: tone colours, durations, pitches, silences, and loudness levels. Controlling and discriminating between these materials inevitably involves skill and aural analysis. Musicians frequently select certain clusters or sets of material to work on. By the same token it seems important for composers to limit available resources to make music manageable – indeed, sometimes to get them started. Thus we have tonal systems, twelve-note techniques, pentatonic scales, Indian ragas, and more limited sets of sound – as we find when Debussy makes a piano prelude out of the interval of the third, or when Bartók writes pieces in his *Mikrokosmos* based on 'fifth chords', or 'triplets in 9/8 time', or when jazz musicians improvise on the foundation of a well-known 'standard' tune, or a blues chord sequence.

Limited sets of materials are invaluable in extending techniques, sharpening discriminations, and emphasizing particular relationships. The music-maker or active listener may focus on materials and techniques and become caught up in the way that certain colours, tones and techniques are handled. Just how does a composer or improviser achieve this or that effect? What types of sound give this music its character?

Control of musical materials presupposes a degree of *delight* in the sounds themselves. Grieg in his later years, recalled his great excitement when, as a boy of six, he discovered for himself the chord of the ninth (Grieg 1905). This piling up of thirds, one on top of the other, was, for him, an impressive sonorous phenomenon, yielding joy which at that stage had little to do with musical expression or structural ordering. And, of course, later in life this particular chord becomes a striking feature of his compositional style, as, for example, in his *Notturno* for piano.

Delight in sound materials as independent entities is also described by Kenneth Grahame, author of *The Wind in the Willows*, as he writes about the childhood experience of 'strumming' at the piano – much better than 'beastly exercises'.

> Those who painfully and with bleeding feet have scaled the crags of mastery over musical instruments have yet their loss in this: that the wild joy of strumming has become a vanished sense. Their happiness comes from the concord and the relative value of the notes they handle; the pure, absolute quality and nature of each note in itself are only appreciated by the strummer. ... And throughout all the sequence of suggestion, up above the little white men leap and peep and strive against the imprisoning wires.
>
> (Grahame 1885: 75)

Many composers of this century have tried to return to this state of childhood grace, starting afresh from sound itself in an attempt to open up new musical possibilities. Take, for instance, Stockhausen's advice to potential performers of *Gold Dust*, from *Aus den Sieben Tagen*:

> for small ensemble
> GOLD DUST
> live completely alone for four days
> without food
> in complete silence, without much movement
> sleep as little as possible
> after four days, late at night
> without conversation beforehand
> play single sounds
> WITHOUT THINKING which you are playing
> close your eyes
> just listen

The following anecdote from Armenia is but one example from Peter Hamel's account of the mystical and magical potential of sound; sound not yet fashioned into music but contemplated for itself, linked with the belief that such meditation leads to insights and enlightenment (Hamel 1978). An Armenian folk story tells of a man who played the cello. Every day he sat, playing the same note, hour after hour. His wife asked him why he did not do as other cellists, move his fingers up and down the strings to make other notes. He replied, they are looking for their note, I have found mine. (Adapted from Peter Hamel in *Through Music to the Self.*)

Such stories remind us of the primordial power of music but they also raise musical and educational issues. What do we think about getting stuck, so to speak, on one note? Is such a minimalist attitude to music a form of arrested development? We all might give different answers; my own view is that a musical and educational perspective that takes into account only this facet of human psychology is simply inadequate. It fails to notice other vital aspects of mind. In particular, by limiting concentration on the impressiveness of experienced sound, it denies another natural desire, to *master* 'the crags' of musical materials, to manipulate instruments, to control as well as to savour sound. There are also *imitative* and *imaginative* elements in the repertoire of human mind, which are part of the rich fibre of musical experience.

IMITATION AND EXPRESSION

The more obviously representational an arts activity is (i.e. the more it refers to events in life) the more it is imitative, having what I would call *expressive character*. Imitation is obvious enough in programme music and in opera but even in the most 'abstract' musical works there are essential imitative gestures. Every performance of a Bach fugue has its own particular universe of gestures, of feeling and emphasis; it has expressive character which can be changed within certain limits by the manner of performance; choice of speed, accentuation and so on. Musical characterization is a direct development of the 'let's pretend' quality of imitative play in early childhood. Fundamentally, and in Piaget's terminology, imitation – expressiveness in music – is an act of accommodation: to some extent we become like the music, taking on a trace of its feeling qualities through postural and gestural *schema*. Imitation is not mere copying, but involves sympathy, empathy, identification with, concern for, seeing ourselves as something or someone else. It is the activity by which we enlarge our repertoire of action

87

and thought. No meaningful music lacks references by imitation to things beyond itself, even if in a highly abstract manner.

> Presumably the notes which we hear at such moments tend to spread out before our eyes, over surfaces greater or smaller according to their pitch and volume; to trace arabesque designs, to give us the sensation of breadth and tenuity, stability or caprice.
>
> (Proust 1913: 288)

Studies of the expressiveness of music tend to run into one major obstacle: any account by people as to how expressive character is perceived will inevitably be *metaphorical*, poetical rather than analytic. The quotation from Proust is an illuminating instance of this.

There is a history of psychological investigation here. One of the earlier attempts was made by Esther Gatewood (in Schoen 1927). She compiled a list of possible effects music might have on listeners, such as sad, serious, amused, rested, longing, patriotic and irritated. People were given a form of questionnaire on which those words were to be checked off in response to short, fairly popular pieces. A comment by Langer in *Philosophy in a New Key* pinpoints a doubtful assumption behind such work:

> The results of such experiments add very little to the well-known fact that most people connect feelings with music, and (unless they have thought about the precise nature of that connection) believe that they *have* the feelings while they are under the influence of the music especially if you ask them which of several feelings the music is giving them.
>
> (Langer 1942: 181–2)

Not only is the language of musical description essentially metaphorical, but there is a distinction to be made between how a person believes music makes him or her *feel* and how the character of the music *itself* is perceived. For example, it would be perfectly possible for a piece of music to be perceived to have about it a general air of 'cheerfulness', but on that account be 'irritating' to a particular listener who may be feeling cynically disposed at the time; or for music to be heard as 'solemn' or 'patriotic' and to make an outsider feel 'amused' by its pretentiousness.

It has been argued that words are able to represent things for us because 'they produce in us some replica of the actual behaviour' (Osgood *et al.* 1957). In music, how is any such 'replica' mediated? What remnant of remembered experience is activated or retrieved when we respond by imitation to the 'content' of music?

An imaginative answer was given long ago by Vernon Lee (1932). In a series of case studies, she investigated ideas people have about music. She divided the responses of her subjects into two main categories, 'listeners' and 'hearers'. 'Listening', she tells us, is 'taking stock of something which is moving and changing and in so far as it is accompanied in him who listens by a sense of high and complex activity'. 'Hearers', on the other hand, tend to day-dream and allow attention to wander away from the music. She makes it quite clear that the division into types is not really a matter of how people listen, but of their *attitude* towards the activity. 'Listeners' know that they are inattentive from time to time and tend to regard this as a failing: 'hearers' 'rarely admit that they have lapses of attention' and in any case, tend not to think of music as requiring sustained concentration.

Vernon Lee found the most positive and illuminating views among her 'listeners', who spoke of music 'chasing away fatigue', bringing the 'keenest inner excitement or exhaltation', a 'strong element of pleasure', a 'special profound emotion'. From this evidence, she is able to build a model to account for those 'replicas' of life situations, drawing particularly upon the work of Henry Head and his concept of '*postural schemata*'. To quote Head directly:

> Every recognisable (postural) change enters into consciousness already charged with its relation to something that has gone before, just as on a taximeter the distance is presented to us already transformed into shillings and pence. So the final product of the tests of the appreciation of posture, or of passive movement, rises into consciousness as a measured postural change. For this combined standard, against which all subsequent changes of posture are measured before they enter consciousness, we propose the word 'schema'. By means of perpetual alterations in position we are always building up a postural model of ourselves which constantly changes.
>
> (Head 1920: 605–6)

Vernon Lee suggests that music activates these *schemata*, (literally 'ghosts') of past movements. In music we can discern an immense range of manner of movement: reaching out, retraction, coalescence, extrusion, integration, disintegration – the rhythms of development and growth which are funda-mental to all living forms. The schemata of a reaction, a stance, a muscular set, an emotion or a gesture are presented in what Hanslick called the 'sounding forms' of music and we empathize with them. We do not need to confine ourselves to thinking about particularly strong feelings or emotional states. Every perception involves an element of muscular adjustment, a modification of kinaesthetic position, and any physical or 'mental' activity will leave a residual postural trace, including the activity we call thinking.

The relationship of posture and gesture with feeling and emotional states has been analysed by Charlotte Wolff (1945), among others. Each gesture is a 'synthesis of many movements' from a basic postural 'platform'. Fundamental gestures include those of forward drive and inhibition, reaching out and withdrawal. According to Wolff, the posture of a 'happy' person is characterized by 'roundness'. The 'flexor muscles become rounder through animated circulation and reinforced tone' (Wolff 1945: 9). There are striking unintentional resemblances between her descriptions of patterns of posture and gesture and the ways in which people say they hear music. Here are just a few examples.

The state of *extreme inhibition*, Wolff tells us, is often characterized by extensor movements, withdrawal, stereotyped and arrhythmical movements, motor unrest, slow motor speed and unnecessary movements. *Depression* may display itself in slow motor speed, non-emphatic gesture, hesitating, tightness of posture and very few unnecessary movements. *Elation* is shown by a wealth of unnecessary movement, fast motor speeds, exhibitionist behaviour, spontaneous, emphatic and rhythmical gesture and self-assertiveness. *Anxiety* is often revealed in unnecessary movement with perseverance, ambivalent motor speed, fidgeting and variable forward impulse. All of these descriptive terms can just as easily be applied to the character of music as to the symptoms of feeling states. For instance, we would be very unlikely to classify as 'exuberant and outgoing' a performance of music with a slow motor speed, non-emphatic gestures, full of hesitations, uncertainties of tempo and repeated fidgeting little figures.

Music is well-adapted to communicate particular kinds of forward motion. Terms like *giusto*, *ritmico*, *a tempo*, *pesante*, and *rubato* serve to point a few parallels, in a relationship recognized by many, including Dalcroze.

> Rhythm, like dynamics, depends entirely on movement, and finds its nearest
> prototype in our muscular system. All the nuances of time – *allegro, andante,
> accelerando, ritenuto* – all the nuances of energy – *forte, piano, crescendo,
> diminuendo* – can be 'realised' by our bodies, and the acuteness of our musical
> feeling will depend on the acuteness of our bodily sensations.
>
> (Dalcroze 1921: 81)

There is experimental evidence of my own to show that music can be described in terms of weight, size, stiffness, outward or inward direction and the degree of activity (Swanwick 1971, 1973, 1979). Such descriptions have been given at a statistically significant level by children as young as seven, in response to simple musical phrases. Correlations were found between crude emotional labels, for instance, that of 'sadness', and the more subtle postural qualities of heaviness, passivity and inward-lookingness. This is hardly surprising. We inevitably use postural metaphors to try to communicate the qualities of affective states. We all know what is meant when someone says that they were made to feel 'small', or were 'weighed down' with care, 'stiff' with fright, 'heavy' with apprehension, 'light as air', 'depressed', and so on. Nor are such expressions unique to the English language. The distinction between 'hearer' and 'listener' has a bearing on this. To give an example; let us assume that a someone attends closely enough to music to recognize at a certain point a particular 'attitude' or 'gesture'. By definition, the 'hearer' is likely to wander off into memories of situations in his or her own life, or perhaps contemplate some bio-graphical detail of the composer or performer, or admire the hat of someone in front. These activities will be regarded as distractions by a 'listener'. Thus George Bernard Shaw found his mind wandering towards remembered Irish funerals whenever he heard the *Eroica* Symphony funeral march:

> Now the sorest bereavement does not cause men to forget wholly that time is money. Hence, though we used to proceed slowly and sadly enough through the streets or terraces at the early stages of our progress, when we got into the open a change came over the spirit in which the coachmen drove. Encouraging words were addressed to the horses; whips were flicked; a jerk all along the line warned us to slip our arms through the broad elbow straps of the mourning-coaches . . .
>
> It is that fatal episode where the oboe carries the march into the major key and the whole composition brightens and steps out, so to speak, that ruins me. The moment it begins, I instinctively look for an elbow strap . . .
>
> (Shaw 1981: 3, 134)

Shaw – very much a 'listener' – tells us that he would then wake up and realize regretfully that he had, for several pages of the score, not attended to a note of the performance.

One of the reasons why music may appear to 'mean' various things to different people, lies in the degree to which specific experiences are associated with music. If we are day-dreaming, then a musical gesture will set off a string of personal and idiosyncratic associations. If we take up the attitude of a 'listener', then, whilst recognizing the character of a particular passage, we will tend to hang on, not to the imagined elbow straps but to the thread of the continuing music and experience the 'exhaltation' of Vernon Lee's 'listeners', a rich fusion of myriad past gestures.

91

The expressive character of a musical passage is thus determined by our perception of its apparent weight, size, forward impulse, manner of movement and other components of posture and gesture. Since such constructs are formulated within the relativities of particular musical contexts, no analysis of physiological change or measurement of isolated aural abilities will help us to understand them. The metaphorical nature of such 'meanings' may account for the power of music to stir and move people, even when there may be no words, no 'programme', and no obvious association with particular cultural values. Metaphorical richness accounts for much of the affective charge of poetry, drama and literature; there is no reason to suppose that music is not also charged, all the more powerfully by being free from the literalness of representation, being fluently *expressive* but not naturally *descriptive*.

IMAGINATIVE PLAY AND MUSICAL STRUCTURE

Anyone who has close relationships with children will know about the assimilative nature of imaginative play, where objects, events and people are transformed into other than themselves, where things are frequently conjured up out of the air. In imaginative play we create a world of new relationships out of the elements around us. In the same way, a new realm is created in a musical composition. If mastery is the element of play that motivates us towards the materials of music, and if imitation is the root of expressive, or referential, character, then imaginative play is the source of musical *structure*. By structure, I mean bringing the expressive elements into relationships, establishing directional tendencies that can lead us on expectantly or be broken off to surprise and delight us. Freud tells this story:

> The Prince, travelling through his domain, noticed a man in the cheering crowd who bore a striking resemblance to himself. He beckoned him over and asked: 'Was your mother ever employed in my palace? 'No, Sire' the man replied. 'But my father was.'
>
> (cited in Koestler 1964: 66)

Here our expectations to do with the relationship of king to commoner are turned right around, within a further relationship to the certain norms of

92

sexual behaviour. As Wollheim says, in humour, 'a moment's mobility is granted to the mind' (Wollheim 1971: 105).

The ultimate distinguishing feature of musical individuality, originality and quality is not found at the level of inventing new sound materials or even in making expressive gestures, but in unique relationships brought about by musical speculation – the imaginative transformation of sound and gesture into musical structure. Unfortunately, the very word 'structure' tends to suggest a fixed *construction* and elicits images of strictly notated pieces or movements in 'sonata form'. Let us be clear: musical structure is simply the effectiveness with which one expressive gesture is heard to relate to another; this applies as much to an improvised jazz solo as to a movement of a symphony.

One influential and penetrating account of how musical structure can be seen as a dynamic process is given by Meyer (1956). Meyer accepts a psychological principle that feeling, or affect, is most intense when reactions are stimulated 'that do not gain expression either in conduct, emotional expression, or fantasy' (MacCurdy 1925). In Meyer's terms: 'Emotion or affect is aroused when a tendency to respond is arrested or inhibited.' He shows how, within a particular musical culture, expectancies are aroused which are fulfilled, delayed or inhibited. Incomplete musical figures set up a desire for completion: for example, passing over a note without sounding it in a known scale series creates a need to hear that note; unresolved chords have us waiting for resolution. From these observations, Meyer generates a theory which identifies important *cognitive* aspects of music, particularly the operation of stylistic norms against which deviations are perceived.

Such a theory owes rather more to Gestalt psychology than to MacCurdy's theory of the emotions, and it is the Gestalt basis that is most helpful in describing the way in which music is structured and perceived. The fundamental act of perception is to see pattern, form or configuration. Perception is essentially the organization of sensory stimulation into meaningful wholes. Simply to survive, we 'theorize' about potentially confusing noises made up of pitch, timbre, duration and loudness; we impose tonality, we hear melodies, counterpoints, imitation, sequences and style, just as Lord Edward did in the passage given at the opening of this chapter. It is a universal human need to make *Gestalten*, to see everything as form. Conversely, the human species has a strong tendency – also necessary for adaptation and survival – to break a mould, to violate a *Gestalt*, to replace one configuration with another. Every good joke reveals this force at work as does every other act of originality, however small. Musical structure arises both from our need to perceive coherent groupings and at the same time from the need to play imaginatively with new possibilities. When participating in music, we can become conscious of this tension. Hans Keller puts it thus:

> The background of a composition is both the sum total of the expectations a composer raises in the course of a piece without fulfilling them, and the sum total of those unborn fulfillments. The foreground is, simply, what he does instead – what is actually in the score.
>
> (Keller 1970)

The Gestalt processes involved in musical perception have been described elsewhere, notably by Deutsch and Sloboda. But they were anticipated long ago by Hanslick, who, sounding remarkably similar to Meyer and Keller over a century later, writes:

> The most important factor in the mental process which accompanies the act of listening to music, and which converts it into a source of pleasure, is frequently overlooked. We here refer to the intellectual satisfaction which the listener derives from continually following and anticipating the composer's intentions – now to see his expectation fulfilled, and now to find himself agreeably mistaken. It is a matter of course that this intellectual flux and reflux, this perceptual giving and receiving, takes place unconsciously and with the rapidity of lightning flashes.
>
> (Hanslick 1854: 98)

Such engagement is impossible if an inadequate 'set' is brought to the experience. Listening for motivic development in much African drumming, for Wagner-like orchestration in Haydn, for tonal tensions in modal plain-song, or for the pitch relationships of Western scales in certain Indian ragas would usually be inappropriate. Expressive characterization lays down a charge of feeling with which we to some extent empathize. But these feeling schemata, these 'ghosts', are vitalized by being combined in new and surprising relationships. Effective music depends not only on *what* is expressed but also on it being *well* expressed, imaginatively structured by the musician. Rewarding listening depends on the ability to 'go along' with particular expressive characterizations and, at the same time, to feel what Bullough called aesthetic 'distance', to recognize that a musical work, whether notated, remembered or improvised, has a life of its own and will at times defy our predictions and expectations. The ability – and it is a considerable ability – to make and respond to music on these terms can only be nurtured and grow from substantial musical experience. Some of

94

this experience may be acquired through education, some more informally in social settings through the process of enculturation. However, the social and cultural context of music also raises a further set of problems for those interested in trying to understand the nature of musical experience and response.

MUSICAL VALUING AND SOCIETY

All that counted was sound and the murderous mood it made. All din and mad atmosphere. Really it was nothing but beat, smashed and crunched and hammered home like some amazing stampede. The words were lost and the song was lost.

(Cohn, cited by Martin 1981: 160)

It is undeniable that our perception of and response to music is influenced by the position it is seen to occupy in a *value framework*. This is probably much stronger than we often suppose and may be regarded as the fourth essential element in the experience of music (the other three being response to sound materials, the identification of expressive character, and the perception of structural relationships). Research and everyday observation suggest that people are not only predisposed to value certain kinds of music for other than musical reasons, but they are likely to perceive the expressive and structural elements of music itself rather differently, depending on the attached value label. For example, the musical value-worlds of regular listeners to Radio 3 and Radio 1 will tend to be sharply isolated from each other, and within these general areas of musical preference there will be further subdivisions of preference and dislike. While the preferences of each individual evolve and fluctuate, there are usually clearly recognizable value clusters: combinations of what we read, how we choose to dress and do our hair, what form of speech we use, attitudes to others, and so on.

Within the field of popular music alone, we shall find distinctive elements of lifestyle across various groups of people whose musical worlds may be centred, around, say, Reggae, Funk, Disco, Soul or Heavy Metal. At times, these lifestyles and the music that accompanies them are so closely bound together that the transmission of contradictory signals is felt as dissonant. For example, recently with a young relative I came across a teenager playing a tape of Led Zeppelin. After the visitor had gone my companion observed that he had been listening to the 'wrong' music. He was not *dressed* appropriately, turned out as he was in a large black coat and topped with blond,

95

possibly dyed hair. He should, I was told, be listening to New Wave or Soul or Funk but certainly not Heavy Metal. If he was really into Heavy Metal he should have been wearing a leather jacket, sporting a pair of dirty jeans and have long greasy hair. The verdict was quite clear: 'he doesn't know his music'. His musical preferences and other cultural signals were discordant; the images were out of line. Perhaps such apparent contradictions are a sign of change, when a value-system is on the move, evolving, crumbling? In any event, unlike my relative, I would regard this breaking of a stereotype as a healthy act of cultural vandalism.

Popular music, rock, jazz and opera are notorious for attracting strong peer-group affiliations, though we should be clear that the processes of labelling music and placing it within a social 'approval' context is universal and can be found just as easily within any category of the Western classical or 'folk' traditions. Frequently, these associations rely on the adhesive of persuasion, the glue of propaganda, the attachment of labels. In an informal 'experiment', repeated several times, I asked groups of thirty to forty students with newly acquired music degrees to listen to a short passage from a recording of Brahms's First Symphony. I then read them a 'review' of this performance, followed by a critique of an alternative recorded version. This second record was then played – exactly the same passage. The musicians were then asked if they agreed with these reviews and an open discussion took place. Some rejected what was said by the 'critics' and a few suspicious people even went so far as to suggest that the reviews had been deliberately wrongly matched to the performances. Others more or less agreed with the critics. No one ever said, during any of these discussions, that they had listened to the same recording twice, though this was in fact the case. A little pantomime had taken place during which the record was replaced in its cover and, by sleight of hand, was taken out again and played on the same equipment, in the same room, at the same level of loudness; all this within five or ten minutes of the first playing.

What is particularly interesting is that many of the comments about the performance were critically quite well-developed, sensitively referring to subtleties of different phrasing, ensemble and speed. Yet, these perceptions could only be said to have resulted from the *value framework* within which the session was conducted: namely that a group of music graduates would be expected to find small and significant differences between performances if alerted by a lecturer to look for such differences by authoritative comments from alleged music 'critics'.

Such responses are similar in kind to those observed during the classic experiments of Asch (1951/1958), when subjects were asked to compare the relative length of lines. The social pressure to conform to the judgements of others was manipulated by a pre-arrangement: having everyone, or nearly everyone else in the group agree to a particular, though obviously wrong, consensus. The level of compliance with the general view was in the order of 32 per cent if no confederate disagreed with the others, in spite of the fact that it seems very clear that the collective judgement was incorrect.

Perhaps one of the most relevant and striking pieces of work in this area is that by Chapman and Williams (1976). Working with thirty-six 14- and 15-year-olds who were all self-declared 'progressive pop' enthusiasts, they assigned them to three experimental groups on a random basis and eventually played to each group a two-minute extract of music composed by Takemitsu, *The Dorian Horizon*. One of the groups was an experimental 'control'. A second group was played two pieces of progressive pop music prior to hearing the Takemitsu work; a procedure intended to establish a particular frame of reference, a label category. This group then listened to *The Dorian Horizon* and were told that it was from an LP by a member of Pink Floyd, 'one of the best, if not *the* best, progressive band in the country at the moment'. The third group was played short extracts of 'classical' music by Bach and Beethoven prior to listening to the work by Takemitsu and were given information along the following lines: 'The piece you are going to hear now is called *The Dorian Horizon* ... a leading Japanese composer of modern serious music. ... He is generally held in high regard by critics of contemporary serious music.'

From the results of this experiment it is clear that those who heard the piece from the labelling bias of 'High Status Music '– that is to say, the group who were led to believe that it was from the area of progressive pop music – evaluated the music more favourably than those who thought the music originated from the contemporary 'serious' tradition, rooted in 'classical music'. The control group tended to be less extreme in their ratings and used the mid-points of scales, seeming to be somewhat adrift on the sea of evaluation without some kind of chart, or labelling system to indicate how they might approach, describe and respond to what was, for them, a new musical experience.

Furthermore, Chapman and Williams found that, between the two main groups, descriptions of *The Dorian Horizon* were significantly wide apart on what they called a 'mood scale' (Joyful/Sorrowful) and on a 'conventionality scale' (Weird/Normal). These scales of mood and conventionality would seem to correspond with what I have been calling expressive and structural elements, and appear to measure not so much levels of preference, but the way in which the music was actually perceived. There are, then, significant changes in perception as well as in value judgements, brought about by differences in prestige labelling.

There is a sense though, in which music can be seen as objective, 'out there', to some extent independent of our particular preferences and prejudices. This is important if we are not to think of ourselves as the mechanical inhabitants of a clockwork universe, where everything conforms to pre-specified and socially determined rules.

REMOVING THE LABELS

Music can be culturally exclusive if the sound-spectrum is strange, if its expressive character is strongly linked with a particular culture or sub-culture and if structural expectations are inappropriate. All of these elements can be amplified by labelling and cultural stereotyping. It is the task of education to reduce the power of such stereotypes through a lively exploration of musical procedures, phenomena which can be relatively independent of cultural ownership.

> An emphasis on individual creators and performers, and a global view of the artistic conventions that they have used and use, are the surest means of developing the artistic consciousness of the nation – Such an enterprise will never succeed if it is multi*cultural*: it must be multi*artistic*. It can only be successful when people are touched by the aesthetic force of the arts and can transcend their social and cultural analogues.
>
> (Blacking 1986: 18)

Writing of his experience among the Venda people of South Africa, Blacking tells us that:

> ... although music making enabled people to express group identities and to experience social solidarity, its ultimate aim was to help them to pass beyond restricted worlds of culturally defined reality, and to develop creative imagination.
>
> (Blacking 1985: 44)

This is a striking observation and challenges any stereotype of 'tribal' music and dance as activities essentially locked into local and limited community values, though this is always a part of the story. What Blacking calls 'transcendental musical experiences' are not gained by staying within the

98

confines of strong and socially embedded idiomatic traditions – the 'authentic' music of the tribe. It is by working with musical *processes* themselves, as though they had a degree of autonomy, that transcendence of these culturally 'restricted worlds' becomes a possibility. Blacking concludes that 'Venda was one of many societies where people freely borrowed, adopted, and adapted songs, dances, ideas, and customs from others without anxiety about their cultural "purity"' (ibid.: 44).

The songs people sing, the tunes they make, the dances they dance stem only partly from extra-musical cultural requirements and conventions. Another determining factor is the materials and structure of musical instruments themselves, which fashion the tonal relationships of certain intervals and scales and particular rhythmic or timbre possibilities; in any culture musicians, given the slightest licence, will go beyond the immediate needs of ritual or community function and decorate, elaborate, 'put bits in'; dancers will invent dance, not simply perform it, a fact evident even in discos. The secret lies in the human aspiration towards playful abstraction and the generation of symbolic forms, such as language, mathematical thinking, music, dance and the visual art. To bring this out clearly I turn to Karl Popper and especially to his concept of self-transcendence.

> The incredible thing about life, evolution, and mental growth, is just this method of give-and-take, this interaction between our actions and their results by which we constantly transcend ourselves, our talents, our gifts. This self-transcendence is the most striking and important fact of all life and all evolution, and especially of human evolution.
>
> (Popper 1972: 147)

Further to this, Popper tells us:

> The process of learning, of the growth of subjective knowledge, is always fundamentally the same. It is *imaginative criticism*. This is how we transcend our local and temporal environment
>
> (ibid.)

Music has its own ways of creating new values transcending both self and immediate culture. Musical procedures can be absorbed and reused over centuries of time, between vastly differing cultures and across miles of geographical space; they are not irrevocably buried in local life-styles, even though they may have birth there. Musical elements (that is to say, the sensory impact of sound materials, expressive characterization and structural organization) have a degree of cultural autonomy which enables them to be taken over and re-worked into traditions far removed from their origins. I give some examples almost at random. An English clergyman visiting Brazil sometime in the middle of the last century, describes the music played in church by the padre/organist:

> He had got, from a friend in Rio, some English music, consisting of country dances and marches, the names of which he did not comprehend; so he applied them to his church services, and it was with no small surprise we heard him begin his andante with 'the Duke of York's march', and conclude his allegro with 'go to old Nick and shake yourself'. This to us sounded exquisitely absurd and even profane, but it was not so to him or the rest of his auditors, who had formed no such association of ideas.

From this account and from my own experience of Brazil, it is apparent that European military marches, fashionable dances and Viennese masses all travelled there in the nineteenth century, eventually to become resident and inspire local musicians to compose in similar styles. The polka, for example, seems to have begun life in rural Bohemia, turning up in Prague in the late 1830s. It was in Paris by 1840, London by 1844 and arrived in Brazil, probably via Portugal, shortly after. These days polkas can be found on tape and disc exemplifying the 'Brazilian' musical heritage along with recordings of church 'orchestras' (which include a choir). These orchestras are a feature of certain towns, notably São João del Rei, about 350 miles from Rio. There, in beautiful Portuguese Baroque churches, they perform home-grown music, influenced by scores from Europe brought inland from Rio by mule during the first half of the nineteenth century, to be studied and emulated by local musicians who would probably never have been to an actual performance of the works which became their models. I had the good fortune to sing with one of these 'orchestras' and know the strength of present day commitment to this music. A church orchestra in Brazil is a group of instrumental players and singers who perform the Mass in Latin alternating with the vernacular spoken Portuguese. There is even a kind of 'band room' specially set aside for weekly rehearsals.

Other examples, again almost at random: the harmonic vocabulary of 'immoral' early jazz, complete with chromatic secondary sevenths, came largely from Victorian hymn books; the Jamaican *Quadrille*, though originating in the upper reaches of European society, has become assimilated into the folk traditions of the Caribbean, thanks to those slaves and servants in the 'great' houses of the planters who observed the social antics of their superiors and were pressed into service to make up dance sets as required; Reggae owes quite a lot to American rhythm and blues (Cross 1984).

Recently on my travels, I came across a Papuan pop song which utilizes most of the *ostinato* from Pachelbel's *Canon* as a repeated bass and chord progression, not the first time that this servicable progression has been put to work since its origins in seventeenth-century Nuremberg.

This musical traffic does not only run from West to East or North to South; nor does it only flow from 'classical' traditions to 'folk'. The drift is in all directions, unstoppable. Western 'symphonic' music (for want of a better term) has always absorbed elements from elsewhere like a great sonorous sponge. Haydn absorbed Slavonic turns of phrase; Debussy was impressed by the 'Cakewalk'; Stravinsky copied 'Ragtime'; Puccini did his homework on ancient Chinese tunes for *Turandot*; Vaughan Williams soaked up modal folk melodies from rural Britain; at some point, 'Moorish' dances became 'Morris' dancing – hence the exotic costumes. In 1987, the composer George Benjamin heard people playing Peruvian flutes outside the Pompidou Centre in Paris; he invited the players inside and systematically recorded them playing all the sounds of which the flutes were capable. Eventually these recorded sounds were to be transformed and restructured with other materials drawn from many differing sources, using the equipment of the *Institut de Recherche et de Coordination Acoustique/Musique* to produce the commissioned work, *Antara*.

Similar transformations can be clearly discerned in punk rock. At its height anti-adult, anti-establishment and anti-authority, to many the music seemed brutal in sound spectrum, lacking in structural cohesion and definitely the territorial property of one social group, complete with dyed hair, scruffy clothes and assorted hardware shoved into the ears and nose. The whole phenomenon was amplified by cultural labelling, especially by the popular press. Notice though, that since the cultural amplification has been switched off, the electronic amplification turned down and the dress conventions and musical tone of voice have lost some of their expressive and territorial charge, some of the elements of punk are more widely received, and have been assimilated into the main cultural stream. Many a 'respectable' person of any age now leaves the hairdresser with a trace of dye and bristle the products of reinterpretation and transformation. The same is also true of the musical elements of the era; they have filtered into the more general language of pop and rock as autonomous devices, carrying with them only a trace, just a flavour of their anarchic origins.

The point here is simply to stress the autonomy that cultural products enjoy once they are freed from the chains of local cultural ownership, media labelling and territorial signalling. Time and use are able to unlock these chains leaving behind what there is of musical value. As a vital element of

101

the cultural process, music is, in the best sense of the term, re-creational – helping us and our cultures to become renewed, transformed. Thus Aldous Huxley's Lord Edward is to some extent a man changed by his encounter with Bach, lifted out of his own time and place.

In this essay I have tried to analyse the components of musical experience and show their psychological roots in play. To this extent music shares its origins with all significant human activities, including science and technology. The three play elements I have discussed – mastery of materials, expressive imitation and imaginative structure – can be seen at work at any level of musical criticism or analysis. Though not always consciously articulated as such, all critical comment falls into one or other of these categories or into a value judgement, the fourth component of musical experience. Research suggests that they also form the basis of musical development in children and emerge in order over time and with experience. (See Swanwick and Tillman 1986; also Swanwick 1988.)

Fused together in musical response, these elements comprise one of the most powerful experiences known to the human race, rooted as they are in the deep instincts of play. Extending playfulness in this way helps to preserve openness, making it possible to have alternative visions of what life can be about.

REFERENCES

ASCH, S.E. (1951/1958) 'Effects of group pressure upon modification and distortion of judgements', in E.E. Maccoby, T.M. Newcome, and E.L. Hartley (eds) *Readings in Social Psychology*, 3rd edn, New York: Holt, Rinehart & Winston.

BENTLEY, A. (1966) *Measure of Musical Abilities*, London: Harrap.

BLACKING, J. (1985) 'Music making in Venda', in *Mana Mag*, October, used with permission of the Music Educators National Conference, from *Becoming Human Through Music, The Wesleyan Symposium*, August 1984, Middletown, Conn.

——(1986) *Culture and the Arts*, Take-up Series, No. 4, London: National Association for Education in the Arts.

BULLOUGH, E. (1906) 'The perceptive problem' in the aesthetic appreciation of single colours', *British Journal of Psychology* 2: 406–63.

CHAPMAN, A.J. and WILLIAMS, A. (1976) 'Prestige effects and aesthetic experiences: adolescents' reactions to music', *British Journal of Social and Clinical Psychology* 15: 61–72.

CROSS, F. (1984) 'From Rhythm and Blues to Reggae', *British Journal of Music Education* 1 (3): 233–45.

DALCROZE, E.-J. (1921) *Rhythm, Music and Education*, published in translation 1967, London: Riverside Press.

DAVIES, J.B. (1978) *The Psychology of Music*, London: Hutchinson.

DEUTSCH, D. (1982) *The Psychology of Music*, New York: Academic Press.

GRAHAME, K. (1885) *The Golden Age*, reprinted 1973, London: Bodley Head.

GRIEG, E. (1905) 'My First Success', an autobiographical sketch published in *The Contemporary Review*, July.

HAMEL, P.M. (1978) *Through Music to the Self*, trans. P. Lemesurier, Wiltshire: The Compton Press.

HANSLICK, E. (1854) *The Beautiful in Music*, published in translation 1957, New York: Liberal Arts Press.

HARGREAVES, D.J. (1986) *The Developmental Psychology of Music*, Cambridge: Cambridge University Press.

HEAD, H. (1920) *Studies in Neurology*, Oxford: Oxford University Press.

HUNTER, H. (1970) 'An investigation of physiological and psychological changes apparently elicited by musical stimuli', unpublished M.Sc. thesis, University of Aston in Birmingham.

HUXLEY, A. (1928) *Point Counter Point*, London: Penguin.

KELLER, H. (1970) 'Towards a theory of music', *The Listener*, 11 June.

KOESTLER, A. (1964) *The Act of Creation*, London: Pan Books.

LANGER, S. (1942) *Philosophy in a New Key*, reprinted 1957, New York: Mentor Books; Cambridge, Mass.: Harvard University Press.

LEE, V. (1932) *Music and its Lovers*, London: Unwin.

LUNDIN, R.W. (1949) 'The development and validation of a set of ability tests', *Psychological Monographs* 63 (305): 1–20.

——(1953) *An Objective Psychology of Music*, New York: Ronald Press.

MACCURDY, J.T. (1925) *The Psychology of Emotion*, New York: Harcourt Brace.

MARTIN, B. (1981) *A Sociology of Contemporary Cultural Change*, Oxford: Blackwell.

MEYER, L.B. (1956) *Emotion and Meaning in Music*, Chicago: University of Chicago Press.

MYERS, C.S. and VALENTINE, C.W. (1914–15), 'A study of the individual differences in attitudes towards tones', *British Journal of Psychology* 7: 68ff.

OSGOOD, C.E., SUCI, G.J. and TANNENBAUM, P.H. (1957) *The Measurement of Meaning*, Urbana, Ill.: University of Illinois Press.

PIAGET, J. (1951) *Play, Dreams and Imitation in Childhood*, London: Routledge.

POPPER, K. (1972) *Objective Knowledge*, Oxford: Clarendon Press.

PROUST, M. (1913) *Remembrance of Things Past*, trans. C.K. Scott Moncrieff, London: Chatto & Windus.

SCHOEN, M. (1927) *The Effects of Music*, London: Kegan Paul; New York: Harcourt Brace.

SEASHORE, C. (1938) *The Psychology of Music*, New York: McGraw-Hill.

SHAW, G.B. (1981) *Shaw's Music*, ed. Dan H. Laurence, London: The Bodley Head.

SHUTER-DYSON, R. and GABRIEL, C. (1968) *The Psychology of Musical Ability*, 2nd edn 1981, London: Methuen & Co.

SLOBODA, J.A. (1985) *The Musical Mind: The Cognitive Psychology of Music*, Oxford: Oxford University Press.

——(1986) 'Cognition and real music: the psychology of music comes of age', *Psych. Belg.* XXVI, 2: 199–219.

SWANWICK, K. (1971) *Music and the Education of the Emotions*, unpublished Ph.D. thesis, University of Leicester.

——(1973)'Musical cognition and aesthetic response', *Bulletin of the British Psychological Society* 26: 285–9.

——(1979) *A Basis for Music Education*, Windsor: NFER-Nelson.

——(1988) *Music, Mind and Education*, London: Routledge.

SWANWICK, K. and TILLMAN, J. (1986) 'The sequence of musical development', *British Journal of Music Education* 3 (3): 305–39, Cambridge: Cambridge University Press.

VALENTINE, C.W. (1962) *The Experimental Psychology of Beauty*, London: Methuen.

WING, H.D. (1948) *Standardised Tests of Musical Intelligence*, revised edn. 1962, Windsor: NFER.

WOLFF, C. (1945) *A Psychology of Gesture*, London: Methuen.

WOLLHEIM, R. (1971) *Freud*, London: Fontana.

The Action Value of
Musical Experience and Learning

THOMAS A. REGELSKI

ACTIVITIES AND EXPERIENCE

The literature of music education is filled with references to the importance of 'experience' for musical learning. In the name of 'experiential
learning' an active approach to teaching music is advocated almost universally. For example, one source states that 'as students are involved in
meaningful musical experiences, their sensitivity to music increases by leaps
and bounds'. By helping students to 'deepen their understanding of music
through conceptual experiences', the teacher is able to expose them to 'a
variety of ways to experience music, and as a result, to increase their
enjoyment of and sensitivity to music as an art' (Hackett and Lindeman
1988: 14).

This coupling of experiential learning with conceptual experience is
widespread. Researchers[1] and authors of music education texts alike regularly specify the need for experience in teaching concepts, usually in connection with so-called elements or qualities of music.

> Once students understand basic musical concepts (e.g., fast and slow, upward
> and downward, beat and no beat), they can apply what they know to all types
> of music and begin to make their own discoveries and decisions about music.
> In order to perceive qualities that are inherent in music and understand how
> they work together, children must experience music.
>
> (Beer and Hoffman 1982: 1)

Formal experiences planned in order to teach 'basic musical concepts' are called 'activities'. However, 'activities are not ends in themselves but are designed to lead to enjoyment, aesthetic sensitivity – and conceptual learning' (Hackett and Lindeman 1988: 12). To foster such goals, the concept-teaching method 'moves through a series of experiences from the specific to the general' (Beer and Hoffman 1982: 88). Quite apart from the theoretical confusion this process represents for teachers,[2] its results are always unpredictable and often undesirable because such generalizing involves a process of abstraction that requires inductive reasoning by students; and 'inductions – quite valid ones – are often in error' (Lee 1973: 164).[3]

While acknowledging a certain advantage of this Activities Approach, as I have dubbed it, over methods where students are passive, I propose, instead, an Action Learning model for music education that overcomes the theoretical and pragmatic weakness of the Activities Approach. A brief summary of Action Learning will provide the foundation for an analysis and critique that identifies and clarifies the inherent weaknesses of the Activities Approach (see also Regelski 1983a: 46; 1983b: 55; 1983c; and 1986: 185).

AN ACTION LEARNING ALTERNATIVE

Action Learning is not a mere synonym for so-called active or 'hands-on' learning. Along with Action Research it participates in the paradigm of Action Theory (see Parsons and Shils 1962) that takes a scientific approach to knowledge acquisition. It is influenced by the philosophy of Pragmatism and therefore judges the value of teaching goals, methods or materials by the tangible consequences that result from each. Being pragmatic, Action Learning seeks to promote tangible results that are applicable to 'real-life' uses of music – the action value of music – and only content, methods and materials instrumental to such ends are employed.

Its scientific approach to knowledge involves treating teaching methods and goals as hypotheses – as presumptions and predictions that must be tested by observing what students are able to do as a result of such instruction. The use of a method to advance some real-life musical pursuit is, in effect, an experiment that verifies (a) the alleged desirability of that pursuit, (b) the skills and knowledge that are claimed necessary to it, and (c) the methods that are intended to bring it to a functional level.

Similarly, concepts are considered to be hypotheses (Piaget *et al.* 1978: 119–21; Lee 1973: 173). If they cannot be or are not used 'in action', then they are useless abstractions, and if they are not regularly put to the test of 'reality' – in the case of music, to real-life musical uses – then they will be neither functional nor learned! When the process of evoking and then testing musical hypotheses in action is facilitated and controlled by the teacher, both students and teacher are constantly aware of the relevance and power or efficacy of the knowledge, skills and attitudes being addressed. And with such modelling of real-life uses of musical learning, the likelihood of a functional transfer of learning from school to life outside after graduation from school is increased.

Action Learning is not a method; it is a comprehensive model by which teachers (1) decide what to teach, (2) plan and deliver instruction and (3) evaluate the suitability of what and how they taught.

1 Goals are decided first. Since Action Learning seeks to promote continuing involvement with music that is satisfying to a significant degree, teachers select goals they hypothesize to be most practicable (a) to teach to a functional level and (b) for people to be able to incorporate into their lives.
2 Then the means of instruction are qualified. Methods, techniques, strategies, activities, lessons and materials are chosen specifically (a) to model the goals, (b) to develop the knowledge and skills necessary to those musical pursuits, and (c) to promote the attitudes, values and rewards that incline people to seek such action values for their lives.
3 Finally, evaluation of teaching success is promoted by accurately observing the degree to which instructional means facilitate discernible progress toward the stated goals – taking into consideration the musical, affective, intellectual and psychomotor readiness of students.

Rather than trying to cover more than students could ever learn or use, Action Learning begins by asking, 'Of all that can be taught, what is most worth teaching?'

The answer is pragmatic. The content of instruction for music in general education[4] should consist of at least the most basic knowledge, skills and attitudes that will be necessary for students to be musically active in life. For Action Learning, less is more. Thus it concentrates on promoting only those skills, knowledge and attitudes that are demonstrably necessary to functional independence (Regelski 1969: 77) in one or more areas of real-life musical involvement.

Such involvements would include those kinds of rewarding musical practices and pursuits typically sought out by musically 'literate' and 'alive' adults who, despite being non-professional musicians, are avidly committed to making music a vital part of the life well-lived. Some obvious praxial roles for such amateur musical involvement in 'real life' include singing in church and community choirs, and community musical theatre; singing in social settings such as ceremonies, clubs, 'sing-alongs', etc.; and playing folk or traditional ethnic instruments for personal enjoyment and recreation. Action Learning also promotes less obvious but increasingly popular musical pursuits such as playing electric or acoustic guitars and keyboards, and recreational performing, composing or arranging using increasingly accessible electronic media such as 'sampling keyboards' and 'musical instrument digital interfaces' (MIDI) with computers.

Unfortunately, not many adults typically seek to participate in large, amateur instrumental ensembles. Since there is not much demand for the creation of such groups, relatively few exist in comparison to the availability of choirs of various types. It is likely that young ensemble players in schools do not acquire the musical competence needed as adults to be able learn their own parts; or – even for those who can – learning a part, then getting together to rehearse with a large group is likely to be too time-consuming for the typical busy adult. Thus Action Learning also promotes musical independence on standard instruments by stressing solos – including the use of recorded accompaniments – and small ensemble literature, such as duets, trios, and other formats for and types of performance that adults are more likely to want and be able to fit into a busy life.

Of course, listening is probably the most accessible manner in which music can contribute meaning to the daily lives of individuals. However, it is clear that too few people value listening enough to go out of their way to seek opportunities – live or recorded – beyond what is all too easily available through the popular media. Schools are so single-minded in inculcating what music teachers consider to be 'good music' that the question of 'What is music good for?' is not sufficiently addressed – especially as regards listening. Not surprisingly, then, students do not learn the value of perceptive listening and thus do not acquire the habit of seeking opportunities to listen with discrimination to a variety of musics. Just as when they are adolescents, they listen passively and mainly to what is readily available. Action Learning takes this into consideration by seeking to model the benefits of discriminating music listening as a mode of more richly experiencing life. Thus, in seeking to savour the essence of life's most significant moments as the 'content' of music, Action Learning incorporates the 'classics' of a wide variety of musics – including multi-cultural musics – that have the greatest likelihood of expanding perceptual skills, cognitive understanding and 'appreciation' enough for the listener to actively seek listening opportunities other than or in addition to here-today-gone-tomorrow popular fare.

Musical knowledge, then, is not approached in the abstract as concepts that are preliminary to such vague ends as 'sensitivity to music as an art' – whatever that means. Instead, Action Learning is conducted in large part by *modelling* the kinds of real-life amateur musical actions and pursuits that are projected as its observable results. Thus, in addition to improving competence, students are more likely (a) to know the existence of such typical musical avocations, (b) to experience the appeal of certain of them, and (c) to appreciate the relevance of the competencies required by those they find most satisfying. Action Learning addresses, then, the need for students to want to use such ability, and accepts that such use will necessarily vary between individuals.

The fact that no musical action has an ultimate state of perfection means that Action Learning's real-life goals are ideals. Such Action Ideals are, however, neither idealistic nor vague. Rather, they are realistic in recognizing different levels and types of musical activity while none the less clearly indicating the improvements that are needed. Thus, they enable both teachers and students to judge the effectiveness of study and practice. Students are thereby rescued from mindless repetition or random effort (Howard 1982: ch. 6). And, unlike those committed to the Activities Approach, the teacher is not deceived into believing that mere enjoyment or participation amounts to learning. The various methods that constitute the Activities Approach – those associated with such 'method formats' as Orff and Kodály, as well as various eclectic methods – all focus so single-mindedly on the 'how' of teaching that the value of the method is an *a priori* assumption. Goals are thus taken for granted or are so vague that no criteria are provided against which ultimate pragmatic effectiveness can be evaluated (Chosky *et al.* 1986: 1–2). Success, then, is presumed to result from the correct choice and proper implementation of the method – because 'it works'!

This criterion, however, is not only false, it amounts to idealistic wish-fulfilment! A method can be said to work only in comparison to some desired outcome. When such intentions are vague or assumed, results will be ambiguous and taken for granted. Thus, claiming that a method works asserts at most that certain activities are capable of being put into practice – are 'practicable' – and not that they have necessarily brought about pragmatic results that demonstrably facilitate a significant and lasting involvement with music.

Furthermore, that a lesson has engaged students actively does not mean that their experience has been *musical*, that 'experiential learning' of concepts has occurred, that any conceptual learning that might result is necessarily musical, or that it is musically worthwhile (i.e. useful in real life). Thus the obligatory references in the literature of music education to 'meaningful musical experiences', 'experiential learning' and 'conceptual experience' only beg the question as to the relevance of experience to music learning and responsiveness; first by failing to qualify the nature of 'experience', then by idealistically assuming the necessity and automatic efficacy of *musical* experience, and finally by treating concepts supposedly taught by experience as sufficient ends of musical instruction.

The following analysis will first clarify the nature of experience, especially musical and learning experience; then the vagueness and unreliability of the Activities Approach will be revealed, and the value of goals that advance more tangible and real-life applications of musical learning will be argued. And, in outlining these conditions, the advantages of an Action Learning paradigm for music education will be demonstrated.

INTENTIONALITY AND RELEVANCE

To avoid having to force instruction on disinclined students, it is necessary that 'initial objectives should be those that students at the time see are interesting and/or meaningful for them to learn' (Tyler 1977: 43). For all but very young children, and especially for early adolescents, this kind of meaning depends on the ability of students to project some personal use for the learning. The younger the student, the more immediate must be such projected use.

This interest is most likely when the kind of real-life uses to which the learning is functionally related is the major means by which it is acquired. Action Learning seeks to bring about exactly such constructive, relevant results – personally engaging amateur uses of music which, unlike 'aesthetic sensitivity', are observable and practical in out-of-school life. 'This means that learners must see the way in which the things they learn can be used, and they must have the opportunity to employ the learned behaviour in the various situations they encounter' (ibid.). At the very least, then, instruction

110

should model or approximate the anticipated real-life use as closely as the formal conditions of school allow.

> The failure to transfer what is learned in school to situations outside of school is a problem that has long been central to educational psychologists. Schools are established to help students acquire behaviour that is important for constructive out-of-school activities. If something is learned in school that is not used by the student in relevant situations outside of school, most of the value of learning has been lost.
>
> (Tyler 1977: 39)

Action Learning seeks to bring about exactly such results – real-life uses that, unlike 'aesthetic sensitivity', are observable and practical. To ensure the likelihood of such pragmatic results, four criteria are observed:

1 Results should be tangible and thus directly observable or capable of being inferred by 'reading behaviour backwards' as evidence of covert processes (Regelski 1975a: chs 6, 7);
2 Results should be capable of serving a useful purpose – an actual or likely application in everyday life – and this purpose should be appropriately modelled at the student's readiness level, enough for the student to savour its rewards;
3 Short-term results should be immediately satisfying while also discernibly advancing competence towards stated long-term Action Ideals;
4 Finally, results should arise through purposive action rather than simply through random activity, simple reaction, or blind obedience or responsiveness to the teacher's directions or extrinsic motivations.

ACTION AS KNOWLEDGE AND INTELLIGENCE

The fourth condition above points to a significant difference between the 'activity' of the Activities Approach and the 'actions' of Action Learning. 'An event is an action if and only if it can be described in a way that makes it intentional' (Davidson 1974: 41). Without such intentionality, activity is random. 'Action', in contrast, 'is different from mere movement because it embodies intentions; it reflects aims and purposes' (Klein 1970: 4).

The intentions of students are therefore the key to whether apparent activity is merely random, or whether it involves actions that benefit musical learning, or that serve some purpose extrinsic to music. This has important consequences for the musical validity of students' responsiveness in ensembles and music classes, for it is their intentions that determine whether or not actions are musical or are instead responsive to other, musically extrinsic purposes.

'Much of the time perception is enmeshed in action providing a basis for doing or not doing something about the events perceived, and guiding us to next steps in relation to these events and objects' (Klein 1970: 56). Because 'perception is an adaptive cognitive act, always rooted in the intentional life of the person, in his motives and aims vis-a-vis the environment' (ibid.: 4), students' perceptions of a learning situation determine their understanding of its value or purpose more than any objective the teacher has in mind. Therefore, what a student 'chooses to take in, either consciously or unconsciously, is what gives structure and meaning to his world'. Furthermore, what the student perceives is 'what he intends to do about it' (Hall 1977: 88).

What a student 'intends to do' with musical 'content' is its perceived action value. It amounts to an orientation for action 'which the actor has of the situation in terms of what he wants (his ends), what he sees (how the situation looks to him), and how he intends to get from the objects he sees the things he wants (his explicit or implicit, normatively regulated "plan" of action)' (Parsons and Shils 1962: 51). Thus, if experience does not evoke musically appropriate action values, the orientation for action of students will be directed by other, non-musical ends.

A teacher can maximize the likelihood that students will profit in ways that involve the musical purposes the teacher has in mind, by being concerned first and foremost with orienting students' intentionality appropriately to the musical knowledge, skills or attitudes that are the content of the lesson. The most predictable manner of promoting such an orientation is the direct use of learning actions that model real-life uses of music and at the same time advance the musical learning and attitudes necessary to such uses.

Action, and thus intentionality, is central to learning, to thinking, and – in the case of music – to musical intelligence. As Piaget has pointed out,

> knowledge is derived from action. . . . To know an object is to act upon it and to transform it. . . . To know is therefore to assimilate reality into structures that intelligence constructs as a direct extension of our actions.
>
> (Piaget 1970: 28–9)

Accordingly, 'intelligence derives from action' and 'consists in executing and coordinating action, though in an interiorised and reflective form' (ibid.: 29). In other words, overt actions that involve transformations of musical materials in effecting intended musical results become interiorized as mental structures – action patterns – and thereafter function as the 'musical intelligence' directing and controlling future musical undertakings.

Subsequent musical actions with newly challenging musical materials, selected by a teacher or encountered naturally, will 'assimilate' familiar variables as part of existing action patterns which are thus cognitively strengthened and become more powerful and more likely to be invoked. The unique variables in new situations – as long as they are not too anomalous – require 'accommodation' of existing mental structures and thus promote change and learning (see Boden 1979: 16).

Unlike mental structures that arise from action, the concepts taught by the Activities Approach originate as verbal abstractions that are prior to and thus outside the child's experience (see Hackett and Lindeman 1988: 10–11). Concept-teaching, then, necessitates filling these otherwise empty abstractions with the kinds of musical experience from which they were originally abstracted. This accounts for the need to advocate 'experiential' or 'active' learning. However, no amount of activity can overcome 'the dead abstraction of mere fact from the living importance of things felt' where, according to Whitehead, conceptual categorizing and labelling 'leads away from the realities of the immediate world' (Whitehead 1968: 11, 39).

STUDENT-FOCUSED AND ACTION-ORIENTED LEARNING

Such dead abstraction is predictable when the study of music is subject-dominated or discipline-oriented rather than student-focused or action-oriented. Subject-dominated teaching is more concerned with conveying the discipline than with whether the student will be able to or want to use such learning in some personally significant way. The learner is not the focus of such instruction, but, rather, music as discipline – music as (1) body of knowledge or achievement, (2) concerned largely with the past, (3) the meaning and value of which is given and, therefore, unchanging.

When content is perceived by students as abstract and impersonal, knowledge in abstraction from action is exalted[5] and students neither see (i.e. understand or foresee) nor experience (i.e. model through use) any action value for their lives. Appreciating no immediate or future action with such content, it is thus inert in its capacity for motivating.

Students who fail to evidence the requisite discipline suffer the ignoble effects of 'being disciplined' in one way or another – which removes them even further from the 'appreciation' – the discipline or 'disciple-ing'[6] – they are supposed to be acquiring. So-called aesthetic education approached through activities that provide experience with abstract concepts and other presumed musical values is so deadening that it might more accurately be called anaesthetic![7] Any interest elicited is short-lived in the case of general music classes or, in the case of performance ensembles, is short-circuited by graduation.

Subject-dominated teaching assumes the inherent and absolute value of such 'content'. Because it sees teaching as a 'conserving' activity[8] for pre-serving the discipline of music, we can acknowledge where many teachers get such notions by dubbing this the 'conservatory approach' to music teaching. One writer, for example, has argued that 'indoctrination of a conservative philosophy of education is most appropriate for music edu-cation'. In this view, 'good music education is not student centred', but rather should be based on the model of the musicologist and, in particular, on an 'intellectual' rather than 'sentimental' contact with 'the best of our musical heritage'. Thus 'moulding the values of students' in accordance with the conservatory model is advocated (Colwell 1987: 43ff.).

In order to indoctrinate such values, other-directed motivation and extrin-sic control are required. And even assuming that students acquire any functional learning, when such controls and motivations are removed – that is, when students are no longer in the class or ensemble – their natural intentionality for other valued pursuits takes over and musical involvement ceases.

In contrast, the student-focused approach of Action Learning bases instruction specifically on (a) student intentionality, (b) the integration of useful subject-matter into student action patterns, and (c) modelling typical and attractive musical pursuits. Students can 'see' and appreciate the con-nection of music learning to life through the foretaste provided by the modelling that constitutes the bulk of instruction. Student-focused learning, then, emphasizes what the student is able and more inclined to do as a result of instruction, and is therefore not to be confused with the 'student-centred' learning criticized by the conservatory approach.

Student-centred learning stems from one extreme philosophy of edu-cation which

114

emphasised the child's interest to the exclusion of all others. Many so-called 'progressive' schools are of this type. But the saner representatives of this movement, under the leadership of Dewey, have attempted to find an adequate adjustment and reconciliation between the two extremes of emphasis.

(Frost 1962: 225)[9]

In contrast to such student-*centred* learning, then, student-*focused* teaching is not a matter of stressing either the student or the discipline but of effecting a dialectical synthesis[10] of the two in order to gain the best of both. Thus, in Action Learning, student-focused instruction is teacher-directed but is not teacher- or subject-dominated. The term 'permissipline' has been coined to refer to the hybrid where instruction is both student-focused as to content and teacher-directed as to organization and control.[11]

The Action Learning teacher cannot abdicate responsibility for selecting and planning subject matter because it is dictated by the real world in which the child must function. Thus, rather than focusing on the discipline in a way that assumes its value is evident to students, selection and organization of content is approached in terms of what the student can do and wants to do of a practical nature with such musical learning. The value of the content for action – its action value *as perceived by students* – is thus what makes instruction action-oriented and student-focused.

PERSONALIZING LEARNING

In order for musical content to have action value it 'must be restored to the experience from which it has been abstracted. It needs to be psychologised' (Dewey 1902: 29). Otherwise, according to Dewey, the subject does not get 'translated into life-terms, but is directly offered as a substitute for, or an external annexe to, the child's present life' (ibid.: 31). It must be personalized through the student using it in some personally meaningful musical way. Thus instead of teaching their own concepts directly, Action Learning teachers use their personal understanding of music to select and organize actions hypothesized to be models or approximations of musical reality.

As a result of reintroducing the benefits and uses of music knowledge into the experience of the child in this way, it is recreated and personalized as though it were of the student's own origin. To thus direct and control learning 'by indirection' (ibid.: 39), the teacher must consider

the ways in which that subject may become a part of experience; what there is in the child's present that is usable with reference to it; how such elements are to be used; how his own knowledge of the subject-matter may assist in interpreting the child's needs and doings, and determine the medium in which the child should be placed in order that his growth may be properly directed. He is concerned, not with the subject-matter as such, but with the subject-matter as a related factor in a total and growing experience. Thus to see it is to psychologize it.

(Dewey 1902: 30)

Use that 'grows into application in further achievements' (Dewey 1902: 30) is necessary, then, for an abstraction to be psychologized as part of a learner's experience.

Dewey is by no means the only thinker to have stressed this connection between action and personal knowledge. Modern experts, too, have stressed that 'all knowing is action' and thus that 'all knowing is personal knowing' because knowing a concept is, so-to-speak, a function of its use. Thus with 'personal participation as the universal principle of knowing', the observer's involvement – an act of knowing – is required for personal knowledge, and thus meaning, to exist (Polanyi and Prosch 1975: 42–5; see also Polanyi 1962).

COGNITIVE PSYCHOLOGY AND EXPERIENCE

'Experience' and 'concept' are empty expressions that have no fixed meaning independent of a theoretical standpoint (Heath 1967: 178; Long 1966: 103). Given the lack of any theoretical delineation, then, 'experience' is not what it is made out to be by advocates of the Activities Approach who prescribe activities designed, for example, to 'experience the concept of high/low' or, stranger still, to 'teach the experience of high/low'. Any such reference to experience in support of a teaching method is meaningless and misleading.

Within the framework of cognitive psychology, for instance, one does not 'experience a concept' since *the concept itself is the experience*.[12] Reference to 'conceptual experience' is similarly redundant. To experience something is already the action of a concept – i.e. is an action pattern giving inward form (in-formation) to sensory data that otherwise would amount to 'non-sense'.[13] Thus, 'to experience a concept' is not only redundant; it would be futile since the abstraction the teacher wishes to teach via experience is already functional to begin with if students are able to 'have' the experience.[14]

Cognitive psychology, following Piaget, approaches conceptualization

116

as a process of active construction where the reality of experience is constituted through the inward form-giving (in-forming), unifying action of the intellect.

> Conceptual thinking can be considered an 'internalized form of sensory-motor action.' Just as a child will fit building blocks together according to some 'plan' of physical movement, so the concept is an internalized plan by which intellect acts on the 'building blocks' of reality data. ... Conceptual thinking is a 'transactive movement' by which our intellect puts together those reality components we entertain or respond to.
>
> (Pearce 1976: 28, citing Furth 1966: 177)

Thus 'concept is a patterned act of intellect, a way by which thinking moves to process reality data into whole events' (Pearce 1976: 223–4). Perceptual experience is therefore not simply the passive reception of sensory data from 'reality' but, according to Piaget, the 'progressive action and construction' (Piaget 1952: 365) of a child's individual conceptual reality.

THE PRAGMATISM OF EXPERIENCE

Progressive educational philosophy misread, then took to an extreme, Dewey's analysis of the need to psychologize abstract subject matter by means of experience. By advocating the 'understanding of music through conceptual experience', the Activities Approach is similarly misguided. Dewey's technical use of the word 'experience' is distinctive to Pragmatism and is far removed from the experiential-learning model of the Activities Approach.

It involves, instead, an interaction where mental energy is 'released, dammed up, frustrated and victorious'; a rhythmic alternation of 'want and fulfilment, pulses of doing and being withheld from doing' (Dewey 1934: 16). Experience, then, involves (1) *intentionality*, (2) the goal-directed *action* of which is (3) frustrated by *problem*, that is (4) subsequently *solved* (ibid.: 36). Experience possesses an enduring unity, an underlying pattern and structure, that 'moves toward a close, an ending, since it ceases only when the energies active in it have done their proper work' (ibid.: 41). It is this sense of unity that permits an experience to have a label (ibid.: 37), such as '*Aida*', 'trumpet', 'fugue', or even 'music'.

117

However, closure alone – that an interaction ends – is not enough to fully constitute an experience. 'The action and its consequence must be joined in perception. This relationship is what gives meaning; to grasp it is the objective of all intelligence' (ibid.: 44). Thus to the four conditions above we must add a fifth: the results of actions must be seen in relation to the ends that were the original focus of intentionality. Without comparing results to intentions, there is neither meaning nor learning! Even in ordinary conversation, people often observe sardonically that some unexpected event was 'a learning experience', thus pointing out that results have meaning only in terms of expectations.

Intelligent experience is consciously exploratory and experimental. Just 'having' impressions is not enough. To have what Dewey called *an* experience, intelligence must reach out with a conscious purpose to act on or with the raw data of reality. 'Some decisive action is needed in order to establish contact with the realities of the world and in order that impressions may be so related to facts that their value is tested and organised' (ibid.: 45).

Observed results need to be related consciously to the facts – which is to say, to the consequences of action judged in terms of the goal which intentionality was acting to bring about. Only then can the value or meaning of an experience be tested and organized as a basis for future experience. 'To apprehend such relation is to think and is one of the most exacting modes of thought' (ibid.: 45).

It is precisely this conscious connection between an action and its consequence that is lacking with respect to the 'experiences' and 'experiential learning' promoted by advocates of the Activities Approach. With the various popular methods constituting such teaching, students rarely have any clear idea as to why they are being directed to be active. They know *what* they are supposed to do, but not *why* it is to be done – why it is worth doing. Without such action values in mind, 'doings' are not directed by intentionality, and 'impressions' are neither unified nor 'in-formed'. Students may appear active but their activity neither constitutes nor guarantees a musical or a learning experience – at least not the kind the activity is supposed to promote.

Two criteria need to be met to qualify experience as being musical. Students must (1) consciously intend some strictly musical consequence of their actions; and (2) be attentive to the relationship between their action and the musical results judged in terms of the intended musical goal. Similarly, for experience to psychologize the teacher's curricular goal, students need to be consciously intending to attain this same learning! Or, they would at least need to become aware of the relationship between their

118

actions and musical results after the fact (i.e. after the 'facts' (in-formations) of the experience); and then, due to the rewards thus modelled, be enticed subsequently to the intention of using such learning in order to bring about those musical results once more.

Judged by these criteria, general music and ensemble classes generally fail to promote strictly musical experiences, or to guide or influence learning experiences to any predictable or significant degree. Intentions guiding students' actions most often involve pleasing or appeasing the teacher, having fun,[15] expending excess energy, showing off or gaining attention, socializing, winning an award, earning a grade, just 'being good' at something,[16] and other non-musical, extrinsic goals. Even if a student does by chance intend a musical result, and thus can be said to have had a 'musical' experience, there is no teacher provision for an orderly progression by which the facts or conceptual 'in-formations' of such an experience can become predictably functional.

The results, then, are haphazard in degree and ultimate effect. This accounts no doubt for the significant drop-out rate of beginning instrumentalists and for the progressive decline of interest and cooperation typically exhibited by general music classes. If their intentions are so oriented, students *may* experience some sense of recreation or diversion. But without appropriate *musical* intentionality such activities fail to promote predictable and systematic musical learning or the kinds of musical rewards that lead people to commit themselves to life-long musical involvement.

In such classes, according to Dewey, 'things are experienced but not in such a way that they are composed into an experience' (Dewey 1934: 35. This distinction is important both for Dewey and for Action Learning. The noun form, *an* experience, refers to a whole that is unified by, as well as characterized in terms of, the focus of students' intentions. The verb form *to* experience, in contrast, involves 'the mere undergoing of this and that, irrespective of perception of any meaning' (ibid.: 45). Lacking the organizing focus intentionality would provide by recognizing (re-cognizing) a relationship between an intention and the results produced, such experiences fail to produce a unified result. The child, therefore, is

> not concerned with the connection of one incident with what went before and what comes after. There is no interest that controls attentive rejection or selection of what shall be organized into the developing experience. Things happen, but they are neither definitely included nor decisively excluded. ...
> There is experience, but so slack and discursive that it is not an experience.
>
> (Dewey 1934: 40)

119

Lacking the unifying presence of intentionality, there are no 'facts' of experience, only momentary 'impressions'. Because no unified mental 'in-formation' results, such experiences fail to promote either musical intel-ligence or meaning. Thus 'such experiences are anaesthetic' instead of aesthetic because they progressively dull the senses (ibid.: 40).[17]

EXPERIENCE AS EXPERIMENT

Experiences involving 'doings and undergoings that were had without control by insight' (i.e. merely 'having' sensations or impressions) Dewey called 'empirical'. With empirical experience 'both the original perceptions and uses and the applications of their outcome in present doings [are] accidental – that is, neither [is] determined by an understanding of the relations of cause and effect, of means and consequences, involved'. Thus, lacking unifying 'in-formation' by intelligence, empirical experiences are 'non-rational' (Dewey 1929: 81–2).

Experimental experience, in contrast, is a matter of 'doing acts, per-forming operations, cutting, marking off, dividing up, extending, piecing together, joining, assembling and mixing, hoarding and dealing out; in general selecting and adjusting things as means for reaching consequences' (ibid.: 156). Experimental experience, then, is the result of intelligence acting to achieve some valued consequence; it compares results to intentions and thereby 'in-forms' a unified meaning.

This is precisely what is missing with the Activities Approach. It evokes mainly empirical experience because the mere presence of 'experience' – some 'activity' to undergo – is not enough to psychologize the abstractions of musical subject matter to a functional level. Such psychologizing results only from experimental experience – experience unified by movement from the motivating effects of conscious musical intentions (action values) to closure, where the student is also conscious of the relation bet-ween actions and consequences. Action Learning, in contrast, fosters such experimental experience by emphasizing intentionality and pragmatic results.

*Experi*ence, *experi*ment and *exper*tise share a common etymological root. Musical expertise, then, results from musical experiments by which students adventurously[18] seek to overcome certain tempting 'problems' – featuring musical variables selected and highlighted by the teacher – that stand in the way of consciously intended musical results. Whether these valued goals are enticed by the teacher's modelling of real-life musical pursuits or arise naturally, the problems are posed to elicit and guide students' musical learning towards the teacher's curricular goals. Musical knowledge is thus 'personalized' by students yet 'controlled' by the teacher.

PROBLEM-SOLVING AND MOTIVATION

To the student, it as though such knowledge is of his or her own origin. And in a manner of speaking it is, since 'a beholder must *create* his own experience' (Dewey 1934: 54). Thinking, then, is 'deferred action' in 'response to the doubtful' (Dewey 1929: 223–4) – a mental action, in other words, involving something problematic or indeterminate. 'The intellectual phase of mental action is identical with an *indirect* mode of response, one whose purpose is to locate the nature of the trouble and form an idea of how it may be dealt with – so that operations may be directed in view of an intended solution' (ibid.: 226).

Thinking is not activated by 'things' such as concepts or facts. Rather, 'thinking is the actual transition from the problematic to the secure, as far as that is intentionally guided' (ibid.: 227). Thus, for example, we typically do not seek knowledge or think about something that is already settled or certain. Instead, intelligence is evoked by the indeterminate or unresolved – which is to say, by 'problems' of various kinds and degrees. To 'inspire' or 'educe'[19] musical thinking, therefore, it is necessary to pose musical problems that focus student intentionality on potential solutions. Musical knowledge arises from overt actions guided towards students' musical goals, with results judged in terms of those goals.

Motivation or interest, then, is a function of 'the identification, through action, of the self with some object or idea, because of the necessity of that object or idea for the maintenance of self-expression'. Such self-expression Dewey saw as aiding 'the self to reach its end' – a kind of existential self-actualization – and interest as 'consciousness of the value of this end, and of the means necessary to realize it'. However, 'both effort and desire exist only when the end is somewhat remote' – that is, when it is a challenge. Most important is intentionality, because for interest to motivate 'there must ... be a consciousness of both means and ends'. Motivation, thus, is a consciousness of 'the hold certain ends or ideals have upon us' and which, therefore, embody the 'active value' called a 'motive (a power inducing to activity)' (Dewey 1896: 217–18, 224, 226, 228, 232).

121

For musical knowledge to evoke such an active (i.e. action) value, therefore, it must clearly exhibit the potential for facilitating certain musical actions students see as 'ideal' – that is, as desirable.

> When the subject-matter has been psychologized, that is, viewed as an outgrowth of present tendencies and activities, it is easy to locate in the present some obstacle ... which can be handled more adequately if the truth [i.e. knowledge or skill] in question be mastered. This need supplies motive for the learning. An end which is the child's own carries him on to possess the means of its accomplishment.
>
> (Dewey 1902: 32)

This kind of teaching is needed to motivate students to practise and to learn, and to psychologize such learning so its value will be functional to such actions.

The appeal of Action Learning comes in part, then, from the attraction of musical action values that are derived from real-life musical pursuits and that are modelled regularly as instruction, thereby invoking an intentionality that is intrinsically musical. Its effectiveness comes from selecting musical challenges or problems that present students with a range of requirements, options and difficulties to be overcome if their individual musical goals are to be satisfied. These tempting opportunities for musical action are structured so that both assimilation and accommodation are evoked – the former to promote the comfortable familiarity that will bring into action and cognitively strengthen existing mental structures, and the latter to provide the novel musical demands that will inspire interest and nurture new or improved mental structures.

A musical activity is a problem only when it presents certain choices or poses certain obstacles that must be resolved because they stand in the way of a personal goal – a conscious goal of musical satisfaction or achievement. So-called 'sequencing' of learning is simply a matter of posing ever more subtle and refined problems. As the conditions of typical real-life uses of music are approximated in incremental stages, new problems are perceived by students as being increasingly realistic and therefore more interesting. Intentionality and achievement provide their own motivation as musical functioning becomes its own reward.

Such learning problems are considerably different from the kinds of 'problems' encountered in connection with discipline-oriented instruction. These typically involve 'assignments' (such as homework or practising) in which students have no interest because the work has no perceived action value – it leads to no foreseeable result or use in which they can become personally interested. Lessons, classes or rehearsals thus become problems where something is done simply because the teacher assigned it. Students' subsequent intentions bring about actions that represent motivational, instructional behavioural and disciplinary problems for the teacher. In contrast, action-oriented teaching enhances self-discipline because students come to regard the learning process – including practising – as its own reward when it regularly leads to greater personally satisfying musical ends.

'WHAT YOU ACHIEVE DEPENDS ON WHAT YOU SETTLE FOR!'

This is a popular way of stating a Pragmatic truism. And because advocates of the Activies Approach 'settle for' so little of a tangible nature, they achieve little of lasting significance. With their sights set solely on methodological rigour (see, for instance, Chosky et al. 1986: 336, 342), they settle for an adherence to recipe-like methods and materials in the belief that correct use amounts to successful teaching. Their prescriptions for 'experiential learning' involving activities designed to teach concepts for the purposes of promoting 'aesthetic sensitivity' and the ability 'to perceive the inner workings of music' have thus beguiled unsuspecting teachers into taking for granted that implementing certain musical activities guarantees valid and valuable results.

Action Learning, instead, begins by explicitly identifying then organizing musical content deemed to be musically valid and valuable because of its demonstrated potential for predictable and prolonged use. This prediction of a personal use for musical learning is its action value. To enhance the likelihood of such use, Action Learning stipulates that teaching methods psychologize that 'content'. Finally, and in almost total contrast to the Activities Approach, its Pragmatism settles for only the musical independence that can satisfy personal musical intentions in the absence of a teacher.

Action Learning remains open-minded as to specific methods and materials as long as they are pragmatic in tangibly and efficiently advancing stated Action Ideals. Teachers will be surprised to discover that many aspects of their teaching can remain comfortably familiar. However, within an Action Learning paradigm, teaching activities, methods and materials are only tools. They are used in connection with 'blueprints' for actions that can and will continue outside formal schooling. Hence they are 'instrumental'[20] in bringing about decidedly different and more predictably controlled results. Thus, Action Learning improves the experience of teaching music as much as it promotes the life-long action value musical experience and learning have for students.

NOTES

1 For example, see Greenberg (1984), for an approving review of several examples.
2 To begin with, what *is* an experience? Is experience the means of acquiring concepts, or are concepts necessary to have experiences? How is the teacher to know the most basic 'specific experience' and be able to relate it 'meaningfully' to other experiences? In what way have experiences been 'meaningful' if students never use 'aesthetic sensitivity' in choosing to be musically active in personally meaningful ways?
3 Wittgenstein points out that induction 'has no logical foundation' (Wittgenstein 1922: section 6.363). Therefore, no algorithm can be taught or used by which valid inductions can be elicited.
4 Music instruction as part of the general education of every student has been called 'general music'. However, this label should not be understood as meaning 'music in general' (i.e. a broad and superficial sample) (see Regelski 1984).
5 Paraphrase of Whitehead (1968: 82).
6 Note that 'discipline' is that quality of appreciation possessed by a 'disciple'.
7 *Aesthetic* is derived from the Greek word for 'sense perception'. Thus *anaesthetic* has come to refer to a loss of sensation – a numbness or lack of any effects or affects from sensation.
8 Although the term is the same one as used by Neil Postman, he does not understand it in the same manner as does the 'conservatory' mentality. He wishes schools to 'conserve that which is both necessary to a humane survival and threatened by a furious and exhausting culture' (Postman 1979: 25). He would no doubt agree that the quest of Action Learning to promote a central role for music in the life well-lived would qualify as a beneficial form of school-induced 'conserving' activity. Individual music-making was, of course, the genesis of all musical activity. And, until the professionalization of musicians, it was a prime pursuit of folk and intelligentsia alike. Whatever else it may contribute, the institutionalization of music as a discipline of professional scholars and practitioners should not detract from the continuing musical activity of non-professional musicians and music-lovers. Such activity must be conserved in the face of the attitude of professional musicians who would have musical activity on the part of the public limited largely to providing audiences enough to earn a living.

9 In *The Child and the Curriculum* (Dewey 1902: 11, 14, 15) Dewey specifically avoided dichotomizing 'the importance of the subject-matter of the curriculum as compared with the contents of the child's own experience'. " 'Discipline" is the watchword of those who magnify the course of study; "interest" that of those who blazon "The Child" upon their banner.' Rejecting both extremes ('common-sense recoils at the extreme character' of both), he asserted the need 'to get rid of the prejudicial notion that there is some gap in kind [as distinct from degree] between the child's experience and the various forms of subject-matter that make up the course of study'.

10 Whereas, as a method of inquiry, dialectics involves an interplay of opposing ideas in a process that seeks to clarify an issue in question, a dialectical synthesis is a continuing state of dialectical tension. Because this tension is positive rather than negative, it is sometimes characterized as a 'creative tension'. For more, see Regelski (1975b: 28).

11 This term was first used in *Time* (21 June 1971: 54). For more detail on the application of this hybrid to music education, see Regelski (1975a: 112–18 and *passim*).

12 Furth (1966: 225). Furth has been a follower and associate of Jean Piaget.

13 That which is so anomalous as to resist assimilation by or accomodation to an existing concept (i.e. schema; hypothesis; theory) will be comprehended only as nonsense. 'Non-sense' is the judgement made when the individual is unable to 'make sense' of sensory data, which is to say, unable to give form to it (i.e. to 'in-form' it). Thus explicated, 'in-formation' is a process by which such 'data' are given meaning and thus become the 'facts' of a theory or concept.

14 Thus to 'have' an experience, in the sense to be clarified in the two sections that follow, is already to 'have' the process of 'in-formation' occur that enables the learner to 'make sense' of the sensory data.

15 That we 'play' music does not mean that just any play in a music class is musical. There is a difference between free play and the purposeful artifice necessary to the arts. (See Hyland 1984: 48, 68–9, 71, 88, 95, 102, 119, 144.)

16 A 'need for achievement' has been identified by D.C. McClelland *et al.* (1953). However, when achievement is sought as its own reward, it remains an extrinsic not a musical value.

17 'Casual' listening and background music illustrate this effect.

18 The 'peri' in 'ex*peri*ment' shares an etymological relationship with '*peril*'.

19 In the view confirmed by contemporary cognitive science, the word 'education' has as its root the Latin *educere*, meaning 'to lead or draw forth'; this should be distinguished from the traditional, discipline-based approach to schooling as 'training', implied by the Latin *educare*.

20 The philosophical term 'Intrumentalism' describes the Action Learning paradigm fairly well, except that the central role of 'action' and 'Action Theory' would not be pointed to and, in music education at least, association of the term with musical 'instruments' would confuse discussion.

REFERENCES

BODEN, M.A. (1979) *Piaget*, Brighton: Harvester Press.

BEER, A.S. and HOFFMAN, M.E. (1982) *Teaching Music*, Morristown, NJ: Silver Burdett Company.

CHOSKY, L., ABRAMSON, R., GILLESPIE, A. and WOODS, D. (1986) *Teaching Music in the Twentieth Century*, Englewood Cliffs, NJ: Prentice-Hall.

COLWELL, R. (1987) 'Education and philosophy', *Bulletin of the Council for Research in Music Education* 90.

DAVIDSON, D. (1974) 'Psychology as philosophy', in S.C. Brown (ed.) *Philosophy of Psychology*, New York: Barnes & Nobles.

DEWEY, J. (1896) 'Interest in relation to training of the will', in *Yearbook of the National Herbart Society*, ed. C.A. McMurry, Bloomington, Ill.: National Herbart Society.

——(1902) *The Child and the Curriculum*, Chicago: University of Chicago Press, reprinted 1967, in S. Dworkin (ed.) *Dewey on Education: Selections*, New York: Teachers' College Press.

——(1929) *The Quest for Certainty*, reprinted 1960, New York: G.P. Putnam's Sons/Capricorn.

——(1934) *Art as Experience*, reprinted 1980, New York: G.P. Putnam's Sons/Perigee.

FROST, S.E. JR (1962) *Basic Teachings of the Great Philosophers*, revised edn, Garden City, N.Y.: Doubleday/Dolphin.

FURTH, H. (1966) *Thinking without Language*, New York: Free Press.

GREENBERG, M. (1984) 'Critique on Linda Patricia Young: an investigation of young children's music concept development using nonverbal and manipulative techniques', *Bulletin of the Council of Research in Music Education* 79: 47–52.

HACKETT, P. and LINDEMAN, C.A. (1988) *The Musical Classroom*, 2nd edn, Englewood Cliffs, NJ: Prentice-Hall.

HALL, E.T. (1977) *Beyond Culture*, Garden City, NY: Anchor Press/Doubleday.

HEATH, P.L. (1967) 'Concept' in P. Edwards (ed.) *The Encyclopaedia of Philosophy*, reprinted 1972, New York: Macmillan/Free Press.

HOWARD, V.A. (1982) *Artistry: The Work of Artists*, Indianapolis: Hackett.

HYLAND, D.W. (1984) *The Question of Play*, Lanham, NY: University Press of America.

KLEIN, G.S. (1970) *Perception, Motives and Personality*, New York: Alfred A. Knopf.

LEE, H.N. (1973) *Percepts, Concepts and Theoretic Knowledge*, Memphis: Memphis State University Press.

LONG, W. (1966) 'Experience' in D. Runes (ed.) *Dictionary of Philosophy*, Totowa, NJ: Littlefield, Adams & Co.

MCCLELLAND, D.C., ATKINSON, J.W., CLARK, R.A. and LOWELL, E.L. (1953) *The Achievement Motive*, New York: Appleton-Century-Crofts.

PARSONS, T. and SHILS, E.A. (eds) (1962) *Towards a General Theory of Action*, New York: Harper & Row.

126

PEARCE, J.C. (1976) *Exploring the Crack in the Cosmic Egg*, New York: Pocket Books.

PIAGET, J. (1952) *The Origins of Intelligence in Children*, New York: International Universities Press.

——(1970) *Science of Education and the Psychology of the Child*, trans. W. Mays, New York: Orion Press.

PIAGET, J. *et al.* (1978) *Success and Understanding*, trans. A.J. Pomerans, London: Routledge & Kegan Paul.

POLANYI, M. (1962) *Personal Knowledge*, Chicago: University of Chicago Press.

POLANYI, M. and PROSCH, H. (1975) *Meaning*, Chicago: University of Chicago Press.

POSTMAN, N. (1979) *Teaching as a Conserving Activity*, New York: Delacorte.

REGELSKI, T.A. (1969) 'Towards musical independence', *Music Educators' Journal* 55 (7): 77–83.

——(1975a) *Principles and Problems of Music Education*, Englewood Cliffs, NJ: Prentice-Hall.

——(1975b) 'A ride on the dialectical seesaw', *Music Educators' Journal* 61 (7): 28–33.

——(1983a) 'Action Learning', *Music Educators' Journal* 69 (6): 46–50.

——(1983b) 'Action Learning versus the Pied Piper Approach', *Music Educators' Journal* 69 (8): 55–7, 64.

——(1983c) *Teaching General Music: Action Learning for Middle and Secondary Schools*, New York: Schirmer Books.

——(1984) 'To be, or not to be.... General?' *Soundings*, Society for General Music, 1 (3).

——(1986) 'Concept-learning and Action Learning in music education', *British Journal of Music Education* 3 (2): 185–216.

TYLER, R.W. (1977) 'Desirable content for a curriculum development syllabus today', in A. Molnar and J.A. Zahorik (eds) *Curriculum Theory*, Washington, DC: ASCD.

WHITEHEAD, A.N. (1968) *Modes of Thought*, New York: Free Press/Macmillan.

WITTGENSTEIN, L. (1922) *Tractatus Logico-Philosophicus*, London: Routledge, section 6.

8

Music as Cultural Text

JOHN SHEPHERD

The idea that music and society are in some way related is one that, on
the surface, does not seem exceptionable. It is an idea that has informed
much work in ethnomusicology, and it is basic to a majority of research on
popular music. In addition, it is difficult to deny that important changes in
musical styles have paralleled important changes in social, cultural and
intellectual life. The musical system of functional tonality, for example, is
one that emerged from the cultural and intellectual fervour of the Renaissance. It is one that also lost a significant degree of creative force towards
the end of the nineteenth century, coinciding with the emergence of new
artistic and literary forms, and the experiencing of crises in religious and
scientific thought.

The notion that music is in some way social has gained considerable
ground in recent years. However, the mechanisms through which the sounds
of music convey 'sociality' are not well understood. In this sense it is
important to draw a distinction between sociality in music, and sociality in
musical life. Although music and musical life are intimately related, social
analyses of the latter have far outstripped social analyses of the former. It
has proved easier to discuss the social circumstances surrounding the creation and appreciation of music (the cultural context) than it has sociality
as manifest in the sounds of music themselves (the cultural text).

This essay explores the idea that the sounds of music convey important
social and cultural messages. These messages, however, are not thought of
as being separate from aesthetic and psychological ones. Both music and
human involvement in its creation and appreciation are thought of as
socially 'mediated'. That is, all those elements traditionally conceived as

contributing to the musical experience – sonic, aesthetic, psychological, physiological and so on – are here conceived as integral aspects of a wider matrix of social and cultural processes. This matrix is thereby implicated, thoroughly and indissolubly, in the creation of significance through music. The idea that music is social in all its aspects differs substantially from received wisdoms concerning its nature and function. These wisdoms rest customarily on the notion of 'autonomy': autonomy both of music and the individuals involved in its practice from wider social and cultural processes. Music has been conceived as a form of expression essentially distinct from the verbal, the literate and the visual. Musicality has been thought of as a special gift, imparted only to the chosen few. And music in industrialized societies, in both its 'serious' and 'popular' forms, has commonly been used as a way of escaping the everyday and affirming individual identity.

However, to claim a social significance for music is not necessarily to imply that music, and the human processes involved in its creation and appreciation, are somehow secondary symptoms or manifestations of 'the social'. Human individuality may continue to be regarded as important, and indeed central, to its practice. Further, it is possible to argue that music has distinctive qualities as a social form. If this essay explores a different way of thinking about music, then it explores equally a different way of thinking about 'the social', and the individual's involvement in the social. And it does this because, ultimately, social, subjective and musical processes are heavily implicated in one another. The problem is not to understand how music and society, music and the individual, and the individual and society relate as separate entities or processes, but rather to understand the character of their involvement with one another as different aspects of one organic process.

QUESTIONS OF CONTEXT AND TEXT

To think of music as a cultural text is to imply that social or cultural elements are contained within or passed through its sonic components. These elements have an origin and existence that are in part extrinsic to the musical experience to which they contribute. This relationship between 'extra-musical' and 'musical' elements has previously been formulated in terms of received wisdoms concerning the nature and function of music. That is, music has been taken to appeal autonomously to the autonomous awareness of the individual. However, the traditional emphasis on positivism that has characterized the study of music since the late 1950s has resulted in the question of the relationship between musical and psychological processes being studiously and sometimes consciously avoided. We cannot forget, argues Palisca,

> that musical aesthetics is not musical scholarship; it is musical experience and musical theory converging upon a philosophical problem. Aesthetics does not rest on documentary or similar evidence but on philosophical and psychological principles tested by experience.
>
> (Palisca 1963: 110)

This avoidance has in turn been entrenched by the way in which an emphasis on positivistic tasks has precluded a meaningful dialogue between the disciplines of musicology and music theory. As Leppert and McClary (1987: xiii) have observed, 'the disciplines of music theory and musicology ... cautiously keep separate considerations of biography, patronage, place and dates from those of musical syntax and structure'. The concentration of musicologists 'on limited positivistic tasks', argues Kerman (1985: 72), has 'had the decided effect of sidestepping "the music itself" '. He continues:

> if the musicologists' characteristic failure is superficiality, that of the analysts is myopia ... by removing the bare score from its context in order to examine it as an autonomous organism, the analyst removes that organism from the ecology that sustains it.
>
> (Kerman 1985: 72)

This separation of contextual from textual matters resonates in a less stringent and more constructive manner within the disciplines of ethno-musicology and popular music studies. The history of ethnomusicology has been characterized by debates between anthropologically- or contextually-oriented scholars such as Alan P. Merriam and musicologically- or textually-oriented scholars such as Mantle Hood. Although these debates have been played out since the late 1950s in increasingly complex and nuanced ways, it is only more recently that ethnomusicology has witnessed the treatment of musical sounds as cultural texts in the work of Blacking (1973), Keil (1979), Ellis (1985) and, most notably, Feld (1982, 1988). Popular music studies, established as a separate undertaking since the late 1970s, has likewise experienced some not unhealthy tensions between sociological and musicological approaches to its subject matter (Shepherd: 1991).

A central problem in understanding significance in music has been that, in their most 'abstract' manifestations, the sounds of music do not obviously

130

refer outside themselves to the world of objects, events and linguistically encodable ideas. In terms of the way in which symbols are commonly understood to have meaning, music emerges either as having 'no meaning', or as having a meaning that is quite distinct and apart from all other forms of meaning. Communication, as Duncan ironically observes, 'must be explained by everything but communication.... it must have, as we read so often, a "referent"' (1968: 31). It is this difficulty which has allowed the appearance of the autonomous nature of music (by which, in this context, is nearly always meant 'serious' music) to persist. The tensions that have existed between the study of the 'extra-musical' and the 'musical' have in no small measure been perpetuated by the genuine intellectual difficulty of understanding how the two may relate.

Only one music theorist has consistently confronted this difficulty in terms of received wisdoms concerning the nature and function of music. Leonard B. Meyer, remarks Kerman (1985: 107), 'has always kept his distance from other [music] theorists'. As 'a genuine polymath of music ... [he] has more or less systematically worked his way through the central problems of aesthetics, theory, modernism, criticism [and] history'. Implicit in much music theory, says Meyer (1956: 33), is the idea that 'the meaning of music lies specifically ... and ... exclusively ... in the musical processes themselves'. Yet there has been a failure 'to state with either clarity or precision ... in what sense these processes are meaningful'. This failure, continues Meyer, 'has led some critics to assert that musical meaning is a thing apart, different in some unexplained way from all other kinds of meaning'. This, he concludes, 'is simply an evasion of the real issue'.

The real issue seems to lie in confusing a form of human expression that does not obviously refer outside itself to the world of objects, events and linguistically encodable ideas with one which makes no appeal beyond itself in the process of generating and evoking meaning. While it can be accepted that music falls within the former category, it cannot sensibly be said to fall within the latter. It is this distinction which allows Meyer to argue that musical processes appeal directly to the logic and flux of mental and psychological processes. Musical meaning is taken to originate and be located within 'psychological constants' (Meyer 1973: 14) presumed innate in humans. There is consequently no need to entertain the notion that music invokes the external, 'objective' world. The ability of music to evoke meaning is facilitated through a conformity between the *structures* of music and the *structures* of the human mind.

Meyer's position is allied to that of Langer, who has argued that the 'inner life' has 'formal properties similar to those of music – patterns of motion and rest, of tension and release, of agreement and disagreement, preparation, fulfilment, excitation, sudden change, etc.' (Langer 1942: 228). This similarity, concludes Langer, allows music to act in relation to the emotional world in the same way that language acts in relation to the propositional world of objects, events and ideas – symbolically:

> If music has any significance, it is semantic, not symptomatic. Its 'meaning' is evidently not that of a stimulus to evoke emotions, nor that of a signal to announce them; if it has an emotional content, it 'has' it in the same sense that language 'has' its conceptual content – *symbolically*. It is not usually derived *from* affects nor intended *for* them; but we may say, with certain reservations, that it is *about* them. Music is not the cause or cure of feelings, but their *logical expression*.
>
> (Langer 1942: 218)

While Langer's work has been philosophical, Meyer's has rested on detailed and persuasive analyses of music in the tradition of functional tonality. Meyer has demonstrated that the best music in this tradition works according to the principle of 'deferred gratification' (Meyer 1959). A piece of music will create expectations that it will proceed to fulfill, but not directly. While the most fundamental of its architectonic levels will, indeed, move sequentially towards a satisfying conclusion, other, higher levels will engage in deviations that detract from the inevitable. The technical characteristics of the music keep the listener in a state of meaningful suspense: meaningful, because fulfilment is not so directly achieved as to render the music banal, and the deviations not so compelling as to render it anarchic and without a sense of direction. In this way the harmonic, melodic and, to a lesser extent, rhythmic elements of the music speak symbolically to the ebb and flow of the inner life.

Meyer has undoubtedly contributed important insights into the structural rather than referential principles according to which music evokes meaning. However, because Meyer's work does not take into account the social ecology that sustains music, these insights do not stretch to an explanation of the mechanisms through which psychological and musical processes are involved with one another. In many instances, psychological and musical processes speak meaningfully to one another because they are grounded in, informed by, and *constituted* through similar sets of social mediations. The substance and logic of the inner life flow from these mediations rather than from 'psychological constants' presumed innate in humans. As a consequence, it is difficult to see also how Meyer's insights could stretch to provide an adequate theorization of the substance of musical meanings. Meyer's analyses of functional tonal music are compelling only because the consequences of social mediations to this tradition are revealed intuitively and through omission. What Meyer identifies as psychological constants appealed to by a particular tradition of music are, in fact, psychological processes specific to particular social and historical circumstances. It is for this reason that Meyer's views on music outside the tradition of functional tonality (or music effectively influenced by that tradition: for example, 'real jazz' (1959: 33)) have at times been ethnocentric and dismissive. Judged in terms of criteria drawn from the aesthetic and technical characteristics of functional tonal music rather than from the social and cultural circumstances of their creation and appreciation, traditional and popular music have emerged, inevitably, as less valuable than music in the functional tonal tradition.

If Meyer theorizes an 'extra-musical' significance for music in a manner which circumvents the traditional problem of referentialism, then he does so without challenging the view that both music and the individual awareness to which it appeals are ultimately autonomous. However, if significance in music can only be fully addressed by reference to the social, then it has to be accepted that social theories for music have traditionally given rise to two difficulties. These difficulties are the result of two assumptions: first – in terms of such theories – that music can have significance only through reference to the external world of people, events and objects; second, that music and the individual creativity responsible for it can amount to little more than by-products of more fundamental social processes. The fear is that, in being reduced to the 'material–factual' world of sociality as it is traditionally conceived, the essential qualities of both musicality and individuality will be eradicated from thought.

To think of music as a cultural text thus raises two issues which remain central to the study of musical experience. The first has to do with the precise relationship of contextual to textual elements. How is it that the 'extra-musical' gets into the 'musical'? The insights provided by Meyer and Langer with regard to the formal congruence of psychological and musical processes may here provide food for thought. The second issue, which follows from the first, has to do with the precise nature of the contextual and the textual. What exactly is 'music'? Is it just sounds? Or is it sounds and the humanly created meanings that are invested in and derived from sounds? Where, in other words, does contextuality stop and textuality begin?

THE STRUCTURAL HOMOLOGY

A framework for answering these questions can be derived from the work of Raymond Williams and the tradition of British cultural analysis. Williams argues that it is counter-productive to think of the sociality of art in terms of the way in which art relates to society:

> We have got into the habit, since we realized how deeply works or values could be determined by the whole situation in which they are expressed, of asking about these relationships in a standard form: 'what is the relation of this art to this society?' But 'society', in this question, is a specious whole. If the art is part of the society, there is no solid whole, outside it, to which, by the form of our question, we concede priority.
>
> (Williams 1965: 61)

The question, therefore, has not to do with the way in which art gains its sociality by reference outside itself to other phenomena that are quint-essentially more social in their processes. It has to do with the way in which the logics of artistic processes *as social processes* may or may not resonate with the logics of other, specific processes (for example, economic, political, educational, familial, religious, legal) which are neither more nor less social in their characteristics. Society is neither a 'thing' nor simply a collection of people, events and objects to which reference can be made by phenomena (such as art) which are inherently 'less' social. Sociality is manifest in structured relationships between people, in structured relationships between people and the worlds they create, and in the structures of the symbolic and cultural forms which arise through and give expression to such relationships. 'Culture', of which 'music' forms an aspect, may be thought of as the processes through which the logics of these structured relationships are made manifest in perceptible forms. The theory of culture, says Williams (1965: 63), may as a consequence be defined as 'the study of relationships between elements in a whole way of life'. A key-word in such study, he continues, is 'pattern': 'it is with the discovery of patterns of a characteristic kind that any useful cultural analysis begins, and it is with the relationships between these patterns ... that general cultural analysis is concerned'.

Williams's concept of 'pattern' is not that far removed from the concept of 'pattern' which informs the work of Meyer and Langer. The one, crucial difference is that the concept is now applied to the entirety of social and cultural processes rather than simply to the psychological processes that form but one aspect of them. It is this way of thinking that has facilitated a number of analyses of music as cultural text. Blacking (1973), for example,

134

has discerned in the melodic structures of Venda music principles of mutuality characteristic of Venda social organization. Keil (1979) has engaged in an analysis of Tiv melodic structures in terms of the metaphor of circles and angles which informs the majority of Tiv life and cultural expression. And Shepherd (1991) has drawn parallels between the harmonic and rhythmic characteristics of functional tonality as a musical system and various features of the social and cultural circumstances in which music in this tradition has been created and appreciated. Such features include the dominant time–space orientation of post-Renaissance cultures, the hierarchical and centre-oriented social structures of industrial capitalism, as well as industrial capitalism's dominant ideological processes. In relation to these ideological processes, it is interesting to compare a 'social' analysis of functional tonal music as articulating the 'ability' of the individual to overcome considerable odds and succeed with Meyer's 'psychological' analyses, resting as they do on the notion of deferred gratification.

The concept of the structural homology has emerged as the theoretical model in terms of which cultural forms may be thought of as giving expression to the structures of wider social processes. That is, there is taken to be a congruent or homologous relationship between the logic of a cultural style and that of the social processes to which it contributes and within which it is embedded. This kind of cultural analysis is best exemplified in the work of Hall *et al.* (1976), Willis (1978) and Hebdige (1979). The principle of the structural homology, like the work of Meyer, effectively circumvents the problem of referentialism with respect to music. However, there are three problems with the way it has customarily been applied to the analysis of cultural forms. First, despite the admonition of Williams, there has been an implicit assumption that cultural styles, including those of music, do in actuality 'give expression' to something outside themselves. Frith (1987: 137) has been critical of this assumption as it has constituted 'the sociological common sense of rock criticism'. According to this common sense, 'good music is the authentic expression of something – a person, an idea, a feeling, a shared experience' (1987: 136). However, observes Frith (1987: 137), 'the myth of authenticity is, indeed, one of rock's own ideological effects'. Second, there is no theoretical protocol in terms of which it is possible to understand the mechanisms through which particular cultural styles resonate with the logic of wider social processes. In this sense, and with specific reference to music, the principle of the structural homology represents no advance over the theories of Meyer in terms of understanding the precise relationship between 'extra-musical' and 'musical' elements. Third, the role of the individual in creating or appreciating the meanings of

135

cultural styles is conceptualized overwhelmingly in terms of the individual's membership of a social group. There is little conceptual space for a theorization of the private, internal world of individual awareness and creativity, and of the way in which this world may connect to the external, public world of shared cultural meanings. The principle of the structural homology speaks almost exclusively to an analysis of this shared, public world.

The principle of the structural homology has one final problem as it relates specifically to the analysis of music – a problem, it must be added, that has much to do with the traditional preoccupations of music theory. The notion of musical structure that the structural homology evokes, in common with the notion evoked in Meyer's analyses, is restricted almost completely to those musical elements that Meyer (1959) has characterized as syntactical. The syntactical in music is comprised of the order of abstract relationships that obtain between individual sonic events. These relationships are conceived as having an existence primarily through the parameter of pitch (the musical elements of harmony and melody) and, to a lesser extent, the parameter of duration (the musical element of rhythm). The presumed primacy of the syntactical in music was first challenged by Keil (1966), who argued that inflectional elements in music – the 'bending' of rhythms and pitches – were as important to the expressive power of jazz (and, by implication, other forms of popular and traditional music) as the more rigidly maintained rhythmic and harmonic frameworks from which they 'deviated'. Keil (1987) has more recently extended these arguments by developing the notions of 'process' and 'texture'. 'To be personally involving', says Keil (1987: 275), '[music] must be "out of time" and "out of tune" '. Keil's notion of texture can be expanded to include tone quality or timbre in music, that is to say, the inherent qualities of sounds themselves. At this juncture, however, it simply has to be noted that an almost exclusively syntactical notion of 'what counts as music' on the part of music theory has allowed little space for the analysis of tone quality or timbre, or of 'inflections' in pitch, rhythm and timbre.

THE RELATIVE AUTONOMY OF MUSIC

The assumption that music may have significance only through an invocation of 'extra-musical' phenomena can be circumvented by establishing the nature of its autonomy *relative* to other social processes. It is clear from arguments advanced by Williams that no artistic or cultural form need *depend* on non-artistic or non-cultural social processes for their significance. At the very least, an 'autonomous' musical sociality (that is, 'autonomous' musical processes as *social processes*) may be thought of as resonating, either harmoniously or dissonantly, with other areas of non-musical sociality. To this extent, the significance of musical sociality may be conceived as having an existence simultaneously intrinsic and extrinsic to 'musical processes' themselves. Conceived in this way, the significance of musical sociality does not necessarily *originate* outside 'musical processes'. However, musical sociality would be of little significance if its internal logics and structures were of no relevance to the logics and structures of other, non-musical social processes – if, in other words, it could find no resonance outside its immediate realm of articulation. It is in this sense that music is relatively autonomous in its relationship to other areas of social process.

This principle of relative autonomy opens up conceptual space for an understanding of the exercise of individual creativity through musical processes. If all areas of social process are relatively autonomous in their relationship to one another, there can exist moments of musical sociality which are purely intrinsic to 'musical processes'. This is because any extrinsic significance may result only from such moments being recognized *subsequently* as of relevance to other areas of social process. It therefore remains possible for people both to create and to know about aspects of their world which may not be accessible to them initially through any medium other than music.

The importance of this point is magnified when it is realized that no social reality to which music contributes has firm and fixed boundaries. The music of a society may say something to that society that the majority of the society does not wish to hear or recognize. This has been the case with much modernist and avant-garde music in twentieth-century industrialized societies. Such music may be thought of as existing only within the cracks and margins or beyond the boundaries of what passes for 'reality' in that particular society. It may then be asked what the difference is between a music which is 'intrinsic' to a society and one which is 'extrinsic' to it where the potential for knowledge and learning is concerned. If there is a difference, perhaps it is of degree rather than kind in the sense that some music is initially closer than others to the particular social reality it addresses.

The principle of relative autonomy is exemplified in the ability of music to communicate cross-culturally. It was argued earlier that, in many instances, psychological and musical processes can speak meaningfully to one another because they are grounded in, informed by, and constituted through similar sets of social mediations. In many instances music has had significance, either because it was appreciated by the very people who created it, or because it was appreciated by people who belonged to the same or a similar social group as the people who created it. These situations have become much less common since the advent of the commodified, mass dissemination of music, and the advent of the portable, cassette playback machine. It is now rare for the musicians responsible for the majority of music appreciated in contemporary industrialized societies to belong to the same groups or even the same times as the people who appreciate it. The circumstances of contemporary professional performers (whether 'serious' or 'popular') in such societies results in them having a minimal experience of the everyday realities of the music-lovers and fans to whom their music speaks. And over the last twenty years it has become increasingly common for 'Third World' people to hear 'First World' music, and for 'First World' people to hear 'Third World' music (Wallis and Malm, 1984). In the words of Swanwick (1984: 53), 'the musics of other cultures and other times [can be] significant, powerful, disturbing [and] moving'. This cross-cultural communication is not, however, made possible by psychological constants presumed innate in humans. It is made possible because the music in question is perceived as having something of relevance to say by the individuals, groups and cultures who appreciate it. There is a very real sense in which music constructs its own truth and its own authenticity.

If music, along with other cultural and artistic activities in modern, industrialized societies, seems to have less importance than economic, political and technological activities, and seems, furthermore, to depend increasingly on those activities for its existence and significance, then that is not because of any innate characteristics of human or social organization. It is because these societies have organized themselves in ways that result in music *appearing* to have this inferior status. In these societies, there has been a tendency to relegate music to the status of 'cultural capital' in the case of 'serious' music (Bourdieu 1977), or to that of 'mere leisure and entertainment' in the case of 'popular' music. In other societies and in other times, music has seemed to play a more explicitly recognized and central role in the maintenance and furtherance of cultural life. Blacking has referred to the way in which music in Venda society has acted as a force for integration after the potentially divisive processes of ensuring material survival: 'the chief function of music', he says (Blacking 1973: 101), 'is to promote soundly organized humanity by enhancing human consciousness'. In a similar vein Keil (1979: 95) has observed that the energy of songs in Tiv society 'seems capable of "solving" all … problems'. Similar instances of the *explicitly* recognized use of music's cultural power in modern industrialized societies has been restricted to dispossessed and marginal groups such as those of black Americans and the youth counter-cultures of the 1960s.

The ability of music to communicate powerfully, both culturally and cross-culturally, has been taken up by Catherine Ellis. Music, she argues, 'can bridge various thought processes ... it can stimulate inter-cultural understanding at a deeply personal level, with the result that a person is no longer a member solely of one culture' (Ellis 1985: 15). According to Ellis, such cross-cultural learning can occur because music is capable of transcending the limits of individual cultures, not by constituting some kind of culture-free, universal language, as has sometimes been claimed, but by giving life to cultural realities in ways that escape 'the prison-house of language'. Against the background of cross-cultural musical communication between members of the Aboriginal and European societies of Australia, Ellis has observed (ibid.: 15) that, 'by being open-minded, a student can become at one with the thought processes of his teacher, irrespective of the cultural barrier which may exist in all other spheres of interaction'. Such a process is not easy, and is often painful for the student. That it can occur at all demonstrates that, if music is social, it is social in some quite distinctive ways that speak directly to its relative autonomy.

SOUND IN MUSIC AND SOUND IN LANGUAGE

A problem with conceptualizing the relative autonomy of musical sociality in terms of its ability to originate and to communicate powerful cultural meanings is that these meanings could then appear to 'belong' to the sounds of music. That is, because the sounds of music can provide an initial and exclusive vehicle for cultural meanings, it might seem as if it is the sounds themselves that 'have' the meanings.

An understanding of the relationship between sounds and meanings in music can best be approached in terms of a comparison of the role of sound in language with the role of sound in music. The conventional wisdom concerning the relationship between sounds and meanings in language is that it is 'arbitrary'. There is no *necessary* connection between the inherent characteristics of the sounds and the meanings that they evoke, although, in the case of onomatopoeia, there may be one in practice. The sounds of words can signify *without* invoking the sonic manifestations of the phenomena to which they refer. 'Birds' can just as easily and successfully be referred to as '*oiseaux*'. In the case of language, it is therefore clear that it is not the sounds that 'have' meanings. Sounds only 'have' meanings in the sense that people, through agreement and convention, put them there.

The same, in essence, may be said about music. However, the relationship between sounds and meanings in music appears to be considerably more complex than it is in language. In traditional, semiological analyses of language, the bare physical fact of a word's sound is termed the 'signifier'. The mental concept with which the signifier is traditionally and conventionally associated (for example, the mental concept of 'birds', as opposed to real, live birds) is called the 'signified'. The signifier and signified then come together in a 'seamless' fashion (a fashion that is normally hidden from view) to form a sign. It is the sign which then refers to phenomena in the real world (for example, real live birds). It is easy to see how meanings in language are the result of social conventions, and how conservative and unassailable these conventions can become when processes of meaning construction are hidden from view, and the conventions thereby rendered 'natural'.

Analysing the syntactical manifestations of musical sounds in this manner is not possible. While the sound 'birds' uttered in isolation will retain the core of the meaning it traditionally carries, a musical pitch, for example, will not. An 'A' at 440 hertz sounded in isolation on the piano carries no musical meaning. Nothing in the physical event of a tone, says Zuckerkandl (1956: 22), 'corresponds to the tone as a musical event'. When we hear a melody, therefore, 'we hear things that have no counterpart in physical nature' (ibid.: 23). An 'A' only evokes a dynamic, musical quality in the context of a structured matrix of other sounds. The 'A' may be perceived as evoking, for example, the dynamic quality of the key-note in A major, the leading note in B♭ major, the mediant in F major, or the dominant in D major. The dynamic, musical quality of a tone changes according to context: harmonic, melodic *and* rhythmic (Zuckerkandl 1956). Its physical qualities do not.

The concept of the signifier is thus of little use as a basis for analysing the relationship between the syntactical manifestations of sounds and the meanings with which they are involved. This is because, in fulfilling their syntactical function, individual sounds *in and of themselves* carry no meaning. However, as Keil (1966, 1987) has argued, there are levels of communication in music other than the purely syntactical. At one of these levels, sounds act not so much in the manner of linguistic signs in referring to actual phenomena in the external world, but as signifiers to evoke the signifieds associated with such phenomena. Sounds at this level may work in one of two ways. Firstly, they may refer to actual sounds in the external world. This reference may be a direct copy, as in the use of drums to signal the mental concept of 'militariness', or a symbolic evocation, as in the case of the 'cuckoo calls' in Beethoven's *Pastoral* Symphony or the 'sounds of the sea' in Debussy's *La Mer*. This use of sound in music is the one that comes closest to the use of sound in language. Such sounds are not, however, capable of denoting actual phenomena in the external world: they refer only to the characteristic sounds of phenomena and not the phenomena themselves. Secondly, there are those sounds which evoke symbolically the inherent structural characteristics of various internal states which are experienced somatically and which derive from conditions and situations in the external world. Shepherd (1991), for example, has argued that, through the mediations of the sound production processes of the body, various characteristic voice types in the field of popular music resonate powerfully with the logics and structures of the different gender identities they evoke. Again, the use of a distant and hollow flute sound to evoke the feeling of a distant and unobtainable love would fall within this category.

Musical sounds of this type, which have been analysed extensively by Tagg (1979, 1991), may legitimately be thought of as signifiers. Their ability to evoke meaning is not context bound. When a black gospel singer begins a performance, for example, the effect upon the congregation, whether positive or not so positive, is instantaneous. There is no need for a continually unfolding context of sounds for the congregation to discern meaning in the timbral characteristics of a particular sound. The broader context of the music may well confirm and augment the original impression, but the voice quality, which the congregation recognizes as coming from 'within the person', signifies in and of itself.

But although these sounds may legitimately be thought of as signifiers, they do not function arbitrarily. Firstly, they always have a structural relationship with their signifieds. Thus, in the case of the drum sounds, the signified is the mental concept of drum sounds in actual military situations, not the mental concept of 'militariness' evoked by actual military drum sounds. The relationship between signifier and signified is structurally tight because the signifier is presumably a direct copy, or a nearly direct copy, of drum sounds in actual military situations. The structural relationship of 'cuckoo calls' and the 'sounds of the sea' to these sounds as they occur in the external world is clearer, as is the structural relationship of the internal characteristics of voice timbres to the logics and structures of gender identities. Secondly, although it cannot be established incontrovertibly, it seems likely that the relationship between sounds in the external world and the second-order signifieds that are evoked through their invocation in music is likewise structural. That is, there may well exist a structural relationship between the internal characteristics of drum sounds and the logics and structures of 'militariness', between cuckoo calls and 'pastoralness', and the sounds of the sea and 'oceanness'. Finally, it seems entirely possible that there exists a structural relationship between the internal logics and structures of these second-order signifieds as musically evoked and the logics and structures of the inner life to which they in turn speak.

Sounds in music therefore seem to appeal 'directly' or 'indirectly' to the logics and structures of the socially mediated inner life, depending on whether or not reference is made to the sounds of the environment. However, it is questionable whether the distinction between 'musical' and 'non-musical' sounds that is customarily made in modern, industrialized societies is a useful one. The music of the Kaluli of New Guinea, for example, is redolent with the bird calls of the rain forest in which the Kaluli live. Further, a musical event for the Kaluli is constituted not simply through the 'musical utterances' of the Kaluli people, but, as often as not, through a dialogue between such utterances and the rich soundscape of the forest and the work environment. The soundscape of the environment is thus as much a musical phenomenon for the Kaluli as the 'musical sounds' they utter, and just as capable of evoking their individual and collective aesthetic sensibilities (Feld 1988). To the extent that the musical traditions of modern industrialized societies refer outside themselves to the sounds of the environment, they are simply inferring an extended frame for what counts as 'music'.

Sounds in music therefore differ from sounds in language in two important respects. Firstly, unlike the sounds of language, sounds in music never refer *directly* to people, events and objects in the external world. They either copy or evoke symbolically the sonic manifestations of those people, events and objects. Secondly, sounds in music seem not to function in a fundamentally arbitrary fashion. They function in a structural fashion that allows them to evoke, directly and powerfully, the logics and structures of the socially mediated inner life.

Categories of analysis drawn from the study of language are, as a consequence, seldom appropriate for understanding the relationship between sounds and meanings in music. It is this problem which has led Wicke (1989, 1990) to use the term 'medium' to refer to the syntactical manifestation of sounds as bare physical facts. Wicke's use of this term recognizes that it is only as integral aspects of a continually unfolding context of sounds that

142

individual sounds in their syntactical manifestations can provide a ground for and resonate with meaning. There seems no reason, however, why Wicke's concept could not apply equally to those sounds in music which can more legitimately be regarded as signifiers. The relationship between the internal characteristics of individual sounds and the meanings with which they are involved seems to be as structural as the relationship between syntactical manifestations and their meanings. Wicke's notion that the sonic medium of music is a structured and structuring template of sounds thus seems to have application beyond its original conception.

The structural manner in which music communicates suggests that an element of necessity exists in the relationship between the 'medium' and the logics and structures of its meanings. This element of necessity has led the Czech semiotician Jaroslav Volek (1981: 246) to observe that 'the semiotics of music, which has to do principally with complex matrices of signs, has of necessity to deal with the structural iconicity of musical works'. However, it does not follow from this principle of structural iconicity that there is a fixed, one-to-one relationship between the structural charac-teristics of the medium and its meanings. The sounds of music no more determine meaning than does meaning determine the sounds. The most that can be said, in all probability, is that the structural characteristics of the medium favour, and maybe even attract, certain meanings, while making it difficult, if not impossible, for other meanings to pass through them. As a consequence, music can only be said to display a *niveau neutre* (neutral plane) (Nattiez 1976, 1988) in shaping the sonic basis for meaning con-struction, not the processes of meaning construction themselves. As Wicke has argued, the medium of music has no meaning in and of itself. It simply offers up *potentials* and *possibilities* for the construction and investment of meaning *on the part of people*.

THE INDIVIDUAL AND SOCIETY

A closer examination of the relationship between sounds and meanings in music points to the central role of the individual in creating and imparting meaning. The inescapability of this role might seem to detract from the idea that music is social in all its aspects and that it is capable of both originating and communicating powerful cultural meanings. This apparent tension in thinking about the individual and cultural dimensions of music can, however, be resolved. This resolution involves further exploration of the idea that the substance and logic of the inner life flow from social mediations rather than from 'psychological' constants presumed innate in humans.

It is a commonplace that people enter into relationships with one another in order to ensure material survival. That is, people enter into relationships to provide food, shelter and clothing for themselves. The nature of this provision can become exceptionally complex, as in the case of contemporary, industrialized societies. Regardless of the level of complexity at which processes of 'material reproduction' occur, however, they necessarily involve processes of 'social reproduction'. Not only is it necessary for people to reproduce themselves materially, they also need to maintain and reproduce the order of relationships that make material reproduction possible.

Reproducing this order of relationships involves people in processes of communication. People, it has been observed, act in terms of the meanings that the world has for them. If they are to act in ways which are more or less consistent with the order of relationships within which they live, then people need to symbolize this order to themselves in consciousness. It is through cultural processes that people represent to themselves in perceptible and symbolic forms the nature of the public, social world in which they live.

The awareness of an individual develops in terms of the ways that the world is presented symbolically to them. In continuing everyday practice, these ways become complex in the extreme. Not only do they reproduce the complexities, inconsistencies and contradictions of the world. They reproduce also the particular interpretations of the world engaged in by those who present it symbolically to the individual. However, the developing awareness of the individual is not simply a palimpsest of the complex ways in which the world is presented symbolically to them. It is a consequence also of the ways in which the individual makes sense of and integrates presentations which are often inconsistent and confusing. The processes through which individual awareness emerges are therefore active rather than passive. Individuals quickly develop a particular logic or more or less coherent set of assumptions in terms of which they assimilate and make sense of new information. While this coherent logic guarantees the individual uniqueness and recognition as a person, it does not give rise to a 'unified subject'. People contain within their own personalities many of the inconsistencies and contradictions derived from the external public world, and become adept at revealing different and often inconsistent aspects of themselves according to the situations they encounter. It is through the often unique and creative ways in which individuals themselves contribute symbolically to the external, public world that processes of material and social reproduction are guaranteed.

Sociality, then, is as manifest in the private, internal world of individual awareness as it is in the external, public world of shared behaviour. The two put each other in motion, and are never static, either in themselves, or in relationship to one another. The indissoluble manner in which the two worlds are involved with one another is highlighted by Bateson when he says that:

> The individual mind is immanent but not only in the body. It is immanent also in pathways and messages outside the body; and there is a larger Mind of which the individual mind is only a sub-system. The larger Mind is ... immanent in the total interconnected social system.
>
> (Bateson 1973: 436)

However, if the symbolism of human worlds occurs both inside and outside the human body, then there is a sense in which the symbolism of the external world can never be definitively known. One person can never have direct knowledge of another person's thought and experience. They can only speculate as to the nature of the other person's thought and experience by interpreting the symbols the other person utters. Human interaction therefore involves a never-ending play of mutual 'reality checks' through which people attempt to ensure that they are, indeed, making sense to one another.

It is in this way that the material media of symbols in the external world act as templates on which individuals map or notate meanings. As Wicke has pointed out in the specific case of music, the material medium of a symbol does not in itself have meaning. Ultimately, it is not symbols which have meaning, it is people. Symbols only 'have' meaning in the sense that people invest in them meanings which the material form of the symbol is capable of 'accepting', either through its conventional range of arbitrarily assigned meanings (as in the case of language) or through its inherent structural characteristics (as in the case of music). Symbols do not therefore 'carry' meanings from one person to another. Were they to do this, there would be the implication of a fixed, one-to-one relationship between a symbol and its meaning. There would be little possibility for the negotiation of meaning on the part of individuals which constitutes such an important aspect of the dialectical relationship between the individual and society, or for the exercise of individual creativity.

Awareness, personality, and a sense of the world are, in the final analysis, created by people. However, there tend to be strong commonalities in the

145

ways in which this creation occurs in any particular group or society. Symbols are not simply passive recipients for the investment of meaning. They carry with them an element of power and influence. Since the creation and perception of symbols is linked to processes of material and social reproduction, symbolic forms in any particular group or society will manifest commonalities flowing from the logics of the relationships implicated in such reproductive processes. Further, although people cannot help but put individual interpretations on to the symbols they perceive, there is a tendency to interpret symbols in ways which seem meaningful to a majority of other people. People are generally fulfilled by making a difference, or by being of significance to other people. Uttering a symbol is therefore, potentially, a politically powerful act, since the form of a symbol will tend to favour the investment of certain meanings over others, and in this way draw people into the range of influence of the person uttering the symbol. At the level of the face-to-face interactions of small groups, such power tends to be distributed more or less equally, since all the people in such groups are capable of both uttering and interpreting symbols. At the level of the greater group or society, however, broad commonalities in symbols lead, it can be surmised, to the creation of broad commonalities in the creation of individual personalities and senses of the world. The common elements in symbolic forms are not, generally, a matter for face-to-face mediation, and people are as a consequence drawn even more into making sense of them in ways which seem to make sense to the majority of other people. Thus, although people are individuals, there are ways also in which the logics of their inner lives become codes for the orders of relationships within which they live.

MEANING IN MUSIC

When an individual invests an aspect of their inner life in the medium of music, therefore, they are probably investing the medium with a meaning which will resonate with the logics of broader social and cultural contexts. It is this resonance which enables music to 'communicate' powerful cultural meanings. However, when a music-lover or a fan invests an aspect of his or her inner life in the medium of music, there is no guarantee that it will match in all its dimensions the aspect of the inner life that the composer or musician may invest in the same medium. Music, like any other symbolic medium, 'communicates' both commonalities and differences. In this way it is capable of mediating powerfully between the individual and society.

To the extent that music can 'communicate' differences, it seems inappropriate to think of the composer investing in music meanings which are then 'passed on' to the music-lover in an essentially pristine fashion. Music-lovers and fans take from music meanings implicit in their inner lives which are capable of being invested in or drawn from the music's sonic medium. If the range and variety of an individual's 'meanings' cannot be invested in or drawn from the particular music they are hearing, then it is unlikely that they will like the music. There would seem to be a need for musicology to concentrate more on field-work and the specific qualities of the sonic medium, and perhaps less on 'biography, patronage, place and dates'.

However, the ability of music to 'communicate' cross-culturally suggests that music acts not only as a medium for the mapping or notating of shared cultural meanings and their individual negotiations. Like other symbolic media, music has an ability to 'instruct' that derives from the social and cultural commonalities which form a context for its creation and appreciation. Yet, in functioning cross-culturally, music also has a potential to 'instruct', the power of which does not derive from such commonalities. As Ellis and Swanwick have in their different ways suggested, music can act as a medium for learning and for the expansion of individual and cultural horizons. This potential derives from the particular capacity of music to speak *directly* and *concretely* to the logics of an individual's inner life, a capacity which derives in turn from the distinctive experiential qualities of sound.

Sound, the structured and structuring medium of music, has properties that distinguish it quite clearly from the sense of vision. Sound brings the world into people from all directions, simultaneously and dynamically. While it is frequently possible to locate the source of a sound, it is a fundamental experiential characteristic of sound that it lifts off the surface of its material source to occupy and give life to the space not only between the source and the listener, but also around the listener. While a sound may have a discrete material source, therefore, it is experienced as a phenomenon that encompasses and touches the listener in a cocoon-like fashion. Since people typically hear not one, but several sounds at once, they are encompassed and touched by a world of simultaneously existing objects and events. And since sound is evanescent, going out of existence at the very moment that it comes into existence, people are encompassed and touched by a world that is constantly in process and dynamic, a world that only exists while it is being articulated through sound.

The attributes of the material world as experienced through vision, on the other hand, do not lift off the surface of that world and come into the observer. They are experienced as inhering in that world, as being insep- arable from and essentially constituting it. Experience and the location of its source become identical. Further, vision is selective. While more than one object or event may occupy the gaze at any one time, vision does not provide an encompassing awareness of the world in the way that sound does. A gaze can be controlled more easily than can hearing, and in this sense the world of vision becomes safer and more permanent than the world of sound. Vision encourages projection into the world, occupation and control of the source of experience. Sound encourages a sense of the world as received, as being revelationary rather than incarnate.

Sound reminds people that there is a world of depth which is external to them, which surrounds them, which touches them simultaneously from all directions, and which, in its fluidity and dynamism, constantly requires a response. Unlike vision, which is the medium of division and control, sound serves to remind people of their tangible relationships to the natural and social worlds. Sound – unlike vision, which is assimilated exclusively and silently within the head – is the only major medium of communication that actively vibrates inside the body. The sound of the human voice could not be amplified and projected were it not for chambers or resonators of air inside the human body (the lungs, the sinus passages, the mouth) that vibrate in sympathy with the frequencies of the vocal chords. Equally, the human experience of sound involves, in addition to the sympathetic vibration of the eardrums, the sympathetic vibration of the resonators of the body. Sound is thus *felt* in addition to being heard. As a consequence, it transcends *actual* tactile sensations in the sense that interpersonal tactile awareness and the *particular* forms of sensory and erotic experience that flows from it is generally an awareness at the surface of the body which then finds internal resonance. Sound, however, enters the body and is in the body. Sound reveals not only the internal properties of inanimate material sources in the external world, but also the inner life of the individual in terms of the way the internal configurations of the individual's body affect the quality of sound production.

Sound is thus ideally suited as a material medium on which to map the somatically experienced inner lives of individuals, the complexly structured and simultaneous interactions of people in the external social world, *and* the fluid and dynamic relations between the two. As a consequence, music shares with other symbolic media a capacity to 'instruct' the individual which lies in part in its basic ability to evoke

148

the social and cultural commonalities within which the individual lives. However, to structure sound into music is to achieve more than this. It is also to create the potential to draw out and influence the structure of the individual's inner life in a manner that does not flow from surrounding social and cultural commonalities. Music, in other words, has the power to 'pull out' of the individual directly and concretely certain 'unprecedented' orders of meaning, and in this way to influence the reproductive processes of the social and cultural formations within which the individual lives.

This power lies in the way in which music brings into play the *inherent* qualities of sound in the evocation of the internal and external social worlds and the order of relations between them. Music reminds people of their inescapable involvement in these worlds. And it does this because, as projected into the sounds of music, these worlds enter into a direct and tangible dialogue with the meanings of the listener's inner life as *somatically coded and experienced*. It is this tangible, bodily interaction between the sounds of music and the meanings invested in them that makes the symbolic awareness of self and society as evoked through music more direct and concrete than that evoked through language or other, visual media of communication.

This potential on the part of music distinguishes it quite radically from language. As speech, language uses sounds to refer to the people, events and objects of the external world as identified, distinguished, and conceptually controlled in a *visual* fashion. The sounds of language cannot, therefore, be linked to the inherent qualities of people, events and objects as thus identified. As a consequence, there exists the potential, with language, for attention to be diverted from the inherent qualities of its sonic signifiers and concentrated instead on the signifieds conventionally and arbitrarily evoked. Indeed, it is the 'cross-sensory' use of sound to communicate essentially visual perceptions that enables language to be completely arbitrary in its manner of signification. And it is this arbitrary relationship between the sounds of language and the inherent visual characteristics of the world to which language refers that gives language its powerful potential to *separate* awareness and thought from the world in which they are embedded. If, therefore, it is difficult for English people to experience the different logic of French culture because they cannot easily understand the code of the French language, then there is a sense in which they may experience the logic of French culture in an immediate, unfettered and direct manner through the sonic media of French music. This is not to imply that French music

149

'possesses Frenchness'. It is to imply that, in creating music, French people will create sonic media consistent with qualities of 'Frenchness'. The inherent characteristics of these media will not only constrain and structure the kind of meanings that English people can invest in them, they may also cause English people to significantly adjust structural aspects of their inner lives in order to 'get into' the music. This is a capacity shared by visually iconic forms of communication, although here the iconicity is mediated in an initially cognitive rather than corporeal fashion, and is therefore not so 'gripping' in its manner of evocation.

Music is capable of evoking cognitive as well as corporeal meanings. However, it does so *indirectly*. Through their syntactical manifestations, in which they in and of themselves cannot 'have' meaning, individual sounds act as demarcators of purely abstract relationships whose appeal is significantly, although not exclusively, cognitive. The impact of such manifestations remains somatic. The derived meanings are cognitive. As Bierwisch (1979: 30) concludes, 'music does not encode conceptual structures; it is not a sign system for cognitive meanings. . . . On the other hand, the conclusion that musical signs do not have cognitive meanings by no means implies that musical utterances cannot have cognitive effects'. In the words of Ellis (1985: 15), music 'is concerned with the education of the whole person'. The success of music therapy in helping emotionally disturbed people can be understood, perhaps, in terms of this insight. Music has the capacity to mediate directly and concretely the relationship between the individual and society by leading people into different conditions of awareness.

The specific power of music lies, therefore, in its capacity both to evoke and to structure symbolically the fundamental immediacy of people's relationships to themselves and the world, and to do this in a manner that is itself direct and concrete. Music has power because, at the moment of impact – at the moment of 'revelation' – it *seems* to gather up and contain within itself meanings that the listener recognizes as his or her own. At its very moment of 'revelation', music hides from apprehension its own social, cultural, psychological and physiological roots. Its iconicity, at the moment of apprehension, is essentially closed and self-referring. There remains a sense, therefore, in which music is 'its own meaning'. As Frith has said of popular music – those musical traditions in modern, industrialized societies which have done so much to reassert a sense of process, texture and the body – 'the intensity of [the] relationship between taste and self-definition seems peculiar to [it] – it is 'possessable' in ways that other cultural forms . . . are not' (Frith 1987: 44).

CONCLUSION

Although recent research in the sociology and aesthetics of music goes some way to answer questions raised through the work of Meyer and the application of the structural homology to the analysis of music, the conclusions of such research are more programmatic than substantive. Work of a substantive nature needs to be undertaken, for example, on the ability of specific sonic media not only to constrain and structure the range of meanings that can be invested in them, but also to constrain and structure the circumstances in which music is appreciated. In this vein, Wicke (1989) has argued that, in emphasizing the syntactical to the relative exclusion of the processual and textural, and in playing down the presence of verbal, visual and motional (dance) elements in music, music in the functional tonal tradition seems to require that people give it silent and isolated attention. The transition from the corporeal to the cognitive requires concentration. In emphasizing the processual, textural, verbal, visual and motional, on the other hand, various traditions of popular music offer up more multifaceted media which allow not only for the investment of a greater range of meanings but also for the music to be enjoyed in a wider range of circumstances. In this respect, work needs to be undertaken also on the relationship between the sonic, the verbal, the visual and the motional in understanding the power of the musical event. It is once again Wicke (1989, 1990) who has suggested that the role of lyrics, images and dance in rock music is to provide referential, and therefore more commonsensical meanings through which fans may conceptualize and, indeed, structure their responses to the music.

Again, there is a need to broaden understanding of the 'relationship' between the individual and society, and the way in which this relationship is mediated musically. Music in modern societies has tended to speak with 'one voice'. Many forms of 'serious' and 'popular' music have been the product of one person (for example, the composer, and, increasingly in popular music over the last twenty years, the producer), and their particular assimilation of the social relationships within which they live. Music spoken with 'one voice' lends itself particularly well to processes of commodification without which the mass production and dissemination of music would not be possible. It can, with some legitimacy, be removed from the 'here and now' of its creation. In many other societies, however, musical events are the result of many voices contributing their own particular 'signature tune' to an event's overall fabric in a live and unrepeatable situation. This fabric is as redolent with the logics of a society's relationships as is a 'piece' of

151

music in modern societies, but in a collective and unique fashion that is tied to the here and now. The logics of a society's relationships are not mediated through the being of any one individual. Hence the ethnomusicologist's traditional problem of where to place the microphone; there is no privileged point of reference. The musical mediation of the relations between the individual and society in these instances emphasizes the importance of individual autonomy and creativity to the social process. As Feld observes in the case of the Kaluli, 'imagine the notion of an anarchistic synchrony as a non-oxymoron and you have an image of how Kaluli work' (Feld 1988: 83). This particular interactional style, concludes Feld, 'maximizes social participation and maximizes autonomy of self' (ibid.: 83–4).

Although the logics of an individual's inner life becomes a code for the logics of relationships within which they live, the nature of the relationship between these logics may vary between different kinds of societies. Aspects of an individual's inner life that in modern societies may be thought of as deviations from and potential challenges to social and cultural commonalities become, in societies such as the Kaluli, crucial contributions to the overall social fabric. Individuals 'rub up' against one another and the overall social fabric through the musical dimensions of process and texture, ensuring that social participation results in the affirmation of the individual, and that the use of music to affirm the self does not require an *individual* withdrawal from everyday reality. Individual autonomy and creativity need not be conceived as being in opposition to social processes. As a consequence, there is no need to think of the role of music in affirming the self as being one that is peripheral and potentially in opposition to social processes. Music need not be mere 'cultural capital' or mere 'leisure and entertainment'. The power of music to pull individuals into the social rather than to isolate them from it has been referred to by Keil (1987) as 'participatory discrepancy'. Keil's observation that 'we still experience much music ... this way' (Keil 1987: 276) seems consistent with the view that music makes its initial impact corporeally and somatically through process and texture. There is clearly a need for music theory to cast off its overriding concern with the syntactical elements of music as encoded visually in the score, and to pay more attention to the full range of sounds as collectively structured in music. The analysis of process, for example, has hardly begun.

To study music is therefore to study a particular and specific way of being human. If, as Knepler (1977) and Bierwisch (1979) have argued, both music and language have developed from the acoustical systems of animals, then they have been implicated *equally* as different, sonically based forms of communication in the development of human sociality. Societies and the individuals who constitute them have been as inalienably and essentially shaped by music as they have by language. It is for this reason that it is not only legitimate but, indeed, also essential to think of musical processes as *in and of themselves* social processes. This shaping of sociality through musicality does not, however, imply any fundamental difference in the substance of what music, language and, indeed, other, visually iconic media may communicate. Musical meaning is not, ultimately, a 'thing apart, different in some unexplained way from all other kinds of meaning'. If language refers disjunctively and cognitively to the visually separable people, events and objects through which social structures are given life, then music may invoke conjunctively and corporeally the immanent social structures through which people, events and objects are held in particular relationships with one another. It is the same world that is being mediated and constituted symbolically. However, if language facilitates the cognitive separation and distancing fundamental to the spectacular technological achievements that characterize modern, industrialized societies, then music cannot help but 'keep us in touch'. The study of music is not *simply* about the study of music, therefore. It is also about the study of a distinctive dimension of human existence. Further research is needed, not just to understand music better, but to understand better an important aspect of the ways in which we have become and remain human.

REFERENCES

BATESON, G. (1973) *Steps to an Ecology of Mind*, St Albans: Paladin.

BIERWISCH, M. (1979) 'Musik und Sprache: Uberlegungen zu ihrer Struktur und Funktionweise', in E. Klemm (ed.) *Jahrbuch Peters 1978*, Leipzig: Edition Peters, pp. 9–102.

BLACKING, J. (1973) *How Musical is Man?*, Seattle: University of Washington Press.

BOURDIEU, P. (1977) *Outline of a Theory of Practice*, trans. R. Nice, Cambridge: Cambridge University Press.

DUNCAN, H.D. (1968) *Symbols in Society*, Oxford: Oxford University Press.

ELLIS, C. (1985) *Aboriginal Music: Education for Living*, St Lucia: University of Queensland Press.

FELD, S. (1982) *Sound and Sentiment: Birds, Weeping, Poetics and Music in Kaluli Expression*, Philadelphia: University of Pennsylvania Press.

——(1988) 'Aesthetics as iconicity of style, or "lift-up-over sounding": getting into the Kaluli groove', *Yearbook for Traditional Music* 20: 74–113.

FRITH, S. (1987) 'Towards an aesthetic of popular music', in R. Leppert and S. McClary (eds) *Music and Society: The Politics of Composition, Performance and Reception*, Cambridge: Cambridge University Press, pp. 133–49.

HALL, S. *et al.* (eds) (1976) *Resistance through Rituals: Youth Subcultures in Post-War Britain*, London: Hutchinson.

HEBDIGE, D. (1979) *Subculture: The Meaning of Style*, London: Methuen.

KEIL, C.M. (1966) 'Motion and feeling through music', *Journal of Aesthetics and Art Criticism* 24 (3): 337–49.

——(1979) *Tiv Song*, Chicago: University of Chicago Press.

——(1987) 'Participatory discrepancies and the power of music', *Cultural Anthropology* 2 (3): 275–83.

KERMAN, J. (1985) *Contemplating Music: Challenges to Musicology*, Cambridge, Mass.: Harvard University Press.

KNEPLER, G. (1977) *Geschichte als Weg zum Musikverständnis: Zur Theorie, Methode und Geschichte der Musikgeschichtsschreibung*, Leipzig: Reclam.

LANGER, S. (1942) *Philosophy in a New Key*, Cambridge, Mass.: Harvard University Press.

LEPPERT, R. and MCCLARY, S. (1987) 'Introduction', in R. Leppert and S. McClary (eds) *Music and Society: The Politics of Composition, Performance and Reception*, Cambridge: Cambridge University Press, pp. xi–xix.

MEYER, L.B. (1956) *Emotion and Meaning in Music*, Chicago: University of Chicago Press.

——(1959) 'Some remarks on value and greatness in music', *Journal of Aesthetics and Art Criticism* 17 (4): 486–500.

——(1973) *Explaining Music*, Los Angeles: University of California Press.

NATTIEZ, J.-J. (1976) *Fondements d'une sémiologie de la musique*, Paris: Union générale d'éditions.

——(1988) *De la sémiologie à la musique*, Montreal: La Presse Université du Quebec.

PALISCA, C. (1963) 'American scholarship in Western Music', in F.Ll. Harrison, M. Hood, and C. Palisca (eds) *Musicology*, Englewood Cliffs, NJ: Prentice-Hall, pp. 87–214.

SHEPHERD, J. (1991) *Music as Social Text*, Cambridge: Polity Press.

SHEPHERD, J. *et al.* (eds) (1977) *Whose Music? A Sociology of Musical Languages*, London: Latimer.

SWANWICK, K. (1984) 'Problems of a sociological approach to pop music in schools', *British Journal of Sociology of Education* 5 (1): 49–56.

TAGG, P. (1979) *Kojack – 50 Seconds of Television Music: Toward the Analysis of Affect in Popular Music*, Gothenburg: Gothenburg University.

——(1989) *Fernando the Flute*, Liverpool: Institute of Popular Music.

VOLEK, J. (1981) 'Musikstruktur als Zeichen und Musik als Zeichen-system', in H.W. Henze (ed.) *Die Zeichen: Neue Aspekte der musikalischen Ästhetik II*, Frankfurt am Main: Fischer, pp. 222–55.

WALLIS, R. and MALM, K. (1984) *Big Sounds from Small Peoples: The Music Industry in Small Countries*, New York: Pendragon Press.

WICKE, P. (1989) 'Rockmusik – Dimensionen eines Massenmediums: Weltanschauliche Sinnproduktion durch populäre Musikformen', *Weimar Beiträge* 35 (6): 885–906.

WICKE, P. (1990) 'Rock music: dimensions of a mass medium – meaning production through Popular music' in J. Shepherd (ed.) *Alternative Musicologies/ Les musicologies alternatives* (special issue), *Canadian University Music Review* 10 (2): 137–56.

WILLIAMS, R. (1965) *The Long Revolution*, Harmondsworth: Penguin Books.

WILLIS, P. (1978) *Profane Culture*, London: Routledge & Kegan Paul.

ZUCKERKANDL, V. (1956) *Sound and Symbol: Music and the External World*, trans. W.R. Trask, London: Routledge & Kegan Paul.

9

Music and the Arts in Pre-Renaissance and Renaissance Worship: A Question of 'Expression'

PETER LE HURAY

In his great pioneering study of Italian Renaissance, Jacob Burckhardt chose to dismiss music with only the scantiest reference to its most superficial social and religious functions. Yet his approach is wholly typical of the way in which music has since been neglected in general cultural studies. R.W. Southern's fascinating book, *The Making of the Middle Ages* (1953) barely pays lip-service to music, whilst most of the great standard general histories are entirely innocent of any reference to it. Perhaps we music historians (or, to use that convenient if isolating Americanism, musicologists) are at least partly to blame, since we rarely venture into the deep waters of cultural history. Recently, though, there have been encouraging signs of a general broadening of vision, and younger scholars have begun to follow the path mapped out by Edward Lowinsky, whose challenging studies of music in Renaissance society have served to open out wholly new perspectives on music in cultural history.[1]

One of the greatest problems that music presents to the general historian of ideas is that it is not 'conceptual' in the way that language is, nor has it a physical presence that can easily be studied. There is, too, the problem of 'maturity'. The discipline of music history is relatively young. Vital sources of music remain untapped, and much archival work has still to be completed before the social and performance history of music can be written. More important still, Western music is in itself a *young* art. By 1200, when the visual arts were beginning once again to show a 'human' face, music had only just begun to formalize a system of rhythmic notation that would make possible a fully-fledged art of 'expressive' music – music, that is, which through the subtle control of harmony, tonality, melodic line, rhythm and texture could miraculously move the human spirit, just as it apparently had done in classical antiquity. Nicola Pisano's sculpture, *Fortitude in the Guise of Hercules* (Figure 9.1), in the Baptistry at Pisa is indeed a stunning example of a thirteenth-century renascence of the human spirit. There were, however, ancient Roman models upon which Pisano could draw, just as there were classical authors for his great literary contemporaries to emulate. Not a note of the music of classicial antiquity, however, had survived. All that medieval man knew was that ancient music had been highly 'affective', and that somehow the Greek 'modes' or scales had been at the root of it all.

Perhaps it was the very lack of classical models that explains at least in part why music seems to have been so slow to catch up with the other expressive arts, for as we shall see below, not until the time of Dufay, in the early fifteenth century, did composers begin to manipulate sounds in a way that unmistakably mirrors the 'expressive' qualities of their accompanying words. But can the explanation be so simple? Indeed, *was* music so very much out of phase with the other arts in the late Middle Ages and early Renaissance? Deep down, the feeling remains that there *are* such things as historical periods – 'distinguishable portions of history', as the *Oxford English Dictionary* neatly puts it – and that each 'period' has unique qualities which can be paralleled in such disparate phenomena as music, the visual arts, literature, philosophy, social and political theory, theology, and so on. As Erwin Panofsky has observed in the masterly opening to his *Gothic Architecture and Scholasticism* (1957), the pursuit of such parallels is hazardous, for an individual can master no more than one fairly limited field, and has to rely on incomplete and often secondary information when venturing outside that field. The attempt to view music within a larger cultural frame may none the less be worth making, if only to identify areas of disagreement that need further debate. It could be, moreover, that interesting parallels emerge, some at least of which may eventually serve to illuminate our musical understanding.

The fifteenth-century theorist and composer, Johannes Tinctoris, was of the opinion that something radical had happened to music during the early part of the fifteenth century – so radical indeed that earlier music could completely be dismissed as primitive and beneath contempt. The sense of living in a new age was not unique to the musician, although as far as

Figure 9.1 Nicola Pisano, *Fortitude in the Guise of Hercules*, c.1260, Baptistry, Pisa

literature and the visual arts were concerned, Renaissance observers tended to draw the dividing lines between old and new a century or so earlier. There was in fact a contemporary and very generally held view that in the late fourteenth and fifteenth centuries there had indeed been a 'Renaissance'

158

or rebirth, and that after a millenium of darkness there had come about another 'golden age', rich enough to rival that of classical antiquity.

The fifteenth-century verdict on the Middle Ages was understandable, if unjust. Indeed, it has taken us a further five hundred years to realize how unjust the verdict was. As research has progressed, the complex pattern of the 'dark' Middle Ages has slowly come into focus. In his virtuosic study, *Renaissance and Renascences in Western Art* (1970), Erwin Panofsky traces the final and irreversible 'Renaissance' of the fourteenth and fifteenth centuries back to a Carolingian 'renascence' of the late eighth and early ninth centuries. The processes of change leading from this 'renascence' to the final one, he argues, went in phases. A further 'proto-renascence' of the late eleventh and early twelfth centuries was, he suggests, preceded and followed by periods of conservative reaction, the boundaries of which depended to some extent on the art in question and on its place of origin. He argues, moreover, that although the processes of change did not by any means travel in a straight line from the 'Carolingian' renascence to a final and irreversible 'Renaissance' five centuries later, they none the less led inexorably from the transcendental to the human. It is this fundamental change that I shall attempt to explore in the following pages, focusing especially on the relationship between music and the Church.

To what extent, then, was the change about which Tinctoris wrote the emergence of a 'human' art from a 'transcendental' one? Does the development of Western music seem to fall into 'periods', and if so, do these periods parallel those that have been observed in the other arts? In what ways (if any) can non-musical concepts, drawn from other cultural disciplines, serve to illuminate our understanding of medieval music?

It was during this period – from the Christianized Roman Empire of the fourth century, to the so-called Carolingian renaissance of the late eighth century – that much of the vast repertory of Christian monody was created – the repertories of Byzantine, Ambrosian and Gregorian chant. Just as from AD 800 the processes of artistic change were to lead (albeit waywardly) from the transcendental to the human, so the reverse processes had been at work during the preceding four centuries. The history of mosaic design may serve to illustrate the point.

Many mosaics dating from the closing years of the 'pagan' Roman Empire are astonishingly 'realistic', so skilfully are the pieces of the mosaic (the *tesserae*) set. There is, for instance the remarkable 'Comedy Scene with Musicians' at Pompeii (Figure 9.2) – a work probably dating from the first century AD, in which shading is used with the greatest skill to create light and shadow; the technique, known as *opus vermiculatum*, causes the figures

159

Figure 9.2 Comedy Scene with Musicians, Pompeii (photo Alinari)

to stand out with extraordinary vitality against their background. In the
'unswept floor' (Figure 9.3), the banquet leftovers have an almost *trompe
l'oeil* effect, due to skilful shadowing that is at once both highly realistic
and exceedingly witty. As time went on, however, three-dimensional plas-
ticity gave way to two-dimensional formalism, a transformation which is to
be discerned in all contemporary art forms. The effect is a change from 'an
outwardly-looking to an inwardly-looking attitude of mind' (L'Orange and
Nordhagen 1966), from naturalism to symbolism, from the imitation of
natural objects to abstract contemplation. Some of the earlier naturalism
lived on, especially in the mosaics of the imperial palace at Constantinople:
in, for example, the wonderfully mobile horses from one of the floor mosaics
there and in the mighty hunter from the peristyle of the palace (Figure 9.4).
Nor is this naturalism entirely absent in mosaics of the early Western
church; the mid-fifth-century representation of the Red Sea crossing, in the
church of Santa Maria Maggiore in Rome, for instance, aptly depicts the
confusion of the pursuing soldiers as they are overwhelmed by the waters

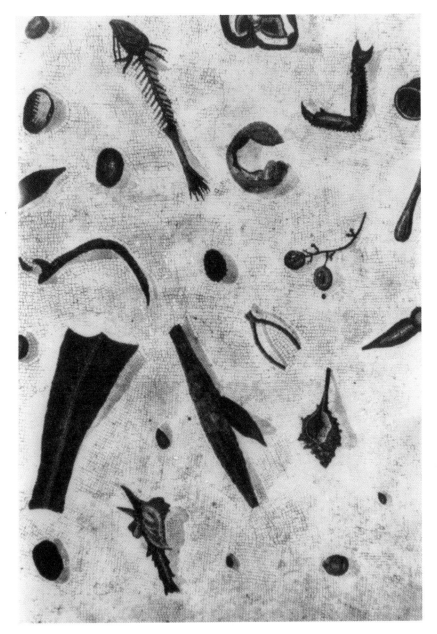

Figure 9.3 Detail of the 'unswept floor' mosaic, Rome

161

(L'Orange and Nordhagen 1966: plates 58–9). Increasingly, however, church mosaics give the impression of withdrawal from the secular world. Various causes have been suggested: disillusion associated with the political decline of the Roman Empire; a resultant concentration of interest on the life to come; a conscious attempt by the use of 'superhuman' symbolism to establish the authority both of Church and state; and the influence of the theology

Figure 9.4 Mosaic from the peristyle of the imperial palace at Constantinople showing a hunter in action (photo D. Talbot Rice)

162

of the Eastern Church, in which the concept of Christ's divinity far out-weighed that of Christ's humanity. The transformation has even been attributed to the 'secular' influence of oriental art, and to declining standards of craftsmanship. Whatever the reasons, the change is unmistakable. It is already apparent in the secular black and white pavement designs that became so popular in Italy during the third and fourth centuries. It is clearly to be seen in the famous sixth-century mosaics of San Apollinare Nuovo in Ravenna. In the church's earliest band of mosaics, running above the clerestory windows, scenes from the life of Christ are represented. The one of Christ healing two blind men (Figure 9.5) is almost abstractly two-dimensional, apart from some outline shading of the garments. Facial features are elongated in a spiritually 'detached' manner; the eyes – those 'windows into the soul' – gaze into infinity. Yet in comparison with the figures in the third band of mosaics, which run the length of the nave walls above the arches, the earlier figures still retain some sense of motion. Only thirty or so years separate the two sets of mosaics; the first however were commissioned by Theodoric, in the period in which Ravenna was under

Figure 9.5   Sixth-century mosaic from San Apollinare Nuovo, Ravenna, showing Christ healing two blind men (photo Trapani)

the rule of the Ostrogoths[2]: the mosaics in the lower band were commissioned shortly after Justinian, ruler of the Eastern Empire, had captured
Ravenna from the Ostrogoths. On the right-hand wall (Figure 9.6 a, b)
moving from west to east, saints in procession

Figure 9.6 (a) Mosaics on the wall of San Apollinare Nuovo, Ravenna, showing saints in
procession, with (b) detail of the above (photo Alinari)

164

float past our eyes, against a background of symbolic victors' palms. They give an impression of being identical parts of an endless row: they are all of the same size and proportions; they all walk with the same length of stride; they all wear the same formal costume; ... all are of a unique type with large serious eyes which those who beheld them in antiquity associated with the concept of the divine man. Thus the faces of late antiquity are modelled according to unchanging patterns of expression which suggest something more sublime and essential than the individuals themselves.

(L'Orange and Nordhagen 1966: 12–13)

This 'Byzantine' style can be traced back to the reign of Constantine the Great (AD 323–37), the founder of Constantinople, capital of the Eastern Empire. It was then that the concept originated of the Emperor as God's chosen representative on earth. From then onwards, church mosaic design became increasingly 'hieratic' (priestly) and remote, developing a Christian symbolism of its own, notably in the Eastern Church. The apse mosaics at San Vitale, Ravenna, vividly illustrate this. San Vitale was built by Emperor Justinian in AD 547 as his Western imperial chapel. In the apse surrounding the high altar – the liturgical centre of the church – he placed panels depicting himself and the Empress Theodora surrounded by court officials and clerics (Figure 9.7). Emperor and Empress are distinguished by their gold haloes, contoured in gold and silver to symbolize their divine status. The style is very similar to that used at San Apollinare Nuovo to represent the saints and virgins in procession (Figure 9.6 a, b).

After Justinian's forces had wrested northern Italy from the Ostrogoths in the 540s the Eastern Empire retained a strong presence in Western Europe for some five centuries. This is clearly reflected in the character of western mosaic designs; in, for instance, the Adoration of the Magi fragment in the church of Santa Maria in Cosmedin in Rome, which was completed at about the time that Pope Gregory the Great was reputedly systematizing the repertory of liturgical chant that now bears his name. It is represented, too, in the superb vault mosaics of the Cappella di Santo Zenone representing Christ, Pantocrator (Figure 9.8). The 'transcendental' quality of the design is immediately obvious from the simplest black and white reproduction. What can never be caught by the camera, however, is the quality of the light that is reflected by the mosaic work. Gone is the smooth, pictorial surface of the ancient *opus vermiculatum* technique. The *tesserae* are now much bigger, and they are set in such a way as to reflect light at many different angles. The best analogy perhaps is with the art of setting precious stones – an art that had recently been introduced from the Orient. As one commentator has observed,

Figure 9.7 Mosaic at San Vitale, Ravenna, showing Emperor Justinian and Empress
Theodora with court officials and clerics (photo Anderson)

Figure 9.8 Vault mosaic in the Cappella di San Zenone,
Church of San Prassede, Rome, representing
Christ, Pantocrator

166

The natural daylight or the light of flaming torches is transformed by the mosaic into something supernatural, refracted and reflected by thousands of separate flashing surfaces ... sacred buildings become transformed into supernatural halls ablaze with the reflected gold and silver of their mosaics.

(L'Orange and Nordhagen 1966: 11)

It is no accident that in one of the Ravenna mosaics the following words are inscribed: '*Aut lux hic nata est, aut capta hic libera regnat*': either light was born here, or captive here, reigns free. This, we should remember, is the kind of environment which also gave birth to the rich repertory of Christian monody.

The transformation from realism to symbolism is also strikingly evident in sculpture. During the period from AD 700 to 900, sculpture almost totally disappeared from Christian art. In the closing years of the 'pagan' Empire sculpting techniques had acquired an astonishing virtuosity. For a brief period, from about AD 230 to 300, individual charactererization emerges with startling realism. The bust of Maximinius Thrax (Emperor, AD 235–8) captures an instant of time: it reveals the 'whole brutality' of the soldier Emperor; its very asymmetry creates a sense of instability, of action (Figure 9.9). From the time of Constantine the Great, the sculpted human face becomes increasingly meditative, increasingly illuminated by a sense of extra-terrestrial abstraction. The process of transformation is fascinatingly demonstrated in the ivory double 'portrait' of a Roman consul, dating from AD 518 (Figure 9.10). The two portraits were originally identical. The second was, however, altered into the figure of a Christian mystic. Not only does the divine flame burn on his forehead, but the receding hair, the bearded face all serve to intensify the mystic gaze. 'The body', said Plotinus (AD 205–70), 'only becomes beautiful when illuminated by the soul'. Here, surely is the visual manifestation of this concept.

Between the fifth and the ninth centuries the Eastern and Western Churches each developed complex repertories of liturgical chant. The repertories were memorized, and only in the ninth century were attempts first made to write them down. In view of this, the precise way in which those repertoires developed before then can only be inferred at second hand from literary and archival sources. The earliest readable sources of music none the less confirm the pre-existence of a substantial repertory of chant. But why, if memory had served perfectly well until the ninth century, was a system of notation *then* developed to codify the chant repertory? Was it because that repertory was growing too big to memorize? Or did notation spring – as Hucke (1980) suggests – from a Frankish desire for greater

Figure 9.9   Bust of Emperor Maximinius Thrax, Museo Capitolino, Rome
(photo l'Archivo Fotografico dei Musei Capitolini)

Figure 9.10 An ivory double 'portrait' of a Roman consul, AD 518

liturgical (and political) unity?[3] Could it be, perhaps, that notation was in part at least developed to establish a certain *manner* of performance?

Questions such as these raise issues that are well beyond the scope of this essay, particularly the issue of chant chronology. Nevertheless the uncertainties have not prevented much heated debate during the past hundred years as to the precise nature of the relationship between words and notes. Two main schools of thought have emerged, one represented by Johner, Treitler and Berry, the other by Apel and Stevens. Johner's description of the Communion chant, '*Vox in rama*' well represents the 'expressive' stance of the first school (the text runs, 'In Rama a voice was heard, and lamentation, weeping and great mourning'). 'The start on the fifth of the mode,' Johner writes, 'the continuing emphasis on the dominant, and the

169

Pressus over the word "ploratus" are expressions of gripping sorrow; they almost sound like a shrill outcry' (Johner 1940: 69). The objection to such an approach is best represented in Apel's discussion of a group of some twenty chants which he describes as 'the Gradual type, "Justus ut palma"' (Apel 1958: 357). Twelve or so melodic phrases are common to the twenty chants, and they form the substance of each one; the melodic formulae are permitted in various configurations. The twenty texts, however, are of widely differing function and mood, ranging from a Requiem text to one sung at midnight Mass on Christmas Eve. On the surface there would seem to be little case for the kind of close word/note relationship that Johner proposed, at least in the '*Justus ut palma*' chants. Liturgical music of this kind, surely, was no more designed to 'express' the emotional and intellectual subtleties of words than were the contemporary visual arts designed to reflect human joys and sorrows. Certainly, in the earliest kind of chant – the simple psalm tone – there can be no question of any close relationship, since the simple formula comprising intonation, reciting note, mediation, second intonation, reciting note and ending is repeated unvaryingly from verse to verse, as shown in Figure 9.11.

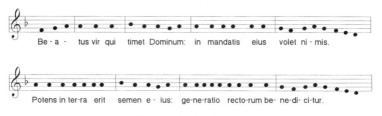

Figure 9.11 A psalm tone

But word/note relationships exist on many different planes, ranging from the purely syntactical to the onomatopoeic. And to understand these relationships the whole question of the role of chant in worship needs to be considered. There is, for instance, the nature of the occasion on which the chant is to be sung; there is the role of that chant within the order of service; and there is the ritual that accompanies the singing of the chant. Consideration must also be given to the more purely 'aesthetic' dimensions of worship: the structure, appearance and acoustics of the building; the positioning of the various participants in the service; even the quality of the vestments and furnishings that adorn the ritual.

From the time of the Carolingian renascence in the late eighth and early ninth centuries the visual arts gradually recovered those human qualities that are so vividly portrayed in the mosaics and sculptures of late classical antiquity. Under Charlemagne vigorous steps were taken to reform secular and ecclesiastical administration on classical lines, and to recover classical learning. Much of what was later known of the literature of classical antiquity, indeed, was known through the copies made by Carolingian scholars. The very lively figures of February, March, August and September (Figure 9.12), for instance, were copied by a Carolingian scribe from a Roman calendar of *c*. AD 350. It was however to be some time before such figures appeared in church sculpture, illumination and painting. The *Libri Carolini*, a central document of Carolingian church discipline and decorum, expressly banned all classical representations from public art, such as naked and semi-naked figures and personifications of the sun and moon. The sinuous Eve from the thirteenth-century doorway of Autun Cathedral is in fact one of the earliest examples of a new humanism in the church arts; not without justification has it been described as the first seductive female since classical antiquity (Figure 9.13).

Hints of the new spirit are none the less to be seen in Byzantine writings of the ninth and tenth centuries, notably in a genre of imaginative meditation that was to be developed with great poignancy in eleventh-century devotional literature. In the following narrative, for instance, George of Nicodemia is concerned to impress the reader with the agonizing reality of the Crucifixion: it is almost as if we are reading a fifth gospel:

> When men believed that Christ was dead, when the throngs had disappeared and the soldiers retired from their meal, then did the Virgin approach the Cross, kiss the feet of her son and the wounds made by the nails, gather the blood that flowed in a stream, and rub it on her eyes and heart. . . . Ah!, she cried, would that these nails had been driven into my own flesh, would, that I had felt all his suffering in my own body!
>
> (Mâle 1986: 28)

It was not until the end of the thirteenth century, however, that the visual arts were to reflect such emotional intensity, and indeed only within the ambit of the Western Church.

To be sure, 'classical' – and thus 'subjective' – qualities are not altogether absent in religious art of the Carolingian 'renascence'. There is a good deal of lively drawing in, for instance, the Aachen Gospels (795–810), which originated in the 'Palace' School of Charlemagne's Court.[4] The figures, however, are restricted to portraits of the Evangelists; there is no attempt to transfer this free-flowing Hellenistic style to the illustration of the Gospel narrative. Contemporary representations of the Crucifixion, for instance, generally convey a medieval quality of poised transcendence above worldly

171

Figure 9.12   Figures depicting the months of February, March, August and September
copied by a Carolingian scribe from a Roman calendar of *c.* AD 350
(Bibliotheque Royale Albert 1er, Brussels, MS 7524/55)

Figure 9.13   Figure of Eve on the thirteenth-century doorway of Autun Cathedral
(photo Bulloz, Paris)

things: the Crucifixion mosaic in San Clemente, Rome (Figure 9.14), well
illustrates this, even though it is a relatively late work, dating from the early
twelfth century. Such representations are akin in spirit to much of the
meditational literature of the early Middle Ages, in which the central events
of the Crucifixion are presented with a coolness that is quite foreign to us
today. Thus, St Ambrose could argue that, standing at the foot of the Cross,
Mary had not wept, for though the Cross outwardly suggested failure, it
was in truth the ultimate victory over death.

It was this spirit, as Moshe Barasch (1976) has so fascinatingly shown,
that underlay the rejection of all violent gesture in Western Christian art
between the sixth and twelfth centuries. Restrained dramatic gestures, such
as hand wringing, begin to appear in Carolingian art of the ninth century,
and are traceable back to classical models. During the course of the eleventh
century a less muted subjectivism becomes apparent in representations of
biblical themes: in one of the scenes from the Gundold Gospels, *c*.1020–
40, for instance (Figure 9.15), the two Marys look up sorrowfully at the
emaciated figure of Christ, hanging from the Cross. A 'profound transformation' in the spirit of the church arts is to be observed, however, from
about 1200 onward, the range of dramatic gesture being extended as far as
self-inflicted injury. The theme of the 'Last Judgement' is one that brought

173

Figure 9.14 Crucifixion mosaic in San Clemente, Rome
(photo Anderson)

Figure 9.15 Crucifixion scene from the Gundold Gospels, *c*.1020–40, showing the two Marys at the foot of the Cross (Württembergische Landesbibliothek, Cod. Bibl. 4° 2)

out particularly vivid gestures of despair. Giotto represents anger and despair in his Arena Chapel fresco of the Last Judgement by showing the damned clawing at their cheeks with their nails (Figure 9.16). Even his angels wring their hands and twist their bodies as they circle round the scene of the Crucifixion (Figure 9.17).

Violent gesture seems increasingly to have been accepted in public life, too, as a symbol of grief. According to the Canterbury chronicler, Gervaise, the destruction in 1174 of the cathedral choir by fire caused amazing public scenes of despair:

> The people were astonished that the Almighty should suffer such things. Maddened with overwhelming grief and perplexity, they tore their hair and beat the wall and the pavement with their heads and hands, blaspheming the Lord and his Saints.
>
> (Frisch 1987: 14)

By the early years of the thirteenth century important funerals in Florence were frequently marked by quite extraordinary and very theatrical outbursts of emotion. The public orator would assemble relatives and friends outside the house of the deceased, whilst inside, the closely-related womenfolk gathered around the bier. Crouching on the floor the women would begin a ritualized lamentation, wailing, tearing their hair and their clothes, and lacerating their cheeks with their fingernails.

It was hardly surprising, then, that such attitudes penetrated to the very heart of religious devotions, and to the Crucifixion story in particular. In this process of 'humanizing' the Christian message, the influence of St Francis of Assisi (1182–1226) can hardly be overestimated.[5]

This is particularly reflected in the immensely popular *Meditationes vitae Christi*, formerly attributed to St Bonaventura but in reality the work of an anonymous Franciscan monk of the early thirteenth century. This poignant Crucifixion scene is a continuation and intensification of the Carolingian 'meditation' quoted above. It stands in stark contrast to St Ambrose's almost offhand account: the soldiers have just returned to pierce Christ's side:

> And therwith one that was cleped [named] longyne (and was that tyme wicked and proude but after[wards] a trewe [be]lever and martir), despisynge [Mary's] wepying and prayeres, with a scharpe spere openede the side of oure lorde Jesu and made a grete wounde oute of the whiche anone ranne to gidre [together] bothe blood and water. And therwith our lady felle adoun in swowne half dede bytwene the armes of Maudeleyn. And then John nought

176

Figure 9.16 A fresco by Giotto in the Arena Chapel, Padua, depicting the Last Judgement

Figure 9.17 Detail of Giotto's fresco showing angels circling the scene of the Crucifixion

mowynge bere that grete sorwe toke to hym mannis herte, and risynge agenst hem saide: Ye wicked men, why do ye this cruelty? Se ye nought that he is dede? Why wil ye also slee [slay] this woman his moder? ... Than was oure lady excited and rose as it hadde bene fro slepe askynge what was done more to hir sone? And thay saide: No newe thing more agenst hym. And after sche hadde kaught spirite and byhelde hir sone so grevously wounded, was also wounded in hert with a new wounde of sorwe.[6]

A similar process of emotional intensification is to be observed in the visual arts of the late thirteenth century. The 'Portail de la Calende' at Rouen Cathedral vividly illustrates this (Figure 9.18). In traditional representations only a few figures are shown at the Cross: the Virgin Mary, St John, and Mary Magdalene with perhaps the sponge bearer, the soldier holding the lance, and maybe personifications of the Church and the Synagogue. Here however there is turmoil. The Jews gather to the left of Christ, dominated by the figure of the centurion; to the right the bent figure of the Virgin is surrounded and supported by the holy women. Even greater extremes of dramatic confusion and despair characterize the Crucifixion scene that Giovanni Pisano carved for the Pisa Duomo pulpit (1302–10). Here everything is crowded together: soldiers on horseback; the onlooker offering

Figure 9.18   The 'Portail de la Calende' at Rouen Cathedral

vinegar; the swooning Virgin; the jeering Jews; and above all the crucified bodies suspended in tortured agony from the crosses (Figure 9.19). If, as Mâle has suggested, the Cross represented throughout the Middle Ages the figure of Christ triumphant, and in the later Middle Ages the figure of Christ the teacher, then by the late fourteenth century the principal theme was Christ the sufferer. The representation of the Passion has moved from

179

Figure 9.19   Crucifixion scene by Giovanni Pisano; detail from the pulpit of the Duomo,
Pisa (photo Anderson)

dogmatic statement addressed to the mind, to emotive imagery which
appeals to the heart. 'From then onward,' Mâle suggests, 'the dominant
aspect of Christianity was to be pathos (Mâle 1986: 82).'

If the 'revolution' was first manifest in Italy, it rapidly spread northward,
direct influence being traceable between major Sienese and Florentine artists
and northern disciples, such as the miniaturists, the Limbourg brothers and
Jean Pucelle, to whom we owe the magical *Petites Heures de Jeanne d'Evreux*
(1325–8). Quite clearly, the model for Pucelle's Crucifixion (Figure 9.20)
was Duccio's representation on the reverse of the great *Maesta* altarpiece,
now in the Cathedral Museum, Siena (Figure 9.21), just as the Deposition
scene in *Les très riches heures* (Longnon and Cazelles 1969) was modelled on
Simon Martini's polyptych, now in the Royal Museum, Antwerp. In almost
all respects the progression towards an emotive naturalism reached its
apogee in the work of the Florentine painter, Masaccio (1401–*c*.1428) (see
Cole 1980). The first of his two great Crucifixions probably originated as
part of the now dismembered altarpiece commissioned for the church of

Figure 9.20 A miniature by Pucelle from the *Petites Heures de Jeanne d'Evreux*
(The Metropolitan Museum of Art, New York, The Cloisters Collection, Purchase, 1954)

Figure 9.21 Duccio's Crucifixion on the reverse of the *Maesta* altarpiece, which served as a model for Pucelle

182

the Carmine in Pisa in 1426 (Figure 9.22). The second and probably later one is a fresco in the church of Santa Maria Novella, Florence (Figure 9.23). A particularly striking quality in both works is the way in which

Figure 9.22   The first great Crucifixion by Masaccio, Carine Church, Pisa
(photo Giraudon)

183

depth is handled. For though earlier artists did in various ways succeed in creating a sense of depth (see below), Masaccio was one of the earliest to make use of Brunelleschi's scientific system of single point perspective. The additional sense of realism is striking. In the Pisa Crucifixion, Masaccio brings the viewer as close as possible to the scene by placing the figures against a bare and shallow 'apse'. We seem almost to be touching Mary Magdalene's robe as we look upward to the figure of Christ. St John gazes in sorrow at her, whilst the Virgin clasps her hands in anguish. Mary Magdalene has been described as one of Masaccio's supreme creations, comparable to those marvellously articulated figures that stand around Christ in Giotto's Arena Chapel. Gesture alone describes here the deepest emotion. Only the awkward foreshortening of Christ's head prevents this from being one of Masaccio's truly outstanding compositions.

The much serener Santa Maria Novella representation is more properly known as the 'Trinita'. Space here is controlled to an entirely different and enigmatic end. We look upward into a large hall, its barrelled vault receding into the distance. The perspective is 'correctly' related to Brunelleschi's vanishing point, and there is a strong geometrical shape to the design. The figures are enigmatically placed, however, within the space. Where does the Cross stand in relation to the imposing arch? Are Mary and John standing outside or are they level with the pillars of the opening? Most importantly, on what plane is the figure of God the Father placed? It certainly rises behind, and it probably supports the Cross – but how much space does it occupy? How far down does the figure extend? Even the lighting, which at first sight seems convincingly naturalistic, is enigmatic. The source of illumination, in fact, cannot be precisely located, but seems to emanate somehow from Christ's body. There is no obvious interaction between any of the six figures, nor are there any signs of subjective responses. Surely, here, Masaccio is using his technical virtuosity to express the mystery of the relatively new complex doctrine of the Trinity, for the fresco has the quality of a theological statement rather than a subjective memorial.

But if its undramatic qualities are uncharacteristic of the age, the fresco does in another sense symbolize an important feature of Renaissance subjectivity: the desire of the contemporary believer to be associated with the subject of the representation. The figures at the bottom right and left of the scene are the fresco's donors. Donors and patrons are certainly symbolized in many earlier religious works of art, but they are almost invariably much smaller than the principal figures, and they are placed in comparatively unimportant positions in the picture. Here, the donors are drawn on the same scale as the other figures; what is more, they occupy one of the

Figure 9.23   Masaccio's second great depiction – a fresco at Santa Maria Novella, Florence
(photo Giraudon)

strongest planes in the total design, the extremes of the base of the triangle. It is as if Masaccio's patrons – the donors – saw themselves at the very scene of the Crucifixion (Pope-Henessey 1964: ch. 6).

The Crucifixion theme in literature, the visual arts and music is sufficient material alone for an encyclopedic study. There is only space here to observe that it gave birth to many closely associated themes, notably those of the Deposition from the Cross, the Pietà (in which the Virgin touches and even holds the dead body in her arms), and the Entombment. These themes were treated in all the available art-forms: statuary, panel painting, fresco, devotional literature, hymnody, and thus music. The influences at work were identical to those that have already been mentioned, the opportunities for dramatic and emotional representation being eagerly seized.

While the literary, dramatic and visual arts may have been moving in a broadly similar direction during the Middle Ages and early Renaissance, the art of musical composition was comparatively slow to respond to the new subjective spirit of the times. This is not to say that the new spirit is absent from contemporary forms of liturgical and devotional composition; indeed it is often strikingly present. That new spirit, however, is conveyed in *words*, not notes. Early in the ninth century, for instance, the practice began of inserting new texts or 'tropes', as they were known, into existing liturgical texts – especially into the sung sections of the Ordinary of the Mass (see Cattin 1984: ch. 23; Apel 1958: 429). In some cases, the new words were set to the melismas of the host chant. Normally, however, both words and music were new. The new words might reinforce the emotional impact of the host text by amplifying the supporting detail, as in the troped Introit, *Hodie Stephanus martyr/ Etenim sederunt:*

Trope	Today Stephen the martyr ascended into heaven; of him the prophet once said, lifting up his voice,
Introit	Princes sat down and spake against me
Trope	The Jews unjustly rose up against me.
Introit	and the wicked persecuted me.
Trope	Full of hate they crushed me with stones.
Introit	Help me, O Lord my God,
Trope	Take up my soul in peace
Introit	for thy servant was exercised in thy justification

(cf. Ps. 119, v. 23)

The trope might act as an introduction to the host text, or it might even add a wholly new dimension to it. An early form of the well-known 'Ave verum Corpus', for instance, was embedded in the Sanctus of the Ordinary of the Mass. The words of the Sanctus extol the greatness and glory of God as revealed in creation. 'Ave verum' expresses the Christian belief in the self-sacrificing love of the creator:

[Sanctus] Holy, holy, holy, Lord God of hosts; heaven and earth are full of thy glory. Glory be to thee, O Lord, most high.

[Ave verum] Hail, true body, born of the Virgin Mary, having in truth suffered and hung on the cross for mankind, from whose side flowed water and blood, be for us our food at the hour of death. O sweet and holy Jesus, Son of Mary, have mercy upon me. Amen.

The phenomenon of troping is a facet of the search for *self*-knowledge (and thus subjective response), which is such a feature of the age. 'Who is more contemptible', asks John of Salisbury in his *Policraticus* (1159), 'than the man who scorns knowledge of himself?' The search for the self is indeed to be seen in every aspect of human endeavour. In the field of religious belief, as Colin Morris has observed, the notion of a collective last judgement and final resurrection were fading away. Within a framework which was in general still that of the Church, decreasing attention was paid to the destiny of the Church, and steadily more to the destiny of each believer (Morris 1972: 144).

Theological concern for the individual manifested itself in a host of different ways: in, for instance, the decision of the Lateran Council in 1215 to establish the practice of annual obligatory confession, to ensure that every Christian regularly experienced the remorse of penitence. Shortly before this the metaphysical doctrine of transubstantiation had been approved, whereby the communion elements of bread and wine came to be regarded as the actual body and blood of Christ. This theological proposition surely had an intention similar to that expressed in the increasingly realistic representations in the visual arts of scenes of the Crucifixion, namely to bring home to all who were present at the Mass the actuality of Christ's self-sacrifice. In lesser ways the subjective spirit flowered in a whole new kind of sermon; in the development of an intensely personal style of devotional literature in the manner of the pseudo-Bonaventura *Meditationes* mentioned above, and in the emergence of a highly emotional style of religious verse increasingly couched in terms of the first person singular.

The role of the trope, as we have seen, was to heighten the impact of the host text. In a more mundane way the practice of troping represents a small shift from collective authority to individual responsibility, for it was – exceptionally – an optional extra within an essentially fixed liturgy, to be sung or not at the discretion of the ruler of the choir. Opportunities for individual choice steadily increased as time went on. The growing importance that came to be attached to votive and devotional celebrations significantly widened the scope for choice, whilst the development in the sixteenth century of non-liturgical devotional music gave the composer unrestricted freedom in the matter of text choice (see Rankin 1985; Sevestre 1985; Kerman 1962).

The sequence was an equally important liturgical and musical form, probably originating not long before the trope. Sequence texts generally comprise a series of couplets, each of which consists of two isosyllabic lines that are sung to the same melody. Each couplet, however, has a different melody, and each normally differs in length from its neighbours. Many of the texts are associated with specific seasons or festivals, and are thus 'propers'. Amongst the better-known sequences are the tenth-century 'Victimae pascali laudes', the eleventh-century 'Veni sancte spiritus', and the thirteenth-century 'Dies irae'. This last example well illustrates the contrast between the dramatic urgency of the verse, and the self-conscious formality of the chant (see Figure 9.24). To be sure, the melodic climax is strategically placed just four phrases before the end, whilst the phrases that follow sink appropriately to the final Amen. It is equally true that the total shape of the melody achieves a very satisfying curve: phrase B moves into higher ground than A, whilst C falls back somewhat though not down to A. Strikingly, too, the climactic phrase E is only stated once, and it occurs at the point where a repetition of D^1 might have been expected. The *surface* shape, however, has little connection with the dramatic shape of the text. Even so, complex long-term and short-term musical repetitions do not necessarily deny the possibility of close musical and textual links; repetitions may deliberately be used to underline connections in the argument that might otherwise have remained hidden. In this sense, then, music can be used to 'express' a text with great subtlety, even though there is nothing inherently 'expressive' in the musical figures themselves. As far as the 'Dies irae' is concerned, it is hard to avoid reading into the music some of the drama of the text. There is no denying, though, that divorced from its text the melody *sounds* much like other trope and sequence chants that are set to texts of very different character.

Figure 9.24

189

Figure 9.24 (cont.)

sequéstra, Stá-tu-ens in párte déxtra. Confu-tá-tis ma-

ledíctis, Flámmis ácribus addíctis, Vóca me cum be-

nedíctis. Oro súpplex et acclí-nis, Cor contrí-tum qua-

si cí-nis : Gé-re cúram mé- i fí-nis. Lacrimósa dí- es

flla, Qua resúrget ex favílla Judi-cándus hó- mo

ré- us : Hú- ic ergo pár- ce Dé- us. Pí- e Jésu Dómine,

dóna é- is réqui- em. A- men.

Figure 9.24 (cont.)

The day of wrath, that day will dissolve the age in ashes, as David prophesied with the Sibyl. / How great will be the quaking when the judge is come, how thoroughly will everything be resolved. / The trumpet, spreading a wondrous sound through the graves of every land will gather all before the throne. / Death and nature will stand amazed when creation rises again to answer the judge. / A book of writings will be brought forth which contains everything for which the world shall be judged. / Thus when the judge takes his seat, everything shall be made manifest; nothing shall remain unavenged. / What shall I, wretched one, say? Whom shall I ask to plead for me when scarcely the righteous one shall be safe? / King of dreadful majesty, who freely saves the redeemed, save me, O source of pity. / Remember, merciful Jesus, that I was the reason for your journey: do not destroy me on that day. / Seeking me, you sat down, weary; you redeemed me, suffering on the cross; let not such great trouble have been in vain. / Just judge of vengeance, give me the gift of redemption before the day of reckoning. / I groan as one guilty, and my face blushes with guilt: spare the supplicant, O God. / You, who absolved Mary and heard the prayer of the thief, to me you also give hope. / My prayers are unworthy, but thou, O good one, show mercy, lest I burn in everlasting fire. / Give me a place among the sheep, and separate me from the goats, placing me on thy right hand. / When the damned are confounded and consigned to piercing flames, call me with the blessed. / I pray, suppliant and kneeling, a heart as contrite as ashes, take my ending into thy care. / That day is one of weeping, on which shall rise again from the ashes the guilty man, to judgement. / Therefore, spare this one, O God; merciful Lord Jesus, grant them rest. Amen

The search for new and more 'human' ways of presenting the Christian message is reflected in the increasing popularity of liturgical drama. Certain tropes came to be presented in simple dramatic form; indeed 'Quem queritis', a trope to the Easter Introit, 'Resurrexi', is arguably the very earliest known liturgical drama. The words are sung and there is a certain simple attempt at characterization, the various characters being identified by differing pitch ranges. There is no evidence, though, that pitch, rhythm or tempo are consciously manipulated to underline the progress of the story or the characters of the protagonists. The Passion story came to be dramatized in much the same way by the simple process of dividing the biblical narrative between two or more singers. By the end of the thirteenth century these liturgical dramas were occasionally if not regularly sung in a highly expressive manner, even though the traditional chant to which the words were sung had no inherently expressive qualities. In his *Rationale Divinorum Officiorum*, for instance, Durandus (d. 1296) suggests that the part of Christ should be sung 'sweetly', and that of the impious Jews, 'loudly and harshly'.

Perhaps the medieval genre which brings the issue of subjectivity most sharply into focus is the Latin 'planctus', about which Janthia Yearley has written:

> The *planctus* in Latin is a lament primarily the creation of monastic composers, containing an utterance of grief at the death of a recently deceased personage, or a person from biblical or classical history, or about the destruction of a city. It is normally characterised by eulogy, usually written in syllabic verse, often in sequence form, and delivered in the dramatic first person.
>
> (Yearley 1983)

The planctus seems to have originated in Carolingian monasteries, perhaps early in the ninth century. It differed from the 'Epitaph' in being a rhetorical expression of grief rather than a formal 'memorial'. Yearley observes that the most specific and apparently 'personalized' accounts of grief are connected with biblical and classical personages. One of the more popular forms of planctus was the *Planctus Mariae*, or lament of the Blessed Virgin Mary, which developed in the late twelfth century, notably in the work of Geoffrey of St Victor. Since the time of St Augustine, writers had meditated on the sorrows of Mary, though not to the extent of imagining the words of her lament. The extant laments vary from the brief, four-stanza 'Cum de cruce deponitur', to the extended 'Flete, fideles animae'. 'Ante crucem virgo stabat' extends for just eight stanzas, and is particularly interesting in that it incorporates the theme of self-mutilation as an expression of great grief, one that has already been discussed in the content of the visual arts (see above, pp. 173–5):

1 The Virgin stood before the Cross / She was thinking about Christ's sufferings / She was lacerating herself / tears washed her face.
2 The Virgin says, 'What have you done?/ What offence have you committed? Why did you climb onto the Cross ?/ Look upon me in my grief.

The complex 'Planctus ante nescia' is a particularly apt *Planctus Mariae* to study in respect of word/note relationships. The structural basis of the chant is the repetitive sequence AABBCC... The repeat pattern is only broadly followed, however, and within each melodic unit there are subdivisions. Thus the musical pattern of the first three verses runs as shown in the following table:

Verse number	Musical phrase
1a	a1, a2, b
1b	a1, a2, b
2a	c, d, e, f
2b	c, d, e, f
3a	g, h
3b	g, h
4a	c, d, e, f
4b	c, d, e, f
5a	g, h
5b	g, h
6a	i(i), i(ii), i(iii), j
6b	i(i), i(ii), i(iii), j

Many of the melodic subdivisions recur more than once during the planctus, but the words differ widely in substance from repeat to repeat: musical subphrase c, for instance (Figure 9.25), is set to the following diverse texts:

Fi - li dul - cor u - ni - ce sing - u - la - re gau - di - um

Figure 9.25

2a Fili dulcor unice, singulare gaudium! (O my son, my only sweetness, my one joy.)
2b Pectus, mentem, lumina torquent tua viscera. (Your wounds torture my heart, my soul and my eyes.)
2c O quam sero deditus, quam cito me deseris! (O how in a late hour were you given, and how quickly do you leave me!)
2d O quis amor corporis fecit tibi spolia! (O what love created for you as a covering of the human frame!)

No one phrase could possibly 'express' (in a madrigalian sense) such a diversity of moods, although by uniting the thoughts expressed in phrases 2a–d, the music certainly adds a powerfully expressive dimension to the text. By 'carrying' the text in this way (Stevens 1986: ch. 8, section vi, 'Sound and Sense') the music can be certainly said to 'express' it. And a case can even be made out for an element of what (for want of a better term) may be called 'madrigalian' expressivity, in certain chants, notably tracts.

If the examples so far discussed fairly represent the relationship that pertained between words and notes during the Middle Ages, the art of musical composition would not altogether have been out of phase with the other arts, and indeed with many aspects of liturgical thinking; even though the technical means that composers then had at their disposal were limited. For as we have seen, the progression from the hieratic to the subjective – from the collective to the individual – was already well under way by the beginning of the eleventh century. *Theoretical* music was certainly in tune with the times, if only because it took its cue from the musical theorists of classical antiquity. Guido D'Arezzo in the fifteenth chapter of his *Micrologus* (*c.* 1050) was indebted to Boethius, who in turn had gone back to Aristotle, Plato and Pythagoras: 'Likewise let the effect of the song so represent its matter that in sad things the neumes are *graves*, in happy things, tranquil, in good fortune, rejoicing, and so on' (see Palisca 1979).

Some fifty years or so later, John Cotton attempted to explain how this should be done:

> The first maxim must be that the chant is varied according to the meaning of the words.... Just as those who aspire to poetic distinction must ensure that actions are matched by words, and that nothing is spoken that is inconsistent with the circumstances of the person concerned, so the aspiring composer must compose his chant in an appropriate manner, in order that it may seem to express what the words say.... [A] composer may be criticised for using a dancing mode for a sad subject, or a mournful mode for joyful words. He must ensure, then, that the chant is ... pitched low for inauspicious texts and high for propitious ones.
>
> (cited in Palisca 1979)

Yet there is nothing in pre-fifteenth-century music to suggest that composers attempted to practise what the theorists preached: neither tessitura nor melodic mode (let alone rhythm or texture, which neither author discusses) were consciously controlled in the ways suggested. Nor, it has to be admitted, were medieval theorists at all clear *precisely* how the desired effects were to be achieved. Musical techniques of composition were not then geared to such ends, any more than two-dimensional techniques of draftsmanship were geared to create the illusion of three-dimensional solids.

Why then was music not more overtly 'expressive', in tune with developments in the other arts? In attempting to answer this contentious question we have to remind ourselves that until the tenth century liturgical music was monodic. Many of the musical elements that were later to be exploited for expressive purposes depended on *vertical* relationships of concurrent voices, notably of course harmony and dissonance. Only during the ninth century were the first tentative steps taken in this direction, and not until five centuries later was a sufficiently flexible technique of musical notation developed to permit a fully systematized control of these elements. Until this had been achieved, no fine-tuning of melody, rhythm, texture and harmony were possible. A simple manifestation of that 'fine-tuning' is the way in which during the fifteenth century an increasing correlation is to be seen between the natural rhythms of words and the rhythms of the notes to which they are set (see below, p. 201). In most large-scale polyphonic compositions of the fourteenth and early fifteenth century, the composer was in no way concerned with making the words audible. Indeed, in many ceremonial compositions for the Church, two or more different texts are sung at the same time. Verbal comprehensibility, then, can hardly have been a criterion of composition or performance, let alone expressive nuance.

So what was music's role in the liturgy? To answer this question it may be helpful to attempt an architectural parallel. Many of Europe's foremost churches were built between 1000 and 1400. Very little was written about architectural theory or practice before 1400 or about the reasons that drove men to attempt such colossal works. It is clear, none the less, that the great cathedrals were an inspiration not only to the religious communities who cared for them but to all who were privileged to enter them (see for instance Gervase of Canterbury's account of the Canterbury Cathedral fire, quoted above, p. 175). In view of the paucity of contemporary comment it is particularly fortunate that one of the witnesses happens to have been a highly influential churchman and statesman: Abbot Suger, of St Denis (1120–55). This abbey was the first great building in which the new Gothic style was successfully synthesized, and it was Suger who initiated the work. Suger would surely have been speaking for his contemporaries when he argued that the function of a vast and complex church was to lift the worshipper out of the everyday world into a truly *ex*-orbitant (i.e. otherwordly) environment:

> Thus delighting in the beauty of the House of God and transferring that which is material to that which is immaterial, worthy mediation has led me to reflect on the diversity of sacred virtues. Then, raised in spirit by the grace of God from this inferior world to higher things, I seem to be living in some strange region of the universe which exists neither in earthly clay nor entirely in the purity of heaven.
>
> (Frisch 1987: 9)

In his extensive account of St Denis, Suger refers several times to the symbolism of light. Over the northernmost door of the west façade, for instance, he placed the following inscription:

> Whoever you are, if you are moved to praise the beauty of these doors, marvel not at their costliness nor at the gold but at the craftsmanship. Bright is the noble work, but being nobly bright it should brighten the mind so that it may travel through the true lights to the True Light where Christ is the True Door.... The dull mind rises in truth through that which is material, and on seeing this light is raised up from its former abasement.
>
> (Frisch 1987: 7)

196

Medieval builders handled the elements of space and light with great skill. The monastic church of La Madeleine at Vezelay, completed just fifteen years before St Denis was begun, illustrates this particularly well. The building divides into three main sections: a darkly lit narthex or ante-nave at the west end; a spacious and more brightly lit nave; and an eastern choir with transepts in which the main services were celebrated, lit by large colourful windows. The dark narthex was where monks and pilgrims would gather on important feast days, before the beginning of divine service. It was there that the ceremony of purification took place, after which the worshippers were ready to pass through the magnificent nave doors (Figure 9.26) into the realm of the serene and luminous church and into the brightly lit choir. The history of church architecture in northern Europe can be seen, indeed, as a quest for light – not, certainly, the cold light of common day, but a shimmering light, filtered through walls of coloured glass. A century or so after the completion of the Vezelay choir, the great windows of Chartres had been glazed (1240). The Sainte-Chapelle in Paris, a veritable hall of stained glass, dates from the same time, and is rivalled only by the unique and much later chapel of King's College in Cambridge, the last great church to be completed before the turbulent years of the Reformation. King's and Chartres remain today much as they were when they were completed, eloquent witnesses to medieval man's preoccupation with space, light and colour.

Space, light and colour are terms that might well be used to describe the qualities that we still admire in the liturgical polyphony of the late Middle Ages and early Renaissance. The very sound of two, three and even four concurrent lines of music must have struck Leonin's twelfth-century contemporaries as altogether *ex*-orbitant. The artistic achievement in sound was every bit as momentous as was the achievement of the great building for which the music was designed.

It is possible to press the analogy between music and architecture even further, for there is an intriguing parallel between the processes of musical and architectural design. In both cases the finished product was a cumulation of creative 'stages'. A rare insight into architectural practice is afforded by the extensive archival material that has survived in connection with the building of Milan Cathedral between 1386 and 1401. Stage one comprised the laying of the foundations. No decisions had yet been taken however about the height of the building or about the style and weight of the vaults and roofs. Nor, therefore, had any firm conclusions been reached about the thickness and design of the supporting pillars and buttresses. During the course of building, at least five alternative plans were considered and at

Figure 9.26 Nave doors of the church of La Madeleine at Vezelay

least eight different European experts were consulted. The building, in fact, grew stage by stage; its final appearance was realized only with the completion of the final stage (see Ackerman 1949).

Milan may have been an exceptionally disorganized example of medieval building practice. The evidence, however, suggests, that architectural planning in medieval times was generally more 'successive' than it was later to become. The essential difference between the medieval approach to architectural design and the approach used by Renaissance architects from the time of Brunelleschi onward centred on the question of unity. Renaissance designs were based upon fully integrated systems of proportion: the larger the building, the more substantial its supporting members. Given the ground plan of a Renaissance church, it is possible to arrive at a fair idea of its total dimension and appearance, whereas a medieval ground plan is by no means as informative.

While it would be wrong to press the musical analogy too hard, it is none the less true to say that a Renaissance motet is considerably more unified than is its predecessor. The medieval composer tended to put together the parts of a composition successively, as did the architect. To begin with he laid a foundation. This commonly took the form of a pre-existent melody or *tenor* upon which a rhythmic 'shape' was arbitrarily superimposed, without regard for the natural phrasing of the melody or the verbal rhythms of its text. Many of the more elaborate pieces were 'isorhythmic' in structure: i.e. the rhythmic pattern (the 'talea') was repeated one or more times either exactly or in some simple proportional relationship to the original values (e.g. 3:2 or 2:1). The melodic line (the 'colour'), too, might be repeated. Stage two involved the addition of a second line against it (commonly named a *'contra'-tenor*), care being taken to achieve a reasonable degree of consonance between the two parts. If a third line or *triplum* was desired, this was then added, ensuring that it was reasonably consonant at each moment with at least one of the two concurrent parts (though not necessarily with both). Only gradually did the final shape of the composition become apparent as line after line was added to the original 'tenor'; and of course with each successive stage it became a little harder to create a singable horizontal line – one, that is, which had a coherent rhythmic pattern and which avoided such awkward melodic intervals as sixths, sevenths and ninths. In composing the opening Kyrie of his *Messe de Notre Dame* (see Figure 9.27), Machaut first laid down the tenor (marked C.F.) by imposing a rhythmic pattern on his chosen plainsong. He then composed a contra-tenor ('against' the tenor), filling in the gaps left by rests in the cantus firmus. Finally he added the two upper parts, possibly in this case conceiving them somewhat simultaneously, though differentiating between them in the use of syncopation and hocket (in the upper part of bar 5 for instance).

Figure 9.27 Opening Kyrie of Machaut's *Messe de Notre Dame*

Figure 9.27   (cont.)

According to the theorist and composer, Pietro Aaron (*fl.* 1490–1545), the 'successive' method of composition gave way gradually during the second half of the fifteenth century to one in which all the separate voice parts of the composition were created 'simultaneously'. No longer did the composer normally begin by laying down a cantus-firmus 'foundation'. Instead, he used musical 'imitation' as his main structural agent. The change marks the point at which 'subjective' qualities start to be observed in music.[7]

The famous *Absalom fili mi* (once thought to be by Josquin) may serve by way of illustration (see Figure 9.28). The Absalom/David theme had long been popular in devotional literature. Abelard's eleventh-century planctus, for instance, reworks the biblical text in a deeply emotive way. There is no question, though, that the monody to which it was then set reflects the mood of the words in any way. This setting proves, in fact, to be one of the first in which the music can be seen to respond in purely musical terms. This is because the technique of musical imitation allows each successive phrase of text to be set to an appropriate melody: the rhythm of the opening imitative point, for instance, reflects in a simple way the rhythm of the words, and the melodic line rises and falls in the way that the spoken voice might well do.

All four voices sing the phrase, one after the other, in 'imitation'. Whilst this element of the compositional process is largely horizontal, the composer is at the same time carefully controlling every vertical relationship in the piece. Note, for instance, the introduction of dissonant notes into the triadic harmony by the technique of 'suspension' (bars 7–8). Such dissonances were then (and still are) found to be particularly appropriate for the expression of darker moods. Dissonance is no longer an incidental by-product of simultaneously moving lines, but a carefully controlled agent for the creation of tension and relaxation.

Figure 9.28 Opening of *Absalom fili mi*

Aaron claimed that the new compositional method was wholly the work of Josquin and a Florentine circle of disciples of the late fifteenth century. There is plenty of evidence to show, however, that composers were already tentatively moving in that direction long before then. There is, for instance, Dufay's remarkable votive antiphon, 'Ave regina coelorum' of *c.* 1464, mentioned above. It must to some extent have been successively composed since it is built on a cantus firmus. Two striking passages in it none the less show that Dufay was in part composing simultaneously: they occur significantly at those moments in the piece at which the composer has inserted his own prayer: '*Miserere tui labentis Dufay, Ne peccatorum ruat in ignem fervorum*', and '*Miserere supplicanti Dufay*' (see Figure 9.29). The mode or key suddenly shifts from the open Ionian or C major to what is effectively C minor – a change that later theorists, such as Glarean and Zarlino would have seen as wholly appropriate to the changing mood of the words.

In a rather different sense, of course, church music has always been expressive, not of particular words but of the liturgical occasion itself: the more important the service, the more elaborate the music. Dufay's motet shows an awakening realization that a quite different relationship was possible. His 'Ave regina coelorum' was however an early bird. The 'expressive' summer of 'subjective' liturgical music was still a century or more away.

Figure 9.29 Extract from Dufay's votive antiphon 'Ave regina coelorum'

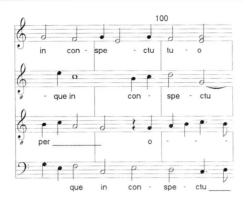

Figure 9.29 (cont.)

NOTES

1 Notably, Lowinsky 1941, 1946, 1954, 1966. For a complete list of publications see, 'Lowinsky, Edward' in the *New Grove Dictionary of Music and Musicians* (1980).
2 Heretics who denied the full divinity of Christ and who were therefore more inclined to the idea of the human Christ.
3 The *Graduale Triplex* (Solesmes 1979) furnishes ample evidence of rhythmic nuancing in early notated chant.
4 Possibly the work of a Greek artist, brought to Aachen by Charlemagne; see Dodwell 1971: pl. 27.
5 Machiavelli acknowledged it thus: 'Christianity was dying: St Francis resurrected it' (Mâle 1986: 83).
6 The text is taken from a translation made sometime before 1410 by Nicholas Love, Prior of the Carthusian Monastery of Mount Grace; see Powell 1908.
7 One of the first observers was the theorist, Heinrich Glarean, in his *Dodecachordon* (1549); see also Miller 1961 and Strunk 1950.

REFERENCES

ACKERMAN, J. (1949) ' "Ars sine scientia nihil est": Gothic theory of architecture at the cathedral of Milan', *Art Bulletin* 31: 84 ff.
APEL, W. (1958) *Gregorian Chant*, London: Burns & Oates.
BARASCH, M. (1976) *Gestures of Despair in Medieval and Early Renaissance Art*, New York: New York University Press.

BECKWITH, J. (1970) *Early Christian and Byzantine Art*, London: Penguin.

CATTIN, G. (1984) *Music of the Middle Ages I*, trans S. Betterill, Cambridge: Cambridge University Press.

COLE, B. (1980) *Masaccio and the Art of Early Renaissance Florence*, Bloomington: Indiana University Press.

DODWELL, C.R. (1971) *Painting in Europe 801–1200*, London: Penguin.

FRISCH, T. (1987) *Gothic Art, 1140–c.*1450: Sources and Documents, Toronto: University of Toronto Press.

GLAREAN, H. (1549) *Dodecachordon*, trans. C.A. Miller in *Musical Studies and Documents* 6.

GROVE, G. (1980) *The New Grove Dictionary of Music and Musicians*, 20 vols, ed S. Sadie, London: Macmillan.

HUCKE, H. (1980) 'Towards a new historical view of Gregorian Chant', *Journal of the American Musicological Society* 33: 437.

JOHNER, D. (1940) *The Chants of the Vatican Gradual*, London.

KERMAN, J. (1962) 'The Elizabethan motet: a study of texts for music', *Studies in the Renaissance* 9: 273.

LONGNON, J. and CAZELLES, R. (eds) (1969) *The 'Tres Riches Heures' of Jean, Duke of Berry*, New York: George Braziller.

L'ORANGE, H.P.L. and NORDHAGEN, P.J. (1966) *Mosaics*, London: Methuen.

LOWINSKY, E. (1941) 'The concept of physical and musical space in the Renaissance', *Proceedings of the American Musicological Society*.

——(1946) 'Music history and its relation to the history of ideas', *Music Journal*, November–December.

——(1954) 'Music in the culture of the Renaissance', *Journal of the History of Ideas* 15: 509–53.

——(1966) *The Renaissance Image of Man and the World*, ed. B. O'Kelly, Columbus, Ohio: Ohio State University Press, pp. 129–77.

MÂLE, E.E. (1978) *Religious Art in France: The Late Middle Ages*, trans. from 5th edn of 1949, Princeton: Princeton University Press.

MILLER, C.A. (1961) 'The *Dodecachordon*: its origins and influence on Renaissance thought', *Musica Disciplina* 15.

MORRIS, C. (1972) *The Discovery of the Individual, 1050–1200*, London: Church Historical Society.

PALISCA, C.V. (ed.) (1979) *Hucbald, Guido and John on Music*, New Haven, Conn.: Yale University Press.

PANOFSKY, E. (1957) *Gothic Architecture and Scholasticism*, New York: Meridian

——(1970) *Renaissance and Renascences in Western Art*, London: Granada Publishing.

POPE-HENESSEY, J. (1964) *The Portrait in the Renaissance*, London and New York: Phaidon.

POWELL, L.E. (ed.) (1908) *The Mirrour of the Blessed Lyf of Jesu Christ*, Oxford: Thames & Hudson.

RANKIN, S. (1985) 'Musical and ritual aspects of *Quem queritis*', *Münchener Beiträge zur Mediävistik und Renaissance-Forschung* 36: 193.

SEVESTRE, N. (1985) 'La place du trope dans le rituel', *Münchener Beiträge zur Mediävistik und Renaissance-Forschung* 36: 193.

SOLESMES, Benedictines of (1979) *Graduale Triplex*, Paris and Tournai: Desclée.

SOUTHERN, R.W. (1953) *The Making of the Middle Ages*, London: Hutchinson University Library, reprinted 1959, London: Arrow Books.

STEVENS, J. (1986) *Words and Music in the Middle Ages*, Cambridge: Cambridge University Press.

STRUNK, O. (1950) *Source Readings in Musical History*, New York: W.W. Norton.

YEARLEY, J. (1983) 'The Medieval Latin Planctus as a Genre', dissertation for the D.Phil., University of York, UK, later to be published by Cambridge University Press.

10

Handel's Ghost:
The Composer's Posthumous Reputation
in the Eighteenth Century

ELLEN T. HARRIS

I t does not surprise us that composers born three hundred years ago have become part of our popular as well as artistic life. Acknowledged masters from Bach to Beethoven to Brahms dominate our musical culture and our concert halls. For those who accept this situation as perfectly natural, the only remarkable feature is that the phenomenon in music is so modern.

Peter Burkholder has argued that the past one hundred years of music composition and performance have been governed by a historicist tradition that has turned our concert halls into museums (Burkholder 1983, 1984). He argues that Brahms is the first 'modernist composer' because he was the first to be 'obsessed with the musical past' and with his own 'place in music history', and because he sought 'to emulate the music of those we call the "classical masters"' (Burkholder 1984: 76–7), and measured the value of his music 'by the standards of the past'. Of course, for the musical past to play such a role in modern music, it has to be accessible, and William Weber has commented on the changes in musical repertoire that occurred in the eighteenth century and observes that these were responsible for slowly undermining what he calls the 'contemporaneity of musical taste' (Weber 1984).

As Burkholder's use of the term 'obsession' implies, this change in repertoire has transformed the role of the composer, who no longer writes for the moment, or, as Weber puts it, to celebrate or amuse, but rather in competition with the musical giants of the past for posterity. Harold Bloom in *The Anxiety of Influence* (1973) has discussed this trend in poetry. He argues that 'the covert subject of most poetry for the last three centuries has been the anxiety of influence, each poet's fear that no proper work remains for him to perform' (Bloom 1973: 48). Poetry has thus become the art of criticism, or, more properly, of misinterpretation. Poets of succeeding generations only succeed by misreading the poems of their predecessors, thereby giving themselves some creative space. Burkholder follows this line of reasoning in his discussion of Brahms: 'This kind of dialectic within music approaches a species of criticism, as if Brahms were writing in his music a commentary on his own experience as a musician, or indeed, given his wide knowledge, a rumination on the entire previous tradition of music' (Burkholder 1984: 79).

Just as Bloom identifies Wordsworth as the first 'modernist' poet, Burkholder identifies Brahms as the first modernist composer. Bloom also identifies Milton as the first 'great inhibitor' (Bloom 1973: 32). By corollary, George Frideric Handel appears as the first Great Inhibitor in musical composition. His ghost was the first to haunt – to compete with and inhibit – the creative skills of those who followed him.

In general, composers who lived before 1750 did not have to live with the past. A great composer would influence composition primarily through his students for one or at most two generations; then he was forgotten. In 1477 the music theorist Tinctoris could write, 'Although it seems beyond belief, there does not exist a single piece of music, not composed within the last forty years, that is regarded by the learned as worth hearing' (cited in Brown 1976: 7). Composers frequently heralded their work as 'new', as in Willaert's *Musica nova* (1559) and Caccini's *Le nuove musiche* (1602). Of course, this is not to say that composers were unaware of the past. For example, Gregorian chant formed the basis of polyphonic music. For centuries, composers began with the original chant, superimposed a new rhythmic structure on the chosen melodic fragment, and composed counter-melodies that would be performed simultaneously. After some time, composers even took polyphonic pieces and treated them as the basis for new composition. This musical process also lies at the heart of many of J.S. Bach's cantatas, in which a Lutheran chorale melody (already more than a hundred years old) serves as the pre-existent material. In this type of compositional practice, however, the old style is seen neither an impediment nor a hurdle; it is, rather, in Bloom's words, absorbed into the new.

It was also common practice for composers pre-dating Handel to imitate an older style.[1] This became particularly popular in the seventeenth century,

209

when the new and old styles were distinguished by such terms as *prima prattica* and *seconda prattica*, or *stile antico* and *stile moderne*. Today we sometimes refer to the older style – which was used especially for sacred music – as the Palestrina style, naming it after the composer whose works are most often taken as models. Where previously the long and unbroken traditions of the Christian Church had been represented in music by the use of pre-existent material, the seventeenth century frequently made this link with the past by using music that was in itself antiquated or anachronistic. This preservation of an older style, however, still did not alter or inhibit modern secular trends. In fact, the new style, the *seconda prattica*, was defined by its separation from the older compositional practice.

It is difficult to say exactly when the term 'new music' acquired a pejorative meaning. Artusi's *The Imperfections of Modern Music* of 1600 may perhaps be the first instance of a trend that has since led to works such as Henry Pleasants's *The Agony of Modern Music* (1955). Without any doubt, in the period between Artusi and Pleasants, composers became more and more aware of the compositional past. For example, in 1751 Charles Avison not only urged historical awareness as a means towards improving contemporary composition, but also recognized that composers should be writing as much or more for posterity as for the present.

> An Improvement of this Kind might be still more easily set on Foot, were there any History of the Lives and Works of the best Composers; together with an Account of their several *Schools*, and the *characteristic Taste*, and *Manner* of each:- A Subject, though yet untouched, of such extensive Use, that we may reasonably hope it will be the Employment of some future Writer.
>
> Painting has long had an Advantage of this Kind, . . . [but] many Professors [i.e. artists] in both Sciences [have] alike employed their Talents in the lowest Branches of their Art, and turned their Views rather to *instant Profit*, than to *future Fame*.
>
> (Avison 1751: 98–9)

By the nineteenth century, composers were actively involved with their predecessors. To take only a few examples, Mendelssohn initiated the rediscovery of Bach's sacred vocal music; Berlioz studied and edited the music of Gluck; Vaughan-Williams participated in editing the complete works of Purcell; Saint-Saëns edited the complete works of Rameau; and Webern edited the complete works of Isaac. One notes that whereas Mendelssohn and Berlioz were concerned with eighteenth-century masters, Vaughan-Williams focused on a seventeenth-century master, and Webern on a sixteenth-century master. This helps to pinpoint the origin of the historicist tradition, for after the past was discovered it quickly grew by extension backwards. Handel was the first composer whose reputation did not have to be revived after a period of obscurity.

Although there can be no doubt of Handel's greatness, the growth of his reputation in the eighteenth century and beyond did not rest solely on his compositional skills. Rather, Handel's continuing posthumous reputation coincided with, and in some ways reflected and largely depended on, a number of important societal trends: (1) the deterioration of the patronage system for composers; (2) the change in the image of the composer from craftsman to genius; (3) the change in musical repertoire due to the rise of music publishing and the growth of the middle classes; and (4) a cultural movement toward neo-classicism in art and architecture, in part as a reaction to important archaeological discoveries. Handel's temporal relation to these four trends contributed greatly to his becoming the first Great Inhibitor in music. Although other composers later played this role, and some of these were to become even greater inhibitors (Beethoven and Wagner are obvious examples), Handel was the first, and from 1759 to 1800 the primary if not the only, composer whose posthumous presence inhibited composers of succeeding generations.

Handel was, for example, one of the first composers to break away from the patronage system, and his independence added to his titanic image. Before his time, and even during and after his life, composers were frequently thought of as craftsmen. They worked for a patron in much the same way as a tailor might: they furnished music on demand. Patrons usually came from the Church or the court, and the composer was generally in the position of having to please an individual – a prince, a king, or a cardinal. Thus Handel, before he was thirty-five, worked at various times and in various capacities for Prince Ferdinand de Medici of Florence; Cardinals Pamphili, Colonna, and Ottoboni of Rome; the Marquis Ruspoli, also of Rome; the Elector of Hanover; and Lord Burlington and the Duke of Chandos in England. After 1720, however, Handel never again worked directly for a patron, although he accepted commissions and support. He became an impresario, founded his own operatic companies, and although he certainly wrote to please his public, he mainly wrote what he pleased. He had no stable position with its attendant benefits; his livelihood depended largely on the box-office success of his compositions.

Handel did not, however, merely pander to public taste. If composers can be thought to compose for patrons, the public, or posterity, Handel can be seen composing for each, sometimes simultaneously. In a letter of 28

July 1743, Handel's primary copyist, Christopher Smith, writes to Lord Shaftesbury that the composer has absolutely rejected a commission from the nobility to compose an opera. He reveals that Handel has chosen instead to write a Te Deum and Jubilate, and he acknowledges that

> This I think perfectly well Judg'd to appease and oblige the Court and the Town. . . . But how the Quality will take it that He can compose for Himself and not for them when they offered Him more than ever He had in His life, I am not a judge and could only wish I had not been employed in it either Directly or Indirectly.
>
> (cited in Matthews 1959: 263–4)

Indeed, Handel did not let public opinion govern his composition, and some of his most remarkable works, notably *Theodora*, were distinctly unpopular during his lifetime. It was clearly with an eye towards posterity and future fame that the composer carefully preserved his manuscripts and left them to Smith in his will.[2] Whenever it was possible for Handel to compose for his patrons, the public and posterity, he did; but he often rejected the first two in favour of the last.

Not only was Handel one of the first composers to break from the patronage system, but he was considered, even in his lifetime, a musical genius rather than a craftsman. Although the concept of a composer as technician, producing on demand, cannot be defended to the exclusion of inspiration and talent in any era (Lowinsky 1964), the composer as craftsman and the composer as genius are, at least to a certain extent, two conflicting perspectives that divide music history at about 1800. Handel became a model of the new aesthetic; his career as well as his music became the stick against which the talents of younger composers could be measured.

In a famous commentary from 1753, for example, Handel is described as a flawed genius who is able to overcome his deficiencies.

> Mr Handel is in Music, what his own Dryden was in Poetry; nervous, exalted, and harmonious; but voluminous, and, consequently, not always correct. Their Abilities equal to every Thing; their Execution frequently inferior. Born with Genius capable of *soaring the boldest Flights*; they have sometimes, to suit the vitiated Taste of the Age they lived in, *descended to the lowest*. Yet, as both their Excellencies are infinitely more numerous than their Deficiencies, so both their Characters will devolve to latest posterity, not as Models of Perfection, yet glorious Examples of those amazing Powers that actuate the human Soul.
>
> (Avison 1753: 50–1)

212

On the other hand, Handel's exact contemporary, J.S. Bach, was criticized during and after his life for writing in an artificial manner and for having an excess of art – in other words, for being a craftsman. In 1737 Johann Adolph Scheibe wrote of Bach that

> This great man would be the admiration of whole nations if he had more amenity, if he did not take away the natural element in his pieces by giving them a turgid and confused style, and if he did not darken their beauty by an excess of art. ... Turgidity has led [him] from the natural to the artificial, and from the lofty to the sombre; ... one admires the onerous labour and uncommon effort – which, however, are vainly employed, since they conflict with nature.
>
> (cited in David and Mendel 1945: 238)

However much one may want to argue with these judgements (and in this century Bach's rigorous aesthetic has earned him the appellation of genius while Handel is sometimes seen as a 'mere' popularizer), they offer an explanation of Handel's posthumous reputation and Bach's relative obscurity during the second half of the eighteenth century. Whereas Bach, the Leipzig Kapellmeister, represented the past by his craftsmanlike approach and his humble position in the patronage system, Handel's persona, his lifestyle, and his music spoke to the future. Indeed, his reputation was evident as early as 1738 when Roubiliac's statue of him was placed in Vauxhall Gardens – an extraordinary happening and, I believe, a first for a living composer. From that time, tributes to Handel's greatness and genius are plentiful; frequently he is equated with Orpheus. It is these judgements, and particularly those that speak of a natural but flawed genius, that form the basis of the critical assessment of his music in the biography by Mainwaring published in 1760 – the year after Handel's death – the first full-length biography and criticism of any composer.[3]

> The merit of Handel's music will be least discerned by the lovers of elegance and correctness. They are shocked with every defect ... while their very character hinders them from entering into those excellencies of a higher nature, in which he so much surpasses all other Musicians: excellencies, which are hardly consistent with a constant regard to those minuter circumstances, on which beauty depends. As taste [or knowledge] ... is of a tender and timid nature, it is apt to consider those bolder strokes and rougher dashes which genius delights in, either as coarse, or as extravagant. However, when it attempts to chastise or correct such passages, it mistakes its province. Art is here not only useless, but dangerous. It may easily destroy the orig-

inality, tho' it cannot create elegance; which if it could be had, would be ill purchased at the expence of the other'.

(Mainwaring 1760: 162–4)

This image of Handel is perhaps best represented by the mythology that sprang up surrounding the actual composition of *Messiah* in twenty-four days.

> Handel is supposed to have sequestered himself in his study ... 'barely touching food', and his servant and the few visitors that were admitted found him alternately weeping or praying, or just staring into eternity.... 'I did think I did see all Heaven before me and the great God Himself', he is said to have declared upon completing the 'Hallelujah Chorus'.

(Lang 1966: 336)

It matters not whether this story is true or false; what matters is that it was widely disseminated and believed. It represents Handel as a genius in the nineteenth-century sense, as a recipient of inspiration from a spiritual source. Although Handel's genius was flawed, it was great. It was polished by, but not dependent on, learned art.

The period of Handel's immediate posterity coincided with the classical revival in the arts that was fuelled by the first important archaeological digs. Herculaneum was rediscovered in 1709; excavations in Pompeii began in 1748. An important expedition in Greece, begun in 1751 by James Stuart and Nicholas Revett, led to the book *The Antiquities of Athens*, the first volume of which was published in 1762. Johann Joachim Winckelmann's more famous book, *Geschichte der Kunst des Altertums* (A History of the Art of the Ancients), was published in 1764. The imitation of antiquity, or neo-classicism, which derived from these discoveries, had its greatest impact on art and architecture, for in these fields direct models could be copied. In architecture, this led to the pervasive use of classic colonnades. In art, the neo-classical movement supported the increased use of historical and biblical subjects and a great reduction in the use of elaborate Baroque ornamentation in favour of purportedly Grecian simplicity of line.

Although music had no surviving classical models to imitate, it too was affected by the neo-classical movement. As in art, music returned to mythological and biblical subjects; even in Handel's music there is a marked shift of emphasis in subject matter in the 1730s from relatively recent, historical, and heroic plots to mythological, biblical, and pastoral plots. The most decisive musical change, however, occurred in the music of Christoph Willibald von Gluck (1714–87), whose chain of so-called 'reform' operas

214

began in 1762 – the same year as *The Antiquities of Athens* – and all have mythological subjects – *Orpheus* (1762), *Alceste* (1767), *Paris and Helen* (1770), *Iphigenia in Aulide* (1774), *Armide* (1777), and *Iphigenia in Tauride* (1779).

Music also reacted to the momentum of the archaeological finds by trying to discover its own past. In 1763, the year between *The Antiquities of Athens* and Winkelmann's *Geschichte der Kunst des Altertums*, John Brown published a *Dissertation on ... Poetry and Music* in which he discusses music in the 'savage State' (Section III), in ancient Greece (Sections V–VIII), among the ancient Hebrews (Section X), and in ancient Rome (Section XI). Only the last forty-eight pages of this 242-page book are devoted to music after ancient Rome and to what modern artists can learn from the classics (Brown 1763). Similarly, Charles Burney begins *A General History of Music, From the Earliest Times to the Present Period*, which was published in London in four volumes from 1776 to 1789, by discussing the music of ancient Egypt and that of the ancient Hebrews, even though, like his predecessor, he had no music on which to base this discussion. Burney addresses this problem directly:

> The subject itself of ancient music is so dark, and writers concerning it are so discordant in their opinions, that every intelligent reader who finds *how little there is to be known*, has reason to lament that there still remains so much to be said. Indeed, I should have been glad to have waived all discussion about it: for, to say the truth, the study of ancient music is now become the business of an Antiquary more than of a Musician. But in every history of music extant in other languages, the practice has been so constant for the author to make a display of what he knew, and what he did *not* know concerning ancient music, that it seemed absolutely necessary for me to say something about it, if it were only to prove, that if I have not been more successful in my enquiries than my predecessors, I have not been less diligent.
>
> (Burney 1782: 111)[4]

Although the historical foundation for musical neo–classicism was, as Burney points out, largely theoretical, it was frequently discussed, in part because it lent a lineage to musical composition that was on a par with the visual arts and literature. When the time came to 'exhibit' examples of ancient music, however, it was necessary to take a more pragmatic approach. Thus 'ancient music' was frequently defined as music composed in or before the seventeenth century. For example, Charles Avison (1751) writes: 'By the Ancients are meant, those who lived from the Time of PAL-ESTRINA to the Introduction of modern Operas' (Avison 1751: 43).

A similar definition was originally used also by The Academy of Ancient Music, an eighteenth-century organization of professional musicians dedicated to the revival and performance of older music. In time, however, this already lenient description of ancient music was further eroded. In a book from 1768 giving 'The Words of Such pieces as are most usually performed by the Academy of Ancient Music, 2nd ed.,' the only two composers whose works are listed in separate sections are Henry Purcell and Handel (who had died only nine years before). At this point, the only necessary criterion for being deemed 'ancient' in music was, apparently, being dead.

Although the Academy continued to perform until 1792, another group, the Concerts of Ancient Music, had sprung into existence in 1776 with the aim of not performing any music less than twenty years old. By 1785 these concerts had gained the patronage of George III, and it seems safe to assume that the success of this organization helped to undermine the earlier Academy. It also seems likely that the two groups were associated in some way, at the very least by their love for the music of Handel. Both organizations performed his music extensively, and it is probably no coincidence that the last president of the Academy, Dr Samuel Arnold, was also the editor of the first Handel edition (1787–97), which was the first retrospective edition of any composer's work. Whereas Burney tried to create a classical past for music, these performing groups solved the problem by fiat: they decided by declaration what was 'ancient music'.

In an archaeological sense, Handel had became an ancient artefact to be treasured, copied, and even worshipped. And this was happening not only in England. Among many landmarks was the first German performance of *Messiah* in 1772, conducted by Thomas Arne; in 1775 it was conducted by C. P. E. Bach. In the 1780s in Vienna, the Baron van Swieten, an important patron of music, introduced the performance of a number of Handel's works. In 1788 Mozart participated in these concerts by reorchestrating Handel's *Acis and Galatea*; he reorchestrated *Messiah* in 1789 and the *St Cecilia Ode* and *Alexander's Feast* in 1790.

In Italy there were performances of both *Alexander's Feast* and *Messiah*. In America performances of Handel's works took place in New York and Boston as early as the 1770s, and in the 1780s the Moravians helped spread the popularity of European choral music in America with performances of Handel and Haydn especially. In 1815 Boston saw the opening concert of the Handel and Haydn Society, a group that is still in existence today.

The Boston Society is but one example of another important cultural trend which emerged in the second half of the eighteenth century towards amateur music-making and a wider music public. The revolutions in France

216

and America, and important social changes in England, were in part caused by and in part the cause of a significant middle class. Individual members of this class did not have the financial strength to hire or commission a contemporary composer, as aristocratic patrons had done, nor, by and large, did they have access to contemporary compositions in manuscript. Therefore, aided by the enormous growth in music publishing and the birth of many amateur choral societies, the idea of a musical repertoire was born – that is, a group of compositions that could be performed repeatedly in cycles. For example, the Three Choirs Festival, which was organized about 1715, and had at its core the choristers from the cathedrals of Gloucester, Worcester and Hereford, first performed Handel's *Messiah* in 1757. According to a history of the organization dating from 1812, 'it was received ... with rapturous applause' and (one assumes because of that) 'has been repeated at every succeeding meeting of the Three Choirs' (cited in Hogwood 1984: 245).

Handel's role as the first Great Inhibitor derived in part from his relation to these various contemporary trends. He was an independent composer who was thought of as a genius rather than a craftsman. As such he stood in the forefront of a change in the conception of what a composer does and was idealized as a model for succeeding generations. He also lived in a period that both rediscovered the glories of ancient Greece and Rome and recreated them in art and architecture. Similarly the musical past was researched as it had never been before, and Handel's music was heralded as ancient. Finally, the eighteenth century saw the rise of the middle class and the development of a musical public that demanded a musical repertoire to hear and perform. Handel not only had the reputation of greatness, but much of his music was published and easily available.

These attitudes were clear immediately after Handel's death. In 1763, an Italian violinist in London wrote to a friend in Naples:

First then, madam, you must know that the English, a very few excepted, neither relish nor understand our music, the German manner has almost universally prevailed amongst them; and such is the force of prejudice, that the ponderous harmony of Handel outweighs, by far, with them, the elegant taste of Italian melody. This, Bach [J.C. Bach (1732–95), Johann Sebastian's son], at first, did not suspect; but finding it, by experience, has prudently changed his style; and now his chorusses roar, his basses thunder, and his airs float in an ocean of symphony. In a word, he has Handelized; and acquired a reputation here.

(Petty 1980: 99)

Four years later, a reviewer wrote of J.C. Bach's *Carattaco* (an opera composed for London in 1767),

> The masterly stile of the music, and particularly the grandeur of the chorusses, makes it to be wished that Signor Bach may meet with further encouragement, as his genius and judgment seem admirably calculated to reform the present corrupted taste of our modern music, and like a second Handel, once again restore that elegance and perfection we have for some time been strangers to.
>
> (Petty 1980: 115)

Gluck is reported by Michael Kelly, a famous English singer in Vienna, to have worshipped Handel:

> One morning, after I had been singing with him, he said, 'follow me up stairs, Sir, and I will introduce you to one, whom, all my life, I have made my study and endeavoured to imitate'. I followed him into his bed-room, and, opposite to the head of the bed, saw a full-length picture of Handel, in a rich frame. 'There, Sir', said he, 'is the portrait of the inspired master of our art; when I open my eyes in the morning, I look upon him with reverential awe and acknowledge him as such, and the highest praise is due to your country for having distinguished and cherished his gigantic genius'.
>
> (Kelly 1826: 252)

In 1791 Haydn travelled to London and while there heard the last of the Commemoration concerts, which had begun in 1784 to celebrate (incorrectly as it turned out) the centennial of Handel's birth on the twenty-fifth anniversary of his death. William Shield, a contemporary English composer, wrote of this event:

> At this last Abbey Meeting, there was present one auditor, of all men the most capable of appreciating its excellence, the immortal Haydn, then on his first visit to this country; and from it he derived a confirmation of that deep reverence for the mighty genius of Handel, which, to the honour no less of his candid modesty than of his judgment, he was ever prone to avow.
>
> (cited in Hogwood 1984: 243)

Haydn reputedly said to the Italian librettist Giuseppe Carpani

> that when he heard the music of Hendl in London, he was struck as if he had been put back to the beginning of his studies and had known nothing up to that moment. He meditated on every note and drew from those most learned scores the essence of true musical grandeur.
>
> (*ibid.*: 243)

Indeed, upon hearing the 'Hallelujah Chorus', he is said to have burst into tears and exclaimed, 'He is the master of us all!' (Geiringer 1968: 121). When Haydn's oratorio, *The Creation*, was performed in London, a number of English critics agreed with this assessment. One reviewer wrote, on 28 March 1800, 'It is certainly a fine composition, in every respect worthy of its great author ... and although not equal in grandeur to the divine compositions of the immortal HANDEL, is, nevertheless, on the whole, a very charming production'. Another wrote, 'It is correctly scientific, for all we know, and certainly not devoid of impressive harmonies; but it breathes no more the sacred inspiration of HANDEL, than KOTZEBUE does of that which immortalized our own SHAKESPEARE!' (cited in Hogwood 1984: 248).

Mozart, who is quoted as saying, 'Handel knows better than any of us what will make an effect; when he chooses he strikes like a thunderbolt' (Hogwood 1984: 247), reorchestrated a number of Handel's English oratorios, as we have seen. The English, showing premature signs of our twentieth-century craving for authenticity, were hesitant to accept these modifications. After the first English performance in March 1805 of one of these reorchestrations, one reviewer wrote,

> We entertain a very high respect for the genius of Mozart, but we also hold the unrivalled powers of Handel in due reverence, and therefore must enter our protest against any such alterations in works that have obtained the sanction of time and of the best musical judges.
>
> (Hogwood 1984: 246–7)

Beethoven is also quoted as affirming Handel's greatness. To Edward Schulz he commented, 'Handel is the greatest composer that ever lived. . . . I would uncover my head, and kneel down at his tomb!' (Hogwood 1984: 248). Johann Stumpff records the following partially written conversation he had with the deaf composer:

> 'Whom do you consider the greatest composer that ever lived?'; 'Handel', was his instantaneous reply; 'to him I bow the knee', and he bent one knee to the floor. 'Mozart?' I wrote. 'Mozart', he continued, is good and admirable'. 'Yes', wrote I, 'who was able to glorify even Handel with his additional accompaniments to *The Messiah*'. 'It would have lived without them', was his answer.
>
> (Forbes 1967: 920)

In 1826, when he finally received his own copy of the Arnold edition of

Handel's works, Beethoven remarked, 'I have long wanted them, for Handel is the greatest, the ablest composer that ever lived. I can still learn from him' (Forbes 1967: 1024).

Throughout the eighteenth century, therefore, and well into the nineteenth, Handel's music exerted an enormous influence on composers and composition. He was revered, emulated, and perhaps even feared. Composers from J.C. Bach to Mozart and Haydn were unfavourably compared to the older master. Since genius was understood as a natural gift that could not be obtained through study, effort was only seen as an impediment to originality. How could a modern composer compete on these terms? As Harold Bloom writes,

> Ben Jonson has no anxiety as to imitation, for to him (refreshingly) art is *hard work*. But the shadow fell, and with the post-Enlightenment passion for Genius and the Sublime, there came anxiety too, for art was beyond hard work.
>
> (Bloom 1973: 27)

The anxiety Handel engendered is already obvious in the last paragraph of the 1760 Mainwaring biography:

> Little indeed are the hopes of ever equalling, much less of excelling so vast a Proficient in his own way: however, as there are so many avenues to excellence still open, so many paths to glory still untrod, it is hoped that the example of this illustrious Foreigner will rather prove an incentive, than a discouragement to the industry and genius of our own countrymen.
>
> (Mainwaring 1760: 208)

At the end of the eighteenth century, however, Charles Burney admitted privately that in England at least this hope had remained unfulfilled, 'I dare not say what I have long thought. That it is our reverence for old authors and bigotry to Handel, that has prevented us from keeping pace with the rest of Europe' (cited in Hogwood 1984: 245).

Handel's posthumous reputation, the societal and cultural trends that nurtured it, and its importance for generations of composers can be easily documented. For example, John Roberts has written about Gluck's borrowings from Handel (Roberts 1987); Haydn's *Creation* also owes an enormous debt to Handel both in its overall shape as well as in specific pieces. Similarly, Beethoven composed variations on 'See the conqu'ring hero comes' from Handel's *Judas Maccabaeus*, and his overture *Die Weihe des Hauses* of 1822 is said to have been inspired by Handel. More examples

220

could be presented from J.C. Bach and Mozart to Mendelssohn and beyond. Influence, imitation, and even inspiration, however, are not evidence of anxiety.

The anxiety that fires creativity is very special, and the quotations given above from Mainwaring and Burney speak rather to the more common type of anxiety that dampens creativity. In his discussion of poets in *The Anxiety of Influence*, Bloom writes, 'My concern is only with strong poets, major figures with the persistence to wrestle with their strong precursors, even to the death. Weaker talents idealize . . .' (Bloom 1973: 5). He goes on to identify six types of 'poetic misunderstanding' that allow a creative poet to overcome the power of his predecessor. The music of the mid- and late eighteenth century offers parallel examples of such revisionist processes, which can be discussed without recourse to Bloom's complex terminology.

Bloom identifies the first category as a misreading or deliberate swerving away from the precursor, who is shown to have gone too far in a single direction. This can be found musically in the mid-eighteenth century in the galant and rococo styles that swerve away from Baroque complexity. Bloom's second category represents a completion of the precursor, who is now shown not to have gone far enough. The musical style of Empfindsamkeit in this way takes up the Baroque concept of emotional expression and makes it both more intimate and more volatile. The third category superficially looks like an attempt to humble oneself before the precursor, but actually succeeds in emptying the precursor's work of its original meaning. Thus, Classical counterpoint of the early 1770s appears to return to Baroque models but actually only uses counterpoint as a texture to demarcate sections or enliven whole movements that frequently are in sonata form, thereby stripping Baroque counterpoint of its meaning as a form-generating process. Bloom describes the fourth process, or 'Daemonization', as the reaching out towards a new and heightened level of power and energy in contrast to the implied weakness of the precursor. The increased dynamic range associated with the Mannheim symphonists and the musical Sturm und Drang exemplify this process. The fifth category offers in contrast a self-imposed curtailment of imaginative endowment that separates the poet from the precursor and simultaneously offers a constricted version of the precursor's achievements. It seems to occur musically in the reform-opera tradition and in the use of folk-song both operatically and symphonically. Finally, the sixth category represents the point at which the poet is able to respond directly to the precursor's work without falling into servile imitation; at this stage the strong poet may even appear momentarily to have written the precursor's work himself at an earlier period. In music this stage is found in the High Classical style of the 1790s.

Bloom's categories follow in an implicit chronological order that appears to occur either within the single poet or in a continuously shifting and endless time frame. This is also the case in music, where the six musical revisionary styles tend to follow one another sequentially throughout the period and also appear in that order in the works of single composers. Haydn's use of the galant style in his Missa brevis in F major from the early 1750s, for example, is followed by his introduction to Empfindsamkeit, which is manifested particularly in his piano sonatas of the 1760s. His flirtation with Classical counterpoint, especially in the Op. 20 quartets of 1772, is then succeeded directly by his Sturm und Drang period, which is particularly well-illustrated in symphonies nos. 45 (1772) and 67 (c. 1778). An 'enforced simplicity' can then be found in many of the 'London' Symphonies of the 1790s, where folk elements play a dominant role. And the final stage is clearly represented in the two last oratorios of the late 1790s and early 1800s. Similarly, in Mozart's career one can point to the differing styles of the Singspiel and *opera buffa* of the late 1760s, the *opere serie* of the 1770s, the breakthrough of *Idomeneo* and *Entführung* in the early 1780s, the 'daemonization' in *Don Giovanni*, the deceptive folk-like simplicity of *Die Zauberflöte* and the final culmination in the *Requiem*. Clearly, one could easily devise a similar pattern for Beethoven.

Even more important than the apparent chronological succession of stages implying a grappling with anxiety and influence, however, is the co-existence of a multiplicity of styles in the late eighteenth century that seems to have no historical precedent. Its most obvious parallel occurs between 1890 and 1930, when styles can also be tentatively identified with Bloom's six revisionist principles. For example, Bloom's 'misreading' can be seen in impressionism, 'completion' in serialism, 'emptying of previous meaning' in neo-clacissism, 'daemonization' in expressionism or primitivism, and 'enforced simplicity' in neo-tonality. In both periods, however, the level of anxiety is manifested not simply in one-to-one musical parallels to Bloom's revisionary processes, but specifically in the multiplicity of co-existing styles and in the clear stylistic shifts evident in the careers of individual composers. Before Haydn, for example, and between 1800 and 1890, it is difficult to name a single composer with similar stylistic disjunctions in his career.[5]

It is not surprising that the two periods in which this occurs were revolutionary politically as well as musically. Furthermore, the musical 'revolutions' of the mid-eighteenth and late nineteenth centuries follow a pattern similar to that described by Thomas Kuhn in *The Structure of*

Scientific Revolutions (Kuhn 1970). In both eras a musically-accepted style or paradigm was rejected, a number of new stylistic 'solutions' proposed, and, at least in the eighteenth century, a new stylistic paradigm accepted. The 'revolution', or the period of transition between paradigms, can be identified, following Kuhn, by the temporary multiplicity of solutions. Whereas scientific revolutions are sparked by an anomalous research result however, artistic change may well be fuelled, following Bloom, by a build-up of anxiety. In the history of musical style, Bloom's and Kuhn's theories interact because the six categories of 'misreading' exist most clearly in two 'revolutionary' clusters rather than continuously. Considering the potentially fertilizing influence of artistic anxiety, it can be no surprise that the first of these periods follows the death of the first Great Inhibitor, Handel, and that the second begins with the first 'modernist', Brahms.

Composers today all work under the shadow of the past, and their anxieties have only grown as the past has expanded. Immediately after Handel's death 'ancient music' was anything more than twenty years old and rarely more than a hundred years old. Today, familiar 'early music' stretches back beyond Handel at least to the Renaissance – five centuries. That is, as the modernist period, defined as beginning with the birth of anxious influence, has lengthened in time, the distant past has expanded backwards almost proportionally. Both the expansion of the musical past and the obsession with this past that Burkholder rightly observes in Brahms's music first began with the impact of Handel's reputation during the fifty years after his death. Concurrent social and cultural changes, including the growth of archaeology, the neo-classical movement in art and architecture, and the crumbling aristocracy, helped fuel Handel's overwhelming posthumous recognition, but it was the spirit of Handel's musical creativity that drove his reputation. Both for musical and historical reasons, therefore, the beginning of the modernist trends in musical composition can be dated to the emergence of Handel's ghost.[6]

NOTES

1 For a discussion of early examples see Brown (1982).

2 For a discussion of Handel's manuscripts and their preservation see Hicks (1985) and King (1967)

3 For further information on Mainwaring's work see Kivy (1964).

4 See also Grant (1983: ch. 5, 'Music to 1450: The Reluctant Historian', pp. 95–124).

5 The mid-eighteenth-century period of multiple styles (about 1740–90) is separated by one hundred years from the late nineteenth-century period (about 1890–1930). It could be argued that a similar period occurred earlier, separated by another hundred years (1690–1740), but I believe this represents more of a unilateral style change typical of the belief, still strong, that 'new is better'. Despite the investigations of the Camerata into the performance of Greek drama, and other such pursuits, there was no generalized preservation or performance of older music at this time that could have caused 'anxiety'. It would, of course, be ridiculous to argue that before the 'influence of anxiety' there was no style change, but rather that in the mid-eighteenth century, anxiety became, for the first time, a prime factor in the process. The multiplicity of approaches, or Bloom's six 'misreadings', at stylistic junctures may be the strongest evidence of this new relation to the past.

6 This article has undergone a lengthy evolution, during which time I presented various versions of it at the University of Chicago, Carleton College, the University of Nebraska (Lincoln), 1986 Conference of the Midwest American Society for Eighteenth-Century Studies, and the 1987 Meetings of the American Handel Society. I would like to dedicate its publication to the memory of David J. Greenstone, Professor of Political Science at the University of Chicago, who heard its first presentation as a paper and was my best critic.

REFERENCES

AVISON, C. (1751) *An Essay on Musical Expression*, reprinted 1753, London: C. Davis.

——(1753) *A Reply to the Author of Remarks on the Essay of Musical Expression*, London: C. Davis.

BLOOM, H. (1973) *The Anxiety of Influence: A Theory of Poetry.* London: Oxford University Press.

BROWN, H.M. (1976) *Music in the Renaissance*, Englewood Cliffs, NJ: Prentice-Hall.

——(1982) 'Evaluation, competition, and homage: imitation and theories of imitation in the Renaissance', *Journal of the American Musciological Society* 35: 1–48.

BROWN, J. (1763) *Dissertation on the Rise, Union, and Power, The Progression, Separation, and Corruptions, of Poetry and Music*, London: L. Davis and C. Reymers.

BURKHOLDER, J. (1983) 'Museum Pieces: the historicist mainstream in music of the last hundred years', *The Journal of Musicology* 2: 115–34.

——(1984) 'Brahms and Twentieth-Century Classical Music', *19th Century Music* 8/9: 75–83.

BURNEY, C. (1782) *A General History of Music*, Vol. 1, reprinted 1935, London: Harcourt, Brace & Co.

DAVID, H.T. and MENDEL, A. (eds) (1945) *The Bach Reader: A Life of Johann Sebastian Bach in Letters and Documents*, New York: W.W. Norton & Co.

FORBES, E. (ed.) (1967) *Thayer's Life of Beethoven*, Princeton: Princeton University Press.

GEIRINGER, K. (with Geiringer, I.) (1968) *Haydn: A Creative Life in Music*, Berkeley and Los Angeles: University of California Press.

GRANT, K. (1983) *Dr. Burney as Critic and Historian of Music*, Ann Arbor: University of Michigan Press.

HICKS, A. 'Handel: the manuscripts and the music', in J. Simon (ed.) *Handel: A Celebration of his Life and Times, 1685–1759*, London: National Portrait Gallery, pp. 18–24.

HOGWOOD, C. (1984) *Handel*, London: Thames & Hudson.

KELLY, M. (1826) *Reminiscences*, London: H. Colburn; critical edn ed. R. Fiske 1975, London: Oxford University Press.

KING, A.H. (1967) *Handel and his Autographs*, London: British Museum.

KIVY, P. (1964) 'Mainwaring's *Handel*: its relation to English Aesthetics', *Journal of the American Musicological Society* 17: 170–8.

KUHN, T. (1970) *The Structure of Scientific Revolutions*, 2nd edn, Chicago: The University of Chicago Press.

LANG, P.H. (1966) *George Frideric Handel*, New York: W.W. Norton & Co.

LOWINSKY, E.E. (1964) 'Musical genius – evolution and origins of a concept', *Musical Quarterly* 1: 321–40, 476–95.

MAINWARING, J. (1760) *Memoirs of the Life of the Late George Frideric Handel*, London: R. & J. Dodsley; facsimile edn, 1975, Buren: Frits Knuf.

MATTHEWS, B. (1959) 'Unpublished letters concerning Handel', *Music and Letters* 40: 263–4.

PETTY, F.C. (1980) *Italian Opera in London 1761–1800*, Ann Arbor: UMI Research Press.

PLEASANTS, H. (1955) *The Agony of Modern Music*, New York: Simon & Schuster.

ROBERTS, J. (1987) 'The "Sweet Song" in *Demofoonte*: a Gluck borrowing from Handel', paper presented at the Annual Meeting of the American Musicological Society, New Orleans.

WEBER, W. (1984) 'The contemporaneity of eighteenth-century musical taste', *Musical Quarterly*, 70: 175–94.

11

On Patronage: 'Musicke, that Mind-tempering Art'

The Role of Patron and Artist as Revealed in the Dedicatory Material in the English Lute-song Books

ANTHONY ROOLEY

Music was believed by many to be nothing, literally, but a motion of the air.
(Finney 1962: 158)

After seven superb and masterly chapters reviewing Renaissance atti-tudes to music, Gretchen L. Finney concludes with this bald statement of the view of music held by English society at the end of the seventeenth century. We are precipitated into the modern world of objective thought where observation and scientific pragmatism hold sway, and provable facts carry more force than intuition and ancient authority.

Gretchen L. Finney has given us here the most penetrating study available of the mental attitudes which prevailed, in relation to music, before the advance of scientific observation. The worlds of sympathetic magic, Neo-platonism and the divine origins of music are examined, using quotations as undeniable proof that, for the Renaissance mind, music was a very different experience and one capable – in opposition to the later view – of bringing about the soul's union with God.

The pragmatic musicologist labours under considerable difficulties when studying the backgrounds to European musical culture before 1650, for the world of thought prior to that date is in direct opposition to his or her training. Modern frames of reference clash, in harsh dissonances, with earlier views (see, for example, Tillyard 1943). Frequently, a selection process is set in motion, whereby data which support a thesis are brought forward, and any which are antagonistic are suppressed; or at best considered to be beside the point. This is especially true of the peripheral, non-musical data which surrounds music publications such as the English lute-song books between 1597 and 1622. There is a history of recent scholarship scouring the dedications and prefaces to these works for scraps of information on biographical details, or for facts on musical performance. These gleanings are deemed important, because they have bearing on the current emphasis upon dates, facts and figures; but the fact that this emphasis is a modern distortion, and that the written material originally had wholly different functions to perform, is overlooked. There is even a note of irritation as the musicologist complains that the original writer spent too much time on 'gross flattery', 'rhetorical clichés', 'stock ideas' or 'vapid Platonism'.

Of course, this prefatory material can yield useful information, and it can lead to creative speculation about matters of musical performance.[1] But this is of secondary importance. The primary intentions of the original writers must be understood, and understood within their own frames of reference. Our knowledge of the history of ideas can be much enriched by such an approach, for the writers indicate – unwittingly almost – the underlying values of their age.

The title of this essay is taken from the dedication to Robert, Earl of Salisbury, in John Dowland's 1609 translation of the *Micrologus* of Ornithoparcus. This dedication, in its use of rhetoric and formality, in its reiteration of tradition and ancient beliefs, is typical of the period. It is of interest precisely because it is so very unexceptional and commonplace:

> Every Plant brings forth his like, and of Musitians, *Musicke* is the fruit. Moreover such is your divine Disposition that both you excellently understand, and royally entertaine the Exercise of Musicke, which mind-tempering Art, the grave *Luther* was not affraid to place in the next seat to Divinity. My daily prayers (which are a poore mans best wealth) shall humbly sollicite the Author of all Harmonie for a continuall encrease of your Honors present happinesse with long life, and a successive blessing to your generous posteritie.
>
> Your Lordships humbly devoted
> John Dowland

Throughout the dedications, with hardly an exception, there is a theme or series of related themes with endless variations. All the dedications have great individuality and wit, but all follow a convention which, for the writers at least and presumably for the dedicatees, had aspects clearly defined and a procedure for unfolding laid down according to tradition.

A brief gloss on the above quotation will help to draw the chief ingredients forward, so that the convention may emerge. The first metaphor is based on the concept of 'sympathy' – that 'like attracts like' – though here clothed in a rather obvious platitude. The 'divine Disposition' of the patron refers not so much to the patron being God incarnate, which would be thought of as blasphemy and over-stated hyperbole, but rather that the position of patronage is one which allows divine inspiration or guidance to flow. To 'excellently understand, and royally entertaine' indicates that, in common with all good patrons, Sir Robert has clear judgement and insight into the art of music in its conceptual or speculative aspect, he provides in bountiful measure opportunities for musical performance.

'The Exercise of Musicke' reveals that music was used not only for entertainment, but was also thought to be a fruitful activity for self-development. The next phrase, 'which mind-tempering Art', states exactly how this development could take place: by strengthening the mind in virtue and resolution. By calling on 'the grave Luther', the dedication enlists the support of established authority which no man would question; and, since Luther 'was not afraid to place [music] in the next seat to Divinity', lesser men should not hesitate to follow his lead. The study of theology must come first; for all knowledge flows from God, but for music to be allowed the second rank shows the esteem in which this highest of arts was held. For 'My daily prayers' we must take Dowland at his word so far as the regularity of his supplications is concerned. The fact that prayers 'are a poore mans best wealth' reflects not material poverty, as we might suppose, but that the position of the artist is poore, or lowly, in relation to the patron. Dowland will 'humbly sollicite the Author of all Harmonie', reflecting his belief in a theocentric universe and the divine origins of music. The 'generous posteritie' wished on the patron reveals the belief that a patron's actions resound long after his death and provide a model of felicity for successive generations. For Dowland to be 'humbly devoted' requires only that he should play the appropriate role of the servant, the mean artist, to his Lord who has shown special favours and grace.

Rather than 'gross flattery', this dedication is a superb example of the time-honoured format, laid down by tradition and venerated by the whole of Renaissance society. It is, in its own way, a work of art, showing as fine a control and craftsmanship as Dowland reveals in his songs. He proves his skill with the language and his intimate understanding of the rules of oratory and the fine use of figures of speech. His is indeed the art of *The Garden of Eloquence*, to borrow the title of a book written by his friend Henry Peacham, printed in 1577. The formalism and balanced rhetoric in this dedication make it a model of its kind, and the content is an inspired reiteration of that which was common to all but a tiny handful of the lute-song books.

The essential theme which emerges from a study of the song book dedications is that music is of divine origin and is made available to all men for their entertainment and improvement. There are clearly definable stages of the journey of this divine gift, and the essential structure lying behind the individual dedications is hierarchical. The hierarchy may be discerned as functioning on seven levels (see Figure 11.1), with the roles of patron and artist placed centrally. This arrangement reflects, of course, the grand hierarchy of the whole of creation, conceived traditionally as 'the great chain

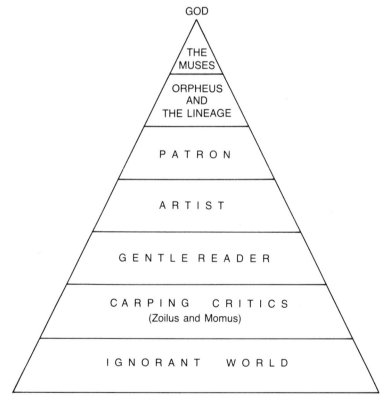

Figure 11.1 The seven levels of hierarchy, as perceived in England in the late sixteenth and early seventeenth centuries

of being', wherein Man (the active agent) and Angels occupied the central places (see Lovejoy 1971). Just as Ptolemy's view of the universe functioned by a moving arrangement of wheels within wheels, so the Renaissance view of creation perceived hierarchies within hierarchies.

Not all the dedications choose to elaborate on the whole architecture: several dwell, understandably, on the role of the patron, since this is central, active and germane to the material in hand. But all the dedications, without exception, have the hierarchical structure as a backcloth to which they refer in varying degrees. A number of them provide as lucid an explanation of the renaissance philosophy of music as one might expect to find (outside a work of philosophy), proving, in passing, that the practical musicians we now admire only for their music were sufficiently conversant with the speculative aspect of music to write beautiful or witty prose, and even on occasion poetry, embodying those subtle ideas.

The general philosophical outline, supported by contemporary authority from a variety of sources, may be revealed as follows.

First, and above all, the divine origin of music was never questioned, let alone denied, and was often referred to: 'God himself is entitled to Musique, it being even his owne spirits most sweet inspiration' (Porter 1632).[2] Sometimes, though, the words would be in pagan guise and addressed to Apollo, the sun-god: 'It is no disparagement to the glorious Sunne, that it discends to fructifie and illustrate the low and humble Vallies' (Attey 1622). That the unassailably divine origin of music was so much a commonplace in Renaissance thought was largely due to the inspiration of the Florentine philosopher, Marsilio Ficino, active at the end of the fifteenth century. His views and teachings were thoroughly disseminated through the whole of Europe by many important writers. The question of music's origin is summed up in his letter 'On divine frenzy':

> The soul receives the sweetest harmonies and numbers through the ears, and by these echoes is reminded and aroused to the divine music which may be heard by the more subtle and penetrating sense of mind. According to the followers of Plato, divine music is twofold. One kind, they say, exists entirely in the eternal mind of God. The second is in the motions and order of the heavens, by which the heavenly spheres and their orbits make a marvellous harmony. In both of these our soul took part before it was imprisoned in our bodies. But it uses the ears as messengers, as though they were chinks in this darkness. By the ears, as I have already said, the soul receives the echoes of that incomparable music, by which it is led back to the deep and silent memory of the harmony which it previously enjoyed. The whole soul then

230

kindles with desire to fly back to its rightful home, so that it may enjoy that true music again.

(Ficino 1495: 45)

Second, and in amplification of the nature of this divine gift, music was seen to embrace Harmony, Concord and Number, all qualities belonging to the Divine and emanating from Him. Each of these three qualities had three aspects and were personified in the Nine Muses. The muses were called on for inspiration, for without them no work of art could emerge. Their inspiration, as a medium for communicating divine inspiration, was vital. The very name of the art reflects, of course, its debt to the Muses, and the 'Lady Music' proved to be a popular and long-lasting personification.

A dedication which suitably illustrates the importance of Harmony is one by William Corkine, in his *Second Book of Ayres*, 1612, where harmony is mentioned six times (six being the number of harmony in Renaissance numerological lore; see, for example, Butler (1970)). The work is dedicated to the brothers Sir Robert and Sir Henry Rich:

> In your truely Noble affections there is an heav'nly harmonie, by the operation of Grace; in your corporall constitution, an harmony of the Elements, by the highest art of Nature; in your heroicall carriage and actions, an harmonie by the worke of wel-discerning Judgement; and, in all, such an highly-commended symphonie each with other, that to no two (as One) could I more properly consecrate the ensuing Accents, comming from and tending to Harmonie, then to you. If then they like you, it argues them most harmonious, sith like loves the like. But howsoever, I humbly referre both my selfe and them, to your favour and good opinion; which with my harts-joy makes such harmonie, as Amphions sweetest straines cannot halfe so much glad mee; Ever remayning, the humble honourer and admirer of your heroicall perfections.
>
> (Corkine 1612)

This rich dedication reveals a great deal. Three kinds of harmony are described; they belong to the patrons and arise out of their several qualities:

1 Heavenly harmonie/through Grace/Noble affections.
2 Harmony of the Elements/through Nature/Corporall constitution.
3 Harmonie/through Judgement/heroicall actions.

These three kinds of harmony interplay and unite in a 'symphonie', making the dedication of a musical work, which itself has three harmonies, an appropriate signification of the patrons' 'Heroical perfections'. To Lucy, Countess of Bedford, Dowland writes: 'as to the worthiest Patronesse, of Musicke: which is the Noblest of all sciences: for the whole frame of Nature,

231

is nothing but Harmonie, as wel in soules, as bodies' (Dowland 1600).

The idea of concord, used frequently in poetry drawing on musical imagery, is – naturally enough in the lute-song books – linked with the marriage of words and music. As Dowland says in the dedication to his first book of songs (1597): 'This small Booke contayning the consent of speaking harmony, joyned with the most musicall instrument the lute'. Again he gives us a clear statement on music as the art of number: 'That harmony (Right Honourable) which is skilfully exprest by Instruments, albeit, by reason of the variety of number and proportion, of it selfe, it easily stirres up the mindes of the hearers to admiration and delight.' Later he amplifies this by drawing in words: 'harmony, naked of it selfe: words the ornament of harmony, number the common friend and uniter of them both'. Thus, in this extract, all three concepts, harmony, concord and number, are united.

At the next stage of the hierarchy, the dedications are unanimous in calling on ancient authority for verification of their claims for the power of music. Classical and biblical exegeses were used in all branches of learning to provide stable reference points, and music was no exception. Both speculative and practical aspects of music are thus supported by 'Antiquitie'. The authorities most frequently cited include King David, Pythagoras, Plato, Linus, Orpheus, Arion, Amphion, Aristoxenus, the Church Fathers, Boethius, and more nearly contemporary opinion, such as we have already seen with Luther. We can trace through this list (which could be extended greatly if we drew on wider sources than the dedications) a line of teachers who pass on a pristine knowledge or awareness of music's divine power. The weight of the ancients' authority could not easily be gainsaid, and the reiteration of their names was tantamount to calling for their aid and protection. The idea of sympathetic magic, of borrowing or drawing power, is not far removed from the roll-call of pristine teachers whose qualities were summoned by their naming. Dowland once more tells us:

> Hence (as all antiquity can witnesse) first grew the heavenly Art of Musicke: for *Linus Orpheus* and the rest, according to the number and time of their Poems, first framed the numbers and times of Musicke: So that *Plato* defines Melodie to consist of harmony, number and words.
>
> (Dowland 1597)

Here we have three authorities mentioned by name; 'and the rest' implies all the other ancient teachers. His patron (Sir George Carey) and his public would have been easily able to complete the list.

The next level, the position of the patron, is understandably the feature which dominates the dedications. That is, after all, what the dedication is there for, so it is no surprise to find the importance of the patron a recurrent theme. What we can find, however, is a far deeper understanding of the conceptual view of the role of the patron in the support of the art of music. Although all seven levels of the hierarchy must be occupied and in operation, and a state of interdependence governs all, it is the middle position which is the active or dominant role and is the point in the world where action is initiated. The patron becomes the mediator, directing the artist's endeavours to higher levels, and the means of communicating the inspiration of the muses, or the knowledge of ancient authority, to the artist. His position is the point of balance, the fulcrum, the insight of the patron allowing the pythagorean concept of the golden mean to be manifest; through his aid, all is in just proportion.

Because things work so differently in our own time, we may be somewhat disbelieving of this all-important role of patronage. Our cynicism would encourage a view of the artist as having the active role, though he might pay lip-service to the patron's greater insight in order to curry favour and advancement. It is probable that by the end of the sixteenth century the hierarchical view of patronage was beginning to deteriorate, and that the integrated, interdependent system known to the Florentine court around Lorenzo de' Medici was already a matter of history. Our desire to find modern attitudes as early as possible in history tends too easily to encourage a modern interpretation. England, in particular, nurtured a conservative view of hierarchical structure, whatever the subject, for considerably longer than the rest of Europe, and we should, perhaps, look upon the Civil War as the watershed of the transition from the old world to the new, with the attendant regrets and jubilations.

It has been shown conclusively that the position held by Elizabeth I as Queen was enough to warrant her divine insight and power. She was clearly very much a woman, and a difficult one at that by the end of her life, but her *position* was seen to allow for the manifestation of divine order (see Yates 1975); it was her duty to fill that role with all the sincerity she could muster. She was, of course, the nation's chief patron, and her largesse, insight and generosity provided a model of conduct for her numerous courtiers. Her tastes dictated the tastes of the court; and, thanks to her penetrating mind, the arts flourished as never before under the patronage of her noblemen. Contemporaries were conscious of this and were extremely grateful; and artists were quick to channel that insight and understanding. Many were the lamentations after the accession of James I, for then patronage was weaker and altogether less intelligent.

The song book dedications reveal the force and value of patronage as it was manifest in the last years of Elizabeth's reign, even though they continued to appear for a further twenty years. Dowland's first epoch-making book of songs set a pattern as much in this as in other aspects:

> This small booke ... I have presumed to dedicate to your Lordship, who for your vertue and nobility are best able to protect it, and for your honourable favors towards me, best deserving my duety and service. Besides your noble inclination and love to all good Artes, and namely the divine science of musicke, doth challenge the patronage of all learning, then which no greater title can bee added to Nobilitie.

> (Dowland 1597)

Though this dedication provided a pattern for lute-song books, Dowland was far from being the originator of the style. His was a refined contribution to the formal artist's address to his patron, modelled, no doubt uncon-sciously, on Ficino's address to Lorenzo de' Medici. Of the many examples which could be quoted to demonstrate the central role of patronage, this, by John Bartlet to Sir Edward Seymoore, sets the tone immediately:

> It is a question hardly to be determined (my most honorable Lord) whether Musicke may esteeme her selfe more graced by the singular skil and exquisite knowledge wherwith your Lordship is indued, both in the speculation and practise thereof: or by the many benefites, and infinite favours your Honour-able bountie hath conferred on the professors of that faculty: in both are the muses greatly honoured, and we (their servants) highly blest; whose vertuous endevours and studious labours, not in this onely, but in many other kindes of Learning, have received their life, growth, and perfection, chereshed and enabled by the warmth your beames have cast upon them.

> (Bartlet 1606)

Bartlet's plan here is quite clear. Seymoore is cast in the role of Apollo by the use of the sun metaphor at the end, thus allowing the conceit that the muses and the Lady Musicke herself are indebted to his insight and understanding. Gross flattery or a fine piece of formal rhetoric? Surely Seymoore, with a fraction of the insight granted him by Bartlet, would have seen through such tasteless flattery instantly – a sure way of *not* receiving patronage one would have thought. But these conventions were employed precisely because they were found to be efficacious; they had currency, they worked and they were believed in. It is not that Seymoore becomes Apollo – that would be a ludicrous idea – but that his position is Apollo-like, and his role as patron is a similitude of Apollo, allowing Apollonian attributes to manifest themselves through him. Seymoore's role as patron would be supported and confirmed by his reading the dedication, for he cannot but have enjoyed the conceit which Bartlet uses with a certain freshness and individuality.

The patron is, by implication, endowed with the following powers:

1   He is granted understanding on the speculative and practical levels.
2   His discrimination and judgement of art come from his own knowledge and the artist hopes he will receive the present work with favour.
3   His lofty position allows him to offer protection to the artist not only materially, but in the sense of a source of inspiration to the artist.
4   His patronage will allow his name to be perpetuated for posterity and will act as an inspiration for future generations of his line.
5   The artist hopes to be allowed to act as the patron's devoted servant so that future works might improve on the quality of the present offering and allow the production of something more nearly worthy of such patronage.

This may appear to us as a rather convoluted way of thinking, but it was a system which worked. Whilst both parties believed in it, the art produced under the system tended towards excellence.

Let us now look at the fifth level: the position of the artist. This statement by Francis Pilkington, about himself, is typical: 'For mine owne part (who am meanest of many which professe this divine skill, though not meanest in good will and humble affection to your Honor) I must confess my selfe many waies obliged to your Lordships familie' (Pilkington 1605).

From a modern viewpoint, such a statement conjures an image of Pilkington as a cringing Uriah Heep character, filled with false modesty and a slippery scheming mind which works by ingratiating through flattery. That Pilkington had more wit than this can be guessed by judging the quality of his songs: they reveal a literary mind and a sharply focused intellect, sensitive to subtle turns of phrase. Such a man wrote such a dedication in full knowledge of the effect his words would have. He is clearly contributing to a convention in making such a statement about himself. That it was not an empty convention can be gauged by the fact that almost all the lute-song book composers subscribed to it; they are simply elaborating on a convention which for them is part of a pre-ordained cosmic order. The 'poor artist', as we might term him, was every bit as important as the 'honourable patron', although lower down the hierarchical scale. He must judge his works 'lowly' or 'never-so-meane', otherwise the grand order will become unbalanced and chaos will ensue. Such phrases as: 'the poornes of my merit holds least proportion with the largenes of your grace' (Bartlet 1606), ensure that the patron and artist keep their due stations. Of course, the artist hopes that others, particularly the patron, will view the works with greater favour than the artist himself, but that must depend on others' judgement.

Writers often show fertile imagination when declaring their position as the 'poor artist':

> I shall esteeme my selfe abundantly graced, if under the Noble protection of your Honours, I may by this meanes but vindicate my selfe from being held a Drone in the mellifluous garden of the MUSES, and contribute but the smallest drop to the immense Ocean of this divine knowledge.
>
> (Attey 1622)

We must surely assume that their originality of expression within the convention was considered part of their artistic merit; that is, they proved their wit and skill by the clever ways in which they expressed their lowliness. Metaphors tend to recur, for the images were themselves meaningful emblems which had wide currency throughout the period. The bee image used by Attey, recurs several times, particularly when the artist speaks of his 'poor labours'. Since the product of the artist was more often spoken of than himself, his 'fruits' are frequently described as being of little worth.

Robert Jones always writes with wit and originality – witness any one of his five dedications – but he creates a particularly clever conceit at the beginning of the dedication of his second book of songs:

> Worthy Sir, and my Honourable friend: I give you this *Child*, I pray you bring it up, because I am a poore man and cannot maintain it: it may suffer much adversitie in my name: your Fortune maie alter his starres and make him happie. Though his Father be alive, I maie call him an *Orphane*, for poore mens *Children* are *Orphanes borne*.
>
> (Jones 1601)

This can hardly have failed to beguile Sir Henry Leonard, the patron. The child image was used, perhaps to less telling effect, by several other writers.

The humility and devotion professed at the close of the dedications before signing the name must also be taken directly at face value. The hierarchical nature of the society, in which every man knew his place, may be abhorrent to twentieth-century liberal thought, but we feel the artist's gratitude at knowing where he stood. Terms such as 'devotion' and 'duty' meant what they said, and to sign oneself as a 'servant' did not imply belittlement, but rather the opposite – a sense of pride in serving so worthy a patron.

Immediately below the humble artist (eager to be servant to his admired, hoped-for patron) was the level of the 'gentle Reader', the judicious purchaser of the volume of songs. Now here is a shift from our contemporary outlook, for in our consumer world the buyer is paramount – modern goods are made first and foremost for selling. Not so for the lute-song volumes, whose prime function was to be a lasting monument to the patron. Economic production can hardly have been possible for either the composer or his printer without a large subvention from the patron – the public took second place. Whilst in the many addresses 'to the Reader' in the lute-song book prefaces the composer is keen to have the good judgement of his reader, the terms of address are very different from those employed for the patron. This new category are gentlemen, rather than nobles, as Jones makes explicit: 'To the Reader. Gentlemen ... my desire is your eares should be my indifferent judges' (Jones 1600). Jones expands on this the following year in his second collection of ayres:

To the Reader.

Reader, I have once more adventured to aske thy counsell, whether I have done well, or no; in taking thus much pains to please thee ... my intent towards thee was good. ... I hold it no shame to crave uprightnesse in thy censure

(Jones 1601)

A hint of abrasiveness might be discerned here, a tendency which becomes wholly manifest as we descend to the next, sixth level of the hierarchy, since there is a real opportunity built into the system for denigration. All above the artist were praiseworthy; all below him could legitimately be criticized. This was done by censure of any critics of the work, and the extreme bitterness of some of these outbursts may come as a surprise after all that has been said earlier. Such is the vitriolic nature of the attacks on critics that modern commentators have often assumed it to have been caused by specific events in the lives of the authors. No doubt there were occasions when this was so; for example, in John Coprario's *Funeral Teares* (1606), which lament the death of Charles Blount. The special circumstances immediately prior to Blount's death had caused society to criticize him rather harshly, and so this volume was used as an opportunity to clear his name and to attack his detractors. But it is something of a special case.

In fact, as with all seven aspects of the dedication formula, the convention of protecting yourself from critics by attacking them first has its roots in antiquity. The first named malignant critic was Zoilus, born at Amphipolis in the third century BC. He was a Greek rhetorician of some small ability who vociferously attacked Homer. The bitterness of his attacks assured him a place in history, and in order to avoid poor Homer's predicament (he couldn't defend himself, for he was long dead), it became the practice to pre-empt any future Zoilus by beating the critic at his own game. This led to some unusual outbursts which, superficially, appear out of character, but are in fact part of the clever game of giving new life to old conventions.

Sometimes the writer mentions possible censure only in passing: 'yeelding my private inventions subject to publicke censure' (Corkine 1610); or 'if your Clemencie shall allowe it favourable roome, I feare not the unequallest front of the sowrest Criticke' (Maynarde 1611). But on other occasions the warding off of criticism becomes the major concern, next to the praise of the patron. Robert Jones takes this feature a step further, and over the course of his five dedications develops an elaborate conceit out of rather unpromising material. One can imagine his public anxiously awaiting yet another book of ayres by Jones, not so much for his songs (they did tend to go off a little towards the end!) but more for the latest instalment of his contrived defence against criticism. One must marvel, as well as smile, at his exotic inventions. This is how he begins in the first book.

> With so none greater enimies to their owne profession then Musicians; who whilst in their owne singuaritie, they condemne every mans workes, as some waie fauty, they are the cause, the art is the lesse esteemed, and they themselves reputed as selfe-commenders, and men most fantasticall. Wherfore if this one censuring infirmitie were removed, these my ayres (free I dare say from grosse errours) would find every where more gratious entertainement. But since even those, who are best seen in this art, cannot vaunt themselves free from such detractours, I the lesse regard it being so well accompanied.
>
> (Jones 1600)

It is clear from this that Jones is playing a game and enjoying it. It would be rewarding to follow his serialization of critical abuse in detail. This preoccupation can be seen even in the heading of the address 'To the Reader'. His first two books are so styled, following formality, and contain much which is censuring horse-play. The third book address is headed 'To the Silent Hearer', the fourth 'To all Musicall Murmurers', and the fifth 'To the friendly Censures'. The contents of all these dwell on what critics are purported to have said of the previous publications, and what Jones would like to say to them if he met them. This is how he greets his 'Musicall Murmurers':

Thou, whose eare itches with the varietie of opinion, hearing thine owne sound, as the Ecchoe reverberating others substance, and unprofitable in it selfe, shewes to the World comfortable noyse, though to thy owne use little pleasure, by reason of uncharitable censure.

(Jones 1609)

His conclusion is even more forceful:

Give me leave to depart, or if not, without it I am gone, carelesse of thy censuring, and fully perswaded thou canst not thinke well, and therefore art curst in thy Cradle, never to be but cruell, and being borne with teeth in thy head, bitst every one harmelesse in this or what else honest industry, makes they eare gossip too. Farewell if thou wilt in kindness, or hold thy selfe from further carping.

(Jones 1609)

Francis Pilkington's use of the same convention seems dry by contrast – '... if it may gaine your gracious acceptation, will fear neither *Zoilus* nor *Momus* his reprehension' (Pilkington 1605), but it does link the convention directly with the classical story.

The seventh stage may be treated briefly, for it is, in a sense, a continuation of the previous point, differing from it only in degree. The critics may be granted some understanding – after all Zoilus was a Rhetorician, if a bad one; but the ignorant majority, the world at large, lie even lower. This lowest of the low was 'the ignorant world' which, through its baseness, could only be expected to react to art with maliciousness, envy and total incomprehension. Dowland separates the sheep from the goats in the following manner:

... so in the house of learning and fame, all good indevourers should strive to ad somewhat that is good, not malicing one an other, but altogether bandying against the idle and malicious ignorant.

(Dowland 1603)

The fear of ignorance and its all-engulfing dark power was a threat of the worst kind to the Elizabethan, who so dearly treasured his education. 'Casting pearl before swine' was probably much more alive in meaning for them than it is for us today.

Finally, not as another stage but more a return to the first, it was the fundamental duty of the servant to pray for his lord. To wish that God would grant long life, happiness and prosperity (and not just so that the artist could have a little) to the patron. Even this formal close to a dedication

was handled with wit, skill and individuality. Dowland, in the final dedication of *The Pilgrimes Solace* (1612) makes this promise to his new patron,
Theophilus, Lord Walden, who was many years his junior:

> In the meane time you shall have a poore mans praiers for your Lordships
> continuall health and dayly increase of Honor.
>
> Your Honours
> humble servant
> John Dowland

As ever, Robert Jones finds an individual solution to this most formal of
closes. His patron for the third book of songs (1605) is the potential future
Myceanas of the arts in Britain, the ill-fated Henry, Prince of Wales:

> Thus praying, that your Highnes may always have an eare able to endure and
> distinguish, the sound of truth, I kneele at your Highnes feet.
>
> Your Highnes in all humble dutie and service
> Robert Jones

Five complete dedications by Dowland, Jones, Corkine and Bartlet are
appended (Figures 11.2–6): they represent the rhetorical art of dedication
writing at its height. In them, the several levels of organization discussed
here can be observed (though hidden with skill and handled with consummate artistry).

What emerges from this inquiry is that, in an age when artists are
generally acknowledged to have flourished (after all, we commonly call this
the English 'Golden Age'), everyone knew their place! The artist was not
alone in his garret; he did not have to sue to an Arts Council bound in
bureaucracy, nor to fly-by-night sponsors demanding their pound of flesh.
Indeed, these artists knew their place in society *and* their potential for
raising essential support. In this, they were no different from their forebears
in the Medici society of fifteenth-century Florence, in ancient Egypt, or in
ancient China. Only today are artists without a social philosophy which
integrates support from above with that from below.

TO THE RIGHT HONO-
RABLE *ROBERT* EARLE OF
Salisbury, Vifcount *Cranborne,* Baron of *Eſſingdon,*
Lord High *Treaſurer* of *England,* Principall *Secretarie* to the Kings moſt
excellent Maieſtie, Maiſter of the Courts of Wards and Liueries,
Chancellor of the moſt famous Vniuerſitie of Cambridge, *Knight*
of the moſt Noble Order of the Garter, and one of his Maiefties
moſt honourable Priuie Counfell.

Our high Place, your princely Honours and Ver-
tues, the hereditary vigilance and wiſedome, wher-
with Hercules-*like, you aſſiſt the protection of the*
whole State : Though theſe (moſt honoured Lord)
are powerfull encitements to draw all ſorts to the
deſire of your moſt Noble protection. Yet beſides all
theſe (*in more particular by your Lordſhips ſpeciall Fauors and Gra-*
ces*) am I emboldened to preſent this Father of Muſicke* Ornithopar-
chus *to your worthyeſt Patronage, whoſe approoued Workes in my tra-*
uailes (*for the common good of our Muſitians*) *I haue reduced into our*
Engliſh Language. Beſeeching your Lordſhip (as a chiefe Author of all
our good) graciouſly to receiue this poore preſentment, whereby your
Lordſhip ſhall encourage me to a future taſke, more new in ſubiect, and
as memorable in worth. Euery Plant brings forth his like, and of Mu-
ſitians, Muſicke *is the fruit. Moreouer ſuch is your diuine Diſpoſi-*
tion that both you excellently vnderſtand, and royally entertaine the
Exerciſe of Muſicke, which mind-tempering Art, the graue Luther
was not affraid to place in the next ſeat to Diuinity. My daily prayers
(*which are a poore mans beſt wealth*) *ſhall humbly ſollicite the Author*
of all Harmonie for a continuall encreaſe of your Honors preſent happi-
neſſe with long life, and a ſucceſſiue bleſſing to your generous poſteritie.

Your Lordſhips humbly deuoted

Iohn Dowland.

Figure 11.2 John Dowland's dedication of his translation of the *Micrologus* of Ornithoparcus
to Robert, Earl of Salisbury

241

TO THE RIGHT HONOVRA-
BLE SIR George Carey, OF THE MOST HO-
NORABLE ORDER OF THE GARTER
Knight; Baron of Hunſdon, Captaine of her Maieſties Gentlemen *Penſioners, Gouernour of the Iſle of Wight, Lieutenant*
of the County of Southt: Lord Chamberlaine of her Maieſties moſt royall Houſe, and of her Highneſſe moſt
Honorable Priuy Councell.

That harmony (right Honourable) which is skilfully expreſt by In-
ſtruments, albeit, by reaſon of the variety of number and proportion,
of it ſelfe, it eaſily ſtirres vp the mindes of the hearers to admiration
and delight, yet for higher authority and power hath beene euer wor-
thily attributed to that kind of Muſicke, which to the ſweetneſſe of
Inſtrument applyes the liuely voyce of man, expreſing ſome worthy
ſentence or excellent Poeme. Hence (as all antiquity can witneſſe)
firſt grew the heauenly Art of Muſicke: for *Linus Orpheus* and the
reſt, according to the number and time of their Poems, firſt framed
the numbers and times of Muſicke: So that *Plato* defines Melodie to
conſiſt of harmony, number, and words; harmony, naked of it ſelfe;
words the ornament of harmony, number the common friend and
vniter of them both. This ſmall Booke contayning the conſent of ſpeaking harmony, ioyned with
the moſt muſicall inſtrument the Lute, being my firſt labour, I haue preſumed to dedicate to your
Lordſhip, who for your vertue and Nobility are beſt able to protect it; and for your Honourable fauours towards me, beſt deſeruing my duety and ſeruice. Beſides, your noble inclination and loue to
all good Artes, and namely the diuine ſcience of Muſicke, doth challenge the patronage of all learning,
then which no greater title can be added to Nobility. Neyther in theſe your honors may I let paſſe
the dutifull remembrance of your vertuous Ladie my honorable Miſtreſſe, whoſe ſingular graces towards me haue added ſpirit to my vnfortunate laboure. What time and diligence I haue beſtowed in
the ſearch of Muſicke, what trauell in forraine Countries, what ſucceſſe and eſtimation euen amongſt
ſtrangers I haue found, I leaue to the report of others. Yet all this in vaine, were it not that your honorable hands haue vouchſaft to vphold my poore fortunes: which I now wholly recommend to your
gracious protection, with theſe my firſt endeuours, humbly beſeeching you to accept and cheriſh them
with your continued fauours.

Your Lordſhips moſt humble ſeruant,

IOHN DOVVLAND.

Figure 11.3 John Dowland's dedication of his first book of lute-songs to Sir George Carey

TO THE GREAT IOY AND
HOPE OF PRESENT AND FUTURE
Times, HENRIE Prince of *Wales*, Duke Of Cornwall.
Earle of the *Countie Palatine of Chester*, Knight *of the Honourable Order of the Garter*, Heyre Apparant to the Realmes of *England*, Scotland, France and Ireland.

MOſt Excellent *Prince, The ſtrength of our Art, (I ſhould ſay, the weakenes,) cannot endure the force of Soueraigne Uertue come neare it, we may,* as neare *as to you , your Eares will yet beare to deale with ſoundes , though not to dwell there, yet to paſſe by them, and by them to learne to tune ſenſes in a riper age. Almoſt all our knowledge is drawne through the ſenſes, they are the Soules Intelligencers, whereby ſhe paſſeth into the world, and the world into her, and amongſt all of them, there is none ſo learned, as the eare, none hath obtained ſo excellent an Art, ſo delicate, ſo abſtruſe, ſo ſpirituall, that it catcheth vp wilde ſoundes in the Aire, and bringes the vnder a gouernement not to be expreſſed, but done, and done by no skill but it owne. There is Muſicke in all thinges, but euery man cannot finde it out, becauſe of his owne iarring, hee muſt haue a harmony in himſelfe, that ſhold goe about it, and then he is in a good way, as he that hath a good eare, is in a good forwardnes to our facultie. Conceite is but a well tunde fancy, done in time and place. An excellent ſentence, is but a well tunde reaſon well knit together, Politie or the ſubiect therof, a Common wealth, is but a well tunde Song where all partes doe agree, and meete together, with full conſent and harmony one ſeruing other, and euery one themſelues in the ſame labour. But now I intrude into your Art, in which all pray (and ſee hopes) that God will giue you a godly and proſperous knowledge, and then all other Artes ſhal proſper vnder it. Our gracious Soueraign (Your Highnes dear Father) hath warmed and comforted ſome great profeſſions already, ſuch little ones as this, looke for it, and beg it of you, your princely nature promiſeth it, which makes my boldnes hope for pardon; Vouchſafe me (moſt excellent Prince) your Protection; whome you allow, all others will commend, their cenſures wait vpon your liking, that otherwiſe wold deſpiſe me. Euen your name in the forefront is a charme for malitious tongus. Thus praying, that your Highnes may alwayes haue an eare able to endure and diſtinguiſh, the ſound of truth, I kneele at your Highnes feet.*

Your Highnes in all humble
dutie and ſeruice

ROBERT

IONES

Figure 11.4   Robert Jones's dedication of his third book of songs to Henry, Prince of Wales

TO THE MOST NOBLE
AND VVORTHY BRETHREN,
S^r. *ROBERT*, AND S^r. *HENRY RICH*:
Knights of the Honourable Order of the
BATH.

 *IN your truely Noble* affections *there is an heau'nly* har-
monie, *by the operation of* Grace; *in your* corporall con-
ftitutions, *an* harmony *of the* Elements, *by the higheft* art
of Nature; *in your* heroicall carriage *and* actions, *an* harmonie *by the* w *rke of* wel-difcerning Iudgement; *and,*
in all, fuch an highly-commended fymphonie *each with other, that to no* two
(*as* One) *coula* J *more properly confecrate thefe enfuing* Accents, *comming*
from, *and tending* to Harmonie, *then to you. If then they like you, it argues*
them moft harmonious, *fith* like loues the like. *But howfoeuer,* J *humbly*
referre both my felfe *and* them, *to your* fauour *and* good opinion; *which*
with my harts-ioy *makes fuch* harmonie, *as* Amphions *fweeteft* ftraines
cannot halfe fo much glad mee; Euer remayning, the humble honourer and ad-
mirer of your heroicall perfections.

William Corkine.

Figure 11.5 William Corkine's dedication of his *Second Book of Ayres* to Sir Robert and Sir
Henry Rich

To the right honorable his fingular
good Lord and Maifter Sir Edvvard Seymoore.
*Knight, Baron Beacham, Earle of Hartfoord, and Lieftenant
of his Maieflies Counties of Somerfet and Wiltes.*

 T is a queftion hardly to be determined (my moft
honorable Lord) whether Muficke may efteeme
her felfe more graced by the fingular fkil & exqui-
fite knowledge wherwith your Lordfhip is indu-
ed, both in the fpeculation and practife thereof: or
by the many benefites, and infinite fauours your
Honourable bountie hath conferred on the profeffors of that faculty:
in both are the mufes greatly honoured, and we (their feruants) highly bleft; whofe vertuous endeuours and ftudious labours, not in this
onely, but in many other kindes of Learning, haue receiued their
life; growth, and perfection, cherefhed and enabled by the warmth
your beames haue caft vpon them. Amongft many, that on the Mufes behalfe doe owe your Lordfhippe the tribute of their pennes, I
muft profes my felf to ftand deeplieft engaged in the debt of dutie, in
that the poornes of my merit holds leaft proportiõ with the largenes
of your grace, and that my vtmoft defert can reach no further, then
humbly to acknowledge, that what delight or fweetenes, foeuer thefe
my fimple trauels may bring to fuch generous and well compofed
fpiritsas beare affection to this quality, was infpired me by no other
power then the influence of your fauour. And though the error of conceite cannot make me fo far ouervalew them, as to efteem
them worthy your Lordfhips iudicious hearing, yet I will confeffe
their want of worth (wherewith my felfe as an impartial cenfurer,
haue already iuftly taxte them) could not diuert my purpofe from
publifhing to the worldthe zeale I beare to thankefulneffe: wher-
in I am ambitious of nothing but your Lordfhippes fauourable acceptance and protection, which if it may pleafe you to vouchfafe to
this firft birth of my Mufe. I fhall then be as farre from fearing de-
traction and cenfure, as I am free from affecting glory and prayfe.

Your Lordfhips moft humble deuoted feruant,

A 2   IOHN BARTLET.

Figure 11.6 John Bartlet's dedication of *A Book of Ayres* to Sir Edward Seymoore

NOTES

1 For example, the important data contained in the oft-quoted prefaces of Dowland, Morley and Campion.
2 See also the preface to Alison (1606), using a poem by Dowland.
3 See F. A. Yates (1975).

REFERENCES

ALISON, R. (1606) *An Houres Recreation in Musicke*, reprinted 1960, London: Stainer & Bell.

ATTEY, J. (1622) *The First Book of Ayres*, facsimile edn 1967, Menston: Scolar Press.

BARTLET, J. (1606) *A Book of Ayres*, facsimile edn 1967, Menston: Scolar Press.

BUTLER, C. (1970) *Number Symbolism*, London: Routledge & Kegan Paul.

COPRARIO, J. (1606) *Funeral Teares*, facsimile edn 1978, Menston: Scolar Press.

CORKINE, W. (1610) *Ayres to Sing and Play*, facsimile edn 1970, Menston: Scolar Press.

——(1612) *Second Book of Ayres*, facsimile edn 1970, Menston: Scolar Press.

DOWLAND, J. (1597) *First Book of Songs*, facsimile edn 1973, Menston: Scolar Press.

——(1600) *Second Book of Songs*, facsimile edn 1970, Menston: Scolar Press.

——(1603) *The Third and Last Book of Songs*, facsimile edn 1970, Menston: Scolar Press.

——(1609) *Andreas Ornithoparcus – His Micrologus, or Introduction Containing the Art of Singing*, facsimile edn 1973, in *A Compendium of Musical Practice*, New York: Dover Publications.

——(1612) *A Pilgrimes Solace*, facsimile edn 1977, Menston: Scolar Press.

FICINO, M. (1495) *Letters Vol. 1*, trans. 1975, London: Shepheard-Walwyn.

FINNEY, G.L. (1962) *Musical Backgrounds for English Literature: 1581–1650*, New Brunswick, NJ: Rutgers University Press.

JONES, R. (1600) *First Book of Songes or Ayres*, facsimile edn 1970, Menston: Scolar Press.

——(1601) *Second Book of Songs or Ayres*, facsimile edn 1978, Menston: Scolar Press.

——(1605) *Ultimum Vale*, facsimile edn 1971, Menston: Scolar Press.

——(1609) *A Musicall Dreame*, facsimile edn 1967, Menston: Scolar Press.

LOVEJOY, A.O. (1971) *The Great Chain of Being*, Cambridge, Mass.: Harvard University Press.

MAYNARDE, J. (1611) *The XII Wonders of the World*, facsimile edn 1978, Menston: Scolar Press.

PEACHAM, H. (1577) *The Garden of Eloquence*, facsimile edn 1971, Menston: Scolar Press.

PILKINGTON, F. (1605) *The First Book of Songes or Ayres*, facsimile edn 1969, Menston: Scolar Press.

PORTER, W. (1632) *Madrigals and Ayres*, facsimile edn 1969, Menston: Scolar Press.

TILLYARD, E.M.W. (1943) *The Elizabethan World Picture*, Harmondsworth: Penguin.

YATES, F.A. (1975) *Astraea: The Imperial Theme in the Sixteenth Century*, London: Routledge & Kegan Paul.

12

Cloverleaf:
A Little Narrative with Several 'Off-ramps'

LOU HARRISON

Increasingly everyone in the USA, either singly or in groups, is continually 'wired for sound'. The electric umbilicus feeds from Mom and Mom is a rock band. Mom is Pop. I am in Los Angeles on a shuttle bus running between an elegant residential college downtown and the campus of the University of Southern California (USC) where I am composer-in-residence for two weeks. The young scholars with whom Bill [Colvig] and I ride the bus assume as a matter of course both the enormous noise of the commute and the loud overlay of speakered pop. I wad cotton, chew and wet it, and press it into both ears. I am saving some of myself for the lectures that I will have to give. The young ones doubtless have excesses of nerve, energy, wit and strength to waste, but their hearing impairments may turn up later.

*   *   *

Electric Amplification

Although it has been found that in some species the grassy sound-receptors of the inner ear will grow back after injury or destruction by too-great loudness, it is not yet known whether this is true in humans. Anyway, the musical falsification of the electronic 'enhancement' is not only almost inescapable in USA public halls, but is indeed preferred now, at least by city people. One supposes that urban ears are so used to industrial abuse that concerts for them must be 'turned up' to be heard.

248

Bill Colvig was given tickets to a San Francisco Opera presentation of Die
Frau ohne Schatten *a few years ago so that he might hear the tuned gongs
which he had made for the production. He remarked to me during the first scene
'this is hi-fi', and I replied 'surely not'. None the less, we finally went to the
men's room, rolled up wet toilet paper, and packed our ears with it. Soon someone
forgot to turn off the mikes and amplifiers during a scene change. The noise was
appalling. Works of mine have been seriously de-shaped by electronicians, and
Stephen Sondheim remembers 'the old days' (before amplifications) in Broadway
theatres in New York. At least one US composer has been sued (sudden loudness
or too-great loudness is physical attack and thus actionable), and the singer Cher
was made to pay a fine by the Las Vegas Musicians Union for pumping volume
too high. I have heard a conductor 'sweep off' into silence a brilliant loud climax,
followed immediately by cathedral echoes – in a tent! Reality ever diminishes.*

*　　*　　*

My two subjects are tuning and world music. The university systems in
California have somehow discovered that the state borders the Pacific Ocean
and that their enrolment is persuasively Asian. USC is a privately-funded
university, and my friend Anthony Vazzana has graciously invited me once
more to demonstrate in what ways I, as a composer, have worked in Asian
music and in what ways used my tuning studies. In a special small series
the Los Angeles Philharmonic has programmed my *Concerto in Slendro* for
performance exactly midway through my stay.

Asian accessibility also stirs studies in tuning. My intense interest in this,
together with my long-time friendship with Harry Partch and my more
recent connection with the Just Intonation Network, centred in San Francisco, underpin my two major lectures on the progress of tuning. The first,
already delivered, concerned (and in fair part made audible) the large section
of history from 1750 BC to the end of the Roman Empire and then through
the High Islamic period.

*　　*　　*

*I began my discourse with the demonstration of tablet U.7/80 (side two) from
Ur, written in Old Babylonian, from the British Museum. However, in many
Western musicians there is a disbelief that intervals exist in any real form anyway.
There are the Twelve Tones, no? – twelve fixed pitches, all equidistant, all
industrial grey. They were fixed in place in the early industrial revolution, and
are pushed by trusting music teachers (all of whom trust piano tuners) and by*

music departments which offer many courses of indoctrination and few indeed of investigation, at least of fundamental things. Michael Baxandall in Giotto and the Orators *says, 'So English has separate names for the colours "blue" and "green" where some other languages have not; linguists say blue–green is an area of experience "more differentiated" in English than in, say, Iakutu.' He also says, 'People who have separate words for the colours "orange" and "yellow" recognize and remember these two colours more efficiently than people who have one name covering both.'*

I think of professional musicians and twelve-tone equal temperament when he says, 'If a group of people is taught even temporary numerical names for each of a set of nine shades of grey, they will discriminate among these shades more efficiently than another group of people who have not been taught the numbers. It is intuitively obvious enough that learning a label for any class of phenomenon directs our attention to the quality by which the class is delimited. Any name becomes a selective sharpener of attention.' My contention is that alternatives ought to be offered. Why not 5/4, 8/7, 3/2, and others, rather than the multiples of a single surd, the twelve-tone equal half-step which can be approximated as circa 10,594,631 : 10,000,000. Why not reality and colour? In the great main music academy of Indonesia one studies ways in which a gamelan may be tuned. There are very few gamelans tuned alike. Truly, the virtues of equal temperament are almost entirely economic. It enables the selling of vast numbers of inter-changeable instruments, all playable with one another in a commercial repertory commercially spread almost planet-wide, appealing to the illiterate, and bypassing cultural history. In raising the basic pitch to A = 443 many serious symphonic musicians give evidence of trying to regain at least some control over basic musical matters.

* * *

During the coming week I will begin in north-west Asia (i.e. Europe) from about 1400, and bring the matter as up-to-date as possible in the time allotted.

* * *

A Further Thought about Kirnberger II

Some years ago, through constant use of our harpsichord and virginals, I began to realize that the third A/ Db in this tuning was surprisingly good, and I observed that it is not directly tuned as 5/4, I had long since discerned that if you use the C Db Eb F G Ab Bb C part of the tuning, you are using a true Ditone Diatonic, and, with the tone A tempered as a slightly wider F/A, an almost perfect

250

Syntonic Diatonic is there on C D E F G A B C. Thus, this temperament embodies a long history of Western music, from the Mesopotamian to the 'common practice'. Now, the 'accidentally-good' major third continued to interest me, and I remembered that some had turned up in a previous completely quintal tuning (years before) of the standard E♭–G♯ series, in which G♯/ C, C♯/ F, F♯/ B♭, and B/ E♭ are quite good. I thought at the time that there must be a way to skew a quintal tuning around so that such thirds would be available in more common keys, but I lacked time to work it out. Well, Martin Tittle's book, A Performer's Guide Through Historical Keyboard Tuning, *revealed to me that from about the fifteenth century the Pythagorean series had been transposed to B–G♭ and, of course, the 'good thirds' are then on A B D and E. In fact, I saw that a good third (only about 1.95 cents, or 32,805/ 32,768 exactly wider than 5/ 4) occurs at every ninth note of a quintal series. Thus, of twelve tones, the last four will form such thirds with the first four. My skewing was now possible. The series D G C F B♭ E♭ A♭ D♭ G♭ C♭ F♭ B♭♭, then, has C/ F♭ (E), D/ G♭(F♯), F/ B♭♭(A), and G/ C♭(B), as good thirds. And a surprise is that the good thirds, on C D F G, are located in exactly the same positions as in Kirnberger II. What's more, if one adjusts the final tone B♭♭(A) equally between D and F♭(E) – so, D A E – one has in effect made a well temperament very, very close to Kirnberger II and in itself a perfectly usable tuning at large. So easy to run up, too. What fun this has been!*

The Kirnberger II well temperament as such is shown in Figure 12.1.

Figure.12.1   Kirnberber II well temperament

Pythagorean Keyboard Tuning

The usual concept of a twelve-toned Pythagorean tuning is shown in Figure 12.2. It is the earliest, being found in the Robertsbridge Codex of 1340, and in the Halberstadt organ book of 1361. The 'good' major thirds here lie, for the most part uselessly, on F♯ G♯ B and C♯. In the quintal series every ninth tone forms a 'good' third.

Next we find that Ugolino (1381–1457), Arnaud de Zwolle (1400–66), and Gaffurius (1451–1522) wrote a transposition to B–G♭ so; B E A D G C F B♭

Pythagorean Keyboard Tuning:
The usual concept of a twelve-tone Pythagorean tuning is:

Figure.12.2   Pythagorean keyboard tuning

Eb Ab Db Gb, which places the good thirds on A B D E. During this same period Anselmi (1386–1440) offered Bb-Gb, which gives the thirds on Ab Bb Db Eb, while the venerated Spanish musician Ramos (1440–91) suggested G C F Bb Eb Ab Db Gb Cb Fb Bb Eb, offering the good thirds, quite usably, on F G Bb C. Finally, one may locate the good major thirds where late Baroque and Classical thought would have them on C D F G by tuning D G C F Bb Eb Ab Db Gb Cb Fb Bb. Any of these tunings may be converted into a well temperament by the simple expedient of 'blunting' the end of the series and so closing it round. Thus if, in the last quoted tuning, the Bb is so adjusted that the fifths D/ Bb and Bb/ Fb (D/ A and A/ E) are to the ear equally dissonant, then the circle has been closed. The result is, very nearly perfectly, Kirnberger's well temperament II. Certainly this is not a completely accurate half syntonic comma temperament because the comma concerned is minutely larger, but it is near enough. If a 'softer' rounding-off is wanted, simply 'blunt' two more adjacent fifths, one on each end, and this will result in a close-to Kirnberger well temperament III. Nota bene: A twenty-tone keyboard would give these major thirds on all twelve tones, but the nineteen-tone one illustrated in Figure 12.3 gives eleven of them.

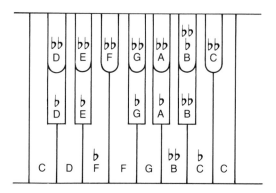

Figure.12.3   A nineteen-tone keyboard, which gives major thirds on eleven of the twelve tones

252

Two phone calls from the Los Angeles Philharmonic came to Aptos before we left. It had been discovered that my *Concerto in Slendro* score contains piano and celeste tuning instructions. Fright. But I allow twelve-tone equal temperament in this piece as a less desirable alternative. 'Do it that way.' 'OK.' Next call. 'But in LA we only have one tack piano rentable from Hollywood supply houses. Could we omit the tacks?' 'No, this is where I draw the line. Borrow a neighbour's old upright; they sound better anyway when tacked.' No complaints from the percussionists about the four galvanized iron washtubs involved. Percussionists never complain; they're interested in music and lack totemic taboos.

The old recording of *Concerto in Slendro* which I used last week in the Schoenberg Institute is in all details correct and handsomely played so that the Gown got the best thing and the Town will get second-best. In the Institute I also explained that now I would use a 'wider' Slendro tuning than I did in 1961 (we can't learn everything at once) and that a recent recording of my *Philemon and Baukis* with the same fine violinist, Daniel Kobialka, uses a wide Slendro in the Gamelan Si Betty (the largest American-built Javanese gamelan, at San Jose State University). In both works Kobialka plays beautifully by depending on his ear. In the Concerto the whole pitch system lies a $\frac{25}{24}$ below A = 440, and in the other piece he plays with the gamelan somewhere between the present D and D♭. After the performance of my Concerto, a well-groomed, courteous, elderly gentleman kindly asked me how a piece of music was generated in the 'The Industry' – did whoever paid for it describe what was wanted? Contract? Rights? In his courtesy he never implied that there is an 'art' of music. We went then to an all-night Russian restaurant, Gorky's as I remember, where one very young man 'entertained' us at high volume with his amplified voice and electric guitar. Every so often, to this end, he would turn round to his stack of amplifiers, press a button, and add electric drum set, and finally a 'big band' background, the whole sound of which in the end caused some of us to flee.

Our lovely Betty Freeman (after whom we named the Gamelan Si Betty) took Bill and me to see her fine exhibit of photos in the foyer of the LA Philharmonic Hall. It is called 'Music People and Others'. The show opened in Milan, Italy, and will later go to the Brooklyn Academy and to the University of California at Irvine. A large number of contemporary composers and some few conductors are celebrated in her moving and sometimes surprising images, as are artists David Hockney, Franco Assetto, and Roy Lichtenstein. Later that day we went to a musicale at Betty's home in Beverly Hills. Alan Rich presided, as always, and first we enjoyed a three-screen silent movie with live musical accompaniment. Actually the movie was shown on a divided single screen, and was titled *Long Gunn but Not Forgotten*. Although fascinated, I did not really know what people in the movie were up to – but I seldom do in real life either. The composer Craig Grady and his friends played charming instruments constructed by himself and Erv Wilson, tuned in Just Intonation. There was a break, then we heard an attractive early piano work by Mauricio Kagel. He himself then introduced the tape of a more recent orchestral piece involving devotions to J.S. Bach. (Why don't they simply canonize him and be done?) The atmosphere was that of a divine service to the composer, and I felt compelled to say (audibly) to my neighbour, 'I'm a Handel man myself.' Franco Assetto offered a wonderful pasta and salad to complete the afternoon. Nicolas Slonimsky was there, amid a number of well-known people; at 94 he is still pert and alert and walks with small precise steps like an Amerindian – soles parallel to the ground – more power to him! It was an unexpected delight to see Erv Wilson. We hadn't had the chance to visit with him in years, and he grows ever fuller of information and loving kindness as the years go by. He continues his botanical work as well as making instruments and studies in advanced musical theory.

Betty told me that Alan Rich had been fired from *Newsweek* magazine because it is no longer going to cover cultivated music. Well, we don't have to buy *Newsweek* anymore. So far as I know there is, then, in the US no national weekly that reviews serious music. The corporations have designed and established a whole 'Pop culture', fully 'Now', fully Commercial, and international in size. All of us who have individual or independent or learned art interests perforce constitute an elite; but then I suspect that we always have.

On the way down to Los Angeles, Bill and I stopped at the California Institute of the Arts (CalArts) to see Pak Chokro and Nick England. Both were in fine fettle and from Nicholas we learned, as elders, to join the American Association of Retired Persons. K.R.T. Wasitodiningrat, as Pak Chokro's present Javanese court rank has it, continues his composing and performing and has just completed the building of a seventeen-unit palace (he's a prince) in Yogyakarta for his family, and typical of him, is beginning another one for artist friends. As always, it was a joy to see this great artist and friend again.

* * *

Gamelan Si Aptos, at our home in Aptos, is being used this semester to teach

Cabrillo College students. Dan Kelley has proved to be a very fine teacher. I regard a music department without a gamelan as essentially handicapped. Along with Henry Cowell I deem it necessary to know well at least one musical tradition other than the one into which one is born. This second acquisition ought also to be 'equivalent'. If Haydn is known, then an equivalent court music should be studied and learned: Javanese Gadon for example, or Chinese or Japanese or Korean court or chamber music. It will not do to extend from Beethoven sonatas to Bluegrass banjo; the social and intellectual contents are largely incommensurate. My pleasure in and advocacy of Javanese Gamelan rises from several sources. Firstly, a fine gamelan is the most beautiful sounding orchestra on the planet. Second, its classic repertory is enormous, and ranges in expression from the thunderously grand to a lyricism of spider-web delicacy. Third, it is a communal music practised by villagers and courtiers alike, and indeed often together. Fourth, in a gamelan there is something to do for almost anyone, from singing, or simply counting and feeling one's way to the striking of a gong, to elaborate and difficult performance at speed, on highly refined solo instruments. The array of musical forms in gamelan music is the most developed of any music and is enough to dazzle or benumb anyone who has only Europe as musical background. You can import or build a gamelan in different metals. You can play classics or compose new music. You can likely never again be bored.

REFERENCES

BAXANDALL, M. (1971) *Giotto and the Orators*, Oxford: Oxford University Press.

TITTLE, M. (1978) *A Performer's Guide Through Historical Tunings*, Ann Arbor, Mich.: Anderson Press.

13

Speculative Music:
The Numbers Behind the Notes

JOSCELYN GODWIN

very art or science – and music is both – has three aspects: a practical
one, a theoretical one, and a speculative one. The practical aspect
concerns its operation in the physical world: in music, for example, it is the
making of organized sound; in painting, the making of pictures; in science,
it is technology. But *ars sine scientia nihil*, at least until the era of artistic
nihilism; in other words, no practice is possible without prior knowledge,
which constitutes the theoretical side of any art or science. To take the same
examples: the musician, whether composer or performer, needs to know how
notes are put together. The painter must know the rules of draughtsmanship,
perspective and the conventions of iconography. Those who work with their
hands follow either rules and traditions of their craft or else the instructions
of someone with theoretical knowledge, such as an engineer.

To the vast majority of people, nearly every human production is divided
simply into practice and theory, a duality reflected in all of our education.
To suggest that there is a third aspect beyond and, in a sense, above them
is to arouse scepticism and even suspicion. However, our initial threefold
definition assumes that this is the case, and that beyond the 'what?' of the
product and the 'how?' of technique lies an even more important question:
'why?'. It is here that the speculative domain begins, and we enter it fully
aware of the dubious reputation that the term has acquired. In common
parlance, if something is called speculative (or most often 'merely
speculative'), it can safely be ignored for all practical and most theoretical
purposes. The engineer does not worry about the 'charmed quarks' and

other particles that fascinate the physicist. The industrial chemist would be astonished to learn that intelligent people are still working in alchemical laboratories. Very few musicians (though I have know exceptions) wonder about the cosmic significance of scales and arpeggios. In short, the speculative domain is non-existent to the practical person, and irrelevant to the theoretical one, and no wonder. Of all the questions that children ask, it is always the Whys that are the hardest to answer, and by the time most people have grown up, they have given up asking them, finding enough to occupy themselves in the Whats and Hows of existence.

The child's point of view is perhaps the best one from which to approach such an unfamiliar subject. A child, starting music lessons, asks why there aren't black notes between all the white notes of the piano. Well, one might answer, it's so that you can find your way around the keyboard and tell the notes apart. That is a practical answer. A theoretical one might be that E to F and B to C are only semitones, so that there's no room in between for a black note. But why should they be only semitones, when all the rest are whole-tones? At this point, the piano teacher will probably change the subject. Few people can answer that question satisfactorily, and the attempt to do so will lead us step by step into the speculative domain.

To restate the question: Why, in the alphabetical sequence of notes, is there only a semitone between E and F, and between B and C? The theory teacher may say that it is due to the nature of the diatonic scale, which is made from five tones and two semitones. By whose decree is this so? Is the diatonic scale just a human invention? Is it adopted by general consent in our culture, while other peoples have invented completely different scales? Or is it some sort of natural law? Why does it have seven notes to the octave, not eight or thirty-one? There is no end to questions like these. To begin with, the answers are fairly straightforward, like the geometrical proofs in Euclid. We will imitate his method, in explaining why the diatonic scale takes the form it has.

To construct a simple scale between two notes an octave apart, C and C':

- Make G, a perfect fifth above C.
- Make D, a perfect fourth below G (by the theorem that an ascending fifth gives the same note–name as a descending fourth).
- Make A, a perfect fifth above D.
- Make E, a perfect fourth below A

The octave C to C' is now filled by the scale

C	D	E	G	A	C'
1	3	5	2	4	1'

It is of course a pentatonic scale that has been created, by taking five successive fifths from the first note. In many cultures, especially the Far East, this scale is considered sufficient for music. Its five notes are separated by two different sizes of intervals, which in our language are called the whole-tone and the minor third.

If we continue the progression by fifths beyond the stage that has given us a pentatonic scale, the sixth term, B, divides the minor third A–C' into a whole-tone and a semitone. The seventh term, F♯, does the same with the interval E–G. The minor thirds of the pentatonic scale have now disappeared, and we have a new scale of seven notes that again uses only two different sizes of interval: the whole-tone and the semitone:

C	D	E	F♯	G	A	B	C'
1	3	5	7	2	4	6	1'

Ingenious as this is, it does not quite explain the set-up of the keyboard, with its white and black keys. Perhaps it would have been better to start not on C but on F, then proceed as before in a sequence of six successive rising fifths (or falling fourths):

F	G	A	B	C	D	E	F'
1	3	5	7	2	4	6	1'

This is satisfactory in that it gets rid of the F♯ and gives seven natural or 'white' notes; but it does not answer the very reasonable objection that most of our music is based on the scale of naturals from C to C', not on that from F to F'. Here it is necessary to explain that the seven-note scale formed by a sequence of fifths is not a fixed scale with a keynote, but a field characterized by a regularly recurring pattern of intervals:

```
...F   G   A   B   C   D   E   F   G   A   B   C   D   E...
     T   T   T   S   T   T   S   T   T   T   S   T   T
```
(T = whole-tone, S = semitone)

This field evidently extends to infinity in both directions, constantly repeating its pattern. Pianos, organs, xylophones, etc., simply present longer or shorter sections of it, adapted to practical use by the human hand or foot.

The diatonic scale, and also the pentatonic, are closed fields in the sense that they repeat the same note-names over and over again, no matter how many octaves one traverses. The series of fifths, on the other hand, is an open field, because each new term has to be given a new name. No matter how far one goes, one will never find a note that exactly replicates one an octave (or a thousand octaves) away. Already, then, we have two musical systems pregnant with philosophical meaning: a bounded system, limited by the choice of a certain number (in these cases, five or seven), and an infinite system which knows no boundaries.

Curiosity may lead us to wonder what happens when we proceed further along this progression of fifths. Continuing from the seventh term, B, we add an eighth term: it will be the fifth above B, namely F♯, and it will land in between the F and the G, splitting their whole-tone into two unequal intervals which we call major and minor semitones. One could pause at this point and consider the possibilities of a scale which used these eight different notes to the octave:

F	F♯	G	A	B	C	D	E	F'
1	8	3	5	7	2	4	6	1'
	s	S	S	T	S	T	T	S

(s = minor semitone, S = major semitone)

However, the F♯ on its own seems like an interloper in this otherwise diatonic scale. It seems to make more sense to continue adding terms in the series of fifths until all the whole-tones are split in the same way as F–G, with the result that, once again, the octave is divided into only two different types of interval, here the major and minor semitone. To complete this process takes exactly twelve terms, and gives us the familiar chromatic scale in which the first seven notes are 'coloured' (from the Greek *chroma*) by the five subsequent ones.

F	F♯	G	G♯	A	A♯	B	C	C♯	D	D♯	E	F'
1	8	3	10	5	12	7	2	9	4	11	6	1'

Our experiment in musical imagination has already shown us an interesting fact: that there are only a few stopping-places in this progression by perfect fifths at which the octave is filled out by only two different kinds of intervals. To summarize:

Terms of the series of fifths	Divide the octave into steps of:
3	fourth and tone
5	minor third and tone
7	tone and semitone
12	major and minor semitone

We will proceed a little further before drawing any conclusions. The thirteenth term, which our limited musical vocabulary forces us to call E♯, lands between E and F, splitting that major semitone into a minor semitone and a very small interval, a 'comma' (c), regarded in most practical music (though not in speculative theory) as virtually a unison (as if E♯ = F). Here is the upper end of our octave, showing this term:

$$
\begin{array}{ccccc}
\text{D} & \text{D}\sharp & \text{E} & \text{E}\sharp & \text{F} \\
4 & 11 & 6 & 13 & 1' \\
 & s & S & s & c
\end{array}
$$

To divide every major semitone of the chromatic (twelve-note) scale in this way would take us from the thirteenth to the nineteenth term of the series of fifths:

$$
\begin{array}{ccccccc}
\text{E}\sharp & \text{B}\sharp & \text{F}^\times & \text{C}^\times & \text{G}^\times & \text{D}^\times & \text{A}^\times \\
13 & 14 & 15 & 16 & 17 & 18 & 19
\end{array}
$$

The division of the octave in this fashion could proceed *ad infinitum*; but still it will be only at certain points of the infinite series that certain conditions are met. The points encountered so far are the numbers 5, 7, 12 and 19, marking the completion of four limited fields or repeating patterns: the pentatonic, diatonic, chromatic and enharmonic.

The child in us might well ask at this point: Why do we have flats as well as sharps? The answer opens up a further dimension of the musical system. We proposed at the very beginning a progression of rising fifths: C, G, D, etc., but we did not at that time define a rising fifth, knowing that any musician would take it for granted. The time has come for more precision.

260

There are two ways to define the interval of a rising fifth. In modern times, when pitches are given as vibrational frequencies, to rise a fifth from a given note is to multiply that note's frequency by $\frac{3}{2}$. For example, a C of 512 Hz (= Herz, cycles per second) will give a G of $512 \times \frac{3}{2} = 768$ Hz. In older times, when there was no means of absolute pitch measurement, relative string lengths were the standard. The string length of the lower note would be multiplied by $\frac{2}{3}$; thus a C-string of 24 inches would need to be stopped at the 16-inch point to sound the G above.

If these procedures are reversed, i.e. if frequency is multiplied by $\frac{2}{3}$ and string length by $\frac{3}{2}$, we get the identical interval, but falling instead of rising, so from C down to F. There is no inherent reason why our genealogy of scales should not have been developed in this downward direction. In that case, the most convenient note to begin with would have been B, for that is where one starts in order to obtain the seven natural notes from seven terms of the series of descending fifths. The resultant scale would be the mirror-image of the one we first constructed, with flats in place of sharps. Here are its first twelve terms, with the numbers beneath the notes again showing the order in which the notes occur in the series:

B	B♭	A	A♭	G	G♭	F	E	E♭	D	D♭	C	B'
1	8	3	10	5	12	7	2	9	4	11	6	1'

Going on to the nineteenth term would bring in enharmonic tones analogous to the sharps and double sharps:

C♭	F♭	B♭♭	E♭♭	A♭♭	D♭♭	G♭♭
13	14	15	16	17	18	19

Now, since our musical system uses both flats and sharps, we must put the two sequences together. It turns out that there are just seven notes common to both systems, and that those are the seven natural notes of the diatonic scale: another confirmation of the fundamental quality of that scale. To the seven naturals are added seven sharps, five double sharps, seven flats, and five double flats, making a total of thirty-one different notes in our system. Since all these notes are available in every octave, they again form a field, characterized by a regularly repeating pattern of thirty-one terms.

Developing the musical system in this way shows that the different scales are by no means arbitrary, but the result of numbers with certain specific properties that occur in the infinite series of fifths: 5, 7, 12, 19, and now 31.

The speculative mind discovers much of interest here, beginning with the very nature of the octave and the fifth that we have been taking for granted. What is an octave? The 'eightness' of its name reflects only one of its aspects, as the boundary of the seven-note diatonic scale. The essential number of the octave is neither eight, nor thirteen, nor any other number but *two*. To make a higher octave, one doubles the frequency or halves the string-length. So it is the simplest of numbers, after one, that creates what our ears know as the simplest interval. Any subsequent division or multiplication by two repeats this identity at a higher or a lower pitch.

Consider, as a parallel phenomenon, the principle of cellular growth, the essential process of physical life. A one-celled organism starts growing by splitting into two. Is this a halving of the original cell? Or has it redoubled itself? The situation is ambiguous. In the same way, a string is halved to produce a higher octave, yet its frequency is doubled. Is the essential number of the octave, then, $\frac{2}{1}$ or $\frac{1}{2}$? One cannot say.

Likewise, the essential number of the perfect fifth is not five – that is merely its position in the diatonic scale – but *three*. Multiplication or division by three gives notes a fifth away from the starting-point (plus an octave which we can discount here since octaves are all equivalent). The entire thirty-one-tone system outlined above has been generated by nothing other than powers of three, reduced as necessary to bring them all within the span of a single octave. What we have been calling the infinite series of fifths is, mathematically speaking, nothing other than the infinite series of powers of three, both positive and negative.

If F is taken as unity, the notes around it are generated by the following powers of three:

...E♭	B♭	F	C	G	D	A...
$\frac{1}{9}$	$\frac{1}{3}$	1	3	9	27	81
3^{-2}	3^{-1}	3^0	3^1	3^2	3^3	3^4

The series progresses to infinity in both directions; but what are these 'directions'? If we are speaking of string length, then they are dimensions of space, expanding to the infinitely large, contracting to the infinitely small. Two galactic strings, tuned in the ratio 3 : 2, would 'sound' a perfect fifth. So would two subatomic particles vibrating in the same ratio.

If, on the other hand, we are speaking of frequencies, then the series will continue beyond our audible frequency range (about 20 Hz to 20,000 Hz) to infinitely long and infinitely short divisions of time. The two ways of specifying musical ratios – as string-lengths and frequencies – turn out to be not just ancient and modern devices, but expressions of space and time, connected in perfect reciprocity. That is to say, as space becomes more and more finely divided (the string gets shorter), the events that fill it become more and more frequent (the vibrations per second increase). Theoretical physicists assure us that subatomic particles vibrate millions of times every second. Contrariwise, expansion into bigger and bigger spaces slows down temporal events, to the degree that a single vibration, or rotation, of our planet takes a whole day, and that of a galaxy, millions of our years.

The whole universe is in a state of vibration; in fact it is a fair speculative position among physicists to say that it is nothing but vibration. There is an unbroken continuum of vibrations running from the infinitely large and slow to the infinitely fast and small, of which we can perceive only a small range with our ears, and an even smaller one with our eyes. These are the vibrations that give us the sensations of sound, and light. We might have been endowed with sense-organs, as doubtless other creatures are, that perceive ranges of vibrations between or beyond these two windows. A creature with a window of perception adjusted to radio waves would have a very different impression of the night-sky from the one our eyes give us.

Approached in this way, our perception of sound becomes something of cosmic significance for us, for in those ten octaves, more or less, lies our richest range of sense-perception. The eye is far less well-endowed, for the slowest red vibrations are less than half the frequency of the fastest violet ones. Hence the eye lacks the experience of the octave, so fundamental to music, and with it seems also to lack a sensitivity to exact proportion in colour frequency. There are no harmonies in colour except in an allegorical sense, because two colours cannot be mixed in such a way that they each remain distinctly perceptible while creating a third entity, the interval. Hence the kind of painting that is based exclusively on colour is extremely limited; some figurative element, some correspondence to the surrounding world is nearly always felt to be necessary, if painting is not to be merely a form of interior decoration. Music, on the other hand, has plenty to say in its abstract mode, exemplified by wordless or pure instrumental music, since it has no difficulty in creating its own spatio-temporal reality.

Long before the scientific discoveries that made it possible for us to conceive of this continuum of vibration, a version of the idea was current in the doctrine of correspondences. The phenomenon of the octave gives our imaginations ready access to this world-view, for in music every octave is identical in pattern, yet differs in plane. Could all the planes of existence be linked in an analogous way, each one reflecting all the others, and all perhaps reflecting some over-arching pattern? This is what the doctrine of correspondences maintains, and there are few cultures in which one does not find it to a greater or a lesser extent. It is noticeably absent in the modern West and other places obedient to the decree that speculation be limited to the physical plane, or else stuffed away in the box marked Religion. Consequently, any purpose or design behind appearances is reduced to the utilitarian, any correspondence dismissed as coincidence. However, such a reductionist approach is quite inadequate to explain the strange behaviour of musicians and music-lovers. Perhaps this is why the tradition of speculative music has never become completely extinct, even in modern times, and why in speculative thought, music has always played such a significant role.

Music's most famous involvement in the doctrine of correspondences is in the 'Harmony of the Spheres', which interprets the dispositions and movements of the planets by indicating musically significant proportions between them. Loosely related to this is the musical explanation given for the order of days of the week, and for the twelve months, governed by the signs of the zodiac. Harmonic proportions have also been used to exemplify the different forms of government, and the harmonic series has been applied both retrospectively and prophetically to historical epochs. The seven colours of the rainbow and the six of the painter's palette, the proportions of architecture, and poetic metre are just a few elements in the other arts whose 'harmony' has received several different musical analogies. More recently, music has been used as an aid to the rational arrangement of the chemical elements, the behaviour of subatomic particles, and the structure of the DNA molecule. The growth of plants and of crystals, the proportions of the human body and its parts, the development of the foetus and the ages of man have all been viewed through the musical analogy. 'Keynotes' have been assigned to perfumes, to trees and waterfalls, to geometrical figures and solids. The elements of alchemy and the aspects of astrology are musically related, as are the incantations of ceremonial magic and the creative words of the gods. These examples must suffice as a sketch of the complex web of interrelated domains to which speculative music has been applied as a key.

We will give one example of the workings of this key. Since antiquity, there have been seven days to the week, named after the seven Chaldaean or visible planets that rule them. These take their place among the innumerable groups of seven found in mythology and sacred writings. Now the order of the planets, based on their periods of revolution around the zodiac and on their presumed distances from the earth, is traditionally:

Moon   Mercury   Venus   Sun   Mars   Jupiter   Saturn

But that of the days of the week is quite different:

Sun   Moon   Mars   Mercury   Jupiter   Venus   Saturn

Why this discrepancy? Surprising as it may seem, the most plausible reason lies in the musical scale. If the planets are imagined as each sounding a musical note, their astronomical order will suggest that the Moon, being the fastest and closest to the earth, sounds the highest pitch, while slow and distant Saturn sounds the lowest. The planetary scale, adapted to the Greek Dorian mode, would therefore be:

Moon	Mercury	Venus	Sun	Mars	Jupiter	Saturn
A	G	F	E	D	C	B

The order of the days of the week might well have been Monday, Wednesday, Friday, etc., had not the theorists of antiquity recognized that the diatonic scale itself is only a secondary phenomenon. As we have shown, it depends for its existence and nature on the series of fifths. More suitable, then, would be an order that reflected this primary series. So, beginning with Saturn and proceeding by descending fifths, we reach the familiar order:

Saturn	Sun	Moon	Mars	Mercury	Jupiter	Venus
B	E	A	D	G	C	F

It only remains to give the Sun pride of place as first day of the week, and to move Saturn to the end.

This is an illustration of how musical laws, themselves derived from the very simplest numbers, are used to articulate a more complex numerical field. One could, perhaps, explain the order of the days on numerical principles alone, but that would not answer the question of why the Ancients should have selected the series 7, 4, 1, 5, 2, 6, 3, rather than any other. This simple example suggests that musical considerations have been present from the very earliest ages of civilization, and that we are still living with the results. In passing, we mention again the other significant numbers of scale-construction, and their coincidence with some other basic measure of time: the *twelve* months of the year, the *nineteen*-year eclipse cycle, and the *thirty-one* days of the majority of months.

Of all the correspondences between music and other systems, we have not yet mentioned the most familiar of all: the harmonic series, derived from the correspondence of pitches to the integer series 1, 2, 3, 4 ... ∞. Like the series of fifths, this is an infinite series with two reciprocal forms. The successive multiples of frequency, or divisions of string-length, by 1, 2, 3, 4, etc. give the harmonic series, while the successive divisions of frequency, or multiples of string-length, by the same integers give the subharmonic series.

The harmonic series, as most musicians know, is a physical as well as a mathematical phenomenon, caused by the tendency of vibrating objects to vibrate simultaneously as a whole and in their aliquot parts (by halves, thirds, quarters, etc.). Different materials and resonators affect the number of harmonics present, and their respective strengths. The first sixteen harmonics of a fundamental C are approximately:

C	c	g	c'	e'	g'	b♭−'	c"	d"	e"	f+"	g"	a−"	b♭−"	b"	c'''
1	2	3	4	5	6	7	8	9	10	11	12	13	14	15	16

(− = slightly flat, + = slightly sharp)

Many of the principles of practical and theoretical music are inherent in this series: the octave is the interval from the first to the second harmonic, and likewise between any harmonics whose numbers are in the ratio 1:2; the perfect fifth is 2:3; the perfect fourth 3:4; the major triad 4:5:6; the dominant seventh chord 4:5:6:7; the whole-tone 8:9 or 9:10; the semitone 15:16. Since we hear some part of this harmonic series in every musical tone (though it goes unnoticed except by the trained ear) many theorists have sought in it the main explanation of musical systems, both ancient and modern. Doubtless these harmonicists are partly right, especially when it is a question of the harmonized music peculiar to Western civilization. If nearly every tone heard instils in the human subconscious the sound of a major triad, no wonder that sooner or later a kind of music emerged that drew on this phenomenon. Yet there are nearly as many aspects of the harmonic series that are rejected in practice, notably the octotonic scale presented by harmonics 8–16, whose intervals gradually narrow from the whole-tone 8:9 to the semitone 15:16. Scale types derived from the series of fifths are clearly preferred to anything of that sort. Moreover, the harmonic series gives only a weak precedent for the minor triad, first encountered only in the combination of harmonics 10, 12, and 15; and no justification at all for the importance of the subdominant note, F. In short, it is only with difficulty that an instrument which plays the harmonic series, such as the natural horn or trumpet, can adapt itself to the diatonic scale and its chords.

Some of these anomalies can, it is true, be explained with reference to the subharmonic series, though since that is inaudible, the explanation is speculative in the purest sense. The subharmonic series is naturally a mirror image of the harmonic one:

c‴	c″	f′	c′	a♭	f	d+	c	B♭	A♭	G−	F	E♭+	D+	D♭	C
1	2	3	4	5	6	7	8	9	10	11	12	13	14	15	16

The subdominant F appears immediately as the third subharmonic, followed closely by the minor triad C–A♭–F, as the inversion of the major one, C–E–G. Curiously enough, there is not a core of notes shared by the two progressions, as was the case with the twin series of fifths; beside the parent note C, the harmonic and the subharmonic series have not a single note in common. Even notes that look superficially the same are not identical in pitch: the seventh harmonic is a flatter B♭ than the ninth subharmonic, and so on. Neither do many of the harmonic notes coincide with those generated by the series of fifths. By mathematical necessity, the only ones that do coincide will be those whose numbers are powers of three, such as C (1), G (3), and D (9) in the harmonic series, and F ($\frac{1}{3}$) and B♭ ($\frac{1}{9}$) in the subharmonic. The next rising fifth, A, is not found until the twenty-seventh harmonic, then E at the eighty-first, far too remote to be sounded on physical instruments.

Herein lies the bone of contention between the two systems, which has been fought over by speculative theorists since antiquity. The most salient result is the difference of their major thirds. For the E reached from C via a series of fifths (C–G–D–A–E) is not the same as the E reached from the same C via the harmonic series. The former E is, as we have said, identical to the eighty-first harmonic; the latter, to the fifth harmonic. To compare them it is only necessary to raise the latter E by four octaves ($5 \times 2 \times 2 \times 2 \times 2$) to find it recurring as the eightieth harmonic. So there is a discrepancy of 80:81 between the two versions of E. This 'syntonic comma' may seem a fraction so trivial that only a speculative musician would bother about it, until one comes to tune a keyboard instrument. Then it is clear that the E reached by way of perfect fifths makes a blatantly sharp major third – sharper even than the wide thirds of equal temperament, and quite unusable in harmony.

The tuning of keyboard instruments is the nearest modern equivalent to working with the monochord, the traditional tool of the speculative musician. Piano and organ tuners usually work by rote, aiming at equal temperament (though there are many subtleties even there), but those who tune harpsichords will often be drawn to experiment with historical tunings. These were devised by the speculative musician in order to provide suitable principles for the practical musician (who could well be the same person), and they always focus on problems which we have illustrated in simple form with the question of the two Es. Tuning, like monochord work, develops concentration on sound, a sensitivity to fine distinctions and to the presence of harmonics.

Reflecting on the two musical systems that we have outlined, the series of fifths and the harmonic series, it becomes apparent that Western music has developed its common language by selecting only a few of the myriad possibilities that each system has to offer. The harmonic series contains innumerable intervals and chords that have never been tried out except by a few contemporary composers. What of the subtle gradation of steps, from the 7:8 interval, a little wider than the whole-tone, through the unexplored territory of the smaller whole-tones 10:11, 11:12, etc., to the semitone 15:16 and beyond into the microtones? One can imagine, theoretically though not yet aurally, a music that worked deliberately with these intervals and their combinations. Atonal music has already proved that music does not have to have a basis of consonance in order to be a coherent intellectual and emotional language, but it has remained shackled to its dogma of twelve notes in equally-tempered tuning. It is this equal temperament that has made possible the versatility of Romantic harmony, but at the same time has desensitized the ear to finer tunings. In throwing over the first, one might hope that composers would begin to re-cultivate the second.

As regards the series of fifths, the limitation of Western music is in using only two of the seven diatonic modes. The diatonic scale generated by seven fifths is a field, or a repeating pattern, in which one can choose seven different starting-points for one's octave. It seems that even in the days of plainsong, the feeling for the individuality of these seven modes was on the wane. It is hard to find a plainsong melody in the D mode or the F mode that does not have B♭s introduced as accidentals, making them merely transpositions of the A and C modes – our minor and major respectively.

Speculative musicians tend to look back to ancient Greece as the source of their art, for it was there that speculative music was carried to its greatest heights, at least in the time for which written records exist. An explanation of the Greek musical system in all its complexity and rational beauty is beyond the scope of this essay. It is enough to say that the Greek theorists did use all these resources: the multiple modes on the one hand, and the subtle intervals on the other, in every combination.

The accepted notion today is that musical theory is largely a codification of practice, and this is correct when modern and even medieval music is in question. However, I would like to suggest that there was a time when speculative theory came first, and practice followed its dictates. Certainly in ancient China, the regulation of music was regarded as one of the ruler's most important functions, while in ancient Egypt, the canons governing the arts remained unaltered for millenia. Any theocracy, or later any dictatorship, permits only the types of music and art that agree with its own ideas. The Greek and Chinese musical systems, together perhaps with the Indian, show every symptom of having been devised theoretically and then applied in practice. We name these three systems in particular because they are most obviously the result of a 'Pythagorean' way of thinking, i.e. one that studies music through number.

In the doctrine of correspondences, numbers are like the warp of a loom, to which the various manifestations cohere like the multicoloured threads of the weft. It is a concept which agrees, up to a point, with that of the modern scientist who believes that All is Number – yet all is not perceived as number, and that is why there is music. Music enables us to perceive directly the numbers that are at the heart of manifestation. Take two of the most common numbers in the doctrine of correspondences, seven and twelve, the numbers of the visible planets and of the zodiac signs. A mathematician can do all manner of tricks with them, but will never know them as intimately as the musician who works every day with the diatonic and chromatic systems. I do not speak figuratively in saying that the musician's knowledge is a direct perception of reality, only it concerns the quality of number, not its quantity.

It is because of music's qualitative approach to number that it has always worked with proportions, that is to say, with comparing one number to another. The mathematician is morally indifferent to the various integers – or if not, then he is a numerologist. But the musician, weighing them in proportion with each other, finds some quite definitely 'better' than others. This finds its proof on the practical level of melody, harmony and rhythm, which are all based on the comparison of one note with another successive or simultaneous one. Compare 1 to 2, and you hear the octave; 2 to 3, and you hear the perfect fifth. Compare 80 to 81, which may seem futile to a mathematician, and you hear something rather disturbing: the syntonic comma. Moreover, by comparing any number to unity, it is possible to assign it a particular note within a given pitch-system.

Let us take as an example the number 360, the number of degrees in a circle. What is the tone of 360? To discover this, one first halves the number as many times as possible, to take out the octaves. Thus $360 \div 2 \div 2 \div 2 = 45$; in other words, the 360th harmonic will have the same note-name as the forty-fifth, only three octaves higher. The pitch of the forty-fifth harmonic is easily defined, since this number is $1 \times 3 \times 3 \times 5$. To multiply a frequency by three, as we know, is to raise it by a perfect fifth, and to multiply it by five is to raise it a pure major third. So if we suppose the fundamental of our system to be C, we can reach the 45th harmonic quite easily by the following route:

$$1 \quad \times \quad 3 \quad \times \quad 3 \quad \times \quad 5$$
$$\text{C} \qquad \text{G} \qquad \text{D} \qquad \text{F}\sharp$$

The tone of 360 therefore sounds an augmented fourth or tritone with the fundamental or first tone.

In the Chinese *Book of Diagrams* we read:

> The aggregate number of the Superior Principle of nature is 216 ... and the aggregate number of the Inferior Principle of Nature is 144. ... The two aggregate Principles of the Superior and the Inferior Principles of nature, added together, make 360, the number of days (generally reckoned) for a year.
>
> *(I Ching*, 'Great Appendix', IX, 52)

Chinese musical mathematics is based entirely on the series of fifths, so it is not surprising that these two numbers also have a place within that series. Taking out the octaves, 216 reduces to 27 (3^3), and 144 reduces to 9 (3^2). Therefore their notes, relative to a fundamental of C, are A for the Superior Principle and D for the Inferior Principle. The two Principles are related by a perfect fifth, and their sum (360) places between them the pure major third, F$\sharp$.

Our year, however, is not 360 days long, 'as generally reckoned', but 365 $\frac{1}{4}$. Its deviation from the ideal is of the order of a musical comma (about 69:70): small enough, but sufficient to require 'tempering' of the ideal 360-day calendar.

This is not the place to draw any conclusions, only to show a method that enables any number to reveal its characteristic interval, and to reiterate that the study of proportions was the very essence of musical research up to the Renaissance era.

The question posed at the beginning, the 'Why?' of music, can now be answered unambiguously. Music exists in order to give human beings knowledge about the universe, of a kind that is inaccessible through other channels. The composer reveals knowledge of emotional states which enrich and educate the listener. The speculative musician discovers universal principles as surely as the mathematician or the philosopher, though since he does not use the medium of words or of pictures, his knowledge is undervalued today, and his discoveries may seem like coincidences or curiosities. That is because of the two-dimensional world in which so many people have been persuaded to live, which prevents them from imagining other layers of reality. The doctrine of correspondences is one explanation of how these other layers interact with the material one, and speculative music is one of the most powerful ways of experiencing the truth of this doctrine.

The fruits of this knowledge are not merely some high-flown intellectual satisfaction, but an understanding of principles that undergird musical theory and practice alike. In themselves, the principles of speculative music are morally indifferent, like those of mathematics. But as soon as they are applied, they take on ethical values, and can affect the destinies of whole civilizations. The same is true of philosophical principles, as applied in government, and of mathematical ones, as applied in technology. At this point of history, it would be futile to wish for a return to the ancient ideal, in which inviolable canons of the arts and sciences are drawn up by those who truly understand their cosmic principles, on the one hand, and their psychological effects, on the other. But ours is a time of scientific and artistic anarchy, and, at least in the case of music, there is no one qualified to draw up such canons. Speculative music is in its second childhood, and its principles have to be sought out and rediscovered from the root up, before anyone can speak with authority about its consequences for theory and practice.

14

Text, Context, Music

ISTVAN ANHALT

onsider this. Someone is seized by fear. What happens? He flees. Or he freezes into a posture, holds his breath; complete silence. He might emit now a hoarse, loud scream. Someone else in a similar predicament might just jabber and giggle helplessly. Or we might hear the distant whine of a child. In another situation someone pants: /ha//ha//ha/ . . . breathy and rhythmical. When there is less threat and more control, we might hear a guttural voice uttering: 'No!' or 'I am scared.' In another context we are members of a congregation that recites in a random cluster of monotones:

> Give ear to my prayer, O God;
> and hide not thyself from my supplication.
>
> Fearfulness and trembling are come upon me,
> and horror hath overwhelmed me.
>
> (Psalm 55: vv. 1, 5)

Or imagine hearing the following in a fictitious song performed in a recital that never was:

Figure 14.1

272

Or, if we hear an exaggeratedly nasal voice intoning with a flourish 'Oh, how dreadful', or, in an opera of the absurd, the tremulous yodelling of a half-clad buffoon complaining about being pursued with evil intent, we would be inclined to think that the message is about quite something else than fear.

In all these experiences, save one, there is sound and within it one or another kind of text (or, in the case of the complete silence of the first one, a telling absence of both). These reflect back on and inform about affect, thought, person and situation.

What is a 'text'? In a narrower sense, in the present framework, one could suggest that 'text' refers to words (normally existing in a written form) set to music by a composer. As this formulation could prove to be somewhat confining, I am suggesting a different one. I will say that a text, uttered, or written, stands for some kind of mental activity, for some kind of experience, which it is able to express as a result of conscious design, reflex action, or instinct, or a combination of these, in a certain situation (context). To this we may add that some texts can, and do, become parts of musical compositions. Now, before we focus on the relationship between 'text' and 'music', let us think of the notion of 'text' in this broader sense.

Two recent experiences of my own will serve to illustrate this concept. A few weeks ago I saw a young woman on the train with Plato's *Republic* held open in her hands. Intermittently, she read and looked up absent-mindedly, or so it appeared. Was it an instance of day-dreaming, or conversely a concentrated dialogue with Plato?, I asked myself. Could it have been a contest between the text of the book and another one, possibly unrelated to Plato, a contest that might have eventually resulted in a written essay on some aspects of the *Republic*, or alternately, in a non-verbal or verbal act that had little or nothing to do with Plato, and which might eventually (or never) be expressed in writing? Or might it have resulted in both?

The second story is about another young woman, a student on our campus, whom I saw sporting an engineering student's jacket with the standard oversize lettering on the back: APPLIED SCIENCE. Not quite a tattoo but akin to a tribal mark, nevertheless; perhaps a somewhat over-eager celebration of belonging. The two stories are unrelated. Yet in both one can see a relationship between a written text, visible to the observer, and another one that goes on in the mind, and which we can only guess at.

However suggestive they may have been, neither of these little scenes included the modality of oral utterance (which was nevertheless present in its 'non-markedness') that constitutes a vital dimension of human experience and of action between individuals and groups, and which often serves also as an intermediate link between thought and feeling on the one hand and a written text on the other.

I would like to pause here and enlarge on this. The way some Jewish thinkers thought about the Bible might be a suitable paradigm for the intimate interconnectedness of these three modalities. Take, for example, Isaac the Blind, the early cabbalist mystic, who lived in or near Narbonne from about 1165 to 1235 and who 'was regarded as the central figure of the Kabbalah during his lifetime' (Scholem 1974: 45). He speculated about the 'three degrees of manifestation of the Torah – the Primordial Torah, the Written Torah and the Oral Torah' (Scholem 1987: 287). Of the Primordial Torah, Isaac wrote: 'In the right hand of God were all the engravings [i.e. the innermost marks, which are, as yet, not real forms] that were destined one day to proceed from potentiality to actuality' (ibid.). Of the other two forms he says: 'the Written Torah cannot adopt corporeal form, except through the powers of the Oral Torah: that is, that the former cannot be truly understood without the latter . . .' (ibid.: 288). We would appear to be justified in reading this as an indication of a deep psychological–epistemological insight, as well as an allusion to the well-known traditional practice of layers upon layers of commentaries upon the Torah accumulating over the centuries, which have, themselves, become a 'companion tradition, an "oral Torah"' (see Urbach 1987: 558). The 'oralness' of the Jewish sacred texts has been considered from yet another point of view by modern bibilical scholarship focusing on literary and historical criticism. Some scholars stressed 'the central role of oral traditions and the accuracy of their transmission in ancient times. They claim that oral transmission influenced the sources even after they were reduced to writing' (Scholem 1987: 358). This is just one example of the many that could be cited in illustrating the interdependence of thought and its transmission, achieved through oral utterance or by writing.

'Language is the Flesh Garment, the Body of Thought', wrote Carlyle in *Sartor Resartus* (Sewell 1964: 47). Garment . . . textile . . . *texo*. . . . My thoughts wander. . . . I move backwards in time. *In illo tempore*. . . . Yes, now I see . . . a woman, seated in front of her loom, weaving. The warp, threads of the woof, more yarn on spindles, uncarded wool in a corner. . . . A timeless picture. How long did it take us to get to that level of civilization? And when did the leaps to metaphor, such as these, occur: from weaving to thinking; from spinning yarn to spinning forth a line of thought; from weaving a length of cloth to weaving an argument; from the threads of a toil to a tale, and, finally, to a text. Already in Roman times *texo* had a number of derivatives. For example, *contexo* meant to weave together; *subtexo* to cover, to draw together under; *praetexo* to weave before, to adorn, to cover, to conceal; and the curious *retexo*, which does not appear to have been preserved in English, French or Italian, meant to unweave, unravel, and also to weave again (Ernout and Meillet 1932: 995–6; *Cassel's Latin Dictionary*, Marchant and Charles 1955). There are numerous others.

A piece of woven cloth, an entire garment worn for the purpose of protection, or concealment, or enhancement, or any combination of these, might also be seen as a symbol: that of the wearer's awareness of his or her own being, his or her own 'thisness' (*haecceitas*), or at the least a significant component thereof. (A double example of this can be seen on a dyptich by Stefano di Giovanni Sassetta, in the National Gallery in London, showing in one of the panels St Francis of Assisi holding a garment in his hands while contemplating becoming a soldier. The other panel depicts him having divested himself of his robe, signifying a complete breaking with family ties, now devoting himself to the Church.)

Spinning and thread are also central metaphors in the myth of the Moiras, who, according to legend, exercised control over the life-spans of humans. Numerous other myths and legends in Greek, Norse, Anglo-Saxon, Slavic, Celtic, Hindu and Persian mythologies also make reference to spinning and the thread, or to bond and binding (see Onians 1951). The word 'text' contains all these relationships and many others besides. Its semantic scope is vast. Since 'text' is none other than an instance of language actualized, what is at hand is 'an inexhaustible abundance of manifold treasures' (Hjelmslev 1961: 3). It (language) is 'the instrument with which man forms thoughts and feeling, mood, aspiration, will and act, the instrument by whose means he influences and is influenced, the ultimate and deepest foundation of human society' (ibid.: 4–5).

How do composers of our time respond to such a vista, such a horizon as this, with respect to the choice of texts (some write their own) to be set in their compositions? It is beyond the scope of this essay to attempt to present a systematic, exhaustive and detailed overview of the various kinds of texts one recalls having encountered in the repertoire. What I am proposing instead is but a brief, provisional and non-systematic listing of certain text-types.

As to objective, theme, approach and/or genre, I recall texts that:

1   expose an idea; tell a story; depict a situation; show a series of actions;
2   praise, criticize, mock, accuse;
3   show identification with a creed, an attitude, an ideology, or an *episteme*;[1]

4 depict the world of dreams, the irrational, or the psychopathological;

5 show archetypes or archetypal situations; enact myth, or engage in mythopoesis;

6 focus on the deictic (that is the space–time) co-ordinates of a situation;

7 search the past; either '*in illo tempore*', the Orphic past, or early historical eras, or ontogeny;

8 employ quasi-magical texts, repeated formulas, slogans, or text deconstructions;

9 are arrived at through collage or assemblage techniques, borrowings;

10 are borrowed from traditional cultures, Western, or non-Western;

11 are documentaries, or pseudo-documentaries, *Hörspiels*;

12 are *ex post facto* text grafts, tropes;

13 are of the kind in which paralinguistics predominate;

14 are vocalizations, and articulatory process-centred works in which body, 'text' and music merge into one.[2]

As to authorship, one notes:

1 adopted texts (sacred or profane);

2 composer's texts;

3 librettist's texts;

4 hybrid texts assembled from diverse sources; and

5 found texts.

As to languages, the repertoire shows:

1 unilingual works;

2 polylingual works;

3 works in a counterfeit language (mimicking a natural language);

4 works in an artificial language; glossolalia;

5 works that are age-specific, class-specific, etc., idiosyncratic utterances;

6 animal language (zoo-semiotic) imitations;

7 onomatopoësis;

8 buccal play;

9 various combinations of the foregoing.

Now a few examples.

Edoardo Sanguineti begins his vast collage-libretto of *laborintus II* for Berio this way:

> In that part, in that part of my memory, in that part of the book, in that part of the book of my memory, *incipit vita nova*.

With this, in one arc of a gesture, he creates the potential for a system of relationships that reminds me of a vast cloverleaf intersection of roadways at the approach to a large city. The complete text appears to me as a large and dynamic assemblage of memory 'places': *topoi* that might have been at the time of composition of some import to the librettist, and to the composer. In it are mingled references to etymology, to historical *loci*, to religious history, including biblical genealogy, and to Dante, himself metamorphosed here into a psychopomp. Diachrony is fused into synchrony, as well as distant conceptual fields to each other, by the sudden appearances of elliptical phrases such as 'from first communion to the Treasury Department: from the darkness which ever surrounds our lives to the 4% profit . . . from the square root to the Trojan horse, from the lapsus linguae to the Russian Revolution'. Then suddenly place names appear: 'to Brussels, to Paris' to 'Mills College, to Santa Fé, to Mass Avenue', channelling into a list of street addresses, presumably of autobiographical relevance (do these stand here as symbols of human relationships?), judging from the inclusion here of 'Via Moscati 7', which I happen to know to have been, at one time, the address of Cathy Berberian, Berio's first wife. At one point, the whole *mélange* suddenly begins to take on the character of an 'insight' into a working mind itself, a mind that acts as a theatre of memories, reminding one, in yet another instance of an epistemological regression, of the numerous forms of a learning device called memory theatre, that was highly prized in the Renaissance as a mnemonic instrument but valued even more as a compendium for one or another *episteme* (see Yates 1966; Foucault 1973).

The very title of the Sanguineti-Berio work puts the listener on guard: here one enters (or descends into) a labyrinth (or is it an inferno?). The figure of the labyrinth is a recurring one in the contemporary repertoire of works for the voice; another notable example of it is Mauricio Kagel's *Anagrama*, the text of which is but a single sentence: *In girum imus nocte et consumimur igni* (We travel in a circle in the night and are consumed by fire). It speaks of loss of direction, and as such contains the connotation of an *aporia*, a theme larger still than the labyrinth. Another feature of Kagel's work is the palindromic structure that brings within itself the flavour of a magical conjuration. All these elements are placed in a setting that features, among other affects, much hilarity (another instance of playing with *topoi*?) (see Chatman 1981: 30). The labyrinth as a metaphor can also be found in the works of R. Murray Schafer, Maurice Ohana and David Keane, among others.

Some composers keep to a theme for a long time, work after work. They seem to be engaged in writing a *carmen perpetuum*. One such composer is

277

R. Murray Schafer, many of whose texts (like some of Erik Bergman's and Harry Somers's) deal with the history of Eastern Mediterranean lands and beyond, and with the influences that shaped the Judaeo-Christian world-view there, including also those of the Cretan, Egyptian, Zoroastrian, Manichean, Tibetan and Hindu cultures. In some of Schafer's texts this theme is woven together with the myth of the labyrinth, particularly with that of Ariadne, the girl of the guiding thread, who appears, dies, and reappears again in various guises in a series of metempsychoses. Numerous other related themes employed by Schafer include alienation and the irrational, with echoes of Novalis, E.T.A. Hoffmann, Rilke, Nietzsche, Freud and Jung, all fusing into a personal, powerful and unified voice.

George Crumb has been occupied for many years painting a large canvas, setting many texts by Federico Garcia Lorca. His works are characterized by great dramatic intensity and an exceptionally wide spectrum of tonal colour. Peter Maxwell Davies, in work after work, gives, with profound empathy, expression to his understanding of and feeling for the spirit of the people who lived and live on the Orkney Islands. John Beckwith's texts come from many sources, but most of them coalesce into a large picture: an individualistic representation – at times dream-like, at times near documentary – of certain facets of nineteenth-century and present-day English Canada. One of his favourite text-types is the collage, and his settings amount to an individual and persuasive blend of directness, *recherché* simplicity and an occasional intentional roughness at the edges, alongside much learned invention. Beckwith's view of his favourite place–time theme also has a characteristic tinge of a play-like contemplativeness, as if allowing an exceedingly bright, precocious, say, 12-year-old to speak out of the mature mind of the adult he has developed into.

Trevor Wishart's *carmen* is a search within the very nature of the musical voice itself, and the compositions that have resulted from this are among the most inventive of their genre. Following his *Anticredos* of 1980, he has been at work on a cycle of six pieces with the general title *VOX*. These pieces show a wide spectrum of compositional techniques related to the voice, specifically including a fairly recently developed one: composing for and with the vocal articulatory process itself as a unified endeavour, instead of conceiving composition as consisting of a pre-existent text and its subsequent setting to music. Complementary semiotic elements in these pieces include *musique concrète* and computer simulations of atmospheric, water and various zoo-semiotic sounds, recorded bird-song and human imitation of diverse animal sounds. One also hears, live, from the members of the small vocal ensemble for which *Anticredos*, *VOX-1* and *VOX-2*, were composed, phoneme sequences, brief utterances in an invented language, as well as imitations of non-Western idioms. The dominant element in these works, however, appears to be human vocal sounds that are produced by extended vocal techniques: vocal processes, timbres, gestures, their relationships to each other, as well as to the other materials present. The composition of these pieces was facilitated by Wishart's experimental work leading to the development of a personal extended vocal techniques repertory and by his own impressive skill in the performance of these techniques. But in speaking of the relative novelty of this approach and the kinds of sounds it produces to compose with, it is essential that we remind ourselves that it is by no means without precedents, some of which are very old, probably even as ancient as humankind.

The great Hasidic teacher, Pinhas of Koretz, for example, taught early in the nineteenth century that

> the holy Torah was originally created as *an incoherent jumble of letters.* ... Only when a certain event occurred in the world did the letters combine to form the words in which the event is related. ... *If another event had occurred in its place, other combinations of letters would have arisen.*
>
> (Scholem 1965: 76–7)

So, once again, the arrow points from the vocal signal back to the feeling or thought that has engendered it. This idea applied to the work of Wishart could perhaps be understood as indicating that he is searching for an artistic pseudo-re-creation of a very early stage of human linguistic competence; a quasi-phonetic, more or less physiologically–emotively conceived or motivated stage that can be regarded as only holding the potential for evolving a broad variety of phonemic, phonological and morphemic repertories that could, and would, develop synchronously and in accord with the evolution of concepts in the mind. In this sense, Wishart's compositional gesture, ignoring the more or less traditional notions of text with its creative constraints in degrees of freedom of choice and opting instead for a quasi-primordial, maximally 'free' repertoire, is a powerful yet, paradoxically, also somewhat constrained one.

This search for the well-springs of expression through thinking in terms of the vocal process itself, instead of in terms of the sign vehicle expectedly produced by it, has other notable antecedents. Homer referred to thinking as speaking and 'located [it] sometimes in the heart, but usually in the ... *phrénes* ... the "lungs" or the "diaphragm"' (Onians 1951: 13). 'It is by his *thymós* (spirit, temper) in this *phrénes*, or by what is breathed into them by some god, that a live prophet divines' (ibid.: 66). Onians cites B. Malinowski's comment that the Society Islanders of the South Pacific conceive of thinking as 'speaking in the stomach'. And about the natives of New Guinea he wrote that

> The mind, *nanola*, by which term intelligence, power of discrimination, capacity for learning magical formulae and all forms of non-manual skill are described as well as moral qualities, resides somewhere in the larynx.
>
> (Onians 1951: 14).

Other similarities can be found in certain shamanistic practices and in Graeco-Egyptian oral magic (Anhalt 1984: 186–96).

There appears to be yet another possible source of influence on Wishart, one that seems to me to be of first importance: early childhood. Roman Jakobson wrote that, in infancy,

> The actual beginning stages of language as is known, are preceded by the so-called babbling period, which brings to light in many children an astonishing quantity and diversity of sound productions.... A child during this babbling period, can accumulate articulations which are never found within a single language or even in a group of languages.
>
> (Jakobson 1968: 21)

There is reason to believe that in Wishart's *Anticredos*, *VOX-1* and parts of *VOX-2* a desire to rediscover some of this articulatory diversity of infancy plays a role, perhaps because of its symbolic connotations.

Now, a new focus: context. How to begin? Perhaps again with a story. Recently, reading the section on travel in a Saturday newspaper, I noticed a photograph showing a handsome couple in one of the beautiful courtyards of the Alhambra, in Granada. The caption read: 'Put yourself in the picture'. It occurred to me that the couple in the photograph could be seen as being its intended 'real text', framed by the suggestive environment which we may term as the 'context'. The composite of these, together with the caption, formed another, compound, text which functioned as an item in the context of the entire travel section, which itself was but one of the several sections that constituted the entire newspaper. The latter's 'text', in turn, could be read in a number of contexts: all the media messages that were issued on that day, etc. What matters here is the process that changes text and its context into a compound new text, which, in turn, is 'read' in some still broader context; and so on, seemingly without end.

A context might expose, point out, confirm and reinforce the primary, obvious, thrust of a text; but it might just as well give it a strange twist that sets up an opposition between the two, sometimes with a startling effect. In eighteenth- and nineteenth-century still lifes one might expect to see objects that were likely to be found, according to assumed degrees of probability and serendipity, on a table in a given place at a given moment. Such assemblages inform and suggest all sorts of extrapolations – that is, contexts. Picasso's and later Kurt Schwitters's collages, and still later Joseph Cornell's boxes, suggest different junctures, contexts. All of these test the imagination. So did Klee when he advised his students in the Bauhaus to collect objects on the street and assemble them into 'works of art'. The exercise appears to have been aimed at weakening the hold of the unthinking response and at mobilizing to a fuller extent the students' imagination. It was based (perhaps with the help of remembering some of Leonardo's thoughts about random visual patterns) on the capabilities of the vast combinatorial power of the mind.

Klee's experiment, alongside similar ones by Dadaists – and especially by surrealists such as André Breton – and *Finnegans Wake* by James Joyce, were among the antecedents that led to the work of Berio, whose preference for collage texts brought forth works like *Passaggio, Sinfonia, Coro*, besides *laborintus II* discussed above.

Combinatorial operations and automatic (random?) writing are at the heart of the mystical discipline developed by the Spanish cabbalist, Abraham Abulafia (1240–after 1292), which he calls *Hokhmath ha-Tseruf* (i.e. 'science of the combination of letters') (Scholem 1954: 130–8). Of particular interest is that Abulafia himself compared this practice to musical composition. He might be considered, with some justification, as having provided an example to John Cage and to Stockhausen in a number of their works. (It is of limited importance whether this influence was direct or indirect.)

Looking at the recent British repertoire, two works, both of which are based on large-scale collage-type libretti, stand out. Tippett's text for *The Mask of Time* is an assemblage of disparate elements, in part borrowed and in part written by the composer himself. The work succeeds largely on account of the unifying power of the music. The strong appeal of the Birtwistle–Zinovieff opera, *The Mask of Orpheus*, is due in some measure to the librettist's and composer's bold conceptualization of a unified new context for a whole array of mythic and philosophical material which they relate to *their* interpretation of the Orpheus myth.

Kagel, in his recent *The Passion of St Bach*, creates a surprising context by positing a number of startling analogies and transformations. This

281

substantial and serious work harks back, of course, to Bach's own Passions, in which the story of the suffering of Christ is the theme and text, and the compositions are the artistic, distanced, context. In turn, the Passions, in their totality, form a part of Bach's total vocal/choral output, the latter being a sort of *carmen perpetuum* in the context of Bach's life, in not only a musical but also a spiritual sense. This life, in turn, has become a theme, a subject for texts; this was realized long ago by historical musicologists and now Kagel has created a work in which Bach himself – the *composer* of Passions – is the central figure, the very 'text' of a passion based on *his* life.

My own *Foci* (1969) is a new context for a fairly wide range of different pre-existent texts in nine languages, uttered live or via pre-recorded tapes by over a dozen singers and speakers. These texts come from a dictionary of psychology, the *Old Testament*, the *Zohar*, the *Genevan Psalter*, the Ishtar legend, and a Voodoo ceremony; to these I added an oath formula, words related to quantification and snatches of colloquial English that I have either read or overheard.

Ben Johnston's *Vigil* has no text at all; at least not one that is to be set and uttered in a performance. The score consists only of the description of an action plan for improvisation by a choral group. The plan calls for the designation of a leader who is instructed 'to undertake an all-night vigil ... on behalf of an oppressed group of people. ... The vigil should entail a mild discomfort.' After the lapse of a certain period of time, this leader is to collect a selection of writings or sayings of 'dedicated members of the oppressed group. ...' These fragments are then studied and meditated upon by the members of the improvisation ensemble, and so on. In short, the work is nothing but a context for a group activity that is expected to produce (or it is hoped it will do so) a satisfactory realization of the idea behind the work.

Bronislaw Malinowski wrote that

> A statement spoken in real life is never detached from the situation in which it has been uttered. For each verbal statement by a human being has the aim and function of expressing some thought or feeling actual at that moment and in that situation. ... Without some imperative stimulus of the moment, there can be no spoken statement ... a word without *linguistic context* is a mere figment and stands for nothing by itself ... an utterance has no meaning except in the *context of situation*.
>
> (cited in Ogden and Richards 1946: 37)

The expanding patterns of interpenetrations between Western and non-Western societies and civilizations during the twentieth century give a new emphasis to Malinowski's statement. Borrowings from non-Western cultures by Western artists are a part of this vast movement of ideas. A recent and interesting example of this is *Choralis I, II, III* by Nigel Osborne, in which he combined Western-type procedures and materials with a Tuareg medicinal chant, a Turkish harvesting song and the Balinese *ketjak* to make an impressive amalgam. He set out to achieve this first by expertly transcribing these models into Western notation. Then he proceeded with imaginative transformations of these transcriptions, ultimately recombining them with other elements into a convincing new whole. The nature of the resulting new work and its context meant that the exorcistic dimension of the *ketjak* could be only alluded to. But this loss of authenticity may be regarded, at least from the vantage point of view of a Western listener, as having been compensated for by the substance of the new work and by the implications of a new context. Similar transfers are also likely to entail the severing of some relationships while bringing about hitherto unthought-of new ones. This can be an intricate and also a rewarding enterprise. Osborne showed boldness in undertaking it, and he succeeded admirably.

In his large-scale mythopoeic enterprises (*Ra*, and *The Princess of the Stars*), R. Murray Schafer has expanded his notion of context to include a predetermined place and a predetermined time of day, and even the number of those who can (must) participate in the performances, which consequently take the form and character of a new ritual. In *Ra* the locale was the impressive modern edifice of the Ontario Science Centre in Toronto. The myth of the sun-god was re-enacted by a fairly large cast and seventy-five co-celebrants (the audience) in a total audio-visual experience that included an Egyptian-style midnight meal, and an hour of rest, the whole lasting eleven hours from dusk to dawn. In *The Princess of the Stars* the legend upon which the work is based is Schafer's own. The work is presented in the open, along the shoreline of a lake. (The première took place in the Canadian Rocky Mountains.) It begins while it is still dark and ends sometime in the morning. Schafer says in the introduction to the work: 'What is the effect of treating nature in this way? By mythologizing it we intensify our experience of it'. By this, I presume, Schafer says that through this process an outer landscape is made to merge with an interior – mythical – scene in the mind; thus, nature and humankind, instead of being antagonists, may be once again integrated into a unified whole.

Contemporary philosophy and linguistics are showing concern for context or situation. This seems to be of relevance to music also. According to Mario Bunge, for example, 'like meaning, understanding is contextual: it does not occur unless a whole constellation of related items is activated'

(Bunge 1985, vol. 7, part 2: 268–9). Hans–Georg Gadamer writes about the 'concept of situation' that represents 'a standpoint that limits the possibility of vision.... An essential part of the concept of a situation is the concept of "horizon" ' (Gadamer 1975: 269). Elsewhere he coins the expression: the 'fusion of horizons' (ibid.: 273). According to Paul Ricoeur in *Hermeneutics and the Human Sciences*,

> What the text signifies no longer coincides with what the author meant; verbal meaning and mental meaning have different destinies, ... the text may explode the world of its author. ... The peculiarity of ... the work as such is ... to transcend its own psycho-sociological conditions of production and thereby to open itself to an unlimited series of readings, themselves situated in socio-cultural contexts which are always different. In short, the work *decontextualizes* itself, from the sociological as well as the psychological point of view, and is able to *recontextualize* itself differently in the act of reading.
>
> (Ricoeur 1981: 91)

and, we should add, in the act of composing also and, subsequently, of being listened to. (Such *decontextualization/recontextualization* seems to be the central idea of Osborne's *Choralis, I, II, III*.)

A fragment from the text of my duodrama for mezzo-soprano and pianist, entitled *Thisness*, can be cited as another instance of decontextualization and recontextualization (and also that of deconstruction and synthesis). It is the fifth of ten parts that constitute the entire text:

5 Vertigo

Reeling
       rolling
                into the cracks ...
    of words ...   worlds ...
Failing
       falling
             along an arc ...

                            *

along an arc ... a long arc ... arc along ...
arca long ... canor arca ... conar ... racon ...
lone agon ... wrong agon ... agonarch ... angor
agon ... racon ...

angor agon, agonal, galga agon, agonarch, galga
arc golag, galga lagōr golag, langōr golag, galga

long glagola golag, galga golag, galga galōr glagola golag, galga galōr glagolag, carna golag,
carna galga golag, glagola galgal golag, glagola gorgōn golag, gorgōn agon golag, carna gorgōn agon, carna agon gonal agolag, archōn agolag, archōn, golag, agonal, archōn, agon golag galac,
golag, glagolag, glogal golag, golan agon, golan
agon, golan agon canān, golan canān agon, galga
canān, agon, angor agon, agon, galga glogal,
can cana agon, cana agon, cana galga agon, angor agon golag, galga lagōr glagolag, galgal
anarch, archōn anarch ... orgōn anarch ... a-
narch ... anarch ... a narc ... a narc ... narc ...
narc ... narc ...

*

narc ... narca long ...

/ɑ/ /ɒ/ /ɔ/ /ʌ/ /o/
/ʀ/ /r/ /x/ /γ/ /χ/ /ʁ/ /ʕ/
/l/ /n/
/h/
o̥
ɔ

*

logar ... arcan logar ... arca long ... a
long arc ...

This text, which, after the first appearance of the phrase 'along an arc ...', uses (apart from the few paralinguistic sounds indicated in phonetic script) the restricted phonemic repertory of this single phrase only, was composed to evoke a number of contexts, through the use of certain 'code-words', or their approximations (such as, for example, 'golag' instead of 'gulag', 'angor' for its meaning in Latin (i.e. pressing together of the gullet, throttling) and also connoting anger, 'agon' standing for contest and also for agony, etc.). If, indeed, this does take place in the minds of listeners, the end result of such a 'creative listening' might be the imagining of alternative superordinate contexts that may be thought of as accommodating many or all the subordinate ones of which the listener has become aware.[3]

From guesses about what might be going on in the mind in some situations we proceeded towards the text. Considerations about the text led us to the context. The next logical step could be one that would lead us to the setting,

285

the composition itself and what the whole weave might mean. Presently, there seems to be no alternative to being idiosyncratically subjective or arbitrarily selective, when contemplating such a huge and complex maze as this one. You would not expect me to produce here a ground plan for this labyrinth, and I shall not pretend that I have one. But what we *do* have are our compositional and critical acts, our preferences and commentaries, and these might have some bearing on what one's own labyrinth, and some of those of one's colleagues, might be like.

Erik Bergman, in his *Noa*, severely reduced the biblical text to a few nouns and the single sentence: 'I am'. This Giacometti-like elimination imparts to the work a starkness and strength. One senses the white spaces between the words as holes, which are filled by Bergman's music to strong effect.

Richard Orton's *Sawlo Seed* is an *arcanum* in miniature. Its text, Shakespeare's Sonnet XII, is concealed in the work through a simple process of overprinting, resulting in a strange-looking script. Here is a part of what Orton says about the process and its purpose:

> I felt there was a mystery involved in the cipher-shapes themselves – of a meaning hidden beyond the façade. . . . Perhaps, one could reverse the earlier process; by overprinting, and the human agency, the print might once again become magical sound, the transforming Word. Thus would the performer become an alchemist, an alchemical musician, transforming the dross of the printed word into a living sound, himself becoming transformed in the process.
>
> (Notes in the score)

Here we have an example of deliberate concealment as potential means for revelation.

Odile Marcel, in a recent article about Maurice Ohana's use of text writes this:

> A partir des années 60, Maurice Ohana se déclare l'ennemi de la langue. Il part en guerre contre elle, dans des oeuvres qui évacuent le mot ou n'utilisent d'éléments linguistiques que pulverisés. . . .
>
> Le discrédit de la conscience et le refus de la psychologie traditionelle justifient qu'on se défie des mots.
>
> (Marcel 1986: 93)

[Since the 1960s Maurice Ohana declares himself to be an enemy of language. He wages war on it in works which empty words of meaning or only employ linguistic elements that are pulverized. . . .

The discrediting of the notion of consciousness and the renunciation of traditional psychology justify that one should distrust words.]

Should Marcel be right, we have here an example for a creative act brought about by the device of text-destruction, the whole signifying perhaps a critique or a protest. (Of course, Ohana and others had before them the example of the Theatre of the Absurd and its diverse antecedents.)

Now we may pose the question: under what circumstances is the use of a surrogate language (drum language, for example), and/or silence, warranted as musical signifiers? For instances of these I shall refer to my opera *Winthrop*, premièred in 1986. The work is about John Winthrop, the founder of Boston in New England. While composing the piece I realized, that, although the story is told from the viewpoint of the settlers, and John Winthrop in particular, *not* to portray the Indians of the colony in the work would amount not to an innocent omission but to conspicuous evidence of bias and falsification. So, they had to be included. But how? Could I ever hope to be able to 'speak' fairly and authentically on their behalf? I concluded that I was unable to do this. What was the alternative then? What I ended up doing was to depict the Indians entirely from the vantage point of the fear and distrust, the relative disinterest, and at times the cruelty, which the settlers felt towards and perpetrated against them. This is, then, what occurs in the work. A mysterious distant drumming is heard by the voyagers as their vessel approaches the coastline of America; this puts foreboding and fear into their hearts. This drumming persists through much of an entire scene (which is the first one of Act II). In a later scene Indian sachems pass by Boston in a wordless cortège, and we hear hostile comments regarding them uttered by the settlers. The march has a droll, pseudo-exotic nature; both music and words convey a mutual lack of understanding, distrust and, on the part of the Bostonians at least, disdain. (The wordlessness of the Indians here is a purposeful act. It is the manifestation of a resolve not to depart from silence. It is a strong gesture.) Lastly, after the Bostonians have attacked and mortally wounded a large proportion of the Pequot tribe in an allegedly punitive raid, we hear the inarticulate sounds of dying men and women. This is followed by a piercing wailing by another group of women, a kind of ululation of grief. These are the sole instances of vocal sounds the Indians make in the opera.

We have considered text and context and touched upon individual works. But a link is missing: those who listen and respond. Michael Polanyi, who seemingly was equally at home in science and in philosophy, propounded a broad view when he suggested in *The Tacit Dimension* (1966) the idea of 'tacit knowing': we seem to understand more than what we think we know, and are able to demonstrate that we know it. We all chart our way in this vast labyrinth of texts, contexts, situations and horizons, and even add a wrinkle or two to it. We compare notes with each other. And while we do this, we also hear voices that say that, basically, we might be alone. Isaac Luria, the teacher in Safed, put it this way:

> every word of the Torah has six hundred thousand 'faces', that is, layers of meaning or entrances, one for each of the children of Israel who stood at the foot of Mount Sinai. Each face is turned toward only one of them; he alone can decipher it. Each man has his unique access to Revelation.
>
> (Scholem 1965: 13)

One reads, and re-reads; listens and listens again. We accept the new on occasions, and on other occasions we refuse access to it. We keep on working on the loom; there is no alternative, as Arachne's example shows. Do you recall Arachne's story as retold by Ovid? The master-weaver girl, the proud one, who did not shrink from the challenge of a weaving contest issued by none other than Pallas Athene herself. Brazen girl, poor, wonderful Arachne; she was turned into a spider by the vengeful goddess with the destiny to spin forever in concert with her descendants. ... Yes we recognize her as one of us, and ourselves as parts of her, and recall also, with a thought that comes from the heart, the theme of the marvellous tapestry she wove for that memorable occasion.[4,5]

NOTES

1 An epistemological field. See Foucault (1973: xxii).
2 Some of these categories would benefit from being looked at from the point of view of the 'speech acts', as conceptualized by J.L. Austin and others.
3 For further comment on *Thisness* see Anhalt (1988).
4 I first wrote this text for, and read it at, The Royal Music Association's 22nd Annual Conference, on 'Words and Music' held on April 10–12, 1987, at Westfield College, University of London. The present essay is a slightly altered version of that original paper.
5 I have continued this exposition and discussion in the closely related paper 'Music: context, text, counter-text' (Anhalt 1989).

REFERENCES

ANHALT, I. (1984) *Alternative Voices: Essays on Contemporary Vocal and Choral Composition*, Toronto: University of Toronto Press.

——(1988) '*Thisness*: Marks and Remarks', in J. Beckwith and F.A. Hall (eds) *Musical Canada: Words and Music Honouring Helmut Kallmann*, pp. 211–31.

——(1989) 'Music: context, text, counter-text', *Contemporary Music Review* 5: 101–35.

BUNGE, M. (1985) *Treatise on Basic Philosophy*, vol. 7, Dordrecht and Boston: D. Reidel Publishing Co.

CHATMAN, S. (1981) 'How do we establish new codes of verisimilitude', in W. Steiner (ed.) *The Sign in Music and Literature*, Austin: University of Texas Press.

ERNOUT A. and MEILLET A. (1932) *Dictionnaire Etymologique de la Langue Latine. Histoire des Mots*, Paris: Librarie C. Klincksieck.

FOUCAULT, M. (1973) *The Order of Things*, New York: Vintage Books.

GADAMER, H.-G. (1975) *Truth and Method*, New York: Seabury Press.

HJELMSLEV, L. (1961) *Prolegomena to a Theory of Language*, Madison, Milwaukee and London: University of Wisconsin Press.

JAKOBSON, R. (1968) *Child Language Aphasia and Phonological Universals*, The Hague and Paris: Mouton.

MARCEL, O. (1986) 'Maurice Ohana: L'Usage de la Parole', in *La Revue Musicale*, nos. 391–3: 87–105.

MARCHANT, J.R.V., CHARLES, J.F. *et al.* (1955) *Cassell's Latin Dictionary*, revised, London, Toronto, Melbourne and Sydney: Cassell.

OGDEN, C.K. and RICHARDS, I.A. (1946) *The Meaning of Meaning*, 8th edn. New York: Harcourt, Brace & World.

ONIANS, R.B. (1951) *The Origins of European Thought About the Body, the Mind the Soul, the World Time and Fate*, Cambridge: Cambridge University Press.

POLANYI, M. (1966) *The Tacit Dimension*, Garden City, NY: Doubleday.

RICOEUR, P. (1981) *Hermeneutics and the Human Sciences*, Cambridge: Cambridge University Press.

SCHOLEM, G. (1954) *Major Trends in Jewish Mysticism*, 3rd edn, New York: Schocken Books.

——(1965) *On the Kabbalah and its Symbolism*, London: Routledge & Kegan Paul.

——(1974) *Kabbalah*, New York: Quadrangle/The New York Times Book Co.

——(1987) *Origins of the Kabbalah*, The Jewish Publication Society, Princeton University Press.

SEWELL, E. (1964) *The Human Metaphor*, Notre Dame, Ind.: University of Notre Dame Press.

SZILAGYI, J.Gy. (1977) 'Arachné', *Antik Tanulmányok* 2: 125–38.

URBACH, E.E. (1987) 'Torah', in M. Eliade (ed. in chief) *The Encyclopedia of Religion*, vol. 14, pp. 556–65, New York: Macmillan; London: Collier Macmillan.

YATES, F. (1966) *The Art of Memory*, London: Routledge & Kegan Paul.

15

On Making Music Out of Music

EDWIN LONDON

This 'essay' crosses the wires of intention by asserting that invention in musical matters is to be understood as nothing better (or worse) than the capacity to embroider pre-ordained and existing structures in a most deliberate manner – a literal-never-ending-litany of the blue in eternal iteration. The attempt to achieve improvisatory freedom (with wilful streaming of freely associated allusion) in a context which otherwise demands discursive order and stricture of linear expository prose, downplays for the immediate moment the considerable and concerted effort of composition. Were we not to possess the Sketchbooks of Beethoven might his method be better understood as a more or less casual diurnal pass over materials with which he, asleep or awake, was willing to identify? While sharpening pencils for another project – 'give us this day our daily bread?' – may he have nonchalantly abandoned Opus 130, perhaps with a hint of 'so-what?' horse sense, in order to get on with the next paying project? Proceeding, then, with a short and respectful paean to Irving Berlin's centenary, the following prose piece reasserts esteem for the rigours of composition by imposing putative form on a ramble through content essentially developed by musical means. One principal aspect of its intent can be said to be the desire to show solidarity with the compositional profession (a holy order of metabolically prone sound wizards), represented through undertonalities of allusive citation. Mention of some well-known members of the guild, past and present, is to be partially construed as a joyful exercise in hearing the sound of 'meaning-loaded' names, even as residues of their oeuvres waft in a colossally polyphonic Symphony Sidereal. It should be kept in mind, too, that the musical effect of this aria might be greater if it were read aloud and/or sung contrapuntally, perhaps with invocation of fugal

290

elements. I leave this option to the intrepid fantasy-prone reader or to gangs of uninhibited operatic empiricists.

I
SPREAD IT WHERE CREDIT'S DUE

Way back, when 'Pound-a-noun-' Stein and Royal Rooster (with strings, no less) came together at the invitation of Perotin, there was an agreement of sorts. As consequence, jet stream widened (whitened?) purview into the century of Berl-in 'wested' (as sainted father ably might say). Himself (IB all alone ohne Emma at the proto forma te-le-fo-no), a virgin transplant, who might croon, in obvious preference to would-be era of ill feeling, 'Always faithful in the So. USA,' he mobilized lyric armies for global combat (GoBLAM).

Civil?
Indeed!

Born, it seems, to cut short (amongst other things) the hegemony of the irascible scion of paunchy de Leon's eon, there was hell to pay (music hath more than soothing charms). Either a burrower at a lender bee, up in the morning, or, yes, still not free of grisly dolphine neon, he joined the Marco Polonius ragtime band (the B's, the beats, the bees' asses stung); meanwhile Thisbe's buskin clawed sinus touted Milenburg joys by bebopping oo-de-busy commerce. This left Troy, at least for the moment, to react intact – not sacked. In fact, only partially blinded by war, as evil eye lay dying (cataract) on mahi mahi armoire of old down home songs, ('six flats unfurnished') a hit, Erl-king lur-king, re-emerged in the left hand. Thankful for this ware were the leaders of D'arbyshille who suffered severely from endemic lie shock syndrome. Would shy Locke (1632–1704) have done St Matthew better? Hierarch's bunker (a dreadful Alexandrine underground) went kerplunk at the mere thought of losing the prerogatives of E-Death intimidation; the welcome mat read in part (corrupt spelling) 'Eire's Choice Voice'. The good folk are all together on this one and latinized, 'Sic semper,' at coarse REB-el temper. (Oy) Sure! This indubitable morality signifies the corporeal nothing of which Shakespeare made note, for (aye) being no prince (a mere herr, sir, and not mine) he (ah) gets no good night suite. But then again, the pedagogue himself, inspired by more than bibliographical vigilance exhorts his wards with orthodox words, not swords, that seem to sound in messy swards of imprecation to say, 'Copy right, copy right, you fools.' There is double edge to the remark, though in this case, the lower of two breeds silence, which may be a more slashing cut and the most unkindest one at that. This VIP manque ran wrinkle, popped on a snapped crackle of Cat's kills and left the author's Iberian forehead paso dobling to no apparent avail as Washington's Irving, shot through with melody, upon seeing the whites of Easter eggs in parade of sky blue Christmas plums played it as it lay. This wan Taiwan Juan won one wand for the yipper: the capitol alive at a hundred.

II

ONE FINE DAY, ALONG CAME GUIDO D'

At this late date, 10,000 years into the epoch of civility (no merrimental behaviour please), a spasmodic census of waste revealed (more or less) complete data (senza sentimento) implicative of a span/scan gamut (almost), silently uttered in dactylic quatrains ranging from scepticemic sceptic/cynic to predisposed na(t)ive idealogue. In so sense innocence; but yet . . .

Fast	Mister	**Yost**	offered	**toast**
Lest	his	**ghost**	crave some	**roast**
Beef	at	**post**	office	**feast.**
Must	this	**boast**	reach the	**coast?**
		(etc.)		

The proem to which is, after all, a stiffed through the sift of graffiti, i.e. a public service announcement of 'mystery-in-progress' as setup. Be prepared, one is warned, for the toughest queries. Individual collective cultural anniversaries and personal clocks run swift current, conjunct, but, alas, sometimes, too, disjointed messages of counter-pointless clucking ducks enraptured by 'Laszlo' Lasso's especial quasi-British labefactation (Arne you glad you're you?). Buddha pressed a book arrest? Well no, not exactly.

His purse excelling, his breadth intending, his lawn intoning, what could he be thinking?

'Two weeks to goal'	he	**shook;**
'Tweak toga,'	he	**rattled;**
'Too weak to go'	he	**rolled**

and staggered away . . . quivering.

Thus, an unrecorded trip ticked into infernal nether land of dissolving Austro-Hungarian empire:

Mahler in **Harlem** again,
but still, like, you know,
superior to **Lehar** in **Lahore**
or **Lear** in **Le Havre**

This reflected the scene for a more deltoid merrie wind sore window than ought possibly to have been mirrored by the nickel eye of spontaneous light laughter. Hosanna shouted at provocative centuries–old international style show themes were incisive addition. Remarked woeful widow Anna Grama Redemptorisottovoce,

'Wear armor Lloyd.'

The sorest purposeful sage (Roget's Le roi d'Isness) allow-lows those in show business debut to make C-noh-te of La (ma-mer-ha-ya-na) sans tyne un-miked. In uttered words if:

(Weber + n) = (Berlioz − lz),

does Shakespeare's comings (eek) obscure the circled eye shade of Carl Maria von Oberon? He, who indirectly lighted the last of Vienna's bassoon/oboe network woodwinds (reeding scripture without the saxophones), was master of Your Ol' Auntie's overtures. It's so implausibly impertinent to summon Tone-man the Carbarian to a no lard or land mass. Alas, a ka-contagious Cyrile-itus spreading to the exposed extremities is in lieu loose but tractable.

293

> itty-bitty Banal-ity
> bitty Banal-ity bitty
> Banal-ity!
>
> (repeat ad libitum)

What became of the berg when the ice melted? In Hector's sector G. Meyerbeer left huge untidy knots of more than just one of those things. Later in Strauss's strassen, the deadly Spazier gang (walking in Heinrich's Shoes) let it be known that 'I am **Chaim**' was no longer grata in **Siam**. The epic dribbler, World B. **Priam**, shouting 'I am the greatest,' mourned over **Miami**, as my American cousin, gorgeous George S. (Alabamy bound) played 'Illinois fell on Azerbaijan.' The supreme sacrifice seemed plausible only to the bounders. Further south, a sort of pragmatic half-baked (Kaff-cough) Alaska was served. One heard 'Mush a due' resonating during rituals of retributive vociferation performed by a band of transplanted gnomes in obvious hilarious reference, one would think, to a rare tragi-comical pair (no doubt the dysfunctional hint, alluding to the upside downturn life had taken over for these unfortunate dimorphs, may fairly be said to be in bad taste). The ears of the victims, filled with the blood pressures of inversion, heard human words for the last time on this earth. The crowd chanted,

'eat	it	when	you	meet	it, ...
heed	it	when	you	read	it, ...
cheat	it	when	you	greet	it, ...'

Forsaken, at peril, salvation denied, there is no fuzz-eye stable heir of theirs racing the hopeful Elba hare after might-have-been escape. Oh no! On the contrary, behind them for whom the belle's toad patiently led researchers to a recently discovered document (it's only a papyrus rune) there was revealed a sanctimonious secular message in the form of a gambeson:

> 'This is not politics,
> This is not religion.
> But is it art?'

(a short interlude)

wholly vowels, a piacere,

A   E   I   O   U
in any order

(about 15 seconds to clear the air)

III
HARD WORK AND AARDVARKS CREATE CASTLES-IN-THE-AIR

Are our immortal souls, pre-existent to our earthly birth, swimming in seas of language formations and depth structures which, when filtered out for temporary terrestrial use, become something specific like English, Ibo or Etruscan? Really now, is it necessary, Junius, to wrestle with this sort of puzzler to cerebrate (if denigration provided by ardent vestigial Wagnerian Aryan provides sufficient provocation) the obvious:

WE ARE LANGUAGE PRONE

Thus we invent nothing but the embroidery of the given

Hello – Meow – A low blow!
Is it difficult, alone,
With aplomb,
To swallow a hollow kilo
Of Cologne jello?

Need we disallow
The Milhaud fellow
A halo whose pillow
Once rested the
Fallow bordello mellow
Plum yellow willow
(not **Othello's**),
Which drowned
The sallow malodorous sailor
Apollo

295

Whose callow cello
Bellowed below
In depth of shallow disputation?

If mad at me, speak Hawaiian; and go plant a monad seed; nail it to the roof; Yeh, Slim, and remember **Mezz, de moaner,** was a licorice stickler! If **Music** (boldly capitalized for the sake of this argument) is language, may it be conceded, there is precious little wrung out of compsymposition save that we are

> making music out of making out music out of making music out of music?
> oobe   dobe ool ya oobe   ool oobe ool ya   oobe   dobe ool ya oobe?

The following, when sung, one might conjecture, to the tune of HOME ON THE RANGE is not necessarily undesirable. H _ _ _   O _ T _ _ R _ _ _ _ is an undiscouraged proteroantecedent tonal ambit making almost-music out of almost-music, in which lyric intent is meant to be illustrative of the inherited longing of the folk for plenty of lebensraum 'neath starry skies above. Yet bury me not contrariwise, if the sung prose has to be excorciated, let it be for the right reasons. Seemly or not, the infernal domain of martyrdom, about which everyone has agreed, at least, to prove that immortality is not retroactive, will justly define inferential performance requirements mandated by stalking hoarseness and the Queen's tall knight. Prepared for rough ride into a rude valley reserved for six hundred (including GoGo-like goners) how can it help but mask manifest demand made on sore throats. **Humpty Dumpty** and **Talking horses?** They speak of cracked eggs and dying men.

(a chorus of motley howls ensues)

IV
HONK IF YOU BELIEVE IN BUNK
(FORD AND MONK)

In the midst of **il mondo della bomba** a refrain is overheard asking a familiar question 'Tennis anyone?' Other mind-boggling conundrums yet

296

to be posed seem to float near the surface of everyday conversation. Example 1 (**Oh-oh- deh-oh** ... an extended levantine **melisma** keyed to generational **grapple** is presently in the foreground). One perceives a long line of **chanting** businessmen 'n' boasting **bubble-gummers** mixing, though not at all very well). ('Teenies anyone?') A daunting pile of them, yes, inquiries, that is, circulate and more flow at each **nervous entry** of new denizens into **the formicary**: (the canons of **orthodoxy** mandate severe clunking and crawly counterpoint). As the bee stings (or the Wasp aunt thereof), **the beast sings** in two parts of open-score surgery without buzz evident. Comanche-onus! A chain of **contravallation** confuses issues between the offenders and the besieged. The **impalpable** speech of dying men recalls to life anguished **Dickens languishing** (languaging in English?) on an invisible table of operation. If there be truth and justice spouting from the purest of hoses let the iniquity of poverty be revealed now without doubtful benefit of added voices in invertible **clerical bewilderment**. Liquidity again –

THIS IS NOT POLITICS
THIS IS NOT RELIGION.

V

PSALM END'S SHANTY LEAVENING
– C'EST LA VIE

With diversity a guiding principle, and perpetual inflective variation on a highly personal base constantly present, a fundamental constituent, Ragtime returns, not as it was, but as it is. Trance scripture (exhibiting the opulence of collective enterprise) is the thing (a new play within an old play on an old theme, with a new song about an old wrong as day ends along a river flowing with troubles and woe) perhaps capturing no conscience or king, but powerful enough to spark an ever-evolving process of communication. This functional identity of past, present, and future enhances an interactive currency backed by the solid principles of generational dynamics. Is my great-grandfather's father my father's son? The world, as Wittgenstein did not bother to say, is an interlocked receptacle of Talmudic commentary, in which the motivated silence of the artist is as respected as would be his/her exclamation points raised in strenuous polyphonic articulation. It's just intonation, nothing more as the wheel is benignly reinvented.

There is a long and honoured tradition of making music out of music. OK. Just as J.S. Bach used traditional chorales to prepare, with infinite loving care,

true **artistry**

and respect for the sources (his fingers in flour kneading, as often as not, dough), a grand series of utilitarian miniature musical gems, for spiritual consumption

so may **we,**
with **humility,**
consciously
utilize **JSB.**

His   commodious   harmonious   melodious   ingenious

recipe
is **redolently**
suggestive **apparency**

in the manifold beatific creation of new and nourishing sustenance. The inherited

legacy
stemming from his musical forbearers, **the**
non-**proprietary**

ownership of which was to be rolled over from other priors (Christian brothers), or prior others (vielleicht Freischütz marksmen), provides, even at this late date, genuine food for thought. Developed with reference to processes of historical reconstruction

(more **embroidery,**
mythology,

298

and mannered ornamentation emanating from the naked), Louis Seize offers anecdotal antidote to

morbidity:

BETTER BUTTER THAN DREAD SILENCE
(a tango)

Why		bread		to		munch
	as		red	Ed	fled	
wry		bred		at		lunch
	to		dead	Ted	fed	
	is		said	as		hunch.
	For			Fred	led	Ned
	to		wed	in-	stead.	
And	my			gin		punch
	was			shed	on	spread.
Lou's			bed	holds		bunch
sans			head	to		crunch

(verse sigh)

for cabbage or king.

The absolution conferred by the processes of historical transferability is, to say the least, an effective means in the commerce fostered by mutual agreement.

LANGUAGE IS EXTENDED, NOT INVENTED.

To say otherwise is to raise false hopes. The cadences of deception have cast an unnecessary submediant cloud over the simplest of life's rituals. Two beat has been implied elsewhere, or not dew bee to be due beet ooze. And why not? Add some words, Dr Johnson, and we can sing it together.

16

Verso-l'uno

WALTER BRANCHI

Matter is the same everywhere.

> Matter of the stars is
> the matter of the earth.
> The kind of light
> they give off carries a
> sort of fingerprint which
> allows us to say that up
> there are the same atoms
> we find on earth.
> The same kind of atoms
> appear in living
> and non-living creatures.
> Frogs are made of the
> same stuff as rocks, but
> with different atomic
> arrangements
> (*R. Feynman*)

All the different atomic arrangements constitute all things and all creatures of the Universe or Nature.

We may wonder: is the Universe the result
of an original matter–antimatter split? It is certain that
at a subatomic level the collision of matter with antimatter is
annihilation: self-destruction and
transformation into electromagnetic radiation
of a pair of particles, positive and negative.
The subatomic particles with opposite sign
are antimatter; that is, positrons (anti-electrons), anti-protons,
anti-neutrons, etc.

Universe is space–time matter distribution

Universe is the aggregate of non-simultaneous and only partially
overlapping, non-identical, but always complementary, omni-transforming,
and weighable energy events.
(*Einstein and others*)

The Universe is the aggregate of all of humanity's consciously-
apprehended and communicated experience with the nonsimultaneous,
non-identical, and only partially overlapping, always complementary,
weighable and unweighable, ever omni-transforming, event sequences.
(*R. Buckminster Fuller*)

Chemical elements are formed
from the smallest particles of
matter, the atom. Solid, liquid
and gaseous organic and
inorganic substances derive
from the various combinations
of the hundreds of chemical
element known today (Periodic
Table of the Elements) and
therefore from the hundreds of
varieties of stable atoms
existing in nature.

Elementary or atomic particles are the units which constitute matter in its
various forms: protons, mesons, electrons, positrons, neutrons and others.

301

Atomic particles tend – in their unceasing movement caused by heat – to reach a uniform temperature and distribution or, as the Second Law of Thermodynamics says, to reach the maximum of entropy. It is obvious, however, that matter in the Universe is non-equally distributed. There are regions of ordered diversity at different levels such as atoms, crystals, stars and galaxies.

Most of these regions have
a characteristic *form* of their own and that form is synonymous with the
       relation among particles according to a certain order
    or *system*

           Every organism
consists of cells, molecules, atoms and other
matter units, but is not from them that
form arises. It is a different category from
matter because form doesn't depend on the
nature of matter particles, but rather it is
the result of how particles relate to each
other within the system. Matter – in the
broader meaning of the word – energy – is
conservative and it always tends towards
uniformity and maximum, entropy.
       On the other hand, form is mutation and creativity.

Energy is the agent of mutation.

Everything is energy; the form and movement of every existing thing are the various concentrations of energy

and the result of transformation.

The amount of energy in the Universe has always been the same and so it will always be.
In its own manner, energy is finite but
infinitely conserved.

302

How much matter a body can contain is its
mass, but mass is energy and therefore
energy is matter equivalent; *energy*
possesses mass and mass represents energy
according to Einstein's formula:

$$E = mc^2$$

where E is energy in ergs, m is mass
in grams and c is the speed of light in
cm/sec. Since the speed of light
is equal to about 30 billion cm/sec,
a small mass can generate a lot of
energy

Einstein once said: 'The more
interesting a theory is, the simpler
are its premises; the more different events it
puts in relation, the larger will be its range
of application'.

Thermodynamics is the study of energy and its transformations.

The First Law
of Thermodynamics or of conservation says that although energy cannot
be created nor destroyed,
it can be transformed
into another form of
energy.

The Second Law
of Thermodynamics says that whenever energy changes from one state
to another, a certain 'toll' is exacted
or better, a certain part
of energy
becomes unavailable,
it disintegrates
or dissipates itself tending
to a concentration loss,
to a randomization and
therefore to
entropy.

303

Entropy comes from the disintegration or dissipation of energy states. Entropy means dissociative energy, disintegration of complex systems into atomic particles which tend, through their unceasing movement caused by heat, towards a uniform temperature and distribution, i.e. presence of equilibrium, absence of order, of limits and therefore of relations.

Negentropy or negative entropy, conversely, comes from the integration of energy states. Negentropy is synonymous with associative energy, of conservation, transformation, energy concentration into atomic particles and synthesis of them to form entities or complex systems, i.e. absence of equilibrium, presence of order and relations and therefore of forms.

Any entity formed by putting together parts according to
a certain order of relations constitutes a *system*
The presence of a system in the Universe (the system of systems)
excludes the Universe outside the system itself,
limits the rest of the Universe which is inside the system
and configures itself in turn as a system.
A house, a book or a piece of music – each are systems.
A system can be both physical and metaphysical.
A thought is a metaphysical system
since it can be seen as a complex of interrelations
among parts the limit of which is arbitrarily chosen
by the thinker as a subdivision of the
universal continuity. Thought is inherently conceptual
and conceptuality is the elaboration and formulation of
one single, isolated image of a thought-system.

Form

It is the perceptible expression of the organization of matter
through a systematic configuration. It is active energy in
space-time. Every form is only one of the many resultants of a
system; my own form W.B. is undoubtedly a man-system
resultant and it differs from other forms of the same system
not on the basis of substance but rather on the
structural relations of substance.

304

Atomic properties are not
reducible to
the properties of all its parts summed
together. If we take the neutron, the
proton and electron of a hydrogen atom
and arbitrarily combine them,
our chances of obtaining a hydrogen atom
are highly improbable. In order to
reconstitute the hydrogen atom it is
necessary to arrange its parts
according to an exact *relation*

A fundamental aspect of form is that the integration of its
energy states is always functionally correlated to its
activity. That is to say, the interrelation among its
constituent parts is basically regulated according to the
various aspects such a form has to assume.

Every system is characterized by constants or *invariants*.
Although invariants are relatively few, systems and their different forms are
almost infinite.

The astronomers and mathematicians J.B. Carr and M.J. Rees
have revealed that the basic features of the physical world are
essentially determined by a few microphysical constants or
invariants which manifest themselves on many different scales,
but which are intimately interrelated. 'Several aspects of our
universe', they emphasize, 'some of which seem to be prerequisites for the evolution of any form of life, depend rather
delicately on apparent "coincidences" among the physical constants [...] The size of a planet is the geometric mean of the size
of the Universe and the size of an atom; the mass of man is the
geometric mean of the mass of a planet and the mass of a proton.'

The form of *Le ali di Angelico* is one of many possible
forms with respect to its generative *system of sound*.
A system of sound is the limiting agent of
imagination in musical creation, or, expressed differently,
the system of sound is limited by imagination and at the
same time it becomes the limiting agent of imagination.

305

The choice of invariants in the system of sound comes
from the composer's imagination according to the
musical dimension he or she wants to create. The same
invariants will limit this imagination while he or she is
giving form to the piece.

Interrelations between different levels of the invariants, which are organized according to compositional strategies, determine the characteristics of
the system of sound, and lead it toward the definition of one of the
perceptible forms it can assume.

Now, if we accept the general idea that a system or whole is characterized
by a set of relations among entities, or sub-systems, and among their
invariants, and that these relations cannot be isolated in accordance with
the linear causality principle, then each whole always becomes a reflection
of the cosmic whole. The greater or lesser communion of relations among
the invariants belonging to many wholes determines the resonance level
they bear in the Universe. The effect that a composition of mine produces
upon the listener is not important *as such*, but rather what is important is
how the composition harmonizes in a complex of systems, where, of course,
we consider people and systems as an integral function of the Universe.

> I am looking for a cosmic music,
> the music of the rising
> planetary culture

> We
> are changing
> The communication revolution is
> changing us. The current invasion of
> communication technologies is clearly
> changing the nature of our
> environment
> and consequently of our behaviour.
> But unlike all previous changes, this
> concerns – for the first time – the earth
> planet in a global sense, people and
> cultures. We are almost living in an
> electronic environment which makes the
> world *smaller and smaller,*
> *included* and *accessible.*

In this dimension, our planet is
nothing more than a 'Spaceship
Earth', as Buckminster Fuller calls it,
and we are its passengers.

'Spaceship Earth' is part
of the solar fleet. The sun exerting its
great gravitational attracting force,
forces the earth, as well as all the
other planets of the fleet,
to rotate around it.

Two bodies are attracted to each other by a force which is
proportional to their masses and inversely proportional to the square of
their distance. (*I. Newton*)

'Spaceship Earth', whose radius is less than 6,000 kilometres, rotates
around the sun at an average distance of about 149 million kilometres and
traverses its path at 108,000 kilometres per hour.

The whole solar fleet, in its spiral movement, travels at 70,000 kilometres
an hour leading to a point in the sky near the bright star of Vega in the
Lyra constellation. During a year its passengers cover 946 million kilometres
around the sun and collectively more than a billion and a half kilometres.

The distances that separate the planets from the sun are absolutely
negligible with respect to the distance that separates the sun from the
nearest star Proxima Centauri which is situated at more than four light
years away (about 10 trillion kilometres).

'Spaceship Earth' with its ten different movements, surrounded by the
gaseous shell which accompanies it, the atmosphere, travels in the absolute
vacuum and silence of space.

Consciously thinking that it is not the sun rising and setting, but rather the
earth that in its rotational movement, completes the night–day cycle
$365\frac{1}{4}$ times a year, is already universal thinking.

307

We are living in an evolutionary process which will bring humanity towards a total integration: self-individuation in the universal dimension and equal distribution of wealth derived by the intelligent exploitation of all planetary energy resources.

The bigger obstacle is represented by politicians. They wish to keep things separated and therefore to retain geographic, economic and other kinds of barriers; this is the only way they can control and wield power. Demolishing barriers and separations would mean their mass suicide.

Politicians are the real opponents and the cause of dissatisfaction; war – never more relevant than today – make the holocaust of all humanity a possibility. The historical role of the politician is now finished since planetary wealth is a technological and not a political issue; more human lives have been saved by antibiotics than by all the meetings of leaders to discuss starvation in the world.

The work of politicians can be more efficiently carried on by a computer. For example, the distribution of wealth at a world level can be actuated *only* through computer control because of the enormous number of variables to consider and compute.

Boundaries and subdivisions consist not only of continents and states, but also of like individuals or circumscribed groups of human beings. Physics and metaphysics are portions.
Specialization is a type of fractionalization that is widespread and strongly encouraged by those in power. Specialization derives from a mechanistic world view (Cartesian, Newtonian) and it leads to a model of knowledge in which every object or event is seen as an apparatus that is in a totally causal relationship with the giant cosmic 'machine'. Specialization produces one-directional minds incapable of considering single events within the context of global interactions. The specialist in one field cannot communicate with another unless there exists a common area of expertise.

308

The unfortunate consequence of such
specialty barriers is that knowledge,
instead of being pursued in depth and
integrated in breadth, is pursued in
depth in relative isolation. Instead of
obtaining a continuous and coherent
picture, we get fragments of remarkably
detailed but isolated patterns.
We are drilling holes in the wall
of mystery that we call nature and reality
in many locations, and we carry out
delicate analyses on each of the sites.
(*E. Laszlo*)

In nature,
unlike the specialistic approach,
every thing and every event are
interconnected, joined together,
and each of them is nothing
but a manifestation of the
same universal integrity.

The specialistic knowledge model
is incapable of understanding how different
events interact when they are simultaneously
subjected to a certain
amount of different
influences.
Almost every event we deal with
it is constituted by a complex of entities
which are multi-dimensionally correlated.

To comprehend the Universe means to be conscious that the characteristics of every whole are not reducible to the mere characteristics of its isolated parts. A whole is such because its constituent parts are interrelated according to a proper order. A whole is, in its turn, related to other wholes to form a larger whole. This holistic view of the Universe is inherent to an *omni-comprehensive* thinking that is just the opposite of the specialistic one.

309

Thinking in terms of facts and events in the context of wholes, forming integrated sets with their own properties and relationships, is the attitude that has to be developed by humanity in order to become a conscious part of the universal wholeness.

To create any whole system, or entity, be it physical or
metaphysical, is fundamentally an
omni-comprehensive type of thinking.
To comprehend the relationships, for example, between
the law of gravitation, thermodynamics and a musical
composition is as important as comprehending the
relations between these same laws and a chemical
compound – and why not? The relationship between a
chemical compound, let's say sugar, and my composition
Dall'angolo di una nuvola.
A musical composition is a dynamic field of gravitational
attraction levels (intervals) among different sonorous
entities. As in the solar system, and also
in a system of sound,
each planet that forms has its own attraction level with
respect to the system's sun.
The unceasing movement of such entities within a system
of sound is the echoing of the movement of the planets of
the solar system.

A musical composition is a set of relations
not of notes!

A musical composition is similar to a sugar molecule
constituted by the interrelation among 12 carbon, 22
hydrogen, and 11 oxygen atoms.

A musical composition is above all imagination which
assumes a form through a system.
The set of internal relations in relation to the set of
external ones, make it an integral part of the Universe.

310

A musical composition is a region of ordered diversity
located in time and space;
it is a concentration of energies
and as such it puts itself in relation with
larger systems
varying with all the different forces which gravitate
around it during the various
seasons, days,

h

o

u

r

s.

It is mutable because those very same forces also
gravitate upon
the listener
modifying
his own
listening

The incredible development of electronic technology and the revolution of the means of communication have set the basis for a planetary unification process. It is almost perceptible everywhere as an associative force within humanity. It is almost interconnected via computers, television, satellites, and it measures itself and inexorably tends towards a global integration (integration being quite different from uniformity). Furthermore, if this process is only just beginning, the sense of being a part of a large eco-system in which a change in even its smallest part inevitably reverberates over the entire system, is already present in our world picture even if not always consciously formulated. The disappearance of fragmentations and disparities will come only on the basis of an equal distribution of all the resources of the world with respect to the entire world population. The development of this attitude and consequent wealth depends above all on the consciousness level that each of us has in being an active part of the earth-system and omni-comprehensive thought. This is the way that will break down little by little, all the geographic, economic, and cultural barriers and political organizations which now hold sway.

We are entering an age of planetary culture
and
planetary culture
implies
planetary thought
and
planetary thought means integral thought
in that it is inherent to all the Universe's constituent elements.

To compose music with the ears of the Universe and not with those of
one's own cultural environment
means integral thought.
Blending in the approach of things and ideas
the scientific knowledge of the West with the mysticism of the East
is integral thought.

Integral thought is
to know and to complete the dynamics of fundamental values
of a culture with those of all others.

Imagination and integral thought are the fundamental agents for the
evolution of humanity on a universal scale.

Through imagination one can put together ideas
and facts in new relations, in new forms,
thus extending the frontiers of methodology.
It is the means of innovation, the quality which
leads men and women to raise themselves from
the lowest level of life to become creators.

Evolution.

Evolution is connected with
transformation
and transformation with conservation.

312

Transformation and conservation are the two
inherent principles of the nature of things.
They occur again and again in every realization
of man whatever the field of inquiry. Nothing
can be real without the presence of both of
them. Mere transformation without
conservation means to pass from nothing to
nothing and mere conservation without
transformation can conserve nothing.

Through a means such as the computer, imagination can find a unique way
to express itself. In musical creation, for example, the composer can imagine
both the limits of the composition (system) and the composition itself
(form). This possibility is totally different from that inherent in traditional
instrumental musical creation, where the composer can easily imagine the
composition. However, in this case, the composition has to be contained
within the physical limits of the musical instrument-system which is necessary for its realization. This limit, together with the performer's own psychomotor limits, defines the nature and range within which traditional
music has been thought and realized. When one uses a computer, the
physical machine doesn't set limits of any sort to one's imagination. But
this doesn't mean that a thought-object, an energy concentration, a musical
form could materialize itself without having been ordered (limited) in a set of
relations (system) which are functionally useful to the composer's imagined
form. One then passes from a physically limited dimension, immutable and
pre-determined with respect to a musical composition, to one whose limits
are determined by a composer according to systems of ideas whose range is
defined only by his imagination. Now, given this possibility, one can naturally wonder: if there are no longer any immutable limits, do these limits
have to be related to anything or not? An answer can be found in the
generalization of music.

To generalize
in mathematics and physics means to single
out principles that are persistently
operative in nature and that show
themselves as true in any special case.
Similarly, one can proceed in music
in order to understand the true principles
in any special case.

313

Barriers between musical cultures which
are determined by their respective limiting
systems, have always made the results
obtained from fundamentals research in music
unusable in practice.
Now, these limits
are intimately connected with the nature of
the musical instruments we are using.
They are abandoned when using a computer
that, in this sense, represents a universal
machine theoretically without limitations
but one which is able to operate within any
limitation.

To generalize the essential elements of music
allows us to find that, independent of instrumental
forms and sound quality, they are common to any
civilization.

Their *adaptation* to the various musical-physical
systems and to their respective operative practices
in a single culture range makes music a separated,
local, geographic, folkloric phenomenon.

To adapt,
in this sense,
means to alter the relationship
between *quantity* and *quality* which
are united in the music,
one being the expression of the other.
When one says 'fifth' or 'octave', one refers to an
intervallic quality, but at the same time to a
quantity, a measure, if we want, of a vibrating
string or air column.

The computer's introduction in music has allowed us
to again unify
this quantity–quality relation
and therefore to operate in the same universal
nature of music,
beyond single systems;
planetarily.

314

Now, it is important to act consciously knowing
that a musical composition is always characterized
by a set of
internal and *external* relations.
Internal relations
give it form (microcosm);
the external ones integrate it with all the
Universe, which is outside it (macrocosm).
To comprehend and harmonize
the internal relations with the external ones mean
to create
cosmic music.

(Burnaby-Vancouver 1984)
English translation
Michela Mollia and Barry Truax

PART 2

The Technology of Music

EDITED BY
Richard Orton

17

Musical, Cultural and Educational Implications of Digital Technology

RICHARD ORTON

The finest musical instruments throughout history have both reflected and focused the technical capabilities of their time and culture. Indeed, those that we most admire as being superlative examples of their type – the Stradivarius or Guarnerius violins, the Flemish or Italian harpsichords, the gongs and other metal instruments of Chinese or Indonesian tradition – seem to raise the art of musical instrument making beyond what could have been predicted, involving an almost alchemical secrecy on their maker's part, to preserve the subtlest details of manufacture from rivals and imitators. The finished objects, the instruments themselves, can be understood to embody considerable musical intelligence and understanding, passed down sometimes over generations to augment, extend and develop the complementary creative activities of performers and composers, contributing in turn to the cultural and educational needs of their society.

Technology has always been an important aspect of music, complementing its skilled performers with an extensive support system of craftspeople, instrument builders and repairers. The knowledge embedded in instrument making of all musical cultures and historical periods is prodigious. In our own time the acceleration of scientific knowledge and technological development has made possible entirely new views of what music is, what it can do, and how it can shape people's thinking. Probably the most important of these new technologies has been that of sound recording. In only one century of development, we can now record and reproduce sound with great veracity, and our ability to do so has created an extra dimension of historical and cultural listening. For many, music is enjoyed primarily through loudspeakers, and the student of music has a vast recorded repertory to investigate.

Sound recording, however, like photography or film and video recording, is not a passive technology. Since the availability of the tape recorder after the Second World War, there has been a growing interest in the idea of the creative use of recorded sound. Starting with the *montage* of recorded sounds of the Groupe de Recherches Musicales and the notion of electronic *synthesis* of the Cologne school, there has been an extraordinary flowering of what has been called electronic or electroacoustic music. While the term may appear clumsy, I have come to prefer the more comprehensive 'electroacoustic music', since it does indicate the electronic mediation of acoustic principles.

The dissociation of recorded sound from its context led to the perception that the *objet sonore* could be consciously placed in a new, synthetic sonic landscape which had been as much composed by an act of will as had the traditional composition with notes on paper. More, the sonic object had to be 'bracketed out' from its original associations in order for its inherent, abstract and 'musical' qualities to be understood, prior to its composition with other sonorous objects and processes.

The ear of the electroacoustic composer is finely tuned and trained in a way quite different from, and complementary to, that of the composer of traditional music. Acuteness of attention to sound quality is an absolute prerequisite of the electroacoustic composer, since sound is actually his or her medium. The medium of the traditional composer, on the other hand, is paper, only the best composers transcending this handicap.

This section of our compendium of contemporary musical thought is not entirely about the implications of electroacoustic music, but this subject inevitably forms a large part. Over approximately the last twenty years an even more important technologically based development has appeared. It has revolutionized the ways in which musicians think, or indeed can think, about sound and sonic expression, and married to the principles of electroacoustic music – or to music in general – forms a mighty alliance which will create the music of the future and transform the understanding of music of the past, will change the ways in which music is performed, and the uses to which music is put. This development, of course, is that of computers and the ways in which the processes of human thought can be captured in them. The very musical processes that composers and performers adopt can be embedded in computer algorithms and replicated at superhuman speeds to produce new forms of creative expression.

Books and works of visual art capture thought in a 'frozen' form, to be held until 'melted' and re-created by a subsequent reader. Works of art that unfold in time, of which musical works are the most highly developed, relive or reinterpret the embedded thought processes, mediated through human action with each performance. With the computer we have for the first time a tool for the modelling of human thought itself, which can re-run the processes of its user-creator's mind. A computer program can, for instance, perform a piece of music in whatever way its composer/programmer/interpreter has intended – including that of not intending, of leaving things 'to chance'.

We can see from all this that we are undoubtedly in an 'age of transition'. The development of computer technology has been extremely rapid, but has by no means run out, and the speed and power of computers, and the discovery of ways to make them more efficient in human interaction, has clearly a long way to go. We cannot therefore know precisely what musical world we are entering. At present our musical culture appears very richly varied, even frustrating in its multiple enticements to the young artist. But from our present perspective it seems that musician programmers are spending, and need to spend, a lot of time and energy codifying their creative thought processes in computer algorithms, laying down the tools for the creative works of the future. Any musical compositions of our time have, for this reason, and quite inevitably, a transient quality because the very tools for the art of the classic age of the future – which will undoubtedly come – are only slowly appearing.

Whereas we now appear to be necessarily concerned with the possibilities of encoding human intelligence by means of computers, I cannot help but feel that the real goal, perhaps for the twenty-first century, is the creation of the intelligent instrument, an instrument that can create any sound or set of sounds we can imagine, that can partner the performer in an act of supreme musical symbiosis. We already hear of musical instruments that appear to be extensions of the performer's personality, so well matched is the mastery of the instrument to the musical intention and its sonic result. The intelligent instruments of the future will be able to reconfigure themselves to the musical and physical needs of their human partners, to achieve a sonic flexibility and musical capability that today can only be imagined.

As an example of one attempt to create an integrated environment for electroacoustic musical composition, I should like to discuss a project with which I have been associated for a number of years. In 1986 other composer colleagues and I founded the Composers' Desktop Project (CDP),[1] which took upon itself the task of providing for composers an affordable yet

321

powerful composing workstation for electroacoustic music through digital recording and playback, and digital sound synthesis. The full story of the CDP has yet to be told, but its beginnings are documented in a number of publications (for example, Orton 1989; Endrich 1989; Malham and Orton 1987). It was designed to be an 'open' project, to which composers could belong and have access to all the system information so that they and programmers could design new ideas and software for it, which would in turn be made available to other users through the CDP organization. At the time of writing, the original aims of the Project have not only been achieved, but have been extended in a number of exciting directions, and five years after its inception some two hundred CDP workstations are installed in eighteen countries, more or less equally divided between individual composers and educational institutions such as universities and colleges.

The CDP Workstation was conceived as an individual composer 'workshop', where, in addition to established techniques being used for electroacoustic composition, experimental methods could be tried. A system of input and output to and from the computer provides links with the outside world – play and record routines capable of dealing with industry audio standards. Here the SoundSTreamer was designed and built, expressly to handle the demanding timing requirements for digital input and output. This achieved, an important goal was to port a large software synthesis package. Richard Moore's CMUSIC, created at the University of California, San Diego, was adopted, soon to be followed by Barry Vercoe's CSOUND, created at MIT. Both are comprehensive systems which provide an extensive set of tools for synthesis and sound transformation.

The next important step was to provide a user-friendly interface for the system. Command-line environments are fine for programmers and developers, but are not nice to use on an everyday basis by composers and users of a recording and playback system. In a command-line environment the user types in the instructions, or 'commands' he or she wishes the computer to perform. Where there is a fixed set of options with a limited number of commands, a graphical version with the equivalents of buttons and special display windows presents a much more approachable face to the novice user. The windows-and-mouse environment popularized by Apple with the Macintosh computer provided a suitable set of graphic tools for the job. Unfortunately, the Macintosh's hard disk routines were not fast enough for sound input and output (the Mac II did not exist in 1986) and so GEM – the graphical environment manager provided for the Atari ST series computers – was used. The first version of the 'CDP Desktop'

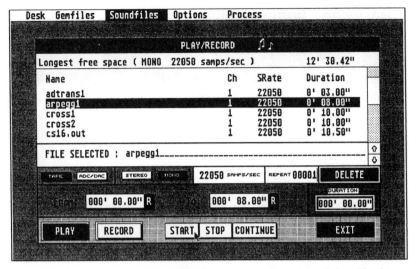

Figure 17.1 A screen of the soundfile directory; part of a program designed by the Composers' Desktop Project

provided a graphical soundfile directory, with buttons for recording and playback of sound, with provision for displaying the contents of the sounds in various resolutions in the time domain (see Figure 17.1). In other ways the Desktop fulfilled the function of a 'shell', i.e. a program which can call other programs listed in a menu, or from a specially designed command-line environment (see Figure 17.2).

These additional programs are usually those providing signal-processing capabilities. An initial set was developed for editing, looping, transposing, filtering and mixing soundfiles, collected together under the name 'Groucho'.[2] The original Groucho routines are currently in the process of extension and improvement. Programs for the extraction and superimposition of envelopes derived from soundfiles, noise gates, controlled harmonic distortion, and so on, have subsequently appeared.

I think the CDP is now well beyond its first phase of development. The original Desktop is being replaced by a new, more efficient interface. The system has been ported on to a faster computer environment, running an order of magnitude faster. The SoundSTreamer concept has been extended and a new version, the so-called 'Intelligent SoundSTreamer', which permits sound processing 'on the fly', is being designed and manufactured. Applications have broadened. An example is the synthesis and control of full Ambisonic three-dimensional soundfields, where individual sounds can

323

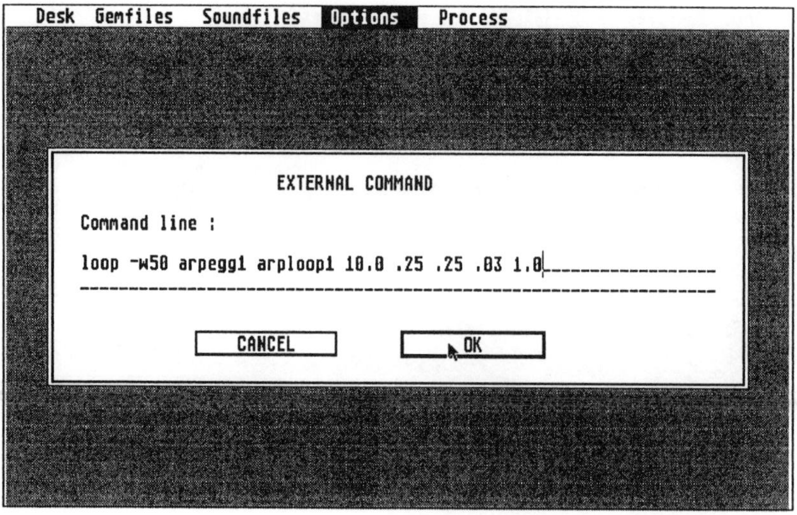

Figure 17.2 Screen showing a command line of the same program

be placed accurately within space, moved at will, and mixed with whole recorded soundfield (see Malham 1990; O'Modhrain 1990). Another is the interfacing of the computer to powerful digital signal processing systems, where the computer is used as the human link to fast, even real-time, musical processing (see Kirk and Orton 1990). Much of the popular conception of 'music technology' is concerned with keyboard synthesizers and with MIDI, the Musical Instrument Digital Interface. CDP has its own set of MIDI programs, many of them experimental or innovative in nature, or providing possibilities for algorithmic composition. Most importantly, there exists an extensive number of ways in which MIDI and the MIDI file standard can be interfaced with the true CDP soundfile and SoundSTreamer environment, permitting two-way communication. So a composer could, if he or she wished, record a MIDI performance, and subsequently realize it using a much more sophisticated and subtle synthesis method.

A consensus that is gradually emerging in computer music is that different representations of music are able to give the composer useful complementary views of his or her material. The time–domain graphic window for soundfiles is required for any editing or other time-based process, but a representation of the spectrum of the sound, giving its timbral evolution over time, is more useful for the composer concerned with formant synthesis, or with the composition of pitched events. The display of the broad control of frequency bands within which pitched events may be allowed to occur, or the filtering-out of events lying within certain frequency regions, may be equally useful to a composer (for instance with the powerful technique known as 'granular synthesis'). Research into the variety of ways that information about music can be conveyed to the composer, and how that information can be efficiently employed, is very pertinent at the present time.

Figure 17.3 shows a number of representations currently available within the CDP. Whilst these are undoubtedly crude in comparison with the best of other graphic systems, they do exemplify the need for complementary representations, and the determination of composers to create means by which these become active 'tools of the trade'. Parts (a), (b) and (c) of Figure 17.3 show increasingly 'coarse' resolutions in time-domain views of a soundfile, showing the transition from the representation of every single sample to windows in which the periodic waveforms may be more clearly seen, to, finally, those in which the amplitude variations, or 'envelopes' of the sound are perceived. Part (d) shows a three-dimensional display of the spectrum of a soundfile, where the evolving timbres of the sound can be analysed in detail. Part (e) shows the graphical display of a CSound software 'instrument', where the unit generators that go to make up a complex synthesis can be graphically organized prior to their use. Part (f) shows one example of the use of my program 'Freehand', which permits both the graphical design of pitch and envelope traces, and in this case is used to control the limits of granular synthesis operations.

Each of these graphical descriptions of sonic events – among many others that are possible – are new types of score, complementing the ones held as 'common music notation', computer programs for which are also, incidentally, increasing in sophistication. A single integrated computer composition environment can provide multiple ways of working, a variety of technical methods which can be tailored for each individual composer's preferred *modus operandi*.

For this section of the *Compendium*, I have been extremely fortunate in assembling able and highly esteemed contributors, all intensely involved with aspects of the central process I have tried to describe; their work is constantly extending the boundaries and applications of musical thinking in our time, and without their efforts progress would undoubtedly be slower, understanding harder to achieve.

(a)

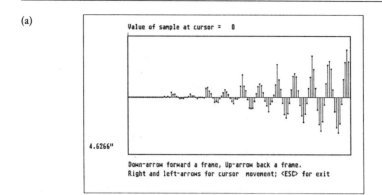

(b)

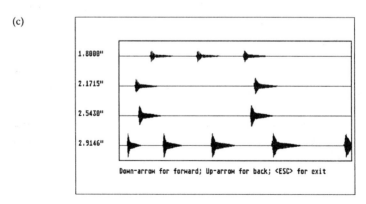

(c)

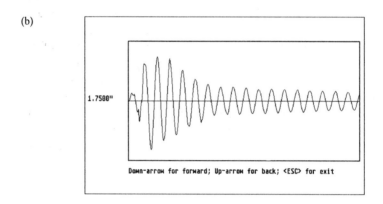

Figure 17.3(a-f) Representations currently available within the Composers' Desktop Project

326

(d)

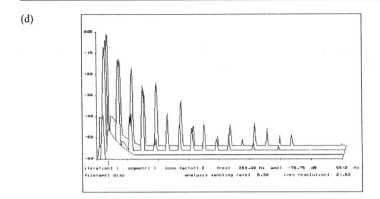

(e)

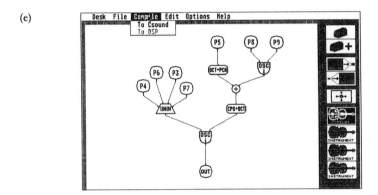

(f)

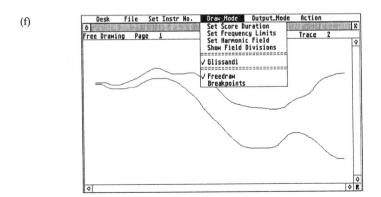

Figure 17.3 (cont.)

327

NOTES

1 The instigators of the CDP were Andrew Bentley, Tom Endrich, Richard Orton and Trevor Wishart. David Malham designed the SoundSTreamer interface, Martin Atkins the CDP Soundfile system, Rajmil Fischman the graphic CDP Desktop.

The CDP provides an interface between a personal computer and sound reproduction systems of professional sound quality, either through pulse code modulation (PCM) or digital audio tape (DAT) technology, whose equipment can be bought 'off the shelf'. More, it provides an extensive and always-expanding range of musical composition software primarily for electroacoustic composers.

Composers' Desktop Project,
Registered Office:
11 Kilburn Road,
YORK YO1 4DF, UK.

2 The original Groucho routines were written by Andrew Bentley.

REFERENCES

ENDRICH, T. 'The organisation and administration of the CDP', in *CDP Yearbook 1989*, York: Composers' Desktop Project.

KIRK, K. and ORTON, R. (1990) 'Midas: a musical instrument digital array signal processor', in *Proceedings of the International Computer Music Conference, Glasgow, Scotland*, San Francisco: Computer Music Association, pp. 127–31.

MALHAM, D.G. (1990) 'Ambisonics: a technique for low cost, high precision, three dimensional sound diffusion', in *Proceedings of the International Computer Music Conference, Glasgow, Scotland*, San Francisco: Computer Music Association, pp. 118ff.

MALHAM, D.G. and ORTON, R. (1987) *Mainframe Music on Microcomputers* (paper presented at the 92nd AES Convention, March), Preprint no. 2479, Audio Engineering Society.

O'MODHRAIN, S. (1990) 'Surroundsound: AB-format sound-field processing program for the Composers' Desktop Project soundfile system', in *Proceedings of the International Computer Music Conference, Glasgow, Scotland*, San Francisco: Computer Music Association, pp. 121ff.

ORTON, R. (1989) 'A brief, informal history of the CDP', in *CDP Yearbook 1989*, York: Composers' Desktop Project.

18

A Technological Approach to Music

F. RICHARD MOORE

INTRODUCTION

Technology – from the Greek *technē* (art) plus *logos* (word or discourse) – is the sum total of ways by which practical and aesthetic goals are realized. New technology allows traditional goals to be pursued in new ways or it allows new goals to be defined. Because technology constantly modifies what goals are possible, it provides a vital and dynamic link between human imagination and reality. Therefore it is often said that technology is far too important to be left to technologists. In other words, important decisions regarding technology should be matters of public policy. One of the most frightening characteristics of today's world, however, is the extent of technological illiteracy. While it is clear that everyone should participate in decisions about technology, most people do not understand even its most basic principles. To make matters worse, the giant technological brush with which we paint contemporary reality often drips in unexpected ways. If experts cannot reliably predict side effects, how can a technologically-naïve public do any better? It is little wonder, then, that so many people fear technology. Nevertheless it is essentially impossible to 'unlearn' what has already been discovered, so we generally cannot decide whether technology exists – only how to use it.

Nowhere is contemporary technology more suggestive of interesting possibilities than in the creative arts. Art and technology have always enjoyed a rich and varied interrelationship, so much so that it is often hard to distinguish between them. Did chemical and optical technologies, for example, create a new art form called 'photography', or is photography a technological response to the visual arts? If photography is a new art form, how is it to be mastered? If photography is a technological response to the human desire to capture visual images (a desire that has existed since before the first cave paintings), what is the new point of painting?

Whether photography is the cause or the result of certain visual art is less significant than the fact that photographic technology has transformed contemporary visual art in important ways. In a landmark 1930s essay entitled 'The work of art in the age of mechanical reproduction', film critic Walter Benjamin noted

> One might generalize by saying: the technique of reproduction detaches the reproduced object from the domain of tradition. . . . It substitutes a plurality of copies for a unique existence. And in permitting the reproduction to meet the beholder or listener in his own particular situation, it reactivates the object reproduced. These two processes lead to a tremendous shattering of tradition.
>
> (Benjamin 1968)

Sound recording technology has similarly transformed contemporary music. One might question, for example, how sound recording is related to music notation, or how the capability to work directly with sounds (rather than symbols on a piece of paper) has affected musical composition.

Sound recording – now over a century old – was just the beginning. Musicians now face a greater array of technological potential than ever before. From a practical standpoint many technological questions remain rather simple, even if their answers are not. In their simplest forms, such questions might be stated 'What possibilities exist?' and 'What does one need to know?'.

The difficulty with basic questions is, of course, that any attempt to answer them precisely results in their immediate disintegration into a plethora of ancillary issues. While complete answers to these questions may be unknowable, the past few decades of technological development in music have revealed interesting patterns, some of which are recognizable as incomplete. It is often the recognition of incompleteness in patterns that shocks us into insights about where to look next.

We begin, then, with the recent history of music technology. Important considerations include both the developments themselves and any patterns of development that can be deduced from them. In so far as these patterns seem incomplete, alternatives for completion may suggest themselves during considerations of how the incompleteness is recognizable. This knowledge can lead to helpful insights into what a contemporary musician needs to learn about technology.

MUSIC TECHNOLOGY: THE STATE OF THE ART

Historical Perspective

In one sense, the modern period of music technology began towards the end of the Middle Ages with the advance of music notation, which cleared the way for a music literature and tradition not based on orality. In another sense, it began during the Renaissance with the advance of mathematics to a point where equal temperament and the anchor it provided for music theory made possible musical instruments that were not only practical to build but compatible with each other, eventually allowing ensembles as large as symphony orchestras to develop. In another sense, contemporary music technology began in the mid-nineteenth century with the pioneering work of Hermann Ludwig Ferdinand von Helmholtz. Helmholtz's investigations into the relationships among physical acoustics, human physiology and human psychology form the basis for the modern science of musical sound, often called psychoacoustics. In yet another sense, modern music technology began in the late nineteenth century with Thomas A. Edison's invention of sound recording in the form of the phonograph, which did for (and to) music essentially what the camera has done for (and to) the visual arts. Regardless of exactly when or where contemporary music technology is rooted, though, there can be little doubt that its present forms rest squarely on the four pillars of music notation, music theory, psychoacoustics, and sound recording.

Electronic Music

Musicologists would probably agree that contemporary music technology began in the mid-twentieth century with the advent of so-called 'electronic music'. While initial distinctions were made between the *musique concrète*

331

of France (based on manipulated recordings of natural sounds) and the German-originated approach to 'pure' electronic music (based on exclusively electronic sound generation and processing), it soon became clear that there was no advantage in keeping such methods distinct from each other. The key to both techniques was the tape recorder. Music had gained a new spatial dimension along strands of magnetic tape, leading some musicians to declare electronic music as another 'new medium'. In statements reminiscent of those of early photographers, electronic music was proclaimed as a 'new art form' not to be confused with – or even compared to – other music. Indeed, much early 'electronic music' sounded quite unlike anything that had been heard before, though this did not necessarily mean that it sounded good or interesting to most people. This was partly because – despite all the theories – the technology of early electronic music was so primitive as to render it virtually impossible to create sounds that resembled traditional music. This encouraged some musicians working in the medium to compensate with extravagant claims about 'new aesthetics'.

Early practitioners of electronic music usually had to compensate not only for primitive equipment but for a nearly complete lack of knowledge of the physical and psychological characteristics of musical sound, as well as a nearly complete ignorance of electronics. This is not to imply that these pioneers were anything other than intelligent, dedicated and creative – only that comparatively little was known at the time about the psychophysics of musical sound – particularly in relation to electronic devices – and the little that was known was not known by most musicians. When suddenly confronted with the capability to design musical sounds from scratch, musicians suddenly need to know a great deal more about sound, hearing and electronics than most music training provides.

Before the establishment of the relevance of electronics to music, music technology changed at an evolutionary pace. New instruments were occasionally introduced as either incremental or quantitative improvements to earlier devices. Most new instruments were developed as the result of some perceived musical need, as when the pianoforte was developed to allow keyboard players a greater range of expression, or the tuba to provide a foundation for the brass section of Wagner's large orchestras. The history of music is rich with tales not only of what instruments were produced, but why.

With the advent of electronics, however, the possibilities for new musical instruments suddenly exploded. Now there were hundreds or thousands of new possibilities both for the production of sounds and for methods by which sounds could be controlled. Music technology now developed at an unprecedented, revolutionary pace. Electronic instruments started to grow not only out of long-felt musical needs for greater expressiveness, but out of the recognition of new technological possibilities as well. The theremin and ondes martenot, for example, provided new ways to accomplish musical feats that were not particularly different from those of the past, but which could be done in entirely new ways. The musical world expanded from one of concert halls, strings, winds and percussion to include loudspeakers, electronics, and psychophysics. Musicians responded, of course, in many ways.

Traditionalism versus Revisionism

The sudden and substantial demands for new skills and knowledge that the new technology of electronic music placed upon its users created a characteristic division in the field of music that persists to this day. One group prefers to concentrate on traditional artistic issues in the context of a new medium; the other prefers to concentrate on new artistic possibilities offered by the new technology. For the sake of discussion I will refer to the first camp as *traditionalist* because of their fundamental desire to absorb new technology into the pursuit of traditional artistic goals. The second camp I will call *revisionist* because of their fundamental desire to redefine artistic goals in terms of new possibilities opened up by technological developments.

Such a division is hardly peculiar to the field of music – it is typical of most fields heavily 'impacted' by modern technology, such as architecture and medicine. Of course, not every architect, physician or musician is, or needs to be, interested in technology *per se*. In architecture and medicine, however, health and safety issues do not allow practitioners to remain ignorant of relevant technological advances for long.

Music, however, is a fine art. In the adept words of Helmholtz,

> the horizons of physics, philosophy and art have of late been too widely separated, and, as a consequence, the language, the methods, and the aims of any of these studies present a certain difficulty for the student of any other of them.
>
> (Helmholtz 1877)

As C.P. Snow has pointed out in his important essay 'The two cultures and the scientific revolution' (Snow 1959), artists and humanists have often tried to divorce themselves from the aims and concerns of scientists and technologists altogether. As the noted humanist and scientist Jacob Bronowski has commented,

> Much of this quarrel between science and soul was trumped up by the religious apologists of Queen Victoria's day, who were anxious to find science materialistic and unspiritual. The sneer that science is only critical came from others. It was made by the timid and laboured artists of the nineties in order that they might by comparison appear to be creative and intuitive.
>
> (Bronowski 1979)

Traditionalists in all disciplines tend to take the view that they should remain aloof from technological concerns so as not to lose sight of traditional values. Revisionists tend to take the opposite view – that only by embracing technological concerns can traditional goals be fully realized. In music, today's revisionist is inclined to think of music technology as a result of musicians' work, while traditionalists are inclined to think of music technology as a result of work done outside the field of music. Just as traditionalists complain that revisionist thinking contaminates aesthetic concerns with irrelevancies, revisionists complain that traditionalists are oblivious to the actualities of the technological world in which they are living. Traditionalists point out correctly that contemporary music technology is not a part of music tradition. Revisionists argue that music technology is – or should be – the result of creative musical thought. Significant disagreements arise over the extent to which practitioners in the field should be involved in the development of the field's technology.

Perhaps more than in other fields, continuing technological developments in music tend to increase the distance between the two camps. One such development has been that of computers.

Computer Music

The electronics revolution that started in the early twentieth century received a considerable boost in the 1940s with the invention of the transistor – the first electronic device to be based directly on new physical insights into the quantum nature of matter. Transistors did not affect which electronic devices could be built so much as their size, complexity and cost. While earlier types of computers, for example, had been made to work, it was really the transistor that allowed the fabrication of computers that could be considered sophisticated (rather than merely impressive) by modern standards.

The most important feature of a computer is that – unlike other machines – its function is not built into it: a computer's function does not inhere in its structure. The function of a computer is determined by a set of instructions – a program – that can be fed into it. A single computer can therefore have many functions, hence many purposes, depending on how it is programmed. Not only can computers have functions their designers did not imagine – their designers intended it that way!

Computers can also be connected through translating circuits ('interfaced') to virtually any other kind of electronic device, making them useful in any circumstance where flexible control is required. Some of these 'peripheral' devices can act as 'sensors', while others may act as 'actuators', allowing computers not only to sense certain characteristics of their surroundings but to take certain physical actions in response to their environment as well. The similarities to living organisms are so compelling that much modern computing terminology is based around anthropic terms such as 'artificial intelligence', 'computer vision', and so on.

Pioneering experiments were carried out in the mid-1950s by Lejaren A. Hiller and others in an attempt to make computers 'compose' interesting music for traditional instruments (see Hiller and Isaacson 1959). When the inevitable circuits became available for 'digitizing' sound, it was not long before people with musical inclinations began to realize that computers could also be used as musical instruments. In 1957, Max V. Mathews, then of AT&T Bell Laboratories (where computers and transistors had both been invented), became the first person to program a digital computer to make musical sounds (see Mathews 1969). At first the resulting music was at least as bad as early attempts to make electronic music, but computer technology was destined to increase in sophistication at an unprecedented rate. Computers offer a level of precision and repeatability that would alter drastically the ways in which musical sounds could be manipulated and studied.

Again there was talk of computers forming the basis of a 'new medium' for music, and panels of experts pondered whether computer music was truly a 'new art form' or not. Such discussions were always inconclusive, of course, but they were held with increasing regularity because, in part, technology itself was increasingly of public concern.

While most early computer music indeed sounded pretty bad, there are certain characteristics of computers that give them more potential as musical instruments than early electronic devices. The poor quality of early computer music was attributed more directly to the ignorance of its makers about the inner workings of musical sound than with earlier electronic music. It was soon realized that, at least in theory, computers can produce any sound that can come from a loudspeaker, putting the blame for poor results more directly on human ignorance than did earlier methods. (This sometimes maddening tendency of computers to reflect the precise state of knowledge (or lack of it) of their users prompted one well-known computer pioneer to call computers 'the inkblot of our age'.) Recognition that the poor quality of many early results coming from computers was determined by their users (also known as the 'garbage in, garbage out' principle) caused John R. Pierce, another well-known computer music pioneer, to liken the computer to a concert grand piano suddenly dropped into the middle of a tribe of Neanderthals (Pierce 1983). Their problem – once they have discovered its function – would have been to learn to play it.

Music Research Centres

The computer introduced truly technologically sophisticated problems for the musician. No longer was it possible to experiment meaningfully with the 'latest and greatest' music technology with virtually no knowledge of musical sound, hearing or technology (uninformed experimentation in computer music more often meets with silence than the at-least-sometimes interesting results than can be obtained without recourse to reading the technical manuals in an electronic music studio). This in turn resulted in a widening of the traditionalist–revisionist gap in music. The means by which computer technology could be accessed are simply too foreign to traditionalist music practice.

As the musical results gradually became more interesting, however, a traditionalist response became increasingly necessary. Objecting to computer music technology as too foreign to the concerns and experience of traditional musicians, traditionalists began increasingly to work with computers through intermediaries. Such intermediaries were typically either 'pure technologists' (such as computer engineers) or junior members of the revisionist camp of musicians. From the traditionalist standpoint, 'pure technologist' intermediaries offered the advantage of being artistically neutral, while junior revisionists offered the advantage of being far more receptive to discuss sophisticated musical issues. In either case the traditionalist supplied traditional musical services with the intermediaries supplying the 'user-friendly' interface. The nature of such collaborations – whether the musical result was successful or not – ranged from symbiotic to exploitive, usually hingeing on the traditionalist's willingness to acknowledge the non-traditional nature of the contribution of the intermediary, and on the intermediary's willingness to relinquish the recognition reserved for the traditionalist musician.

Providing a context for such collaborations became one justification for forming music research centres such as the Institut de Recherche et Coordination d'Acoustique et Musique (IRCAM), established in the early 1970s by noted composer/conductor Pierre Boulez with extensive support from the French government. Originally conceived as an institution where the *crème de la crème* of music, science and technology could be brought together in order to better understand and create music, IRCAM was an attempt to forge a traditionalist–revisionist alliance on a grand, international scale. With Max Mathews as its first scientific advisor, it is not surprising that IRCAM's commitment to computer research into musical questions was assured from the outset.

Other institutional responses to the artistic problems and opportunities offered by contemporary technology include the Center for Music Experiment and Related Research (CME), also formed in the early 1970s under the leadership of composer Roger Reynolds at the University of California, San Diego. Unlike IRCAM, CME has been led by a succession of directors (including the author), each of whom has taken a decidedly different approach to music research and the role of music technology. Computer-based research into musical questions did not become a priority at CME until 1979, when I founded the Computer Audio Research Laboratory (CARL) project there. Other important research centres for computer music include the Center for Computer Research in Music and Acoustics (CCRMA), led by John Chowning at Stanford University, and the Electronic Music Studio (EMS) led by Barry Vercoe at the Massachusetts Institute of Technology. What is surprising, perhaps, is that despite such substantive institutional undertakings, little progress has been made in creating any real alliance between musical traditionalists and revisionists. These research centres act rather as 'neutral turf' where scientists, artists and technologists work perhaps nearer to each other than usual, but interact only rarely in more substantive ways because 'the language, the methods, and the aims of any of these studies present a certain difficulty for the students of any other of them' (Helmholtz 1877).

The primary function of the research centres has therefore been to supply technical resources for various kinds of music research. Because technological advances now allow serious research to go on practically anywhere, research centres today serve the two primary functions of providing a social context in which extra-traditional alliances can form, and of supplying expensive or exotic equipment. As relevant equipment becomes cheaper, the mission of these research centres increasingly gravitates towards networking and education.

'Digital' versus 'Analogue' Technology

Developments in computers were based on the use of transistors in one of their characteristic operating modes: as switches that can be turned on and off very rapidly by electronic control signals. If we think of the two states as representing the binary digits 1 and 0, we can see that properly inter-connected transistors can store and process information represented as binary digits. Binary digits – dubbed 'bits' by a well-known mathematician – are the basis for so-called 'digital' electronics.

Transistors can also be operated so that their output is made to follow, or 'track', an electronic input signal, much as one end of a see-saw moves in response to the other end bobbing down and up. The motion can be made more forceful, for example, by placing a fulcrum – or pivot point – closer to one end than the other, forming a kind of crowbar. This action corresponds to amplification of the strength of a signal. Since the output of such a transistor varies in an analogueous way to its input signal, this mode has come to be known as 'analogue'. 'Digital' and 'analogue' circuits thus demonstrate how the same underlying technology can be used in two usefully different operating modes.

Combining the ever-decreasing size and cost of transistors with the design of electronic music studios would in itself have permitted suitcase-size, personal electronic music studios. But using electronic signals to control electronic devices also makes it possible to build practical electronic music instruments that can be played in real time. Based on techniques developed earlier in the context of analogue computers, Donald A. Buchla and Robert A. Moog pioneered in the construction of so-called 'voltage-controlled music synthesizers' during the 1960s.

The real-time operation of these devices addressed a major complaint of many musicians – particularly traditionalists: because it was impossible to play most early electronic devices in the traditional musical manner, much of the spontaneity of live performance was missing in electronic music. This often made the resulting music sound 'stilted', 'contrived', or otherwise unlike performed music. One classically revisionist response to this complaint was that electronic music *should* sound different from other music. After all, the logic went, there was no reason to expect non-traditional instruments to sound like traditional ones, and any effort to make them

338

behave more like traditional instruments could easily overlook significant new possibilities. In most cases, though, the traditionalist complaint tended to gather as much momentum since the music at hand did indeed sound contrived.

There was a concomitant rejoicing over the real-time capabilities of analogue music synthesizers, for they gradually admitted electronic music into the traditional arena of live performance. Early voltage-controlled synthesizers were too delicate and unwieldy to be taken directly on-stage, but the attachment of real-time capabilities to electronic music techniques increased the productivity of electronic music studios enormously. Instead of laboriously splicing together hundreds or thousands of pieces of magnetic tape – a technique common in early electronic music – or laboriously typing hundreds or thousands of detailed instructions on a computer terminal – a technique common in early computer music – musicians could now interconnect a few voltage-controlled modules and control the result by playing in real time with a piano-like keyboard.[1] It was even possible to demonstrate the performance of traditional music on electronic synthesizers, as Wendy (*née* Walter) Carlos so amply demonstrated by publishing *Switched-on Bach* – a recording which soon outsold any other recording of classical music in history. Morton Subotnick and others rapidly produced a number of charming voltage-controlled synthesizer works that were published on records, such as Subotnick's *Silver Apples of the Moon* and *The Wild Bull*. Electronic music had become productive on a major scale.

The main result of this large increment in productivity was that electronic music could be exploited commercially. As electronic music synthesizers became smaller and more reliable, commercial musicians began to recognize that their combination of 'roadworthiness' and novelty could sell records and tickets to concerts – particularly rock concerts. Voltage-controlled synthesizers began to infect commercial music like a successful virus. Though they were certainly limited in many ways (one spoke until the early 1980s of 'monophonic' or 'polyphonic' synthesizers, depending on whether or not they could produce more than one note at a time!), many performers became adept at playing on the keyboards, ribbon controllers, pitchbend wheels, joysticks, and myriad other devices used to translate simple human actions into time-varying voltages.

The commercial success of voltage-controlled analogue music synthesis had several noteworthy effects. It increased public awareness of electronic music, albeit in ways that were as limited as the early synthesizers themselves. It attracted the attention of a few powerful commercial manufacturers to the electronic musical instrument field. It suggested to many students of music that electronic music techniques would not remain esoteric in the future, but would form an increasingly important part of what every practising musician was expected to know about (the resulting student demands created some difficulty for many schools of music – students often wanted to learn about a musical subject about which they already knew considerably more than their professors!).

Despite the commercial success of voltage-controlled synthesizers, the revisionist camp now complained that the use of the technology of electronic music in the commercial milieu was too trivial compared with its true potential. Simply because it was now possible to synthesize simple tonal harmonies in front of a live audience did not mean that the potential of electronic music had been fulfilled. All it showed, in fact, was that electronic music techniques could be used in the service of traditional music. Fundamental progress in technological music-making was yet to be made. But commercialization had only just begun.

Digital Audio

By about 1980, transistor-based technology of music allowed significant improvements in sound recording. The self-same sound digitizing devices that had formed the basis for computer music now allowed digital sound recording, which has several advantages over analogue recording techniques. Some of these advantages are clearly audible in the quality of the recorded sound, others reside in improved robustness of recordings. At first digitally-mastered recordings had to be distributed via traditional magnetic tape and vinyl disc media. By 1983, lasers and integrated circuits – more recent forms of transistor-based technology – allowed compact disc (CD) players to be sold commercially. Compact disc systems allow direct playback of digitally mastered recordings without the intermediary distortions introduced by magnetic tapes or vinyl discs. So-called 'hi-fi' suddenly got noticeably 'hi-er'.

Digital audio technology was not limited to playback of commercial recordings. Analogue voltage-controlled synthesizers, which tended to drift out of tune as they warmed up just like analogue radio sets, were replaced by digital synthesizers which functioned internally according to processes that had been worked out within the context of computer music. Following the work of computer music researchers, new digital synthesizers were introduced commercially in the early 1980s that did not drift out of tune and were more flexible than analogue synthesizers (while costing considerably less). Digital synthesizers became immensely popular, soon outselling all other electronic musical instruments combined. The Yamaha D X-7, introduced commercially in 1983, and other Yamaha synthesizers produce sounds using the frequency modulation technique worked out by John Chowning in the late 1960s and patented by Stanford University around 1971.

The final nail in the coffin of electronic music as an esoteric art form was the commercial introduction of the personal computer. Just as compact disc units and digital synthesizers were appearing on the mass market, computer manufacturers started to produce home computer systems that were superior in many ways to the 'giant electronic brains' that had been objects of technological and economic reverence only a decade before. Enormous resources were expended on the development of 'user-friendly interfaces' aimed at making the computer as useful as possible to the non-specialist. Commercial 'user-friendly' software has been developed specifically around the (traditional) needs of artists and musicians, allowing many people without traditional artistic training to wield considerable computing power in the production of visual art and music. A simplified and standardized interface called the Musical Instrument Digital Interface (MIDI) – which allows computers or digital synthesizers to communicate in real time – allows such devices to be combined in useful ways.

The current state of the art of music technology can be characterized as the age of the digital micro-chip. Hundreds of thousands of transistors (or their equivalent) can be etched onto thin wafers of crystalline silicon the size of a human thumb-nail. Hardly a month goes by without the announcement of another commercial offering of yet another electronic music device. The electronics-based technology of music, whatever else it has done, has grown from an esoteric concern of a few musical revisionists to a major – some would say the primary – concern in music today.

OBSERVATIONS ON THE STATE OF MUSIC AND ITS TECHNOLOGY

Commercialization

Transistor-based technology is perhaps the only valuable resource that is getting cheaper as time goes by. Digital technology in particular is getting cheaper so quickly that its continued proliferation is virtually guaranteed for the foreseeable future. To such well-established and often-cited phenomena as 'Moore's Law', which implies that the cost of any given computation will be cut in half every two years, we must now consider such phenomena as 'Joy's Law', which states that the speed with which a given computation can be done will double every year. In essence, the cost of computing is diminishing so rapidly that computing power may soon become the first virtually limitless free resource. The social implications of virtually free resources are enormous.

The most significant recent development in music technology has been its extensive commercialization since the early 1980s. The marriage of music and electronics technology has been a commercial success without precedent. Computing devices of both the special-purpose and general-purpose varieties have shown themselves to be the most popular musical instruments yet devised. Commercial software is available to address many musical problems, including composition, music notation and education. Present computing speeds usually require real-time operations to be implemented in the form of limited-purpose devices such as digital synthesizers, reverberators, recording and playback devices, mixers, and so on. General-purpose devices have limited real-time capabilities but are far more flexible in their operation. Programmable digital signal processing (DSP) microcircuits promise to ameliorate the inflexibility of real-time operations, or, conversely, to enhance the real-time capabilities of fully programmable systems. The ideally inexpensive, fully programmable real-time music system has yet to be built, but there is little doubt that it will soon be feasible.

It is reasonable to expect that in the relatively near future the distinction between a real-time and non-real-time device will be more a matter of choice than necessity. Some musical operations – such as live performance – 'naturally' occur in real time, while others – such as composition – 'naturally' occur outside real time. Certain types of sound processing are better suited either to real-time or non-real-time operations. Current digital signal processing techniques allow, for example, the duration of a sound to be altered drastically without changing its pitch. While it would be possible to change a sound's duration by a small amount over a brief duration in real time, it takes but a moment's thought to realize that in general it is not possible to alter the duration of sounds in real time.[2]

So-called 'real-time composition' or improvisation is a highly specialized type of musical performance with its own special set of advantages and limitations. Composition in general, of course, requires the ability to make earlier portions of a composition dependent on later portions as well as vice versa. Another example in which real-time processing is not desirable is during fixed or automated processes such as removing the background noise from a sound recording. In such cases the processing needs to proceed as quickly as possible rather than in real time. It would be of clear benefit in such cases to go faster than real time if possible.

To understand the effects of commercialization it is necessary to have some grasp of the forces that drive it. The successful commercialization of technology has depended primarily on packaging that accomplishes at least four things: broad marketing appeal, low market price, ease of use by the average customer, and protection of the seller's intellectual property. In order to survive in the commercial arena, someone wanting to market music technology must therefore consider the following four questions.

1 What type of music technology will appeal to the greatest number of people? Is there a danger that a given product might appeal only to a small number of people?

2 What type of music technology allows individual units to be sold profitably at a relatively low price? Contemporary marketeers are quite knowledgeable about the ranges of price that are associated with such marketing phenomena as 'impulse buying', 'status symbols', and so on.

3 Will a product be easy for the 'typical' – that is, technologically naïve – customer to use? The ideal product is, of course, a device that does exactly what everyone wishes it to do without its having to be told what that is. A common technique used by salespeople involves convincing potential customers that what a device does is exactly what everyone was waiting for, even though they might not have known it before.

4 Will a successful product or its function be easy to replicate? If so, the manufacturer is in trouble, for competition will soon appear to participate in the profit-making process. Ideally, therefore, products are hermetically sealed 'black boxes' that self-destruct if anyone tries to understand their function, thus protecting the intellectual property of the seller.

After considerable development, devices passing all of these tests – some with flying colours – began to appear in the commercial market-place around 1983. Many more have appeared since, as the profitability of commercial offerings in the music technology market-place continues to attract the attention of hi-tech industry.

Despite enormous proliferation, however, it is not clear that this commercialization has done anything to change – let alone improve – the general quality of music-making. Popular music – the arena in which new music technology has been most readily adopted – has remained about the same in form and content as it was before the great commercialization of music technology. Art music – the context in which most new music technology has originated – has been very slow to explore new technological possibilities. The very rapidity with which technology has been changing does not imply that its full potential is being realized at the same rate. And especially in artistic fields such as music, the inevitably more numerous traditionalists are usually not well prepared to exploit new technological possibilities, even when they are inclined to do so.

The Mass Production of Clichés

Commercial television programming in the United States is strongly influenced by a well-known 'ratings' system that is simultaneously sound business practice and artistic anathema. The basic purpose of this system is to assure that the first provision listed above – making the product appeal to a large number of people – is satisfied. Under this system, many programmes are shown experimentally on the commercial channels at the beginning of each programming season. A sophisticated statistical sampling method is used to determine how many people actually watch each programme, thus rank-ordering the programmes according to an objective measure of 'popularity'. The more people watch a given programme, the more advertisers are generally willing to pay for advertisements woven skilfully into its fabric. Because television programmes are invariably expensive to produce, only the ones that get the highest ratings survive beyond the experimental period. Others are quickly discontinued, and the ratings are measured again several times each year. This all makes what is known as 'sound business sense'. The result is what is called 'commercial American television', which, while undeniably profitable, is a famous disaster by almost any aesthetic criterion.

Why there should be such a wide gap between what is commercially and artistically successful is an interesting topic in itself, if only because this rule has interesting exceptions. There is, however, a strong likelihood that commercial and artistic criteria will normally differ for a very simple reason: *artistic potential tends to depend strongly on what is not common while commercial potential tends to depend strongly on what is.* Subjective evaluations among large numbers of people on such issues as the agreeableness of television programmes tend to define a bell-shaped curve of preference which I call the 'normal curve of taste'. This curve reaches its zenith at its average value, where the largest number of divergent tastes – or subjective preferences – coincide. A television programme's probability of surviving the commercial ratings system is determined not by its overall quality but by the difference between its perceived quality and this average perceived quality. Programmes of much higher or lower quality than this average stand little chance to receive high ratings, and hence have little chance of commercial survival. While one might argue that this eliminates the best of the possibilities along with the worst, the operators of commercial television defend the practice by pointing out that they cannot survive as businesses without maximizing proliferation – even if it comes at the expense of eliminating high quality – because of competition in the market-place. In other words, if one competitor doesn't do this, another will because no business rule prevents it. Commercial success is thus like natural selection – in the short run, what is average tends to survive better than anything else. Or, conversely, what survives better than anything else becomes the average.

A negative form of support for this theory can be found in the colourful history of musical invective, in which the pattern of consistent rejection of artistic works later recognized as masterful is almost comical.[3] Whatever else is true about criteria of artistic quality, immediate popular acceptance – hence commercial success – is not among them. Moreover we cannot conclude that because it achieves popular acceptance a given work is of high artistic quality. Popularity and artistic quality are simply independent issues. In the context of music technology, commercialization has necessarily followed sound business practice in the sense that it has favoured devices that would be popular rather than those of any particular artistic quality. While popularity in itself does not rule out the possibility of high artistic quality, the tendency in business is nevertheless to favour the average rather than the uncommon. Thus the commercialization of music technology has generally concentrated on devices that match traditional applications.

Side-effects of Commercialization

While it might seem that the exploitation of new technology in the pursuit of traditional artistic goals is well served by this process, it is important to observe that side-effects of commercialization, which occur whenever new technology is substituted for old, tend to limit the effectiveness of the traditionalist approach. I call these the 'oleomargarine' and 'fireman' effects.

The usual reason for the substitution of newer technology for old is cost, which in classical economic theory is the inverse of scarcity, or uncommonness. The 'oleomargarine' effect occurs when newer technology does not equal or exceed the quality of older technology, as when oleomargarine was introduced as a substitute for scarce butter during the Second World War. The 'oleomargarine' effect is generally most noticeable when the newer technology is in a relatively immature state, as it was, for example, during the early period of electronic music. Many new technologies fail because of this effect, even though they may have great potential for later development.

If the cost saving is too small or the 'oleomargarine' effect too great, new technology is usually rejected in the marketplace. If it clears this hurdle, however, the second side-effect becomes relevant. The 'fireman' effect occurs whenever new technology results in the elimination of jobs. The 'fireman' effect is generally noticeable soon after the 'oleomargarine' effect disappears, and is typified by insistence that people with certain types of jobs continue to receive pay even after their services have become obsolete. It is the very success of the newer technology in providing an acceptable (or better) result at a lower (or much lower) cost that causes people to lose jobs. The insistence that displaced people be neither retrained nor dismissed then creates the 'fireman' effect, as when the need for people to shovel coal on locomotives (the 'firemen') was eliminated by the introduction of diesel and electric engines. A refusal to adapt to new circumstances would constitute a true triumph of traditionalism. In the long run, however, change invariably proves more powerful than that which resists it.

Traditionalists could resist the anathematic effects of change by resisting the commercialization of technology. Because costs are difficult to set arbitrarily, the primary traditionalist weapon against successful commercialization of new technology is 'oleomargarinization' – drawing attention to ways in which new products are inferior to previous ones. If the 'oleomargarine barrier' is small enough, or the cost pressure high enough, however, successful commercialization of new technology is very difficult to stop. Traditionalists are then forced to survive in one of two ways.

One traditionalist survival route involves becoming curators of museums. In music there is considerable evidence that this is a fair depiction of the contemporary state of so–called 'classical' music in general, especially opera. In the United States in particular, public support of symphony orchestras and opera houses has shrivelled considerably over the past few decades into a relatively steady state that appears to match that for museums fairly well.

Traditionalists can undoubtedly expect to find support for traditional goals within such contexts, albeit severely limited support.

Ultimately, however, traditionalists survive by changing the definition of 'tradition'. This necessitates revision of aesthetic objectives according to new possibilities created by new technology, i.e. acceptance, however partial or reluctant, of the tenets of revisionism. A healthy aspect of this approach is that it does not necessarily mean that traditional objectives must be rejected altogether. Rather, it implies (1) that traditional objectives must be augmented to include the implications of new technological possibilities, and (2) that it is necessary to learn to use new technology in an effective way. In addition, if the traditionalist wishes to affect what new possibilities come into existence, it is necessary to learn (3) how to affect the development of the technology itself.

This brings us, finally, to a consideration of what contemporary musicians need to learn about contemporary music technology.

A TECHNICAL APPROACH TO MUSIC

A typical traditionalist approach to technology is (1) to assume its existence, (2) to use it, and (3) to remain otherwise as aloof from it as possible. A typical revisionist approach to technology is (1) to learn as much as possible about it, (2) to use it, and (3) to improve it.

By definition, traditionalist approaches can always be shown to have been successful in the past. A music traditionalist approach fails, however, when music technology changes so that it becomes impossible to practise music in traditional ways. Each time a pianist sits down before a concert grand, for example, the instrument is essentially the same. This makes it possible for the pianist to proceed beyond some recently developed level of mastery of the instrument. The level of mastery can thus be made ever-increasing, at least until fundamental physiological and cognitive limits are approached.

Musical instruments based on contemporary technology (such as computers) differ from traditional instruments in that they change much more rapidly. It is important to note that technology-induced (as opposed to commerce-induced) changes are usually not matters of mere fad or fashion. Most computers are replaced within a few years because it literally costs more to maintain older machines than to replace them. With proper care, a piano is just as useful and valuable twenty years after it was

347

purchased as when it was new. With any amount of care, a twenty-year-old computer is virtually useless and worthless (except perhaps as a museum piece). Consider, for example, that a personal computer costing less than the average 1990 automobile is potentially more powerful than the largest computers available (at any price) in 1970. Not only was the earlier computer more expensive, but its electrical and maintenance requirements would probably now exceed the cost of its replacement.

The situation in current music technology is actually somewhat worse than this. If it were possible to maintain a stable technological environment for, say, only a few years before it had to be changed, then considerable practice in the traditional music sense would still be possible. An added factor, however, is that hardware changes are less disruptive than software changes, if only because the latter occur more or less continuously, with ever-greater disruptions occurring every few years. This pattern of nearly continuous change will continue for the foreseeable future.

In addition, we must add the obfuscatory effects of competition in the market-place. Before its great commercialization in the early 1980s, musicians interested in using music technology had to be concerned primarily with changes introduced by new technological possibilities. Commercialization adds the important element of puffery[4] and subtracts the element of reliable information about how products work. The first is simply a fact of life in a free market; the second arises from a perceived need to protect 'intellectual property' from falling into the hands of competitors 'disguised' as customers.[5]

Recognition of the intimate relation between knowledge and power is a factor many marketeers would prefer consumers to forget. We can easily find examples of marketing emphasis placed on the validation of ignorance as a desirable state of being. The message to individual customers from the commercial market-place is, in effect, 'Buy this product because (unlike inferior products that make demands on your understanding) it will satisfy your needs without requiring you to learn anything'.

There is, of course, nothing illegal, immoral, or even particularly objectionable about all this when products have a mundane or utilitarian function like making toast or displaying television signals. After all, a great benefit of the Industrial Revolution was precisely that obtaining certain results (such as making toast) could be broken down into simple steps (such as pushing a button). Almost all the problems associated with contemporary technology arise from the fact that there is a profound misrepresentation associated with connecting a simple push-button to a complex result. In what ways this misrepresentation may be objectionable, immoral or illegal depends on the particular circumstances.

Few people could become confused enough to think that playing back a compact disc recording had anything to do with creating the music itself. But if the buttons that play back the recording are piano-like keys on a sampling synthesizer such confusion becomes more likely. It seems that simply sitting at a piano-like keyboard is enough to create an impression of 'making music', however false that impression might be. Manufacturers have used this tendency to commercial advantage for some time in the form of automatically-generated accompaniments for 'one-finger' melodies and similar technologically impressive (but musically irrelevant) instruments. The musical irrelevance results from the fact that the user of the device is only playing a recording, albeit a dynamically changing one. (In order to participate in the music-making process, it would be necessary for the user to be able at least to make the recording in the first place.)

A similar situation obtains in the case of computer software. Home computers are often portrayed as repositories for software of various types. In effect, home computers allow software to consumers on an 'add-a-purpose' basis. But a strictly prefabricated piece of software is to the computer user the logical equivalent of a sound recording. In this case the recording is the set of instructions in the prefabricated software. As with a sound recording, the result may be useful, entertaining or even satisfying to a certain degree. But prefabricated software typically does not permit the user to access the most important feature of a computer: its programmability. In order to access the real power inherent in a computer, it would be necessary for the user to be able to program it in the first place.

There is, of course, nothing wrong with not wanting to make one's own music or programs, just as there is nothing wrong with wanting to use music or programs made by others. The question only becomes relevant when we consider the proper relation of a creative artist to an artistic tool. Any musician who wishes to use computers in a creative way needs to learn how to read and write computer programs just as much as he or she needs to learn how to read and write music notation. Fortunately, learning to program is trivial compared with the formidable task of learning music notation. Unfortunately for the musician, commercial forces conspire with artistic traditions to make it appear much more difficult than it is for an artist to learn programming.

Elements of a Technological Approach

In order to contend with the relatively easy task of learning about music technology, the more difficult task of overcoming the traditional injunctions against doing it, and the truly formidable task of using our most advanced technologies in a creative way, it is necessary to take steps. While there are undoubtedly many possible paths to any goal, I suggest that there are four necessary conditions that must be met by any path leading to an artistically expressive technology. In addition to these conditions there are a few considerations peculiar to music in particular. Taken together, these constitute what I call a 'technological' approach to music.

The first condition is that it is necessary to reject the notion that learning is associated with being a beginner. If nothing else is clear about the state of contemporary technology it is that it is in a constant state of flux. The task of learning about it is therefore never truly finished. Some changes are only incremental, allowing us to add a new element to a well-established direction. Many changes, however, require learning about qualitatively new directions of technological development. Until recently, for example, the physics of optics did not seem particularly relevant to digital audio processing. Optical storage devices such as the compact disc introduced a new type of technology to musical relevance. Magneto-optic technology now promises to become a primary direction for digital storage of all sorts, not merely for musical sound. There are many other such examples.

The second condition is that one must fully reject the tenets of specialism. The hallmark of specialization is depth of knowledge in a particular topic. The hallmark of specialism is rejection of breadth of knowledge. The fundamental assertion of specialism is that the only useful way to increase one's knowledge is by restricting its scope. While a focused view of knowledge has obvious benefits and increasing necessity as knowledge grows, survival requires both well-functioning central *and* peripheral vision. In addition, most complex tasks require a continual shift of focus rather than a myopic insistence that it is necessary to look in only one direction to perform any real-world task.

The third condition is that one be willing and able to adopt the best possible learning strategies. If one is to accept both the necessity of learning and the necessity of variable focus, the relevance of efficient means for acquiring new information and insight becomes obvious. Traditional methods of learning – such as reading books, which is relatively slow, and repetitive practice, which is even slower – must be augmented by more efficient learning schemes. The very technology about which we are trying

350

to learn provides at least some solutions to this problem in the form of dynamically searchable databases, interactive presentations (essentially 'books' that can answer questions), and so on. The main challenge is not simply to develop such methods, of course, but to use them.

The fourth condition is that one must adopt an extreme-inward approach that alternates between top-down and bottom-up. In effect, the 'top-down' approach starts with overall objectives and proceeds to develop the necessary means for their implementation, while the 'bottom-up' approach starts with available technology and proceeds to examine the problems whose solution inheres in what is already possible. The top-down approach is fundamentally traditionalist – the bottom-up approach is fundamentally revisionist. Neither approach alone is sufficient to realize fully the potential benefits of technological development, and much of value has been lost by unnecessarily conceiving the approaches as contradictory. The value of the traditionalist approach is that it keeps technological evaluations rooted in past – which is to say psychological – reality, while the benefits of revisionism lie precisely in its ability to keep tradition from degenerating in galling stagnation.

Applying these principles as guides results in a few steps that I would recommend to anyone who is interested in developing a useful cognizance of contemporary music technology.

The first step in learning about any subject is to learn as much as possible about the language in which information on that subject is expressed. The basic background for music technology consists of the four 'pillars' mentioned at the beginning of this chapter: music notation, music theory, musical psychoacoustics, and sound recording. The broader and deeper one's preparation in these four subjects, the more efficient will be one's apprehension of both the reasons underlying contemporary music tech-nology and its methods. Traditional music training typically includes only half of this information (music notation and theory, including the ancillary forms of ear training, sight-singing, harmony, counterpoint, and so on). Because musical psychoacoustics is itself an interdisciplinary subject involv-ing music, psychology and physics (and a certain amount of human physiology), useful preparation in this area is relatively rare in academic institutions. Sound recording and the related issues of digital audio and digital signal processing are likewise uncommon in university curricula. Academic rarity means only that a student must take a greater share of the responsibility for organizing his or her own learning about a given subject.

Given a reasonable amount of preparation in the four 'pillars', the only remaining background topics needed to apply most contemporary

351

technology effectively to music are computer programming and music synthesis techniques. Computer programming is necessary in order to be able to take advantage of the only feature of a computer that distinguishes it from other devices (its programmability) and the fact that creative applications of computers are much more likely than others not to be supported by pre-existing commercial software. Music synthesis techniques are peculiar to musical applications (at least so far), so they too must be considered basic to the contemporary technology of music.

Virtually all the remaining information needed by the contemporary musician is in a category that I would call 'volatile' in the sense that it is likely to become rapidly obsolete. It will take some effort to learn to distinguish between the traditional methods that remain useful and those that do not. The full realization of both the traditional goals of music and the potential of its ever-changing technology will be possible only for those who reject neither music's past nor its future.

NOTES

1 It is also possible to generate the analogue control signals with a digital computer. This was the basis for the world's first real-time computer music system – called GROOVE – created by Max Mathews and the author in 1969 at AT&T Bell Laboratories.

2 If one were 'stretching' sounds by a factor of ten, for example, it would take 10 seconds to listen to a 'stretched' 1 second sound. If this process were being done in real time, a performer would have played an additional 9 seconds of sound before work on it could begin. The amount of memory needed would grow without bound! Similarly, if the sound were being compressed rather than stretched in time the problem is even worse: the time compression operation would be required to look further and future – a task known to be difficult at best!

3 One account of the beginnings of Ludwig van Beethoven's *Fifth Symphony*, for example, includes the following characterizations:

> Criticism of this symphony, upon its first presentations, was somewhat divided; Jean Lesueur, a famous French composer and theorist, found it such exciting music that he felt it shouldn't even exist; Louis Spohr, in his Autobiography, finds the theme of the first movement wanting in dignity, the Trio of the Scherzo too grotesque, and the last movement replete with unmeaning babel. The London Philharmonic Orchestra members thought the opening was intended to be humorous on account of the shortness of its theme.
>
> (Wier 1935)

4 'Puffery' is a legal term referring to the natural – and legally excusable – tendency of salespeople to exaggerate the benefits associated with purchasing their products.

5 In fact, the only difference between a customer and a competitor is whether the customer also sells (or resells) a similar product. The usual way to make sure that a customer cannot do this effectively is to make sure that the customer cannot easily learn how to make an improved product. The best way to make sure the customer cannot improve on a product is to encourage him or her to learn as little as possible about a product except from a users' point of view. Essential information about how a product functions is regarded as 'intellectual property' of the seller and is generally kept as secret as possible.

REFERENCES

BENJAMIN, W. (1968) 'The work of art in the age of mechanical reproduction', in H. Arendt (ed.) *Illuminations*, New York: Schocken.

BRONOWSKI, J. (1979) *The Common Sense of Science*, Harvard University Press.

DODGE, C. and JERSE, T.A. (1985) *Computer Music: Synthesis, Composition and Performance*, New York: Macmillan.

HILLER, L.A. and ISAACSON, L.M. (1959) *Experimental Music: Composition with an Electronic Computer*, New York: McGraw-Hill.

HELMHOLTZ, H.L.F. (1987) *On the Sensations of Tone as a Physiological Basis for the Theory of Music*, reprinted 1954, trans. and ed. A.J. Ellis, New York: Dover.

MATHEWS, M.V. with the collaboration of Miller, J.E., Moore, F.R., Risset, J.-C. and Pierce, J.R. (1969) *The Technology of Computer Music*, Cambridge, Mass.: MIT Press.

MATHEWS, M.V. and PIERCE, J.R. (eds) (1989) *Current Directions in Computer Music*, Cambridge, Mass.: MIP Press.

PIERCE, J.R. (1983) *The Science of Musical Sounds*, New York: W.H. Freeman.

SNOW, C.P. (1959) *The two cultures and the scientific revolution* (The Rede Lecture), London: Cambridge University Press.

WIER, A.E. (ed.) (1935) *The Nine Symphonies of Beethoven in Score*, New York: Harcourt, Brace.

FURTHER READING

APPLETON, J.H. and PERERA, R.C. (eds) (1975) *The Development and Practice of Electronic Music*, contributions by O. Luening, A.W. Slawson, G. Ciamaga, J. Chadabe, J.E. Rogers and G. Mumma, Englewood Cliffs, NJ: Prentice-Hall.

KNUTH, D.A. (1968) *The Art of Computer Programming*, Reading, Mass.: Addison-Wesley.

MOORE, F.R. (1990) *Elements of Computer Music*, Englewood Cliffs, NJ: Prentice-Hall.

ROADS, C. (ed.) (1985) *Composers and the Computer*, contributions by H. Brün, J. Chowning, J. Dashow, C. Dodge, P. Hamlin, G. Lewis, T. Machover, J.-C. Risset, C. Roads and I. Xenakis. Los Altos, Calif.: William Kaufmann.

ROSSING, T.D. (1990) *The Science of Sound*, Reading, Mass.: Addison-Wesley.

STRAWN, J. (ed.) (1985) *Digital Audio Signal Processing: An Anthology*, contributions by F.R. Moore, J.O. Smith, T.L. Peterson, J.A. Moorer and J. Strawn, Los Altos, Calif.: William Kaufmann.

——(ed.) (1985) *Digital Audio Engineering: An Anthology*, contributions by J.F. Mcgill, R. Talambiras, P.R. Samson, F.R. Moore and J.A. Moorer, Los Altos, Calif.: William Kaufmann.

XENAKIS, I. (1971) *Formalized Music*, translated from the French by Butchers, Hopkins, Challifour and Challifour, Bloomington: Indiana University Press.

19

Towards a New Age in the Technology of Computer Music

PETER MANNING

The development of facilities for computer music has advanced at an almost breathtaking pace since the early 1980s, largely as a result of the revolution in digital technology which has brought the power of the institutional computers of a decade ago to the desktop of the individual. This particular application has highlighted many complex issues which require careful consideration, not least due to the fact that the required partnership between artists and scientists involves the linking of disciplines which in many respects have little in common. Composers and performers of traditional music have primarily been concerned with the subjective characteristics of sound-producing agents, rather than the physical principles involved in their excitation, and this special regard for matters acoustical extends to the development of music notation and the teaching of subjects such as harmony, counterpoint and orchestration down the centuries. To a scientist, the identification of a musical event involves determining its precise physical content in terms of the evolution of frequency and amplitude components with respect to time. Both are seeking to understand the nature of sound, but the subject is investigated from very different points of view. A further dimension becomes apparent when one considers the involvement of psychologists who are primarily concerned with the way in which we react to sound stimuli. The seeking of common goals thus requires great understanding and sensitivity if rewarding partnerships are to be achieved, and unfortunately this has not always proved to be the case. In particular there has been a marked tendency for scientific and commercial considerations to outweigh those of a musical origin, and as a result, despite some good intentions and much industry, the creative development of the medium has been erratic and at times disappointing.

The study of this ever-growing sphere of music technology is a daunting prospect, especially for the artist with limited scientific training. Indeed the field is now so large and volatile that even the experienced computer music composer or researcher cannot expect to become acquainted with more than a small range of facilities drawn from a much larger spectrum of possibilities. Whilst the capabilities of one system are being mastered and applied to a particular compositional project it is not unusual to discover that an improved or radically altered version is under construction, requiring the expenditure of further time and effort in studying new techniques before they may be incorporated in the compositional process. Such instability is unknown to instrumental composers who can rely upon a stable and well understood range of acoustic resources for their works. It is perhaps significant that an increasingly pointed controversy has arisen over the degree of technical training that should be considered a prerequisite to any serious use of the electronic medium. On the one hand it is argued that the study of music technology should be accorded the same consideration and commitment as that associated with conventional compositional training, if the creative results are to match expectations. On the other hand the instability of the technology itself is seen as a major disincentive for many composers who quite reasonably expect a positive and long-lasting return for any substantial investment of time and effort in developing new methods of working. Engineers in any branch of the applied sciences will generally define their objectives in terms of producing systems that will carry out set tasks in a more efficient manner, measured in terms of speed, economy of cost, and/or physical characteristics; in other words, they seek to optimize the performance of available tools whilst at the same time advancing the technology itself. Such an outlook, if not carefully qualified, does not inspire a natural partnership with the creative artist, and taken to an extreme can give rise to serious disagreements. Whilst it is true that factors such as speed, compactness and affordability are major considerations for a composer, it is the ability to relate to and interact with a particular system that will ultimately determine its value as a tool for creative work. Methodology that may make perfect sense from a musical standpoint will not necessarily translate into efficient and economical machine processes, and if the design of the system militates against or even specifically excludes such modes of operation, then the interests of the composer are not best served.

The evolution of computer music has gone through a number of phases, developing from a highly specialized and little-known offshoot of main-stream electronic music during the late 1950s and early 1960s to become the central focus of attention by the end of the 1980s. A considerable debt is owed to Max Mathews for the pioneering work he carried out in digital synthesis at Bell Telephone Laboratories, New Jersey, from the late 1950s onwards. His MUSIC series of software synthesis programs has inspired a whole lineage of derivatives, still used extensively in studios throughout the world, and has served as the starting point for many of the hardware systems available today. Basic to all these systems lies the traditional musical concepts of an orchestra and a score, the orchestra providing the basic definitions for one or a number of individual instruments, and the score the data for their performance. The instruments are assembled from a series of function statements known as unit generators, representing the component pro-cedures required for sound generation and processing. These are derived in the first instance from conventional analogue devices such as oscillators, filters and reverberators, but over the years their functional versatility has been greatly extended to include techniques such as the processing of externally produced sound material and the synthesis of both speech and vocal sounds.

A primary feature of these programs has been their non–real-time mode of operation, and prior to the 1980s their dependence on large institutional computers. The latter restriction severely restricted access to the composing community at large for many years and the former has forced composers to adopt a highly formalized approach to the production of their works. The reasons for this latency between supplying instructions to the machine and hearing the results are primarily to do with the large amounts of computation required for all but the simplest of sonological events. It is quite usual for a standard general-purpose computer to require many times the actual duration of a synthesized extract to calculate the corresponding digital wave function, and in such circumstances it is necessary to employ an intermediate storage device such as a computer tape or disc to accumulate the information over whatever period of time proves necessary. Then, and only then can the results be output via a suitable digital-to-analogue converter.

For many composers this lack of any interactive contact is a major drawback, but there are a number of important compensations. Firstly, the choice and disposition of unit generators to create instruments is limited only by the availability of computer memory and, in the case of especially complex procedures, the computing time the composer has at his disposal to run the program. Secondly, every aspect of the sound generation process is precisely programmed with assistance from special function-generating routines which carry out such important tasks as calculating wavetables or shaping the dynamic envelope of individual sounds. It is thus possible to specify a number of concurrent synthesis tasks, the task of scheduling the component processes being left to the program. In addition, the computing environment opens up the possibility of programming aspects of the compositional process itself, for example employing rule-based procedures or statistical functions to generate performance data in response to more general specifications as to the overall evolution of events. This 'top-down' method of working has proved attractive to many composers who wish to control and modify composite sound models rather than construct each and every event entirely from first principles. Granular synthesis (i.e. creating sound from statistical distributions of spectral grains) has emerged as an important application in this context, building to a considerable extent on techniques first explored in depth in the POD (Poisson Ordered Distribution) programs of Barry Truax. Since the late 1970s specially fabricated signal processing systems such as the DMX 1000 have been available for emulating some features in real time, but it has taken a further decade for the goal of running comprehensive software packages such as CMUSIC or CSOUND in this manner to become a distinct possibility. The advent of new computing technologies such as parallel processing is offering for the first time the prospect of sufficient processing power to meet such a challenge at a realistic cost.

It is the programming aspects which highlight perhaps the most significant differences that existed between software synthesis systems and traditional electronic studios in the 1950s and 1960s, the latter being almost entirely dependent on the manual control of devices at every stage of the compositional process, with consequential delays in many respects no less significant than those of the digital studio. The primary compensation here was the ability to interact with the equipment, and thus craft each and every aspect of the sound directly. On the other side of the equation the practical limitations of adjusting knobs and faders by hand, and the laborious nature of cutting and splicing innumerable lengths of recording tape led to considerable frustration and a growing desire for more user-friendly facilities. The solution that emerged, known as voltage control technology, signalled the start of the first commercial revolution in electronic music, pioneered by manufacturers such as ARP, Buchla, EMS and Moog from the mid-1960s onwards.

A primary feature of these systems is the ability to use the output from one modular device as a voltage function for controlling the input of another.

For example, it becomes possible to construct simple frequency or amplitude modulators by merely connecting the signal generated by one oscillator to the frequency or amplitude control input of a second. In such an arrangement the frequency of the first oscillator determines the speed of modulation, and its amplitude determines the depth, providing at one extreme a simple pitch or amplitude vibrato and at the other a wealth of rich timbres as a result of the generation of spectral sidebands. Similarly, voltage-generating keyboards can be connected to any number of device inputs to create complex sequences of events in response to individual keystrokes. Basic voltage control networks, nevertheless, still suffer from a number of limitations. To give but two examples, the control of a number of functions from a keyboard is inevitably constrained by the dexterity of the performer, and the addition or substitution of automatically varying functions such as the voltage outputs from sub-audio oscillators, whilst ensuring a constantly changing sound spectrum, invariably leads to cyclic patterns of events which can quickly destroy any sense of organic growth and development. The very ease of use was to prove deceptive for many composers and as a result the quality of works produced using these synthesizers has been distinctly variable. Ironically some of the most successful pieces have been those fashioned in more popular idioms, for example, the *Switched-on Bach* realizations of Wendy (formerly Walter) Carlos, which established a very distinctive, if somewhat stylized image of electronic music in the public eye as early as 1968. By this time, however, the first steps had already been taken to improve the control facilities for these synthesizers with the introduction of elementary sequencers, and attention quickly focused on the potential of adding more sophisticated control facilities, driven by a computer.

As time passes the significance of these hybrid designs is all too quickly being forgotten. Some of the better systems of this type offered facilities for serious composers which have yet to be fully surpassed by modern real-time, all-digital systems. The ability to work directly with the synthesis equipment, investigating and selecting different combinations of devices and device settings, combined with an ability to transfer data to and from the computer for editing and performance, provided in many respects the best of both worlds. Further, since the computing requirements were generally not as demanding as those of software synthesis it proved possible to use smaller and cheaper machines, in many instances dedicated entirely to the application. Computer music, in this broader definition, thus became no longer confined to the computer laboratory where it hitherto had to endure a shared existence with other scientific applications. In time even software synthesis programs were to be exported to such smaller machines (MIT released MUSIC 11 for the PDP 11 range of minicomputers in 1978) but it was hybrid technology which blazed the trail for music systems with dedicated computer facilities almost a decade earlier.

The four most important hybrid studios of the time, all custom built, represented a wide spread of institutional and compositional interests, namely a radio station (Stockholm), an academic institution for music and sonology (Utrecht), a commercial synthesizer manufacturer (EMS, London), and a communications research centre (Bell Telephone Laboratories, New Jersey). Whilst hybrid systems combined many of the more attractive features of software synthesis systems and traditional electronic music studios, it was inevitable that they should also incorporate some of the disadvantages. In terms of versatility and reliability, for example, they could not match the performance of a MUSIC program. Not only was the choice of equipment totally fixed since this involved actual devices rather than computer simulations, the performance of the analogue components was affected by constraints such as long-term stability and the speed and accuracy of response to computer commands.

The seeds for a better approach to real-time system design, known as mixed digital technology, were sown by the invention of the microprocessor, which heralded the start of the final stage of the transition of computing power from the institutional mainframe, via the minicomputer, to the single board processor. It has been noted above that mainframe computers of the 1960s and 1970s were incapable of generating more than the simplest of sounds in real time, and the earliest microprocessors offered only a fraction of the computing power of a large machine. Whilst this situation was to change significantly in due course, there were, nevertheless, from the outset a number of engineering short cuts which could be taken to reduce the amount of computing required. Inevitably penalties were incurred as regards musical quality and compositional flexibility, and these have been more significant than some commercial synthesizer firms and media commentators would lead us to believe.

Fidelity was treated as a secondary consideration by many manufacturers, with some quite devastating consequences. In software synthesis systems the accuracy of conversion required between a digitized representation of the audio wave and its equivalent analogue voltage function is invariably regarded as a critical consideration, and few studios of any significance pursuing this particular technology have been prepared to accept any shortcomings in this respect. The critical factor here is the number of binary locations or bits used to represent the numerical value of each waveform sample. In approximating the values of waveform samples the numerical accuracy or quantization determines the purity of the sound: the poorer the resolution the greater the residual noise content. Today, 16-bit resolution, representing a quantization range of 65,536 steps, is considered the minimum for high quality audio, and various techniques are being developed to raise this standard still further. At the beginning of the 1980s, 16-bit converters were still relatively expensive, especially for any competitively priced commercial system, and there was an additional incentive effectively to double the throughput by using just eight bits to represent each sample, matching the basic data unit of most microprocessors of the time. Eight bits, however, can represent a range of only 256 quantization steps, a startling reduction on the resolution of 16-bit formats which results in a much reduced audio quality, particularly at lower amplitude levels. Despite this drawback sythesizers offering only 8-bit resolution became commonplace, even in the so-called 'professional' sector of the market.

The other factor that directly affects fidelity concerns the number of waveform samples used to represent the audio information as a function of time. As a simple rule of thumb it is necessary to generate samples at a rate that is at least twice the frequency of the highest spectral component to be synthesized. Given the ear's ability to hear sounds up to about 18,000 hertz (some psychoacousticians contend that components considerably higher than this affect our subjective response), it is thus desirable to work at rates of at least 36,000 samples per second. For high quality digital audio the recording industry has established even higher standards, typically in the range 44,100 to 48,000 samples per second. These rates double for the generation of stereo information since this involves the interleaving of samples from two independent channels of information. In marked contrast, synthesizer manufacturers have been content to use rates as low as 20,000 samples per second in order to gain further valuable computing time between samples. This has led to significant restrictions in many systems since it is necessary to suppress all frequency components in excess of half the sampling rate to avoid signal errors, which otherwise appear as spurious tones reflected back into the main audio spectrum. Whilst this economy can be partially disguised if the synthesizer is restricted to the generation of carefully regulated synthetic sound material, defects become all too apparent if material from the natural sound world is to be processed.

The first generation of sampling synthesizers, which (as the name suggests) are devices that rely exclusively on sampled extracts of acoustic sounds, suitably digitized for manipulation and resynthesis, were generally of a poor quality as a result of such economies, and manufacturers were quickly forced to raise their standards both as regards sampling and also quantization. Whilst economies such as the above considerably reduced the load on the computing engine, the main key to processing economies lay in modifications to the synthesis process itself. Direct synthesis programs employ a number of special techniques to maximize computing efficiency, in particular the use of wave tables for oscillators, calculated in advance and then scanned at the desired frequency.

Unfortunately this technique is not as straightforward as it might seem at a first glance since at a fixed sampling rate simply reading every one, or every second, or every third sample only generates a series of fixed frequencies in a particular harmonic series. Some synthesizers have been built where the sampling rate is varied for each oscillator as a means of directly controlling frequency, but the resulting asynchronous signals create major problems in signal mixing and digital-to-analogue conversion. With a fixed sampling rate the generation of a full spread of frequencies requires the use of incremental values for table pointers other than integers, and it is thus necessary to introduce mathematical routines to extrapolate each sample value for a theoretical point that may lie anywhere between two adjacent table values. For the cleanest results such values should be properly interpolated, but this requires significant computation. Rounding to the nearest stored value is much faster, but the resulting errors are quite significant unless the wave tables themselves are particularly large, perhaps 4096 values for each basic waveform pattern rather than the more normal 512. Computer memory was still relatively expensive in the early 1980s and the temptations to economize on table sizes were thus considerable, with an inevitable effect on the resulting sound quality.

In a digital synthesizer devices such as oscillators are usually implemented in hardware, and these can be specially engineered to ensure maximum operational efficiency. Wave tables, for example, are usually stored in permanent read-only memory banks with hardwired address generators for fast access. The gains, however, have hitherto been more in percentage terms than a quantum leap in performance, and the pressures to achieve further processing economies remain substantial. If the synthesizer is keyboard-orientated then some advantage can be gained by restricting the entire system to tempered pitches, but in so doing the possibility of working with freely moving frequency spectra is immediately precluded. Similar considerations apply to the next stage in the synthesis chain, the superimposition of a dynamic envelope to allow the articulation of individual notes. In an ideal design each sample should be multiplied by an audio rate scaling function, capable of providing values between zero and the maximum

362

amplitude permitted by the system, with a numerical accuracy to match the resolution of the converter. In processing terms such a requirement is almost as demanding as that required to generate the oscillator function in the first place, and is in addition to it. In software synthesis programs the result is merely a proportional increase in the overall computing time. In a real-time environment the amplitude function has to be either streamlined significantly or transferred to a second, independent processor which can work concurrently with the first. Such multiprocessor environments are relatively new developments and will be discussed further later in this chapter.

In the field of professional recording, designers of digital mixers now consider it essential to update fader settings at the audio rate, and are still wrestling with the problems of handling multiple channels in this manner. Although the requirement here is the overall regulation of amplitude, rather than the short-term enveloping of individual sound events, the ear is so sensitive to imperfections in digital signal processing that very few economies in performance are now considered acceptable. This example illustrates all too clearly the caution which must accompany the prevailing view that digital systems are naturally superior to the analogue ones which they replace. Such a goal is probably achievable, but the development of the necessary technology is still far from complete.

Most synthesizer manufacturers have sought economies in their facilities for amplitude control, using techniques such as updating the scaling factor every ten or twenty samples and rounding the scaling values themselves to the nearest table entry rather than interpolating. Reference has already been made to the relatively high cost of computer memory in the early 1980s, and with an eye to manufacturing costs the incentive to keep such tables as short as possible was understandably great. It was thus quite usual to use tables of as few as sixty-four different scaling values to control the entire amplitude range. The price paid in terms of musical quality as a result of these economies was a distinct roughness in sounds of a modest or quiet amplitude, and a pronounced distortion in the transients of sharply articulated material.

Further opportunities for design economies, to be traded against quality and versatility, exist at all subsequent stages in the synthesis and processing chain, and in a highly competitive market situation few manufacturers have failed to exploit them. Financial success, however, has encouraged a number of the more enterprising companies to invest directly in digital research, not least in the development of custom-designed very large scale integrated chips (VLSIs), each capable of containing hundreds of logic gates which may be specially configured for a particular application. The introduction of the Yamaha DX7 synthesizer and its derivatives in the mid-1980s, based on a custom-designed VLSI audio generator chip, signalled the dawn of this new era in the design of real-time commercial systems, which others have been quick to emulate. As composing and performing tools such synthesizers still have their limitations – for example, the DX7 and its relatives rely exclusively on frequency modulation techniques for the synthesis of audio spectra, with no user-adjustable filters or other signal modifiers. Further, most of these products are designed in the first instance as performance instruments, offering few facilities for programming compositional procedures. Internal memories are often available for storing a generous selection of parameter settings, but without external assistance most machines will respond only to manual keystrokes. An obvious partner is to be found in the desktop computer, which can be programmed to provide powerful facilities for generating performance data in response to higher level compositional procedures.

In 1983 a historic agreement was reached between leading manufacturers over a standard communication protocol for digitally controlled equipment, known as the Musical Instrument Digital Interface or MIDI. As a result, synthesizers and associated equipment can be coupled together via a simple chain of connecting cables to create an integrated system. It thus becomes possible via MIDI to use a single keyboard to control a number of synthesizers, or to add a programmable control system, running on a general purpose microcomputer. Suitable MIDI interfaces are now available for many popular microcomputers, and in some instances, such as the Atari ST series of machines, included as a standard facility.

As a digital protocol MIDI can carry up to sixteen different channels of control information, each directed to a specific item of equipment, or indeed in some instances to different voices within a single synthesizer. Each channel transmits a complete set of operating instructions for a sequence of musical events, a significant advantage over voltage control networks, which require separate control leads for each function. Information is transmitted serially (that is, each item of data is passed along the wire bit by bit rather than in parallel, whereby entire bit patterns are transmitted in a single step). A major advantage of this method of transmission is the convenience of a single control line for the entire protocol. A parallel system would have required bulky and expensive multi-core cables with one wire for each data bit, plus some additional wires to carry signals to control the transmission itself. The main disadvantage is a proportional reduction in the transmission speed which results from sending data piecewise down a single wire rather than in in a single step across parallel links. Whilst for many years the computing industry has tended to regard serial protocols as more suitable for medium- and low- speed communications, recent advances in digital technology have led to the development of ultra-fast transmission facilities which largely overcome this particular disadvantage.

Unfortunately the combination of a failure to predict back in 1983 the extent to which MIDI control would be applied within digital networks and the still developing state of interface chip technology contributed to a decision that established 31,250 bits per second as the transmission speed for all networks. By today's standards this is not exceptionally fast and is already causing a number of difficulties as systems develop. By the time special control bits have been added to check that data is correctly transmitted and received, the maximum rate of data transfer reduces to just over 3,000 elements per second. Whilst this is clearly more than adequate for conveying simple pitch and duration information from a keyboard to a single bank of oscillators, given just ten fingers to play notes at any one time, the density of information increases significantly if more complex control information is transmitted with every keystroke.

A closer look at the MIDI protocol reveals that each string of elements is not merely composed of data values but includes embedded control codes, identifying which parameter is to be updated, followed by one or a number of arguments for the parameters themselves. Further, if several different channels are in use simultaneously and the traffic of information is dense, the bandwidth per channel drops proportionally. To the user the first obvious signs of MIDI saturation is an unpredictable delay in response, particularly from devices furthest away from the controller. By the time this lack of synchronization becomes apparent other more subtle effects will have occurred, for example alterations to the articulation of polyphonic sound material as individual note attacks become displaced by varying delays, which can be as short as a few thousandths of a second. The dysfunctions of MIDI and their significance have commanded increasing attention amongst commentators as the limitations become more generally recognized and better understood. With so many manufacturers committed to the current standard, however, the likelihood of a new super-MIDI standard seem rather remote at present.

There are other fundamental characteristics of MIDI that present particular problems for the serious composer. These concern the nature of the control data that may be transmitted via the protocol, in turn a reflection of the design considerations that influenced the original agreement. The focus for such an accord lay in the primary markets for volume sales of digitally controlled synthesizers, which were universally seen to be the rock and pop music industries. This outlook contrasted sharply with that of the pioneers of commercial voltage-controlled synthesizers who directed their products towards the educational sector in the first instance. The unease of many institutional studios and centres of research and development surfaced at such august gatherings as the annual International Computer Music Conferences of the mid-1980s. Here champions of MIDI found themselves repeatedly subjected to close and sometimes overtly hostile questioning over the suitability of the protocol to support equipment for serious composition, and this led to spirited but in the end quite constructive debates on the future of computer music as a whole. More recently this spirit of confrontation has softened to one of cautious co-operation, encouraged to a significant extent by a realization on the part of many manufacturers that support for fundamental research at institutions, including the direct injection of funds, would lay firm foundations for their own future prosperity.

In considering the virtues and limitations of MIDI, a distinction has to be made between music that is essentially note/event orientated, and more often than not tied to the conventions of the tempered scale, and what might best be described as abstract music, concerned primarily with the texture and the shaping of complex sound models. Whilst it is true that software synthesis programs were modelled on traditional concepts of music writing in the first instance, such was their versatility that they readily adapted to more mathematically demanding concepts. The nature of MIDI precludes this adaptability to a significant extent, and whilst some composers have devised ingenious procedures for overcoming such limitations the protocol remains fundamentally unsuitable for the transmission of information such as glissandi within individual spectral components, or the density of events required for granular synthesis. In the case of a network of smaller synthesizers, based on relatively simple internal architectures, the influence of MIDI will clearly be substantial. This characteristic may not be so apparent when more elaborate digital synthesizers are involved, including many of those custom-built by institutions. Here the sophistication of the internal technology provides the composer with a powerful layer of control quite apart from MIDI itself. Any further development in this area, however, is restrained by the limits of current technology, pointing once again to a fundamental need to increase the power of the computing engine by several orders of magnitude. Then, and only then, will it be possible to construct and operate the kind of human–machine interfaces which will allow the creative development of the medium to be driven by artistic considerations rather than technical constraints.

In striving towards such objectives there are a number of musical issues that must be considered. Some of these have been alluded to above, but they now need to evaluated more fully in a broader context. Even a superficial study of working methods in an all-MIDI studio on the one hand and a traditional software synthesis studio on the other reveals sharp differences in working practices, the former being to a significant extent interactive and intuitive and the latter predetermined and objective. Whilst it is perfectly true that a composer can approach either system with a fully notated score or an equivalent set of synthesis instructions, it is in the formative stages leading to such specifications that the above differences become most apparent. The transition from non-real-time towards real-time operation in the field of software synthesis composition has been progressive, and it is interesting to observe how attitudes have changed over the years. In the early days the delays between supplying synthesis instructions and hearing the results were measured in days rather than hours, and the preparation of material was thus regarded in much the same light as the preparation of a typescript for publication in a book or journal. In the same way substantial alterations rather than minor corrections to such a document invariably incur financial penalties so the composer was firmly discouraged from reworking much material on the grounds of computing cost, let alone the personal frustration of yet further delays. As technology steadily improved so delays of hours became delays of minutes, leading to a growing sense of contact with the synthesis system itself. This aroused interest in more powerful tools of communication such as mouse-driven computer graphics using icons to represent the components of the orchestra and direct data entry devices such as music keyboards or knobs and faders for the input of score information, developments that in turn increased the pressure on system designers to reduce the latency still further.

As this circular pattern of development has gathered pace so the musical significance of such major changes in the working environment has become distorted, for there would appear to be an underlying assumption that the ultimate goal of all computer music composers is to work exclusively in real time. This is demonstrably not the case for it denies the relevance of musical arguments developed away from the machine as part of the pre-compositional process, as apart from free improvisation and experimentation which do revolve around an immediate relationship between the intuitive responses of a composer and his or her performance tools. It is the ability to move freely between these two modes of operation and the musical continuity that can be achieved in the process which together establish the creative value of any such system, not a misplaced assessment of the

367

superior qualities of one particular method of working. The hybrid systems discussed above provide formidable bench-marks against which to measure the performance of all-digital systems from both a technical and a musical point of view. In the same way there is no reason why MIDI systems should not include programmable facilities to assist the compositional process; the same argument may equally well be applied in reverse to the addition of interactive tools for software synthesis systems.

Traditional programming techniques generally involve analysing problems into partitioned procedures, each of which consists of a series of computing statements, processed sequentially. Special branch instructions, sometimes containing conditional arguments, control the flow of processing both within procedures and from one procedure to another. Some applications require the specification of procedures that are to be processed concurrently. In traditional computing architectures, however, such parallel operations have to be simulated since, given a single processor, only one operation can be executed at a time. If, for example, a composer specifies a polyphonic texture for a single instrument in a MUSIC program, as many copies of the instrument as there are concurrent notes must be loaded into memory. Whereas in older versions of the software the composer had to type in these multiple specifications explicitly, modern versions such as CSOUND generate the copies automatically. Synthesis of the desired texture then proceeds by calculating a few samples for the first copy, typically 256, which are stored in a special memory buffer. The same number of samples for the second copy are then calculated and added to the temporarily stored values of the first, and so on until all the component strands have been synthesized and aggregated. The results are then written out to disk and the process starts all over again with the next block of samples. Thus it may be seen how the load on the processor increases in direct proportion to the number of simultaneously sounding events. A parallel, ironically, can be drawn with the problems of MIDI control signals discussed above, where, despite a more modest requirement in terms of the rate of data flow, essentially the same criteria apply, i.e. the greater the number of active channels the slower the response. For real-time software synthesis the challenge is thus not merely to raise the basic processing speed to cope with a single voice of audio information, but to find ways and means of coping with the generation and manipulation of several voices simultaneously.

The problems encountered in using standard computers for sound synthesis are by no means unique to musical applications. Similar processing bottlenecks are encountered within the general area of digital communications, and this has encouraged manufacturers to develop hardware architectures specifically for signal processing. The DMX 1000 processor mentioned above (p. 358) was one of the first commercial systems of this type to appear on the market at the end of the 1970s, based on bit-slice hardware. The most significant feature of this particular technology is the ability to construct an entire processor, including the internal arithmetic and logic unit responsible for time-critical computations, from powerful and ultra-fast building blocks which may be connected together with relative ease. A major consideration is the ability to pipeline processes, allowing a number of linked operations to be carried out concurrently, rather than one at a time. This chaining of operations is similar to that employed on a car production line where all of the workers are kept fully occupied all of the time, each contributing to one aspect of assembly whilst a continuous succession of cars moves down the track, step by step acquiring all the necessary parts.

A number of custom-built audio processors based on other architectures were constructed during the 1980s, one of the best known being the 4X, built at IRCAM. The design for this system evolved around networks of logic gates, the most elementary building blocks available for constructing any digital system. Whilst designs such as 4X come close to the optimum in terms of a dedicated computing engine the engineering challenge is not to be contemplated lightly. Bit-slice technology has allowed signal processing research to proceed at a considerably less complex level with only a marginal loss in flexibility and efficiency. The growing demand for such tools encouraged hardware manufacturers to fabricate further processing devices at the VLSI chip level, and since the mid-1980s increasing numbers of research centres have concentrated on designing computer music systems around them. Known generically as digital signal processors or DSPs, these products are designed specifically for the generation and manipulation of numerical data at high speed, using an instruction set that is deliberately focused in compass to ensure maximum computing efficiency. These devices are particularly suitable for repetitive computations, a major feature of audio processing, and can manipulate data at quite remarkable speeds if the programmer is economical in coding the required procedures. For the system to operate in real time all the computations for each audio sample must be completed within the short time frame that exists between samples. To put this in context; at 40,000 samples per second the computing time available between samples is only 25 microseconds. If the DSP runs at a typical clock rate of 100 nanoseconds, a maximum of 250 processor cycles are generated between samples. Whilst several of these will inevitably be used up simply transferring data in and out of the processor a substantial percentage will remain available for the processing function itself.

The internal architecture of a DSP is specially configured to ensure that the maximum computing efficiency is extracted from each processor cycle. In a conventional processor the number of machine cycles required to process each instruction varies considerably according to its complexity, ranging from less than five for a simple addition to perhaps a hundred or more for a multiplication. Most DSPs are designed to execute most if not all instructions in one or two cycles, greatly increasing their processing speed. Notwithstanding such performance characteristics, system designers still face a number of problems. The biggest constraint is the challenge to ensure that at no time will the number of processor cycles used exceed the maximum permissible between samples, otherwise the system will simply stop. Programming techniques have been developed to modify instruction sequences if processor saturation is approached but these inevitably result in some form of signal distortion. By the late 1980s a number of DSPs could sustain about eight real-time oscillators, and the very latest processors expand this capacity by several orders of magnitude. The addition of any refinements such as adjustable filters to shape the resulting timbres reduces the capacity to only about two oscillators per DSP unless sacrifices are accepted in the audio fidelity. The performance statistics, nevertheless, compare very favourably with those obtained from the very best commercial systems using custom-designed VLSIs, and are superior in at least one important respect: the procedures are achieved by means of software which can be readily modified and improved at any time. With a VLSI approach much of the processing architecture is permanently fabricated, thus limiting the user to a fixed choice of characteristics.

Until such time as another quantum leap in processing speed is achieved, networking provides the only practical means of increasing the power of DSP systems, connecting processors both in series to take advantage of pipelining and also in parallel to allow the distribution of concurrent tasks. Unfortunately such an application is far from straightforward; and there are major stumbling blocks to further development of this technique which have yet to be satisfactorily overcome. In the same way that voltage-controlled or MIDI synthesizers require a control system to pass information between individual devices, so a network of DSPs requires a sophisticated management system to ensure the integrity of the system as a whole. In terms of the rate of information transfer the combination of processor control instructions and audio data require a transmission speed many times that of MIDI, supported by a sophisticated communication protocol to ensure that each device correctly receives and processes information within the permitted time interval. The latter requirement frequently requires complex and computationally expensive arbitration routines which inevitably reduce the overall efficiency of the system. Whilst looping techniques can provide a means of buffering the effects of small transmission delays, they can themselves lead to an equally fatal condition known as deadlocking, where each of two interdependent operations enters an infinite wait state pending instructions or data from the other.

Problems of communication manifest themselves here in a more fundamental respect, undermining efforts to solve problems such as those just discussed. DSPs are normally connected together via conventional computer buses, i.e. high-speed parallel communication lines for transmitting instructions and data over short distances between hardware devices, the components for the latter being mounted on printed circuit cards which plug into special multi-pin sockets attached directly to the bus itself. Notwithstanding the parallel environment the transmission speed is finite, and has to be shared between all the devices attached to the bus. Since DSPs receive and transmit a high density of information, each additional processor has a major effect on the performance of the system as a whole, and experience has revealed an important constraint on the number of processors that can be efficiently networked in this manner. Adding a second DSP to a bus will almost, but not quite, double the processing capability. This loss in capacity is due to overheads incurred in multiplexing the control system and ensuring that the operation of the system as a whole is correctly synchronized. This effect becomes more marked if a third processor is added, the further improvement in overall performance over the two falling significantly short of the expected 50 per cent. Addition of a fourth processor makes only a marginal improvement, and by the time a fifth or sixth is added the overall performance actually starts to decrease, for the volume of data and control signals begins to exceed the available bandwidth on the bus. Most DSP systems are thus currently optimized for at the most three or four processors pending an efficient solution to the problem just described.

One promising line of research into architectures that avoid this particular impasse concerns the transputer, a British product from INMOS which is specifically designed as a building block for the construction of massively parallel computing systems. This device is essentially a complete computer on a chip with a central processor, some local memory and, unusually, a set of serial links for the communication of data and instructions. The latter, usually four per transputer, can be configured as input or output lines as required. Two input and two output links provide a balanced throughput. Alternatively one input and three output links provide a higher rate of output in return for a reduced rate of input, an arrangement highly appropriate to an application such as a digital oscillator. The serial environment allows for a greatly simplified communication protocol involving direct connections from one transputer to another rather than via a common bus, with the result that arrays of transputers can be freely configured to achieve a performance that closely matches the degree of parallelism employed. Thus whilst a single general-purpose transputer will generally under-perform the audio processing capacity of a typical DSP, the situation reverses quite dramatically once several are networked together. Despite the use of a serial protocol for communications, the very high speed of transmission – typically 20 or 30 million bits per link – ensures a bandwidth more than adequate to cope with high quality audio data, providing the processing load is distributed intelligently across the network. As faster and more sophisticated members of the transputer family become available so the prospects for transputer-based synthesizers are becoming more attractive. Another related line of development showing considerable promise involves replacing the conventional bus system for networking DSPs with a transputer-based control system, thus capitalizing on the signal processing performance of the former whilst overcoming the bandwidth problems described earlier.

One of the biggest problems encountered in designing interactive facilities for the operation of digital synthesizers is the very different nature of the world that lies outside such systems from the one that exists within. The former is only partially predictable and essentially asynchronous. A good interface must allow the composer the freedom to choose the most suitable range of tools for his purpose with no unreasonable restrictions over the manner in which they may be operated. By contrast, the world within systems is highly organized, synchronous, and capable of responding only to logical and precise instructions. With so many sensors in a sophisticated human-machine interface, major problems are frequently encountered in scheduling the flow of information to and from an already heavily loaded central processing system, and great ingenuity has to be used if the system is not to respond unpredictably to new commands, or at worst stop due to a failure to keep up with the flow of information. Once again the architecture of transputers offers particular properties that make them highly attractive devices for the dedicated control of sensors, well able to handle, prioritize, and schedule incoming and outgoing information for a central processing network of further transputers, or transputers and DSPs in an ordered and efficient manner.

Such is the pace of technical development that there can be little doubt that the 1990s will bring further dramatic improvements in the design of computing architectures, and all the current indicators point to a growing emphasis on multiprocessor networks such as those discussed above. Computer scientists are only just beginning to grasp the significance of a concurrent processing environment, in particular the need to adopt fundamentally new approaches to system design both in terms of hardware and software. Now more that ever before it is vital that the partnership between scientists and musicians is reaffirmed and strengthened if the potential benefits of these new frontiers of technology are to be reaped by composers, in whose hands alone lies the creative future of the medium.

FURTHER READING

MANNING, P.D. (1985) *Electronic and Computer Music*, Oxford: Clarendon Press; revised edn forthcoming (1992/3).

MATHEWS, M.V. and PIERCE, J.D. (eds) (1989) *Current Directions in Computer Music Research*, Cambridge, Mass.: MIT Press.

MOORE, F. (1989) *Elements of Computer Music*, Englewood Cliffs, NJ: Prentice-Hall.

ROADS, C. (1989) *The Music Machine*, Cambridge, Mass.: MTP Press.

ROADS, C. and STRAUM, J. (eds) (1987) *Foundations of Computer Music*, Cambridge, Mass.: MIT Press.

20

Electroacoustic Music and the Soundscape: The Inner and Outer World

BARRY TRUAX

The relation of music and technology is becoming increasingly para-doxical. Within musical thought, computer technology allows the composer to conceive musical ideas from strikingly new perspectives. At the same time technology allows music to be increasingly embedded within the 'media environment' as a commodity with more exchange value than use value. Music frequently functions as a surrogate environment that interposes itself between us and the external world, imposing a relationship instead of expressing it. Music as an expression of the human spirit is locked in a struggle with music as the product of corporate control.

This chapter will examine the contemporary role of music first from the outside, in terms of music within the soundscape, and then from the inside, in terms of the soundscape within the music. In the first section I will trace how the traditional and complex relationship of the listener to the environment has been transformed by the social production of the electroacoustic listener as a consumer within a surrogate media environment. What originated as a complex relationship in the acoustic world reflecting a coherent unity has evolved into a merely complicated relationship based on inherent contradiction in the electroacoustic world. This evolution poses a dilemma for both the contemporary listener and composer, namely how to live with contradiction.

In the second section, I will explore the new soundscape that is evolving within the practice of music and technology. Most of this presentation will be based on my personal experience as a composer whose creative work is intimately entwined with the development of software systems for composition and sound synthesis (Truax 1985). This experience has led me to conclude that what is significant about the composer's use of technology is its ability to change the process of compositional thinking, not merely its output. One example of this will be illustrated by my experience both with interactive computer music composition systems and with the domain of granular synthesis. This unusual method of sound construction links the micro-level world of sound 'grains' at the millisecond level with the macro level of perception and results in new compositional concepts relating sound and structure (Truax 1988).

The practice of electroacoustic music is producing, at least in some of its manifestations, a new kind of listener and a new soundscape, while simultaneously being equally concerned with producing consumer-orientated music and products. However, I see the more positive role of electroacoustic music as a search for unity and coherence within an electroacoustic environment based on inherent contradiction. Whether music can resolve such contradictions and lead us into a more balanced relation to our environment remains to be seen; it is this quest that will concern us here.

MUSIC WITHIN THE SOUNDSCAPE

Listening and Acoustic Communication: Complexity within the Acoustic Environment

From the contemporary perspective of ecology we can understand the traditional soundscape (i.e. the acoustic environment prior to industrialization and electrification) as a balanced ecosystem. Unfortunately it seems that we are only able to conceptualize that balanced relationship as an ecological one because we have since lost it. We are now confronted with such obvious incongruities in the soundscape that we are able to understand what it was we once took for granted. The necessity of the ecological concept springs from the context of loss, or at least from the present threat to survival. The question for us now is whether a new balance can be regained. Can we – with consciousness – be part of a new ecosystem?

The conscious awareness we seek can be encapsulated by the term 'design'. It comprises the models, the knowledge and the techniques that we understand and can put into practice. Murray Schafer characterizes soundscape design as a compositional challenge that involves everyone, not just composers (Schafer 1977). In my own view, design must also include contemporary technology, the same technology that is largely responsible for the imbalanced situation we now find ourselves living in. Technology is the external embodiment of our knowledge, and we are only hiding from our responsibility for its effects if we blame it for our problems. At this point in the helix, we must choose between trying to reverse direction – an impossibility in my view, given that consciousness cannot be reversed – and using our awareness and our technology to bring about that return but on a different, more conscious level.

Our concepts of design must be informed by an understanding of the past. That past cannot be regained, only re-created by a conscious restructuring of relationships. But the process of restructuring can benefit from a knowledge of how the soundscape functioned prior to industrialization and electrification, even if we cannot restore those conditions. Based on the foundation work of the World Soundscape Project (1973, 1977a, 1977b, 1978a, 1978b) at Simon Fraser University, Burnaby, Canada, in the early 1970s to document and study the acoustic environment, I have evolved a 'communicational model' to describe how soundscapes function (Truax 1984). Unlike the models of the traditional disciplines that study sound, which are based on concepts of energy transfer and signal processing, the communicational model is based on the concept of information exchange.

At the centre of the acoustic communicational model is the listener, because listening is the primary interface where information is exchanged between the individual and the environment. The auditory system may process incoming acoustic energy and create neural signals, but listening involves the higher cognitive levels that extract usable information and interpret its significance. Listening is also multi-levelled because it can involve various degrees of conscious attention. We normally think of listening as always attentive, and in fact this is the most analytical form that listening takes. However, most of the time, we process acoustic information more at a background level without attention being focused on it. This information provides the environmental context of our awareness, the ongoing and usually highly redundant 'ground' to our consciousness.

However, background listening is still a sophisticated cognitive process, involving feature detection, the recognition of patterns and their comparison to known patterns and environmental 'signatures'. Moreover, background listening can trigger conscious attention to be focused on an incoming sound when there is sufficient need or motivation from the listener. We have all

376

experienced the recognition of a particular sound, such as a voice, footsteps, or a car door closing, even when we are not listening for it. The sound attracts our attention either because it is unfamiliar ('who could that be?') or instead, precisely because it is familiar and because it has significance ('oh, I need to talk to that person'). I call this situation 'listening-in-readiness' because it involves both background and foreground listening strategies. It requires a favourable acoustic environment for information to be available (a good signal-to-noise ratio in technical terms), and an active cognitive processing of patterns and their comparison to known ones.

These different levels of listening involve analytical attention being paid to short-term details in the foreground case, and holistic or Gestalt pattern recognition in the background case. These two complementary strategies are often described as the respective provinces of the two hemispheres of the brain, and music is known to involve either or both such strategies, depending on the listening context and the listener's training or competence (Bever and Chiarello 1974). But I suspect that our traditional experience with environmental sounds predates the development of these cognitive abilities with music, both for the individual and the species as a whole, and therefore soundscape experience is fundamental to all forms of listening. However it is understood, listening is at the centre of the complex relationship between the individual and the environment.

I have suggested elsewhere that instead of listening being the end stage of a series of linear energy transfers from source to listener, we can understand it within a system of information exchange where sound mediates the relation of the listener to the environment (Truax 1984). In the traditional soundscape, that mediation entwines the listener in a unity with the environment. Hildegard Westerkamp has characterized the relationship as a balance between input and output, impression and expression, listening and sound-making (Westerkamp 1988). The information we take in as listeners is balanced by our own sound-making activities which, in turn, shape the environment. Acoustic ecology mirrors and complements the social and biological ecology in traditional societies.

At the conclusion of its study of five European villages, the World Soundscape Project postulated that the soundscape of each, to the extent that it reflected its traditional function, was characterized by variety, complexity, and balance (World Soundscape Project 1977b). Variety characterizes the amount of potential information in the environment, complexity the processing of that information by the listener which determines the listener's relationship to the environment, and balance the set of constraints that regulates and stabilizes the system. The result is the acoustic community, a communicational system in which sound plays a formative role. Music is an intense and specialized form of sound-making, both individual and social, through which that coherent relationship to the environment can be expressed.

Attali (1985) suggests that music reflects the need for order in the face of the violence of noise and affirms that 'society is possible'. He also points out that the control of music – and hence of all sound-making – is the concern of those in power, those responsible for social order. Music therefore reflects the prevailing economic order. Even more dramatically, Attali hypothesizes that changes in music-making may predict and precede changes in the economic order! Could the mediating role of sound mean that new forms of acoustic communication presage a new social order?

In addition to Attali's dialectical relationship of music and noise, there are other implications of noise on the acoustic ecosystem. Traditional acoustical engineering approaches have concentrated on the negative effects of noise, ranging from the physiological damage it can cause, to psychological effects, disruption of communication, and social trauma. Within the acoustic communicational model, we can understand noise as a destabilizing force. Instead of the traditional objective definitions of noise as an aperiodic waveform or a sound with high intensity level, or the subjective catch-all of noise as 'unwanted sound', we can focus on its role in disrupting or obscuring acoustic information. The simplest way in which it does this is by masking, that is, by making other sounds more difficult to hear.

Within our model of the acoustic community, noise is anything that upsets the balance of the system or its constraining forces. It is anything that reduces variety and increases redundancy, anything that obscures the clarity of a sound or reduces the definition of the acoustic environment. It is anything that simplifies or weakens the relationship of the listener to the environment, anything that reduces the desire to listen or the opportunity to make sounds. In practice what noise creates is an information-poor environment, one in which there is little desire to listen because there is so little that is meaningful to listen to. In the worst case, noise impairs the physical ability to hear and stresses the physiological functioning of the entire body. More commonly it simply reduces the meaningfulness of the aural experience and the sense of self and place.

Perhaps most significant of all is the way in which noise as the cause of degeneration of an acoustic community paves the way for profound changes, at both the individual and social level. Faced with the destruction of meaning from one perceptual source, the individual seeks a replacement in another, usually the visual. But the visual sense has developed to complement the auditory, not to replace it. It objectifies and detaches, contrary to the auditory sense which involves and connects. By the end of the nineteenth century, the forces of industrialization and urbanization had profoundly changed the social and economic order of Western Europe and North America. They were also threatening to change the acoustic environment of most communities irrevocably, not only with the sounds of industry but also with those of motorized vehicles, both on the ground and in the air. Into this acoustically precarious situation a radically different type of sound phenomenon was about to be introduced – electroacoustic sound. Music and the soundscape would never again be the same.

Electroacoustic Communication:
The Listener as Consumer within the Surrogate Environment

It has been claimed that the introduction of the phonetic alphabet was a major turning point in the history of communication. By allowing speech sound to be objectified and stored, it eroded the oral tradition and paved the way for literacy (Ong 1982). Although literacy has had a profound effect on human consciousness in that it allowed and encouraged inner speech, together with the development of abstract thinking and the concept of the self as an individual separate from the environment, it has not had a comparable effect on the soundscape. On the other hand, the electroacoustic revolution has had a profound effect on both. By allowing any sound to be objectified, stored, and reproduced in any other context, electroacoustic communication has not only eroded literacy but has also paved the way for a complete redefinition of what constitutes the acoustic environment and the listening experience.

Whereas industrialization changed both social conditions and the sounds that populated the soundscape – both of which threatened the balance of the acoustic community – electroacoustic communication provided a completely new element: contradiction. In the natural environment, contradictions cannot occur; a species in contradiction with its environment simply dies out, unless of course it can adapt. Within electroacoustic communication, contradiction is an inherent and inescapable fact.

The essence of the electroacoustic process is that it transforms acoustic sound, with all its physical characteristics and limitations, into a different energy form, namely an electrical signal which has very different characteristics (such as travelling at the speed of light) and none of the same limitations. In other words, the electroacoustic process breaks all the

379

constraints of the physical acoustic world, but in so doing it creates all its contradictions.

In the acoustic world, sound is constrained by being tied to its context, in relation to which it derives at least part of its meaning. In the electroacoustic world, sound can be taken out of its original context and put via a loudspeaker into any other, where its meaning may be contradictory to that environment. The contradiction in any electroacoustically reproduced sound is that it exists in this time and space but it is from another; it exists in this context but is not necessarily appropriate to it. The sound comes from an inanimate source, the loudspeaker, but can we treat it as an inanimate environmental sound if we recognize it as speech or music? It is both, and the contradiction cannot be resolved. Schafer (1969) termed this phenomenon 'schizophonia' to indicate its 'aberrant' quality.

In the acoustic world, sound can only last a certain time before its energy dies away; it can only travel a certain distance, or have a certain loudness and, in general, certain timbral qualities. In the electroacoustic world, none of these constraints apply. With amplification and electronic sound synthesis, the behaviour and characteristics of sound are almost completely arbitrary. It can travel nearly any distance, be many places simultaneously, sound arbitrarily loud and be transformed in timbral character until it is unrecognizable.

One of the most significant contradictions in electroacoustic sound, in terms of its implications for the listening process, is the ability to repeat a sound exactly. Attali (1985) sums up the most essential characteristic of both monopoly capitalism's stockpiling of commodities and music in the twentieth century with the same word: 'repeating'. In the natural acoustic world, a repetition of a sound is never exactly the same, nor can a sound overlap itself; to do so would be a contradiction. Variety and difference are inherent in the acoustic process, and since information is based on the perception of difference (Bateson 1972), the acoustic world is full of information. Exact electroacoustic repetition, which is not only possible but commonplace, eliminates difference and hence reduces information. In the mixing studio it is a simple matter to repeat a sound exactly or combine it with itself up to an arbitrary density of layers. What kind of sense is the brain supposed to make of what previously had been a contradiction in acoustic terms?

When such 'contradictory' phenomena as the radio, telephone or gramophone record were first experienced, the wonderment at the 'magic' of technology in breaking normal constraints seems to have overpowered any uneasiness at the underlying contradiction. When we consider how poor

380

the quality of early forms of sound reproduction was, we may wonder why listeners were so convinced they were hearing the original. Was it simply because there was sufficient resemblance or could they not analyse the difference? Since then both scientific and aural analysis have been based on the electroacoustic reproduction and repetition of sound. As a result, our sense of 'sound quality' is conditioned by the fact that, thanks to electroacoustic technology, we have heard many poor as well as good examples of reproduced sound.

Today, frequent exposure to electroacoustic sound – and a survey of my students indicates that they hear in excess of fifty hours per week of reproduced sound (Truax 1984: 154) – has lessened the sense of magic and made the contradictions at least conventional if not actually banal. The same seems not to have occurred on such a wide scale with new forms of electroacoustic music unless the music imitates conventional instruments and musical styles. Known sounds that are reproduced become conventional fairly quickly; new electronic sounds seem strange when first introduced (e.g. tones replacing bells in telephones) but again, they too become quickly accepted, presumably because their meaning is already known. However, non-derivative electroacoustic music finds much slower acceptance because it requires the development of a new frame of reference, a new language, in short, a new system of communication.

What has been accepted with remarkable ease is electroacoustic sound as an environment in daily life. Whether it is the ubiquitous background music (rapidly becoming foreground music) in public places, the radio or television as accompaniment to daily activities in the home or car, or the Walkman and portable radios as an accompaniment attached to your person, electroacoustic sound, including a lot of music, is seldom far away. Already in the early 1960s, Mendelsohn (1964) found that among New York City radio listeners, the majority used radio as an accompaniment to daily activities, as a way to bracket the day and 'lubricate' social relations by having common experiences to talk about, as well as to influence mood and behaviour, a trait that the Muzak Corporation has been exploiting since the 1930s (Cardinell 1948).

I suggest that this use of electroacoustic sound as an everyday accompaniment creates a 'media environment', and I suspect that it functions as a surrogate environment for most people, one that seems richer and more meaningful than the alternative 'natural' one which may be noisy, lonely, boring, uninformative or alienating. Into these 'gaps' in life comes sound that will at least seem to fill the deficiency, the radio that will get you through the rush hour while you are trapped in traffic, the record player that masks the sounds of neighbours, the television that provides distraction for the tired and bored and 'company' for the lonely.

The problem with such surrogates is, first, that because they don't alleviate the real problem, they create a psychological dependency on its antidote, and secondly and more seriously, that most of these media environments are intimately connected to the commercial world. As a result, the listener becomes the recipient of countless advertising messages as well as the consumer of audio products and services. As part of the same process, music becomes a commodity like any other, with more exchange value than use value. On the broader political-economic level, American popular music also becomes the forerunner and most significant symbol of American products and values in a world increasingly dominated by corporate interests.

Interestingly enough, even if few composers seem to have learned anything from environmental sound experience, it appears that advertising designers have. Most of their audio advertising techniques, even if not consciously designed to work like environmental sound, certainly seem to act the same way. We have already noted the importance of background listening in the traditional soundscape where sounds common to an environment can be processed without conscious attention being focused on them. The frequent repetition of advertising works in much the same way, even when the listener is not actively attuned to it or the sound itself is low level. The frequent presence of background music in a particular environment builds up much the same pattern of association.

I call this type of listening where attention is focused elsewhere 'distracted listening' (Truax 1984). The problem for the advertiser is how to communicate to a person in this kind of situation. Factual information cannot be conveyed with any reliability of recall, hence advertisements seldom include such specifics. Instead, advertisers surround their product name with the desired image, supported by stereotypical music and voices, with attention 'hooked' by easily recognized tunes, motifs, slogans, rhymes and other 'catchy' items. These sounds and images strike what Schwartz (1973) calls the 'responsive chord', in that the listener supplies the appropriate meaning or association. After many repetitions, the product will be embedded in the listener's memory with a variety of images and emotions attached to it. When a need arises or when a decision to buy is being made, the sight or name of the product is sufficient to evoke the appropriate response. All of this occurs, indeed best occurs, without analytical attention or logical thought being applied (in fact, paid attention to, an ad usually seems absurd and the listener may become defensive about the message).

With the rise in environmental noise and the loss of community as a source of meaning, electroacoustic sound has fertile ground in which to operate as a surrogate. Once commoditized, music has become inextricably linked with this process and the multi-billion dollar industry that goes along with it. The individual's psychological dependence on the media environment and industry's continual need for new products and services guarantees that the electroacoustic relationship will be long-lived, even if imbalanced. Yet Attali and others claim that a crisis is developing, both economically and socially, and change is inevitable. He even suggests that certain developments in contemporary music foretell this change: 'Music, the ultimate form of production, gives voice to this new emergence, suggesting that we call it composition' (Attali 1985: 134).

From the Complex to the Complicated: A Crisis for the Composer and Society

The electroacoustic revolution has completely transformed the traditional soundscape and the role of the listener within it. Impressed by the scope of technological development, we are often tempted to say that we live in a 'complex' age. We assume that technological sophistication leads to progress and then are surprised when that technology creates more problems than it solves. The nuclear arms buildup and the problems of environmental pollution have convinced many that this 'progress' has brought us to the edge of destruction of the planet.

Instead of regarding our technological age as being complex, I think it is more appropriate to understand it as being complicated. The essential difference between the two descriptions is that, to me at least, the term complicated implies contradictions, a lack of coherence that complex systems exhibit. To be complicated, a system poses problems, perhaps unresolvable ones, and if so it is unstable. Such instability may lead to adaptive behaviour if the system can reorganize itself, but it can also lead to breakdown if it doesn't.

Technology poses problems, and electroacoustic technology, as I have shown, by being based on inherent contradiction, poses some quite difficult ones. One of the most difficult stems from the fact that we do not wish to give up what we perceive as the positive effects of technology, which we have come to depend on, even if they are accompanied by negative implications. In fact, the technological 'habit' of most people is such an integral part of their 'life-style' that any criticism of technology is often taken as a personal attack. It is difficult to stand back from such personal involvement to gain the larger perspective and perceive alternatives.

I have argued elsewhere (Truax 1984: ch. 13) that two key factors in any solution are the need to regain control and the need to experience alternatives. The crisis is similar for both the public and for the professional composer – the lack of personal control and the lack of alternatives. The two are closely related. The audio industry and the mass media, by gearing their products to the widest possible audience (or 'market' in their terms), ignore the needs of the individual. Two familiar problems for most electroacoustic composers are, first, the lack of access to the media and to other means of distribution, and second, the dependence on the companies that manufacture computer music instruments for the means of production. Despite the inherent flexibility of software and programmed control, the currently available computer music products exhibit a depressing degree of similarity and closed or 'black box' design.

The personal computer has been developed and marketed with a strongly democratic appeal; likewise, personal computer music systems have promised to bring the power of large-scale digital music systems into the realm of personal ownership. To a certain extent this has happened, but the new products (and one is always waiting for the 'next' one) invariably come with musical limitations and a 'closed system' mentality. The reasons seem to be two-fold, the first being the necessity of the mass market-place to base its products on the lowest common denominator of market appeal, and the second being the proprietary secrecy that stems from the competitive nature of the industry. The result seems to be that, with the worldwide spread of the same 'democratic' technology, everyone has the 'freedom' to sound the same!

The situation is particularly ironic with digitally based technology because of its inherent flexibility. Hardware costs and limitations are quickly ceasing to be the most constraining factors for users; ironically, it is the software that poses the greatest limitations because of the conventional musical models it implements. Software by its very nature is open-ended and flexible. It is notoriously difficult to standardize, to transport to other hardware configurations, to copyright or to profit from, but the industry has managed to do all of those things. The root of the problem is that if companies provided truly open-ended software, they would go out of business – they would no longer be needed. Individuals could become self-sufficient because they would have the means to evolve and develop their own ideas, instead of being the user of others'. For industry to prosper, it must reduce differences and perpetuate dissatisfaction.

On the other hand, I'm not sure that most individuals actually want that kind of open-endedness. It would mean taking a great deal of responsibility for one's own development. It would mean active involvement and participation, taking an initiative, constantly being in a state of learning, and worst of all, risking failure. We have not been conditioned by the marketplace to accept this scenario readily. However, if we do not embrace this path, we will continue to live, with a greater or lesser degree of discomfort, with contradiction in a society that is increasingly vulnerable to breakdown. At this critical juncture does music itself provide a glimpse of any answers?

THE SOUNDSCAPE WITHIN THE MUSIC

We have seen in the first part of this chapter that music is increasingly a part of the everyday environment. In many cases it becomes the key feature of the soundscape, even if it is not meant to be listened to. It works its effects on us wherever we go and becomes associated in our memories with environments and products. In essence, it becomes the 'ambience' of the media environment. Once habituated to its omnipresence in public, we purchase it for private use in order to duplicate its effects or to signify our social role. The more serious stockpile the commodity in the hope that time will be found to listen to it in future. In the microcosm of our personal lives we replicate the macrocosm of the social and economic world.

It is interesting to consider the music that resists this incorporation into daily life, music that refuses to become ambient, music that demands involvement, music that we cannot passively consume but which requires us, even as listeners, to construct its meaning. The fact that such a music still exists gives us hope that music as a human phenomenon remains alive, that music has not become merely environment. For each person, the music that serves this function will be different. It is a personal discovery and may be found anywhere, in the conventional or in the experimental, in the wilderness or in the city, outside our culture or within it, with technology or without, through sound-making or listening in depth. Wherever it is found, it will involve thinking through sound.

For me the most vital form which that music takes is electroacoustic music, because it is in that medium that I am simultaneously composer, performer and listener. The mingling of what were traditionally these three separate functions gives this type of musical experience an intensity which is less present for me in other forms. I propose to examine the soundscape within this music in order to discover in the microcosm the characteristics of the new macrocosm that we seek.

Technology and the Compositional Process: Changing the Instruments of Thought

The practice of electroacoustic music leads us back to first principles. It is constructed from the ground up, as it were. Nothing is given, everything must be reconstructed and reconceptualized. As a result, everything must be done with knowledge and conscious awareness. The world this music creates is artificial but it is still a world, and to function properly that world must be coherent. Contradiction arises most often through the interface of the electroacoustic world to the real world.

One of the most fundamental characteristics of electroacoustic music is that the composer designs the sounds themselves, their organization into larger forms, and ultimately the space or environment which the composition creates (Emmerson 1986). That space is inherent at all levels of the composition, in the sounds and their organization, as well as in the performance or 'diffusion' of the sounds in an acoustic space. This latter aspect is often a source of contradiction – the space implied by the sound structure is inconsistent with the quality of reproduction and the acoustic characteristics of the space in which it is performed. The art of diffusion is to make the inner and outer spaces coherent and complementary.

Likewise, if electroacoustic sounds create space, they also create time. By comparison to the traditional view that sounds exist in time, contemporary ideas about cosmology suggest that the movement of objects creates our sense of time. Sound, possibly more so than visual phenomena, has always had the dynamic role of creating time, and music can be thought of as a particular means of organizing and shaping subjective time. The electroacoustic composer has the unprecedented ability to control time at the micro as well as the macro level.

Constructing the electroacoustic world requires knowledge, a great deal of knowledge. I have already described technology as embodying human knowledge, and the most powerful embodiment today is in the computer. It is one of the paradoxes of electroacoustic music that it would not exist without such external embodiment, hence its profound appeal to the inner world of imagination. I suspect that our age-old fascination with technology has a lot to do with that interplay of the inner and outer world that it represents. Technology as the embodiment of knowledge (whether in the 'soft' form of the ancient I Ching or the 'hard' form of the modern computer) is a mirror of human consciousness. We are simultaneously drawn to it and fearful of what we might find, and so it is not surprising that the computer today provokes such strongly ambivalent reactions.

The computer is a powerful tool for controlling complexity. It does so on the basis of a specific model of a given complex task and this model is implicit in the software used to address that task. Therein lie two critical questions: what is the source of the model, and what is the locus of control? Both questions challenge us in fundamental ways. The model reveals how we conceive of the task at hand. If we rely on traditional models of how music is constructed – for instance, according to instrumental music practice – then we shouldn't be surprised if the music that is produced is an extension and reflection of that practice. There may be some pragmatic value in using a machine to produce that kind of music, but all that it reflects back to us is what we already know. In many cases even that may not truly belong to us because it has only been inherited, not revealed as the result of our own search.

The issue of control similarly reflects our preconceptions, tinged in this case with psychological implications. We need the computer to control complexity, but we are afraid of losing control to it. However, the computer brings our need for control to a crisis point by showing that it leads to absurdity. Even if we decide to specify all events in a composition, the computer demands that we specify all parameters of those events. And then if we specify all parameters, the complete digital specification of the audio signal requires many thousands of sound samples per second – clearly an absurdity to control directly. The computer ultimately reduces to absurdity the traditional linear model that music originates with an all-powerful composer, passes through an obedient performer, and ends its journey as a communicated message to the passive listener. To escape the inherent contradiction of this model, the composer must rethink what the process of composition means with a computer.

What the computer does is to allow us to change the process of thinking with sound (Truax 1986). It becomes a new instrument for musical thought, not merely for new sounds. It provides a framework, an extendible one, for thinking about music. By virtue of its open-endedness, it allows the experience gained from its use to be channelled back into further software development. Whether the strategies used are deterministic or stochastic, whether the process is top-down or bottom-up, whether the details are determined by algorithms or by direct specification, the computer must be guided by the composer as to whether the results are musical. The concept of control by the composer gives way to the role of musical guidance, the composer as a musical strategist with the tacit knowledge to evaluate the musicality of the results of the process.

The result of this different approach to musical process is inevitably a new musical language and a new electroacoustic soundscape. Its characteristics implicitly reflect the new system of elements which have resulted in its birth. It has been evolved and negotiated by the composer, not imposed. It creates its own sense of space and time. Its imagery may have some basis in the real world but in general it seems as if a curtain has been drawn aside to reveal a different and completely coherent universe, to which the composer is but a conduit. The music is not a static entity, but within technical constraints may have a dynamic existence such that it changes from performance to performance and may even be adapted to a different medium. It creates an environment that requires the listener's involvement to establish its meaning, a meaning that is at once collective and personal. By contrast, the masterpiece tradition of the nineteenth century constructed an immutable musical edifice, solidly grounded on the foundation of tonality and to be visited in reverence in order to receive a reflection of the composer's inspiration. Today's successful electroacoustic work resembles more a participatory environment in which information is exchanged between listeners and the soundscape.

From Micro to Macro: Complexity and the World of Granular Synthesis

The digital technique that, in my experience, goes back the furthest to first principles is granular synthesis. It has been suggested as a computer music technique by Xenakis (1971) and Roads (1978) and is based on the production of a high density of small acoustic events called 'grains' that are less than 50 milliseconds in duration and typically in the range of 10–30 milliseconds. Typical grain densities range from several hundred to several thousand grains per second. Such high densities of events have previously made it difficult to work with the technique because of the large amount of calculation required, and therefore until recently few composers have experimented with it. Using a digital signal processor controlled by a microcomputer, I have been able to implement the technique with real-time synthesis and incorporate it within an interactive compositional environment (Truax 1988).

In taking us back to first principles, granular synthesis questions what

388

those principles really are. It challenges the traditional Fourier model of sound, which states that any periodic waveform may be reduced to the sum of a set of harmonically related sine waves each with a different amplitude. The first problem with the basic Fourier theorem is that it ignores time; it implies that the constituent sine waves have infinite duration. In order to deal with actual musical sounds, each cycle of the sound may be analysed to establish the time variance (or envelope) of each component harmonic (Mathews and Risset 1969). However, such sounds are not periodic as they begin, having instead an 'attack transient' or burst of noise as the instrument is set in motion. It is interesting to note that this short period of time as the sound begins, when the amount of acoustic variation is the greatest, is the most critical for the identification of the sound. It is also the part that contains the greatest amount of information. If that part of the sound is cut off, the rest is barely recognized as coming from the instrument in question.

The second problem with the Fourier model is that it corresponds poorly with the psychoacoustic reality of how our auditory system actually processes musical sound (Roederer 1975). Although we can perform Fourier analysis, i.e. distinguish separate harmonic components, we can do so only for the lower harmonics whose frequencies are sufficiently far apart, and only under conditions where the sound is prolonged such that we have time to focus on those harmonics. In other words, we have to simulate the unchanging conditions implied by the Fourier theorem for it to be applicable. In more realistic situations, with sound densities in music involving several notes per second in a melodic line, possibly combined with chords and various accompanying instruments, the auditory system uses much more efficient means to identify and track particular instruments.

In 1947 the British physicist Dennis Gabor proposed an 'acoustical quantum' as the fundamental unit of sound that incorporates both frequency and time because 'it is our most elementary experience that sound has a time pattern as well as a frequency pattern' (Gabor 1947: 591). In other words, the quantum is the shortest duration of sound that will activate the auditory system. It is an 'event', not merely a fixed stimulus. Although the techniques of granular synthesis depart from the ideal Gabor grains, they still involve the principle of building complex events from seemingly trivial micro-level, enveloped quanta called grains.

In fact, what is most remarkable about the technique is the relation between the triviality of the grain (heard alone it is the merest click or 'point' of sound) and the richness of the layered granular texture that results from their superimposition. The basic characteristics of the grain are preserved in the macro-level texture, and changes to the basic shape or content of the grain will alter the resulting texture. However, the macro-level is also more than the sum of its parts because of the way in which the grains are organized with respect to each other. For instance, if the component grains all have a similar frequency, the result is a musical pitch, but as the frequencies of the grains are spread over a larger range, the result becomes a broad-band noise, much like the natural textures of wind and water. These sounds create a remarkable sense of space and volume. Similarly, if the durations of the grains are all similar, the frequency spectrum and timbre of the resulting sound is much richer because of the phenomenon of amplitude modulation. In addition, when a short delay is placed between grains and then increased, the fused granular texture begins to 'pull apart' as isolated events emerge perceptually from the texture and eventually establish rhythmic relations. Once global amplitude contours are added, we have replicated all of the basic acoustic properties of sound.

One of the primary characteristics of granular synthesized sound is its dynamic quality. A static, unvarying sound is virtually impossible to achieve. It is the exception, not the rule. This quality is reminiscent of the natural soundscape in which everything is in a state of flux. It was not until the electroacoustic revolution that an entirely static sound was produced by the electronic oscillator. Predictably, such sounds fell on the ear only to produce boredom. The auditory system is oriented towards change and quickly habituates to redundant stimuli. The result of this habituation, a process called adaptation, is that the loudness of a steady tone decreases until theoretically, with infinite exposure, the sound disappears! We also react to steady, high-frequency tones with irritation. They seem piercing and unnatural. Nature has fortunately provided for transience in such sounds (such as birdsong) and a pattern of decreasing energy in the upper frequency range to make them palatable.

In terms of the issues of compositional control raised earlier, it is clear that granular synthesis requires a shift in thinking. It is obviously impossible for the composer to specify each individual grain, given that there may be thousands of them per second. Hierarchic levels of control are absolutely necessary, and at each level the composer simply specifies key control variables on the basis of which all of the specific data is calculated by the program. Interestingly enough, the structure of the software that realizes the technique is different from conventional programming approaches that tend to be linear and deterministic. The granular software, in contrast, more closely resembles an organic system in which parallel processes are working independently, linked by access to common variables representing 'the state of the world' and by messages passed between processes. The standard debugging technique of stopping the program and stepping through its instructions one at a time is meaningless in this case; once stopped, the program loses its most essential characteristics, its time behaviour and the interaction between levels. In this kind of system, the user functions as the source of control messages that guide the overall process without directly determining it.

There are also many fascinating parallels between the world of granular synthesis and the subatomic level of physical matter. First, of course, is Gabor's idea of the quantum of sound, an indivisible unit of information from the psychoacoustic point of view, on the basis of which all macro-level phenomena are based. However, more specifically, Gabor postulated that the parameters of this quantum were frequency and time. The student of acoustics is often taught that these are two distinct and unrelated parameters, but of course, on a deeper level of understanding they prove to be reciprocal to each other, both physically and psychoacoustically. There is also an 'uncertainty principle' relating them, analogous to Heisenberg's uncertainty principle about particles at the subatomic level. He demonstrated that the more precisely you determine the position of an electron the less you know about its velocity, and vice versa. This is because velocity is the rate of change of position. Similarly, the smaller the time window in acoustics, the larger the uncertainty (i.e. bandwidth) in frequency. Frequency, as the rate of change of phase, is the reciprocal of time.

In another analogy to quantum physics, time is reversible at the quantum level. The quantum equations are symmetrical with respect to the direction of time, and, similarly, the quantum grain of sound is reversible with no change in perceptual quality. That is, if a granular synthesis texture is played backwards it will sound the same, just as if the direction of the individual grain is reversed (even if it is derived from natural sound) it sounds the same. This time invariance also permits a time shifting of sound derived from the real world, allowing it to be slowed down with no change in pitch. Grains are taken from the sound sequence at specific points but the rate at which these points advance through the sequence need not be at the original clock rate. When 'clock time' is stopped, the grains can move backwards through the sound with no difference in sound quality. All of the characteristics that establish the directional experience of time occur at the macro level. Granular synthesis is in a unique position to mediate between the micro and macro time worlds.

The basis of granular synthesis in the seemingly trivial grain has had a powerful effect on my own way of thinking about sound and music. It clearly juxtaposes the micro and macro levels, as the richness of the latter lies in stark contrast to the insignificance of the former. Moreover, the range of densities obtainable, from the low levels associated with human gestures through those perceived as rapid and virtuosic, culminating with entirely fused textures, suggests a compositional continuum ranging from human scale to abstract. Finally, in terms of sound and structure, it is clear that the two are inseparable with this technique. The macro-level structure can only be described in terms of its component sounds, and the resulting sound complex is definable only in terms of the structural levels that characterize its organization.

To date, I have composed three works using the granular synthesis technique. The first, *Riverrun* (1986), was based on synthesized grains (Truax 1987b). The fundamental paradox of granular synthesis – that the enormously rich and powerful textures it produces result from its being based on the most 'trivial' grains of sound – suggested to me a metaphoric relation to the river whose power is based on the accumulation of countless 'powerless' droplets of water. The opening section of the work portrays that accumulation, as individual 'droplets' of sound multiply gradually into a powerful broad-band texture. The dynamic variation implemented by changing variables continuously allows the piece to create a sound environment in which stasis and flux, solidity and movement coexist in a dynamic balance similar to a river, which is always moving yet seemingly permanent. The piece, I find, also captures some of the awe one feels in the presence of the overpowering force of such a body of water, whether in a perturbed or calm state, and as such it seems to create a different mode of listening than does conventional instrumental or electroacoustic music.

Two more recent works, *The Wings of Nike* (1987), for computer images by Theo Goldberg and two soundtracks, and *Tongues of Angels* (1988), for oboe d'amore, cor anglais and four soundtracks, are based on the granulation of sampled sound using very short fixed samples. In the case of the first work, these are male and female phonemes, and in the second piece the samples are derived from the live instruments involved in the performance. Despite the brevity of the source material, very rich textures and complex rhythmic patterns can be obtained from it. The pitch and timbre of the resulting sound are determined by the source material unless the grain duration is too short, in which case a broad-band spectrum results. However, the overlay of up to twenty simultaneous versions of such sound, each with its own variations, produces a 'magnification' of the original sound, as well as the possibility of gradual or rapid movement through its micro-level characteristics.

The degree of magnification involved can be appreciated when it is

392

realized that three of the four movements of *The Wings of Nike*, lasting approximately 12 minutes, were derived from only two phonemes, each about 150 milliseconds long! The stereo tape is a mixdown from an eight-track original which includes four stereo pairs of the granular material, and therefore the vertical densities of sound are around eighty at any moment, and the horizontal densities range from quite sparse through to 8,000 events per second at the very end. The sounds are heard at approximately their original pitch combined with versions an octave up or down, except towards the end of the first movement where a slow downward glissando is heard.

In the case of the male phoneme ('tuh'), timbral changes are possible as the grains move from the aspiration at the beginning of the sample, through the consonant to the pitch of the voiced vowel and finally past it. Microscopic timbral changes that normally go unnoticed become evident with the repetition of the overlapping grains. The analogy in the work is between the sampled visual image of the statue (the Winged Victory, or Nike) that forms the basis of the computer-generated images and the sampled vocal sound as the source of the tape. Each is based within the human dimension but the transformation techniques extend them towards the supra-human, as at the end of the first movement (Album).

In the second movement, the Scherzo, the statue is given a rather androgynous head, and the phonemes in the tape part are detached and realistic. However, each image accumulates again into more elaborate patterns that mask the source. In the third movement (The Illuminated Nike), frequency modulation grains are used. Just as the image of the statue undergoes colour variations in illumination, different types of modulation 'colour' the carrier frequencies of the tape sounds producing timbral variations. In the last movement, the Coda, both the visual and aural elements are progressively multiplied (the wing feathers and drapery in the visual case, and the syncopated phonemes in the musical accompaniment) until they fuse. A new kind of machine emerges that releases the earth-bound images into upward flight.

Speed, rhythmic patterns and density changes such as gradual accumulation or evaporation of the sound are other compositional strategies that granulation makes available. Speed and density, for instance, can change from isolated events, through to fast repetitions (each with slightly different timbral characteristics), and finally result in fused textures. Stochastic patterning of the grains can occur over the same range of densities as well, giving the sense that the sound is coalescing or evaporating.

In the interaction of the tape with the live performer in *Tongues of Angels*,

393

this progression from speeds and patterns within the performance range of the instrumentalist to those achievable only by the computer creates much of the underlying dramatic tension of the work. We sense the struggle of the performer to match the virtuosity of the tape part and to transcend the limitations of human performance. The transcendence finally materializes at the end of the work when, after a gradual accelerando in both parts from syncopated rhythms through to fused textures and continuous gestures, there is a dramatic downward glissando on the tape. Despite the fact that all material was derived from the instruments heard live in the performance, the effect is suddenly that of a choir of voices, a transcendent image that inspired the biblically derived title of the work. Perhaps it could also be a metaphor for the technique of granular synthesis that seems to break into a new sonic domain.

I have described these compositions in some detail to give a sense of how dramatically this synthesis technique has changed both the musical thinking process and its results. The computer is an absolutely essential element in the system that has allowed this to happen. It is an interesting footnote to the granular synthesis story to consider why I should have been the first to implement it in real-time synthesis and hence to explore its potential with ease. It was technically feasible to do so about ten years earlier than my 1986 implementation, even though it is still technically impossible with most commercially produced MIDI-controlled synthesizers. I suspect that the main reason is the shift in basic concept which the technique demands. Technology always seems to be limited most by our own preconceptions and in turn it limits what is 'thinkable' with that technology. There is no precedent for the granular concept in instrumental music, hence a mind-block to its implementation. One wonders how many other techniques we have similarly excluded.

Resolving Contradiction:
Towards a Re-integration of the Inner and Outer Soundscape

In the first part of this essay I argued that music in the outer soundscape has become devalued as a result of the electroacoustic revolution. Functioning primarily as a commodity and a surrogate environment, it is situated within a system based on complication and inherent contradiction. In the second part I argued that the inner soundscape of non-derivative electroacoustic music has resulted from the same revolution. That soundscape, as a new system of acoustic communication, is based on complexity and inner coherence. The task facing us now is to re-integrate the inner and outer sound-scapes.

The search for complexity is an attempt to resolve contradictions and to seek unity and coherence, whether in the musical or social worlds. The technique to be used is that of design. I would like to think that composers could take a guiding role in that search because of their technical knowledge and because of their deep awareness of the aural experience. Perhaps the simplest place to begin is to see the act of composing as an analogy to and expression of that search, with the composition as its dramatization. The experience of such works could resonate within other individuals for whom the search is slightly below the surface of their awareness. That experience within the controlled environment of music could lead outwards to become applicable to, by analogy, the problems of the external world.

However, I do not see many composers being concerned with such matters. No matter how paradoxical the situation becomes, they seem to have little concern for the acoustic environment or the effects of media, preferring instead to complain about their victimization by these forces or about the lack of interest by the public in their esoteric concerns. From the ghetto of the new music community we hear a squabbling over crumbs that alternates with a mood of despair. Most indicative of all, we see an attempt to bring about a return to 'old values', to tonality and harmony, the principles that once worked and that presumably are the only ones that can still communicate to an audience that, in the meantime, has become accustomed to tradition as another commodity.

For composition to have any relevance to the problems I have described here, it must be based on a different world-view, a different educational process, and a different relation to technology. The purpose of all of these is integrative not exclusive, and it requires a change in our system of values. For the composer it may mean forgetting about the primacy of 'concert music', the most difficult shift of all in values. Our need for more concert music is surely less than our need for trained people to work in education, in media and technology, or in social and environmental areas involving sound. And yet we resist such departures from the field of 'pure' music because we have been taught to think of these other applications as second-class. Who has taught us to think that way?

In other words, I think we know what the answers are but we resist them psychologically. We need equality but we cling to the power and privilege to be found in hierarchy and inequality. According to the old ways of thinking, concert music is better than popular, instrumental better than electroacoustic, composing better than teaching, art more important than environment. Even if we resist those values, they are still embedded in our psyche as much as any other form of ideology. Unfortunately they link up with the much more untenable values of racism, sexism, patriarchy and imperialism that are similarly based on power and domination. These are the values that have brought society to the brink of collapse and they must be eradicated.

The alternative is subtle. By equality we do not mean the reduction of complexity found in liberalism's equation that everything is the same, that all ideas and cultures have equal value, and that music is the 'universal language'. This philosophy gives the appearance of a lack of prejudice while maintaining the status quo of power. It reduces difference instead of acknowledging it. The differences between cultures, ideas, and men and women are real and can never be eliminated. What must be eliminated is the notion that one is superior to the other. We can start by acknowledging that fact in music. Power and dominance was expressed in nineteenth-century music through the hierarchy of the tonal system, in which conflict had to be resolved by a reassertion of the tonic. Our music can reflect other models, such as the yin–yang concept of the complementarity of opposites, in which musical energy can derive from the interplay of difference, not its annihilation (Truax 1982, 1987a).

Attali characterizes his vision of the new social and economic order by the term 'composing'. He sees a decentralized economic system in which a network of individual and small group efforts replaces the monolithic, centralized forms of modern capitalism, the musical precursors of this change being the musics found on the fringes of the commercial mainstream. As a composer with a typical lack of understanding of abstract economic matters, I found his formulation surprisingly true to what I observe happening among musicians today, particularly the more technologically orientated. There is little reliance on government, institutions or business because of their inflexibility in dealing with individual needs. Instead, self-publication, self-promotion, home studios, and even software development in some cases, are becoming commonplace. Communication links are informal, though often global in scope, and sensibilities are highly regional, though often sophisticated in outlook. Large institutions are suspect and organizations tolerable only to the extent that they serve the network of individuals, not the accumulation of power. There is no centre; music has moved elsewhere.

Attali, however, underestimates the role of technology in this process, seeing it only as the expression of power. I have tried to show that music technology, and the computer in particular, while being the present servant of power, has another, more subtle side to it, one leading to freedom. Using technology is by no means the only way to proceed and I am not sure that we really understand all of its implications yet. But I am convinced that it does show a path forward.

The inherent contradictions of electroacoustic technology cannot be resolved, but they can be transcended. The initial effects of technology are disruptive of traditional systems of acoustic communication, and the power that technology wields has been appropriated by dominant institutions. Our task now is to regain control of technology at the individual level and through conscious design to reintegrate it into our lives and our environment. Only then will it become a liberating force and an extension of our consciousness.

ACKNOWLEDGEMENT

This essay is based on a series of talks given at the conference, Musica/Complessità (Music/Complexity) held in August 1988 in the convent of SS. Annunziata near Amelia, Italy. I would like to thank the organizers of this conference, Michela Mollia and Walter Branchi, for the opportunity to synthesize the diverse aspects of my work in music, technology and the soundscape, as well as all of the conference participants for the interaction and enthusiasm that gave it life. My attendance at this conference was supported by the Department of External Affairs, Ottawa, and the equivalent agency in Italy to whom thanks are also due.

REFERENCES

ATTALI, J. (1985) *Noise: The Political Economy of Music*, Minneapolis: University of Minnesota Press.

BATESON, G. (1972) *Steps to an Ecology of Mind*, New York: Ballantine.

BEVER, T.G., and CHIARELLO, R.J. (1974) 'Cerebral dominance in musicians and nonmusicians', *Science* 185: 537–9.

CARDINELL, R.L. (1948) 'Music in industry', in D. Schullian and M. Schoen (eds), *Music and Medicine*, New York: Schuman.

EMMERSON, S. (1986) 'The relation of language to materials', in S. Emmerson (ed.) *The Language of Electroacoustic Music*, London: Macmillan.

GABOR, D. (1947) 'Acoustical quanta and the theory of hearing', *Nature* 159 (4044): 591–4.

MATHEWS, M. and RISSET, J.C. (1969) 'Analysis of musical-instrument tones', *Physics Today* 22 (2): 23–30.

MENDELSOHN, H. (1964) 'Listening to radio', in L.A. Dexter and D.M. White (eds) *People, Society and Mass Communication*, London: Macmillan.

ONG, W.J. (1982) *Orality and Literacy: The Technologizing of the Word*, London and New York: Methuen.

ROADS, C. (1978) 'Automated granular synthesis of sound', *Computer Music Journal* 2 (2): 61–2; reprinted in C. Roads and J. Strawn (eds) *Foundations of Computer Music* Cambridge, Mass.: MIT Press, 1985.

ROEDERER, J.G. (1975) *Introduction to the Physics and Psychophysics of Music*, 2nd edn, New York: Springer.

SCHAFER, R.M. (1969) *The New Soundscape*, Vienna: Universal Edition.

——(1977) *The Tuning of the World*, New York: Knopf.

SCHWARTZ, T. (1973) *The Responsive Chord*, Garden City, NY: Anchor.

TRUAX, B. (1982) 'Timbral construction in *Arras* as a stochastic process', *Computer Music Journal* 6 (3): 72–7.

——(1984) *Acoustic Communication*, Norwood, NJ: Ablex.

——(1985) 'The PODX system: Interactive compositional software for the DMX–1000', *Computer Music Journal* 9 (1): 29–38.

——(1986) 'Computer music language design and the composing process', in S. Emmerson (ed.) *The Language of Electroacoustic Music*, London: Macmillan.

——(1987a) '*Sequence of Earlier Heaven*: The record as a medium for the electroacoustic composer', *Leonardo* 20 (1): 25–8.

——(1987b) *Digital Soundscapes*, Cambridge Street Records, CSR-CD 8701, 4346 Cambridge Street, Burnaby, BC, Canada V5C 1H4, and Wergo Records WER 2017–50. Note: this Compact Disc includes *Riverrun*.

——(1988) 'Real-time granular synthesis with a digital signal processor', *Computer Music Journal* 12 (2): 14–26.

——(1990) 'Composing with real-time granular sound', *Perspectives of New Music* 28 (2): 120–34.

——(1991) 'Capturing musical knowledge in software systems', *Interface* 20 (3–4): 217–33.

——(1992) 'Musical creativity and complexity at the threshold of the 21st century', *Interface* 21 (1): 29–42.

WESTERKAMP, H. (1988) 'Listening and soundmaking: A study of music-as-environment', unpublished MA thesis, Simon Fraser University, Burnaby, BC, Canada.

WORLD SOUNDSCAPE PROJECT. The Music of the Environment Series, R.M. Schafer (ed.), Vancouver: A.R.C. Publications.

(1973) No. 1 *The Music of the Environment*.

(1977a) No. 3 *European Sound Diary*.

(1977b) No. 4 *Five Village Soundscapes*.

(1978a) No. 2 *The Vancouver Soundscape*.

(1978b) No. 5 *Handbook for Acoustic Ecology*.

XENAKIS, I. (1971) *Formalized Music*, Bloomington: Indiana University Press.

21

Composition with Machines

CURTIS ROADS

The earliest computer music activity – *computer-assisted composition* (see Hiller and Isaacson 1959) – is still misunderstood by the public. This essay traces some experiences with machines programmed to represent musical structure and execute compositional processes.

Computer-assisted composition implies the existence of software tools that aid the composer in creating and manipulating representations of music. In the past, computer-assisted composition referred to large composition programs written for batch processing computers. The composer would specify a set of initial data, and the program would generate an entire score according to the initial data and encoded musical rules.

Today, with interactive machines, the concept of computer-assisted composition has broadened. A composer can choose from a catalogue of programs that lend assistance with any number of musical tasks: from transcription systems that convert a keyboard performance into music notation, to sequence recorders that recall and manipulate a stored phrase, to interactive patch editors used to tune a digital synthesizer to digital sound mixing systems that are conducted via graphical scores. Furthermore, one can program the machine to assist with a specific compositional task. This labour can be made more efficient by a programming language that contains the appropriate musical constructs and interaction tools.

Underneath the languages and the graphics of the machine is a thick layer of intercommunicating automated procedures that manipulate representations of music. The procedures and underlying representations define the musical games that are possible with the system. As we shall see, every machine-assisted composition develops from fundamental assumptions about a music that has been encoded within the machine.

WHY COMPUTER ASSISTANCE?

The traditional composer – sitting at a piano or scribbling on manuscript paper – would appear to have no need of assistance, save for a music copyist when the time comes to prepare the parts of an orchestral score.

But when we:

1 allow the musical palette to incorporate an expanding catalogue of musical colours (timbres), and
2 allow for the arbitrarily variegated 'brushes' (sound envelopes) with which to apply the colours (for detail at the level of elementary sonic grains to global control of sound blocks, masses, and clouds), and
3 admit the possibility of programmed machine performance (for example, to permit the auditioning of multiple-part scores that would be impossible to perform by a human being), and
4 accept the machine as a musical *idiot savant* – capable of rapidly carrying out specialized compositional calculations, such as searching for certain sound objects or compositional calculations, computing variations for later selection, or taking on a variety of subtasks that would be overly time-consuming for mortal hands

– in short, when entering into the musical universe of what Varèse called 'organized sound' (Varèse 1971), then machine assistance is not only welcome, it is a necessity.

This essay chronicles some experiences with music machines past and present. As the text explains, I began to write programs to generate scores as a music student, and I realized these scores in electronic music studios. By 1976, however, my attitude toward programs that generate entire compositions changed. My interest shifted from 'composition programs' *per se* to more flexible and interactive systems.

AUTOMATED COMPOSITION PROGRAMS

3–S

From 1972 to 1974, composers at California Institute of the Arts (Cal Arts) had access to a single-user minicomputer system (a Data General Nova 1200). The only peripherals attached to the computer were a teletype terminal and papertape reader. No disk storage drive or digital-to-analogue converter (DAC) was available. Digital sound synthesis was not feasible, so I concentrated on writing score-generating programs.

3–S for string textures (1972) was my first attempt to apply algorithmic methods to composition. The second and third movements made use of the output from a small computer program. Durations of events in the second movement were determined by a probability distribution referenced by the program. The frequencies of a sine wave fed into a ring modulator were determined by a related program. Since a ring modulator takes two input signals, the other input to the ring modulator was a collection of recorded string textures (both solo and ensemble sounds).

COLLIGATION 1 AND 2

Colligation 1 (1973) is an electroacoustic tape composition, realized according to a score generated by a program called MC-1. This program modelled the behaviour of Markovian stochastic automata. That is, each musical variable (duration, frequency, amplitude, etc.) was represented in the program as a separate *stochastic automaton*. The term 'Markovian' meant that the behaviour of a musical variable at any point was influenced by its immediate past behaviour.

The MC-2 program was an extension of the basic ideas in MC-1, and resulted in the tape composition *Colligation 2* (1974). In MC-2, *inter-dependent* stochastic automata served as the generators of musical process. 'Interdependent' means that some of the automata were linked with one another. In the linked automata, values computed for one musical variable (such as frequency) could influence the behaviour of another variable (such as duration).

This influence between variables was never a simple linear mapping. Rather, the 'stability' of one variable influenced the stability of another variable. 'Stability' simply means that the value of a variable does not vary much over time. For example, if frequency and duration were linked, then

401

the stability of the frequency variable would cause the durations of successive events to be similar. Figure 21.1 is a diagram of two directly linked variables. In this figure, the immediate past behaviour of variable A directly affects variable B. The lower diagram demonstrates an inverse link. The immediate past behaviour of variable X causes variable Y to behave in the opposite manner.

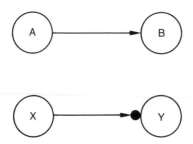

Figure 21.1. Linkage of one musical variable with another; (a) direct link (b) inverse link

The MC-2 program was a first attempt to incorporate *analysis procedures* into the composing process. Rather than following a pre-set Markovian pattern, in which probabilities for future behaviour are read from a fixed table, MC-2 used *time series* analysis to track overall trends in its past output. This information was used to alter the probabilities associated with the program's future musical behaviour.

To realize *Colligation 1* and *Colligation 2*, the alphanumeric printouts from the MC-1 and MC-2 programs were transcribed into graphic scores. Since computer sound synthesis was not available at Cal Arts, *Colligation 1* and *Colligation 2* were completed using electroacoustic studio techniques.

PROTOTYPE

prototype (1975) for computer sound was realized according to a set of procedures worked out by hand. These procedures were expanded and later coded as the PROCESS/ING program (described on p. 405).

The idea of interconnected automata is the conceptual basis of the piece. But instead of the fixed links between a few variables embodied in the MC-2 program, *prototype* assumed that all variables could be interlinked, and that the links changed over the course of the piece, producing different patterns of musical behaviour. Twenty different interconnection networks among the musical variables form the 'background' structure of the composition. Figure 21.2 shows four of the interconnection networks used in the piece.

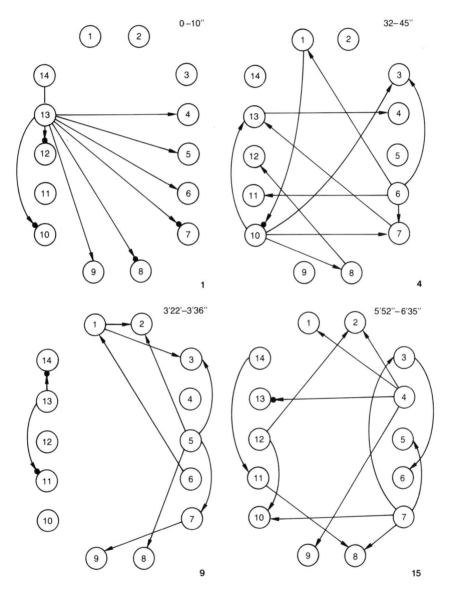

Figure 21.2. Four interconnection digraphs of *prototype*

403

The sound for *prototype* was computer-synthesized using a technique called granular synthesis. With granular synthesis, thousands of brief 'sound particles' are massed together to form pitches, chords, glissandi, and rich spectral clusters (Roads 1978a, 1988a). The grains are grouped into events that can be drawn in the form of a graphic score, as shown in Figure 21.3.

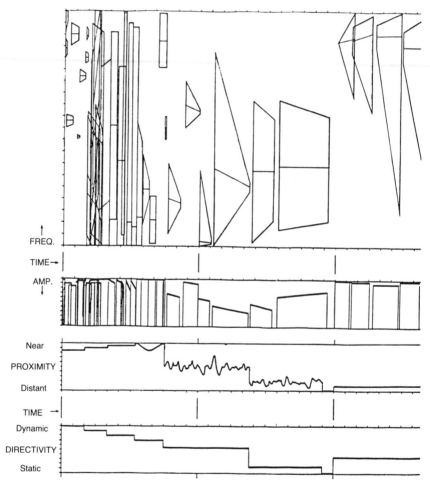

Figure 21.3 Score example from *prototype*, showing frequency versus time in the top part and 'proximity' (amount of reverberation) and 'directivity' (amount of spatial panning) in the lower two graphs

THE PROCESS/ING PROGRAM

The PROCESS/ING program (Roads 1976) was written at the University of California, San Diego (UCSD) for a large mainframe computer. This composition program was based on a generalization of the notion of inter-dependent automata explored in the program MC-2 and the piece *prototype*. PROCESS/ING was the culmination of my efforts in using stochastic processes for composition.

As in the scheme for *prototype*, interconnections between musical variables in the PROCESS/ING program were continuously variable from − 100% to + 100%, that is, from fully inverse to fully direct. At each sound event, the interconnections among the musical variables were reassessed and possibly changed. Thus, the musical logic was not fixed, but rather evolved according to specific constraints.

Figure 21.4 shows the interconnection scheme behind the computation of one musical event. Twenty-six musical variables are shown (labelled 0 to 25). Note that variable 22 is completely independent, while variable 25's behaviour is directly linked to five other variables, and inversely linked to one other variable. In turn, variable 25 directly influences three variables and inversely influences one other variable.

The PROCESS/ING program incorporated three levels of analysis and control. The results of the analysis were fed back into the system to ensure that the musical logic did not remain static or fall into repetitious behaviour. With three levels of analysis and control, the system could not only change its behaviour it could also change the way it changed the behaviour, and even change the way it changed the way it changed. The output exhibited clear patterns and correlations between variables that shifted (usually asynchronously) over the course of several sound events.

My control over the processes embodied in the PROCESS/ING program was global, and was set before the program was run. It was not possible to specify the placement or character of individual events, but only the overall balance of processes and their development. Several scores were generated by PROCESS/ING. One serves as the basis of the unfinished composition, *Plex*.

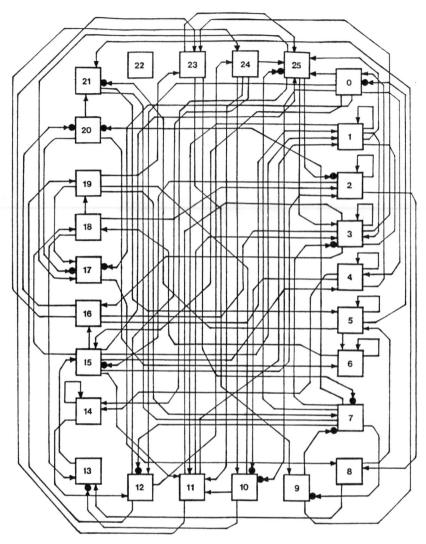

Figure 21.4 Digraph of the interconnection scheme for one event generated by the
PROCESS/ING program

FROM BATCH COMPOSING TO INTERACTIVE COMPOSING

By late 1976, my interest in composition programs *per se* had waned. It
appeared to me that the notion of a non-interactive, fixed-strategy

406

composition program was an artefact of batch computer technology of the 1950s and 1960s. In batch composing systems, all the composer's decisions are formalized into a program written in a compiled language. The composer submits all these decisions *en masse*, and an execution of the program yields a score for an entire composition.

The design of such composition programs as Project 1 and Project 2 by G.M. Koenig (1970a, 1970b), and Lejaren Hiller's many programs such as PHRASE (Hiller 1981: 7–21), presumed that the output of the programs was almost sacred. The composer could select from the outputs of several runs of the program in choosing one to realize in sound, but to edit the output was seen as a violation of the aesthetic contract of using the program in the first place. For example, Hiller has said that he never edits the output of his composition programs. If he wants to change something, he changes the program, recompiles it, and runs it again (Roads 1981a). Koenig allowed the composer flexibility in interpreting ambiguities in the print-out, but did not expect the composer to significantly alter the data printed by the computer (Koenig 1979).

Such an 'all-or-nothing' strategy has major drawbacks. Composition programs embody compositional decisions, but why should a decision made while editing a score be any less sacred than one that has been coded in a programming language?

Two of the major justifications that are usually given for using batch composition programs are *consistency* – the output of the composition program is the result of a fixed set of formalized rules, and *originality* – the output of the composition program follows a rigorous logic and so avoids the familiar clichés that composers sometimes fall into. The program can generate 'surprises' that composers probably would not have produced on their own.

Even if these two criteria were the most important factors in creating interesting music (and I am not sure they are), no existing program can guarantee that the listener will detect consistency or originality in the resulting composition. This is because the notion of consistency and orig-inality embodied by such programs is often shallow and formalistic. Simply because a certain aspect of a piece obeys combinatorial invariants or some parameter follows a probability distribution is no guarantee that the listener will find it consistent or original. Musical consistency and originality are cognitive categories for which little theory yet exists.

Not all composers who have used such programs feel that an extreme all-or-nothing position is necessary. For example, Iannis Xenakis did not feel bound in interpreting the output of his Free Stochastic Music (FSM) program (Xenakis 1971). His composition *ST/10–1, 080262* contains numerous examples of selective use and rearrangement of the program output (Roads 1973). Paul Berg extended his PILE language for waveform generation – another 'all-or-nothing' system in its original incarnation (Berg 1979: 30–41) – into an interactive real-time performance system. In the version of PILE for the DMX-1000 synthesizer, the composer can enter new values into the running program through the alphanumeric keyboard, or feed in acoustic signals through the analogue-to-digital converters attached to the synthesizer. His recent work involved building a flexible Lisp toolkit for algorithmic composition (Berg 1987).

INTERACTIVE SYSTEMS FOR COMPOSITION

For all these reasons, my interest has turned to more flexible and interactive systems for composition. This is not to suggest that large-scale composition programs are useless. Composers may find interesting possibilities in them, especially if their output is treated with some flexibility. They can also be potentially valuable research tools in scientific projects aimed at modelling music cognition (Minsky 1981).

The need for flexibility was reinforced in my studio work. From 1976 to 1981 I realized a series of electronic and computer music compositions: *Construction*, *Object*, *nscor*, and *Field*. These pieces were organized on an intuitive basis, rather than on the basis of a pre-set system of procedures (Roads 1985a). In these works, I was interested in a kind of polyphonic timbre flow that could be organized only by careful listening, and for which there is as yet no formal theory or coded procedures. Experiences with these pieces led me to think about interactive tools to assist in organizing the materials of composition. One major goal of these tools would be to help composers explore many more possibilities than they could ever hope to try without a computer.

An interactive system for composition does not preclude the use of rules for consistency or originality on some level. But its principal advantage over a fixed composition program is its *strategic flexibility*. With strategic flexibility, the composer can choose, at any moment, the material to operate on and the operations to perform. In the ideal case, these decisions can be made in the presence of sound, by listening to the material at hand. Intermediate results can be saved, and the generated material can be edited.

By applying a series of operations in an order chosen by the user, users of an interactive system can quickly expand a set of basic material into a large-scale structure. Transformations can be applied to these structures and listened to before further manipulations are performed. The composer can 'backtrack' from a dead end or repair minor flaws in an otherwise interesting composition.

The rest of this section describes several approaches to interactive computer-assisted composition.

Parameter List Manipulation: The CL Language

A working alternative to the notion of a batch composition program became possible for me in 1976, with the availability of the interactive digital sound synthesis system Timbre Tuning System (TTS). TTS was designed by Bruce Leibig of the Center for Music Experiment (CME) at UCSD. This program, running on a dedicated computer at CME, was one of the first interactive digital synthesis systems in existence. High-level composing tools were needed, since specifying data for the software instruments in TTS was a time-consuming effort. The most interesting instrument required the composer to type twenty-four numbers (one for each parameter field) for each note of a piece.

Bruce Leibig, Robert Gross and I formed the CME Composing Language Project to address the issue of providing interactive composing tools. These tools were to cut down on the amount of typing required of the composer and provide strategic flexibility in composing. After discussions among the three of us, I designed an interpreted language called CL, short for 'Composing Language', for generating and manipulating parameter field data (Roads 1977).

Here is an example of the how CL could be used for interactive manipulation of lists of parameter field data. We begin with a collection of three sets of pitches and call the sets X, Y and Z. We want to end up with a new set in which the pitches in X, Y and Z are reversed (XR, YR and ZR) and merged (draw one from XR, one from YR and one from ZR, then begin again, until done). Given the three pitch collections (A B C), (D E F), and (G A♭ B♭), we want to produce the collection (C F B♭ B E A♭ A D G).

409

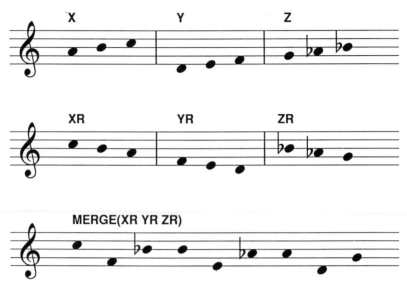

Figure 21.5   Manipulation of three sets of pitches, X, Y and Z

Figure 21.5 shows the manipulations. (All notes are in the treble clef.) The following is the CL code to produce the intended result:

Define the pitch sets:

X = A B C
Y = D E F
Z = G A♭ B♭

Reverse the pitch sets:

XR = retro (X)
YR = retro (Y)
ZR = retro (Z)

Merge the pitch sets:

Result = merge (XR YR ZR)

CL could also be used to manipulate dynamic markings (*ppp pp p mp f ff fff*), as well as lists of durations and other symbolic and numerical parameters.

Fortunately, it is now possible for virtually any composer to use such a language in manipulating score data. CL is similar in its semantics to many of the list-manipulation functions in the LISP language. A number of groups have recently extended LISP and its popular cousin LOGO for musical purposes (Coral 1986; Orlarey 1986; Desain and Honing 1986; Boynton *et al.* 1986; Laurson *et al.* 1992).

Experiments with Formal Grammars

In working with the sound synthesis language TTS one creates individual events and short phrases. Composition with TTS could be split into two stages: (1) creation of sound objects, and (2) organization of the objects into a composition. Early in 1977 I began research on the notion of using formal grammars as a kind of compositional shorthand to organize the sound objects created by TTS and by other means. This research resulted in the design of two related languages – Tree and Cotree (Roads 1978b).

Tree was a grammar specification language. It allowed a composer to specify a compositional grammar – a hierarchical structure that stipulates the way individual sound events can be grouped into high-level syntactic structures called *tokens*. Tree did not specify a single composition, but rather the syntactic rules behind a family of compositions realizable in the grammar.

By contrast, Cotree was a language for expressing the order of tokens in a particular composition. All of the tokens specified in a Cotree expression had to be defined by grammar expressed in Tree. The job of the software was to generate all the events in the proper order by referencing the Tree grammar. Since a complete composition containing hundreds of events could be specified by only a few high-level tokens, manipulating Cotree expressions (i.e. adding a token, deleting a token, or rearranging the tokens) was akin to changing the overall architecture of a composition.

Figure 21.6 is an example of a simplified grammar expressed in the Tree language. The !* and *! delimiters enclose comments. In the rules, the colon (:) indicates a rewrite rule. Commas indicate sound objects in succession, while a division sign (/) indicates objects to be played in parallel. A full point between two tokens indicates a conditional *or rule*, in which one object is selected out of several by a *control procedure*. The s() tokens are silences, with the duration specified in milliseconds between parentheses.

A graphic notation exists for expressions in the Tree language. Figure 21.7, part (a), shows three simple expressions, demonstrating (1) parallel, (2) serial, and (3) conditional or rules. Part (b) gives their graphical counterparts.

A Cotree specification is a shorthand description of a piece, so it is typically concise. It consists of a list of top-level tokens woven together

```
tree begin

        !* The name block identifies the grammar *!
        name begin

                name := Zyra;
                version := 1.0;

        end

        !* The specif block contains the grammar *!
        specif begin

                !* Specifies the control procedure for any or-rules *!
                globalcontrol = decider_29.;
                !* Top-level structures *!
                SECTION_1 : A, B;
                SECTION_2 : C/D;
                !* Middle-level structures mapped onto terminal tokens *!
                A : object1 . s(500)/object2;
                B : object3/object4, s(1000), object5;
                C : s(750), object6, object7/object8;
                D : object9/object10 . object11;

        end

end
```

Figure 21.6   A musical grammar specified in the Tree language

with flow-of-control structures (**if-then-else**) and other linguistic structures for algorithmic composition. The goal of the language was to make it easy to specify a variety of expressions quickly, allowing a composer to audition various complex forms of polyphony without enumerating all their details every time.

A prototype implementation of Tree and Cotree was developed. Soon after the appearance of published descriptions of the designs, several other systems along the same lines were developed. GGDL (Holtzman 1981: 51–64) and Prod (Green 1980) are examples. Kevin Jones (1981: 45–61) implemented an interesting stochastic grammar composition system employing Markov-chain rewrite rules.

Although Tree and Cotree were designed to work in conjunction with a library of synthetic sounds, it is now conceivable that a grammar-based system such as this could be part of a music workstation organized around a large database of digital sounds, of both synthetic and natural origins.

(a)

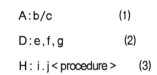

A:b/c (1)

D:e,f,g (2)

H: i.j< procedure > (3)

(b)

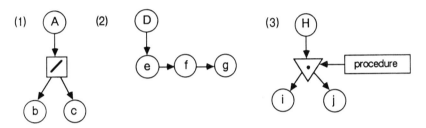

Figure 21.7 Two representations of a musical grammar: (a) three simple rewrite rules expressed in the Tree language exemplifying the parallel, serial, and conditional cases, (b) a graphical representation of the three rules

Interaction with the SSSP Musical Workstation

The Structured Sound Synthesis Project (SSSP) at the University of Toronto, developed in the late 1970s and early 1980s, was one of the first interactive workstations for composition. The SSSP workstation combined powerful interactive graphics techniques with real-time digital sound synthesis – a unique combination at that time.

Some of the sound material used in *nscor* and *Field* was created during a visit to the SSSP in 1979. The SSSP workstation provided the composer with a graphic score editor and a collection of commands for quickly transforming score fragments or subscores into larger structures. These include splicing, merging, deleting, stretching, shrinking, reversing and other operations. The sequence: 'transform, play, transform, play ...' occurred over and over in my work. Within minutes, I could 'telescope' a simple subscore into an enormous and complicated structure, because transformation could be applied to entire scores or phrases as easily as single notes.

413

Interactive Orchestration

In the past, when composers worked mostly on paper, the only way for them to check their work was to play out a reduced version on a piano, or try to imagine the sound of dozens of instruments playing simultaneously – a form of guesswork, depending on the complexity of the score. One of the advantages of computer music systems is the possibility for a composer to audition parts of a score as they are created. Interactive score editors and real-time digital synthesis renew the subject of orchestration, and a number of creative approaches to the subject have been explored recently.

For example, the SSSP musical workstation contained a graphic score editor that allowed composers to enter note events using a mouse. One could display a score in one of eight different types of notation. These display formats varied from common music notation to an iconic representation without staves. In order to orchestrate a score with synthetic instruments for later playback, one pointed at an instrument name in a menu and then tapped the note (or icon) on the screen. The note was then assigned to that instrument.

The UPIC system developed by Iannis Xenakis and his associates at the Centre d'études de mathematiques et automatiques musicales (CEMAMu), Paris provides another kind of orchestration facility. Instead of manipulating note events, composers change the waveform assigned to an *arc* – a line drawn in the frequency/time space. The waveform reassignment occurs *en masse*. That is, all arcs associated with a given waveform A are assigned to waveform B. Figure 21.8 shows a score fragment from my composition *Message* (Roads 1988b). Although the arcs are similar in shape, they actually represent several different sampled sounds.

The SSSP workstation and the UPIC system provide a direct means of exploring different orchestrations of a score. But neither system has any knowledge of orchestration that could help composers in this process.

When a music system 'knows' musical rules about the objects it manipulates and can apply this knowledge under the direction of the composer, we can call it a musically intelligent system. One of the ways of making computers more effective in musician–machine interaction is to develop systems that serve as musically intelligent *composer's assistants* (Roads 1981b). The goal of such systems is a deeper and more flexible musical interaction than has been commonly the case in electronic music studios. This should aid composers in the most creative phases of composition, when they are conceiving and trying out new ideas.

One system that incorporated codified musical knowledge was Ios

TRAVAIL   PAGE   1

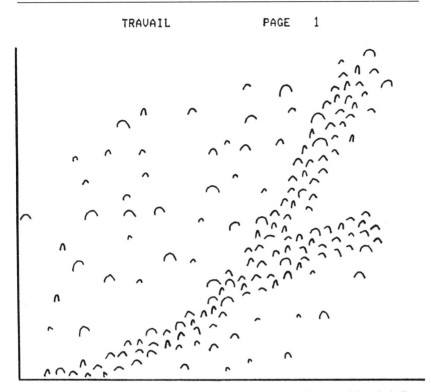

Figure 21.8. A score fragment from the composition *Message.* The arcs, although similar in shape, represent several different sampled waveforms.

(interactive orchestration system) (Roads 1982). Ios was not a complete composer's assistant system but rather a specialized assistant for orchestrating a composer-supplied score from a set of rules specified by the composer in an interactive way. The programs making up Ios were designed and implemented in the LISP language during 1982 for a Symbolics computer. The basic idea is that the composer provides a score and a set of *orchestration rules* to the computer. These rules are in the following abstract form:

(feature instrument transform)

A typical rule looks like this:

(top-line-in-phrase alto-saxophone trill)

The computer analyses the score and searches for the *feature* specified in the rule, for example top-line-in-phrase. If the feature is found, Ios associated it with the *instrument*. The *transform* is an orchestration technique applied to the feature, such as an ornament or mode of articulation. With digital synthesis, the transforms can include modulation or colourations of the sound such as vibrato or reverberation.

The specification of orchestration rules was mediated by a menu–oriented user interface to Ios called Ioq (interactive orchestration query; see Figure 21.9). No typing was required of the composer, and – unlike a textbook – the rules could be quickly changed at will.

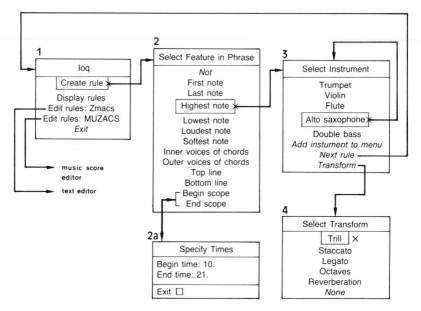

Figure 21.9. The arrows show a sequence of menus for interactive orchestration. A typical sequence is (1) Create a rule, (2) Select a feature, (2a) Specify the beginning and ending time of a rule's scope, (3) Attach an instrument to the feature, (4) Apply a transform to it. The first menu reappears automatically.

ORGANIZING THE SOUND DATABASE

Recently the economics of digital hardware and the computational demands made by music software have converged to make *digital audio workstations* (DAWs) the control centre of the modern electronic music studio. The hardware of a DAW consists of a personal computer combined with analogue and digital interfaces that record sound on a random-access storage medium such as a magnetic or optical disc. The software includes programs for accessing, mixing and editing *soundfiles*. After mixing and editing using graphical methods, the hardware can convert the digital audio information back into sound or transfer it to a portable medium (such as digital audio tape (DAT)) for storage or transportation. This digital audio information can be transferred without loss to a mastering system for compact discs or another distribution format.

To the electronic music composer, the digital audio workstation serves a role analogous to the writer's word processor. Large-scale compositions can be assembled piece by piece; different sound combinations can be tried without destroying the original soundfiles.

The AD-MIX and the Studer Dyaxis System

From 1985 to 1990 my efforts at Studio Strada centred on the compositions *Message* and *Folly*. These pieces were organized with the Audio + Design AD-MIX digital mixing system and the Studer Dyaxis – a digital audio workstation that connects to an Apple Macintosh computer.

The AD-MIX machine works in conjunction with a modified Sony PCM processor. It layers two new channels of digital audio onto an existing two-channel signal, using two video-cassette-recorder decks. The AD-MIX remote control unit provides a high-quality linear fader and several push-button controls for real-time processing of the mix. Once a mix tape has been completed, the overdubbing process can start again by inserting the resultant 'sound-on-sound' mix tape into the playback deck. This can be layered with another two channels of sound, and the new mix can be layered yet again, creating the possibility of an arbitrary number of overdubs. The final mix can be transferred digitally to the Dyaxis system for editing.

In practice, the 'infinite overdubbing' possibilities provided by the AD-MIX system boil down to three commonly applied musical operations:

1 creation of dense layered sound masses;
2 creation of intricate, ornamented contrapuntal lines;
3 adding no new sounds but reshaping the amplitude envelope of an existing sound mix by using the fader.

The AD-MIX system provides real-time control of a mix and relies on serial media (video-cassettes) for playback and recording. In contrast, the

417

Dyaxis is a non-real-time mixing and editing system (following a 'do-then-play' model) that uses a random-access digital audio medium (a large-capacity magnetic disc). The functions it performs, used in conjunction with software running on the Macintosh, are illustrated in Figure 21.10. and can be listed as follows:

1 digital recording and playback of sounds to and from hard disc (tape recorder mode);
2 storage and playback of soundfiles created by commercially-available synthesis programs;
3 digital transfer of sounds to and from digital audio tape (DAT) recorders and video-cassette-based pulse-code modulation (PCM) processors;
4 mixing of an arbitrary number of soundfiles using graphical methods;
5 editing (cut, paste, splice) of sound files using graphical methods;
6 synchronization of sound file playback with SMPTE and MIDI-controllable devices such as videocassette recorders, synthesizers, and samplers;
7 centralized control of MIDI synthesisers and effects.

In addition to these two hardware components, a variety of synthesis and sound analysis packages run on the Macintosh, some developed by the author.

In 1991 we replaced the AD-MIX system with a more flexible digital signal processor called the Lexicon 300. It performs the same mixing functions as the AD-MIX and also allows programmable spatialization of sounds.

CONCLUSIONS

The Role of the Machine in Composition

The introduction of machines into the practice of composition can lead towards at least two extreme poles. On the one hand, instant compositions can be produced with the operator having only the barest responsibility for the generated piece. Some commercial computer games embody this mode of operation for familiar musical styles. To some extent, this justifies the fear surrounding the introduction of the computer into musical life – that the composer's role is trivialized by compositional procedures.

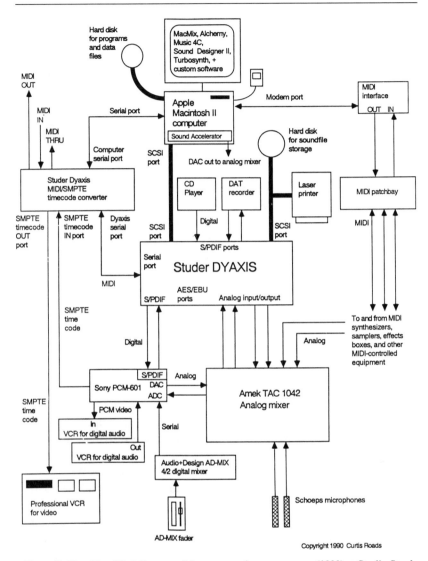

Figure 21.10. Simplified diagram of the composer's current setup (1990) at Studio Strada, Boston

419

On the other hand, interactive algorithms can be used to embed compositional decisions deeper into a work than would be possible without computer assistance. In this case, rather than eroding the composer's role, algorithms actually extend it. Here are a few examples of how algorithms can expand the scope of compositional decisions:

1 controlling the microfrequency variations among the partials of a given tone;
2 sifting through massive amounts of data to select a specified sound or sound combination;
3 sending sounds on elaborate and precise spatial paths computed according to composer-specified rules;
4 interpreting a composer's gestures through an input device to effect changes in the musical process being produced (Chadabe 1984: 22–7);
5 generating variations of sound materials to provide the composer with several alternatives to a given sound or series of sounds;
6 generating complex polyphonic textures that would otherwise be impossible to control.

No Composition Without Representation

Thirty years ago batch composition programs demonstrated the musical potential of machine automation. The interactive utilities of today let us work more selectively to apply a tool at any point in the composition process. But much work remains in bringing together these disparate utilities to create an integrated system.

We can take a cue from the world of commercial music. Wealthy film and 'show business' composers can hire a dozen or more subcontracting composers to create a musical soundtrack. The integration of their results is co-ordinated by high-level subcontractors acting as managers for those who subcontract beneath them. This work is usually routine, such as grinding out variations on a theme for later selection by the maestro, conforming a musical section to the duration of a scene, or orchestrating a piano score for a multi-voiced sampling synthesizer. The bulk of this level of musical knowledge could be formalized and encoded into a machine that accepts musical assignments and provides alternatives for the human composer to choose from. Such a music machine might provide less wealthy composers with some of the same efficiencies as their counterparts in the entertainment industry.

420

A number of specialized assistant programs have been developed, and we have witnessed the first generation of commercially available interactive composition systems. These programs record short keyboard patterns played by the composer, and repeat and mutate the patterns according to a 'style template' specified by the composer. Although they have been moderately successful from a commercial standpoint, these programs are musically limited in that they deal exclusively with MIDI data (primarily equal-tempered pitches and metered rhythms). Their facilities for timbral and spatial control are crude. A more fundamental problem from a compositional standpoint is that they are not extensible.

At the core of the problem is the need for more powerful representations for music that support multiple viewpoints. The lack of any path between the two poles of MIDI pitch/time data for scores on the one hand and soundfile data for audio signals on the other highlights the problem of one-dimensional representation for music.

The issue of flexible and extensible machine representations for music is a continuing one. Over twenty years ago Herbert Brün observed that computer music systems are not musically neutral (Brün 1969). Every system constrains the composer to a restricted set of operations; every 'view' provided by a music system is a filter that biases the viewer's attention to a particular perspective on the piece.

This chapter has displayed a variety of views on compositions. A piece such as *Message* makes use of many representations, from traditional music notation to graphical UPIC scores to MIDI data to SMPTE-striped video-tape to sampled sound files. I have built Studio Strada as a system of interconnected machines to try to support multiple representations. Of necessity, I have used commercially available devices and mostly com-mercially available computer software.

The connection between scores and actual sounds, which is supported by a thin thread in the MIDI world, must be strengthened. Between the composer's working score and the sound stand an infinity of intermediate representations. Recent advances in digital signal processing point to models of musical sound that combine time–domain and frequency–domain rep-resentations with other information (De Poli, Piccialli and Roads 1991). For example, experiments have already shown how granular signal rep-resentations can suggest new paradigms for musical organization (Roads 1978a, 1988a).

In the future, machines must be given more knowledge about musical structure and musical sound. They must use this knowledge to act more like a human musician; that is, to draw inferences from partial descriptions, and to view and manipulate musical data from several perspectives (Roads 1981b, 1985b). When they do, we can hand them more, not less, responsibility. But we must always be wary of their hand-coded limitations. A programmer's mind creates the machine, and in this sense, after all, machines are only human.

REFERENCES

BERG, P. (1979) 'PILE – a language for sound synthesis', *Computer Music Journal* 3 (1): 30–41; revised and updated version in C. Roads and J. Strawn (eds) (1985) *Foundations of Computer Music*, Cambridge, Mass.: MIT Press.

——(1987) Personal communication.

BOYNTON, L., LAVDIE, P., ORLAREY, Y., RUEDA, C. and WESSEL, D. (1986) 'MIDI-LISP: A LISP-based environment for the Apple Macintosh', in P. Berg (ed.) *Proceedings of the 1986 International Computer Music Conference*, San Francisco: Computer Music Association, pp. 183–6.

BRÜN, H. 1969. 'Infraudibles', in H. Von Foerster and J. Beauchamp (eds) (1969) *Music by Computers*, New York: John Wiley & Sons.

CHADABE, J. (1984) 'Interactive composing: an overview', *Computer Music Journal* 8 (1): 22–7; reprinted in C. Roads (ed.) (1989) *The Music Machine*, Cambridge, Mass.: MIT Press.

CORAL (1986) *Object Logo Reference Manual*, Cambridge, Mass.: Coral Software.

DE POLI, G., PICCIALLI, A. and ROADS, C. (eds) (1991) *Representation of Musical Signals*, Cambridge, Mass.: MIT Press.

DESAIN, P. and HONING, H. (1986) 'LOCO: composition microworlds in Logo', in P. Berg (ed.) *Proceedings of the 1986 International Computer Music Conference*, San Francisco: Computer Music Association.

GREEN, M. (1980) 'Prod: a grammar-based computer composition program', in H.S. Howe, Jr. (ed.) *Proceedings of the 1980 International Computer Music Conference*, San Francisco: Computer Music Association.

HILLER, L. (1981) 'Composing with computers: a progress report', *Computer Music Journal* 5 (4); reprinted in C. Roads (ed.) (1989) *The Music Machine*, Cambridge, Mass.: MIT Press.

HILLER, L. and ISAACSON, L. (1959) *Experimental Music*, New York: McGraw-Hill.

HOLTZMAN, S. (1981). 'Using generative grammars for music composition', *Computer Music Journal* 5 (1); reprinted in C. Roads (ed.) (1989) *The Music Machine*, Cambridge, Mass.: MIT Press.

JONES, K. (1981) 'Compositional applications of stochastic processes', *Computer Music Journal* 5 (2).

KOENIG, G.M. (1970a) 'Project 1', *Electronic Music Reports 2*, Utrecht: Institute of Sonology.

——(1970b) 'Project 2', *Electronic Music Reports 2*, Utrecht: Institute of Sonology.

——(1979) 'Protocol', *Sonological Reports No. 4*, Utrecht: Institute of Sonology.

LAURSON, M., ROADS, C. and DUTHEN, J. (1992) *Patchwork: A Programming Environment for Music Composition*, Paris: IRCAM.

MINSKY, M. (1981) 'Music, Mind, and Meaning', *Computer Music Journal* 5 (3).

ORLAREY, Y. (1986) 'MLOGO – a MIDI composing environment for the Apple IIe', in P. Berg (ed.) *Proceedings of the 1986 International Computer Music Conference*, San Francisco: Computer Music Association.

ROADS, C. (1973) 'An analysis of the composition *ST/10* and the computer program free stochastic music by Iannis Xenakis', Los Angeles: California Institute of the Arts.

——(1976) 'A systems approach to composition', unpublished BA thesis, La Jolla: University of California, San Diego.

——(1977) 'Preliminary report on the CME Composing Language Project', La Jolla: Center for Music Experiment, University of California, San Diego.

——(1978a) 'Granular synthesis of sound', *Computer Music Journal* 2 (4); revised and updated version in C. Roads and J. Strawn (eds) (1985) *Foundations of Computer Music*, Cambridge, Mass.: MIT Press.

——(1978b) 'Composing Grammars', in C. Roads (ed.) (1978), *Proceedings of the 1977 International Computer Music Conference, La Jolla, California, USA*, San Francisco: Computer Music Association.

——(1981a) 'Report on the IRCAM Conference: the composer and the computer', *Computer Music Journal* 5 (3).

——(1981b) 'An intelligent composer's assistant: a proposal for a knowledge-based system', unpublished proposal for MIT Experimental Music Studio, Cambridge, Mass.

——(1982) 'Interactive orchestration based on score analysis', in T. Blum and J. Strawn (eds) *Proceedings of the 1982 International Computer Music Conference, Venice, Italy*, San Francisco: Computer Music Association.

——(1984) 'An overview of music representations', in M. Baroni and L. Callegari (eds) *Musical Grammars and Computer Analysis*, Florence: Leo S. Olschki Editore.

——(1985a) 'The realization of *nscor*', in C. Roads (ed.) (1985) *Composers and the Computer*, Madison: A-R Editions.

——(1985b) 'Research in music and artificial intelligence', *ACM Computing Surveys* 17, 2.

——(1987) 'Esperienze di composizione assistata da calculatore', in S. Tamburini and M. Bagella (eds) (1987), *I Profili di Suono*, Rome: Musica Verticale-Galzeramo.

——(1988a) 'Introduction to Granular Synthesis', *Computer Music Journal* 12 (2).

——(1988b) 'Sound structure in *Message*', in C. Lischka (ed.) (1988) *Proceedings of the 1988 International Computer Music Conference, Cologne, West Germany*, San Francisco: Computer Music Association.

423

ROADS, C. (ed.) (1989) *The Music Machine*, Cambridge, Mass.: MIT Press.
——(1993) *Computer Music Tutorial*, Cambridge, Mass.: MIT Press.
VARÈSE, E. (1971) 'The liberation of sound', in B. Boretz and E. Cone (eds) *Perspectives on American Composers*, New York: Norton.
XENAKIS, I. (1971) *Formalized Music*, Bloomington: Indiana University Press.

APPENDIX:
LIST OF COMPOSITIONS MENTIONED

3–S (1972) for string textures; strings of the Cal Arts Orchestra, Gerhard Samuel, conductor; realized at California Institute of the Arts; remixed at ID studios, Hollywood. (Available: *Tape, Working score, Documentation*) Premièred June 1973, 1750 Arch Street, Berkeley, California. (13:34)

Colligation 1 (1973) electroacoustic tape music; score generated by a Nova 1200 computer program: MC-1; realized at California Institute of the Arts; remixed at the Village Recorder, West Los Angeles. (Available: *Tape, Score, Documentation*.) Premièred January 1974, California Institute of the Arts, Valencia, California. (16:10)

Colligation 2 (1974) electroacoustic tape music; score generated by a Nova 1200 computer program: MC-2; realized at California Institute of the Arts; remixed at the Village Recorder, West Los Angeles. (Available: *Tape, Score, Documentation*.) Premièred March 1974, California Institute of the Arts, Valencia, California. (19:00)

prototype (1975) computer sound; samples computed on Burroughs B6700 computer system at University of California, San Diego (UCSD); digital-to-analogue conversion at the Center for Music Experiment, UCSD, La Jolla; remixed at the Village Recorder, West Los Angeles. (Available: *Tape, Score, Documentation*.) Premièred May 1975, Mandeville Centre for the Arts, UCSD, La Jolla. (8:00)

Construction (1976) electronic sound; realized at UCSD, La Jolla; remixed at the Village Recorder, West Los Angeles. (Available: *Tape, Remix, Score, Documentation*.) Premièred May 1976, Center for Music Experiment, UCSD, La Jolla. (13:50)

Plex (1976) computer-generated score: PROCESS/COMPUTER program, extensive editing of the score; unfinished study.

Objet (1977) electronic and computer sound; samples computed on the Burroughs B6700 computer system at UCSD; realized at UCSD, La Jolla; remixed at American Zoetrope Recording, San Francisco. (Available: *Tape, Documentation*.) Premièred September 1978, International Gaudeamus Musicweek, Bilthoven, The Netherlands. (14:00)

nscor (1980, revised 1986) computer sound; sounds produced at the Centre for Music Experiment, La Jolla, Institut voor Sonologie, Utrecht, the Structured Sound Synthesis Project, Toronto, and the Experimental Music Studio, MIT; realized at the Experimental Music Studio, MIT; remixed at Suntreader Studios, Sharon, Vermont. 1986 revision at Studio Strada, Cambridge. (Available: *Wergo compact disc, Tape, Documentation*.) Premièred October 1980, Musei Civici, Varese, Italy. (8:45)

Field (1981, revised 1985) computer sound; realized at the Experimental Music Studio, MIT, Cambridge, and at Century III Studio, Boston. 1985 revision at Studio Strada, Cambridge. Commissioned by the Council for the Arts at MIT (Available: *Tape*, MIT/*Sony compact disc*.) Premièred December 1981, Auditorium, University of Massachusetts at Boston, Park Square, Boston, Massachusetts. (5:00)

Message (1986–1990) composition for alto saxophone, computer sound, and computer graphics projections. Images by David Em (Los Angeles), saxophone textures by Earl Howard (New York). Realized at CEMAMu, Paris, and Studio Strada, Cambridge, Mass.. Commissioned by Mobius, Boston, in conjunction with the Massachusetts Council on the Arts and Humanities. (Available: *Tape, Documentation*.) Premièred June 1987. Mobius, Boston. (12:00)

22

Artistic Necessity
Context Orientation
Configurable Space

CRAIG R. HARRIS

Contemporary artists from many disciplines are exploring the potential of incorporating computer technology into their creative realm. The art work, the tools used to create it, and the creative environment are inextricably linked. The use of computers offers possibilities for artistic expression which extend far beyond just the development of new tools to perform traditional tasks in traditional ways. This suggests a re-evaluation of the relationship between the artist, the art work, and artistic processes and materials.

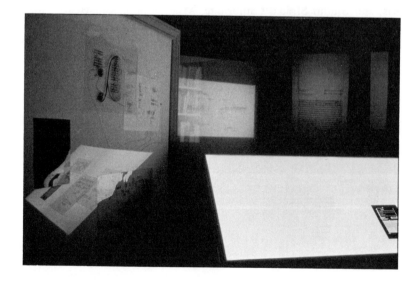

Current working methods and the products that ensue are strongly affected by concepts developed in a paper-based technology. In order for new musical instruments and tools to be developed that do more than apply former modes to a new medium, the computer technology needs to be clearly understood, and the fundamental assumptions upon which current systems are built have to be identified and examined. Similarly, artists' creative processes need to come under scrutiny so that the requirements of art can play an appropriately central role in the development of these new vehicles for expression. During this re-evaluation and reconstruction, some principles which form the foundation of our conceptual framework will evolve, some will recede, and new foundations will develop.

In contrast with traditional instruments, a unique characteristic of computer-based technology is that there are no inherent sounds or intrinsic sound manipulation processes. This amorphous characteristic permeates and influences every level of process and product. The assumptions about sound and process are imposed by the humans designing and using the machine. A work environment designed with such a flexible medium has a dramatic impact on both creativity and productivity.

Environment has a wide range of components, including the physical work space, the mechanisms and processes with which one works, and the sounds and types of events that form the many layers of activity in a composition.

This presentation is a simulation and description of a composer's studio of the future, the materials used, and processes and concerns regarding the manipulation of the materials in that environment. The subsequent text and images follow a composition in progress, and represent suggestions of concepts for consideration and contemplation.

CONNECTIONS
BETWEEN IDEA AND REPRESENTATION

Clear, clean, open space. Unencumbered space.

Flexibility. Malleability.

Begin with blank space and no assumptions. Build the space only with what is required, with the tools that are most appropriate for the task.

A motion. A gesture. Broad strokes.

Create shapes to denote concepts of aural and structural characteristics and design. Manipulate them in a complex web of relationships which expand upon every gesture and articulation on virtually any layer.

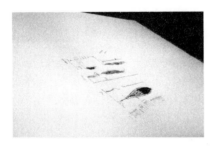

Shapes appear, reappear, and transform in various constructs in a variety of contexts. Connections are revealed and need to be represented in a manner that is meaningful to the artist. The representation may not have to mean anything at all to anyone *other* than the artist, and may not even bear resemblance to an end product or a fixed, preconceived method of notation.

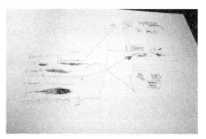

Experiment with a variety of styles for representation; freeze a layer for specific types of operations; impose conceptual models at various levels of structure and detail; connect or link ideas, layers and sketches in dramatically different ways.

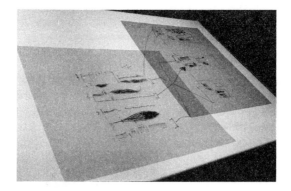

Lay out the work environment. Map out the surfaces, the tools, and the ambience, all according to the artistic requisites of the moment.

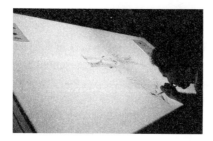
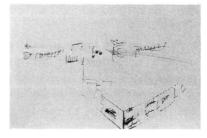

Block out main space, sketching spaces, auxiliary space. Block spaces for digression – space to research related ideas, to investigate other works, or to explore some aspect of another topic.

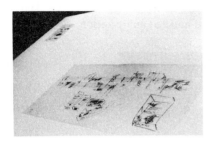 

Display an image of a page, a book, a bookshelf, or a picture that represents an important connection between a concept and the current focus of the work. In many cases it isn't even necessary to see detail. A mere symbolic reference may be enough to maintain a connection with a creative source.

CONNECTIONS
BETWEEN DEGREES OF SKETCHES

Details undergo massive transformations; structure is contorted and turned upside-down and inside-out. Some elements carry through from raw sketch to more refined sketch, and finally to the finished composition.

Others follow established principles of construction, but detail falls away in favour of something that results from evolution. Specification of structure and detail is at times more representative of relationships and reference than it is of specific notes, harmonies, rhythms, or principles of organization.

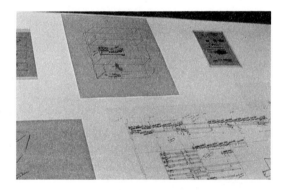

Explore the *malleable* display table and wall – the manoeuvrability of material, the placement and angle of the large blank surface. Record and process a specific artist's textual and graphic activity, whether hand-written, typed, spoken or drawn.

Bring sketches back and *throw* them onto the wall, expanding work space and field of vision.

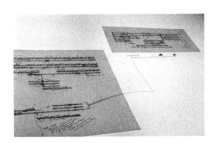

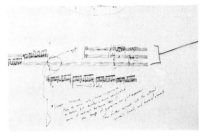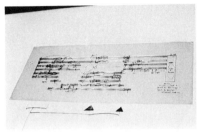

Zoom in. Sketch on top of this and massage any aspect of the material. Refer to features in this sketch and related representations.

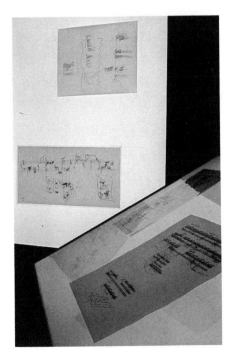

Assign symbols or tags to carry with a developing concept within and between representations, so that exploration and refinement at each stage accumulates knowledge about history and characteristics.

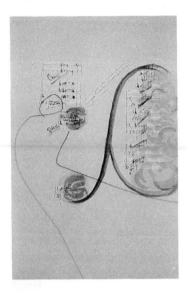

Define size and scale. Choose viewing styles with sensitivity to the processes taking place, and the individual doing the viewing.

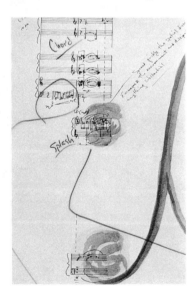

434

Design views with appropriate element shading, according to specific contextual requirements. Alter it at any stage to suit new requisites.

Emphasize low 'C'; make a note of particular harmonic relationships and the repetition of a specific chord. Mark and loosely describe significant events that have a particular character, including any known details about the sound.

Specify correlations between local and structural levels without being locked into having to know every level of detail, and without being forced to work in a predefined mode. Merge and integrate components from various sketches.

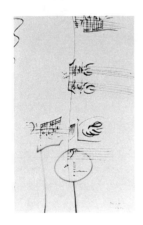

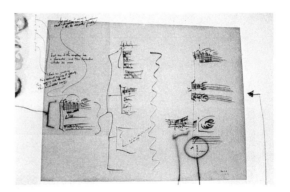

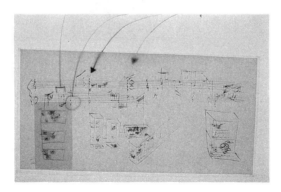

Sketches may contain notations for which direct aural correlations can be made. These accompany the still-to-be-defined raw elements, along with text, *margin* notes, drawn links, and other relevant methods for representing the current state of work. Create with tools for representation and generation that span a vast range from the very primitive to the very refined. Work to the degree of specificity and the rate of activity required by the context.

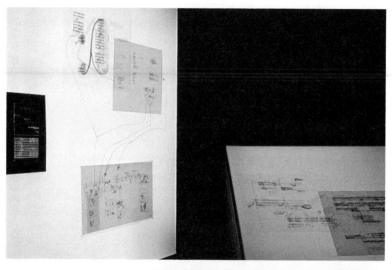

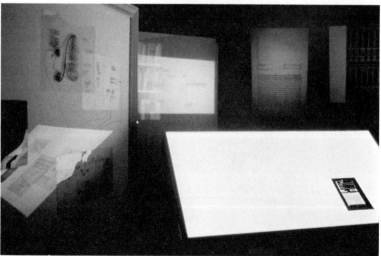

CONNECTIONS
BETWEEN LEVELS OF DETAIL

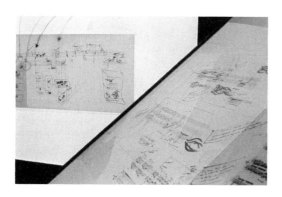

As music exists in time, so do the processes that create it. These processes are not purely linear. Ideas occur spontaneously; operations take place simultaneously. Development of elements within sketches do not progress at the same rate. Tools designed to support creativity must fundamentally follow both the nature of the activity and the natural flow of the specific artist.

437

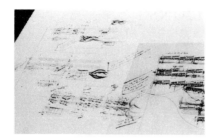

Reconstruct the layout of the physical workspace. Reallocate objects to strategically useful locations and alter their appearance for use in new contexts. Follow a train of thought to develop a two-minute gesture, and a separate one to explore new techniques for representation while refining a single element.

Draw, grab, drag, link, highlight.

Shrink, zoom, condense, overlay, extrapolate, formulate.

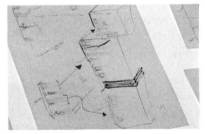

Manoeuvre easily between macrocosm and microcosm. Move among a set of different concepts on several planes and be able to peruse all simultaneously.

438

Enlarge selections to envisage sizes and highlight specific elements. Shift the view; rotate the image. Take advantage of aerial views, back-shadowed projections, reverse-negative images, single still snapshots or animated images, transparent overlaid images with different levels of detail, shading and colour, and varying degrees of focus.

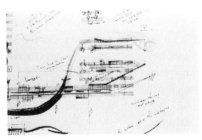

Select regions, layers, or groups of layer. Characterize objects as separate entities on one level, and as a group at another level. Build links between ideas, sections, sketches, and their various representations. Manipulate and transform them in local and global ways according to dynamically assigned specifications. Make comparisons, adjust alignments of different layers.

Experiment with new ways to work with and represent traditional issues. Explore new ways to manifest sound objects and processes that have yet to be defined.

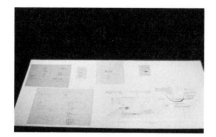

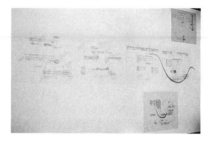

For a context that requires that a sound move in space while the room transforms in shape, construct appropriate mechanisms to describe, to generate, to analyse in musical or scientific terms, and even to perform it.

Draw upon reference elements to investigate the nature of vocal sounds and how they might apply to spectral characteristics. Perform a spectral analysis on a recorded low 'C' of a piano; investigate the envelope of each harmonic and how they might individually map onto spatial location trajectories, relative amplitudes of voices, and durations of sections in the composition.

Display long gestures to enhance the perception of large-scale motion. Modify room ambience, step back, and view the current state from another vantage point.

Flow naturally between concepts, versions and structural layers, respecting an internal sense for spontaneity and continuity.

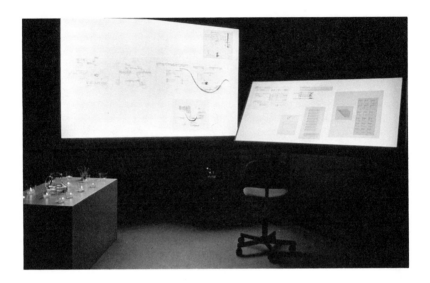

CONNECTIONS
BETWEEN DIFFERENT VIEWS OF THE SAME THING

The notion of a single representation for a composition is obsolete. There are specific visual and aural requirements and processes for performance, conducting, music analysis, musicological research, and education. There are further unique notational and procedural imperatives which support the compositional process from the sketching stages through to completion.

Construct displays specifically for performance. Build analysis space, research space, areas for working with orchestration or sound generation. Fabricate customized full-score representations for conducting and completed compositions.

Use general representations or score reductions; display levels of fine detail to analyse, generate, modify and explore.

441

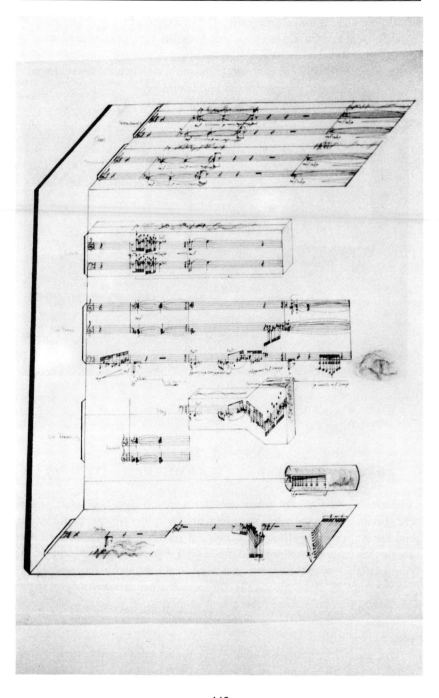

442

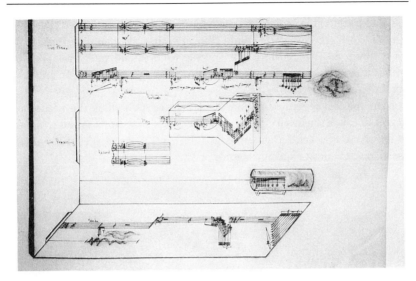

Shift the viewer's focus while still maintaining a connection with the preceding images. Explore the relationship between orientation and representation. Work on different aspects of the project without having to disassemble the room for an hour's or an afternoon's work.

Build a contextually derived, reconfigurable play environment. Based on specific contexts, customize sound realization in ways that will produce the most direct results. Select parts, specific timbres and intensities, relative amplitudes, designated level of structure. Play specific parts or create an aural sketch of a section.

Map the visual representation of play space, as well as the nature and degree of touch sensitivity. Segment a portion of space for a sound template, in the shape of a hand as an envisaged design. Design shapes that embody the characteristics of specific sounds and processes.

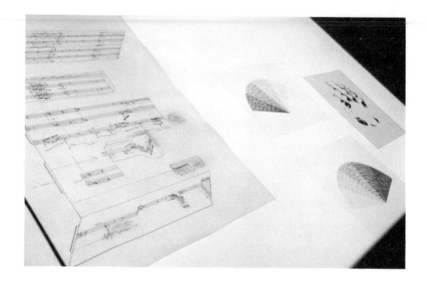

For a sound realization of a particular section, define a post-processing technique to apply to all *strike* tags and highlight their appearance; over the course of the selected phrase, map all tags marked *chord* to have specific timbral characteristics, selecting among a specified set of pitches.

Redesign and reassign the sound template. Interact with collections of databases containing sounds and procedures. Play fragments, phrases, voices and entire compositions. Match traditional or innovative representations with appropriate types of sounds and processes. Refine sound realizations as concepts become clarified.

444

Clear an entire wall. Pull together several related representations into coherent constellations. Quickly sketch out their placement and relationships; then slip the finished representations into place.

Freeze the image and once again step back to view the totality.

445

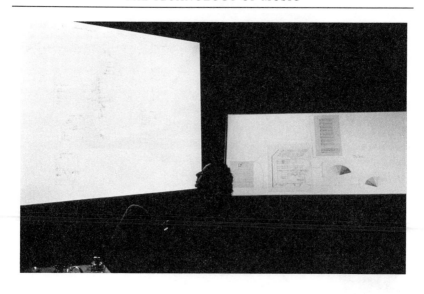

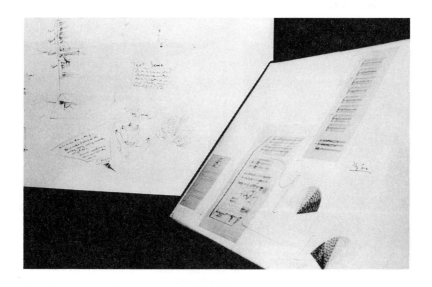

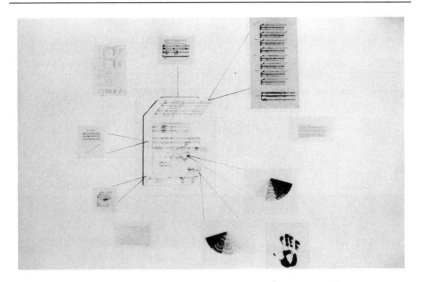

Achieve direct interactions among sound, sight, action, and process.

CONNECTIONS
BETWEEN DIFFERENT ROOM VIEWS

Save the current state of the room view – the images on the table and wall displays, associated sounds and music, the room ambience.

Mutate it. Manoeuvre between various combinations of room views. Allow the environment to evolve around the artist's dynamic requirements, rather than binding the artist to fundamentally fixed notions about creativity and artistic processes.

Record actions and processes so that the sketches can be rebuilt. Display and perceive differences between various sketches and versions. Retrace and reconstruct the steps and procedures that follow from, or are dependent upon, changes at any level of the hierarchy.

Generate a complex of diverging tangents, branching in different directions from a common point. Observe attributes; investigate their implications. Return to the nexus, and integrate anything relevant for the work in progress. Save potentially useful material gained from the pursuit for use in other circumstances.

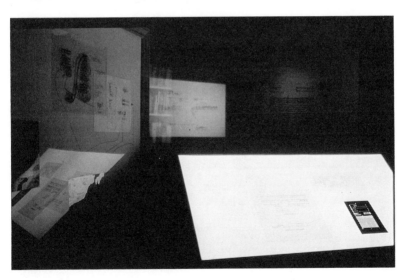

Configure the history of the composition's progress. Define the nature of the history itself, indicating the extent and type of information to retain – which processes and commands to follow or ignore, and which ones to mark for special attention. Explore and control the impact of changes on all affected levels of activity.

Construct combinations of room views that are meaningful in relation

to one another. Investigate the maze of paths and decisions that led to a particular stage in the composition.

Design the character and modes of transitions between timed sequences of room views – still views, slow dissolves, and animation.

Preserve stages, sequences of states, and the nature of transitions between states. Build scenarios of room views designed to enhance creative orientation and to stimulate artistic momentum.

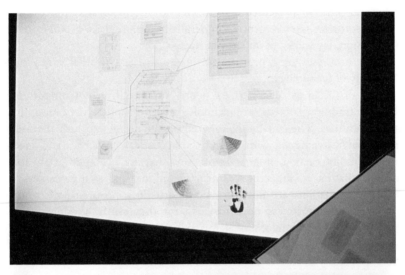

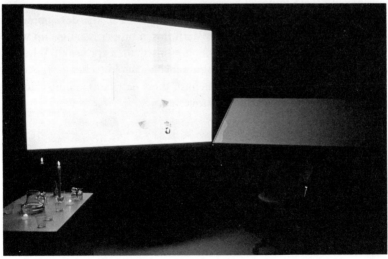

CONNECTIONS
BETWEEN HISTORICAL VIEWS

The connection between art and technology is so strong that it is difficult to examine them independently. However, in order to gain an understanding about the nature of the artistic process as it relates to technology, the interplay between conceptualization and actualization needs to be investigated.

Several concepts presented here are not new to the creative process.

Conceptualize, sketch, process in parallel, develop ideas. Develop structural design, lay work out on large surfaces.

These processes are representative of creative activity that exists independently of technology.

Some of the ideas suggested are poorly supported, or not supported at all by the traditional, fixed-form technology, with its underlying assumptions and capabilities. The constraints inherent in the use of paper, or the use of traditional instruments, with their fixed acoustical properties and mechanisms for interaction, impose limitations that are not appropriate for a medium that has no inherent sounds or sound manipulation processes.

These limitations are not intrinsic to artistic expression and creative processes, and no longer need to exist, for they are by-products of the application of a technology of a former period. A technology that fully supports the dynamically configurable environment provides the artist with the opportunity to extend his or her artistic resources substantially, and to move beyond these imposed barriers.

The requisites of art must be the driving force in the development of new musical instruments and tools. With this, a proper relationship will be achieved between art and the technology used for expression. When the fascination with technology, or an adherence to an old technology, becomes the dominant force in the development of these new tools and instruments, fundamental artistic concerns are subverted.

BIBLIOGRAPHY

BAISNEE, P., BARRIERE, J.B., *et al.* (1988) 'Esquisse: a compositional environment', *Proceedings from the International Computer Music Conference*, pp. 108–18, San Francisco: Computer Music Association.

BUXTON, B., *et al.* (1979) 'The evolution of the SSSP score editing tools', *Computer Music Journal* 3 (4): 14–25.

——(1982) 'Objed and the design of timbral resources', *Computer Music Journal* 6 (2): 32–44, Cambridge, Mass.: MIT Press.

DECKER, S., *et al.* (1986) 'A modular environment for sound synthesis and composition', *Computer Music Journal* 10 (4): 28–41.

HARRIS, C. (1987a) 'A composer's computer music system'. *Computer Music Journal* 11 (3): 36–43.

——(1987b) 'The missing links – a studio report', *Proceedings from the International Computer Music Conference*, pp. 73–9, San Francisco: Computer Music Association.

LERDAHL, F. (1987) 'Timbral hierachies', *Contemporary Music Review* 2 (1): 135–60, London: Harwood Academic Publishers.

POPE, S.T. (1986) 'The development of an intelligent composer's assistant', *Proceedings from the International Computer Music Conference*, pp. 131–44, San Francisco: Computer Music Association.

ROADS, C. (ed.) (1985) *Composers and the Computer*, Los Altos: William Kaufmann.

ROADS, C. and STRAWN, J. (eds) (1985) *Foundations of Computer Music*, Cambridge, Mass.: MIT Press.

SCALETTI, C. (1987) 'Kyma: an object-oriented language for music composition', *Proceedings from the International Computer Music Conference*: pp. 49–56, San Francisco: Computer Music Association.

ACKNOWLEDGEMENTS

Artistic, production, and graphic assistant: Mary T. Faria
Photographer and design consultant: Marion Gray
Producer, layout design, original graphics, art direction: Craig Harris
Sound template illustrations and graphic design assistance: Jim Kozlik
Production and artistic assistant: Candy Kuehn
Set design and construction: Tom Proost, Cynthia Sumner
Editorial assistance: Patricia Riposo

23

Flying Through a Musical Space:
About Real-Time Composition

JOEL CHADABE

We must throw wide the windows to the open sky.
(Debussy, under the guise of 'Monsieur Croche')

ABOUT FLYING

Since the earliest days of poetic history, freedom has been sought through flight. From Icarus on, the romantic dream was to soar through the air, where there are no roads, no constraints, where you can go wherever you like, where you can decide from moment to moment where you want to go next. As Leroy Jenkins put it, in the context of musical improvisation, 'you're thinking as you go'.

By 'flying' I mean composing as you perform. Your instrument is your plane. Your universe of musical possibilities is the space through which you fly. Your composition is your flight path.

ABOUT MUSICAL SPACES

Earle Brown portrayed one of the imaginary musical spaces through which one might fly. The score to *December 1952* is a single sheet with straight lines of varying widths and lengths drawn horizontally and vertically. The

454

lines in their nonspecificity represent imaginary sound objects suspended in an imaginary musical universe, 'the score [is] a picture of this space at one instant, which must always be considered as unreal and/or transitory' (Brown 1961). We encounter sounds as we travel in any direction through this space, moving to the 'right, left, back, forward, up, down and all points between ...'. I have always imagined myself as the pilot of a spaceship flying through that musical universe, going wherever I want to go, encountering sounds in whatever order I choose, realizing a limitless variety of musical forms.

Edgard Varèse said, in 1959:

> There is an idea, the basis of an internal structure, expanded and split into different shapes or groups of sounds constantly changing in shape, direction, and speed, attracted and repulsed by various forces. The form of the work is the consequence of this interaction. Possible musical forms are as limitless as the exterior forms of crystals.
>
> (Varèse 1959)

Varèse was describing Earle Brown's musical universe, albeit from a slightly different perspective. But then Varèse had already made his flight, in 1958, in *Poème Electronique*. The sounds in *Poème Electronique* are provided by snare drums, gongs, melody instruments, sirens, electronic tone generators, and voices. The sound objects include percussive single strokes, often with grace notes; repetitions of single strokes forming rhythmic figures; rolls, shakes, fast repetitions, flutters, buzzers; short pitched sounds, detached, grouped in brief melodic fragments; sustained tones that sometimes change timbre but not pitch; portamentos to pitches; and glissandi, as in sirens. Occasionally these sound objects are linked as groups forming larger constructions, as, for example, the rhythmic repetition of a gong sound, or the grouping of several electronically generated pitches into a chord, or the alternation of a flutter and a hollow drum sound. Each sound object is self-contained and complete in itself and, in the sense that one might imagine these sound objects as suspended in a space swept by 'various forces', one might imagine *Poème Electronique* to be a flight through the universe represented in Earle Brown's score.

ABOUT MUSICAL STRUCTURES

The idea of musical flight is antipodal to the concept of a classical musical composition as a fixed, complete structural object, and to classical musical values which espouse the virtues of proportion, balance and symmetry. The structures of classical music are symmetrical. When the chordal progressions of a tonal composition are charted, they appear to be symmetrical around a point in time. Every tonal structure is a two-part form where chordal progressions lead away from a tonic chord at the beginning and back to it at the end, completing the form. The symmetrical chordal structures of tonality can be equated with the symmetry of time in the context of Newtonian determinism. An orrery is a clockmaker's model of the New-tonian solar system, with planets and their moons revolving in different cycles and at different speeds around the sun, each motion synchronized to one central gear through a hierarchy of gears and mechanical arms. The planets and moons of an orrery move in predetermined tracks, their future positions seen well in advance of their present positions. In such a pre-dictable framework, time becomes symmetrical: 'the music of the spheres is a palindrome', in the words of Norbert Wiener (1961: 31).

The cranking of the orrery's central gear can be reversed, and the lines that connect past to present to future can lead backwards as well as forwards. From the centres and turning points in the symmetrical structures of tonal compositions, as from the point of the present in Newtonian time, we can look equally easily to the right or the left, ahead or back, and move with equivalent predictability. In other words, classical musical structures are rooted in a deterministic way of thinking about music. You know where you're going. You see the whole as you make the parts, so you can make the parts fit. The idea of musical flight and its lyrical evocation of freedom, on the other hand, is based on impulse, caprice, on-the-spot decision-making; in a word – indeterminism. You don't know where you'll turn next.

ABOUT MANOEUVRABILITY

Musical flight requires manoeuvrability, and manoeuvrability requires an immediacy of control. Your manoeuvrability will depend upon the link between your composing gestures and the musical variables. Max Mathews's Conductor Program, written in 1976, is a *performing* solution rather than a *composing* solution to the problem of controlling a musical process, but it

456

illustrates clearly – and in traditional musical terms – the link between pilot and plane. Max Mathews, F. Richard Moore and Jean-Claude Risset described it in the following way:

> To avoid limiting the capabilities of the system to what could be accomplished by a person controlling a sound synthesizer directly, a new concept in control is necessary – what we call the 'conductor' concept. Simply stated, it is that the relation between the performer and the computer is not that between a player and his instrument, but rather that between a conductor and an orchestra.
>
> (Mathews *et al.* 1974: 267)

The Conductor Program operated in three stages: (1) an entry stage, where notes were input into the computer's memory with a keyboard, (2) a 'rehearsal' stage, where the phrasing, accents and other characteristics of each voice were added to each voice individually, and (3) a 'performance' stage, where all of the voices were played back together. During the performance-stage playback, balance and loudness were controlled by a three-dimensional joystick and tempo was controlled either by turning a knob or by beating time with a key. The Conducting Program is a performing rather than composing solution because the important musical decisions, in this case the notes and phrasing, were made before the performance took place. You are in control, but there's little room to maneouvre – there *are* roads, there *are* constraints, you *can't* go wherever you like, and you *can't* decide from moment to moment where you want to go next.

The SAL-MAR Construction, built between 1969 and 1972 by Salvatore Martirano and others at the University of Ilinois, is a *composing* rather than *performing* model of controlling a musical process. The SAL-MAR Construction is a large, complex instrument, consisting of sound generators controlled by special-purpose digital circuits, a performance console with 291 touch-sensitive switches, and twenty-eight loudspeakers arranged throughout a performance space. The instrument automatically generates sounds with different timbres, pitches and loudnesses, and automatically routes the sounds along four paths through the arrangement of loudspeakers, but the processes by which the instrument functions are controlled by a performer. In other words, Martirano is conducting an 'orchestra', but his conducting consists of telling the orchestra how to improvise. 'In performance', Martirano wrote, 'I can change my relationship to the sound by zooming in on a microprocess, fiddle around, change the process or not, remain there or turn my attention to another process.'[1] Now here's a pilot who can manoeuvre his plane.

ABOUT *M* AND RANDOMNESS

Intelligent Music's program *M* appeared in January 1987 as an interactive composing and performing environment. The idea behind *M* was the creation of a musical plane that anyone could fly. In fact, the first items to be implemented in the development of the program were the conducting grid and the baton, the inspiration for which came from a flight simulator for the Macintosh, i.e. the joystick. Because of its automatic procedures, *M* has been widely discussed in the press as an 'algorithmic' composing program, a program which composes music *for* you instead of *by* you. That's not at all what *M* is about. *M* is about real-time composing. Further, the identification of *M* as an algorithmic composer echoes the criticism so often directed against John Cage that, by relying upon automatic – and even worse, *random* – methods for making musical decisions, the composer abdicates his or her responsibility.

Cage composed *Birdcage* in 1972 with my assistance. He arrived with three groups of pre-recorded tapes. Group 1 consisted of bird sounds recorded in aviaries. Group 2 consisted of recordings of Cage himself singing his *Mureau* in a kind of chanting voice (he observed that 'it makes the birds seem less ridiculous'). Group 3 was the wild track, consisting of environmental sounds. During the first day of working together, we copied samples from the tapes that Cage had brought with him onto another series of tapes. He used a table of random numbers to determine the duration of each sample and the order in which the pre-recorded tapes would be sampled. In all, twelve new tapes were made, each a different ordering of samples of varying durations. The following day, we electronically modified the sounds on the new tapes, playing them back through filters, ring modulators, and other audio processing devices, producing yet another series of tapes. The choice of processing method and the duration for which each method was employed were determined by random numbers. Our work, finally, resulted in twelve tapes, each consisting of a random sampling of bird sounds, Cage's singing voice, and environmental sounds, all of which were randomly processed in one way or another. The performance space for *Birdcage* is an open space through which people may freely move, and the twelve tapes are played back in such a way that the sounds are mixed and directed to different loudspeakers around the hall – in Cage's words, '*Birdcage*, twelve tapes to be distributed by a single performer in a space in which people are free to move and birds to fly.'

The point is that the art of Cage's composing lies not in the use of the random numbers themselves, but in his choice of sounds and in the way he applies the random numbers. Cage, in other words, poses questions. What sound will be on what tape? And for what duration? Which method of processing will be used? And for what duration? It is the *questions* that define the composition. The random numbers merely provide interesting variation. That is also true with M.

The random numbers in M simulate the complexity and unpredictability of improvisation. After all, the intuitive acts of an improvising musician might be thought of as 'random' – 'thinking as I go', in Leroy Jenkins's words. Although there are reasons of taste, habit, physical reaction, psychology, and so on, underneath the improviser's action, the reasons are underlying and elusive and you can't predict exactly what's going to happen. You can predict a *range* of behaviour, but not the details. To whatever extent you direct it to do so, and in whatever way you direct it to do so, M 'improvises' on your musical material. In Renaissance Florence, the masters in the art workshops would paint the outline of a landscape and their assistants would paint in the leaves – perhaps even adding some improvisational details of their own. Well, M provides you with assistants who improvise your details, leaving you free to concentrate on where you're going as you fly through your musical space.

If underlying and elusive causes lead to unpredictability and 'randomness' in improvisation, it might be worth looking for a moment at the mechanism of a random number generator, just to verify that underlying and elusive causes are in fact the basis also of random numbers and that, consequently, random numbers properly applied might do quite well as a simulation of improvisation.

Starting, for purposes of this example, with a row of four figure 1s, the leftmost and rightmost number of the row are combined according to the exclusive-or (XOR) truth table ($1 + 1 = 0$, $0 + 0 = 0$, $1 + 0 = 1$, $0 + 1 = 1$), as shown in Figure 23.1, producing a new leftmost number for the next row.

The numbers in the first row are then shifted one position to the right, allowing the rightmost number to drop off and disappear, as shown in Figure 23.2. The numbers are then dropped down to the next row, so that the first row's leftmost three numbers become the second row's rightmost three numbers.

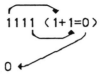

Figure 23.1 An example of random number generation, following the XOR truth table

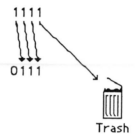

Trash

Figure 23.2 After the first stage of generation, the rightmost number drops off and the three remaining figures form the rightmost end of the row below

The exclusive-or operation, the shift right, and the dropping down are performed repeatedly to generate a series of rows.

1111
0111
1011
0101
1010
1101
0110
0011
1001
0100
0010
0001
1000
1100
1110
1111

It is obvious that there is nothing random about this procedure. The operations are cyclic, mechanical and predictable. Another cycle begins in the sixteenth row, and clearly any arrangement of 1s and 0s will lead predictably and mechanically to the next. But those operations are so underlying and elusive, even ridiculous, that the logic of the series could not be perceived if the series were presented in, say, decimal notation, and without explanation. Who would guess that the next number in the series 15, 7, 11, 5, 10, 13, 6, 3 ... is 9? Yet there are rules, or causes, behind the series. And because the causes are not evident in the numbers they produce, the numbers appear to be random. In *M*, they appear to be the result of intuitive, improvisational decisions. They cause unpredictable variation within ranges.

ABOUT FLYING WITH *M*

In using *M*, you begin by entering basic musical pitch material whether a tune, chords, scales, whatever. Then, while hearing your music play, you define the nature of *M*'s improvisations on that material – you can define cycle length, loudness variation, accent pattern, rhythm, articulation, note density, time distortion, transposition, timbre, note ordering, and so on with all of *M*'s variables – thereby defining the links between your performance gestures and their musical results. You are 'tuning up' your plane. Here are three examples of specifying aspects of *M*'s improvisation. Note that they are independent variables – but that they all affect the music simultaneously.

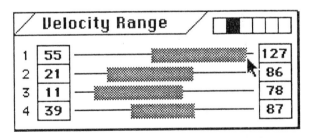

Figure 23.3   The Velocity Range edit window of *M*

1   The Velocity Range edit window, as shown in Figure 23.3, contains four *range bars* which let you define ranges within which a MIDI velocity value will automatically change. To change the range setting of a range bar, first

position the mouse arrow at the high or low end of the range you want to define, then drag the grey area to the other end of the range. MIDI velocity values extend from zero, which is silence, to 127, which is loud. For each of *M*'s four voices, you can set a range of automatic variation by dragging the cursor on the screen, as indicated by the arrow. Every note that *M* plays will be at a loudness somewhere within that range, simulating the variations in loudness with which an improvising musician plays.

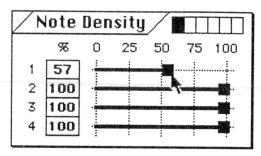

Figure 23.4 The Note Density edit window of *M*

2   The Note Density edit window, shown in Figure 23.4, contains four sliders which let you set values by dragging 'handles' left or right to determine the percentage of notes which will be left out of the material you've recorded. In Figure 23.4, Voice 1 is playing 57 per cent of its notes, or, to put it another way, *M* will play each note with a 57 per cent probability. The Note Density control simulates the rhythmic and textural decisions made by an improvising musician.

3   The Note Order edit window, shown in Figure 23.5, lets you mix different types of note ordering to transform your pitches into different degrees of improvisation or variation. The *original order* is the order in which you initially recorded the pitches. The *cyclic random* order is a scrambling of the pitches into another order, but stored in the computer's memory so that the scrambled order will repeat. *Utterly random* means that the pitches you recorded will be played back in a continually changing, unpredictable order. When you mix different types of note ordering, you're stating the percentages of time that the pitches played by *M* will be ordered in a certain way. In Voice 1, as shown in Figure 23.5, you'll hear the original ordering of pitches 35 per cent of the time, you'll hear the scrambled order 44 per cent of the time, and you'll hear randomly chosen pitches 21 per cent of the time.

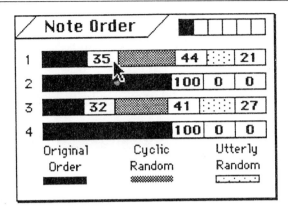

Figure 23.5   The Note Order edit window of *M*

Once you've defined the links between your gestures and their musical results, you fly. With the mouse as your control device, you're pointing, clicking, dragging, choosing one process, then another, then several together. You can use *M*'s Mouse Advance feature which allows you to phrase melodies with a continuous movement of the mouse. Or you can use the Robot Conductor to automate certain processes while you perform others. You can use the Velocity Range edit window as a performance mixer, dynamically balancing the voices. You can click on a Snapshot and change all of the variables together. In short, you can act at any level of a control hierarchy, from control at the detailed level of changing one variable in one voice to control at the highest level, where you're changing any number of variables in all the voices. *M*'s main screen, shown in Figure 23.6, is the control panel of your musical plane, and the mouse – whether you're using the version for Macintosh, Atari, Amiga, or IBM – is your joystick.

The variety in the types of gestures you make with the mouse, and your interactions with their musical results, creates a unique performance environment. In David Zicarelli's words:

There are different kinds of interaction one experiences in performing with *M*, and they are distinguished by the types of physical gestures a performer makes with the mouse. One often interacts with *M* by *guiding it* – making discontinuous gestures, such as pointing and clicking, which re-orient the music in a particular direction. But one can also be involved in the physical articulation of the notes as they play. The movements here are smooth, and the performer's attention is directed towards continuous re-orientation. Decisions are not made consciously, yet one cannot say that the performer

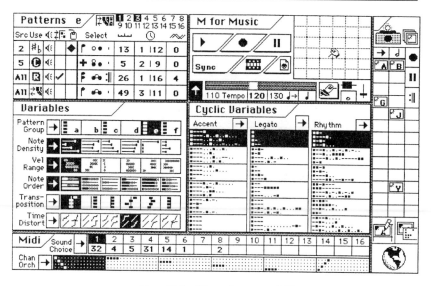

Figure 23.6 The main screen of *M*

has no control over the situation. It is a mistake to think that we always act by evaluating our situation and then deciding a course of action. Music made with *M* has a human quality because the program's musical output reflects the performer's musical choices and gestures. In the first case you might say that the performer is controlling the macrostructure of the music, and in the second case the microstructure, but it is not really a clear-cut division. Often the single adjustment will have more effect on the details than the whole, and continuous gestures will often provide transitions from one place to another, even as they participate in revealing the other place that one might want to go.[1]

Because of *M*'s complexity of musical variables and their aggregate effect on your music, as well as its use of random numbers, *M* gives you back more than you put in. Flying with *M* is not only about flying and freedom, not only about real-time composing, it's also about the discoveries you'll make in exploring new musical spaces.

NOTE

1 Taken from a personal communication.

REFERENCES

BROWN, E. (1961) *Folio*, New York: Associated Music Publishers.

DEBUSSY, C. (various) *Monsieur Croche the Dilettante Hater*, a series of short music-critical articles, included in *Classics in the Aesthetics of Music*, 1962, New York: Dover.

MATHEWS, M.V., MOORE, F.R. and RISSET, J.C. (1974) 'Computers and future music', *Science* 183 (4122): 263–8.

VARÈSE, E. (1959) 'Rhythm, form and content', lecture at Princeton University; excerpts published in 'The liberation of sound', in B. Childs and E. Schwartz (eds) *Contemporary Composers on Contemporary Music*, New York: Rinehart & Winston 1967.

WIENER, N. (1961) *Cybernetics*, Cambridge, Mass.: MIT Press.

24

Music and Image on Film and Video: An Absolute Alternative

DAVID KERSHAW

Recent computer-based advances in the synchronization of sound and image on film and video have encouraged young, technologically aware musicians and artists to experiment with these remarkable resources at professional and, increasingly, at amateur level. The generation and organization of music and graphics with the assistance of computers is becoming commonplace, to the extent that relatively cheap machines and sophisticated programs are now affordable by schools and colleges, and by the individual for home amusement. Such has been the rapidity of development in this field, however, that attention is still focused upon coming to terms with the 'nuts and bolts' of synchronization, with less awareness of aesthetic potentials.

Musical accompaniments to narrative film – for example, in the context of features, documentaries, cartoons and commercials – ultimately serve the story being told; they are shaped to a visual 'programme', with the composer's skill being evaluated primarily according to his sensitivity in mood-matching. But film itself can escape this narrativity, and become, like much concert music, 'absolute', structurally and aesthetically autonomous. Released from subservience to narrative, both film and music can forge a new identity, an identity which will be unique to the medium.

Early in the twentieth century, avant-garde artists and film-makers were already exploring the possibilities of creating an absolute visual language in analogy to music. Later, with the coming of sound-on-film, they experimented with the relationship of sound in conjunction with the absolute

466

image. An awareness of the achievement of these experimenters and later figures suggests potentials of sound–image relation which have only now become realizable through computer technologies.

Speculation and experiment in the correlation of absolute visuals and sounds have a long if rather discontinuous history. It is only in the present century that, initially through the medium of cine-film, it became possible to articulate complex, precisely synchronized temporal interrelations between music and dynamic coloured forms. The new art of cinema, whose early years were spent travelling the fairs and garish booths of the 1890s, lost no time in flaunting itself as a nickel-peepshow for the masses, disgorging narrative extravaganzas in the form of fantasy, travelogue, melodrama and comedy capers. Cinema's narrative appeal persisted through the years of live sound-accompaniment, and with the coming of sound-film, this form of entertainment was (as it still is, whether on film or video) popularly esteemed as the most lavish and compelling story-telling medium available.

It is not surprising that visual artists were at first loath to have anything to do with cine-film. In the first years of the century the art-film house was unknown, and the audience for the programmes of Louis and Auguste Lumière was no prospective audience for a cinematic presentation of modern art. But, considering the contemporary interest in virtual movement,[1] it is surprising that by the mid-1920s so few artists had even considered the possibility of painting 'in time', if not that even fewer had actually completed short abstract films. For the technical demands of animation were foreign territory to canvas painters, and the almost total inaccessibility of the new medium to the individual artist made the prospect of 'animating' his or her drawings distant indeed.

Around the turn of the twentieth century visual artists had become increasingly preoccupied with two areas of investigation – time and mysticism. The philosopher's ponderings on the reality of time became a shared concern of the avant-garde, common to Futurists, Cubists, and Constructivists. Their canvases sought to represent past, present and future in a contracted simultaneity; or they sought behind relative exterior phenomena for absolute values poised in a timeless dynamic equilibrium. There was an underlying belief (recently fuelled by Wagner-mania) that in music could be found the key to life's mysteries. Through its ambiguous precision – enmeshing self-expression and sense-impression within an autonomous statement – music mediated between man's subjective realities and the objective phenomenal world. The canvas painter, his or her former assumption of the validity of graphic representation lately undermined by

467

camera-art, might now seek spiritual rejuvenation in a pictorial mode resonating to music's (time-based) autonomy.

The intangible, mystical unreality of time bewildered and intrigued visual artists. Intoxicated by their own daring in trespassing on music's terrain, many eagerly embraced the new theosophical movement which offered release from the mundanity of an imperfectly perceived, imperfect world, and a glimpse of the incorruptible higher planes of existence granted the exalted few. Representational canvas painting was coerced into abdication in favour of its natural heir, narrative cinematography. Simulacra of the external world could now be provided by the camera, thus relieving artists of their mimetic subservience to the perceived. Reality became internalized. That which was exterior should be transformed, interpreted, abstracted or ultimately outgrown as the artist's inner eye evolved its own para-reality of absolute 'thought-forms'. Fascinated by, yet at the same time ultimately dissatisfied with, their grasp of this new dimension, time, artists vied with each other in wooing it away from music to the visual arts – none ultimately with more tenacity or courage than the makers of absolute films, where a preparedness to confront time 'head-on', to wrestle with an unfolding temporal flux, marked them out from the majority of canvas-painters who were still concerned with the instantaneous representation of change through virtual movement.

A sensitivity to the workings of time and an inclination towards the transcendental stimulated the creativity of the vast majority of absolute film-makers, from the Swedish Viking Eggeling,[2] and the Germans Walther Ruttmann and Hans Richter in the early 1920s through to the American brothers John and James Whitney in the 1940s and later. Paradoxically, this extra-temporal mysticism was often sought in a medium that impresses upon the animator the utter artificiality of an apparent dynamic continuum (which is actually conflated from a concatenation of discrete 'stills').

Composers of music were not unmoved by current theorizing on time – the natural carrier of their art. The relatively articulate ambiguities of eighteenth and early nineteenth-century chromaticism had become over-faceted with the accretion of increasingly distant partials; pivotal chords had swept into a maelstrom of vertiginous rotation, where the stabilizing properties of a coherent tension–relaxation flow had become exhausted through a harmonically non-functional chromatic surge.

In the expressionist outpourings of composers and artists the spontaneous and feverishly inchoate gesturings of the hypnagogic state welled up; the flood-gates of time burst open, overwhelming the senses in an engulfing excess of sensation. The periodic cadencing of earlier arts – the poise of linear design, the resolution of acoustic disharmony in consonance – was replaced by a prolonged deferral of closure, even to the point of its absence. Completion was no longer a prerequisite for art. To this degree had time eaten away at the discreteness of the artefact.

Throughout the 1930s and 1940s, and into the 1950s, there were still few experimenters in abstract and absolute film, for cameras (and film-stock) were prohibitively expensive and almost exclusively at the disposal of major production companies. Only with the revolution into substandard gauges – the introduction of 16 millimetre and 8 millimetre equipment for amateur use – did the medium of absolute film slowly begin to grow as a by-product of the flourishing home-movie market. By the 1980s the growing availability of video as a medium for animation and the rapidly increasing flexibility of computer animation programs quickly gave the community video workshop and even the lone worker access to a graphic sophistication previously unavailable to all but commercial studios.

INTERRELATION OF SOUND AND IMAGE

The term 'audio-visual counterpoint' (meaning some form of asynchronism) was much bandied about in film-music aesthetics between the two World Wars, the assumption appearing to be that it was of itself desirable, and that other, more conventional uses of sound in films were correspondingly weak and uncreative. Whilst it may have been necessary at that time – especially during the emergence and establishment of sound-film between 1927 and 1930 – to protest against the restriction of musical accompaniment to a psychologically supportive role, today the question of the function of sound, and more pertinently of music in film, can be less polemical. For it will be acknowledged that in commercial, narrative-driven film this use of music feels as natural to us as it did to the first generation of silent-film pianists.

What can a normative interrelationship between sound and visual image be in absolute film? It would seem perverse wilfully to reject the fundamental relationship found in narrative film – that of psychological reinforcement. Whether the dominant mood-message is conveyed by aural or visual means is immaterial; it is a question of intuitive supplementation of the one by the other, either running both media continuously or requiring the one to act in a supportive, but also commentative role at selected points. The contention that a mere embellishment, or extraneous duplication, results from

469

the yoking together of sound and visual image in harness, as it were, is not supportable. Raymond Spottiswoode rightly argued that audio-visual parallelism was actually impossible, citing Clive Bell's opinion that 'two artistic media cannot convey exactly the same impressions; and if this be true, the limit will be approached asymptotically and never reached' (Spottiswoode 1935: 180). Conversely, Spottiswoode observed how

> sound and sight are said to contrast when they convey different impressions. Here also the limit is difficult to determine; for though the visual film might convey the concept 'Force' and the sound factor 'Lethargy', the inevitable penumbra of peculiarities attaching to the use of a particular medium would blur the opposition until it had lost its precision.
>
> (Spottiswoode 1935: 181)

Admittedly one may weary of the clichéd conventions of hurry-music, horror-music, love-music, and so on, but this distaste is not evoked by the relationship itself; it is caused, rather, by the outworn nature of the musico-dramatic entity. Eisler's successful scoring to *14 Ways of Describing Rain* is a case in point; here he provided an unusual form, but still a form, of instrumental onomatopoeia to the visuals, while at the same time continuing to provide a musical ambience conducive to a fuller concentration on the screen.[3] To borrow Paulo Milano's terminology, music was here serving at once a neutral, rhythmic, illustrative and limited psychological function (Milano 1941: 89–94).

Similarly, in absolute film it would seem foolish to attempt to establish a compositional method based on 'contrapuntal' interplay, such that one would conceive of intermedia relationships primarily in terms of asynchronous 'collisions'. Such collisions, the very spice of the film medium as musical dissonances are within a broadly consonant context, can only function at full strength within a field in which sound and visual image are otherwise in closely sympathetic relation. This enhancement of audio or visual 'dissonance' through its incorporation within a generally 'consonant' context is overlooked in Spottiswoode's otherwise valuable observations.

Although those synchronous relationships that commonly occur in nature are few, they must be accounted the strongest of all binding forces. As will later become apparent, these can all be translated into absolute terms and then readjusted or even disputed at will.

1   Synchronous occurrence, or 'attack', of image and sound: as in the 'snap' of finger against thumb.

2   Visual rise and fall equated with pitch rise and fall; owing primarily to vocal-cord sensations of muscular tension and relaxation.
3   Speed of movement equated with pitch-level: as in the whirring of a swung rope.
4   Distant (small) image equated with distant (soft) sound; near (large) image equated with near (loud) sound. Size is related to amplitude.
5   Large image equated with low-pitched sound: as with the diameter of drum-heads; hence small image equated with high-pitched sound.

In addition to these, there are two isolated, rather more rare natural phenomena which, although exploitable, perhaps evoke their realistic source too strongly to be much use in the context of absolute film.

1   The Doppler effect: as when a sounding image, moving at constant speed past the spectator, appears suddenly to drop in pitch.
2   Time lag: as when distance is sufficient to render apparent the difference in transmission-speed of sound and light.

Whilst these are all observable phenomena, there is another field of learnt audio-visual interconnection which cannot be neglected. This derives from the language of human communication, and can be summarized as follows.

1   Abrupt, angular gestures are associated with harsh, short words (sounds).
2   Expansive gestures are associated with broad, long-phrased declamation.
3   Easy, fluid gestures are associated with a conversational or warm tone of voice.
4   Stillness of body and silence both convey introspection, or non-communication.
5   Extreme bodily activity is associated with rapid speech (sounds).

These relationships, of course, neglect the strong associations of absolute imagery and sound perceived independently. For example, consider how the angular image connotes variously unease (facial distortion), attack (bodily rejection), asceticism (Christian symbolism of thorns, cross), and how falling sounds may connote spent energy, lamentation and finality. But these are all readily understood, and retain their associative potency to some degree however much abstracted. (It becomes clear from this that the term 'absolute' is one of convenience; there can, assuming human mediation, be no such thing as an absolute, universal art-form representing incorruptible verities. If one cannot embrace the synaesthetic mysticism of Wassily Kandinsky and his generation, absolute imagery is no substitute for tran-substantiation. Our glimpse of 'reality' is partial at best, conditioned by age, sex, temperament and environment.)

Absolute sound-film can depart markedly from the conventions of narrative film in the following ways:

1 'Mickey-Mousing' (point-by-point synchronization) of music and visual movement may be the prime temporal link.
2 The shape of the film may be strongly conditioned, or even dictated, by 'musical' considerations.
3 Synchronism and asynchronism and every variety of contrapuntal inter-play may be shaped in a musical way, involving phrase-repetitions, polyphonies, and the gamut of tension/resolution, anticipation and gratification associated with musical structuring.

There is no convenient graph of psychological effect to be plotted when considering audio-visual synchronism and asynchronism. Furthermore, in dealing with absolute film one is denied access to the most valuable weapon in the armoury of the composer for commercial narrative film: association. Within mainstream cinema the composer can, and nearly always does, rely upon the associative capacity of his material to elicit the immediate response demanded by a medium whose products probably receive – for any one consumer – a once-only exposure. The message must be clear and unam-biguous, assimilable without conscious effort. Thus whether syn-chronization of mood or the less common asynchronization is desired, identification by association is the rule. The old compilation-manual mood-musics of the silent film pianists and orchestras are thus effectively still being exploited, albeit periodically updated.

How does absolute film stand in relation to this? Unless one creates images to music gleaned from the standard repertoire, as the experimental animator Oskar Fischinger did,[4] or one is content to write a pastiche-compilation, one is denied the emotive resonances of known musical styles, and thus the synchronous and asynchronous modes must be conceived in different terms. Since, however, it may be anticipated that a short absolute film would be viewed – on home videotape or videodisc or in an art-film cinema – several times, the necessity for instant 'effectiveness' is removed. Consequently, one can approach the structure of the film in much the same way as many composers would nowadays approach the structuring of a piece of music, namely – in this disintegrative world – from unique premises, individual to their oeuvre, or perhaps even individual to the particular work.

That is to say, the shaping of interrelationships in an absolute film might be defined for that film alone; forms of synchronism would be established and dissolved in wholly absolute terms. That this lays great stress on viewers' preparedness more actively to evaluate the audio-visual complex of activity before them cannot be denied. However, it is not proposed to present viewers with some arcane cypher for decoding. Given an adequate technique and imaginative capacity, the film-maker should have designed a piece which, like most successful 'high-art', can be experienced at several levels of familiarity and sophistication. An immediate intuitive grasp of structure, of tension-patterns, should be available on first screening; and this, then, should serve as the catalyst for future explorations of deeper layers of meaning within a film.

A PRESCRIPTIVE NOTATION

It was the very absence of a specific vocabulary with which to discuss absolute film that obliged the early artist film-makers to appropriate from musical terminology words such as rhythm, counterpoint, polyphony, orchestration, tone, overtone and cadence, in many instances overworking and overextending these terms until their metaphorical vigour became exhausted. Numerous artists and film-makers strove to promote graphic abstraction as an autonomous language, with animators having recourse not only to the terminology of music but to music itself, in an effort to lend credence to what might otherwise appear a goalless kaleidoscopic divertissement.

From its earliest years the composition of absolute film has been hindered by the unavailability of a workable prescriptive notation, some shorthand mnemonic which might 'fix' the most characteristic attributes of mobile shape prior to full graphic realization and filming. Such attempts as were made – notably those of Werner Graeff in his *Filmpartituren I* and *II* of 1922 – were made at the expense of any graphic flexibility. Here a timed succession of squares and rectangles, cloned from the screen format itself, constituted the entire subject matter. As in Richter's more complex *Rhythm 21*, a temporal 'orchestration' was sought, independent of any 'limiting' graphic design. Given that such a gross reduction of means cannot for long satisfy the artist, how may any more flexible scoring of visual activity be achieved? And if this problem can be overcome, how then are the visuals to be related to that most absolute of musics, electronic music – which

473

similarly wants for a notation? (A conflict must arise if instrumental or other 'concrete' music is used in conjunction, and in synchronization, with absolute film-visuals. A double location is then proposed for the sound: the primary inescapable 'live' source, and the secondary grafted source imposed through synchronism. The illusion of unity in this instance can never be total, the recollection of instrumental gesturing ever vying with the intended 'manufactured' synchronism.)

In commercial cartoon animation, where unambiguous character definition has always been the primary goal, comparable 'scripting' problems do not arise; for given a troupe of familiars – a Donald Duck, a Goofy, or a Bugs Bunny – their interactions may be presented in terms of a ludicrous parody of human behaviour; thus personalities are created, stock-responses defined, and whatever the situation, however fancifully 'unrealistic', empathy is assured through a psychological veracity of behaviour. As fear, greed, cunning, anger, the lust for revenge – these and a host of other human emotions – are condensed into the cartoon Lilliput, and so distanced, we can mock our own emotional frailties. Through the use of a simple graphic *story-board* – the name itself points to the crucial dominance of narrative in such work – only the key points in the action are depicted, as in a magazine strip-cartoon, relegating further elaboration of gesture and movement to a secondary role which at all times must contrive to enhance the anthropomorphism of activity.

Denied this easy identification, absolute film-imagery can only function in terms analogous to those of absolute music; its internal argument, its ability to refresh itself, to regenerate continually, to contemplate its own being – this is the new arena.

By 1954 Ralph Potter, Director of Transmission Research in Bell Telephone Laboratories, in an excellent article, 'Abstract Films', could still observe that 'a written language for the scoring of abstract color-form compositions is still to be evolved' (Potter 1954: 85). And indeed a major handicap to any close analysis of absolute film composition is still the unavailability of a 'score'; the interested viewer, intent upon understanding the compositional detail of such a film, is reliant upon repeated viewings and on what written elucidation may be forthcoming from the film-maker himself. But words cannot substitute for the comparative precision of a film-score any more than they can in the case of a music-score; thus the film-works of Viking Eggeling, Hans Richter, and Oskar Fischinger, for example, can now only be analysed from viewings, and whilst this is not inherently unsatisfactory, it is regrettable that later film-makers cannot profit from an understanding – aesthetic rather than technical – of the criteria which conditioned the spatio-temporal organization of visual activity.

'ABSOLUTE' RELATIONSHIPS

With regard to the correlation of sound and visual image, Potter's approach is quietly realistic: tacitly repudiating the idiosyncratic concoctions of synaesthetists, he stolidly avers that 'we can follow two performances *only* when the two become one. And this means one to the audience – not the artist. The fact that two things may seem related to the artist who combines them is not a reason for them to seem so to others' (Potter 1954: 85). The unity, or oneness, of sound and image must be self-evident, incontrovertible. Flying in the face of all those whose effusions on the supposed identity of colour, shape and sound have swollen the annals of colour-music theory, he remarks:

> There aren't many things in visual abstractions that have any convincing relationship to music. One possible relationship is the indirect tie between the mood incited by color and the mood incited by the accompanying music. At best it is feeble, and in itself entirely unconvincing. The *forms* in visual display bear little relation to the sounds of music.
>
> (Potter 1954: 86)

This summary rejection of the accretions in audio-visual analogy, succinctly dismissive, smacks of common sense, and offers a welcome antidote to the confused, perfumed superabundance of Theosophical metaphysics. In conclusion, Potter defines the one vital connecting link between moving image and sound: 'Actually, the only bond of any consequence is MOVE-MENT' (Potter 1954: 86), by which should be understood the dancing *rhythm* of visual abstraction as it derives from the tempo and rhythmic gestures of the accompanying music. Visual and sound movement fuse best in rapid tempo (note the helter-skelter pace of cartooning) and least well in slow tempo. But fast visual rhythm is a bar to its assimilation; 'the eye cannot perceive detail when the details are in rapid motion' (Potter 1954: 86). (Thorold Dickinson has remarked, though, how audio-visual unison assists concentration, enabling assimilation of material faster than is normally possible (see Dickinson 1971: 59).) Whilst Potter regards this blurring of detail as an unwanted confusion, clearly it can equally well be treated as a compositional ploy within a scale of comprehensibility.

Only very few correlations, borne out by research into the psychology of perception, are recognized by Potter. Drawing upon evidence in E.D. Adrian's *The Physical Background of Perception*, Potter can assert that 'a change in the pitch of a tone is the equivalent of visible movement *across* the field of view. And changes in the loudness of sounds are equivalent to changes in visual movement *toward or away from* the observer' (Potter 1954: 88). Beyond this stating of the obvious, though, he is unwilling to venture, and his guarded approach must be applauded, even at the cost of apparently impoverishing the scope for audio-visual unity.

Mantle Hood, drawing on the researches of Theodore F. Karwoski and Henry S. Odbert (Dartmouth College, 1936), nominates these and other relationships and associations, a few of which are generally recognized, but most of which (d. to j. below) have actually been experienced only by a minority of subjects:

> There may be postulated certain general relationships of photisms to special aspects of music:
>
> a. a rise in pitch is relative to an increase in brightness;
> b. accelerated tempo increases brightness;
> c. pattern in music is related to pattern in the photism, smooth music producing graceful lines, staccato or syncopation producing jagged lines;
> d. variation in pitch sometimes produces a change in position and direction in the visual field;
> e. in some cases the first note or the key of the selection is correlated with background colour;
> f. striking music may produce third dimension;
> g. volume increase may expand the area occupied by the photism;
> h. turns or trills may cause movement round a center mass;
> i. different instruments may be represented by lines [of] different color, rising and falling with changes in pitch;
> j. the mood of pleasantness of the music may evoke fitting colors.
>
> (Hood 1951: 53)

Hood argues that colour and music may, by association, appear unified, but denies any common physical identity. For all but those individuals who enjoy synaesthesia, the link must be through association or analogy. Whereas Potter dismisses other, *artificial* interconnections such as relating a pitch rise with a receding visual image, on the grounds that 'education is practically out with non-captive audiences' (Potter 1954: 88), it can be argued that just such structured correlations, albeit not consciously perceived by the spectator, can make new, fruitful interconnections which, once having been confirmed in

476

any specific work – that is, having been given time to establish their symbiotic nature – may be dislocated by various means, and the degree of disconnectedness 'played-upon' as a melodic Gestalt might be deconstructed to generate separate rhythmic and pitch cells. The danger of obfuscation inherent in such contrivance must always be borne in mind, of course. So few are the *equivalents* in sound and visual image, as Potter has suggested, that it becomes incumbent on the composer/film-maker to do just this: to *make* connections, not in the fond belief that they express some eternal verities, that they grant access to esoteric vibrations which it is the composer's mission to divulge to the less sensitive and well-endowed, but to make connections as any composer of music must when interrelating his or her own materials – extending, curtailing, expanding, contracting, varying, confirming, contradicting – treating experiential time as something infinitely malleable, which, by his or her intervention, can be shaped into a simulacrum of his or her sensibility.

Potter does however concede that, after an exploratory stage in audio-visual composition, it may be possible for the film-artist to depart from unison; but it is necessary first to be 'able to translate freely from one language to the other. We must know equivalents in the two languages, even though there is no intention to employ them *in unison*' (Potter 1954: 88). He seems to suggest that equivalents other than those dependent on a rhythmic identity may be *discovered*, whereupon an audience will enjoy 'a much more convincing experience than visual motion or audible motion can provide singly' (Potter 1954: 88). The suggestion that 'audible motion', alias music, may at some stage be superseded by a 'more convincing' synergistic *Gesamtkunstwerk* is inflammatory, and patently improper! It is not a question of 'better than' but of 'different from'. That new *equivalents* may be discovered seems unlikely; *invention* is the key to the world of audio-visual interplay, an invention unhampered by the limited and limiting 'correspondences' erected by the shamans of colour-music.

Whilst one sympathizes with Potter's unwillingness to compare visual form with musical sounds, it can however be maintained that although melodic 'shape' can in no direct way be related to visual shape, nor dynamic to spatial volume, it is through *gesture* (i.e. rhythm of movement) that the spatial and temporal arts are linked. That is, since any visual image cannot but exist in *time*, and since any music must inhabit some *space*, the two do share a common temporal–spatial universe, albeit working within it to different ends. In *gesture*, the physical gesture reinforced by vocalization – the sigh, the scream, the command – a common expressive source is found. Whereas in the visual arts it is the spatial characteristic of the gesture that is presented, in music it is the sounding characteristic. This is not to suggest that a translation from one to the other can be made, for these gestures have in both cases become highly stylized symbols whose very distance from their original physicality renders them the more available as 'artistic' expression. By their use, expressivity is re-presented; the painter/composer 'gestures' whilst creating an art-object, but this gesture is a recollection – personal or communal – of the archetypal instinctual gesturing of primitive humans.

As Susanne K. Langer confirms, '... if the content [of art] be the life of feeling, impulse, passion, then the symbols which reveal it will not be the sound or actions that normally would *express* this life; nor associated signs, but *symbolic forms* must convey it to our understanding' (Langer 1957: 223–4). Langer, drawing upon Jean d'Udine's *L'Art et le geste* (1910), contends that all the arts aspire, not towards music, but towards *dance* – in other words, towards the gestural, which by various modes of transformation may become manifest visually or in sound. 'Every feeling contributes, in effect, certain special gestures which reveal to us, bit by bit, the essential charac-teristic of Life: movement. ... All living creatures are constantly con-summating their own internal rhythm' (Langer 1957: 227).

VISUAL TENSIONS

In passing, one may note David Rothenburg's research (both theoretical and applied) into an intermeshed audio-visual language, where he has advanced certain equivalents in terms of dissonance level. (He designed and constructed an image-generating keyboard which took advantage of the then most up-to-date (1974–5) computer-graphics display facilities.) Rothenburg asserted that acoustic dissonance might properly be paralleled with the visual 'dissonance' of, for example, Moiré patterns and strobe lights, both sound and visual image producing sensations of greater or lesser tension.

> Acoustic dissonance derives from the receipt of impulses which are in the same order of frequency as the refractory period of the auditory nerves. Similar, and more powerful, visual effects occur when there is an interference pattern with the refractory period of the optic nerves or with the alpha rhythm of the brain. ... Note that the interfering families of curves forming a Moiré pattern need vary very little in order to produce blinding interference patterns. This resembles a musical dissonance in which the frequency of the tones

forming a chord vary little, but the total effect is far more than the combination of component tones. Similar analogues to tonality, timbre, etc., exist.

(Rothenburg 1975: 140)

One doubts whether such visual dissonance will ever become as contextually conditioned as is intervallic dissonance in music; for dissonance, unlike discordance, has only relative not absolute value, seeming now weak, now strong, dependent upon environment. Furthermore, sounding dissonance – as long as its constituent voices can be recognized (thereafter it jells into a noise-band) – is a many-layered phenomenon, implying a multiplicity of entry and exit points suggested by centuries of use in widely differing contexts. Can one expect visual dissonance to convey such a wealth of implication? Attractive as it may appear to equate sound and visual image in this manner, the fact remains that acoustic disequilibrium (for this is what is meant by dissonance) can be represented visually by many means other than interference patterns. One has only to consider Piet Mondrian's work, where dissonance and consonance, thesis and antithesis, 'sound together', reconciled in delicate balance, in 'dynamic equilibrium'. Set temporally, visual disequilibrium can as well be denoted by spatial imbalance as by the grosser means of retinal irritation advocated by Rothenburg.

One consequently remains equally unconvinced by John Whitney's extended essay on computer-generated visuals in his *Digital Harmony: On the Complementarity of Music and Visual Art*. Here he optimistically hypothesizes that:

the attractive and repulsive forces of harmony's consonant/dissonant patterns function outside the dominion of music. Attractions and repulsions abound in visual structures as they become patterned motion. This singular fact becomes the basis for *visual harmony* with a potential as broad as the historic principles of musical harmony.

(Whitney 1980: 5)

In positing close analogies between visual and aural harmony in this way, Whitney joins with the numerous colour-music inventors of Skriabin's day; even whilst corroborating his predilections with scientific evidence, his efforts at determining correspondences remain idiosyncratic. Indeed, at one point he makes no claim that the analogies plotted are in any sense absolute: 'whether my efforts constitute a final valid grammar is irrelevant' (Whitney 1980: 6), and he freely admits to being 'neither authoritative nor professional in matters of music' (Whitney 1980: 10).

Whitney holds that computer graphics provide the long-awaited key to

479

a new audio-visual world unified by a common harmony. Like several earlier film artists he is seeking a complementary grammar, a 'thorough-bass' of visuals in motion. By 'harmony' he 'refers to the physical fact of orderly ratio in both its horizontal and vertical [linear and simultaneous] meaning' (Whitney 1980: 5). In translating such harmonic ratio, interference and resonance to the visual plane (using the media of film, video-tape and, ideally, video-disc) he relates sound-wave 'modulation' of the air to modulated light, claiming that 'we can create integral aural/visual compositions in a domain of harmonic continuity' (Whitney 1980: 16).

Although currently fully occupied with visual organization and generation alone, Whitney, like Oskar Fischinger before him, foresees the day when the artist will compose complementary sound and visual image in one; a more sophisticated interactive digital system will ease the creative process by permitting instantaneous real-time playback. For the time being though, he is happy to 'settle for whatever music I might find for each new graphic composition' (Whitney 1980: 44) – a disappointing retreat from the radical audio-visual serialization attempted in the earlier *Film Exercises*.

In pursuing the musical analogy, Whitney activates graphic elements at speeds proportional to the intervallic ratios of the harmonic series in such a way that, for example,

> If one element were set to move at a given rate, the next element might be moved two times that rate. Then the third would move at three times that rate and so on. . . . This is harmonic resonance, and it echoes musical harmony, stated in explicit terms.
>
> (Whitney 1980: 38)

Rather than simulate naturalistic perspective, Whitney visualizes a rhythm of pattern, whereby a repertoire of elements could be orchestrated according to a generative harmonic plan. At a later stage of his research, three crucial terms were defined:

> . . . *differential, resonance* and *harmony*. First, motion becomes pattern if objects move *differentially*. Second, a resolution to order in patterns of motion occurs at points of *resonance*. And third, this resolution at resonant events, especially at whole number ratios, characterizes the differential resonant phenomena of visual *harmony*.
>
> (Whitney 1980: 40)

In working towards and beyond such consonant points, Whitney argues an analogy with the processes of tension accumulation and discharge in tonal music, firmly believing that on the visual plane such structured motion is as potent a begetter of emotion as it is in musical composition.

He ingenuously aspires – as did Eggeling and Richter before him in their quest for 'universality' – to 'a visual world of harmony to which there must be innate human responses' (Whitney 1980: 42).

In this he surely betrays his mishearing of his avowed model, tonal music (he distrusts twentieth-century non-tonality as an unfortunate, passing aberration) as a steady-state communicative system, an incorruptible and hence non-progressive language which, although undeniably the product of a specific set of social conventions, can now somehow be construed as defying mutability, as valid for all time. His impatience with the bland stasis of computer-graphic 'video-Valium' (which in fairness often operates within the terms of reference of an oriental, not occidental philosophy of time) further encourages his pursuit of a tensional expressivity founded upon the inherent force-fields of the harmonic series. Nor does he find the immobile electronic music of the 1960s and 1970s to his taste, for it also similarly relinquished control of functional harmonic structure.

Whitney's acknowledgement of music as mentor to his explorations in visual graphics does, of course, commend his research to serious investigation; that he is no naïve is testified by the densely argued *Film Exercises* of the 1940s, although his apparent enduring ignorance of Eggeling's and Richter's fruitless search for a mobile graphic universality does rather diminish the significance of his belated revelations.

In the course of *Digital Harmony*, Whitney details several recently completed 'harmonic' films, devoting an entire chapter to the analysis of his *Arabesque* of 1975, a seven-minute film accompanied by improvised Santour music performed by the Iranian Manoocheher Sadeghi. Earlier pieces, for example the three *Matrix* films, were similarly compromised by 'borrowed' music-tracks, namely sonatas by Antonio Soler (*Matrix I*, 1971), and music from Terry Riley's *Rainbow in Curved Air* (*Matrix II* and *III*). It is revealing that *Matrix I* and *II* actually display the same computer graphics, but employ such radically different sound-tracks. This surely confirms Whitney's insensitivity to audio-visual interrelations.

Like Rothenburg, Whitney conceives moving visuals in terms of a scale of beat-frequency nodes, and similarly points to acoustic parallels with the perceptual interferences aroused by 'dissonant' Moiré patterns. His visual dynamic is propelled along its course by a concatenation of graded collisions between consonance and dissonance, order and disorder, tension and resolution. Entertaining as his thesis is, the aesthetic limitations of overlooking all but one interpretation of the word 'dissonance' are evident: fluid transformations of stellated and other geometric graphics can hardly challenge the multi-planar 'corporeality' of music – corporeal in its literal acoustic three-dimensionality, and also in its textural layering, which by establishing hierarchical perspectives incarnates the phenomenon of audition.

As observed above, when rebutting Rothenburg's equations, there is more to 'dissonance' than beat-patterns, aural or visual. Understood as a metaphor of conflict, disorder, disequilibrium, or interference, it may encompass every kind of asymmetry, both temporal and spatial. Whitney's visual translation of musical dissonance is by no means invalid, but it is undoubtedly limiting. His researches do not advance our understanding even as far as those of Eggeling and Richter, whose comprehension of visual music appears far more generous and mature than Whitney's. For these men both recognized that, in the medium of mobile graphics, dissonance was essentially a function of temporal organization, not of spatial configuration. Hence Eggeling's *Symphonie Diagonale* and Richter's *Rhythm 21* create tension-fluctuation by montaging and faceting their material rather than by subjecting it to fluid transformation. By so graphically energizing time, periodic and aperiodic rhythmic trajectories were launched, and it is through *their* cumulative interferences, *their* curtailment, congestion, prolongation or rupture that visual 'dissonance' is generated.

TEMPO INTERRELATIONSHIPS

We must know how to grasp the movement of a given piece of music, locating its path (its line or form) as our foundation for the plastic composition that is to correspond to the music.

(Eisenstein 1943: 131)

The Japanese have shown us [an] extremely interesting form of ensemble, the *monistic ensemble*. Sound-movement-space-voice here *do not accompany* (nor even parallel) each other, but function as *elements of equal significance*.

(Eisenstein 1951: 20)

The most important means of macro-structural control resides in the 'orchestration' of *tempi*. Whether one chooses to term this a control of tempi or of rhythms is immaterial, since at root they are one and the same; for without an implied tempo rhythm cannot be articulated, and without rhythm, tempo is non-existent. Tempo is perhaps the better term since it suggests a steady periodic pulsation, a background throb against which foreground rhythms operate. The plural 'orchestration of tempi' is used advisedly, for whilst the singular 'orchestration of rhythm' may have sufficed for Richter's essentially silent studies, it cannot satisfactorily do so once music is introduced in parity with the visuals. The persistent unity of tempo between sound and visuals in the films of Oskar Fischinger and Norman McLaren is their gravest limitation; it seems not to have occurred to these film-makers to set off visual against aural tempi. But only by so doing can the 'equality' of the media be maintained, and their individual temporal trajectories preserved. It is vital that each medium be permitted to develop according to its own 'inner necessity', not for ever constrained and inhibited by the onward flow of the other. It may be imagined how, when the tempi are allowed to act in a controlled interdependence, their coming together at moments of maximum synchronism (as they would tend to do) may be construed as the height of tension, both being obliged to regard the developmental needs of the other, and to accommodate accordingly. This is a far cry from the music-dominated visuals of Fischinger or the image-dominated music effects of a Disney cartoon-short, where such is the imbalance of media that creative intermedia tensions can only fortuitously arise.

The location of tempo is problematic; it resides not simply in frequency of attacks, but issues – in music – from a conditioned response to a complex of metric, rhythmic, harmonic, dynamic, registral and timbral factors, all of which contribute towards temporal pattern perception. The establishing of a metronome mark is no guarantee that any notated tempo will actually be experienced as such. The tempo of activity – whether it be visual or aural – need not necessarily be equated with the tempo at which the activity is notated. For example, a music notated *Presto* may actually sound as though the activity were no more dynamic than the blandly changing patterns of a kaleidoscope. Tempo is only meaningfully assessed as it sounds to the ear, or appears to the eye – not as it stands in notation. The intangibility of tempo, however, does not annul the fact that it is the very vehicle of music, within whose flux all else must operate. If quantitatively closed to evaluation, 'temporal numerosity' is qualitatively clear for all to hear.[5] Visual tempo in film is yet more fugitive, image erasing image (frame by frame) to a degree unknown to sound succession in music. Here again, though, the pulse of a visual sequence can be felt, despite the difficulty – especially in mapping out sequences of absolute animation – of anticipating the screened result. As in music, visual tempo is the product of a complex of movements, being further affected by whatever qualities of virtual rhythm are to be found in the shapes employed. The nature of montage, the mode of movement of shapes, colour-balance, texture – all these will combine in conveying the sense of tempo.

'Interferences' of visual and aural tempi should of course be created, and can probably only be provisionally evaluated empirically at a 'line-test' or equivalent early stage, running the visuals in synchronization with the already completed sound-track. With considerable experience in the new medium it is possible that calculation could play a greater role in this, thus avoiding the time-consuming need to re-cast extended visual sequences that are found to relate unsatisfactorily with the music.

It is tempo that subsumes all other activity in the composition of absolute animated sound-film. How else can interrelationships be controlled? If one takes exception to Mickey-Mousing of the Fischinger manner, if one abjures the narcissistic 'structure-is-all' film, and censures as too idiosyncratic any synaesthetic marriage of sound and visual (of the order: blue *is* C major), then one is indeed hard pressed to find any means other than that of tempo by which to manage the play of activity.

The conventional means of tempo-control in nearly all films (notoriously in the 'Mickey-Mousing' of cartoons) is for sound and visuals to conform to the same temporal trajectory. That is, if the cat chases the mouse, the music runs fast and furious; if the mouse tiptoes stealthily away, the music matches each step with a stocking-footed aural ghosting. Here there is a simple identity of visual and aural tempi.

Now consider a situation where, in absolute animation, the visual activity pelts along, whilst in complete contrast, the musical activity defines a slow tempo. Conditional upon the exact nature of the activity, the tempi will interact one upon the other in a variety of ways. Visual images will not necessarily appear to 'speed' the sounds (as if in forced resonance), nor will the sounds necessarily 'slow' the visual. Indeed, the comparatively static nature of the sound might even serve to heighten the visual frenzy. Or the sound tempo might, if synchronization of beat occurred not infrequently with the visuals, act as marker-points to the visual activity, demarcating passages of the visual flux. The fact that concurrence of two dissimilar tempi can result in a range of very different psychological effects (being entirely dependent on the precise nature of the material conveyed by these tempi) does not invalidate the premiss that tempo-control is fundamental to solving the problem of simultaneously thinking in terms of the two media, sound and visual. Indeed it is evidence of the wealth of variety obtainable even within the framework of just two contrasted and relatively 'dissonant' tempi. Not that there need always be only two tempi in operation at a time. Certainly one can conceive of a situation where several tempi might inhabit the same time-span, the level of 'confusion' of superimposed tempi being as controllable by pitch, rhythmic, and textural differentiation as the tempi themselves. These tempi should not be thought of as audible click-tracks, as necessarily 'pitched'. Indeed it is likely that in many instances the tempi would not 'surface' at all, or need be felt over any extended period, but that – as in the medium of music alone – a tempo might be implied by a diversity of foregrounded rhythmic gestures, which might only retroactively acquire a verifiable metrical or tempo-ral context.

The virtue of so concentrating on tempo admits the inescapable fact that our perception of visual and aural rhythm is very dissimilar. Just as there is no universal equivalence of hue and pitch, so there is no equivalence of sounding rhythm and seen rhythm. A visual image, even a still image flashed on the screen for just three frames (one eighth of a second), can carry within it its own viewing-path; the eye is guided along curves, across the frame, up and down. In the sound world there is no equivalent for this. Instead, the process is reversed; for do we not hear (after the event) as a 'moment' the whole melody which, in first audition, we were obliged to hear as a succession of pitches? In imagery, the literal visual moment is extended temporally by the eye's viewing path; in music, the temporal expanse of a statement is afterwards traced as a unit, as an expanded moment. Two such incompatible perceptual modes cannot attempt any simplistic one-to-one relationship without the one becoming a mere embellishment, a condiment to the other.

Working empirically, one finds that tempi can be articulated by a wide variety of means, some obvious, some subtle. A few are described below.

1 The concurrent presentation is possible of dissimilar tempi articulated by dissimilar activity – in short, two events, apparently unrelated.

2 The concurrent presentation is possible of dissimilar tempi articulated by similar activity. Here, for example, one might find rhythmic augmentations and diminutions, although as already argued, rhythmic imitation of this kind could be no one-to-one process. For example, the pitch-material in Figure 24.1, part (a), might be approximated in visual, rhythmic imitation not by three visual bleeps and a long-held image, but by only two shots as shown in part (b).

This example merely serves to illustrate that consecutive sounds (later recalled as a 'moment') should not necessarily be complemented by rhythmically echoic visuals. The above visual image will probably be read left-to-right, and will thus 'feel' the same as the sounds, more so than would three visual bleeps; for visuals share no common acoustic

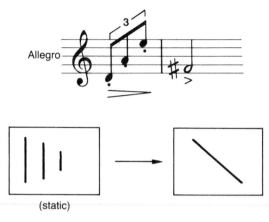

(static)

Figure 24.1   (a) This pitch–material of three short notes and one long might be approximated in visual, rhythmic imitation (b) as two shots

as do sounds, and since it is their shared acoustic that holds sounds together, visual activity similarly treated would fall apart.

3   Cross-media tempi articulation – deliberately sounding or imaging one by the other – is also possible. (This may superficially seem to offend against the principle of perceptual distinction argued above; however, such trespass may be sanctioned, for here it is the pulse, not any specific rhythmic gesture, that is being exchanged.) For example, establishing a sounded rhythmic pulse and then switching it over to the visual plane and back to the aural, as shown in Figure 24.2.

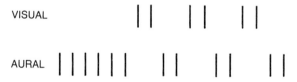

Figure 24.2   Cross-media tempo articulation: a rhythmic pulse is established aurally, transferred to the visual plane and back to the aural

Against this, other tempi polyphony (articulated by rhythms) could appear, either within the one medium, or again crossing from one to the other. At this level of complexity, the structuring of this section would no longer be perceptible on viewing/audition; not that this matters in the least, there being nothing more limiting than an art-form reliant upon the perception of its construction in order for it to communicate.

486

4 Pulse could be given by one medium, rhythmic interjections by the other.

5 The losing of audio-visual synchronism could be employed for its capacity to disorientate the audience temporarily by exceeding their limited audio-visual channel capacity and hence their tension-tolerance.

It remains to note five additional audio-visual correlations independent of tempo, all of which may be assumed to have only local validity:

1 Only a temporary identity may be established between pitch-timbre and a hue. There is no correlation between a particular sound frequency and that of colour.

2 There is a possible link between timbre and saturation. As the accretion of overtones modifies, so the saturation changes; but this remains as artificial as any other arbitrarily chosen matching.

3 For acoustic and dimensionality, one might match two-dimensional imagery with synthesized sound and three-dimensional imagery with concrete sound. But it is questionable how meaningful this would appear.

4 To identify high/low pitch with high/low position on screen would be ludicrously limiting. However, the screen-format does allow for clear visual retrogades and inversions, as shown in Figure 24.3.

R	**Я**
ᴚ	**ᴚ**

Figure 24.3 Visual retrogrades and inversions can be obtained on the screen to echo musical pitch

Each of these areas could as well be 'characterized' by aural timbral differences (for example), as by matched aural retrogrades or retrograde-inversions, etc.

5 Image freeze in the full course of an action or at its natural cadence could have, respectively, an arresting or a restful effect. Still moments permit viewers to respond more actively to the imagery which no longer 'holds' them in its flux, but allows them to stand back and assess the past events, the import and balance of the frozen present, and to speculate on which of the many possible future extensions of activity will be adopted. During the image freeze, of course, the sound-activity can take on any function – recapitulatory, anticipatory, supportive,

disruptive. These points of freeze might last from a half-second up to twenty seconds or longer. (A loose aural equivalent to visual freeze might be the tape-loop.)

A prescription for absolute sound-film composition might read: plot the intermedia tempi-concurrences and juxtapositions, articulate them rhythmically, clothe these articulations in shape, colour, pitch, timbre and dynamic, and trust to intuition to guide the point-by-point activity.

GRAPH OF CONCURRENCE

Rhythmic unison binds the seen and the heard with such conviction that an audience cannot but identify the sound as somehow emanating from the visual image. To be more precise about the rhythmic liaison: it is the synchronous attack which binds. What follows is comparatively immaterial. (As in the case of live-action lip-synchronization, should synchronization not be secured, a jarring irritation occurs; the viewer is ever trying to draw the two together again. In terms of absolute film this need not always result in an undesirable situation, for a controlled 'interference', an intentional 'out-of-tuneness' between sound and visual image may enhance the eventual slipping into synchronism.)

If this synchronous attack is the most unifying device, without which the artificiality of the medium becomes obtrusive, how might it be structured into a film-composition? For non-stop attack-unison throughout a film would become wearisomely simplistic, on the level of a light-show where sound-impulses translate directly into light-patterns. Such fawning dependence of visual image on sound is quite antipathetic to an art-form, the *raison d'être* of which is to interweave the auditory and the visual whilst each observes its inherent developmental needs. However, the complete absence of synchronous attack gives an equally flaccid impression. Visual activity, however frenetic, pales before the acoustic vigour of sounding rhythms; it lacks the 'edge' which sound enjoys, for it has no transient bite. In short, visual rhythms are comparatively insubstantial; to speak with authority, to command attention, they require aural amplification. Thus enhanced, they spring forward from the screen with a quite remarkable immediacy, vitalized, dynamic and organic. Absolute graphics – previously unmotivated and drifting mutely – become imbued with intent; they become purposive; it seems that it is not only we, the spectators, who hear them, but they who, sounding, can also necessarily hear. Thus a bond is

488

forged; we see, they 'see', as they interact within a landscape of absolute visuals; we hear, they 'hear', as they emit or respond to sound. So without resorting to gross anthropomorphism, without endowing 'characters' with behavioural attributes, it is possible to promote empathetic audience response through this simple contrivance of synchronism.

Not all graphics need be so 'sounded'. Stationary elements – inanimate scenery – may be left silent, or may be complemented by a concurrent acoustic ambience – a continuum or an ostinato perhaps. Nor need all mobile shapes be sounded, for this would soon cloy, becoming tiresome. Rather some form of 'graph of concurrence' should be devised which might plot the density of synchronous activity. This could be taken as a preliminary to further elaboration and inflection, preceding consideration of the relative rhythmic emphasis to be bestowed upon such synchronous points. It might be established irrespective of, and preceding, more detailed considerations of the exact timing of these points, or even considerations of their expressive function. The graph would have but little limiting effect on the nature of the music and visuals regarded independently, but would act throughout as a controlling agent upon the potential synchronous interrelationships. Where a high frequency of synchronization was felt desirable, considerable discreteness in note-attack would be required of the music. The visuals too would need to be strongly marked, either by 'montage' techniques, or by such means as 'pop-ons' or the clearly articulated movement of figures. At other times, though, the attack-level of the one medium could be the polar opposite of the other; extremely discrete articulations of the one could be complemented by a seamless continuum of the other. Thus, an audio-visual film might be provisionally structured by initially determining the tempi and required density of synchronism within various sections, prior to the determination of either music or imagery. This radical departure from conventional film-scripting constitutes a most important point, crucial to a successful intermeshing of the media, for only by virtue of such a preliminary balance being struck can there be any hope of a satisfactory resultant 'give and take' between them; by which is meant a shifting of emphasis, so that the audience will now be more aware of the visual, now of the sound activity – even though such transference of attention will generally only be marginal, operating *within* an overall receptivity.

This is not equivalent to applying one compositional principle to both image and sound, as has sometimes been done. When abstracting from live-action, such a systematized interpenetration of stimuli may prove valid – for the 'identity' of image and sound need not be questioned. Mauricio Kagel's *Antithèse*, *Solo* and *Match* are composed in this way. A shared programme can ensure compatibility of sound and visuals only if perceptual differences are properly understood and taken into account. As Frits Weiland has observed: 'an apparent solution is to restrain the visual impressions in order to allow the ear to register more. However, the reciprocal effect between eye and ear does not permit such a simple shift in the presentation of visual and aural signs' (Weiland 1971: 83). Nor is it acceptable to map visual and auditory rhythm according to the same compositional pro-ramme. It might initially appear that such a procedure were innocuous, but it fails to account for the dissimilar nature of sound and visual images, both of which will require a 'reading-speed' peculiar to their own interior structure and moreover to their contextual significance.

The theoretician Noel Burch has argued that, whereas 'cinema dialectics cannot be expressed or written down in purely arithmetical terms . . . musical structures ultimately can be' (Burch 1973: 51–2). He rightly suggests that one's estimate of shot-duration is virtually a function of its legibility, such that any uncluttered shot will seem longer than a cluttered shot of the same duration. Hence the organization of perceptible durations is a complex and empirical process.

> Any given cinematic rhythmical pattern will never be experienced in the same way as a musical pattern, unless it consists of nothing more than a simple alternation of black and white frames. If the images involved are at all complex, this rhythmical unit remains little more than a pure abstraction, and is not at all perceptible as a coherent pattern.
>
> (Burch 1973: 51–2)

Whilst fully concurring with Burch in his circumspect attitude towards visual rhythm, one may likewise caution against too facile an understanding of musical rhythm, the perception of which is also conditioned by its 'legibility'; that is to say, as rhythms are 'voiced' by pitch, and as those pitches succeed one another within (and sometimes without) a metrical scheme, so a hierarchical system of 'weightings' is established, whereby certain rhythmic elements are foregrounded at the expense of others. Agogic accentuation is only one means of lending 'stress' to a note or chord; its metrical placing within the bar, its relative dissimilarity within its surroundings, and its structural role will all accord it a prominence – and hence a significance – not apparent on the page. Psychological time is as unquantifiable in music as it is in film. Music's notation may pretend to an arithmetical exactitude, but this is mere appearance. In audition it is the fundamental melodic–rhythmic shape which, in conjunction with harmonic

490

rhythm, underpins an entire movement, and against the background of which all surface detail is experienced and subconsciously evaluated. Furthermore, each work, spatial or temporal in design, requires of us a concurrent (whilst experiencing), a projective (expectant), and a retrospective comprehension according to its own 'intrinsic time'. This latter is a function of the density of argument, and is independent of the clock-time taken up in perceiving the work. (It may explain, for example, Webern's gross overestimate of the duration of some of his works which, however slight they may appear on paper, actually teem with condensed musical arguments that demand multiple 'scans' before they yield up their beauty.)[6] Musical rhythm is thus vastly more complex than Burch allows, and further confirms the impracticality and futility of attempting any total rhythmic organization (serial or otherwise) of visuals and sounds.

Interestingly, Burch develops his discussion of visual rhythm to propose that a dialectic may be effected between shot-duration and legibility. Snatching a shot away from the viewer before its necessary reading-time is fulfilled creates tension (and enhanced attention, as the makers of commercials well know) through deprivation, whilst prolonged retention of a relatively empty shot creates tension through satiety, as the eye repeatedly tracks the same limited landscape. 'These constitute the poles (or rather the vectors) of a true dialectic of durations, capable of generating visual rhythms ultimately as complex as those in contemporary music' (Burch 1973: 53). The informed listener will not need reminding that such a dialectic has itself been elevated to a self-sufficient compositional practice since 1950, with the polar extremes being explored by integral serialism and process-music. The inordinate discontinuity of the one, and the equally extravagant continuity of the other, explore the very perimeter of a territory inhabited by more conventional musical languages which seek a richer and subtler dialectic between disjunct and conjunct statements.

All that has been established so far is the frequency of interconnection between sound and visual images. It is important to determine this at an early stage, since it conditions to an extent the very nature of the musical and visual material, in so far as – in sequences of exact synchronism – both media must accept considerable constraint on their own natural temporal trajectory, each accommodating to the needs of the other. Conversely, in sections of loose synchronism, the media can exploit the very different tensions arising through their apparent independence of each other, and the composition of each can proceed less circumspectly, trusting to the 'inner necessity' of each medium's onward thrust to 'charge' the resulting audio-visual confluence.

What is not established by this approach is the degree of rhythmic emphasis given to the selected points of synchronism. It is only the frequency of such points that has been determined. The nature and degree of emphasis is a dimension which can then be overlaid on the chosen points, and in practice it may be found that at times the media will share the emphasis, whilst at others one medium will voice a synch-point strongly whilst the other remains weakly articulated.

The decision to elevate tempo and synchronism to the role of major structural determinant arose through a refusal to acknowledge that small-scale rhythmic interrelations could be relied upon to communicate. Whereas in music a high degree of polyrhythmic complexity can be comprehended by a trained ear, the intermingling of two media would require an ability on the part of both film-maker and audience somehow to translate from one to another in coming to terms with an audio-visual nexus. From the evidence afforded by the Whitney *Film Exercises* it seems unlikely that this is possible, unless one were so to impoverish one's material that composition became no more than an arid permutational game, with sounds and shapes serving to 'voice' abstract rhythmic articulations. Arbitrary decisions equating such-and-such a shape with such-and-such a sound are too facile, resulting in a cold intellectualism devoid of organic energy. A bolder approach must be adopted, whereby local interactions are as much the product of intuition as of calculation. Perhaps in time a wider language of audio-visual correspondences might evolve from much experiment in perceptual psychology, but at present the obvious 'felt' connections remain those few already noted.

BEYOND THE FRAME

One of the great aesthetic advances encouraged by the introduction of sound-film at the close of the 1920s developed from the ability of sound to suggest to the mind's eye that space surrounding the framed image: 'off-screen space'. Its potential could work against the autonomy of the image in that the projected picture frame no longer enjoyed the respect formally accorded it as strictly defining and delimiting the visual play of shape (figurative and non-figurative alike) bound within its borders. The aesthetic (as distinct from the economics) of screen proportion could no longer remain a burning issue once it was appreciated how relatively 'accidental' and 'incidental' the framing of a scene must appear when off-screen sound could blur the edges to the extent that – in the spectator's imagination – the sound-activity off-screen might seem more 'present' than the image actually offered to the eye. In virtually all areas of film-making today the ability of sound to 'push-out' the frame line in this way, or to counterpoint an off-screen location with that screened, is exploited almost unthinkingly; it has become standard practice, and arouses no feelings of disquiet amongst the sophisticated image-literate viewing audience of the 1990s. Sounds can vastly enrich the repertoire of on-screen camera angles and editing techniques with an invaluable array of implied visual manoeuvres off-screen, suggesting the ongoing existence of objects (anticipating their appearance, and persisting after their removal) and even their metamorphosis once they have disappeared from view. It thus aligns cinema more closely with our own forms of mental awareness, as our attention is drawn to activity both seen and heard, both near and far. Sound at all times conveys to us a sense of the spatial context encompassing the limiting frame area of visual activity, for one infers from its acoustic – its reverberation characteristics – the nature of the space occupied.

Electronic music offers the facility of infinitely variable acoustic, from the most 'two-dimensional' dryness to a strongly three-dimensional prolonged reverberation. By varying this reverberation time, either imperceptibly or to shock effect, the spatial context of the same visuals can be radically altered, and the audience drawn into the action, or encouraged to contemplate it dispassionately. To this latter end the incorporation of 'stills' and action-freeze can contribute; the internal tensions of a figure can be explored, a potential metamorphosis anticipated by the spectator, and this conjecture confirmed or contradicted by the film-maker. The mechanics of delineating off-screen activity by sound presume, however, a degree of familiarity and identification with the subject matter which, although universal in the case of narrative live-action materials, is rarely if ever available in the case of absolute graphics.

If one ponders the achievements in absolute animation, it soon becomes apparent that very few films – either silent or sound – have grappled with this problem. A remarkable self-imposed limitation by makers of absolute films has been their ignoring of off-screen space, as evidenced by the ubiquitous use of the 'static' camera-view. Rarely does the camera become the subjective eye, operating *within* the filmic environment instead of viewing it soberly at a distance. (Movement of the camera, apart from tracking in and out, is actually illusory in most animation; it is the art-work which is either physically moved by increments, or which metamorphoses graphically.) Even the strongly rhythmic articulations of classic montage techniques are under-used: the dramatic intensity of cutting from long shot to tight close-up – similarly implying a mobile camera – is unexploited, even though in cartoon animation the gamut of such live-action editing formulae is run. An acknowledgement of off-screen space realized by the use of a simulated mobile camera is one immediate means of enriching absolute film. In the silent films of Eggeling and Richter the camera remains as stationary as Lumière's; in *Symphonie Diagonale* the action obliges by confining its evolution entirely within the frame-boundary; in the *Rhythmus* films, expanding shapes do encroach upon off-screen space, but have no independent reality there; one can assume their existence 'out-of-sight' but cannot know for certain that they live, or whether they continue to metamorphose, or remain in a limbo of 'suspended animation' until called into play again within the screen. Unless the viewer can 'characterize' the thing seen, can attribute to it certain constant features, or – in the case of living things – behavioural responses; unless the viewer can comprehend the thing's nature, purpose, or general mode of operation, it will remain alien, unpredictable, hence unsympathetic. In the field of live-action, or in the derived, parodistic world of the cartoon, visual activity remains largely true to our experience only in so far as it operates according to, or with reference to, known laws of cause and effect, extreme and whimsically improbable as it may appear.

In narrative film-making of all kinds, the veracity of psychological response invariably preoccupies the film-maker and his or her critics to the extent of conditioning all other profilmic considerations of tempo, chiaroscuro, temporal manipulation in editing, etc. The treatment of a story-line *using film* – this is what commercial cinema is all about. People and places are represented; however stylized a treatment of a story, certain constants remain, in the absence of which communication can hardly begin. On screen, people behave – 'naturally' enough – rather as people do behave: they are motivated, they interact. Objects behave like objects, they are inanimate, and by association are more or less under the control of people.

Such a bald, inconclusive and colourless statement of the obvious is only proffered to demonstrate the enormous gulf existing between commercial cinema and absolute animation, for the latter boasts no people, nor can one distinguish between animate and inanimate with any certainty. And whereas superficially similar absolute imagery on canvas ('still' and 'framed') is set within a vigorous painterly tradition which has always asserted its communicative purpose (namely, its capacity to draw out of the flux of life a synthesis of elements which find sanctuary there in a temporary reprieve from change), the absolute film is necessarily about change, without which it is nothing, and being about change, it is about life-forms; therefore it

494

concerns us to know the how and the why of their evolution, although we begin wholly ignorant of their *raison d'être*.

Narrative cinema is able so fruitfully to exploit off-screen space precisely because this space is inhabited by the familiar. To the extent that on-screen activity is familiar, so will off-screen activity be predictable, and this space will become available. Further, if an identity between on-screen visuals and associated sound can be established, the retention of such sound in the absence of 'its' visuals will encourage an imaginative restoration of the visual complement by the spectator. As an obvious example take the conventional reverse-angle shooting of a conversation between two speakers; it is unnecessary to see-hear each speaker in turn. The common practice is to incorporate 'reaction' shots where the addressee is shown listening to an (unseen) speaker. In absolute animated film, however, no such familiarity can be assumed; indeed the medium precludes it, eschewing as it does the easy bond of anthropomorphism. If familiarity is precluded, how then may off-screen space be used, if at all? Can it expand the screen-format, can off-screen sound here comment meaningfully on the visible? Within an electronic sound-track is it possible to find any equivalents for the several mixed tracks of a narrative film – synch speech, synch effects, unsynched location sound, voice-over and music-track?

It is perhaps not so remarkable that, in the sound era, absolute animated films have overlooked, or perhaps shied away from, the potential of off-screen audio-visual activity, for it poses thorny problems. Off-screen space has commonly been used as a 'dump' for unwanted imagery; shapes fulfil their on-screen destiny, and if they do not escape by recession, or 'pop-off' unceremoniously, then they make a transverse exit, discreet or precipitate, into a limbo out of sight, out of mind. If they should be identified with diegetic sound,[7] this may just serve briefly to sustain their imagined presence, but the identity is weak, and will soon sunder. Identities between the seen and the heard must, in absolute animation, be constructed; they are not 'given' as is the case in narrative film. Such artificial constructs can readily be accepted, but it is less straightforward to attempt meaningful inflections of an identity once established, nor will image and sound necessarily evoke their complement when perceived in isolation. Any liaison is imposed, and prone to rupture. Unless continually forced into a synthetic oneness, the elements re-assert their own identity, their autonomy, resisting symbiosis.

On-screen interrelationships of shape and, by implication, sound (which will also be read as on-screen) are, then, easily generated and maintained; the point-by-point evolution of either or both elements can be assimilated without effort. Concurrent activity will commonly be understood as occupying the same time and space, since the alternative of a robust off-screen reality cannot yet be substantiated. Any synchronous activity will confirm the identity of elements; the shape seen is understood to be 'making' the sound heard.

It does appear that absolute animation suffers from this marked limitation, compared with live-action film: what is out of sight is, by and large, lost to the compositional argument. Sound will usually be heard as emanating from within the picture-plane, and only with difficulty can it be made to stand outside, especially when in a non-diegetic commentative role. Perhaps the limitless malleability of sound and shape in this medium necessarily result in an impoverishment of the off-screen world. When infinite metamorphosis of both sounding and visual form is possible, individual identity must yield to a celebration of the process of change itself. Arguably the gain is as great as, or greater than, the loss.

In conclusion: a number of recommendations have been set down pertinent to a compositional method in absolute sound-film. These have posited that an overall control of the medium cannot be attained without due regard being paid to the interrelation of audio-visual tempi, and to the graphing of rhythmic synchronizations. The problem of negotiating off-screen space and sound has also been explored, with the conclusion that this remains a refractory area, one that requires sensitive handling if it is to be accommodated within a developed aesthetic of absolute sound-film.

NOTES

1 'Virtual' movement occurs wherever 'it is the artist's avowed intention to create a sensation of movement through transparency, arrangements of line and colour etc.' (Popper 1968: 93). The origins of kinetic art can be traced to a common fascination in the 'temporal canvas' from Manet and Degas through to Post-Impressionism, Expressionism, Futurism, Cubism, and more recently to Op-art. Early interest was spurred by the time-lapse photography of Eadweard Muybridge and J.-E. Marey, and of course by cinematography.
2 Of the three contemporary innovators Eggeling, Ruttmann and Richter, only Eggeling has been thoroughly documented. Louise O'Konor's pioneering and meticulous doctoral study of 1971 is limited only by the absence of some primary source material withheld by Hans Richter, Eggeling's co-worker in the early 1920s. Eggeling's ascetic *Symphonie Diagonale*, first screened in 1925, grew out

of many years' experiment with scroll-drawings. Richter's *Rhythmus 21* and *Rhythmus 23* films are, in comparison, graphically crude, but are nevertheless remarkable – like Werner Graeff's unrealized film-scores – for their shunning of any graphic tradition in favour of an 'orchestration' of the screen-format itself. Ruttmann's technically sophisticated film *Opus I* was the earliest to be shown with synchronized (live) musical accompaniment (with a specially written score by Max Butting), but it seems to anticipate Oskar Fischinger's aesthetic through a reliance upon anthropomorphic association. His later *Opus* films (*II, III, IV*) are progressively more 'absolute' in conception.

3 In 1940 Hanns Eisler became director of the Film Music Project. With the support of a grant from the Rockefeller Foundation this unit, part of the New School for Social Research, undertook practical experiments into new methods of putting music to the motion-picture. By way of illustration Eisler presented a detailed analysis of a sequence from *Fourteen Ways of Describing Rain* in the appendix to *Composing for the Films*. He also provided a (now notorious) counter-example: a brief sequence by Prokofiev to Eisenstein's *Alexander Nevsky* (Eisler 1947: 148–65).

4 Fischinger's many short animated films were extremely popular in the 1930s and 1940s, and are the most polished of all absolute animated films before 1950. As a professional animator Fischinger was wooed by Disney to work on *Fantasia*, but his style was rejected as being too abstract. Some silent studies, such as the early *Orgelstäbe* sequences of 1923–7, and the *Radio Dynamics* fragment of 1941, show that popular or classical music was not always an essential spur to his imagination. See William Moritz's fine appreciation of Fischinger's lifetime achievement (Moritz 1974: 37–188).

5 'Temporal numerosity' is the name given to the perception of the number of events per time unit accomplished 'without counting' (Spender and Shuter-Dyson 1980: 405). See 'Rhythm, Temporality, Tempo', II, 3, section 4: 403–10 within the New Grove article 'Psychology of Music' for a relatively recent overview of the perception of tempo.

6 See Souriau (1949) for a fascinating dissertation on 'intrinsic time'.

7 Diegesis: a narrative. 'Diegetic sound: Any voice, musical passage, or sound effect presented as originating from a source within the film's world.' 'Non-diegetic sound: Sound, such as mood music or a narrator's voice, represented as being from a source outside the space of the narrative' (Bordwell and Thompson 1979: 409, 411).

REFERENCES

BORDWELL, D. and THOMPSON, K. (1979) *Film Art: An Introduction*, 3rd edn 1990, New York: McGraw-Hill.

BURCH, N. (1973) *Theory of Film Practice*, London: Secker & Warburg.

DICKINSON, T. (1971) *A Discovery of Cinema*, London: Oxford University Press.

EISENSTEIN, S. (1943) *The Film Sense*, ed. and trans. J. Leyda, 2nd edn 1948, London: Faber & Faber.

——(1951) *Film Form*, ed. and trans. J. Leyda, London: Dobson.

EISLER, H. (1947) *Composing for the Films*, British edn 1951, London: Dobson.

HOOD, M. (1951) 'Color music: a new art form', *New Outlook* 2: 52–4; 3: 54–6.

LANGER, S.K. (1957) *Philosophy in a New Key*, Cambridge, Mass.: Harvard University Press.

MILANO, P. (1941) 'Music in the film: notes for a morphology', *Journal of Aesthetics and Art Criticism* 1 (1): 89–94.

MORITZ, W. (1974) 'Brief critical appreciation of the achievement of Oskar Fischinger', *Film Culture* 58–59–60: 37–188.

O'KONOR, L. (1971) *Viking Eggeling 1880–1925, Artist and Film-Maker: Life and Work*, Stockholm: Acta Universitatis Stockholmiensis.

POPPER, F. (1968) *Origins and Development of Kinetic Art*, trans. S. Bann, London: Studio Vista.

POTTER, R.K. (1954) 'Abstract films', *Films in Review* 5 (2): 82–9.

ROTHENBURG, D. (1975) 'Visual music – a new art form', in J. Grayson (ed.) *Sound Sculpture*, Vancouver: A.R.C. Publications.

SOURIAU, E. (1949) 'Time in the plastic arts', *Journal of Aesthetics and Art Criticism* 7 (4): 294–307.

SPENDER, N. and SHUTER-DYSON, R. (1980) 'Psychology of music', in S. Sadie (ed.) *The New Grove Dictionary of Music and Musicians*, London: Macmillan.

SPOTTISWOODE, R. (1935) *A Grammar of the Film: An Analysis of Film Technique*, London: Faber & Faber.

D'UDINE, J. (1910) *L'Art et le geste*, Paris: Alcan.

WEILAND, F.C. (1971) 'Relations between sound and image', *Electronic Music Reports* 4: 66–91.

WHITNEY, J. (1980) *Digital Harmony: On the Complementarity of Music and Visual Art*, Peterborough, NH: McGraw-Hill.

FURTHER READING

CURTIS, D. (1971) *Experimental Cinema*, London: Studio Vista.

CURTIS, D. and FRANCIS, R. (eds) (1979) *Formal Experiment in Film 1910–1975*, London: Arts Council of Great Britain.

KERSHAW, D. (1983) 'Tape music with absolute animated film: prehistory and development', unpublished D.Phil. thesis, University of York.

LAWDER, S.D. (1975) *Cubist Cinema*, New York: New York University Press.

LE GRICE, M. (1977) *Abstract Film and Beyond*, London: Studio Vista.

RICHTER, H. (1971) *Hans Richter on Hans Richter*, London: Thames & Hudson.

RINGBOM, S. (1970) *The Sounding Cosmos: A Study in the Spiritualism and the Genesis of Abstract Painting*, Abo: Abo Akademi.

SITNEY, P.A. (1974) *Visionary Film*, 2nd edn 1979, Oxford: Oxford University Press.

25

New Musical Instruments
in the Computer Age:
Amplified Performance Systems and
Related Examples of Low-level Technology

HUGH DAVIES

There is a very natural tendency to view recent history from today's viewpoint rather than in its true chronology. Where technology is concerned, it is clear that each successive stage of its creative application has been almost entirely dependent on scientific and technological advances, although there are a few instances where an artist has been 'ahead of his time' by using more primitive resources to achieve with difficulty something that subsequent developments made much more straightforward. A brief historical outline of the relationship between music and electrical technology is thus helpful in establishing the background for this chapter (see also Davies 1984).

During the second half of the nineteenth century the application of electricity and electromagnetism to all areas of communications and sound grew very rapidly. Initially the technology was primarily digital, but changed to being primarily analogue, especially as a result of the two most significant inventions in the field (both of which occured in the mid-1870s) – the phonograph and the telephone. A century later, in our own time, it became necessary for the cycle of alternation between digital and analogue to continue with a change from analogue electronics back to a more soph-isticated digital form. It is likely that at some time in the not-too-distant future a new super-analogue will, in turn, become essential for opening up new areas for further development – or else our present forms of digital will be expanded to incorporate analogue on equal terms.

The first serious applications of electricity to the production of musical sounds date from around the 1880s; they involved early forms of electric piano that used special microphones, which we would now call contact microphones. These electroacoustic instruments were followed during the 1890s by the earliest instruments to produce sounds electro-mechanically (based on technology first devised some fifty years earlier), in which the varying electrical voltages created in an electromagnet by the rotation of a nearby toothed or profiled disc or cylinder were used to activate a loudspeaker. Such instruments (including the Telharmonium and parts of the contemporaneous Choralcelo, both of which took around a decade to plan and construct) were enormous, and required one or more rooms of machinery that must have resembled small power stations. Only thirty years later, in the original Hammond organ, similar mechanisms were completely contained inside the instrument's console.

It is the third category of sound generation that has become of greatest significance: to distinguish it from the others it might be called 'fully' electronic. It did not come into being until around 1920, since it depended on the invention of the electronic valve (1904–6) and its commercial pro-duction during the First World War. The valve also formed the basis of the electronic amplifier, which – together with appropriate loudspeakers – was perfected in the mid-1920s, immediately becoming an essential feature of all instruments that were based on electrically or electronically generated sounds, as well as of all electrical sound recording and broadcasting equipment.

At this juncture it is important to establish the precise meaning of the terminology used so far. I differ from some of my colleagues who refer to all music reproduced over loudspeakers as 'electroacoustic'; for a variety of reasons I prefer the term 'electronic'. Typically, neither is completely accurate. The three types of instruments can be defined in the following way (Davies 1988):

electroacoustic	instruments whose sound sources are derived from vibrating objects, equivalent to acoustic instruments, but influencing an electrical circuit by means of special transducers (microphones) and often (deliberately) pro-ducing a minimum of acoustic sound.

electromechanical instruments whose sounds result from a rotating mechanism (that produces no acoustic sound) influencing an
electrical circuit.

electronic instruments whose sounds are created by an electrical
circuit that consists of electronic components and has
no moving parts.

The two latter categories require a power supply and can be called 'active'
circuits, the former does not and is 'passive'. Further variants of terminology
include in particular the more commercial and everyday replacement of the
term 'electroacoustic' by 'electric' (as in electric guitars and pianos). When
classifying the instruments in this way, those in the first category must be
seen from the viewpoint of the associated electrical circuitry (which is
an integral part), whereby the vibration of the sounding object and the
microphone together form an electrical sound generator, while in other
contexts they are compared with existing acoustic instruments and principles
of sound generation, especially in terms of their physical construction.

Thus the whole field is described by different people in terms of either
'electroacoustic' or 'electronic', extrapolating from one or the other extreme.
Since this overall term is applied not only to musical instruments but also
to taped and live 'electronic' music, it might seem that too rigorous an
adherence to the classification of the instruments (which is the subject of a
major research project by the author) is of little relevance to the newer field
of experimental music. But sound recording and reproducing equipment is
included in the same classification system: gramophones are electroacoustic,
tape recorders, CD players and computer disk drives are electro-mechanical,
and computer memory (whether permanent or temporary) is electronic.

Today's partial separation of the two areas of electronically generated
sound – electronic instruments and electronic music – came about largely
because of the hiatus that the Second World War caused in artistic life;
wartime reduces artistic activity while intensifying technological progress.
During the 1930s, 'electronic music' (and equivalent terms) described the
exploration of the possibilities of new electronic and electrical instruments,
and (more rarely) the composition of music for them. Post-war electronic
music had as its medium the tape recorder, which was perfected in the late
1940s as a result of wartime improvements and became for the first time a
tool of reliable quality that composers discovered to have creative possibilities. It also matched the preoccupations of many of the more advanced
young composers and indeed enabled them to pursue ideas that had resulted,

in Germany and elsewhere, from a concentration on rigorous serial techniques distilled from a study of Webern's music, and in France as an extension of the atmospheric creations of radio drama. Indeed, had the tape recorder not become available at that precise time, it is likely that the earliest post-war electronic music would have involved live electronic techniques.

Electronic instruments continued to be developed, primarily in a commercial context, and only a few such instruments found their way into early electronic music studios as specialized sound sources. The two areas remained basically separate until, in the mid-1960s, the first synthesizers were designed specifically for use in electronic music studios. Only several years later did they start to be more widely seen as live performance instruments, opening up new possibilities in rock music and becoming of less interest for serious composers. Digital technology has now introduced a greater rapprochement once again, enabling compact composition systems (equivalent to a complete electronic music studio) to be produced, first of all in the form of the top-of-the-range computer-synthesizers like the Synclavier and Fairlight and, more recently, in the use of personal computers (especially the Apple Macintosh and Atari ST) to control and co-ordinate a variety of commercial synthesizers and samplers. The functioning of the multi-track tape recorder is increasingly being mimicked in the software of such systems.

All this has not entirely replaced one of the two remaining original areas of sound generation, that of electroacoustic (or electric) instruments. Contact microphones (especially in the more sensitive form based on piezoelectric ceramic crystals, first introduced around 1930) have continued to be used today in electric pianos and some types of electric organ, together with electromagnetic microphones, such as are best known in the electric guitar. It may at first seem surprising that in our era of digital synthesis there are increasing commercial applications for such analogue devices; their role is to convert into varying electrical voltages (and then into MIDI signals) the vibrating sound sources of those types of synthesizer controllers that call upon the techniques of traditional wind, string and percussion instruments. By the end of the 1980s successful MIDI controllers had been developed that were based on all such instruments: beginning with drums, somewhat later guitars, then wind, bowed strings, keyed percussion and finally pianos.

Thus, in the computer age, there is still considerable need for specialized transducers, which may or may not be actual microphones. New materials are being developed for a variety of non-musical purposes that could also be applied to musical instruments, especially involving the piezoelectric effect of pressure-sensitive devices; the first piezoelectric cables have recently been devised, so that in the future it should no longer be essential for the transducer to consist of a fragile object. There is thus still an interesting future for amplified instruments; just as 'mechanical' instruments (all the traditional ones) are not rejected by computer music specialists, so electroacoustic ones (new versions of traditional instruments as well as newly invented ones) are likely to have a significant role to play in the future development of today's various musics. And as synthesizers are increasingly being designed with greater flexibility in tuning subdivisions (including the possibility of microtonal scales with more than twelve divisions of the octave), it seems likely that more experimental MIDI controllers will also be devised.

The use of advanced computer-based equipment is, of course, no guarantee of musical quality or sophistication. As recently as the mid-1980s, some thirty years after the first computer music was composed, I heard two works, created with the latest technology, which reminded me of nothing so much as an early computer-generated tape piece and the simplest of live electronic transformation techniques, both from twenty years earlier. Some computer music specialists seem to view low-level electrical technology as quaint and folkloric, yet do not reject the more old-fashioned established conventional instruments; furthermore, there is a tendency to judge everything from a technological viewpoint, without applying basic musical criteria to computer music itself.

Since the Second World War, with roots in different areas of more experimental composition from earlier decades of the twentieth century, various approaches have been adopted that enable the composer to escape from the limitations of traditional instruments and notation. Those that concern us here are in the fields of timbre (including 'noise'), tuning and variable pitches, as well as the spatial movement and positioning of sounds. These avenues have been explored by many composers who have sought to expand the capabilities of existing instruments by such means as preparations (in the sense of John Cage's prepared piano) and multiphonics, or, more radically, in the creation of tape music in the studio, in the performance of live electronic music, in computer music (produced both live and in the studio) and in the use of specially constructed instruments and found objects. All of these permit a wider range of timbre, divergences from tempered tuning (not necessarily cast in alternative tuning systems) and pitch inflection possibilities (from portamenti to small pitch-bends and glissandi, as favoured by Percy Grainger in his more experimental mood). Such emphasis on an individual sound world is not of itself a guarantee of musical quality, but at the very least it provides an antidote to the current trend of undifferentiated rhythmic monotony and melodic repetition which dominate both 'minimal' music and much rock music. Rich and complex timbres, unusual tunings and pitch inflections (as in the pan-pipe music of Eastern Europe) tend to catch my ear among the vast blanket of all kinds of music that is available at the touch of a button to today's listener at home.

Timbre has taken on an unusually important role in much of this music, especially since the 1960s. This is because, for the first time in musical history, we are offered sounds that have fundamentally different characteristics from those that been the basis of all previous music. What our ears are used to are sounds that contain many types of imperfection on a microscopic (or perhaps microsonic) level. No performer (especially of a non-keyboard acoustic instrument) can guarantee to play a sequence of notes constant in loudness, timbre, vibrato rate and (except with keyboards) pitch. When two or more players play in unison they are to some degree out of tune with each other, there are clashes and beats between the pitches, vibrato rates, attacks and so on. On an even more microscopic level the frequencies of the pitches they play will be out of phase with each other. These elements, minute as they are, make up the interest in the quality of the sound of traditional instruments. For example, a solo violin, even playing quietly in its middle or low register, can cut through the much louder and higher 'unison' notes of the massed orchestral violins because its sound is clean and not 'blurred'.

Electronic sounds, by comparison, are always precise and regular in all their attributes, and considerable effort is necessary to modify this effect to match the qualities of acoustic instruments – as in the design of electronic organs for churches, where every idiosyncrasy produced by pumping wind through pipes (such as the attack 'envelope' and the variable length of time that different pipes take to 'speak') is mimicked by special circuitry. In analogue and digital tape music there are, of course, methods of creating more complex electronic sounds that, by avoiding the qualities of traditional instruments and music, can produce new and vital sound qualities. None the less, even with the most advanced techniques, works continue to be composed in which the impoverishment of the electronic sounds is only too evident, and the listener's ear tires more quickly. One can only assume that such composers are overly concerned with pitch relationships at the expense of timbre.

The inventors of new acoustic and electroacoustic instruments have, on the whole, shown a greater than average concern with timbre (Panhuysen 1987). Indeed their approach can be compared with that of a composer who works with 'concrete' rather than electronic sounds. In both cases the first stage is identical – searching for sound sources that can form the basis of the final sound material; these are then either expanded to form an instrument or processed further in the studio. Many of these inventors have, consciously or unconsciously, sought to achieve richer timbral qualities than are available in our orchestral instruments. Such conventional instruments have undergone several centuries of development and improvement, such as in terms of greater control and flexibility, wider pitch range, louder sound capability, greater ability to project the sound in larger halls, and better blending with other instruments. But the question never seems to be posed: have all these gains been at the expense of anything – such as timbre?

Rich as conventional instruments may sound, alone or especially in combination, their timbre in the course of their development has become blander. Compare the basic timbre of the piano with that of the harpsichord, or, even closer, with that of a fortepiano. Robert Cogan, in *New Images of Musical Sound* (1984), shows highly detailed spectrograms, produced by newly developed equipment, of a wide range of pieces of music, including a movement from a Beethoven piano sonata played on both a twentieth century piano and a fortepiano from around 1820, which Beethoven himself originally owned. Although the latter produces a softer sound, its spectrum includes a whole octave at the top of the register and nearly as much at the bottom that is totally lacking on the piano.

The fact that instrument builders are normally classed as craftspeople rather than artists is in part irrelevant, since the invention and design of a completely new instrument certainly comes more into the domain of the artist. Furthermore, the inventors are normally also composers as well as their own interpreters, thus combining in a single person the roles of creator, interpreter and craftsperson. The visual aspects of such new instruments are also significant, and some musicians have explored this sufficiently to have created instruments, sound sculptures and sound installations for exhibition spaces or open air sites. Some of these new instruments (not only amplified ones) visibly relate to existing instruments or principles, others do not, although ultimately they can all be classified according to the standard categories.

Visual, sometimes also theatrical, elements are often called into play in the performance technique required for a new instrument, and are implicit in its construction. It may require the performer to stand, sit on the floor or walk around while playing. The size of the instrument may be unusually large or small, and the implements that are used to excite the sound objects on it may also be unconventional – specially made or selected percussion sticks of various sizes and materials, feathers and needle files (as bows), and natural elements such as sun, wind, rain and ice (Leif Brush's very highly amplified outdoor Terrain instruments), and a gas flame (Richard Lerman).

The activity of many of the inventors of new instruments who work regularly with amplified sounds arose from an involvement in working in the electronic music studio, and, sometimes, in live electronics. Here the sounds of conventional instruments, other objects (producing both 'sounds' and 'noises') and, occasionally, electronic oscillators or environmental sounds are electronically treated in real time by means of devices such as filters, ring-modulators, reverberation units, 'chopping', tape delays and potentiometers (for loudness control). In my own case these methods were particularly explored in the group *Gentle Fire* (1968–75), in which the music was heard over two or four loudspeaker channels. A similar interest in the control and distribution of sounds in the concert space has also been reflected in many of my invented concert instruments; some of the earliest (going back to 1968) are stereophonic, and since 1980 several have been quadraphonic (with a single exception built as early as 1969).

The decision to become an instrument inventor, however unconsciously arrived at, is one that depends on several factors. These include preferences for live performance involving the kind of sounds otherwise created in the studio, as well as for acoustic, albeit amplified sounds over electronically generated ones, however intricate their treatment. Individuality of timbre is always important, and this often implies an adherence to older technology. Such a 'low-tech' approach could in many cases (as least as far as the actual hardware is concerned) have been employed fifty or even a hundred years ago – but wasn't. Amplified instruments can also explore different sound qualities equivalent to those used in live electronics, such as effects that resemble modulation, from the interaction of the vibrations of two adjacent sounding objects, and reverberation, by careful positioning of two or more microphones. Filtering can be approximated by placing several microphones (sometimes ones with different frequency response characteristics) in different positions, individually selectable and mixable, as well as by interposing materials with different absorption qualities between the vibrating object and the microphone, or, as with the 'instrumental loudspeakers' of David Tudor, by inserting such materials between a small loudspeaker and a microphone, both of which are fitted inside a container.

Typically, as in my own case, such an involvement does not necessarily exclude occasional compositional use of complexly generated or processed electronic sounds (including computer music), motivated by an interest in exploring less obvious possibilities of the equipment concerned, sometimes

507

unforeseen even by its designers. This enables me to bring the perspectives of my work as a builder of new electroacoustic instruments to bear on the electronic music studio; indeed this approach can also be seen in my works for traditional acoustic instruments.

In order to design a live performance of computer music that is visually convincing, the composer-performer also needs to design an 'instrument', which will in fact be a specialized synthesizer controller, in the manner of the existing commercial types of MIDI controllers listed above. A few of these did, indeed, start out as inventions by practising musicians, such as Nyle Steiner's trumpet-like Electronic Valve Instrument, recently revamped as the Akai EVI synthesizer controller (together with its new sibling, the saxophone-like EWI), and the Grid, a MIDIfied version of Emmett Chapman's electric-guitar-like Stick. Several of these controllers were originally marketed by their inventors in the mid-1970s on a small scale; Chapman's is still available.

Controllers developed in the mid-1980s include several string and wind instruments, newly invented or adapted; but the most original of all, Michel Waisvisz's Hands, is more unusual and extremely ergonomic. As shown in Figure 25.1, two plates containing various types of switches and variable controls are strapped around the performer's hands; they function like parts of the control panel of a synthesizer, sending streams of MIDI information to several digital synthesizers and/or samplers under computer control. The performer is free to make any arm or body movements and to walk around the stage (with the sole limitation of an umbilical multicore cable). Waisvisz's system and the resulting music, carefully tailored to suit each other, have achieved the first great successes of live computer music, perhaps of computer music generally. The Hands system was developed at a unique centre in Amsterdam, STEIM, where several other specialized MIDI controllers have been produced for individual composers, including ones for the Americans Ron Kuivila and Nicholas Collins (whose earlier modified trombone controller is highly ingenious). Such successful combinations of different stages of technology augur well for the future.

The main area under consideration in this essay is, however, one in which the sound sources are not electronic. The 'classic' early composition that falls into both the live electronic and amplified instrument (or, in this case, object) categories is John Cage's *Cartridge Music* (1960), in which various small objects are amplified by means either of contact microphones or of old gramophone record cartridges. The latter, first used by Cage in 1939, have holes for the insertion of a stylus – or preferably larger, for a needle, which is held in place by an adjustable screw – and usually contain similar

Figure 25.1   Michel Waisvisz's instrument 'The Hands'

piezoelectric crystal units. Another early classic work in the field is Karlheinz Stockhausen's *Mikrophonie I* (1964). This is a live electronic work which, in its use of hand-held microphones moved around in front of the surface of a giant tam-tam that is excited by a great variety of unusual implements, does not quite qualify in the context of invented or modified electroacoustic instruments with built-in microphones; but, certainly in the case of my own early work, it provided a direct inspiration in that direction.

509

Of the composers who came to prominence in the 1950s it is Mauricio Kagel who has been most involved as an instrument inventor. Few of his instruments involve built-in amplification, but the *Rahmenharfe* (= frame harp), built for his composition *Unter Strom* (1969), exemplifies one of the visual aspects mentioned above, in being very large, measuring 6 by 1.5 metres. Another composition from the late 1960s for which its composer created a substantial instrumentarium is Annea (formerly Anna) Lockwood's *Glass Concert* (1967–8; retitled *Glass World* for its issue on gramophone record), which includes the amplification by means of air and contact microphones of small pieces of glass in various forms. Amplified instruments and objects were also a feature of the work of two European improvisation groups of the period, AMM and Musica Elettronica Viva. The latter included Frederic Rzewski's photoelectrically controlled manual system for distributing sounds over four loudspeakers; similar devices also devised by composers were Lowell Cross's 'Stirrer' and Stockhausen's 'Rotation Mill'.

In 1967 I began to construct both amplified instruments and simple electrical devices for processing live sounds, the latter primarily for use in the group *Gentle Fire*. These were extremely simple, avoiding electronic circuitry; for example, sounds were 'chopped' simply by inserting an old-fashioned 'wind-up' telephone dial into the amplification chain, using two terminals leading to the switch that is operated when the wound-up dial is released, interrupting the continuity as many times as the number shown on the dial; some noise is added as an attack each time the contact is restored, and a small capacitor connected between the signal and earth leads filtered this to the desired amount. Some electronic qualities were obtained by producing difference tones and by acoustic feedback (howlround). For performances on my earliest electric instruments I started out using a set of pedals which provided a filter, ring-modulator (with built-in oscillator), phase shifter, fuzz distortion and loudness controls; before long I replaced the wider range of sounds that they provided with newer invented instruments. An interest in earlier electrical technology has also led me to devise a sound installation of an imaginary electronic music studio from the 1930s (if anyone had thought of such a thing at the time), using technology equivalent to what existed then, and music theatre compositions that, on one level, are live performances of a silent film and of a 78 r.p.m. gramophone record.

Among amplified instruments there is a wide panorama between totally new inventions and those that, like the electric guitar, are basically an amplified version of an existing instrument and require only a slight modification of performance technique. The Chapman Stick explores guitar technique further, as do the instruments built by Fred Frith, Ivor Darreg's Megalyra family and Glenn Branca's harmonics guitar. In the case of the Stick, on the neck there are two parallel sets of strings, treble (left hand) and bass (right hand), which are activated not by being struck at the lower end of the instrument but by the fingers 'hammering' onto the strings in the appropriate fret positions. Other new amplified string instruments are more radical. Max Eastley's Bow (his principal instrument in concert performances) is a large monochord some two metres in length which is bowed, plucked and struck. An electronic oscillator 'drives' the string in Peter Appleton's Blue Drone, which also has a lever for altering the string's tension. In Hans-Karsten Raecke's Blas-Metall-Dosen-Harfe a saxophone mouthpiece and tubing with several finger-holes is combined with a plethora of amplified plucked strings.

Specific techniques restricted to a single instrument matter least of all with percussion instruments, since a player with a pair of sticks can play on any object that makes a sound; with amplified instruments, fingers are a viable alternative. Tom Nunn's percussion boards, including the Earwarg and Mothra, feature a variety of different metal objects attached to a flat table-like surface, as do, in miniature, my own two Shozygs. Some of the instruments built by the Sonde group, which include various percussion elements, are multi-person instruments, a recent phenomenon more often found in new acoustic instruments. Chris Brown's Gazamba is a nearly totally rebuilt Wurlitzer electric piano, with the keyboard controlling the activation of a selection of sounding objects that combine the timbres of the prepared piano with those of a gamelan.

More unusual playing methods are used for Mario Bertoncini's various Aeolian harps (the largest of which is 7 metres high) and 'gongs', which are blown on by means of hand-held jets of compressed air. Among other performance techniques, the strings of Dieter Trüstedt's Ch'in family of instruments are blown by the performer's breath. My own Concert Aeolian harp (see Figure 25.2) is also, in addition to other techniques, mouth-blown, sometimes directly and sometimes through tubing of various diameters. Instead of strings stretched inside a frame I use fretsaw blades that are clamped more or less centrally, giving two unequal lengths and thus pitches; in a quadraphonic version these are mounted in two long parallel rows, with a contact microphone at the ends of each row. Even further removed from traditional techniques are those systems in which the sound is controlled from a distance, such as in Godfried-Willem Raes's *Holosound*, in which physical movement within a circle drawn on the stage controls electronic

Figure 25.2   The Concert Aeolian harp, designed by Hugh Davies

sounds, and Gordon Monahan's spatial distribution of taped sounds in *Speaker Swinging*.

My own most frequently used sound source is the coiled steel spring in all its forms, fifty of which (all different) were collected for the quadraphonic My Spring Collection, and several identical springs are stretched like strings in the family of a dozen Springboards (see Davies 1981). Here there was a development from an electric-guitar-like parallel layout in the earliest models to a fan-shaped arrangement in which all the springs (fourteen in one model) meet at a single point, through which the vibrations of any spring are – unless manually damped – passed on to all the others, providing a limited form of built-in variable reverberation.

Some of the most unusual 'instruments' and performance methods are found in the very different installations, based on highly amplified sounds of the human body, of Jeanette Yanikian (*Aorta*) and of Stelarc, and in the amplified costumes of Laurie Anderson and Harry de Wit. In the work of Richard Lerman, piezoelectric pick-ups are attached to flexible, often suspended, materials such as thin sheets and strips of metal, including aluminium foil, copper and wire gauze, plastic and paper, such as rice paper and banknotes. His work is divided between installations and performances, which of their nature have a prominent visual and theatrical element. One of the most unusual of these involves using the flame from a small hand-held gas jet to heat up thin metal sheets, causing them to bend and flex.

In the present context the use of special microphones or other transducers built into new instruments has been isolated from the even larger area of newly invented acoustic instruments (and related sound installations and sound sculptures) to which it is otherwise indissolubly linked. As with live electronics, these instruments have enabled many musicians (including, a point not further explained here, visual artists and a few architects, poets and physicists) to find their way into performing in concerts that in most cases would otherwise not have been available to them. Ultimately the greatest attraction of performing one's own specially designed musical instruments (whether amplified or acoustic) or synthesizer controller is the wide range of unusual and rich sound qualities that are potentially available, selected personally rather than for commercial reasons. This has all the advantages of tape music, in that the composer has full control at every stage in the production of the music, in addition to the excitement and tension of performing in front of an audience; and it is not only the composer-performers but also the audience who benefit from this and appreciate the reintroduction of the performer into electronic music.

REFERENCES

COGAN, R. (1984) *New Images of Musical Sound*, Cambridge, Mass., and London: Harvard University Press.

DAVIES, H. (1981) 'Making and peforming simple electroacoustic instruments', in R. Orton (ed.) *Electronic Music for Schools*, Cambridge: Cambridge University Press.

——(1984) 'Electronic instruments', in S. Sadie (ed.) *The New Grove Dictionary of Musical Instruments*, London: Macmillan.

——(1988) 'Elektronische instrumenten: classificatie en mechanismen', in exhibition catalogue *Elektrische Muziek*, The Hague: Haags Gemeentemuseum.

EXPERIMENTAL MUSICAL INSTRUMENTS (since 1985). Many articles in this journal will be of interest.

PANHUYSEN, P. (ed.) (1987) *Echo: The Images of Sound*, Eindhoven: Appollohuis; incl. H. Davies, 'A survey of new instruments and sound sculpture'.

26

The Listening Imagination: Listening in the Electroacoustic Era

DENIS SMALLEY

The extensive range of sound sources admitted into music via the electroacoustic medium has initiated a revolution in the sounding content of musical works, appealing to a variety of listening responses not fully encompassed in previously existing musics.

Potential sound materials extend over a far-flung territory. In one category we find sounds snatched, borrowed, captured by microphone from nature or from culture, sounds that prior to their capture had no musical purpose; in a second category are those sounds specially created for musical use: instrumental and sung sounds. In a third category are those electroacoustic sounds (whether they are synthesized or heavily transformed natural sources matters little) seemingly remote or divorced from the familiar sounds of voices, instruments, nature or the identifiable sounds of our culture. Moreover, whatever 'instrument', device or agent has brought these sounds to life may be both invisible and unknown to the listener. Therefore, at one extreme of the sound-field are sounds whose source can be identified, but at the other are sounds whose source the listener may well not be able to deduce.

The apprehension and contemplation of invisible sources may take place alone in the privacy of the home or collectively in a public place. In a public space there could be performers among the loudspeakers (sources visible and invisible), and the performers' actions might seem to have little correlation with the articulation of the sounds. Thus sources can equivocally be visible yet invisible.

Such are our possible encounters with this acousmatic medium where the provenance of the materials is screened from our gaze.[1] It is my purpose in this chapter to uncover the listening strategies involved in responding to electroacoustic music, implying that the electroacoustic medium, far from being a mere extension of vocal and instrumental resources, needs rather to be celebrated, emphasized, and developed for its originality and imaginative revelations of human experience.

WAYS OF LISTENING

Hearing and Listening

Music listening at its most intense is quite different from everyday listening. In English the verbs 'hear' and 'listen' identify two common modes distinguished by *intention*. To 'hear' implies an involuntary act, that a sound penetrates consciousness, almost that one cannot help hearing, whereas to 'listen' signifies an intention on the part of the listener who consciously apprehends a sound. If we talk about 'listening' to music we describe an intentional act, but if we talk about 'hearing' music we mean that the music exists outside any act of intention to listen on our part. Thus we can hear a piece of music and as a result decide to listen to it, and we can apply this transformation in listening attitude to any sound if we are so inclined. This process involves a change in *focus* and *attention*. 'Hear' and 'listen' cover the basics of listening but need considerable amplification in order to be comprehensive. We need to know, for example, what we are listening to, what we are listening out for, and why we are listening.

The Schaefferian Listening Modes

Pierre Schaeffer, in delineating the listening process (Schaeffer 1966), identified four modes. The first mode is an *information-gathering* one where we are occupied with the provenance of the sound and the 'message' it carries: our attention focuses on the occurrence or event attached to the sound. For example, in hearing a car coming along the street or someone coming up the stairs we are interested not in the sound itself but the information it conveys – perhaps that the car is travelling too fast or that the person

515

coming up the stairs is trying not to be heard; we wonder what the consequences of travelling too fast might be, who is coming up the stairs, and the motive behind their stealth; in the case of the car we are an outside observer; in the case of the person on the stairs we are likely to be directly involved in the consequences. We interpret these messages from the spectro-morphology of the sound,[2] based on our accumulated knowledge of people, occurrences, environment, and the sounds associated with these experiences. In mode one, sounds are an index to a network of associations and experiences; we are concerned with causality; it is a question of living and acting in the world, ultimately of survival.

The second mode identified by Schaeffer emphasizes *passive reception*, where the listener cannot help hearing a sound: there is no intention to listen. Because of the sound's impact or suddenness, its unusual features, or for contextual reasons, the listener cannot blot it out: the intrusion of a ghetto-blaster, an explosion, a symphonic chord which calls the listener to attention, a cry. This listening category is less satisfactory as a separate mode and is certainly not self-contained. The examples of the car or footsteps described above are apprehended passively in mode two but initiate active thought processes which accompany the closer probing of the sound and its messages by the listener. The main difference between modes one and two is that while mode two concentrates on subjective impact (my reaction to the sound), mode one concentrates on the object of my attentions (the occurrences outside me). Mode one therefore centres on the object, on the source of the sound, and in this sense is called by Schaeffer *objective*. Mode two, being at least initially centred on me, the subject, in an analogous sense can be considered *subjective*.

Modes three and four are concerned with music listening, more specifically with the processes of *responding to a musical language* as opposed to the sounds of everyday life. In mode four we find musical works, which are purposely created for listening. They can loosely be regarded as specially selected sounds encoded in a structure that has a sense and meaning for those listeners who share the code (though we may be very hard pressed to say what that sense or meaning might be). What the listener responds to is the musical sign[3] as opposed to the index of mode one. As with mode one the focus is on the object of perception, in this case the musical work.

Mode three represents the intentional process of *appreciating and responding to attributes of sounds* ignoring any mode one messages they might contain. It is a selective process where some sounds are preferred at the expense of others. These preferences are based on certain spectro-morphological criteria which appear to the listener to be more attractive, interesting or significant than others. For the composer this listening process could ultimately lead to pertinent values being abstracted,[4] providing the first steps in the construction of a musical code which might result in a mode four work.

If we take the car sound mentioned in discussing mode one and consider it in all four modes, the contrasts in listening attitudes can be highlighted. In mode two the speeding car impinges on our consciousness. In mode one we wonder what will happen given that it is a busy street; we might recognize the type of car, and so on. If we then ignore the context of events and consider only the sound, for example its dynamic shape, the intonation of acceleration, the changes in the timbre and grain of the sound, then our listening focus and attention intentionally shift to a selective perusal (and enjoyment) of attributes in mode three. If these observations were to instigate both a wider and closer examination of criteria we might be able to create a network of signs and meanings from which a mode four musical work results. This hypothetical work may not attain the state of abstraction implied in mode four: it could be open to multi-modal listening responses. If the actual sounds of cars were retained and composed into a car-scape one can imagine that mode one would remain dominant for most listeners: it would take a listener practised in shutting off mode one responses to escape such a *response weighting*. If, on the other hand, our new-found criteria instigated an instrumental work, any mode one links might be more ambivalent, elliptical, or even absent altogether, at least to the conscious ear. Being an instrumental composition it would introduce a quite different network of listening attitudes, those associated with instrumental gesture.

None of the modes, therefore, is exclusive. One can imagine varieties of modal shading and shifts during the listening process even in a work thought to be 'abstract'. Our music listening mixes all four modes, crossing between them in differing doses depending on our attention and focus, and on our competence and experience as listeners.

I have freely elaborated Schaeffer's modes because they represent a serious and useful attempt to understand the listening process as a whole. Faced with the influx of new sounds, Schaeffer was preoccupied with establishing criteria for building a new musical 'language'. His modes implied how this might be accomplished, principally by abstracting values observed in mode three. Most important for this discussion is the contrast between modes one and three which epitomizes polarized listening practices important to electroacoustic music. Mode one takes the listener outwards from the sound itself, reaching out into wider relationships with the objects, events and experiences beyond. Mode three draws the listener into the sound itself, into a contemplation of its sounding shape. The crux of the mode one–three relationship is the continuum between reaching outwards and being drawn inwards.

Autocentricity and Allocentricity

Ernest Schachtel[5] diagnosed the relationship between subject-centred and object-centred perceptual activity in ways which complement Schaeffer's modes.

The *autocentric* or subject-centred senses focus on basic responses and feelings of pleasure and displeasure. The emphasis is on subjective reaction to something. Taste and smell, the thermal sense, proprioceptive perception (tension and relaxation of muscles, joints, etc.) are clearly autocentric. For example, reactions to the taste of food, to perfume, enjoyment of a hot bath, or the rewards of stretching on getting out of bed do not normally require interaction with and examination of an object of perception. Autocentric perception is primitive and basic and it is no coincidence that it is associated with the child's first relationships with the world.

The *allocentric* perceptual mode is object-centred in that it involves perceiving something independent of the perceiver's needs. The relationship between the qualities we perceive and any feelings of pleasure or displeasure we may have is less direct or less pronounced. Indeed, pleasure or displeasure in the manner of autocentric reaction may even be irrelevant. It is a process of active and selective focusing on an object, being able to discern distinguishing features in a non-partisan way. Visual and aural perception are capable of achieving the highest degrees of allocentricity. No wonder, then, that these two senses form the basis of art forms.

Autocentric attitudes to music and sound are common. At its most primal, musical autocentricity is concerned with positive/negative emotional reaction to sounds. Indeed listeners often actively seek to use music specifically to induce well-being or change a mood from negative to positive. This element of utilitarianism, where music is considered a thing to be used, often forms part of the autocentric attitude as is the case with Muzak, where music is purposely harnessed to induce a mood or attitude for commercial gain. A universal autocentric attitude occurs in reacting negatively to an unwanted sound which undesirably disrupts one's mental state.

Allocentric attitudes to sounds encompass the apprehension of musical structure (Schaeffer's mode four), and our appreciation of sounds outside musical contexts in the manner of Schaeffer's mode three. The allocentric mode is a direct encounter with sounds, an affirmative interest separated, at least temporarily, from any desire to turn the object of perception into a need-satisfying tool. Such a listening strategy is one of openness to discovery developed through interactive 'play', with no particular purpose in mind and no primary goal of basic gratification.

Autocentricity and allocentricity exist in parallel. While the autocentric examples above give the listener little option as to attitude, there are many situations where the balance may be tipped either way depending on the individual and the context. Such circumstances commonly involve a response focusing on emotions associated with the object of perception rather than adopting the option of a more allocentric investigation. In other words, the qualities of the object of perception could be perceived and appreciated in an allocentric manner by one listener, while another type of listener will leap immediately to an autocentric interpretation. It is particularly significant in electroacoustic music when sounds are regarded as strange. For example, autocentric responses can be related to fear or apprehension initiated by the exaggerated magnification of the dimensions of realistic sounds (transformed Schaeffer mode one messages), the ways sounds approach the listener and are perceived as objects existing in the space, and the bombarding of sounds at high intensity. On the other hand the practised allocentric listener might find such autocentric responses rather crude and clichéd. But primarily allocentric listeners can also be quite snobbish about such responses, pushing them into the background in preference to the intellectually more respectable objective stance. Shifts between autocentric and allocentric attitudes are thus a fundamental part of the listening process.

Subject–Object Listening Relationships

I can now propose a synthesis of the Schaeffer and Schachtel modes designed to summarize the basic relationships between the listener and sounds, between the subject who is perceiving, and the objects of perception. The term 'relationships' is preferred to 'modes', as it hints at impermanence and shifts in perception. The entire sound-field must be accounted for since any sound can become part of an electroacoustic work. The following three relationship-types are retained.

The *indicative relationship* represents Schaeffer's mode one: sound as message, or information about environmental action, events, occurrences.

It is object-centred and can be either actively or passively apprehended depending on whether the sound impinges on our consciousness or whether we are actively seeking it (waiting for a signal, for example).

The *reflexive relationship* is taken from Schachtel's autocentric mode. It is subject-centred and is concerned with basic emotional responses to the object of perception. The object has no real identity separate from the subject's emotion. This type of relationship can be active or passive but has a strong tendency towards passivity since there is little or no exploration of the object of perception, only response to it.

The *interactive relationship* embraces Schaeffer's modes three and four, and Schachtel's allocentric mode. It involves an active relationship on the part of the subject in continuously exploring the qualities and structure of the object. In this sense it can be regarded as interactive. No pre-formed expectation is sought by the listener. The interactive relationship embraces structural hearing, aesthetic attitudes towards music and sounds, and Schaeffer's concept of *reduced listening*.[6] It is possible to have an interactive relationship with any sound, although naturally some sounds will be more fruitful than others.

The indicative and reflexive relationships are the most prevalent. As far as listening to music is concerned the reflexive relationship popularly dominates, and as far as Western art music is concerned there should ideally be a partnership between the reflexive and interactive. Clearly an interactive relationship is necessary for the fullest appreciation of Western art music. All three relationships are subject to perceptual shifts which are within the focal gift of the subject, although not all listeners are equally gifted.

The remainder of this chapter concentrates on elucidating the different types of indicative relationships, and the shifts and shadings among them.[7]

INDICATIVE FIELDS, INDICATIVE NETWORKS

Introduction

Indicative relationships as described above, while forming a major aspect of our use of the auditory sense, are largely regarded as a trivial and inferior attitude to sounds when it comes to considering the sounding materials of the art of music, where interactive relationships are considered psychologically more rewarding. However, if we do not confine the notion of the indicative relationship to mere messages, events and information but extend it to include a wider frame of references to experience outside and beyond music, we immediately penetrate both more extensively and deeply into the relationship between musical experience and our experiences of living. The sounding materials within a composition cannot be solely or even primarily self-referential. The apprehension of musical content and structure is linked to the world of experience outside the composition, not only to the wider context of auditory experience but also to non-sounding experience. Approached from the multiple perspectives of life outside music, the materials and structure of a musical composition become the meeting-place of sounding and non-sounding experience. Electroacoustic music, through its extensive sounding repertory drawn from the entire sound-field, reveals the richness and depth of indicative relationships more clearly and comprehensively than is possible with other musics.

The concept of the *indicative field* and the *indicative network* has been created to explain the links between human experience and the listener's apprehension of sounding materials in musical contexts. The term 'indicative' signifies that the musical manifestation of a field refers to or indicates related experiences in the non-sounding world. Nine fields are identified. Three are archetypal: gesture, utterance and behaviour. These fields are original universals. Human utterance and the consequences of gesture have traditionally provided the fundamental sounding models for music. The behaviour-field is concerned with sounding relationships in space and time, which can be considered analogous to certain modes of human relationship, observed relationships among things or objects, or human–object relations. The six remaining fields are energy, motion, object/substance, environment, vision and space. A single field is not autonomous and does not exist either inside or outside music without overlapping other fields. Gesture, for example, is inevitably linked with certain aspects of all the other fields. Whereas the term 'field' is used when referring to any one of the nine areas as a separate entity, 'network' is used to refer to a central field in its relationship with the satellite fields that form its full character. The nine fields were identified through empirical enquiry based on experiences of decision-making during the compositional process, and on assessing the reactions and interpretations of listeners to electroacoustic music in both teaching and concert contexts over a number of years. This kind of enquiry into the listening imagination does not lend itself easily to a more 'scientific'

521

investigation. The calculated prompting of a limited number of listener-subjects could easily verify the existence of some aspects of the fields, but could satisfactorily probe neither the totality and extent of less conscious aspects of the fields nor the complex interdependence of the networks. In this essay I rely on triggering the reader's dormant knowledge of listening experience.

The fields must lie within the perceptual experience of the listener, and must therefore be rooted in communal experience, however unconscious such knowledge may be. This is not to say that the musical guise of the fields will always be easily accessible to the inexperienced perceiver, since the sound language may be unfamiliar. The indicative fields cannot include compositional models based on scientific, mathematical, statistical or other theories, regardless of any universal validity. This is because these models cannot be 'understood' without explanation, and even then they may have little apparent connection with the listener's natural interpretation of sound materials. However, such models may well be spontaneously embraced within the *field-view* of, for example, a scientist-listener who has developed specialized indicative habits. Although my aim in this essay is to uncover fields which may be considered more universal, we should not forget that a variety of personal indicative shadings fan out from communal indicative bases.

The notion of the indicative field/network comprehends relationships that are considered mimetic. Mimesis[8] in music is the conscious and unconscious imitation or representation of aspects of nature and culture. However, the indicative field/network concept is not concerned with all aspects of representation as is clear from the mention of theories and models above. Furthermore, the electroacoustic medium can appropriate materials directly from the sounding world; strictly speaking this is neither imitation nor representation. The space-field poses a similar problem since its indicative significance has to take into account the relationship between the composed musical space and the actual listening space: again not simply a question of representation. Other indicative terms like 'metaphor' and 'trans-contextuality' will occur to the reader, and these are useful in considering some indicative relationships but not all. Finally, the indicative field/network can be considered as a musical branch of semiotics since quite clearly there are signifiers and signifieds at a variety of levels and orders. The tangle involved in redefining existing terms or borrowing terms from other disciplines is often unsatisfactory and is inappropriate in this case where a new term is needed to express a conceptual package that is particular to music listening.

Gesture

Traditionally musical gesture involves a human agent who, sometimes using mediatory implements, acts physically on sounding bodies by fingering, plucking, hitting, scraping and blowing. These gesture-types harness energy and motion through time: a controlled, physical motion at a varying, energetic rate results in the excitation of a sounding body and the shaping of a spectro-morphology.

Everyone has daily experience of gestural activity and is aware of the types of consequences of the *energy-motion trajectory*. Gestural activity is not only concerned with object play or object use but also enters into human relationships: it is a gesture that wields the axe and it is a gesture that expresses the intimate caress. The energy-field can vary between extremes of force and gentleness, and in the temporal domain can be very sudden of motion, or evolve more slowly. Broadly defined, human gesture is concerned with movement of the body and limbs for a wide variety of practical and expressive reasons; it is bound up with proprioceptive (kinesthetic) perception of body tensions and therefore with effort and resistance. However, the indicative field does not stop with a physical act since tension and resistance also concern emotional and psychological experiences. Thus in music there is a link between the energy-motion trajectory and the psychological apprehension of sounding contexts even when physical gesture is not present.

In instrumental and vocal music there is always real human gesture and actual human presence: the directness of the link is apparent. However, this is not so in all types of electroacoustic music. I have previously (Smalley 1986) introduced the notion of *surrogacy*[9] to demonstrate the existence of new types of sounds which are more remote from physical, gestural origins than was previously possible. Human experience of physical gesture provides the basic, pragmatic model. These sounding gesture-models can be recorded as they occurred in their original, cultural context and be incorporated in a musical work. Instrumental gesture, however, is more specialized, and is a *first order surrogate*, a stand-in for non-musical gesture, one step removed from the model. In electroacoustic music, as long as an instrumental sound-source is identifiable it remains a first order surrogate. If human gesture is detectable behind object-based sound sources, these also are first order surrogates. For example, if I intentionally scrape two objects together so that the type of gesture is apparent and the types of materials can be identified (metal, wood, etc.), that is tantamount to a first order instrumental gesture: there is musical purpose lurking behind it. (Of course in this example the object/substance-field is also invoked.) If I use a synthesized sound which, to all intents and purposes, sounds like a known instrument, then it too remains a first order surrogate because it is apprehended as if it were a real instrument. (Such is the case with most of the pre-set sounds from commercial synthesizers.) If, however, I start to create spectro-morphologies that have no apparent links with an identifiable source then I move a step beyond the instrument into *second order surrogacy*. For example, my new morphology might sound as if it were created by a hitting action, but after the initial impact its spectrum behaves in such a peculiar way that I cannot imagine what kind of material or sounding body it could be, nor what could make it behave in such a way. Thus in second order surrogacy there are vestiges of human gestural activity which are surmised from the sound, but I cannot find a realistic explanation for everything I hear.

Beyond second order surrogacy the links with potential physical origins are further masked, finally reaching a state where neither gesture-type nor source can be surmised. Here we reach *remote surrogacy*. But the links with gesture need not be entirely lost. The gesture-field operates in the psychological domain, and in remote surrogacy the indicative link can be forged through the energy-motion trajectory alone, without reference to real or surmised physical gesture or an identifiable source. The listener is thus called upon to exercise and enjoy maximum gestural imagination. Of course in a state of remote surrogacy the indicative relationship may easily shift to other fields that share indicative attributes with the gesture-field. This is very probable since the sounds involved are likely to be highly ambiguous because they are not firmly rooted in known sounding gesture. Thus the energy-motion trajectory belongs not only to gesture but to all types of energetic motion related to phenomena in the object/substance-field, the environment-field, the kinetic area of the visual-field, and the space-field. Whether or not gesturally remote energy-motion trajectories will be apprehended in the gesture-field is dependent on their time-scale and type of spectral energy content. For example, the more a gesture is stretched out in time the more it begins to lose the energetic impetus associated with its physical origins, and the less it is linked to the source of energy that instigated the motion. Moreover, if a highly stretched gesture is to offer any auditory interest, it will need internal spectral motion, which may either reinforce or contradict the external gestural motion, providing rival attractions for the listener. Under these circumstances one can easily imagine a wide range of field-shifts and a variety of indicative mixes. Perhaps all that will remain of the gesture-field will be the psychological and proprioceptive responses of the listener, which will largely be pushed into the background of consciousness as stronger, foreground fields take over. Thus the energy, motion and expression of musical gesture have an automatic, extensive and deep indicative relationship with non-musical experience, making the gesture-network powerfully pervasive. I suggest that if the listener does not discover some gesture-field attributes in a musical work then the music will seem to be distanced from the more intimate, internalized domain of personal experience; the listener may feel as if 'observing' invisible phenomena displayed on a screen or in a space.

Utterance

Utterance is the second archetypal indicative field, and like the gesture-field it is directly linked to the human body.[10] Gesture and utterance are not distinctly differentiated fields. At a psychological level they can be synonymous because both are articulated through the energy-motion trajectory, and both are concerned with proprioceptive perception. Hence the term *vocal gesture*, which expresses this shared indicative significance. However, the spectro-morphologies of language-utterance and para-linguistic utterance sound very different from instrumental gesture. But even here there is common ground because language-utterance and instrument-gesture have traditionally been closely associated in song. The nature of the text–music relationship and the mutual pull between the two fields is a vast subject that is beyond the scope of this essay; it suffices to make the reader aware of the overlap.

The fact that the sounds of utterance are generated from within the body, and that they are the essential vehicle of personal expression and communication, makes utterance intimate and emotionally charged. Therefore the listener's relationship with utterance is often reflexive rather than indicative. This is evident in most popular vocal music, where the music is widely interpreted as the personal utterance of the performer, thereby encouraging the listener to respond reflexively. The fact that most popular music is vocal demonstrates the predominance of the reflexive relationship over wider indicative interpretations.

In electroacoustic music the voice always announces a human presence, perhaps in a sounding context that is not regarded as directly human. This presence alters the significance of the context, redirecting the listener's attention to centre on indicative meanings associated with the perceived utterance. Thus the satellite fields will be interpreted in the light of the energy-motion trajectories of vocal gesture. The utterance-network as a whole can only be decoded by reference to the third indicative archetype, the behaviour-field.

Behaviour

The placing of sounds in a context automatically ensures that some kind of relationship must exist among them. The term 'behaviour' has been chosen to represent these relationships. It may refer to human behaviour deduced from the utterance-network, to relationships in and among the networks of object/substance, environment or vision. The fields of energy, motion and space are inevitably strongly implicated. The behaviour-field can first be defined by discussing two pairs of oppositions: *dominance/subordination*, and *conflict/coexistence*. Naturally there are continuously mediating positions between the polar extremes.

Dominance/subordination is concerned with the (in)equality of participating morphologies and is related to three interlocked ways of interpreting the idea of foreground and background: spectro-morphologically, spatially and indicatively. Since spectro-morphology is concerned with temporal shaping, the fields of energy and motion are activated. In the behaviour-field context space is concerned with proximity/distance and mobility/immobility, but these dimensions can seldom be separated from the types and groupings of spectro-morphologies. Thus some spectro-morphologies will be considered more dominant than others in certain contexts due to a variety of factors: dynamic shaping, changes in spectral richness, rapidity of spectral motion, rate of spatial displacement, and so on. A simple, obvious example would be bright, spatially present, impact-attack morphologies superimposed on a sustained, relatively distant, spectrally inactive morphology. Finally, the indicative impact of a sound can affect its dominance: we are already aware of the voice's focal pre-eminence. Identified sources will also dominate the unrecognized.

Conflict/coexistence is intended to highlight temporal relationships within the behaviour-field. On the one hand sounds can exhibit competitive tendencies, and on the other they can exist in a reciprocal, confluent environment. Again, spectro-morphological factors are determining, but so also are types of temporal coordination and density organization. Synchronicity reflects a consensual behaviour as does the erratic, asynchronous, discontinuous behaviour exhibited by a texture of like morphologies or morphologies displaying a familial resemblance. Conflicting behaviour requires simultaneous or successive contrast of spectro-morphologies whose dynamic shaping and temporal activity reflect forceful displacement, but not all such contrasts are conflicting. For example, high densities of contrasted events could be interpreted as coexistent, and even lower densities can indicate coexistence if the behaviour continues long enough to establish a quasi-permanent *modus vivendi*. Thus a conflicting behaviour can settle into coexistence if given enough time. In addition, a textural behaviour can reveal conflicting and coexistent tendencies simultaneously, though at different structural levels. For example, the spectro-morphologies at the interior of a texture can conflict on a low level while the motion of the texture as a whole exhibits an external coherence through co-ordinated contour change, dynamic shaping or spatial displacement: internal conflict is thus at odds with collective coherence. Conflict/coexistence detected in the utterance- and environment-fields will tend to inspire a dramatic interpretation closely linked to reality.

The third major area of behaviour is *causality* which, although it exhibits attributes of the two paired oppositions, needs separate consideration. Causality in this context does not refer narrowly to physical gesture. It is more concerned with one sound's acting upon another, either causing the second event to occur or instigating change in an ongoing sound. Causal relationships may be synonymous with the real world when human utterance, environmental or cultural sounds are incorporated in a work. But in less realistic contexts musical causality is freer and may be perceived as weak or strong. It is then linked to the fields of gesture, energy, motion, and object/substance, and besides contributing to notions of dominance/subordination and conflict/coexistence, tends to add impetus to the forward motion of musical structure. This type of causality is surmised rather than known: visual or experiential knowledge cannot verify the relationship or test it by recreating the temporal sequence. It is possible for causality to be surmised purely from the temporal proximity of two different sounds if the sequence is insisted upon through repetition. Even if the time-gap between the two sounds is varied to a certain degree, causality can still result. This would be weak causal behaviour allied to signalling. More often it will be the shaping of the energy-motion trajectory which adds strength to the relationship aiding a more confident causal diagnosis. If the second event responds spectro-morphologically to interference from or impact with the first event, the causal relationship will be perceived even more strongly.

Energy and Motion

The energy and motion fields are intertwined in the spectro-morphology of sounds and have already been discussed in defining the significance of the energy-motion trajectory. There cannot be sound without energy in the spectral domain and there cannot be energy without motion. The energy-field is distributed in pitch-space creating a *spectral texture* which can vary between compaction and dispersal. It is associated with the creation and release of tension which, as we know, is at the source of the gesture-field. The listener can deduce the style of energetic physical action from the spectral behaviour of a sound, and even where the sounding body is not known or real, energetic tensions and releases are conveyed through spectral change.

The energy-field depends on the motion-field which exists on a variety of time-scales and at a variety of structural levels. Motion can be detected both in external contour and internal, textural behaviour. Since motion is integral to temporal experience all types of non-musical motions can have musical counterparts, although sounding motion is open to far greater imaginative licence than is possible in reality: musical motions do not have to be real or plausible. I have catalogued the types of motion elsewhere (Smalley 1986: 20–4) and merely summarize the essential points here. Musical motion will be interpreted as moving forward if a directional tendency is sufficiently strong and/or is maintained for an adequately long time-span. Directionality is related to goal orientation and growth as in converging/diverging, ascending/descending contours, and accumulative/ dissipative and diffractive/conglomerative growth. Circular motions can be created by spectral recycling or reinjection, and the experience of relative stasis can be created through recycling processes or through planar motion. The widest possible repertory of motions is possible in electroacoustic music because of the spectro-morphological freedom of the medium which allows both an extensive variety of attitudes towards (dis)continuity and conjunct/disjunct motion, and an unrivalled elasticity of temporal flux. Finally, it needs to be emphasized that the spatial dimension of motion can be created spectrally without actual spatial movement, although clearly a trajectory or cyclic motion can be enhanced or qualitatively altered by adding an actual spatial dimension.

Object/Substance

The word 'object' is commonly used in the term 'sound object' although it is used somewhat loosely. The sound object was originally a Schaefferian concept related to objective/subjective approaches to listening, and emphasized a sound as the object of perception in mode three. In the object/substance field the popular sense of 'thingness' is intended.

How can a sound be a thing when it has no material existence? First because actual sounding materials can be used, simulated or alluded to. Thus there is an extensive indicative repertory of material-like qualities – stone, glass, ceramics, woods, metals, skins, etc., which can be subject to gestural play. Second, objectness can be deduced from types of motion that suggest analogies with the motion of objects. For example, attributes of the spinning motion can be imaginatively represented spectro-morphologically without duplicating the sound of a real spinning object; here the qualities of a visual object are transferred to a sounding object-structure; the sounding manifestation may evoke impressions and memories of observed spinning objects as well as suggesting imagined non-existent images related to the motion-type. In this case, objectness is one of several possible indicative choices. Third, objectness can be attributed to morphologies without reference to real materials as long as there is some semblance of a plausible gestural origin. For example, sharp attacks or a series of granular scrapes could be regarded as objects even if their matter is seemingly unreal as long as an attack- or scrape-gesture is diagnosed. An individual object is necessarily coherent in spectral behaviour. The examples so far referred to imply both a temporal identity and internal spectral compactness: the way in which a sound occupies the pitch-space is influential in ascribing objectness. If the spectral texture of a sound is widely dispersed or diffuse it is less likely to be regarded as an object because of its unwieldy dimensions unless it is felt that an exaggerated magnification has taken place: it depends on the vestiges of compact objectness. The impression of dimension gleaned from the spectro-morphology is therefore important, and is particularly significant with relation to the listening environment. A spectro-morphology can often be regarded as an object if its projected spatial presence is 'quasi-graspable': it is on a human scale.

The examples used above, apart from skins, are of solid materials. This is not to say that objects are all inflexible. The substance end of the field emphasizes malleability and fluidity and refers primarily to textural motion. The fluid analogy is apposite, referring as it does to low-level spectro-morphologies which coagulate into flexible, temporal flows at higher levels. There are environmental as well as visual correlations, and the greater vagaries of substance permit a more ambiguously adventurous approach than is possible with objects.

Environment

The incorporation of environmental sounds into music via the recording medium has led to a greater appreciation of the musical qualities of sounds outside the immediate human orbit. Common ground between human and animal utterance has been opened up to exploration, and the sounding objects and textures of the environment have found common cause with contemporary approaches to instrumental texture. Equally important are both the spatial expansion implied in drawing the environment into music, and the spreading out from music towards the environment. The environment-field will be further considered when discussing sounding models, and it will form an important part of consideration of the space-field.

Vision

Every field discussed so far contributes to the visual indicative network. It is true to say that vision is at the very basis of the gesture-field, and that the energy-motion trajectory is unimaginable without its visual cor-relatations. This would imply that music, and electroacoustic music in particular, is not a purely auditory art but a more integrated, audio-visual art, albeit that the visual aspect is frequently invisible. That in turn suggests some kind of synaesthesia.[11] This is true, but it would be wrong to regard the vision-field as hallucinatory or as a strong, involuntary type of syn-aesthesia like that of 'colour-hearing'. Rather, it is a weaker, voluntary, associative synaesthesia which will vary in consciousness and activity among listeners. The vision-field embraces both kinetic and static phenomena. For example, the textural design of textiles or rock formations could easily form part of a listener's indicative reference-bank. Musicians, because of their interactive relationship with sounds and sound-structures, tend to regard the vision-field as extrinsic to music, but our discussion of the indicative networks reveals pervasive intrinsic qualities. Thus vision must be accorded the status of a network.

Space

References to the space-field have largely been withheld until now in order to avoid a fragmented approach. We still await an authoritative investigation into this, the newest and most innovative indicative network, and this section can only hope to outline the relevant criteria. For many composers it would seem logical to separate discussion of the space-field into three areas. The first area – the use of space to articulate sounds and musical structure – is a constant preoccupation and is commonly thought of in a relatively objective way as part of the interactive listening relationship. A concentration on this area can mean that the composer regards space primarily as an enhancement or reinforcement of sounding properties inherent in spectro-morphologies and structural relations, and in practice this is often the case. The second area concerns sound diffusion – the articulation of the composed spatial content in public performance – commonly recognized as a problem since it concerns adapting the composed musical space to an unpredictable listening space. The problem results from the public space's undermining of the articulatory shaping considered so important (and dealt with so carefully) by the composer working more intimately in the studio-space where the work was created. The third area concerns the affective interpretation of space – how the listener experiences and feels about space. This last area is the most neglected (often unconsciously) by the composer, although for the listener it overshadows the other two simply because the listener is not involved in the first area, and cannot know about problems in the second. In this chapter it is this interpretative aspect that concerns us – the indicative relationships with space, which in practice cannot be separated from perceived spatial articulation as apprehended in a listening space.

A musical space is not empty and cannot be separated from its sounding content. Thus it is the relational structure of spatial content, the connectedness of space, which is important. Conceptually (not actually) there are three categories of relational structure. The first is the relationships and behaviour among sounds within the composed musical space; the second is the movement between successive spaces, or the transformation of space in the work; the third is the interaction between the musical space and the listening space that for the listener will be fused with the first two. The *composed space* possesses an *acoustic topology* – an elastic continuum – which may vary between a reflective, enclosed space, and a freer, non-relective space as can be experienced in the environment. The *listening space* theoretically encloses the composed space within it. Thus perceived musical space is always a *superimposed space*. This ultimate spatial setting, which can vary between listenings, usually lies outside the composer's control. It may be a large, public space where groups of people share the listening experience, or a more intimate, private space at home. In both cases the dimensions and acoustic of the listening space are likely to be different from the original (controlled) acoustic context in which the work was created, not to mention the differences experienced in social and physical terms. The spatial transference brings to the concert hall or home sounds which otherwise would not be heard there. This superimposition of spaces can create 'consonant' or 'dissonant' relationships between composed and listening environments changing indicative interpretations to an extent often not envisaged or even considered by the composer; bringing the intimate into the large, the large into the larger, the vast into the small, must be influential.

The opposition between intimacy and immensity,[12] or, to express it slightly differently, confinement and vastness, is the most important indicative property of musical space. This opposition is fundamental to human experience. We are constantly aware of a personal space within the orbit of our practical daily activities or personal relations, while we also experience a relationship with the more open environmmental spaces outside and beyond. These divergent dimensions are reflected in our experience of acousmatic, electroacoustic musical space, and the effect of their indicative contribution depends primarily on how well the composer circumvents the confinement of the superimposed, listening space. In other words, is the listener transported to a real or imagined environment beyond the immediate walls, or is the listener in the midst of musical activity within the space? Is it a case of 'reaching out' or of 'closing in'? Is the listener an involved participant or an impartial observer? Do sounds confront the listener or is the listener drawn into the sound-field? Therefore, is the musical context psychically close or is it remote?

Answers to these questions depend fundamentally on the type of musical content as filtered through the non-spatial indicative networks. Psychic closeness, for example, is strongly dependent on the harnessing of the three archetypal fields, since they have the most direct human links; human utterance, proprioceptive perception of physical gesture, and a social interpretation of the behaviour-field, in collusion with spatial setting, can draw in the listener. If the listener encounters a very high proportion of heavily processed sounds or sounds in remote surrogacy that do not spark off archetypal indicative links, then a certain psychic distance is bound to occur. However, it should not be assumed that distant spaces or vastness are in themselves psychically distant. Paradoxically, distance and spaciousness can be intimate if they are perceived physionomically. For example, the listener faced with a vast aural space might adopt a reflexive relationship, associating the perceived space with states of mind that could be experienced in it, such as loneliness, being alone, feeling sad, feeling insignificant faced with vastness. The scale of the space in relationship to the perspective of the content is indicatively fundamental. For example, assume that a gesturally based sound or utterance is 'recorded' intimately so that to the composer in the studio it appears to be living in the space; if you distance yourself from this same sound in a collective listening environment the intimate spectral qualities will become masked, and the sound's activity will take place at a greater distance; psychic impact is altered by spatial distancing. This would seem to indicate there can be correlations between psychic and physical remoteness, and that, in the case above, a personal listening space would be preferable if a certain intimacy is to be preserved. Certainly public spaces do not inspire intimate contact. The impression of thingness in the object/substance-field is similarly dependent on collusion between the perspective of the auditory image and the use of space.

By contrast, musical contexts of an environmental-type scale can expand the listening space, either transporting the listener beyond the listening space or creating a larger space for the listener to inhabit. Such experiences are achieved through the relationship of indicative content to the spectral texture of pitch-space, to spatial texture, spatial orientation, and temporal space. This does not mean that these four areas are of no consequence to the preceding discussion; it is just that they can be more appropriately approached here. The height/depth occupancy of the pitch-space affects the impression of dimension, not only through the distance between registral extremes but in the way the intervening pitch-space is filled. A certain continuity in internal/external energy-motion behaviour will also be required, with the emphasis on minimal external evolution. Spectral texture will be mediated via *spatial texture* which concerns the topological content of the real/imagined space – its size, the relationships of the dimensions of sounds to their localization, the density of distribution of sounds, the connectedness of the sounds in space (spatial continuity/contiguity), and actual spatial movement. The spatial texture does not have to be set in the distance; it can be present, embracing intimate content. In public listening where the speaker system is well designed and used, an imported environment can seem comfortably suited to the listening space. This would be a case of a consonant relationship between the composed and listening spaces where any reflective properties perceived would be attributed to the acoustic of the listening space. The same environment encountered in a personal space over a pair of loudspeakers, while perhaps allowing more intimate definition, would rely on the indicative power of the music to overcome the disparity between composed and listening spaces.

There is obviously a difference in *spatial orientation* between the two listening spaces just described. Sound within the visual field, sound confronting from ahead or stealing up from behind, sound flying overhead or circumferentially enclosing, all have a real and symbolic significance for us. These broader aspects of spatial orientation are more important than certain details of movement, not all of which are indicatively significant: for example, whether lateral movement is on one side as opposed to the other, or whether a sound moves from left to right rather than from right to left. An environmental 'feel' can be achieved by combining circumferential orientation with an impression of spatial continuity. *Temporal space* is an impression of space created through stability and continuity in time. For example, ongoing, sustained spectral textures showing very slow or no signs of longer-term evolution can be perceived spatially if the listener becomes less aware of forward motion and the lower levels of time passing. In other words, continuing existence can approach a quasi-permanence analogous to the contemplation of the visual permanence of a landscape.

An acousmatic work does not have to confine itself to a single space-type. Indeed, in the light of the expressive possibilities discussed above it would seem positively advantageous if it did not. Thus spaces can themselves be transformed: they can be subject to graduated or interpolatory shifts, and the same sounds can appear in different spatial contexts. This I call *spatio-morphology*. It is clear that fluent, idiomatic, topologically elastic spatio-morphology is the unique property of the acousmatic electroacoustic medium. It is equally clear that the circumstances of the superimposed space make the indicative space-network somewhat fragile. We have yet to arrive at a stage where the space-field can become totally 'holosonic', or at least where such technological control of space-field becomes a practicable proposition for composers. Even then the problems of the public and private superimposed space will still be with us. Indeed they will be magnified.

SOUNDING MODELS

What discussion of the indicative fields and networks reveals is that musical materials are linked to non-sounding experience, and vice versa. Until the electroacoustic era, music could only be made using real, sounding models. We should now enquire further into these models, which still remain the principal cultural determinants of musical materials, investigating how the electroacoustic medium has influenced our thinking about and use of the available sounding world.

Sounding models for musical sounds are traditionally found already existing in the outside world. Some may be transferred directly into music, as is the case with simple percussion. Usually, however, some kind of adaptation and elaboration is necessary, and thus sounding models form the basis for the development of instruments and repertories of sound morphologies which can eventually become quite remote from the model-source. The available conceptual categories of sounding models are summarized in Figure 26.1 which we shall first examine from the perspective of traditional (mainly Western) practice.

Accepting that the indicative significance of sounds is culture- or community-specific the diagram has at its centre the culture of the listener who will have a particular attitude to the sounds of nature. The double arrow between 'native culture' and 'other cultures' indicates the ethnocentricity, even parochialism, of the listener, and recognizes that other cultures will have their own models based around human utterance and human agency. This bifurcation separating the voice from human action is fundamental, all cultural sounds being produced either as utterance or as a result of human agency.

Utterance in daily life consists of the interplay between speech-language and paralanguage both of which provide the basis for vocal gesture in music. The doubled-headed link with vocal gesture signifies that for the music listener the traffic travels in the opposite direction: no matter how heavily stylized a vocal music may be, it is a manifestation of human utterance. Music thus indicates non-musical utterance.

The sounding products of *human agency* are divided into those sounds created intentionally for a specific use or function, and those that are accidental by-products of human activity. Sounding signals abound in contemporary life, and as a result of electronic sound there are many more than there used to be. They may be divided into functional genres ranging from warning signals (horns, sirens) to calls to attention (sounds heralding an announcement, signals demanding silence in public gatherings), start-

535

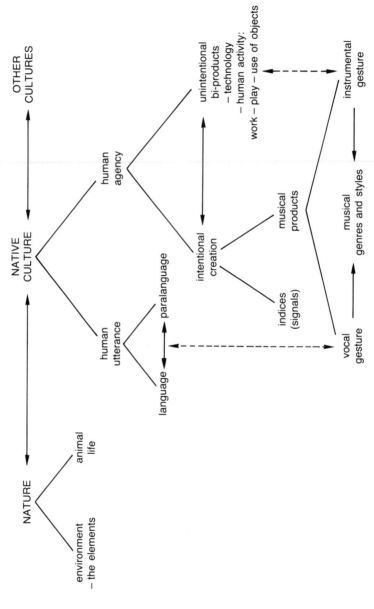

Figure 26.1 Sounding models

stop/arrival signals (pedestrian crossings, lifts), and information provision (time signals, computer tones, slot machines). However, sounding signals are a subcategory of signals in general which are manifest in a variety of kinetic and static visual guises including human gesture. If we regard signalling as a type of structural function we find it has a wider musical application in association with weak causality. If one sound event becomes associated with a particular type of consequence, such that the first event seems to announce or warn of the imminence of a following event, then a signalling relationship is created. Thus it is not the actual sound of the signal that acts as the model but the behavioural relationship of the two sounds. Unintentional by-products may unwittingly act as signals: the signal itself can thus be an unintended by-product. A common example occurs when an unexpected change in the sound behaviour of a mechanical device warns the user that things are not as they should be. This application has no musical significance.

While some unintentional sounds, like those of machinery, may be unavoidably incidental, others are of greater significance since they can provide the inspirational source of intentional musical exploration. Such evolutions result from our interaction with objects during work or play: the act of hollowing out a log which leads to the log drum, the gourd which becomes a resonator, blowing on a reed or down a tube, and so on. Human interaction with sounding objects lies behind traditional *instrumental gesture*. The passage from object experimentation to the creation of a musical instrument involves the increasing refinement of hitting, scraping or blowing, such that sophisticated and detailed techniques of control are consciously elaborated as a result of the performer-listener's conscious exploration of the interactive relationship. Gradually a performance practice evolves. However refined, specialized or rarified the instrument, its mor-phologies and associated techniques may become, the primal hit, scrape or blow never fades from the listener's mind. It is a knowledge possessed by everyone, and its sophisticated instrumental guise is something all can appreciate.

The notion of virtuosity and the admiration occasioned by technical prowess are based on identifying a consummate control of the articulation of morphologies. Instrumental and vocal gesture involve more than the production of single morphologies: the energy-motion trajectory of phrase-gestures is formed from the groupings of note-gestures. The word 'phrase' suggests links with language, and the use of the breath to control and articulate wind instrument morphologies provides the direct instrumental correspondence with vocal gesture in that the human airstream is the shared means of control. One important change in contemporary musical styles (even music involving voices) is that airstream-determined phraseology and cadencing practice have waned as other indicative networks have grown in influence. Those most basic of human activites, utterance and physical gesture, have traditionally met and collaborated in music.

Musical compositions at the style, genre or work level can themselves become sounding models when they are borrowed for or composed into a new musical composition. While this has become widespread in modern polystylistic composition, reference to styles or genres outside the immediate composition or cultural context is a centuries-old practice.

Since music is traditionally a human activity the sounds made by *nature* could not themselves be directly harnessed for musical use prior to the electroacoustic era (although I have pointed out that a listener can have an interactive relationship with the morphologies and sounding behaviours of the environment in a manner analogous to the interactive relationship with musical materials and structure). Thus the listener can now apprehend the sounds of nature as if they were a compositional creation, although the indicative sense behind the sounds is of quite a different order from the human-based indicative messages of gesture or utterance. Gesture and utterance lie within human control. The sounds of nature traditionally have not. But the sounds of nature have acted as models in a mimetic sense. Certain attributes of their morphological behaviour may be imitated exactly or stylized to be articulated by vocal or instrumental surrogates. The most interesting musics resulting from this mimetic process are found in the musics of non-Western cultures.

SOUNDING MODELS
IN ELECTROACOUSTIC CONTEXTS

For most people the instrumental and vocal performance of sounds defines what music is. That is, utterance and physical gesture are all. Not surprisingly, therefore, any attempt to shift from these primal sounding models is likely to meet with a certain incomprehension. If you take away or weaken the tangibility of the known, visual, gestural model and the direct, universal articulations in utterance, then you undermine the stability of the conscious and unconscious reflexive relationship that the listener seeks.

The electroacoustic medium is unprecedented in that, unlike instrumental and vocal tradition, it permits access to the entire sound-field. It is free to develop sound repertories that are not confined to the notion of the instrument or voice, and it does not have to construct its sounds from material sounding bodies. Consequently it need not be limited by the human practicalities of real-time execution and live performance practice. Of course, electroacoustic music can remain wedded to instrumental and vocal gesture as it does with much MIDI-based popular composition, where the synthesized or sampled sounds are either convenient substitutes for known instruments or else they deviate very little from the instrumental gestural model. The design of most high-street music technology and the marketing strategies adopted are naturally based on feeding the tried, common cultural denominators.

Instrumental Gesture

The activity of the electroacoustic musician who discovers sound sources by experimenting with the myriad available cultural objects continues the tradition of generating instrumental gesture from object-play. But although instrumental gesture is the means of exciting the found sounding body, the end-goal is not necessarily the creation of a new 'instrument' which will eventually become ubiquitously integrated into the culture.[13] In many cases the discovery will only be used in one composition and then discarded. This can be because its distinctive character becomes quickly exhausted. But there are more complex reasons associated with the idea of instrumental identity. Our new sound may resist a full instrumentalization because too few of its spectro-morphological attributes can be varied only within narrow boundaries with the consequence that the rich network of relationships needed for a more pervasive instrumental function cannot be created. In other words, normal instrumental practice requires the careful control of timbral identity over a sufficiently broad, striated pitch-space. Many electroacoustic sounds, whether synthesized or developed from recorded sources, resist any consistent scalic organization which could permit sophisticated and detailed registral play. For example, imagine that our new sound possesses a type of spectrum containing a variety of different components which, spread over a wide pitch-space, create an audible internal texture. Transpose this sound to different pitch-levels and you will affect the internal identity, weighting and focus of the components. This action could create groups of sounds quite different from each other so that when we contrast one group with another it is difficult or impossible to relate them all to an identical source or mode of gestural activity. Thus it becomes impossible to identify a common source across the pitch-space. The traditional notion of the instrument rests on this concept of causal permanence,[14] which requires that variations over a broad pitch-space do not destroy the identity of the source: in spite of differences in articulation, timbre and dynamic shaping throughout registers we should still recognize the sounding body and the type of gesture that excited it. With many electroacoustic sounds this is clearly not the case.

The electroacoustic medium allows us to use sounds that – unlike instrumental sources – have, or appear to have no real, material existence. They may be sounds unrecognizable in their recorded form, sounding objects in highly transformed states, or inventively synthesized sounds. They may weave between material reality and non-existence. In the most interesting and original electroacoustic music, the traditional notion of the instrument, so fundamentally linked to causal identity and so intimately tied to human agency via gestural activity, no longer provides such a dominating and fundamental indicative link. It is often not so much a case of stretching (or contracting) the notion of 'instrument' but of discarding it altogether.

Utterance

Traditionally, types of stylized singing have been the only acceptable musical voice. Now all aspects of human utterance are available to be used directly, as uttered, or as models for sounds and sound structures. (The language-stream, for example, can provide a structural model.) The repertory of vocal sounds is set out in Figure 26.2. The base-line represents the vocal continuum between language and music; parallel with the base-line are three further reference-planes representing a potentially increasing remoteness from the base-line; expansions of paralingual activity and the use of the voice to imitate non-vocal sounds, or even to suggest gestural energy-motion trajectories, soon bring utterance into close contact with other indicative networks. We find this in contemporary vocal music. For example, the voice is central to text–sound composition, where the most rewarding encounters are found in an interlocking of indicative and semantic factors; the voice conveys semantic content as well as providing a reservoir for indicative interpretations allied to vocal qualities and behaviour. Extended vocal techniques also run the gamut between language-utterance and environment. If we then add in the potential of the electroacoustic medium for revealing vocal micro-sounds, for creating new voices, and for surpassing natural limits, then the vocal repertory can merge into the indicative networks more idiomatically than was previously possible.

UTTERANCE REPERTORY

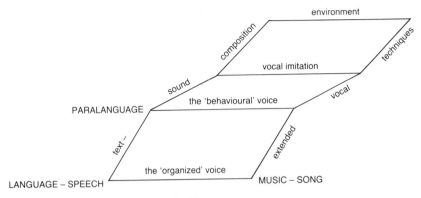

Figure 26.2 The utterance repertory

The presence of the voice in an electroacoustic context opens up a wide range of indicative situations. The moment a voice is perceived in a sounding context the listener's ear is drawn to it and interpretation shifts to focus on the unseen human presence, trying to decode the meaning of its utterances and the relationship of the person to the sounding environment. Thus a musical context prior to the vocal entry may have had quite a different indicative perspective: a human presence where previously there was none changes everything. The unexpected entry of a musical instrument, or for that matter any unexpected sound-type whose causal origin is identified, can create a similar indicative shift, but none is as immediate, powerful or universally recognizable as the voice. It is not only the expanded utterance repertory that is significant for electroacoustic music but also the potential relationship of the human being to new environments. The invisible electroacoustic medium, relying on auditory images alone, can thus become a unique, original window on human experience.

Nature, Culture, Transcontextuality

In the electroacoustic medium the sounds of nature can at last come into their own. Prior to the invention of recording they could exist only through imitation on an iconic level, where certain attributes of the spectro-morphology or syntactical behaviour of natural sounds were mutated into a stylized form suitable for articulation either by human utterance or instrumental gesture. Once the microphone provided convenient *direct access* to sounds previously beyond human control then the sounds of nature could be integrated more closely into musical contexts, and thus potentially exert a stronger influence on musical language. For the first time sounding models beyond human intervention could be drawn into music to be used either as they are or to be subjected to the same transformation processes as other sounding materials.

Where the sounds taken from cultural activity or nature are used as recorded, or where transformation does not destroy the identity of the original context, the listener may become involved in a process of *transcontextual interpretation*.[15] We should include here any recorded sound event where we are simultaneously aware of two (or more) contexts. We may therefore include such cultural sound events and activities as fly-on-the-wall recordings where the participants are not consciously 'performing', sound documents of historical events, recorded extracts from other musics, and so on. In *transcontexts* the composer intends that the listener should be aware of the dual meanings of a source. The first meaning derives from the original, natural or cultural context of the event; the second meaning derives from the new, musical context created by the composer.

Where sounding cultural activities are involved the second meaning is commonly concerned with inducing a particular attitude towards the material. This may form part of some kind of critical commentary, whether serious or ironic, social or political. Successful transcontextual interpretation is dependent on shared norms and meanings. It is therefore possible to use recorded materials with strong or well-known cultural implications as the basis for a composition that is entirely parochial, which would have little meaning outside the cultural group within which it was composed. Such pieces, involving little manipulation of the directly accessed materials beyond the mixing or juxtaposing of recorded sequences, sit on a borderline between sound-documentary and music, contrasting sharply with the other end of the electroacoustic medium where sophisticated technology permits the creation of richer, more elliptical indicative networks from highly manipulated, covert sources. Transcontextuality does not concern sources which, although identifiable, seem to the listener to possess no real-life context. If I use a recording of cutlery being cleared away after a meal, that is transcontextual; it refers to a real cultural context. But if I used from the recording a single, metallic, knife-scrape, this is less likely to be principally a transcontextual event because the context has been excised. I say 'less likely' because for a certain type of listener the identification of the knife

542

and ideas and images associated with knives may dominate the interpretation. But the more interactive listener may connect the knife-sound more
closely with an instrumental-type gesture and the networks of indicative
interpretations based on metallic materials, friction and motion. If an actual
knife is not identified as the source then these wider interpretations must
take over. The composer could, of course, exploit all these indicative
possibilities. It is therefore quite clear that the decoding of transcontextual
meanings can be a very personal and fragile affair.

As far as nature is concerned second meanings are different. Although
the sounds of nature could be harnessed to make an ecological statement,
the indicative possibilities are frequently liable to be more comprehensive.
As we noticed in discussing the environment-field, the textures of environmental recordings can have much in common with contemporary attitudes
towards musical texture, which may in turn be closely analogous to visual
experience of texture, whether kinetic or static; the sounds of animal life
can be linked to the environment and life outside human existence on the
one hand, and yet be linked to human utterance on the other. Nature, then,
is subject to wide-ranging indicative shifts, much more so than sounding
cultural activity.

The transcontextual process makes it possible for the musical composition
to embrace the sounding world outside human control. Yet this cannot be
achieved without human interference. The act of recording in itself involves
decisions about the sound image to be captured, in particular, decisions
concerning spatial focus and image. When a recorded environmental
sequence is placed in a musical context, or if the sequence itself becomes a
musical work without further intervention, the composer must still make
transcontextual decisions related to temporal context: where to place it, how
to approach and quit the sequence, the choice of start- and end-points, and
so on.

By definition, the source must have existed prior to its transference
although the new context does not necessarily make the listener aware of a
diachronic dimension. For example, environmental sounds possess this
'spatial' dimension rather than an 'historical' one. They also have a special
temporal quality since we understand them as continuing (perhaps even
infinitely) into the future after the musical work has run its course. At this
stage we should recall that the concept of the superimposed space, discussed
above under the space-field, can be a manifestation of a formative spatial
transcontextuality.

The concept of transcontextuality is a useful way of understanding an
indicative process since it is obvious that something outside the musical

543

context is indicated. Transcontextual relationships are included within the notion of the indicative field and network, which is more comprehensive and involves links with experience which may be deeper, more covert or more remote. We might therefore say that transcontextuality is more superficial, although this should not be taken to mean that it is unimportant since the issues raised or experiences evoked may indeed be fundamental. But transcontextuality is not necessarily a simple question of black and white. The more the composer intervenes in the spectro-morphology of an identifiable source the more vestigial that source will become. Its directness will decay so that dual contextual interpretation is less certain as ambiguity increases, until the sound is eventually divorced from any audible relationship with its origins. When transcontextual identity becomes less clearly defined the ear relies more on alternative indicative interpretations, and the composer remains the sole guardian of a dual knowledge.

MODEL SHIFTS, INDICATIVE SHIFTS

Prior to the electroacoustic era the sounding models on which musical works were based remained fixed within the musical repertory of the culture. This meant that the listener could automatically assume before even listening to a piece of music that it would be rooted either in the instrumental gesture model, or human utterance, or both. In the case of the combined gesture-utterance model (accompanied vocal music), even if the voice does not enter at the outset, its potential presence is announced clearly in advance by the title of the work and list of performers, or by the visual, physical presence of the singer-in-waiting. So, traditionally, the indicative framework and boundaries of a musical work were not only pre-determined but, as far as the culture was concerned, permanent. The listener's rewards lay in discovering how this archetypal indicative framework would be fleshed out by the composer's manipulation of the pitch-rhythm system, revealed through performance-gesture and performance-utterance.

Since electroacoustic music is not restricted to the model of utterance and a model of gesture that is entirely instrumentally determined, it cannot rely on the assumptions outlined above. Instead it actively cultivates and encourages greater exploratory uncertainty as the basis of the listener's interpretative strategies. Rarely can the listener have pre-knowledge of the total sound repertory of an electroacoustic work. This is obvious in the case of totally acousmatic works, where there are no visible, live, real-time sounding sources: everything remains to be revealed by the composer and discovered by the listener. That is both an attraction and a problem. The attraction lies in the openness to maximum imaginative potential which can shift and drift flexibly among indicative networks. The problem lies in the composer's determining and harnessing the fields of indicative operation. Moreover, not only must the fields of operation be chosen, but the sounds themselves must be created, and if they are to be synthesized they have to be created from scratch. Given so much choice it is not surprising that it is often a more fruitful strategy to let the sounds themselves suggest the fields and networks of operation.

Because the acousmatic nature of the electroacoustic medium does not require the selection of a fixed, limited number of sound sources for any one work it is possible to shift among sounding models and sound types in flexible and unique ways. Such model shifts will instigate shifts in indicative interpretation and can permit unusual mixes. The composer can work in several indicative networks simultaneously or successively, either permitting an element of focal choice for the listener or directing a stream of successive shifts. A shift can be sensitively shaded and graduated, or brutally interpolatory. The *graduated shift* is based on shared spectro-morphological attributes, while the *interpolatory shift* ignores common attributes and emphasizes dramatic differences. Of course, a shift could contain elements of both types. As far as focus is concerned we should recall that vocal presence dominates, but that in the case of other sounds focus is determined by indicative-interactive listening abilities, habits and strategies. Of particular importance, therefore, are ambiguities which shift in and out of the direct human presence. For example, noise-based contours permit graduated shifts among environmental models (such as air and wind), an utterance model (the human airstream) and an instrumental gesture model (wind-controlled instruments); shifts could be created among the percussive morphologies and noise-like or nodal spectra of vocal consonants, varieties of struck objects based on the struck instrumental gesture model, and related sound-types drawn from the environment. Similarly, the textural behaviour of an environmental source could shift to a vocally based texture exhibiting analogous behaviour patterns.

Under acousmatic conditions it is possible to imagine the vast possibilities of shifts based on the graduated and interpolatory principles, moving among indicative shadings which may be evident, ambiguous or polyvalent, and which appeal to interactive and indicative relationships.

545

INSTRUMENTS, VISION, INDICATIVE
SHIFTS

The problems and attractions discussed above are also involved in partially acousmatic works, where there is a both a visible, live performance presence, and an invisible acousmatic component – the known combined with an unknown. Many composers choose a solution that lets the instrumental gesture-model confine the acousmatic imagination so that the work as a whole remains tightly within a sector of the gesture-field and its associated, instrumentally-based morphologies. In such situations neither the electroacoustic medium nor the traditional instrument is explored to its full imaginative potential. More enticing is the prospect of creating sound environments where the instrument, while remaining at centre-focus, is placed in contexts where new or ambiguous indicative interpretations are encouraged. Naturally, not all instruments lend themselves equally well to this expanded approach because their repertory of sound morphologies and sound types lacks the chameleon-like adaptability necessary for shifting among the indicative networks; traditional instruments, after all, were not developed with this mobile life-style in mind. However, much can be achieved through a very refined attitude to amplification of the instrumental source, accompanied by the performer's being prepared to achieve an increasingly fine control of sound articulation. Most wind and bowed stringed instruments are relatively adaptable. Other instruments, like the piano and individual percussion instruments, do not lend themselves to this flexibility because their morphological types are restricted to attack(-resonance) models. Groups of instruments carefully selected for their orchestrational possibilities can permit a more inventive sound repertory, but the increase in direct acoustic presence may technically and musically restrict or prevent the use of the subtleties offered by amplification. Furthermore, as the group increases in size so are new perceptual problems introduced. The more performers there are, the more varied the visual physical activity becomes, eventually achieving a state where the visual aspects of instrumental gesture compete with and overwhelm the purely acousmatic component.

Then there is the question of silences. The simultaneous 'visual silence' of many players weighs heavily, affecting the perception of structure by axing the music into visually active and inactive periods. Add to this the pleasures of source-spotting: the more original the sound repertory, the more likely it is that the listener will play games with source identification. Thus sheer visual force can relegate the acousmatic component to a subordinate role, always dragging indicative interpretations towards the gesture-field. These problems cannot always easily be solved by 'choreographing' the physical activities and silent periods of groups of performers because playing periods and gesture are often bound to sounding, orchestrational requirements.

As we have realized, the question of the instrument's remaining at centre-focus in not just a matter of sound but also of visual activity. The visual relationship between the seen instrumentalist and unseen acousmatic material is important on a dramatic level and it influences how sounding relationships are apprehended by the watching listener. We all know how much the performer's demeanour (which is seen to reflect sound articulation at a variety of structural levels) can affect the reception of the music. Those listeners relying entirely on a reflexive relationship look to visual activity at least to reinforce their emotional reaction, and at times even largely to translate the music into the appropriate reflexive emotion. In a pure instrumental work, sounding gestural relationships are always paralleled by an active human presence, whereas in the partially acousmatic work the electroacoustic component is invisible. The consequences are that the composer must include a certain dosage of gesture-based content in the acousmatic component in such a way that the desired human sector of the behaviour-field can be activated by both parties. Thus while a partially acousmatic work can explore the extended possibilities of instrumental play within the newer indicative networks, there must always be a proportion of acousmatic content acting within both the gesture-field and the behaviour-field if the two parties are to be regarded as equally significant. Indeed, since the acousmatic component is competing with the visible it must have a strongly articulated presence. The success of a partially acousmatic work is determined by the inventiveness with which the gesture- and behaviour-fields are exploited.

There are times, even in pure instrumental ensemble music, where the composer successfully achieves broader indicative interpretations, and the listener is less conscious of the gesture-network and the human-oriented sector of the behaviour-network. For example, these conditions are brought about in textures where the feeling of time passing stretches out beyond the reach of the more directive influence of gesture so that individual instrumental events are subsumed in a collective behaviour. The behaviour-field invoked can then become associated with the indicative networks of object/substance, vision, environment and certain aspects of space. The success of such textural contexts is not entirely a question of the composer's skill; it is also a question of listening attitude. The composer immersed in his sounding world can easily push aside the habits of source identification and gesture detection, but it is not so natural for other listeners to forsake such links. However, the practised interactive listener need have no problem, and the listener who habitually thinks extramusically about musical materials can adapt as long as the wider indicative interpretations are already appreciated outside music, and are considered, consciously or unconsciously, to be appropriate responses to music. It is worth noting that the breakdown of tonality, striated pitch and metrical rhythm as the prime organizing forces inevitably brought instrumental music closer to a wider indicative framework, particularly after the Second World War, during the period when electroacoustic resources began to spread.

The arrival of computers, MIDI-controllers and live signal processing on the concert stage has introduced a new problem related to gesture and visual focus. There is an increasing ambiguity between what is seen and what is heard, leading to ruptures in the links between the sounding and visual aspects of gesture. Computers are used on stage for accessing material and cuing sequences; MIDI-controllers can break the gesture link by permitting the performer to articulate sounds that are not the idiomatic property of the 'instrument' (percussion from a wind-controller, environmental sounds from a guitar-controller etc); MIDI-controllers permit the remapping of parameters so that the watching listener may be confused about or oblivious to the sound–gesture link; signal processing can transform a sound so far that it is no longer connected to its visible, instrumental source. Thus we can arrive at a situation where sounding spectro-morphologies do not correspond with perceived physical gesture: the listener is not adequately armed with a knowledge of the practicalities of new 'instrumental' capabilities and limitations, and articulatory subtlety is not recognized and may even be reduced compared with the traditional instrument (creating what I call a *minus-instrument*). The puzzled listener can be forgiven for not knowing whether to ascribe perceived musical deficiencies to a minus-instrument, the performer, or the composer.

What are the consequences? The causal connection between gesture and sound is undermined or destroyed, and performance gestures previously visible become invisible. Thus we witness a shift even in live performance towards the acousmatic. This is at once an enticing and dangerous prospect. It is enticing because of the potential expansion in the notion of the instrument and its musical language capacities. It is dangerous because at an extreme, in *live acousmatic performance* the word 'live' becomes redundant and meaningless. These are serious questions for the performer and composer: if you stay too close to the traditional gesture-model, electroacoustic

548

potential is not explored; if you go too far away you destroy the notion of 'performance'.

All the problems encountered above largely evaporate when a work becomes totally acousmatic, as it does when listened to in a recorded format. The visual sense, while still contributing to the listener's indicative relationship with sounding materials, is not activated by seeing a performance. Thus a recording of a partially acousmatic work is totally different from a seen performance. We all know that a live performance of pure instrumental music is not the same as a recording, for social, acoustic and technological reasons. But the transference of a partially acousmatic work to a totally acousmatic version is much more drastic, so drastic that the dominance of instrumental gesture can be reduced and absorbed into the acousmatic fabric. The problems raised above, if not entirely eradicated, are at least substantially transformed for the better. Of course, source recognition and instrumental gesture are not negated, but they are no longer directed by actually seeing the performance. Thus if instrumental and electroacoustic spectro-morphologies are aurally allied to the point of ambiguity, indicative interpretations gleaned from a recorded version can be substantially different from a seen performance. This is even more likely since recording permits questions of detailed equilibrium, relative presence and spatial perspective between the acoustic and electroacoustic components to be finely controlled, enhanced and even improved. The partially acousmatic work can therefore exist in two quite different guises. While the live performance may still be a rewarding experience if the relationship among musical, technological, spatial, visual and social components works, such a marriage has become increasingly complex and unstable. It is above all the acousmatic versions of works that reach an audience and that are today more significant for human experience. The acousmatic work and the acousmatic representation of the musical work should be in prime focus at the forefront of contemporary music activity.

CONCLUDING REMARKS

Adopting a perceptual approach I have attempted to find ways of explaining the special attractions of electroacoustic music, revealing how its sonic imagery expands beyond, and ultimately transcends the gesture- and utterance-based heritage of Western music. My primary concern, however, is with questions of musical signification. In identifying networks of indicative fields I hope to uncover mechanisms used by listeners to construct meanings from electroacoustic musical works, thereby contributing to discussion of musical signification generally. Any attempt to construct generally applicable theories of signification must take electroacoustic music into account. Moreover, the broad continuum of its sound world, stretching between the imagined and the real, provides the most comprehensive basis for studying human relationships with sonic phenomena.

Nattiez (1990: 102–29), in a comprehensive discussion, points out that historically, theories of musical signification oscillate between extremes that may exist concurrently. Simply defined, the intrinsic approach emphasizes formal relations within a work ('music is itself'), while the extrinsic approach concentrates on relations with non-musical experience. It might seem that my position in this chapter is heavily weighted towards the extrinsic, and indeed I consider that it is impossible for music to be purely intrinsic. I agree with Susan McLary when she sensibly affirms a faith in 'the public's pragmatic knowledge of musical signification', regardless of the attempts of academic disciplines, 'to insist that music is only music, that it cannot mean anything else' (McLary 1991: 21). If you inquire into a listener's response to a sound or musical work, trying to elucidate what it is that attracts or repels, it is impossible to avoid extrinsic references, such is the nature of verbal communication. However, identifying extrinsic relationships will not of itself uncover the meaning of a sound–event or work. In order to explain extrinsic workings and qualities we shall need to focus our attention on an intrinsic analysis of spectro-morphological features and their structural context. In other words, the extrinsic is determined by the intrinsic and vice versa – it is a reciprocal relationship. I regard musical experience as simultaneously extrinsic and intrinsic.

It is not a perverse indulgence which leads the electroacoustic composer frequently to ignore indicative signification, becoming immersed in the interactive relationship with sounds in order to refine spectro-morphological details. Interactive listening is the very means of penetrating the intrinsic qualities which determine the power both of the indicative networks and of the reflexive listening relationship. But interactive immersion frequently leads to drowning when the composer becomes incapable of surfacing to rediscover what was the fresh, indicative impact in the sound that provoked the immersion in the first place. Repeated focusing on minutiae easily prevents the composer from retaining a pragmatic perspective.

The interactive listening relationship is indeed a specialized acquisition which lies beyond the competence of most listeners. Yet it can be acquired by non-composers who become familiar with electroacoustic styles, and who are prepared to deepen their acquaintance with a work through repeated listenings which draw the attentive ear into interactive searching once the indicative essence can be taken for granted. But how often does the expert listener, including the composer-listener, get that far into a work? I regret to say that as a listener I rarely do or feel the need to do so, and I suspect that in the end the composer is an interactive listener for his or her own music but less so for the music of others. I therefore sympathize with Nattiez (1990: 95) when he states that the interactive relationship (he calls it 'concentrated hearing', a free translation of Schaeffer's *'écoute réduite'* – reduced listening) is 'hearing *as experienced by a composer, who hears sounds with extreme attentiveness before integrating them into a work'* (his italics).

The participation of technology in the compositional process has encouraged the spread of a listening attitude that approaches music more as a demonstration of a technical or technological process than an auditory experience. What is 'perceived' is technological progress: the ability of the technology or computer program to carry out a process or manipulative feat that is considered new, interesting in some way, or an improvement on existing means. This listening attitude belongs to the music technology subculture (composer, researcher, technician, manufacturer) and is encouraged by proliferative innovation and rapid obsolescence. Listening to technology is a necessary pursuit for those seeking new and improved musical means, but it is disquieting to realize that music that is not perceptually viable is too frequently presented as if it were. Composers (not only electroacoustic composers) often fruitfully conceive their music following processes, ideas and systems that are not perceptually determined; but the composer who ultimately refuses to confront the perceptual consequences abdicates cultural responsibility. Regrettably there is too much electroacoustic music that demonstrates a disdain for listeners' indicative needs and the spectro-morphological means of achieving them.

There remains a barrier between those listeners who can accept and enjoy full indicative relationships and those who are unable to break free from the immediate visual and physical nature of gesture and utterance as represented by instrumental and vocal tradition. This is apparent not only among 'ordinary' listeners. It is more seriously entrenched among educated musicians. Sometimes this is because they all too rarely come across a rewarding work, and are not motivated to pursue or take risks with new experiences. Professional musicians unfortunately often propound a closed ideology which sets stringent limits to what is acceptable as 'music'. Call it sonic art or sonic sculpture if it makes you any happier, but it is still a sounding art, and music was ever that. Even if these cultural barriers did not exist, it is inevitable that electroacoustic styles that seem to imply radical shifts away from both the prevailing 'classical' heritage and the 'popular' mass market will only gradually find wider acceptance. But the spread is inevitable as increasing numbers of young electroacoustic composers committed to indicative breadth filter through the culture, and as an increasing repertory becomes more widely disseminated on that ideal medium, the compact disc.

NOTES

1 The word 'acousmatic,' now widely accepted, was used by Pierre Schaeffer to refer to any listening circumstance where the source of the sound cannot be seen. It applies to all music heard over loudspeakers, but particularly to the electroacoustic music listening context. The term originally referred to the Pythagorian situation where lecturers spoke to their pupils from behind a screen in order to eradicate any visual distraction which might detract from language communication.

2 I invented the term 'spectro-morphology' to represent the dynamic shaping of the pitch-spectrum of a sound or sound-structure. (See Smalley 1986.)

3 'Sign' is used here in its semiotic sense. It is often impossible to identify musical signifiers with certainty, although there is more hope of doing so in traditional, note-based music, where there is a consistent low-level significant unit.

4 'Abstract' and 'abstracted' are discussed in Emmerson (1986a)

5 See Schachtel (1984). This book is concerned with psycho-analytic and psychological theory. Although music and sound are discussed, Schachtel clearly felt unable to examine them in as much depth as the other senses. Nevertheless, the musician-reader will find many concepts which can readily be expanded.

6 Reduced listening requires the listener to examine sound interactively, blotting out any indicative interpretation. (See Schaeffer 1966 and Chion 1983).

7 Smalley (1986) and the present chapter should be considered as parallel and interlocking texts, the present chapter elaborating indicative principles merely suggested in the former publication which was primarily concerned with interactive relationships. However, the two cannot easily be separated, and the reader will notice changes in thinking.

8 See Emmerson (1986a: 17–20) for a discussion on mimesis related to electroacoustic music.

9 I have decided that this term is best confined to an understanding of gesture. Applying it generally results in different and confusing systems of 'order'.

10 The most useful discussion of utterance in music is in Wishart (1985). The present chapter can only touch the surface of the subject.

11 Synaesthesia can be defined as 'the process whereby secondary sensation in one field is produced by a primary stimulus in another' (Sack 1980: 132).

12 The idea of 'intimate immensity' is developed in Bachelard (1964: 183 ff).

13 The integration of a new 'instrument' into a culture is not a purely musical question, but depends on the socio-economic climate and a lengthy period of time for full assimilation. The possibility that a new electroacoustic 'instrument' could become established is extremely remote due to the dual factors of rapid technological redundancy and commercial competition. Indeed, in our current socio-economic climate the prospect for such an occurrence seems fanciful. It should be noted that a synthesizer is not an instrument. It is a collection of potential instruments.

14 The concept of causal permanence is Schaeffer's. See Schaeffer (1966) and Chion (1983), or, for a discussion in English, Dack (1989).

15 Transcontextuality, mainly related to visual arts, is discussed in Hutcheon (1985). The ideas are more interesting than her musical references, which are confined to 'quotation music' and stylistic imitation.

REFERENCES

BACHELARD, G. (1964) *The Poetics of Space*, trans. M. Jolas, New York: Orion Press.

CHION, M. (1983) *Guide des Objets Sonores*, Paris: Editions Buchet Chastel/INA GRM.

DACK, J. (1989) 'Electro-acoustic musical thought and instrumental thought: the significance of Schaeffer and the Cologne School', unpublished Ph.D. thesis, Middlesex Polytechnic.

EMMERSON, S. (1986a) 'The relation of language to materials', in S. Emmerson (ed.) *The Language of Electroacoustic Music*, London: Macmillan, pp. 17–39.

——(ed.) (1986b) *The Language of Electroacoustic Music*, London: Macmillan.

HUTCHEON, L. (1985) *A Theory of Parody: The Teachings of Twentieth-century Art Forms*, London: Methuen.

MCLARY, S. (1991) *Feminine Endings: Music, Gender, and Sexuality*, Minneapolis: University of Minnesota Press.

NATTIEZ, J-J. (1990) *Music and Discourse: Toward a Semiology of Music*, Princeton, NJ: Princeton University Press.

SACK, R.D. (1980) *Conceptions of Space in Social Thought*, London: Macmillan.

SCHACHTEL, E.G. (1984) *Metamorphosis: On the Development of Affect, Perception, Attention, and Memory*, New York: Da Capo Press.

SCHAEFFER, P. (1966) *Traité des Objets Musicaux*, revised 1977, Paris: Editions du Seuil.

SMALLEY, D. (1986) 'Spectro-morphology and structuring processes', in S. Emmerson (ed.) *The Language of Electroacoustic Music*, London: Macmillan, pp. 61–93.

WISHART, T. (1985) *On Sonic Art*, York: Imagineering Press.

554

27

Composers and Audiences:
New Relationships in the Technological Age

BRUCE PENNYCOOK

MOTIVATIONS

In 1986, I published an article which examined the courtship and marriage of technology and composition in college-level music education (Pennycook 1986). I predicted then that the accelerating growth of computer-based commercial music products would lead to a general disenchantment with electroacoustic music by serious composition students and professional composers. I also predicted that even the most generally accessible electronic instruments such as the Yamaha DX7 would not foment a repertoire in the way that the piano had in the previous century.

I was both right and wrong.

My bases for these predictions failed to take into account the extent to which audiences as consumers shape the concerns of composers and of musical activities in general. Powerful technologies have reshaped the mechanisms by which music of all descriptions is delivered to listeners. The forces of global enterprise have promoted a uniform musical face to market their goods and services and, at an unprecedented rate, the differences among these products are diminishing toward a common state of *sameness*. Composers and audiences of new music cannot remain immune from these trends.

To imagine that contemporary music and, more important, that the audiences, both real and potential, of serious music-making can survive and flourish against such pressures without a major shift in the visibility and presence of the *demand* for this kind of artistic expression could only result from a failure to observe major changes in the mechanics of the global electronic age. At an unprecedented rate, differences among consumer products marketed throughout the world, via expanding networks of electronic communications systems, are diminishing toward some unknown state of *sameness*.

Just as sameness is dominating the global market place through the pervasive neutralizing forces of media advertising, the range of styles of popular music has been diminished by the omnipresence of electronic and computer music equipment and by the domination of the development of these devices by a few international firms. More and more people are receiving music with less and less sonic variety. Although there exists a bewildering array of sophisticated computer-based music gear, the trend in commercial music (including film soundtracks) has been towards artificial replication of standard acoustic instruments. Leading manufacturers such as Yamaha, Roland, and eMU Systems are well aware that timbral experimentation remains the domain of the minority of buyers and that digital instruments and devices that faithfully replicate many other instruments are preferred by the majority.

Nevertheless, the few buyers who do appreciate and exploit the capabilities of these new instruments attempt to project a richer acoustical world than commercial music tends to provide. Only universities, schools of music or heavily subsidized public institutions offer the facilities necessary for these pursuits. While the commercial music industry continues to expand worldwide, deploying marketing techniques and resource manipulation similar to those used by Coca-Cola or General Motors, the public venues and media distribution channels for contemporary music are crumbling from lack of funding and diminishing audiences.

Despite the pressures of commercial forces, composers are composing, performing and making records and compact discs of their music at a rate that seems contrary to the realities of public interest in and support for their work. Who are the intended audiences for these pieces? What influences are being exerted by the expansion of commercial music distribution and by the thriving electronic/computer music industry? Are there observable changes in the general orientation of young composers and audiences?

To focus the discussion, I have prepared two (unpublished) concert reviews, one of a concert that took place during the 1988 *International Festival du Jazz de Montréal*, and the other of a new-music concert I recently attended in Toronto. The music presented at these concerts is relatively typical of many other presentations. More important, however, is that the audiences can be considered to be representative of the general interest in and awareness of the two musical styles.

Review of a Jazz Concert: The Montréal Jazz Festival, 1988

Salle Wilfred Pelletier, the largest and grandest hall in Montréal's Place des Arts, had sold out weeks in advance. Unlike the quiet solemnity of the patrons of the Orchestre Symphonique de Montréal, the theatre's home ensemble, the audience was in flux, activated by the steamy July heat-wave, cold beer, and a week of live jazz.

The famed Ballets Jazz de Montréal presented two new works by jazz-guitarist, Pat Metheny, who enjoys a nearly mythical status from his triumphs at previous Montréal Jazz Festivals.

One of the works, *Adieu*, had been commissioned especially for the Festival combining Metheny's unique style with Richard Levi's choreography. The piece presented a gentle, seamless flow of lyrical duets and ensemble settings plus the fluid improvisations of Metheny accompanied by pre-programmed material from a Synclavier digital music system.

Both the music and dance existed in a kind of torpid dream-world – pastel chiffon and streams of sonorous jazz-folk harmonies which very gradually increased to a swirl of colour on stage and deep, thick synthesized sounds ornamented by Metheny's improvisations. After the climax the music slipped away to quieter moments, eventually disappearing with the lighting and activity on stage following the gradual decay.

After the final chord, the audience seemed completely spellbound, waiting several moments before launching into a thunderous standing ovation. The dance and the music had touched them. Pat Metheny appeared on stage alone, shy but visibly appreciative. The night had been a triumph for both new jazz and contemporary dance.

Outside on the street, the bluesmen, the fusion–rock–jazz groups, the Latin-salsa bands and the twenty-piece big bands sparred for their place in the Festival soundscape. Thousands of people filled the bars and the open sections around the elevated band stands listening, dancing, and cheering on each soloist no matter how repetitive the playing or poor the sound-system. Everyone had come to witness first-hand jazz-legends and unknowns alike and to enjoy live, improvised music in a carnival atmosphere.

Review of a concert given by Vivienne Spiteri and Joseph Macerollo at the Music Gallery

On 21 April, 1989, the Music Gallery in Toronto sponsored a joint concert featuring Montréal harpsichordist Vivienne Spiteri and the internationally renowned accordian virtuoso, Joseph Macerollo. The concert included works for harpsichord alone – *What's in a Name?* by Roderik de Man, *Fantasmagoria* by Ka Nin Chan, and *Fantango* by Jukka Tiensuu; works for harpsichord and interactive computer system – *the desert speaks* by Bruce Pennycook; harpsichord and 12–string electric guitar – *Doubling* by Timothy Brady (who also performed the guitar part); accordion, live electronics, and tape – *Sticherarion* by Larry Lake; accordion and tape – *Earth Cycles* by Alexina Louis, and *In the Beginning Was the End* by Hope Lee, for harpsichord and accordion, commissioned especially for this concert. All of the composers with the exception of de Man and Tiensuu are Canadians.

A small but appreciative audience enjoyed an evening of superb playing by the two soloists and nearly flawless technological support from the Music Gallery, even though the mix of traditional acoustic and synthetic timbres caused a kind of auditory confusion.

The works ranged from the translucent pointillism of *Fantasmagoria* to the jazz-influenced style of *Doubling* – a kind of study in presto unison playing. The Lake work intermingled electronically altered sounds from the accordion with sustained, rich sonorities from the tape. Here, Macerollo's mastery of extended techniques effectively bridged the gap between the reedy sounds of the concert accordion and electroacoustic music.

Each of these reviews has been written intentionally in a style that reflects its likely readership – the jazz review might have appeared in a daily newspaper whereas the new music review could have been found (if at all) only in a speciality newsletter or scholarly circular. They have been invented for this article to illustrate certain differences and similarities between the two events in terms of musical content, audience demographics, venues, funding, and the role of electronics. From these discussions some generalizations regarding the current and future states of contemporary music-making will emerge.

MUSICAL CONTENT

The musical language of Metheny and other rock-influenced jazz musicians has emerged from a synthesis of the back-beat drum styles of American soul music, country–folk–rock guitar and modal blues. (This style is familiar to nearly everyone since many of the acoustical and rhythmic aspects of jazz–rock 'fusion' now appear in watered-down form as 'environment' music seeping out of loudspeakers all over the industrial world.) Jazz musicians and contemporary composers have been deeply influenced by this fusion partly because of the merging of electronics and virtuoso playing but also because of the blending of rock and jazz rhythmic styles. For example, Timothy Brady's *Doubling* for electric 12–string guitar and amplified harpsichord utilizes similar harmonic and motivic materials to Metheny's compositions, but presents a more unified and consistent structure. The harmonic language and driving repetitive rhythms are familiar but the form in which they are presented is much more challenging than the predictable chorus–solo–chorus format of most jazz tunes. In my opinion, Brady's piece is successful because it presents familiar, accessible territory yet demands a degree of attentiveness and concentration from the listener beyond most jazz releases.

A comparison of the two concerts reveals another important similarity. Like many contemporary jazz artists, Metheny utilizes a subtle blend of several processing devices in his works. He also uses a computer audio system to expand his compositional resources. For the performance of *Adieu*, a Synclavier,[1] a very expensive digital sampler-sequencer, provided all of the accompaniment material. Similarly, many composers of electroacoustic contemporary music are exploring computer-assisted accompaniment and utilizing complex arrays of sound-processing devices. Concert set-ups for these two styles are beginning to look very similar. In some cases they are also beginning to sound alike.

A much more pronounced contrast exists, however, between the language of fusion jazz and works by university-trained composers such as Chan and Lee which are derived from the angular, dissonant language of serialism. There have been moments in jazz history when the language of the post-war musical avant-garde attracted adventurous composers and musicians such as Cecil Taylor, a pioneer of the 1950s Free Jazz movement, and widely acclaimed saxophonist Anthony Braxton. In fact, had the *Ballets Jazz* commission been awarded to a modern disciple of Free Jazz, the comparison of these two concerts would have taken a totally different tack.

I am not suggesting here that the aleatory improvisational styles of Braxton and others can be equated with the highly controlled methodical post-serialism that we loosely call 'academic' composition. I will venture, however, that to an untrained ear, the consistently dissonant harmonies and

559

jerky rhythms of Free Jazz and contemporary composition sound uniformly grey and generally unappealing.

Perhaps this reality has influenced some of the pioneers of the post-war avant-garde. Although it would be difficult to attribute the shift away from the very dissonant and unmetred orchestral sound clusters of Penderecki's *Threnody* (1958) to the modal and strikingly motivic language of his more recent *Concerto for Viola and Orchestra* (1987) to any direct influence from American jazz, one must wonder what kind of forces *have* contributed to Penderecki's return to less adventurous ground.

It is my contention that many composers, both young and established, have elected to alter the relationship that they wish to foster between their music and the audiences to which it is directed. For many composers, the period of radical experimentation (and intentional audience alienation) belongs in the past. It is just too lonely.

AUDIENCE DEMOGRAPHICS

The huge enthusiastic crowds that stars like Miles Davis, Pat Metheny, Wynton Marsalis and Luciano Pavarotti enjoy are rivalled only by the attendance at rock concerts and professional sports events. Such idolatry has existed prior to the present era of course; Liszt, Verdi and Wagner are obvious examples from the nineteenth century. The forces that contribute to such widespread recognition are fuelled by public visibility, informed discussion and, in the modern world, 'media coverage'. Unfortunately, news coverage and serious criticism of contemporary music are extremely rare.

The apparent lack of interest in and critical understanding of contemporary music among learned professional artists outside the music community is very distressing. An examination of critical review magazines in North America such as *Harper's*, *Atlantic Quarterly* or *Canadian Forum* rarely reveals a single reference to the activities and concerns of composers or the concepts and devices of composition. This cannot mean that the authors and critics who read and contribute to these publications have no interest in music; I am certain they do. But it could mean that the music they receive does not convey matters of significance or inspire informed discussion. It could also mean that when they *do* seek out contemporary musics, they are equally disenchanted.

It would be convenient and soothing to assume that the non-musicians are simply uninformed – that they are the product of a shoddy education lacking in any substantive musical training. It may be, however, that contemporary composers are not speaking to anyone outside the institutions that shelter them and that modern musical discourse has become so insular and private that outsiders cannot hope to decode the messages. Have composers been led to the emperor's tailor and come out naked?

Consider for a moment the standing-room-only crowd at the jazz festival and the tiny gathering at the new music concert. It is reasonable to assume that the audience at the Metheny/Ballets Jazz concert was comprised of a wide spectrum of music and dance consumers, many of whom were probably discerning listeners or perhaps professionals in other art disciplines. Overall, the people at that concert reflected the make-up of the Festival audience in general – 25–45 years of age, multi-racial, and roughly even in proportion of males and females. The fewer than sixty people who attended the concert at the Music Gallery were primarily musicians and, as with nearly every new-music concert I have ever attended, the audience was almost exclusively white and at least 80 per cent male, 25–45 years old. Probably, many had received or were in the process of undertaking formal music training. This is a familiar situation; small audiences most of whom are involved with the venue, the institution, the artists, or their own creation of similar works, attending what will possibly be a first and last performance of a concert which, given the usual complexity of modern music, probably consumed countless weeks of preparation.

Herein lies the most troubling aspect of this discussion and the central theme of the article. Many practitioners of new music have sunk into the worst kind of relativism and have consequently become the least capable people of judging the value (as opposed to technical quality) of their works. Fragmentation and stylistic chauvinism are reducing the audiences to private clubs and secret societies. At the same time, the rest of the world is enjoying Pat Metheny, Mozart, King Sunny Adé, Pt. Shiv Kumar Sharma or whoever, and not paying any attention to musical styles that are intentionally remote and seem to pursue the singular aesthetic of complexity. I will return to this problem shortly.

Regardless of the size and make-up of audiences, it can be assumed that live performances retain a unique strength that cannot be wholly replaced by electronic means. The many hundreds at the jazz festival and the handful at the new-music concert both enjoyed the fleeting experience of live human expression. Unfortunately, the availability of live music, especially contemporary music, is very limited.

I noted with interest a survey undertaken in England by Bernard Barrell

561

of the number of performances of works by living British composers by major professional orchestras throughout the country (Barrell 1986: 1–5). In brief, Barrell showed that the principal orchestras throughout Great Britain have almost abandoned the living composer. Similar surveys taken in Canada assessing the frequency of works by living composers indicate that, while the number of recordings and broadcasts of Canadian orchestral performances is increasing, the number of performances of Canadian-composed works is rapidly declining.

Barrell does not question the reasons behind these trends. I submit that the same factors that are diluting the audiences of contemporary music are also forcing conductors and music directors to mount works drawn primarily from familiar, pre-twentieth-century repertoire. As public funding is reduced (rightly or wrongly), the burden of financial accountability is forcing a more conservative attitude among programme directors. The assumption is that audiences only want that which is familiar and pleasing and that fulfilling this assumption will generate increased ticket revenues and there-fore sustain the concert venues.

The two concerts I have been discussing occurred in very different venues. *Place des Arts* survives by mixing profitable events with government-financed presentations. The Music Gallery, on the other hand, like so many similar small venues in North America and Europe, struggles to retain its place as a centre for experimental musics of all kinds. It survives through the leonine efforts of its administrators to secure annual operational funds, but it may not survive the increasing pressures towards conformity and profitability.

The major venues can increase the percentage of money-making shows without appearing to have abandoned their cultural obligations. The smaller experimental venues would become totally different institutions if they shifted their artistic policies in favour of commercially viable activities. Once again, market imperatives will dominate and the production of and access to highly specialized artistic activities will decrease.

These conditions will intensify over the next few decades. The strength and global pervasiveness of multinational firms will increase exponentially. More and more fringe activities like experimental music, dance and film will be squeezed out as public and corporate benefactors search for profitable ways to sell the 'look and feel' of caring.

For many concert-goers, a shift toward the familiar will be welcome. The key point is, however, that there may be a totally different and substantially larger audience which will not be remotely affected by the life or death of the traditional music establishments. It is this 'other audience' to whom composers should consider directing their work through alternative means.

COMPOSERS, AUDIENCES AND TECHNOLOGY

It is clear that the age of unfettered financial subsidies for the arts is drawing to a close. Coupled with decreases in public (and corporate) funding for experimental art is the obvious disinterest towards it by an increasingly educated public at whom it is probably directed.

Without question, music audiences exist. The continuing growth of the music industry and strong concert attendance proves this. Equally without question is the increasing global access to music through electronic distribution mechanisms, and it is through these mechanisms that contemporary music composers in the future could cultivate new audiences. The 'other audience' *is* listening and, in my opinion, growing weary of the uniformity and intellectual paucity of popular music. Young composers are exploring musical styles that are both musically rich and appealing to the untrained listener by absorbing the sonorities and, most important, the energy of jazz, rock and many other popular styles. It is very unlikely that 'academic' composition, with its emphasis on sonic extremes and so-called musical experimentation, will ever capture the interest and critical appraisal of the hundreds of thousands of educated and culturally sophisticated listeners who are inseparably connected to electronic media. I am certain that the vitality and relevance of contemporary film and literature which serious composition enjoyed a century ago can be regained. Composers must realize that music-as-nuclear-physics may produce learned approval but will never capture and stimulate the vast and truly worthy audience starved of artistic fulfilment.

The technological means to reach audiences worldwide are now being installed. Composers can address this audience by responding to the growing need for vital and relevant musical expression. Or, they can remain cloistered and ignored.

NEW AND REVISED PREDICTIONS

My prediction that instruments such as the ubiquitous Yamaha DX/TX series (over 3,000,000 sold) would engender a new repertoire of contemporary music was correct. But although there *are* many compositions that utilize this technology, other devices can usually be substituted. In other words, these instruments are to contemporary music as the wide variety of keyboard instruments were to the Baroque composer – fully interchangeable and equally correct. The concept of a generic instrument has been extended even further with the introduction of digital samplers. These devices are the 'Polaroid' of music; brief moments of any sound can be captured and replayed with surprising realism but, like instant photo-developing, without the intricacies of the manual developing process. Yet they offer unprecedented performance (or perhaps I should say re-performance) capabilities which have significantly extended the composers' and performers' timbral palette.

My other prediction, that composers would not adopt the same technologies as commercial and jazz musicians, was clearly wrong. As each new wave of devices emerges, composers and performers in all fields are benefiting from and exploiting the advances in digital audio engineering.

It is with this revised assessment of the marriage of technology and serious musical endeavour that I offer my new prediction that the presence and importance of serious composition will reattain a position of public visibility and cultural prominence. This will happen because there is a widespread demand for profound musical expression and experience and because composers will capitalize on the mechanisms of global communications technology through the creation of works that reflect the musical realities of the people with whom they are communicating.

I hope that I am right.

NOTE

1 New England Digital Corporation, White River Junction, Vermont.

REFERENCES

BARRELL, B. (1986) 'Concert analysis, orchestral concerts 1984–85', *Composer* (Journal of the Composer's Guild of Great Britain), Winter.
PENNYCOOK, B. (1986) 'Electro-acoustic music: a new paradox', in S. Emmerson (ed.) *The Language of Electroacoustic Music*, London: Macmillan, pp. 119–40.

28

Music And Technology:
Problems And Possibilities

TREVOR WISHART

INTRODUCTION

Music and technology have always been intrinsically bound up with one another. All musical instruments are technological extensions of our ability to make sounds by blowing, scraping, hitting or otherwise exciting materials in the world around us. More fundamentally, the development of the Greek tradition of mathematics and physics was initiated by the Pythagorean discovery of the relationship between the lengths of vibrating strings which produced consonantly related tones.

The evolution and perfection of the violin in the sixteenth and seventeenth centuries is a good example of the crucial importance of technological advance in the development of European Art Music, while the nineteenth century saw the more systematic development of mechanical instrument technology through both the technical genius of instrument makers like Adolphe Sax and the musical demands of composers like Wagner.

The twentieth century has brought about a much more intense relationship between music and technology. This is partly due to the development of cheap and easily accessible electrical power, and the subsequent evolution of electronic and digital technology and its application to musical problems. More significantly, however, the phenomenal rate of technological progress and the growth of our knowledge about all aspects of the physical world have penetrated most aspects of our existence, and music is no exception.

As a result we have seen a veritable explosion in the development of new musical instruments whose sound sources are electronic circuits or magnetically stored sound data. More fundamentally, the mushrooming of the science of information technology has brought about a qualitative change in our ability to handle and manipulate musical data of various kinds.

These developments are at once full of artistic promise and beset with pitfalls, and in this essay I aim to address both of these aspects of the current relationship between music and technology.

THE POTENTIAL

Musical Knowledge Acquisition

Technology promises to revolutionize the process of musical learning in its broadest sense. At the most obvious level, the advent of musical recording has made more kinds of music available to more people than was ever before possible. The ability to hear (and re-hear) any specific piece of music at any time has immense repercussions in the field of music learning. We can study a score, *and* a realization of that score in performance, over and over again. We can study a recording of our own performance, and hence gain insight into our strengths and weaknesses as performers. We can listen to the music of other cultures, and other epochs, without waiting for the special public occasions on which these might be played. Although to some people, this accessibility of recorded music is a threat, to me, coming from a low-income, working-class family in an industrial town in the north of England, it was my high road to serious music.

Accessible technology also has much to offer in the more conventional areas of music education. Simple aural training, which can be a drudge for both students and teachers alike, can be transformed using interactive computer programs, in the manner of computer games, which the student can adjust to his or her level/needs, leaving the teacher free to deal with higher level concerns. More significantly, using a computer sequencer/score-writing program and synthesizer provides a direct link between the action of playing notes and the appearance of a score. Being able to see immediately the notation of a phrase or chord played on an instrument can short-circuit the learning problems of people who have difficulty with musical literacy.

At a more advanced level, the task of appreciating the nuances of orchestration has in the past involved a long study of the existing literature, aided in the present century, perhaps, by listening to records and cassettes. Even this, however, can only be a guideline for a composer who is attempting to do something new with orchestral resources. When I was a music student there was a story circulating, possibly apocryphal, that at the University of California students heard their orchestration exercises played immediately by the University Orchestra. Whatever the truth of this rumour this was certainly not the case at my college and the idea of attempting to write new orchestral music knowing that the first aural confirmation (or denial!) of one's intuition would be at the first performance was extremely intimidating. Having become accustomed to working with sounds in detail by listening to them in the studio, the situation in regard to orchestral works had, for me, become more rather than less daunting!

Suddenly, however, the advent of the cheap polytimbral synthesizer and the computer-based sequencer means that instrumentation ideas can be tested, in rough, using synthesized sounds approximating instrumental analogues; they can also be varied at will, almost at the touch of a button, to improve or completely alter an initial conception. Orchestration, at least in its initial stages, becomes an interactive learning experience, and, for me, this is a qualitative change in the music-learning experience. Also, ironically, such developments make the task of composing for traditional instruments much more accessible, a fact that I hope will counter some performing musicians' fears that the new technology will destroy their craft. This is not to say that we will all necessarily become better musicians, but merely that the task of acquiring essential musical skills is much simplified and we should expect to see basic musical ability spread more widely in the community at large.

At the level of the generation of musical structure, technological means, in the form of sequencer/synthesizer or just using a domestic multi-track tape-recorder, open up the possibility of immediate aural feedback of the musical structures we are developing. The elaboration of a satisfying formal scheme for the generation of musical events can involve the composer in a great deal of time and effort. In the past, it would be difficult to know if a slight change in the assumptions or the details of that structural idea would have produced a more effective musical result. Also, after investing a great deal of intellectual energy in deriving a formal scheme and producing a score it is exceedingly difficult to admit that the aural results are not as exciting as one might have hoped for. (It's easier to blame the performers, or perhaps the listeners!) Electronic

567

technology allows us to adopt a heuristic approach to building musically effective structures. Build, test by listening, rebuild. This ability will, it is hoped, reduce the temptation to construct impregnable ideological postures to defend our compositional procedures.

A simple example of this heuristic approach is provided by my own work, *VOX-3* for four amplified voices,[1] in which the singers are asked to sing in different metres and/or tempi mutually co-ordinated in a very precise manner. This co-ordination is achieved by providing each singer with a click track, the four click tracks having being generated in precise tempo-relations by a computer program. In this manner I hoped to be able to explore the counterpoint of different, clearly delineated, rhythmic streams. (The ways in which accents synchronize, or fail to do so, between the simultaneous streams provided a second-order level of rhythmic organization, inaccessible without the precision of the computer-generated synch tracks.) Rather than taking for granted the effectiveness of my experiments (or just hoping for the best), I sang all the parts onto a domestic multi-track tape-recorder to convince myself of the efficacy of the polyrhythmic counterpoint, before committing a final version to paper. In this way a theoretical insight into new musical structures was tested, aurally, long before it reached the concert hall.

The combination of computer-sequencer and synthesizer has a particular bearing on rigorously formalized compositional procedures. These are ideally suited to being programmed. Furthermore, programs can be parameterized in such a way as to permit variation of the structure in detail or in essence by the exchange of a few parameters in the program. Each alternative structure may then be aurally tested, at least in rough, using a MIDI synthesizer. The advantages the technology offers in this regard, however, rely on the willingness of composers of this rigorous persuasion to allow the concept of aural testing into a world which can often seem a closed circle of compositional method and textual analysis, untouched by human ear.

The same heuristic approach to musical formation can be applied in other fields. A simple example is the application of multidimensional scaling techniques to sets of new, or unique, sounds which a composer wishes to use in a composition. The composer can define any quality he or she feels to be important in the perception of the sounds, either traditional (pitch, loudness, brightness) or personal (fuzziness, stability–instability, recognizability, etc.), and then assign values to the sound objects along perceptual dimensions according to his or her perception of these properties. In this way one should be able to build up a useful perceptual map of the properties of the sound world one is working with, and this could become an important pre-compositional tool.

Score Production

From the traditional composer's point of view, the availability of 'music-processing' along the lines of the word-processor, although it may not (as yet) be intrinsically faster at the level of notating the score than the traditional pen and manuscript paper approach, should offer a number of significant advantages. For example, it should be possible to extract and print parts *automatically*, and to produce single scores or parts on demand.

This in its turn makes self-publication a viable proposition, and we may expect to see music publishers in the future acting more as agents for their associated composers' works, rather than investing large sums in costly print runs. Because of the lower investment costs involved in taking on new composers, we might also hope to see more adventure and risk-taking among the large publishing houses.

Not all the technological problems of 'music-processing' have been solved, however. There are still subtleties of layout, even in the most traditional of scores, that have not been satisfactorily formalized. More significantly, any composer who, as I do, chooses to use non-standard notation from time to time, will have a hard time finding suitable computer-graphic tools. It is certainly possible to imagine a graphic environment in which arbitrary visual icons can be created, and their dimensions and characteristics modified in a rule-governed way appropriate to a time-based notation system. But it seems unlikely that any major commercial software house is going to spend a lot of time time developing it. The problem here is not a limitation of the technology, but of the commercial environment in which it evolves, and this will be discussed more fully below.

Musical Instruments

The original archetype of the electrically powered instrument was the electronic organ. The wind-powered organ on which it is modelled is a relatively ancient instrument and strangely untypical of the contemporary instrumental pantheon, in that it requires a power source to provide air pressure independent of the *performing* actions of the player. (The performer may have had to provide air pressure by pedalling bellows but this was separated from the activity of playing the keyboard; a similar separation occurs in the bagpipes.) Electricity to drive the air-pump was an obvious and unremarkable innovation here.

But the organ has another unusual characteristic in that it provides a set of different, quite distinct sound qualities from its many rows of pipes which are, however, all activated by the same playing action (fingers pressing keys). In more conventional instruments, the timbre of the instrument is intrinsically bound up with both its particular mode of excitation (blowing, plucking, striking, bowing) and the action of the performer in exciting this mechanism. Particularly where the performer's sound-making action is continuous (as in bowing or blowing) the performers physiological control of action through time has a profound effect on the nature and evolution of the instrumental sonority.

The advent of both electrical sound-reproduction, via amplifiers and loudspeakers, and the development of electronic oscillators, made it possible to develop an electronic analogue of the organ. Although the quality of the sounds was (especially in the early stages) not comparable with traditional organs, in a certain sense this did not matter. The concept of a set of contrasted timbres, accessible through stops from the same keyboard(s) was sufficiently organ-like for the new instrument to be quickly accepted for what it was.

However, the electronic organ concept has dogged thinking about the development of new electronic musical instruments ever since. Many so-called 'synthesizers' available on the commercial market are little more than electronic organs with a broadened pallette of stop sonorities. (I will refer to these instruments as 'synthetic instruments' to differentiate them from true, general purpose sound synthesizers which I will discuss below.) This development has distinct drawbacks. The organ is a very special type of instrument; the separation of the performing action from the sound-generation procedure, the clear-cut delineation of pitch and sonority, and the division of sonority into a set of distinct fixed classes or stops are, in a wider musical context, both excessively rigid and creatively limiting. In particular, it strongly reinforces the simplistic notion that music is essentially pitch-structures in time, to which 'timbre' is added, in a kind of colouring-book way. This problem will be discussed more fully below.

Furthermore, if the organ concept is taken as the paradigm of a musical instrument there is little incentive to delve deeper into the perceived 'musicalness' of the sonority of more typical traditional musical instruments. We can simply go on providing endless new arbitrary stop settings, substituting abundance for subtelty.

Fortunately musicians have demanded more, and most synthetic instruments are now at least touch-sensitive in one or more ways – to key-pressure or key-velocity – and, significantly, to aftertouch, meaning that the player can influence the continuing evolution of a sound once it has been initiated, as is always the case on traditional bowed or blown instruments. The limitations of such systems as exist are not chiefly due to any limitation in the underlying control concepts, but more to do with the fineness with which this control data is encoded and the particular way it is linked to the sound-production mechanism. The advent of the MIDI protocol (for transmitting musical data, within or between synthesizers or computers) is again, in principle, to be welcomed. A lack of fineness of discrimination, and the system's willingness to lose control-data information in favour of pitch/loudness information in an overcrowded channel, could all be overcome if the data transfer rates and certain other aspects of the protocol were upgraded.

Linking performance action in a subtle and convincing way to timbral variation is a more complex problem and will most probably remain as much a craft in electronic instrument design as it was with traditional instrument manufacture (though we now have the possibility of making this linkage programmable!)

The increasing refinement with which we can now model natural sounds, and manipulate those models, also gives us another insight into the development of more lively synthetic instruments. The original keyboard-synthesizer assumption was that a particular waveform would suffice for a single instrumental voice (or stop) over its whole range. This is clearly an inadequate model, but it is more difficult to define *precisely* what it is that makes us recognize the quite wide range of timbres we hear from piano notes (or, in fact, organ pipes) in different registers as belonging to the same class, and being different from sounds from even a different kind of piano. By carefully synthesizing sets of closely similar sounds, whose differences we can clearly define in acoustic terms, we can set up controlled psychoacoustic experiments to examine such questions and hence develop better acoustic models of what constitutes a 'musical instrument' in the traditional sense. This insight may then be generalized and applied to the design of a whole new field of potential synthetic instruments.

Although the electronic organ concept has been limiting in many ways, and currently exerts a strong conservative influence on even electroacoustic music education (see below), in another sense the organ concept may prove to be revolutionary. The very separation of performance action from the sound-producing mechanism at the heart of organ technology has led, by a

571

circuitous route, to interest in the technological separation of 'excitation-transducer' and 'sound-source', which in turn is leading us towards a redefinition of what a musical instrument is.

Using sophisticated electronic sensing techniques it is (or will be) possible to detect, very accurately, subtle nuances of, for instance, embouchure, breath pressure, and tongue motion, to encode these electronically, and then to redirect the sonic outcome of this physiological control data in a programmable way. Broadly speaking, tongue motion might control noise content, embouchure the spectral brightness of the sound, breath pressure the pitch of the sound, or any other association of action with sonic properties we care to program. Furthermore, we may 'fine-tune' the effect a particular physiological action may have on any of these properties of the sound. Thus, not only is the sound itself determinable separately from the mechanics of production, but the way the player physiologically controls that sound is open to redefinition. In this way we retain the detailed subleties of instrumental technique but apply them in as yet unheard ways.

Meta-instruments

Our understanding of the multidimensional nature of 'timbre' has advanced more since the development of sound-recording and the advent of computer technology than in the whole previous history of acoustics. The ability to capture sounds in their totality and examine them, as it were, under an aural microscope, led to the first detailed phenomenological classification of sonic properties, by the *Groupe de Recherches Musicales* in Paris. The ability to perform detailed spectral analyses over sequences of very short time-windows, using computers, has taught us both how immensely rich in detail a single natural sound can be and how limited our preconceived notions of timbre and the relationship between pitch and 'timbre' have been.

Helmholtz's nineteenth-century study of 'musical tones', rooted in a traditional classification of musical parameters, tended to confirm pre-conceived categoric distinctions between musical and non-musical tones, percussion, and not-percussion, and above all the notion that timbre (or, more acutely, all those properties of a sound that are not pitch, duration or overall loudness) was a fairly simple and secondary aspect of our musical perception.

Helmholtz's theory, though correct in broad outline, was both limited in scope (dealing only with 'musical tones' as defined by nineteenth-century practice) and in fine detail. Timbre was seen to be primarily a function of the relative loudness of harmonic partials within the spectrum of a sound (and here Helmholtz was necessarily dealing with time-averages, as his analysis techniques did not permit the fine windowing of the sound now available to us thanks to electronic computing power and digital sound recording) and the overall variation in amplitude of the sound (the loudness 'envelope'). The opposite to this ordered state of affairs was noise, in which the spectral components were extremely disordered over frequency and time.

This leads us to a consideration of a central new development in twentieth-century music, the synthesizer proper. The true concept of the synthesizer is not that of an instrument in the traditional sense, but of a universal sound-producer, a meta-instrument. With the development of electronic circuits that would produce sinusoidal oscillations at audio frequencies, it seemed that it should be possible to construct such a meta-instrument along lines suggested by Helmholtz's analysis of sounds. If all sounds were truly made up of sine-wave partials, then it should be possible in principle to construct any sound whatsoever by combining such sine-waves and imposing an appropriate envelope on the resulting combination (the concept of additive synthesis).

The principal flaw in the over-optimistic early development of the synthesizer was, however, theoretical rather than practical. Helmholtz's analysis lacked fine details, and so did the sounds produced by the early synthesizers. To produce anything approaching the 'liveliness' of a natural sound, we need not only to control the relative loudness of the partials, but also their phase relationships, the individual loudness envelope of each partial through time, subtle pitch-shifts of the partials and so on.

It needed the advance in our acoustical understanding, and the development of large general-purpose synthesis languages on computers, before anything approaching the inner richness of natural sounds could be generated directly by such additive synthesis techniques. The only true synthesizers (with this degree of generality) have been, until recently, large programs running on mainframe computers, and taking some considerable time to compute their results. These 'synthesis engines' are about as far removed from the vernacular understanding of a synthesizer as one could get, yet the programs are very close to the ideal of the meta-instrument we have outlined.

Recently these powerful programs have become available on cheap computers (such as the Composers' Desktop Project system), and the rapid advance in hardware technology means that the speed of computation is

573

rapidly advancing. There do exist purpose-built hardware synthesis engines that will do (at least most of) the synthesis in real time, and we can assume that such speed will soon be available at an affordable cost.

We should not, however, be fixated by the goal of real-time operation. Certainly, for most music-performance operations, a system that operates in real time is essential. But musical composition has never been a real-time occupation, and we should not be surprised if producing a complex sound or sound-sequence, through synthesis or analysis and spectral shaping, takes a certain time! Computers can certainly take some of the drudgery out of the compositional process. But the development of new ideas always takes time.

The potential of a meta-instrument also throws up difficult aesthetic questions. The composer working with such a powerful tool can produce sounds literally arbitrarily. If we can do anything, what should we choose to do? The traditional grouping of orchestral instruments in terms of mode of sound production is not purely whimsical. These may provide us with some initial guidelines. But the flexibility with which we can define sound-events challenges the traditional frameworks in which we think about timbre (in subjugation to a pitch-based musical argument). The Groupe de Recherches Musicales' classification of sounds in terms of certain perceived properties provides one possible categoric system for dealing with sonority.

The real compositional problems thrown up by the general-purpose synthesizer are therefore to comprehend the sonic potential of a new sound in terms of its perceived properties, and hence to be able to use it effectively in a musical context (whatever that may be), and, more radically, to work through our understanding of acoustics towards the construction of new sounds whose properties we have already perceived in our sonic imagination.

As an example, my own as yet uncompleted *Fluxor* project aims to model some of the properties of fluid flow in sound. The idea here is not to make the sounds of fluids, but to produce sounds that exhibit laminar or turbulent flow, granulation, helical motion, and so on, which are some of the phenomena we observe in flowing fluids. My sonic imagination tells me that such sounds may prove musically interesting. However, there is certainly no *a priori* assumption on my part that this is necessarily so, and the crucial test of this synthesis experiment will be the listening experience. The computer provides the only means by which such a sonic experiment can be conducted, permitting me to build models of fluid flow using perceived properties of sound-streams, and to provide myself with many 'handles' to be able to adjust the nature and interrelationship of the sound-parameters involved in the model. For me this project unites very satisfyingly the scientific discipline of hypothesis and experiment with musical creation.

Music as a Plastic Art

Another area where technology has expanded musical possibilities is in what is known as signal processing. The most common example of this is filtering of sounds, used even in the humblest domestic sound-reproduction system. Particularly in the rock music world, the real-time manipulation of electrically transmitted sound signals has become standard practice, using various 'effects units' to add reverberation, echo and distortion of various kinds, and to flange or phase sound signals. Digital technology has improved the quality and flexibility of most of these 'effects' and added some new possibilities, in particular the pitch-shifting and chorusing effects of the 'harmonizer'. Computer control of such devices increases the subtlety and flexibility of their use in performance.

More radical than this development, however, is the fact that the combination of digital sound-recording and computer analysis of sounds provides us with another completely new compositional discipline. We can now literally take apart any recorded sound, using programming techniques such as the Phase Vocoder or LPC, and then reconstitute the data in any way we wish before resynthesis, to produce a new, transformed sound.

In this context, sound materials become like clay in the hands of a potter, and music becomes a plastic art, where sonic objects of any origin can be moulded to the particular shape required by the composer. The aesthetic implications of this new world of possibilities are discussed more fully in my book *On Sonic Art*.[2] Again the computer provides the means to produce arbitrary transformations of the material, and compositional skill lies in both an understanding of musical acoustics – giving an insight into what kind of transformations will lead to what type of results – and aural judgement of those results.

For example, in my *VOX-5*, in which the utterances of a voice metamorphose into various recognizable sounds, a central aesthetic aim was to make the metamorphoses seamless and 'natural'. Seamlessness meant that there should be no perceptual glitch in the metamorphosis where perception suddenly switched from voice to, for example, crowd sounds. 'Naturalness' is less easy to define but implies that the technological means of metamorphosis should never become apparent in the sound result (which might occur if at any intermediate stage the sound became recognizably synthetic in origin).

Both synthesis and sound-recording/sound-sculpting fundamentally challenge the notion of instrument and instrumental streaming (the division of musical space into bands of 'fixed' timbre). The *Fluxor* project defies musical analysis in terms of instrumental streams, because the 'instruments' can be in a continual state of metamorphosis and may merge into one another or emerge from one another in this process. Sound-sculpting in particular permits us to introduce the concept of representation, and more importantly its subtle manipulation, into the musical realm. This is a quite radical departure in music. Whereas the visual arts were traditionally thought of in representational terms, so that the radical twentieth-century break was into abstraction, music has always been regarded as quintessentially non-representational. The possibility of representation in music therefore leads us to question and re-evaluate our habits of musical thinking. In *VOX-5* (a pure electroacoustic work with no performers, but forming part of a larger work *VOX*, with live vocalists), the listener hears a single 'supervoice' placed at front centre-stage uttering syllables which travel spatially out into the auditorium. As they do so, they transform into recognizable sounds of the natural world (variously crowds, bees, a horse, bells). The piece is a musical work (a dramatic arioso section between the frightening vocal theatre of *VOX-4* and the dance music of *VOX-6*) but both aesthetically and technically rests upon (sonic) representation, as in traditional visual art. We therefore experience a kind of sonic animation, akin to visual animation, though with very different aesthetic qualities because of the different natures of the sonic and visual media (for example the different cues we require for recognition of a source in each medium).

Of course, the purpose of technological innovation is not necessarily imitation. Nevertheless, the imitation of nature gives us a standard of detail and subtlety to aim for in building our computational and our musical/acoustic methods.

Musical Performance: Interactive Control Structures

I have mentioned above the impact of new technology on our very conception of what a musical instrument is. Information technology is also beginning to revolutionize the nature of performance interaction. In the simplest sense, the co-ordination of live performers with pre-recorded or real-time synthesized sounds has until recently been predicated on the idea that the performers must take their timing from the pre-recorded or synthesized part. Much recent research, however, has gone into building intelligence into sound-reproduction/synthesis technology, so that the computer can follow the performer or conductor.

Thus a program might follow a score and the sound of the performer(s), and assess the performer's position relative to the score, taking into account not only performance 'rubato' but also performer errors or omissions. Alternatively, through movement sensors, the computer may be 'taught' to follow the gestures of a conductor. In this way, pre-recorded/synthesized material can become responsive to the exigencies of a particular performance.

The computer science involved in solving such problems is at the forefront of information technology research. Using more elementary systems, however, we can establish 'listening links' between performers (especially if they are using the MIDI protocol to transmit data) to allow synthesizers to respond conditionally to data being transmitted. Thus performers may automatically cue synthesized events, or changes in the nature of a co-performer's events, by, for instance, playing a particular pattern of notes which a program recognizes. In fact, extremely complex sets of relationships between live performers, and between performers and pre-planned synthesizer patches, can be programmed, allowing the elaboration of complex musical interrelationships in a situation where, nevertheless, the performers are free to improvise the material that they directly perform. Again the ability to build intelligent musical-gesture sensors (either in software or hardware) is critical in this developing field.

THE PROBLEMS

Commercial Pressures

In many cases, the initial development of technology for artistic applications involves advanced and expensive machinery, and a great deal of research investment. With one or two important exceptions, the financial resources to pay for this are available only in the commercial arts sector. Hence in certain respects technological innovation tends to be led by the commercial arts world. Although this has the obvious advantage that large capital investments in research and machinery are feasible, it has the disadvantage of skewing the development of the technology towards more conventional aesthetic preoccupations.

Similarly, any company involved in developing complex software packages to run on cheap microcomputers, or sophisticated synthetic instrument hardware, must aim for high volume sales if it is to recover investment costs and make a profit. This means that systems tend to be targeted at the average consumer. So a lot of professional computing expertise goes into developing traditionally based music tools, but very little into considering the more generalized tools the serious composer might require.

This is a problem throughout the world of music technology at the present time. It means that more traditional approaches to music are made easier, while more radical approaches remain as difficult as before; this inevitably has a strong influence on student composers. In particular, the radical innovations of electronic and *musique concrète* composers of the past forty years, all critically inspired by new technological developments, are still difficult to come to terms with intellectually (to those imbued with a traditional school music education) in terms of both knowledge (the detailed understanding of musical acoustics) and technique. The sheer awkwardness of the original technology (tape-splicing, synthesis with oscillators) forced composers to rethink their traditional approaches to music-making and, in the process, to develop important new musical ideas. Many of these insights and advances have since become realizable in a much more rigorous way through the use of general-purpose computer technology.

However, the keyboard-centred MIDI systems developed in the 1980s, which look so very much like the pianos of the traditional classroom, invite an easy-going pre-electronic traditional approach to the new technology, as traditional assumptions tend to be built into their design. Often it is necessary to defeat the assumptions of the system to achieve a more radical approach to sound-materials. More importantly it is probably crucial for the composer to become to some degree technologically competent, as a programmer, or possibly a hardware designer/builder if he or she wishes to realize the potential of digital technology to the full. With the computer almost anything is possible if you know how to program, or if you have access to sympathetic programmers. If you have to rely exclusively on commercially available software your musical horizons will necessarily be limited.

Furthermore, the development of mass-market music tools is biased by the impact of the marketing imperative. It is advantageous for a company developing, say, a new synthesizer, to make its sound-producing algorithms closed and inaccessible to the user, and to go for 'product differentiation' to ensure that the particular product can compete in the market place. In this world, technology can easily becomes sonic fashion – one must use a Protea 2000 synthesizer or an Upjohn sampler to be 'in'. The chasing of fashion in this way has the danger of generating technological ephemera, sounds or possibilities which are, literally, here today and unavailable tomorrow. What digital technology should offer us is completely open access to sound generation and manipulation, and the permanent reproducibility of digitally encoded data or algorithms.

Technical and Musical Excellence

Another dangerous attitude is to mistake technological advance for musical progress. It is an easy game to dismiss whole categories of music-making because the technology with which it was produced was 'underdeveloped'. One finds this even among computer music professionals, some of whom dismiss 'tape-music' as being of necessity inferior because the available technology was inferior to that we have today. But this is just a confusion of categories. There are masterworks of music produced with tape-recorder techniques, and dreadful works of music produced using the most advanced computer technology, and vice versa. A similar comment applies to the critical stance, 'isn't it amazing to be able to do this with a computer?' applied to a work that could have been done with a piano accordion and would even then have been considered banal. Excellence of modelling technique or software sophistication does not necessarily add up to musical excellence.

From this viewpoint it is very important to develop categories of analysis and criticism based on the perceived phenomena (the music as sonic experience) and separated from the technicalities of production. This is an underdeveloped sphere, as, until the late twentieth century, musical analysis has, of necessity, been musical-text based. This means both that music whose structure is not focused on the traditional text-visible parameters of pitch and duration is undervalued (if not ignored) by traditional analysts, and that a critical dialogue about the music as music can be difficult to establish. This is very important also in relation to the individualist/romanticist view of artistic production persisting in Anglo-Saxon cultures, which focuses upon individual 'inspiration' and 'personal taste' or fashion, rather than upon artistic skill and agreed critical criteria.

For the public at large the naïve perception is often that there are clear criteria for technological excellence but, partly due to the existence of conflicting musical discourses in our pluralist society, there are no solid criteria for artistic excellence (it's purely a matter of personal expression, mysterious 'inspiration', and individual taste). Despite this, the romantic associations of art in the popular consciousness still bestow a very high status on artistic creativity, so that it can be seen as a good deal more glamorous than technological creativity. In a highly specialized world, experts in one field often hold the naïve public conception of what is needed in another field. Thus, unfortunately, most musicians would think twice about launching into the development of signal processing software, whereas technological experts with no previously developed advanced musical skills often feel strongly attracted to dabble in musical composition.

It is important that this relationship be got right. It is certainly possible to be gifted in both the technological and artistic sphere, but this is not common. However, it is possible for most musicians to acquire some technical skills that will allow them to expand the possibilities of technology, made available to them by technological experts, for their own personal use.

Similarly it is possible for technologists with some musical skills to produce musical examples that exemplify new technical procedures, for the illumination of serious composers. We should, however, clearly distinguish between what is a technical demonstration of musical potential (a kind of proto-music) and what is a polished musical artwork, to avoid bringing technologically based music into disrepute with the musical public. The problem with the latter is that, in the ethos of conferences dedicated to music and technology, or computer music, and which are technology-research orientated, the criteria for selecting the scientific papers are rigorous while those for selecting the musical works *as music* may be very vague indeed.

The technological ethos can have a more direct impact on composers working with new technology. The ethos of technological research is future possibilities – the gossip is always of what we will soon be able to achieve in terms of machine speed, memory, power, flexibility, interactivity. One can be easily embroiled in the excitement of using the latest, fastest, most powerful, most interactive technical system as a substitute for broader aesthetic goals, or in putting off the realization of some cherished artistic aim 'until the technology becomes available'. Artistic production is not merely about what is possible, but about what is 'worthwhile', 'valuable' or 'authentic' to human experience. If this were not so, artistic production would be both easy and entirely programmable.

The Technological Imperative

In a world where scientific and technological progress is regarded as a central concern, and the arts as a peripheral matter, it is not easy to establish some kind of even-handed relationship between art and technology. This is particularly true within institutions of research and learning. The institutional budget for scientific/technological research is always much greater than that for the arts and humanities. It is frequently difficult to justify the allocation of resources to music technology, except where it can be shown to be significant in terms of computer science or electronic-technological concerns.

Technological preoccupations can turn out to have unexpected spin-off for musicians, and it is certainly true that a different, technological/scientific mode of examining the world and conducting research can have a leavening influence within the musical world. I found this to be one of the most important aspects of IRCAM, the state-supported centre for computer research in music and acoustics in Paris, directed by Pierre Boulez. Fortunately it is also the case that many of the problems in high-speed processing of data and establishing flexible and responsive networks of control which interest serious musicians are also interesting problems for scientists and technologists.

However, this need not be the case, and there is the constant danger that the technological imperative will swamp the artistic imperative. Is a project being pursued because it has great musical potential or because it is technologically fascinating, or even merely because funds are available in this area, for technological reasons? Often, music institutions may have to compromise on such matters, or even bluff, if they are to have access to the financial resources needed for music-technology research.

Furthermore, the need for a research-orientated institution to keep abreast of the latest technology, something that (compared with the average composer!) it can afford to do, is good for both research and for students. How this relates to the composer/performer in the outside world is a different problem. Something (a powerful new machine, a new language, etc.) may be fascinating from a research point of view, or for the realization of a particular musical work *in situ*, but how can it interface with the real world of music-making beyond the institution? If the composer or performer is presented with a completely new instrument before each new piece it becomes impossible to develop any deep knowledge or skill about making music with it.

What musicians need are music-technology systems that are generally

581

available: i.e. cheap (they can therefore own them, and become as familiar with them as, say, a domestic piano), compatible with more powerful, institution-based facilities (implying that institutional facilities must therefore be compatible with them!), and 'upwardly mobile' in the sense that the system is capable of open-ended development. At the moment this, to my mind, implies software-based systems running on cheap micro-computers and using, as far as possible, 'universally' accepted data-structures; such as, presently, the MIDI protocol and standard soundfile storage conventions. As far as possible software should be open, so that tools can be upgraded (rather than new hardware having constantly to be bought), and built upon for personal applications. Furthermore, certain commercially available black-boxes (especially effects units) that have stood the test of time, and whose algorithms are generally well-understood, will probably stay in the technological kit of the non-institutional musician, as 'standard repertoire instruments', so to speak.

Music-technology institutions therefore need to preserve a balance between innovative research and the practical interface with the music-making world. They need to think in terms of 'downwards compatibility' when developing new systems!

Finally, there are some problems that are not so easily dealt with. The first of these we have already touched upon: the need for time to absorb the new technical possibilities into the more general background of cultural and musical knowledge, so that the technology becomes the servant of our artistic ideas, and not the master. Technology makes possible new things, but these are not therefore *necessarily* interesting in a wider perspective.

Last of all there is the question of musical judgement and how it is to be defined and exercised in a world where information technology allows us to define and realize with relative ease almost any procedure, no matter how obtuse or 'complex'.

NOTES

1 Wishart, T. (1988) *VOX* (1–6), Virgin Classics CD; score available from Alfred A. Kalmus.
2 Wishart, T. (1985) *On Sonic Art*, available from Trevor Wishart, 83 Heslington Road, York Y O1 5A X.

29

Composing Sounds with Computers

JEAN-CLAUDE RISSET

THE HISTORICAL CONTEXT: TWO AVENUES FOR NEW MUSIC, AND THE ADVENT OF ELECTRICITY

Throughout the twentieth century, new music has been in quest of novelty. Earlier, the tonal syntax was not even questioned by Western musicians. Yet it was insidiously weakened by their subversive imagination, which took advantage of each and every expressive resource it could offer, stretching the rules to the limits of rupture. Going back to restore a stronger sense of tonality looked like a beaten path for most composers; rather they sought new avenues for their art.

Traditionally, composition consists of putting together pre-existing elements – notes – as they will be played by the instrumentalists from a score where they are assembled. The tonal syntax established a strong hierarchy between the twelve tones of the chromatic scale. During the nineteenth century, the cadential strength of tonal gravitation had gradually been eroded by chromaticism and by the very refinement of modulations. Many composers tried to renew the grammar in various ways. A radical way was proposed by Schoenberg: suspending tonality, then avoiding its re-emergence through a compositional system ensuring the equality of the twelve tones. This was pushed further by Babbitt, Messiaen, Boulez and Stockhausen, up to a highly precise and detailed determination of the parameters of the musical events. Such an extreme degree of organization, upsetting usual continuities, can make the music sound complicated, even disorganized. Cage took the radical approach of 'composing' disorganized

583

music through the injection of randomness – or by submitting the parameters to precise but arbitrary laws (taken from extrinsic fields: from the stars, from James Joyce, from a train timetable ...). Xenakis and Ligeti selected processes such as stochastic composition or polyphonic weaving, managing details in order to control global effects in their music, instead of submitting elements to local grammatical constraints that would be lost in the overall result. Composers such as Berio and, in other ways, Donatoni capitalized on pre-existing syntaxes of music – recent or not – to achieve some kind of personal synthesis. All this consideration given to the relations between the elements of music, all this elaboration of syntax, grammar and 'language' is well in the line of the Western tradition, which has for centuries simplified or decanted the sound material so that it lends itself to classification, hierarchies and complex combinations. (For instance, the simplifying choice of the equally tempered tuning permits more varied and complex games with tonal modulations.)

In contradistinction, Varèse has been the first to propose his music as 'organized sound'; to focus his compositional effort on the elaboration of the material; to compose the sound itself rather than to compose *with* existing sounds. Such a preoccupation can often be recognized in non-Western music, where the sound is often carefully elaborated. It was pursued by Schoenberg himself in his Opus 16. With his *Sonatas and Interludes* for prepared pianos (completed in 1948), Cage opened a non-tempered universe accessible from the piano keyboard, usually thought of as quintessentially well-tempered. A few composers have followed this path, including George Crumb, Toru Takemitsu, Jean-Claude Eloy, Dao, Gérard Grisey and Tristan Murail.

Looking back to the nineteenth century, one should remember that in around 1875 two discoveries were made which led to gradual yet profound changes in our relation with sound. Sound recording, invented by Edison, made it possible to consider sound as an object, to measure or analyse it, to reproduce it, to modify it. And the electrical handling of sound, pioneered by Bell, who invented the telephone, made it possible to escape mechanical constraints and to benefit from the power of electricity for sound reproduction – and also for sound production, as was demonstrated a little later. At the turn of the century, Cahill built an extravagant electrical instrument, the Dynamophone, a genuine electrical power station for music synthesis: it used dynamos to produce electrical vibrations. This machine was impractical; the resources of electronic technology were not available yet. But this attempt to manufacture sounds electrically struck the imagination of Varèse, who first envisaged electricity as an essential resource to open a new world of sound. In the words of Hughes Defourt, 'the electrical revolution' was under way.

Applications of electricity for sound reproduction rapidly developed after the invention of the triode by Lee de Forest in 1906. (Few people realize that the triode was also called the 'audion', and that de Forest meant to use it to manufacture electronic instruments.) The omnipresence of electrical, or electroacoustic, sound – that is, sound emitted by loudspeakers – changed the musical perspectives. Earlier, it was extremely unusual to be exposed to a great variety of types of music. Debussy was strongly impressed by the Indonesian orchestras he heard at the Universal Exhibition in 1889 – a rare event. Now, recordings make available to everyone a host of different kinds of music: music from remote places, from ancient times. The availability of all these different musical expressions is taken for granted by the young generation; it has smeared the clear sense of perspective that one had about the evolution of Western music.

The use of electrical technologies to *produce* music rather than just to *reproduce* it never seemed a major preoccupation. Between the two world wars a few pioneers developed electronic instruments, but most of the time they thought of adapting them to the existing repertory. Leon Thérémin – or Termen – played his 'singing antenna' to Lenin in 1921. This instrument is still used 'conventionally' by virtuosos, who can control it somewhat as a singer controls his voice, but it has also been used in more avant-garde music. Varèse's *Ecuatorial* (1934) requires two theremins or ondes martenot. In Cage's *Variations V* (1963), the dancers of the Merce Cunningham Company are supposed to produce part of the music by dancing close to the Theremin antennae. Boulez occasionally played the ondes martenot when he was musical director at the theatre company Renaud-Barrault; hundreds of musical scores call for the ondes, notably from Honegger, Messiaen, Jolivet and Murail. There are two ondes in the Ensemble d'instruments électroniques de l'Itinéraire, for whom I wrote in 1982 *Aventure de ligne* – in this piece, the electronic instruments dialogue with a computer-generated tape.

Electronic instruments, despite their possibilities, have generally been conceived with a traditional approach. But *musique concrète*, electronic music and tape music – all three of them based on new possibilities offered by the electrical technology – were much more radical and innovative. Pioneers of electronic music, such as Eimert, Goyevaerts and Stockhausen, came from the serial school: in 1950 they hoped that the precision made possible by technology would permit them to realize accurately rigorous and complex serial scores, unplayable by human hands. On the other hand, *musique*

585

concrète, pioneered by Pierre Schaeffer and Pierre Henry starting around 1948, and tape music, started by Ussachevsky and Luening in 1950, focused on renewing the sound material of music by resorting to recorded sounds without restriction to 'legitimate' musical instruments, and elaborating them in new ways, through editing, looping, filtering, reverberating, and so forth. The achievements of *musique concrète*, electronic music and tape music have been substantial, and their influence has been important, even for composers who still write only 'conventional' instrumental music. 'Acousmatic music', as advocated by François Bayle, has grown as an original and different art form. Yet it has remained marginal; it has not really made its way into the mainstream. For instance, György Ligeti, after working very hard at realizing *Artikulation*, abandoned electronic music because it did not afford him the precise possibilities he longed for. Actually the medium was not neutral; the equipment used was not originally designed for the creation of new music, and the different aesthetic attitudes of the practitioners of both musique concrète and electronic music were crystallized by the respective technical limitations of the kind of sound material they used.

The development of the digital computer was a decisive step in the progress of electronics. It is not a tool, built for a specific purpose, like an oscillator or a filter; it is, rather, a kind of boundless workshop, which helps in the design and construction of new tools – for instance a flexible software musical instrument with as many oscillators as desired. The computer can perform intellectual tasks in conjunction with material tasks. Thus one may program an 'intelligent' musical instrument, which will completely change its timbre depending upon the context. The computer can take complex logical decisions, and it can apply these decisions to the manufacturing of very contrived images or sounds.

In my opinion, the intervention of the computer in music, a process pioneered by Lejaren Hiller and Max Mathews, is a turning point in the electrical revolution. It brings within reach an infinite wealth of possibilities, which previously one could only hope for without being able to achieve them. The limitations are no longer technical, due to hardware problems, but rather intellectual, having to do with the software, the databases, the problems of conception, knowledge and know-how.

Historically, the logical possibilities of the computer were the first to be taken into consideration in music. In the nineteenth century, Lady Lovelace worked with Babbage, who built the Analytical Engine. This remarkable mechanical precursor of the computer lacked only the proper technology to become practical. Lady Lovelace had clearly envisaged potential applications to musical composition. Around 1950, John Pierce and Elizabeth

Shannon experimented on stochastic composition. (In stochastic music, the compositional choices are made by random selections governed by the laws of probability.) But the main exploration of automatic composition by computers was conducted by Hiller, who reported them in his book *Experimental Music*, written jointly with Isaacson. Basically, Hiller's method was to use computer symbols to designate the musical elements – note pitches, durations, etc. The computer 'composed' by selecting symbols at random and then screening them, using a grammar of musical rules: those elements that, added to the previous ones, led to ungrammatical combinations were dropped and the random search was continued. This research laid the ground for the work of some dedicated composers (mainly Pierre Barbaud and Gottfried-Michael Koenig; also James Tenney, Denis Lorrain, Otto Laske, and others) who tried to elaborate a grammar that would lead to compositions they would accept as legitimate. Xenakis, too, resorted to this approach in some of his pieces. However, the influence of these experiments has not been widely influential; by and large they have not greatly changed the musical landscape.

On the other hand, the use of the computer and of digital techniques for sound synthesis and processing, which owes a lot to the work of Max Mathews, has permeated the musical scene much more, as witnessed by the impact of IRCAM, a musical institution centred on this field, as well as by the increasing popular success of MIDI digital synthesizers, keyboards and modules. Although I am myself critical of some uses of digital sound, I may be prejudiced in evaluating its impact when compared to that of the computer as an aid to instrumental composition. I have dedicated much of my time to developing, exploring and demonstrating the possibilities of the computer to 'sculpt' sound, and I have endeavoured to link it to other ways of making music. (I have also written pieces for instruments, voice and orchestra, without any intervention of modern technology.) But I elected to do so because of my interest and faith in the refined possibilities of the computer and digital techniques to extend the compositional control to the level of the microstructure of the sound.

THE FIRST STEPS OF COMPUTER-ASSISTED COMPOSITION

While there are historical precedents for automated composition going back to the eighteenth century, we focus first on the work of Hiller and Isaacson, whose book *Experimental Music* gives details of the musical experiments performed, which in turn imply aesthetic options. Inevitably, the very idea of automated composition raises questions about the act of composing.

A computer can easily be programmed to select and assemble symbols chosen among a given repertory, following rules and constraints implemented in the program. The compositional rules cause a certain order to prevail over the original chaos. This implies a conception of composition close to that expressed by Stravinsky in his series of lectures, published under the title '*Poétique musicale*'. Hiller used a 'Monte-Carlo' method in which musical symbols and parameters are associated with numbers. The computer picks numbers at random and then screens them through acceptance tests, which implement compositional rules and constraints, retaining a set corresponding to 'music' that follows the rules. These experiments resulted in a piece, the *ILLIAC Suite* for string quartet (ILLIAC is the name of the computer used), which is more interesting as a demonstration piece than as a genuine composition.

This process also inspired Xenakis to realize pieces such as *ST4, ST10, Atrées* (1962), using the computer program ST to generate the scores. According to Xenakis, the program is the 'objectivation' of the musical form, since it defines a minimal set of rules and constraints to structure the music (Xenakis 1971). Between 1962 and 1964, James Tenney realized several pieces – *Stochastic quartet, Dialogue, Phrases* – where he specified the broad lines of the composition, letting the computer fill in the details. The specifications given by the composer – the 'score' – consisted essentially of graphs that stipulate, as a function of time, the range within which the computer may pick at random certain parameters – pitches, durations. These pieces were also directly realized into sound by the same computer (see Tenney 1968; Risset 1987). Denis Lorrain has also realized several pieces of computer stochastic music and has written an article on stochastic processes (Lorrain 1980) which is of great interest since it also gives explicit algorithms.

Most composers, however, did not stay with computer-assisted composition very long. For instance, Xenakis now very rarely resorts to computer-assisted composition – and one may argue that the 'hand-made' *Pithoprakta* (1957) advocated stochastic music more convincingly than his computer-composed pieces. There are, though, a few exceptions; certain composers have been deeply impressed by the concept of computer or automatic composition. Lejaren Hiller and Janine Charbonnier have produced numerous pieces composed with the help of the computer. Above all, for some composers – I think in particular of Fausto Razzi, Michel

Philippot, Pierre Barbaud, Gottfried-Michael Koenig – the important point is the absolute rigour of the computer in the realization of a process. For some of his pieces, Philippot has forced himself to apply with complete rigour the compositional rules he selects as though he were using the Monte-Carlo method. Barbaud, a dedicated pioneer, composed music with the help of the computer for thirty years. His compositions are genuine experiments of artificial creativity, since he refused to correct the output of the composing program. His music is not often played – it is not always appealing – in part because he had such a purely Apollonian, anti-Dionysiac concept of music: he scorned the use of dynamics, crescendos, accelerandos and other expressive features, claiming that they concern theatre rather than music. Also he realized certain compositions into sound with collaborators who were sometimes co-authors, but he claimed no interest in the sonic realization – a position that can hardly be recommended, in so far as one considers that music must be heard. However, some of Barbaud's pieces are impressive, as is his solitary attitude. Koenig spends a long time writing elaborate programs, which he calls projects, and which produce mostly instrumental pieces. At the Institute of Sonology in the Netherlands, he is also producing computer-synthesized pieces – such as *Funktion Blau* – with the same demands. In the wake of his work with early electronic music and extremely rigorous serialism, Koenig is pushing to the utmost the preoccupation of formulating rules that will be complete enough to determine the music he wants to come out.

Koenig's position is extreme, but it corresponds well to the logic of programming a computer to compose music. If the composer chooses this process then he must delegate to the program his compositional choices, which must then be made completely explicit. (This was relatively easy in some instances of stochastic music.) However, most composers do not abide by these constraints when they compose. Even when they are quite rigorous, the strict formalism is not usually sufficient; important choices are made, and the composer would have trouble stating them in advance to add rules so that the computer could replace him. *Le marteau sans maître* by Pierre Boulez was composed with extremely precise formal constraints – to the extent that the musicologist Le Kublyakov could restore them twenty years later simply by analysing the score. It is clear that these constraints are no more than a skeleton of the piece; that the freedom of the composer has exerted itself beyond them; that many of his decisions are hard to explain; and that they are part of the process of invention and would have been impossible to specify in advance.

Even existing compositional rules are insufficient. Hiller implemented the rules of strict counterpoint as described by Fux in his *Gradus ad Parnassum* (1725); this experiment produced strange results, which did not violate the rules but were rather alien to the spirit of counterpoint. This drew from Milton Babbitt the remark that 'The rules of counterpoint tell [you] what not to do, they do not tell you what to do.' The composer does not work by filtering random choices through explicit rules. In fact, human imagination seems incapable of producing true randomness; it comes out with structured fragments rather than minimal elements.

These difficulties may explain the dissatisfaction of many composers with the computer as a compositional tool. There are many processes that we perform satisfactorily but without yet being able to program them – even simple actions like image interpretation, or face or word recognition. Composition is an extremely complex activity, far from being well understood. If one knew how to include in a program all the criteria of compositional choice, then indeed one would know a lot. It is hard to believe that one can ever quantify and even make explicit one's implicit aesthetic criteria. The meaning or the value of a formalism, of a syntax, is contingent upon the context and the compositional purpose. And the creative process may be more vivid in the invention of new rules than in the exploitation of existing ones. As Debussy said, 'Works of art make rules, but rules do not make works of art'.

So it is problematic to resort to the computer as a relay to the composer's decisions – unless the composer is willing to correct the output of the computer and make his or her own final decisions about the validity of the musical output. In fact, it is wise to expect less intelligence and musicality from the computer, and to give it an ancillary role. Certainly the logical and combinatorial power of the computer can be very helpful to the composer during the phase of 'pre-composition', when he or she builds specific musical materials which must embody certain constraints. Music input languages (such as Pla by Schottstaedt, Formes by Rodet) provide features to manipulate phrases and to perform certain operations on musical contexts. This can be seen as an extension of the role of notation, which has in the past suggested musical processes such as inversion or retrogradation. Similarly, object-orientated languages facilitate the manipulation of 'objects' which are characterized by specific data as well as by specific procedures for transforming them. Logical programming, introduced by Alain Colmerauer, who developed PROLOG at Marseille-Luminy, should help to experiment with a set of rules. And one may hope – although music is so complex – that the composer will be able to take advantage of expert systems that can react to orders expressed in a 'declarative' form. This is much easier to formulate than an algorithmic form, which would demand the prescription of every step the computer should take.

These developments are still in their infancy, but they are promising for music; and music is such a demanding domain that it should help develop and test them. So the landscape has not been upset by computer-aided composition; but geological revolutions are very slow, yet eventually upsetting. The logical and combinatorial powers of the computer are being used in ways that may not be visible. In particular the computer is often called for in digital synthesis – for developing arpeggios or other sound structures; for shaping the sound in ways that are often unconventional; and for controlling aspects of the sound that are not accessible with instrumental sound. In fact, it is somewhat artificial to separate the computer as a brain and the computer as a tool; its unique value lies in the fact that it is both.

COMPUTER SOUND SYNTHESIS

The Programming Problem

In 1958 an unusual concert took place at Cooper Union in New York. At the request of Edgard Varèse, two atypical pieces were presented. One was *Two Sounds* by La Monte Young, lasting forty minutes. The other lasted only one minute. This was *Pitch Variations*, synthesized on the computer by Newman Guttman, who had collaborated with Max Mathews and John Pierce in the early work at Bell Laboratories on computer sound synthesis. The first sounds had been synthesized in 1957. At the same time, Mathews and his collaborators had also realized the first digital recording of sound – a process now used commercially for compact disc and DAT cassettes.

In principle, any sound that could be produced by a loudspeaker could be synthesized by the computer – given the proper program. The first problem to be solved in order to take advantage of this potentially limitless resource was the *programming problem*. The process would be impossibly tedious if a user had to write a new program for each new sound. Mathews designed programs that could be used to generate a variety of sounds: MUSIC I, MUSIC II, MUSIC III, MUSIC IV and MUSIC V. A basic concept – modularity – was already present in MUSIC III (1959). As in

591

Lego or a Meccano set, the user has a menu of basic modules – called unit generators – which are segments of programs, but which can (mostly) be thought of as performing a certain operation, just like a piece of equipment in a studio. Among these modules would be oscillators, adders (mixers), filters and envelope generators. The user could select and assemble at will any of these modules to define a certain process of sound generation – called an 'instrument' by analogy. Then the various 'instruments' could be activated by instructions called 'notes', specifying action time, duration and whichever parameters in the instruments had been left open. Waveforms, envelopes and complex temporal evolutions may be defined as stored numeric functions, which can be defined mathematically in various ways or drawn from a graphic tablet (they can also be extracted from the analysis of sounds). The user could always add his or her own modules or supplementary features. Far from simulating the modular voltage-controlled synthesizers built by Moog and Buchla around 1965, the concepts of MUSIC III preceded and probably inspired them.

MUSIC III had many descendants: MUSIC V (1967), which followed MUSIC IV. The latter was the starting point for other widely distributed programs: MUSIC 10 (Poole), MUSIC 360, MUSIC 11, CSOUND (Vercoe). Its principles have influenced the design of many digital synthesizers, capable of computing in real time sounds of a certain complexity. Software synthesis, using programs such as MUSIC V, cannot usually work in real time, except when producing rather simple sounds on fast computers. In fact, MUSIC V is not designed as a real-time program. But software synthesis has great advantages. A program like MUSIC V has no limit in complexity; unlike real-time synthesizers, it can always compute more complex details if one is ready to wait. It is flexible; it can produce virtually any sound, given an objective description of its physical structure. It is transportable and its results are reproducible. It can of course mix any number of sounds by simple addition. It can produce stereophonic or quadrophonic sound. The 'recipe' – the data for the synthesis program – is at the same time a thorough description of the physical structure, expressed in a language specific to the program. Such descriptions can be communicated, so that the results of sonic exploration can be cumulated between users and over time. Thus, after having explored some synthesis possibilities, I assembled a few 'recipes' together with the recordings of the sounds and some explanations in a 'computer sound catalog' (Risset 1969): this document has proved useful, as have others of a similar nature (Chowning 1973; Moorer and Grey 1977; Lorrain 1980; Haynes 1982; Morrill, forthcoming).

The Psychoacoustic Problem

The early years of computer synthesis were productive but also disappointing. A number of pieces were realized, notably by Mathews, Pierce and Tenney, often using ingenious compositional algorithms (as the records *Music from mathematics* and *Voice of the computer* show). However, the sound quality was often dull, certainly not as varied and exciting as one could have hoped from a process that theoretically had no limits. By varying at random the parameters of synthetic sounds, one obtained sounds that lacked identity: although physically different, they were not very different to the ear.

These early experiments revealed the *psychoacoustic problem.* The word psychoacoustics refers to the relation between the physical structure of the sound, which must be specified to the computer if it is to produce that sound, and the perceived aural effect, as the listener experiences it. Now the psychoacoustic relation between physical parameters and their perception is much more complex, much less transparent than was originally believed. This was not a complete surprise. Pierre Schaeffer, the pioneer of *musique concrète*, had on the basis of his own experience, advocated musical research to develop a *solfège* of sound – a *solfège* of effects, not causes. And several studies (Leipp 1971) had insisted on the complexity of musical sounds and musical phenomena, usually described in a very schematic way.

The foolproof test of synthesis confirmed these points of view. Changes in a sound stipulated in terms of physical parameters did not always translate into the expected auditory effects. Hearing is highly idiosyncratic, for reasons that have less to do with music than with information and survival (see Gibson 1966; Risset 1973, 1988; McAdams and Bregman 1979). To take advantage of the potential of computer sound synthesis, one must take these idiosyncrasies into account, and develop a body of psychoacoustic knowledge, concerning complex sounds in musical contexts.

We may object that such problems concern sounds rather than music itself, which is not about sounds, but about the relations *between* sounds. However, the most exciting possibilities of computer synthesis lie in the exploration of novel sounds that may lend themselves to novel types of relations and novel sonic architectures. And the musical relations between sounds should not only be on paper – music is meant to be heard. Working with computer synthesis, the composer will set structural relations between physical parameters, but the significant relations are those that our mind will recognize aurally.

Let us take the example of pitch. When one prescribes frequency relations, one expects that they will translate into analogous relations between pitches – a frequency ratio of $2:1$, $3:2$, etc. will correspond to musical intervals of an octave, a fifth, etc. This is so for most 'usual' sounds – except for those above 4000 Hz or so, where precise intervallic identification collapses. This limit corresponds to the higher notes used in the high instruments – piano, piccolo – and this is certainly not a coincidence. But perception gives much more unpredictable results with sounds that are 'inharmonic': that is, not made up of harmonic components. Inharmonic sounds often do not have a clear pitch, but they may have: for instance, bells, tuned gong, or the low notes of the piano. In such cases, the frequency relations map in a complex way into the heard intervallic relations.

I gave an extreme example of this when, in 1968, I synthesized sounds whose pitch appear to the listeners to go *down* when all their frequencies are *doubled*! Here the physical octave does not map into a subjective octave; it sounds more like a descent of one semitone. Admittedly this is an extreme case, but it demonstrates that the relations intended within subjective qualities of tones – like pitch – can be distorted and misrespresented if one specifies them in terms of physical variables – here frequency – which are traditionally associated with these qualities (Risset 1971). More recently I realized an even more heretic example: a sound with rhythmical beats, which seem to *slow down* when one *doubles the speed* of the tape recording (Risset 1986). A physical acceleration can be heard as slowing down. Clearly, auditory perception is not always transparent and intuitive, and it is essential to understand it to ensure that the conceived relations are not distorted by their embodiment into sound.

The above examples used specially contrived physical parameters. By contriving them in other ways, one can exploit these oddities of perception to generate acoustic illusions, paradoxes, 'impossible' effects. For instance, I extended Roger Shepard's 'staircase to heaven' – twelve semitones in chromatic progression that seem to go up for ever when they are repeated. I generated endlessly descending glissandi, or sounds that seem to go down the scale when they are repeated – pitches that go down locally but go up globally. These are not mere curiosities; the effects make audible fundamental hearing mechanisms that are basic to music perception: for instance, the similarity between octaves, recognized by musical notations that give the same name to notes an octave apart. I incorporated a few of these auditory paradoxes, implemented with the computer in some of my compositions. In *The Fall* from *Little Boy* – one of the first extensive pieces entirely synthesized by computer (1968) – descending glissandi never reach the bottom; this was an impression I wanted to convey, but I also used such sounds for their plastic value (see Cogan 1984). In *Moments newtoniens*, gliding sounds first give an impression of rotation but as they slow down, they are heard as falling sounds – an allusion to Newton's discovery that falling bodies and orbiting planets can be ascribed to the same physical interaction: gravitation. In that same piece, I presented paradoxes in both the pitch and the rhythm domain – sounds that go up but eventually get lower, with a beat that speeds up yet gradually gets slower. I also attempted to mimic endlessly descending pitches with the voices of a chorus in *Dérives*, for chorus and computer-generated tape (1985), and with the instruments of the symphonic orchestra in *Phases* (1988). However, there are limits, since paradoxical sounds must in many cases be contrived in a specific way, within a certain range of speed, for instance. Out of this range, the paradox loses its strength or simply does not work. Also the effect is basic, so it may appear as an *object trouvé* if one recognizes it from one composition to another. In fact, I first presented my pitch paradoxes as 'minimal art' or 'conceptual' pieces.

Other composers have capitalized on the oddities of perception and the fine control over the sound structure afforded by computer synthesis. An outstanding example is John Chowning's illusory movements. The ear relies on certain fine features of the sound to infer that it comes from a moving source: varying amplitude, varying direct- to reverberated-sound energy ratio (this is an important clue to the distance of the source), and the Doppler effect. By synthesizing sounds with these features, Chowning guides the ear – and the mind – into reconstructing an inner representation of the world coherent with the aural data. In this representation, it seems as if the sources of sound are moving, whereas in truth the sounds are emitted by fixed loudspeakers. In Chowning's piece *Turenas* (1973), the music carves its own space.

Taking advantage of the refinement of computer synthesis to exploit the properties of perception makes it possible to suggest through music an illusory world, devoid of material constraints, without any physical counterpart, yet deeply anchored into perception. In my piece *Songes* (1979), by departing from realistic instrumental sounds and gliding gradually into an imaginary world, I tried to evoke the departure from the real world as happens in dreams.

IMITATION OF MUSICAL INSTRUMENTS

It is possible to produce synthetic sounds that emulate musical instruments, that have presence and identity, even though they do not come from an existing source and they have not been produced through the physical

595

process they suggest. But this is not easy. Early attempts to imitate the sounds of musical instruments from the data given by acoustic treatises were unconvincing; they even failed completely for certain types of sounds such as brass tones or bowed string tones.

Thus some studies were made to try to imitate instrument tones. The goal was not only academic, checking by synthesis the validity of the analysis, but also aesthetic, trying to understand what makes the richness, the life and the identity of certain instrumental sounds. This information might help to avoid the monotonous 'electronic quality' stereotype, and to inject into synthetic sounds personality and character. I myself did some early research on brass tones, which uncovered a relation between the amplitude and the spectrum – the higher the amplitude, the wider the spectrum, the brighter the tone. This feature demonstrated the importance of spectral variations, whereas classical models assumed a fixed characteristic spectrum for a given musical timbre. It also showed the interest of internal relations between parameters of sounds to suggest some robust identity. John Chowning, who invented a powerful technique of synthesis by audio rate frequency modulation (see Chowning 1973), thus related the modulation index to some other variation in the sound.

CLOSE ENCOUNTERS: INSTRUMENTS AND SYNTHESIS

There are good reasons why instrument-like sounds should be included in the palette of computer sounds. They have proved musically useful; the musicians and the listeners have a long experience of them, and many composers are interested in 'close encounters' between instruments and synthetic sounds. Instrumentalists bring with their playing scenic presence, life, variations and danger. The synthetic world may come close, if one knows how to imitate instrument tones by synthesis, yet it is basically different: 'presence of absence', with no physical counterpart; great ease of playing accurately any pitch scale; weaker identity and greater flexibility.

I stage such close encounters in my piece *Dialogues* for four instruments and computer-generated tape (1975). As the title indicates, the instruments and the computer sounds are on the same level. The two worlds merge and even fuse at times, the computer answers the instruments, the instruments respond to the computer. Later they contrast and prolongate each other. The computer sheds harmonic clouds which are related to the harmonic structure of the instrumental part; specified harmonics of the notes played by the instruments sound and then die out (see Figure 29.1). When the succession of harmonics is regular, from bottom to top or vice versa, one gets a kind of 'spectral analysis of a chord', as though it were heard through a frequency window moving up or down. (Here I used specially written sub-routines to generate the individual harmonics from the proper global specifications: the computer also helps in completing the score needed for synthesis.)

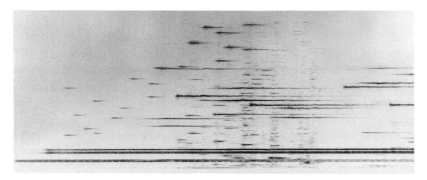

Figure 29.1 This is a sonogram – a kind of sound photograph – which portrays a 'harmonic cloud' synthesized by computer for my piece *Dialogues*. Time runs from left to right – the picture shows about 2 seconds. Frequency increases toward the top. Each horizontal line corresponds to a frequency component. A computer subroutine helped the composer specify the dispersion of the components in time.

At some point in *Dialogues*, a certain chord played by the instruments is echoed by a gong-like tone which the ear cannot really analyse but which is a kind of shadow of the chord: the ear recognizes that the same harmony underlies both. I also used this prolongation of harmony into timbre at the very beginning of *Mutations*, for computer-synthesized tape (1969). Actually, this 'gong' was composed in just the same way as the chord: its sine wave components had the same frequencies as the fundamentals of the chord. A composer cannot request an orchestra to provide a gong with a specified internal harmony. Although the instrument-like synthetic timbre is nothing new, the fine control of its harmonic dimension is quite novel.

In *Traettoria* by Marco Stroppa, the computer part, which heard alone would not appear so appealing, skilfully enhances a very imaginative piano part. In *Prisms* by Stanley Haynes (1977), a pianist dialogues with synthetic sounds which at times merge in intriguing ways with the piano. In *Aber die Namen* by Gerald Bennett (1979), the singer on stage is echoed by a remote voice, literally disembodied, since this voice is not the voice of anyone. At the end of my piece *Passages* for flute and computer synthesized sound (1982), the flute player sings into his flute, while a synthetic flute-like sound gradually acquires a vocal quality. Here, identities vacillate, as in *L'autre face* (1983), where here the soprano dialogues with an invisible, imaginary sonic world; amidst this unreal world, an illusory soprano appears as a ghost.

SYNTHESIZING VARIANTS

Computer synthesis allows considerable flexibility. It has the interesting possibility of producing *variants*. Once a certain synthesis model has been defined and implemented as an 'instrument' in a program such as MUSIC V, the parameters of this model can be changed without changing the process of synthesis. This produces transformations that can be intriguing in that they are close to the original sound in some ways and very different in others. Similar effects can hardly be obtained with acoustic instruments, which have a rather inflexible structure.

I have exploited the capacity of the computer to perform intimate sonic transformations in several pieces. In *Little Boy*, in *Mutations*, and most substantially in *Inharmonique* (1977), I could transform bell-like sounds into fluid textures by changing just the shape of one curve, controlling the time contour of the individual frequency components (in inharmonic relation). A curve with a sharp attack and a resonant decay suggests a bell. The synchronous attack helps the ear to fuse the components and to give the impression that the sound comes from a single object – a bell. If the curve gradually swells and decays, one hears a fluid texture with the same harmonic content as the bell. Due to the asynchrony of the envelopes, the sound is now dispersed and, just as a prism disperses white light, one can distinguish the individual components more easily. Thus the composer can by changing certain aspects of the sound induce listening to be synthetic or analytic, focalized or distributed. In *Inharmonique*, this transformation is effected onto polyphonies of bell-like sounds, which are 'melted' into smooth or bouncing textures. The underlying harmony – or inharmony – is unchanged, but the morphology is upset, as in a change of physical state of the same substance.

In *Archipelago* (1984) Roger Reynolds has used a similar process, explored by John Chowning and Steve McAdams; imposing the same frequency micromodulations onto a subset of the harmonics of a given tone destroys the fusion and causes this subset to stand out aurally as a separate entity. If a subset comprises the even harmonics of an oboe-like tone, the oboe will split into a clarinet-like tone – the odd harmonics – and another tone, one octave above – a powerful effect. Here one should be aware of the role of perceptual organization, the behaviour of which can be guided by specific constraints imposed upon the sounds.

Other composers have exploited the capacity of computer synthesis to produce variants. Instrumental ranges can be exceeded by simulated instruments, for instance the synthetic trumpets in Dexter Morrill's *Studies for Trumpet and Computer* (1975). John Chowning has synthesized beautiful imitations of the singing voice. In his piece *Phonē* (1981) one can hear a 'basso profundissimo', suggesting a singer with a huge chest and neck. But this vision is evasive, since the low tones undergo slow metamorphosis into completely different sounds. Continuous metamorphosis of a timbre into another one cannot be achieved with instruments, except by the equivalent of fade-in/fade-out: but one then hears a double sound during the transition. Chowning had already achieved gradual transitions between two timbres – from dry percussion into brass, for example – in *Sabelith* (1971) and *Turenas* (1972). In these pieces, a few functions of time controlling the spectra, through frequency-modulation parameters, and the dynamics, suffice to define timbral trajectories running across different timbral families.

Such trajectories suggest a continuous space of timbres. One can picture instrumental timbres as familiar islands; synthesis gives us access to the ocean of timbres. Can one resort to maps or compasses on this ocean? Continuous timbral trajectories suggest the idea of a timbral space, going in between our familiar timbres and extending beyond. The fact is that maps of the timbral space already exist – not arbitrary maps, but multi-dimensional representations which portray the subjective similarities or dissimilarities between different timbres in terms of distances between the points representing them. As David Wessel says: 'A timbre space that adequately represented the perceptual dissimilarities could conceivably serve as a kind of map that would provide navigational advice to the composer interested in structuring aspects of timbre' (Wessel 1973).

John Grey (1975) and David Wessel (1973, 1978) have provided experimental models of timbral spaces including several instrumental families – strings, woods and brass. Constructed from ratings by subjects of dissimilarities between pairs of tones, these models reveal two dimensions. One appears to be associated with brightness or tone height, determined by the position of the centre of gravity of the spectrum along the frequency axis – which reminds one of Schoenberg's statement that pitch is one dimension of timbre. The other dimension seems to relate to temporal features. Here, just by asking subjects *how much* certain timbres differ, one gets information about the *ways* in which they differ. Moreover, the process of looking at the localization of certain timbres within the timbral space, with due regard to its dimensions, allows us to make useful predictions about how these timbres will behave in context – to predict, for instance, whether a string of tones with different timbres will give the feeling of continuous or discontinuous lines, and whether two rapidly alternating timbres form a single melodic line or 'segregate' into two distinct lines. Around 1977, David Wessel and Bennett Smith implemented a program by means of which a composer could draw his or her own timbral space with whichever sound objects interested him or her. Such representations suggest various movements through timbral space, various ways to control and structure timbre.

COMPOSING THE INTERNAL STRUCTURE OF SOUNDS: FUNCTIONAL SPECTRA

Most instrumental tones – sounds with a distinct pitch – are made up of harmonic components – sinusoidal sounds of frequencies f, 2f, 3f, 4f, 5f, 6f, etc. (the frequency f is that of the fundamental or first harmonic, 2f is that of the second harmonic etc.), corresponding to pitch classes C, C, G, C, E, G, etc. Low piano tones depart slightly from this harmonic structure. The main exception is bells. But, as explained above, bells – or gongs – have a certain inharmonic structure that the composer cannot tamper with. Computer synthesis affords him or her this possibility: gongs or inharmonic textures can be composed just as chords. In my piece *Little Boy*, a specific harmonic structure – going up, G♯, E, G♮, E, B, A♯ – is present beneath the surface. Imposing a strong modulation upon such sine wave components with frequency ratios corresponding to this structure causes them to be fused by the ear. As we saw, with percussive envelopes, one can get a gong-like sound with the harmony as a watermark; the very spectrum assumes a harmonic function. I also imparted slow frequency glides – glissandi – to such a group of sine waves, while maintaining a constant difference between their frequencies (a constant ratio would be needed to maintain a constant frequency interval). This again helps auditory fusion, so that the underlying harmony turns into a specific tone colour. I have accumulated such groups – I call them *klangs* – in certain frequency areas. In *Little Boy*, *Mutations* and

Songes, I have assembled klangs, transposing them with frequency ratios that are the same as those that govern the harmonic structure within the klang – this is a recursive, multi-stage structure: chords of chords, or rather klangs of klangs. Figure 29.2 shows an example of this structure in *Little Boy*.

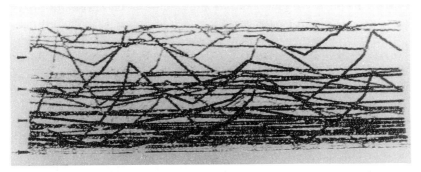

Figure 29.2 Accumulation of 'klangs' made up of parallel gliding sine waves in different frequency registers (from my piece *Little Boy*). This uses the same kind of representation of sound as Figure 29.1.

Frequency ratios usually define melodic scales and harmonic chords. However, in so far as fusion takes place, it becomes hard to sort out lines or voices; the ratios act as a kernel to determine spectra, tone qualities, timbres. In spectral music spectra are the basic elements. They play an organic role when they act internally, but they are also truly functional. Inharmonic spectra can be exploited with precise control, going beyond the erosion of well-tempered frequency scales, as Cage's prepared piano or wind instrument multiphonics. As mentioned above, one can act upon various factors that influence analytic or synthetic listening, so that one inharmonic complex can be heard either as one or as several entities. But we also have the liberty to select the component frequencies of inharmonic tones so as to differentiate intervallic relations between such tones in specific ways. Although the issue is still discussed, the privileged status of these intervals in Western tonal music is unlikely to be independent of the fact that the intervals between the fundamental and the low-order harmonics are the octave, the fifth and the third. According to Helmholtz (1877), Plomp (1976) and Terhardt (1974), these intervals are more consonant if the sound is made up of harmonics, but this is not necessarily so if the sound is not made up of harmonic components. One may object that these scientists consider sensory consonance and dissonance, and disregard their cultural,

601

quasi-linguistic significance within a given musical syntax. None the less, in 1966 John Pierce suggested that the harmonic affinities between inharmonic sounds depend in a partly predictable way upon their internal structure. Thus the composer has the option of choosing this internal structure (Pierce 1966, 1983) so as to manage new relations, new attractions, a new 'pitch sociology', as Edmond Costère puts it (Costère 1962).

Many pieces using computer synthesis are based on inharmonic tones; examples are my own *Inharmonique, Songes, Contours* and *Profils*; *Senza voci 2* by Guido Baggiani and Gorgio Nottoli; *Androgyny* and *Arras* by Barry Truax; *Mycènes-Alpha* by Iannis Xenakis; *Désintégrations* by Tristan Murail; and various pieces by Teresa Rampazzi, James Dashow and Philippe Manoury. In the synthetic part of *Little traveling music*, for piano and computer by Loren Rush (1976), the sounds seem to swing in space; synchronously they sway between harmonic and inharmonic content. In *Stria* (1977) John Chowning resorts to textures that are harmonically structured according to certain intervals based on the golden mean. The same intervals govern the frequency transposition of the textures, so that these rich sounds can be mixed without roughness, as though two solid bodies could go unchanged through each other. The internal sonic structure relates to the scale – and also to the proportions, to the form of the piece.

SCULPTING SOUNDS – REAL AND SYNTHETIC

Electronic music was very primitive in its way of controlling temporal contours. Computer synthesis permits the specification of evolutions in time in a very detailed fashion. A MUSIC V 'note' can as easily last a tenth of a second as five minutes; it can take many notes to compose an event, but one note can also compose many events – or no salient event at all, just a quiet, living flux. One can play with sounds in time, but also play with time inside a sound. The latter is exemplified in *Interno* by Walter Branchi, *Black it stood as night* by Denis Lorrain, *Chreode* by Jean-Baptiste Barrière, *On crossing the river* by Johannes Goebel, *Jardin secret I* by Kaija Saariaho, *Pain* by Takayuki Rai, *Against the silence* by Tom DeLio, and *Kyokata* by Gerald Bennett. A sound can be single or multiple; the frontier is fuzzy, and the composer can displace it, as Chowning does in *Phonē*.

Any curve can be used *a priori* to mould a synthetic sound. I had the computer calculate complex and supple curves using defective Fourier synthesis (see Figure 29.3): I used these curves to modulate the frequencies of sine tones moving in space at the end of *Songes*. In *Earth's magnetic field* (1970) Charles Dodge has made variations of magnetism measured in a laboratory audible through quantized pitch contours. Working with Curtis Bahn, he has resorted to fractal curves in more recent pieces such as *Profile*, which often yield very smooth and unnaturally natural qualities, as Mike McNabb also noticed. Amplitude or frequency contours were extracted from a recording by Irène Jarsky of a poem by Claude Minière; Michel Decoust has taken advantage of these contours to sculpt the synthetic sounds of his piece *Interphone* (1977). Some rhythms from the recording govern the timing of a synthetic part. The piece also resorts to excerpts of the recording filtered by computer; this is no longer synthesis.

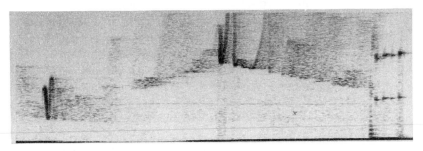

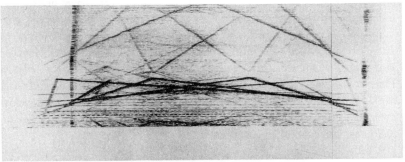

Figure 29.3 Top: curves modulating the frequencies of mobile sine tones at the end of my piece *Songes*. These curves are computed by defective Fourier synthesis.
Bottom: symmetrical glissandi from my piece *Little Boy*.

Why indeed limit oneself to synthesis? In an avant-garde concert held in 1965 in New York, with Malcolm Goldstein, James Tenney and George Flynn, I had played an experimental piece called *computer concrète*. I was interested in the process, in the hybridization, even though the result was by no means accomplished. It was not even genuine computer *concrète* –

recorded sounds processed by computer – but rather a mix of 'wild' computer synthesis and recorded sounds processed by analogue means. Probably the first experiments in computer *concrète* were those which resulted in Vladimir Ussachevsky's *Computer Piece No. 1* (1968). This piece comprises computer sounds – harmonic arpeggios I had generated by scanning the harmonics of a chord, processed by the composer using analogue means, such as mixing and frequency-shifting – but also digitized sounds that were processed by a rather primitive program called SUPER-SPLICER. Ussachevsky exploited the program to generate rhythmic events that would have required a lot of tiny splices – he brought to that piece his artistry and tape craftsmanship, using a know-how that would be precious to many computer musicians.

Mathews had anticipated sound processing in addition to pure synthesis in his design of the MUSIC V program. The necessary modules were added at IRCAM in around 1977. Vercoe also included this possibility in his MUSIC 11 synthesis program. Computer processing and synthesis were used in York Höller's *Arcus* (1978), in my *Mirages* (1978) and *Songes* (1979). Jonathan Harvey's *Mortuos Plango, Vivos Voco* used recorded material consisting of a child's voice – the composer's son – and of bell tones; the sounds were transformed, mixed, laid out together with the MUSIC V program, yielding a very appealing, expressive and successful piece.

The use of the computer is often difficult, and it requires a lot of expertise and ingenuity. Frequently, composers are helped by assistants whose contribution can be really creative. In fact, the best are usually composers. Daniel Arfib's skilled contribution to Decoust's *Interphone*, Stanley Haynes's hard and brilliant work for Höller's *Arcus* and Harvey's *Mortuos Plango*, Thierry Lancino's assistance to Roger Reynolds for *Archipelago*, and Scott Van Duyne's collaboration for my *Duet for one pianist*, discussed below, were all critical to the successful completion of these pieces within the deadlines, and more than just that.

A number of pieces unite analogue and digital synthesis or processing. Among them, *Tides* and *Clarinet threads* (the latter for clarinet and tape) by Denis Smalley, *Desert tracks* by Michel Redolfi, *Vox 5* by Trevor Wishart, *The vanity of words* by Roger Reynolds, *Erosphere*, a floating fascinating poem by François Bayle, and the lively and humorous *Don Quichotte Corporation* by Alain Savouret. Mike McNabb's *Love in the asylum*, uneven or hybrid musically, achieves at times an extraordinary atmosphere, both vivid and unreal. From the start, *Les filles du sommeil*, by Georges Boeuf, using many sounds from the Synclavier synthesizer, carries the listener into a hardly resistable whirl.

However, processing usually does not bring the same flexibility and the same control over the sound as synthesis does. Most processing is global and exterior; when it operates on sounds with a strong identity, this identity remains throughout the transformations, and it is hard to escape the pitfalls of collage. To bridge the gap between analysis and synthesis one may try to find a specific synthesis model that will simulate the original sound; then one can benefit from the flexibility of synthesis. But this may be very hard – a genuine research problem. Another way is to resort to analysis–synthesis processes. There are certain functions in terms of which any sound can be analysed and then reconstructed from the analysis. By altering the parameters between analysis and synthesis, one can perform quite intimate transformations of sounds.

Moorer has explored analysis–synthesis processes such as linear predictive coding and phase vocoder. Thanks to these processes, one can change the rate of recorded speech without getting the famous Donald Duck effect (normally speeding up speech sounds also moves the spectra upwards). Paul Lansky has skilfully used predictive coding in several successful pieces. Moorer's *Lions are growing* is an impressive piece of 'concrete poetry', where the originally recorded poem is submitted to a number of transformations, for instance slowing down as far as a factor of 27. Moorer has also performed cross synthesis, which had first been realized with vocoders, by using the excitation data of one sound and the resonance data of another. Tracy Petersen also took advantage of cross-synthesis, which was recently implemented on a Synclavier synthesizer at Groupe de Musique Expérimentale de Marseille by Richard Kronland, David Hagège, Jacques Diennet and Jérôme Decque.

I used cross-synthesis in my piece *Sud*, realized at the Groupe de Recherches Musicales in Paris in 1985, with linear prediction programs implemented by Benedict Mailliard. I thus hybridized sounds of pianos and metal chimes, cellos and birds, harpsichords and sea-waves. My musical incentive was partly to try to evoke hybrids, chimeras, but mostly to imprint onto certain recognizable sound textures energy contours and fluxes issued from other types of sound (for example, to suggest 'waves of harpsichords').

Actually, in *Sud*, the energy flux of the initial sea-wave sounds permeates various aspects of the composition. The natural sounds, initially very distinct, tend to merge gradually with the synthetic sound. I tried to achieve this in several ways – through conventional mixing, of course, but in a more unusual way which I might call substractive cross-synthesis. While many natural sounds (the sea, the wind) have a continuous frequency spectrum, I used synthetic harmonic arpeggios and scales with sharply defined pitches (in particular a major-minor scale, G, B, E, F♯, G♯, B, E, F♯, G♮, B, E, F♯, G♯ . . .). Then I used resonant filters tuned to these pitches to filter natural sounds. If the resonance is damped, it merely colours the original sounds which retain much of their identity. If the filters are sharply tuned and thus resonant, one gets the feeling of a harp tuned to those pitches and set into vibration by the sounds, which only leave the trace of their energy flux. Thus, in the third movement, there is a 'bird's raga'; the bird's song is sharply filtered, and only the 'raga', the pitches of the scale, remain with rhythms and quantized frequency contours originating from the bird's song.

I also used such resonant filters, implemented by Daniel Arfib in his IBM-PC version of the MUSIC V program, to filter Michel Portal's clarinet in my piece *Attracteurs étranges*, realized in Marseilles in 1988. In the same piece, I took advantage of two analysis–synthesis processes that are being developed in Marseilles and which are already quite useful. One of these analysis–synthesis processes is Gabor analysis–synthesis in terms of basic sound 'grains', oscillations with a duration limited by a bell-like envelope. Gabor, the inventor of holography before lasers permitted its implementation, published this idea in 1946. Analyses in terms of these grains have been proven mathematically complete, permitting faithful reconstruction. Xenakis (1971) had been inspired by Gabor to compose in terms of grains of sound; he made some suggestions for the use of those grains for computer sound synthesis. Although his proposals seemed to be problematic (see Smith 1973), they motivated Roads (1978) and later Truax to perform granular synthesis of sound. This was not analysis-synthesis, though.

It was probably Daniel Arfib who performed the first analysis–synthesis in terms of the Gabor grains. The reconstruction, quasi-perfect, lends itself to intimate modifications. For instance, by increasing the grain separations, Arfib could slow down a speech utterance without frequency transposition – which he did up to a factor of 128. I took advantage of these developments in my already-mentioned composition *Attracteurs étranges*. The clarinettist Michel Portal (also a brilliant jazzman and composer) recorded a number of pre-written musical phrases and sound effects. Some recorded segments were transformed in various ways – complex editing; spatialization, filtering and mixing through Arfib's augmented version of MUSIC V; and adding echoes, spatialization and harmonization, implemented by Pierre Dutilleux on the SYTER real-time audioprocessor. But in a number of places I also used spoken phrases or clarinet sequences speeded up or slowed down using Arfib's technique with Gabor grains.

A recent and promising method for analysis–synthesis of signals is the wavelet transform (Combes *et al.* 1989). It looks like a derivation of the

Gabor method, but it offers better numerical convergence and stability. Moreover, the formalism of the method is still valid with a variety of different basic wavelets. The method goes beyond sound signals and time-frequency representation; it truly provides a time-scale representation. In Marseilles, Richard Kronland-Martinet has taken advantage of the speed of the SYTER audio-processor to make a broad exploration of the wavelet transform, in collaboration with Alex Grossman. Kronland realized some interesting musical transformations: for instance, one akin to wave dispersion. So did Frédéric Boyer, who performed granular wavelet resynthesis with many channels (whereas the reconstruction can work well with only one channel per octave, provided the bandwidth of the analysing wavelet is over one octave). For instance, using twelve channels per octave, Boyer has performed analysis–synthesis of the spoken voice; for the resynthesis, he dropped many channels, keeping only those forming, for the instance, a perfect chord (or a diminished seventh chord, or whatever), thus giving the strange impression of a voice with a specific musical harmony embedded in the vocal chords.

INSTRUMENT–COMPUTER DIALOGUES AND REAL TIME

As I mentioned above, a number of pieces use live instruments in dialogue with computer sounds. One of the first historical precedents for this, Bruno Maderna's *Musica a due dimensioni*, had a flautist play together with a tape recording of the electronic sound. Such had to be the case for early computer and instrument 'mixed' pieces, when computer synthesis could not be done in 'real time'; it had to be produced in advance, since the computation took longer than the duration of the music. However, the recording imposes its strict tempo, since one cannot change its speed without altering the frequencies; the instrumentalists have to follow the machine; and often they must follow a stop-watch. The interest of performing computer-generated sounds in real time, just as instrumental sounds, is obvious: it permits the performer to introduce performance nuance while listening to the musical result of his gestures. This is important to impart naturalness and musicality to otherwise stiff computer material.

In fact, real time offers a way of taking advantage of the precious know-how of virtuoso instrumentalists. Pure virtuosity is musical virtue; it injects into the gestures complex features materializing a sense of style and musical direction. This gestural expertise can be diverted to the control, on a real-time computer system, of parameters very different from those of the instrument. Although one might favour the approach of designing entirely new digital instruments, which would call for different gesture capturing devices, this approach is problematic, since it takes years of hard work to master an instrument, and one is unwilling to undertake such investment for an instrument that has no repertory and that may be abandoned because of some technical or commercial avatar.

In 1974 Jon Appleton and Sydney Alonso designed the *Synclavier*, the first real-time digital synthesizer. This consisted of a special purpose digital processor, a kind of computer that was less general, less flexible, but somewhat specialized in order to speed up certain operations – those that are involved in computing sound. The processor must be controlled by a computer, but the computer is relieved of most of its computational load. The controls for the performer are mainly an organ-like keyboard, a spring-loaded knob and a number of push-button switches. The way these controls operate is ingenious: the designers have taken advantage of the experience of Mathews and Moore with GROOVE, mentioned below. Jon Appleton has given many concerts performing live on the Synclavier. He did not have to produce all the notes heard at a given time; some could come from a pre-recorded sequence triggered by the performer.

Since then, a variety of real-time digital processors have been developed, including the 4X at IRCAM, and more recently the popular Yamaha DX7. It is hard to compare them since there are many different types, from the inexpensive to the extremely costly. Some, much more than others, are open to different possibilities, and they also demand more of the user.

In Pierre Boulez's *Répons* (1981), masterful instrumental music is amplified and spatialized by the powerful and expensive 4X machine. Similarly, Luigi Nono's *Prometeo* (1987) uses real-time audio processors to expand the instrumental and vocal parts. (Andrew Gerszo was the assistant for *Répons*, and Sylviane Sapir for *Prometeo*.) It is indeed of interest to use digital processing to give a symphonic dimension to a chamber orchestra, since a dedicated chamber orchestra will play demanding contemporary music better and more readily than a symphonic orchestra. But, in the case of *Répons*, the 4X performs relatively simple processing of the instrumental sounds. Most composers demand a complexity which goes beyond the processing limits of present synthesizers; a number of pieces resorting to real-time systems are composed as successive recorded layers, which prevents the control of tempo during the performance.

Until recently, real–time systems were delicate, often bulky, and expensive to travel with – only a few courageous composers such as Ed Kobrin, Jon Appleton or Bill Buxton hit the road transporting their digital performance systems with them. The present generation of processors promises to be powerful and compact. However there is no unanimity about the preferred design, so there cannot be any standardization – in fact there will be competition between various centres or various companies developing real-time musical systems. One may think this is appropriate: let the best one win! But there is a serious problem. It is a big time investment to realize a piece with a particular real-time machine. Now technological progress makes such machines obsolete, updated by 'better' ones (while recorded tape pieces can easily be transported on a newer recording medium). Unfortunately, this means that the pieces composed for a given machine risk obsolescence – it is hard and uninspiring work to adapt such a piece to another machine, and the composer would rather produce a new piece. Quite a few pieces composed a few years ago can no longer be heard, not because the pieces themselves are obsolete but because they require equipment that has since been abandoned.

As Appleton remarked, this situation does not encourage the composer/performer to deepen his or her work, since it risks being short-lived; it prevents the constitution of a repertory, as well as the establishment of a tradition of performance. It is hoped that some future synthesizers may be 'upwardly compatible' with the present ones, but this is unlikely to happen, unless the problem is confronted seriously. In fact, the issue is more intellectual than technical. To make a composition for real-time devices durable, the operations implied in the composition should be described in terms of certain procedures. Then one can endeavour to make these procedures portable from any machine to its successor.

There are other limitations to real time, which is too often considered a universal panacea. It is more suited to performance or improvisation than to composition – in fact, it is often so irresistible that it tends to induce a dominantly empirical attitude rather than a masterful control of the unleashed sound material. Also, some processes are inherently incompatible with real-time operation; so the composer longing for specific tone qualities, and confronted by the psychoacoustic problem mentioned above, should not believe that real time will permit him or her to 'tune' timbres to his or her satisfaction empirically, by hand and ear. In a given setting of a real-time system, the timbres that the composer will be able to scan will be samples of the synthesis or processing processes – of the specific sound models – set on the machine ahead of real-time operation. And it is more difficult to change sound models on real-time systems than with software synthesis.

Yet, clearly, real time has a lot to offer. One of the earlier computer-controlled real-time systems was GROOVE, designed by Max Mathews and F. Richard Moore in around 1968. Different kinds of controls were used: electric organ keyboard, computer keyboard, switches, knobs, even a three-dimensional 'wand' permitting control of several parameters at the same time. The assignment of this or that gestural input to these or those parameters was arbitrary, and stipulated to the control program. In fact, an elaborate algebra of time functions made it possible to combine different controls, or to have a gesture inflect a pre-established sequence. A lot of thought had been given to the extent of desirable real-time control: if the user controls everything in real time, the computer does not really help and leaves the user with a difficult task demanding high virtuosity, just like on an ordinary instrument. Mathews has proposed a number of ways to use GROOVE as different types of 'intelligent instruments', ranging from the 'tape-recorder mode' – minimal demand, minimal control – to the 'organ mode' – the other extreme, demanding one gesture for each sound. In between, there are many possible modes, corresponding to different types of control. In the 'music minus one' mode, the performer plays only one part against other parts prepared in advance; the pre-established parts can be synchronized to the performance instead of being played in an inflexible tempo as would be the case in 'music minus one' with a tape or a disc. In the 'conductor' mode – which Mathews tried with Pierre Boulez – the performer does not play any note, but controls the tempo and the balance between pre-established parts. The 'sequential drum' mode enables the performer to trigger a new note or a new sequence each time he or she hits a drum sensed by the computer (the order of the sequences has to be preset). A number of pieces have been realized on GROOVE by F. Richard Moore, Max Mathews, Laurie Spiegel and others. Emmanuel Ghent has written music for *Phosphones*, a ballet danced by the company of Mimi Garrard. The sequences for the stage lights were controlled by a punched tape prepared on the computer together with the audio tape; this meant that flashes of light briefly showing the dancers in the middle of a jump could be perfectly synchronised with rhythmical chords, a new and impressive effect.

However, GROOVE was the only system of its kind, and it was dismantled when the computer – a Honeywell 224 – became obsolete. Fortunately, since 1983, the MIDI format, a norm for exchanging control information between digital modules – keyboards, synthesisers, samplers,

610

sound processors, reverberators and also computers – has fostered the multiplication of such modules; a genuine commercial jungle now exists where many emerging products are stereotyped and of limited musical value. However, a number can be of interest, and the industrialization of digital modules is making them cheaper and more available, so that the individual user can have access to digital sound processing. This has occasioned a proliferation of real-time music activity of diverse interest, including highly individualized, even 'wild' practices, which may be a salutary reaction to the normalizing weight of large institutions. Composers like Reiner Boesch have exemplified this liberation of digital sound. Musicians coming from jazz, such as George Lewis, or from theatre, like Michael Waisvisz, have defined personal live systems which give a musical echo to their improvisations or their gestures.

The availability of the MIDI has permitted me to realize an idea I had formed with Max Mathews in the early 1970s: to 'marry' GROOVE and MUSIC V operation. Real time is invaluable for the introduction of performance nuance. But real-time sound synthesis is inherently limited by the computing capacity of the hardware synthesizer, unlike software synthesis. In 1987, Frédéric Boyer wrote a MIDI sequencer with an interface converting MIDI data into MUSIC V input format. So one can play sequences on a MIDI synthesizer introducing nuances with real-time feedback. The performance data can then be communicated to the MUSIC V program, which performs complex synthesis without the limitation of real time, while preserving the nuances introduced in real time. The MIDI pitch numbers do not have to refer to equally tempered frequencies for the synthesis; programming makes it easy to convert them into any desired scale. I exemplified this real-time specification of a non-real-time computer part in *Voilements*, for tenor saxophone and tape (1987). In this piece, I also used the SYTER real-time audio processor, designed by Jean-François Allouis, to alter saxophone recordings in various ways – echoing, reverberating, filtering, harmonizing and accumulating: the piece is about the changing relation between the saxophonist and his or her artificial shadow.

The concepts illustrated by Mathews and Moore in GROOVE remain valued and important. Mathews has devised a transportable instrument based on his sequential drum in association with a IBM-PC-compatible computer and a MIDI synthesizer; he has also interfaced his electronic violin with a synthesizer. Richard Boulanger, Maureen Chowning and Janos Nyegesy have demonstrated the possibilities of these systems, which are expressive and theatrical. Tod Machover has developed a similar approach with his hyper-instruments. The use of MIDI gear and ingenious programs

611

by Joe Chung extend and amplify the role of the performer: the gestures trigger actions and musical developments – arpeggios, chords, etc. – which are sensitive to what is being played.

Working initially with the flautist Larry Beauregard around 1983, Barry Vercoe has programmed a *synthetic performer*: a program that analyses what the flautist is doing and tries to follow and accompany him or her on a real-time synthesizer in a truly musical fashion, respecting the nuances and the tempo fluctuations. This is work in progress, which has musicological significance – to better understand the correlates of musical performance – but it is also promising to revive the interaction between instrument and digital sound. *Jupiter* (1987) by Philippe Manoury, implements this close interaction in an elegant way: the flautist triggers or influences the music produced in real time by the 4X processor, which gives a convincing suppleness and musicality. A similar interaction is implemented in Manoury's *Pluton* (1989) for piano with MIDI output and 4X sound. The MIDI output translates the notes played by the piano into MIDI code so that the computer can follow it – an easier task than in the case of the flute.

REAL-TIME PIANO–COMPUTER INTERACTION: A DUET FOR ONE PIANIST

As a final example, I would like to elaborate on a recent work of mine (1989), because it inaugurates a new process. It is called *Duet for one pianist*. There are indeed two parts: the first one is played by a pianist; the second is played on the same acoustic piano, but not by a pianist. It is not pre-recorded either – one could of course play live on the keyboard when the rolls on the player piano were being played back, but these are not the rules of the game here. Actually, the pianist is followed by a computer program, which 'plays' on the acoustic piano in ways that depend upon what the pianist plays and how he or she plays it.

This requires a special piano, with MIDI output, so that the computer can know what the pianist is playing (which keys are depressed, when, how loud and how long), and MIDI input, so that MIDI signals can cause piano keys to be pushed or released (each key can be played from the keyboard, but it can also be activated by an electric solenoid within the piano, which can push them down or release them). I used a Yamaha Disklavier piano, which was available at the MIT Media Laboratory, where Barry Vercoe had already used it for his work on the synthetic performer discussed above.

The piece also requires a computer with a MIDI interface – here a Macintosh II. The software used, as in Manoury's *Pluton*, is the MAX program, completed by Miller Puckette at IRCAM. This is a very remarkable program, which allows the user to build his or her own 'patches' specifying the various real-time operations performed. Other pianos or computers could be used, provided they offer similar possibilities.

This process of live piano–computer–piano interaction had never been implemented before, and serious difficulties were encountered initially. The first was some kind of feedback problem. Assume the computer is required to perform a symmetry operation: each time a note – say an E – is played by the pianist, the program should generate the MIDI code corresponding to the symmetrical pitch with respect to a given note – say middle A. So it does, and the piano will play a D. Then the MIDI output will signal that D to the computer, which will then generate the code for the symmetrical pitch – the original E. And so on in a loop. The problem was solved by Scott Van Duyne, who built an 'anti-feedback filter' which tries to retain the MIDI messages issued from notes played by the pianist and to eliminate input MIDI messages that are likely to reflect the note just triggered by a MIDI command. (This will however prevent fast repeated notes.)

Another problem is inescapable on acoustic pianos. Between hitting a note and hearing it there is a delay – and this delay depends upon the loudness of the note, which is related to the key's velocity. Hence this delay can range between about 20 milliseconds, for loud notes, to 200 milliseconds and more, for very soft notes. This will cause erratic and objectionable rhythmic deviations. For instance, a string of MIDI commands corresponding to a regular rhythm with a crescendo will be heard as accelerating (and crescendo). Van Duyne wrote a program of compensation, based on statistical measures he made of the delay as a function of loudness. Such compensation is provided in the Disklavier, which is more often then not just used as a player piano; but it is probably crude, and the standard setting imposes a fixed delay of 500 milliseconds between the command and the actual tone – which clearly permits only delayed interaction, not real-time interaction.

With these problems solved, it was possible to design patches to specify which interaction would take place. A given patch determines the way the computer will select the notes it will play – the choice of process it will use depends upon the notes played by the pianist. I did not use any stochastic degree of liberty; for the patches I used, the computer plays notes that depend in a predetermined way upon what the pianist plays and how he or she plays it. I acknowledge the highly competent help of Scott Van Duyne, whose efficiency and insights were invaluable.

I elected to explore and demonstrate different relations between the pianist part and the computer part. Hence the *Duet for one pianist* was articulated into eight different 'sketches', each of which calls for a different kind of live interaction. I shall describe them briefly to give a more precise idea of what relations could be set between the pianist and his or her computer-controlled ghost partner. A new patch, corresponding to a different sketch, has to be loaded from the disk into a computer core memory, which is done from the computer console; but once it is loaded, all the changes are triggered by the pianist from the piano, without any intervention of the computer operator.

Double. The pianist plays alone. Then, on the repeat, the computer adds ornaments. These are pre-recorded: they are called when the pianist plays certain notes; their tempo can be influenced by the tempo of the pianist.

Mirrors. Each key played by the piano is echoed by a key stroke, symmetrical with respect to a certain pitch – a process used in Webern's second *Variation*, Op. 27, quoted at the beginning (and also at the end, with time reversal). The symmetry centre and the response delays are changed throughout the piece to vary the effects.

Extensions. To the arpeggios played by the pianist, the computer adds additional notes transposed in pitch and more or less delayed.

Fractals. To each note played, the computer adds five notes spaced approximately – but not exactly – one octave apart. If the intervals are stretched octaves, when the pianist jumps one octave higher, one will get the sensation of a semitone descent, as was mentioned in the paragraph on the psychoacoustic problem. Thus the pitch patterns played by the pianist are distorted in strange ways. In places, the texture sounds as if it were not well-tempered.

Stretch. Pitches are added, as in *Extensions*, but the intervals are not merely transposed: they are stretched by a factor ranging between 1.3 and 2.7. This extends the harmony as well as the melodies played by the pianist.

Resonances. At the beginning and the end the computer plays long sustained chords. In the middle section the pianist plays mute chords: the strings are set in resonance by the sequences played by the computer.

Up Down. Quasi octave arpeggios are triggered by the pianist, whose few

614

notes can thus generate many notes. The tempo of the arpeggios is set at first by the tempo of certain patterns played by the pianist; later by the pitch he or she plays; then by the loudness – this is a most unusual type of control.

Metronomes. This sketch begins with a short canon: the computer echoes the pianist on transposed pitches and at different tempos. Later it plays simultaneously different sequences at different tempos. Then (an allusion to Ligeti's *Symphonic Poem for One Hundred Metronomes*) it repeats the same pitches, but again at different tempos, either preset or set by the pianist.

The MIDI data could be made to control MIDI digital gear as well as MIDI pianos, and I do plan to make an 'orchestrated' version. However, it is interesting to set up an interaction between the performer and the machine which would take place within the acoustic domain – the only way, for instance, to use the acoustic resonance effects – yet mediated by the computer. Here one is no longer composing sounds. Rather, the computer is used as a composing/performing tool, sensitive to what the pianist is doing, turning the piano into an intelligent instrument – and the ghost accompanist into a musical partner. It is clear that many other kinds of interaction can be programmed, which could be of great interest, especially if improvisation is involved.

PARTING REMARKS

The electric revolution and the computer age have hardly begun. Yet most music heard today comes from loudspeakers. The digital domain is expanding; with technical progress, computers and digital systems should get more and more user-friendly, inexpensive, and affordable to the private user. Many people fear the intrusion of the computer in our lives, since it appears as a fearful instrument of normalization. Yet it does not have to be so. Art music has been and should continue to be a strong resisting force against the temptations of triviality and mercantilism, against the appeal of stereotyped and quickly exhausted gadgets. In the domain of musical sound the refinement of digital synthesis and processing opens wide new territories, offering different points of view, suggesting novel thoughts. It shows that the computer can be – and should be – a tool of liberation and personalization. Only a tiny part of these new territories has been explored so far; most of it is still unknown, '*terra ignota ubi sunt leones*', as in the ancient and incomplete maps of the earth. But the avenues open are already more than promising.

My own tendency is to try to bridge gaps, to relate various domains – the computer synthesis world and the instrumental world; real-time and non-real-time operation; computer-controlled sound and computer-aided composition – generally speaking, to view the digital domain as an integral and integrated part of the mainstream of music with all its faces.

I evidenced my reservations about computer composition, which I myself approached only with caution. Music is so subtle and complex, whilst artificial intelligence is as yet so primitive. Computer composition may in fact have played a substantial and visible role in changing the perspective over highly formalized processes of composition. The invention of photography took the function of representation away from painting; this probably helped painters liberate themselves from imitation and set new criteria for invention. Similarly, the ease with which the computer can perform extremely complex combinations may have helped change the outlook toward formalism and enabled us to consider the issue in less naïve, more advanced ways.

One should be cautious about one's own defiances, even towards computers' 'intelligence'. Evolution has ceased for humans, yet it goes on – in cultures, in libraries, know-how, computer programs and data bases. We are only in the first era of our dealings with the computer, a developing and changing concept. It is likely to be a challenge for several generations to find how to manage, learn, work, create, and live in efficient synergy with the new intellectual tools provided by science and technology. Music has marked the early ages of the computer; it should remain an advanced field of thought, pointing toward harmonious trades with the machines.

REFERENCES

CHOWNING, J.M. (1973) 'The synthesis of complex audio spectra by means of frequency modulation', *Journal of the Audio Engineering Society* 21: 526–34, reprinted in Roads and Strawn (1985).

COGAN, R. (1984) *New Images of Musical Sound*, Cambridge, Mass.: Harvard University Press.

COMBES, J.M., GROSSMAN, A. and TCHAMITCHIAN, P. (eds) (1989) *Wavelets: Time-frequency Methods and Phase Space*, Berlin: Springer Verlag.

COSTÈRE, E. (1962) *Mort ou transfigurations de l'harmonie*, Paris: Presses Universitaires de France.

GABOR, D. (1946) 'Theory of communication', *Journal of the Institute of Electrical Engineers* 93: 429–57.

GIBSON, J.J. (1966) *The Senses Considered as Perceptual Systems*, Boston: Houghton Mifflin.

HAYNES, S. (1982) 'The computer as a sound processor: a tutorial' *Computer Music Journal* 6 (1): 7–17.

HELMHOLTZ, H. (1877) *Sensations of Tone*, trans. E.J. Ellis, New York: Dover, 1954.

LEIPP, E. (1971) *Acoustique et Musique*, reprinted 1984, Paris: Masson.

LORRAIN, D. (1980) 'A panoply of stochastic canons', *Computer Music Journal* 4 (2): 53–81, reprinted in Roads (1989: 351–79).

MCADAMS, S.E. and BREGMAN, A.S. (1979) 'Hearing musical streams', *Computer Music Journal* 3 (4): 26–43, reprinted in Roads and Strawn (1985: 658–98).

MOORER, J.A. and GREY, J.M. (1977) 'Lexicon of analysed tones', Part I: 'A violin tone', *Computer Music Journal* 1 (2): 39–45. Part II: 'Clarinet and oboe tones', *Computer Music Journal* 1 (3): 12–29.

MORRILL, D. (forthcoming) *The Little Book of Computer Musical Instruments*, Los Altos, Calif.: W. Kaufman.

RISSET, J.C. (1969) 'An introductory catalog of computer synthesized sounds' (with sound examples), Bell Laboratories Report, Murray Hill, NJ: Bell Laboratories.

——(1971) 'Paradoxes de hauteur', *International Congress of Acoustics* 20S10.

——(1973) 'Sons', in *Encyclopedia Universalis*, Vol. 13, pp. 168–71.

——(1987) 'About James Tenney, composer, performer, and theorist', *Perspectives of New Music* 25: 549–61.

ROADS, C. 'Automated granular synthesis of sound', *Computer Music Journal* 2 (2): 61–2.

SMITH, S. (1973) *Perspectives of New Music*, Fall 1972/Spring 1973: 269–77.

TENNEY, J.C. (1968) 'Computer music experiments, 1961–1964', *Electronic Music Review* 1: 23–60.

TERHARDT, E. (1974) 'Pitch, consonance and harmony', *Journal of the Acoustical Society of America* 55: 1061–9.

WESSEL, D. (1973) 'Psychoacoustics and music. A report from Michigan State University', *Bulletin of the Computer Art Society*, 1930.

——(1978) 'Low dimensional control of musical timbre', IRCAM Report no. 12 (with sound examples on cassette), Paris: IRCAM.

XENAKIS, I. (1971) *Formalized Music*, Bloomington: Indiana University Press.

FURTHER READING

BENNETT, G. (1981) 'Singing synthesis in electronic music' in J. Sundberg (ed.) *Research Aspects of Singing*, Stockholm: Royal Academy of Music, pp. 34–50.

CADOZ, C., LUCIANI, A., and FLORENS, J. (1984) 'Responsive input devices and sound synthesis by simulation of instrumental mechanisms: the Cordis system', *Computer Music Journal* 8 (3): 60–73.

CARTERETTE, E.C. and FRIEDMAN, M.P. (1978) *Handbook of Perception, IV: Hearing*, New York: Academic Press.

CHAMBERLIN, H. (1980) *Musical Applications of Microprocessors*, Rochelle Park, NJ: Hayden Book Company.

CHOWNING, J.M. (1980) 'The synthesis of the singing voice', *Sound generation in winds, springs, computers*, Stockholm: Royal Swedish Academy of Music.

CHOWNING, J. and BRISTOW, D. (1986) *Frequency Modulation: Theory and Applications*, Tokyo: Yamaha Music Foundation.

——(1986) *FM theory and applications*, Tokyo: Yamaha Music Foundation.

COGAN, R. and ESCOT, P. (1976) *Sonic Design – The Nature of Sound and Music*, Englewood Cliffs, NJ: Prentice-Hall.

Computer Music (1980), UNESCO report, Canadian Commission for UNESCO.

DE POLI, G. (1983) 'A tutorial on sound synthesis techniques', *Computer Music Journal* 7 (4): 8–26.

DEUTSCH, D. (ed.) (1982) *The Psychology of Music*, New York: Academic Press.

DI GIUGNO, G. and KOTT, J. (1981) 'Présentation du système 4X', *Rapport IRCAM* 32, Paris.

DODGE, C. and JERSE, T.A. (1985) *Computer Music: Composition and Performance*, New York: Schirmer Books, Macmillan.

DOLANSKY, L.O. (1959) 'A novel method of speech-sound analysis and synthesis', Ph.D. dissertation, Harvard University. See also *IRE Trans. on Audio* AU-8, 6 (1960), p. 221.

DOLSON, M. (1986) 'The phase vocoder: a tutorial', *Computer Music Journal* 10 (4): 14–27.

DUFOURT, H. (1991) *Musique, Pouvoir, Écriture*, Paris: C. Bourgois.

ERICKSON, R. (1975) *Sound Structure in Music*, Berkeley: University of California Press.

GREY, J.M. (1975) 'An exploration of musical timbre', unpublished thesis, Stanford University, Calif.

GREY, J.M. and MOORER, J.A. (1977) 'Perceptual evaluation of synthesized musical instrument tones', *Journal of the Acoustical Society of America* 62: 454–62.

HARTMANN, W.H. (1985) 'The frequency-domain grating', *Journal of the Acoustical Society of America* 78: 1421–5.

HARVEY, J. (1981) '*Mortuos plango, vivos voco*; a realisation at IRCAM', *Computer Music Journal* 5 (4): 22–4.

HAYNES, S. (1980) 'New developments in computer music synthesis', *Music and Musicians* 28 (April): 20–22.

——(1980) 'The musician–machine interface in digital sound synthesis', *Computer Music Journal* 4 (4): 23–44.

HILLER, L.A. and ISAACSON, L.M. (1959) *Experimental Music: Composition with an Electronic Computer*, New York: McGraw Hill.

618

HILLER, L. and RUIZ, P. (1971) 'Synthesizing sound by solving the wave equation for vibrating objects', *Journal of the Audio Engineering Society* 19: 463–70.

LANSKY, P. and STEIGLITZ, K. (1981) 'Synthesis of timbral families by warped linear prediction', *Computer Music Journal* 5 (3): 45–9.

LAWSON, J. and MATHEWS, M.V. (1977). 'Computer program to control a digital real-time synthesiser', *Computer Music Journal* 1 (4): 16–21.

LOY, G. (1985) 'Musicians make a standard: the MIDI phenomenon', *Computer Music Journal* 9 (4): 8–26.

MATHEWS, M.V. (1969) *The Technology of Computer Music*, Cambridge, Mass.: MIT Press.

MATHEWS, M.V. and KOHUT, J. (1973) 'Electronic simulation of violin resonances', *Journal of the Acoustical Society of America* 53: 1620–6.

MATHEWS, M.V. and PIERCE, J.R. (eds) (1989) *Current Directions in Computer Music Research*, Cambridge, Mass.: MIT Press. (With compact disc of sound examples.)

MORRILL, D. (1977) 'Trumpet algorithms for music composition', *Computer Music Journal* 1 (1): 46–52, reprinted in Roads and Strawn (1985).

Music and Technology (1971), Paris: UNESCO and La Revue musicale (disponible aussi en français).

Musica e Elaboratore (1980), L.I.M.B. Biennale di Venezia.

Nuova Atlantide: il continente della musica elettronica (1986), L.I.M.B. Biennale di Venezia. (With two cassettes of musical works.)

OPPENHEIM, A. (1969) 'Speech analysis–synthesis system based on homomorphic filtering', *Journal of the Acoustical Society of America* 45.

PALEY, R.E. and WIENER, N. (1934) 'Fourier transforms in the complex domain'. *American Mathematical Society Colloquium Publ. XIX*, New York.

PETERSEN, T.L. (1976) 'Analysis–synthesis as a tool for creating new families of sound', *Preprint No. 1104 (D-3), 54th Convention of the Audio Engineering Society*.

PIERCE, J.R. (1983) *The Science of Musical Sound*, Freeman, San Francisco: Scientific American Library. (With discs of sound examples.)

PLOMP, R. (1976) *Aspects of Tone Sensation*, New York: Academic Press.

RISSET, J.C. (1966) 'Computer study of trumpet tones' (with sound examples), Bell Laboratories Report, Murray Hill, NJ: Bell Laboratories.

——(1978) 'Paradoxes de hauteur', *IRCAM Report No. 10*, with cassette of sound examples, Paris: IRCAM [See also Pierce (1983)].

——(1985) 'Computer music experiments 1964–', *Computer Music Journal* 9 (1): 11–18, reprinted in Roads (1989: 67–74).

——(1986) 'Musical sound models for digital synthesis', *Proceedings of the International Conference on Acoustics, Speech, and Signal Processing*, Tokyo, pp. 1269–71.

——(1986) 'Pitch and rhythm paradoxes: comments on "Auditory paradox based on a fractal waveform"', *Journal of the Acoustical Society of America* 80: 961–2.

——(1988) 'Perception, environment, musiques', *Inharmoniques* 3: 10–42.

RISSET, J.C. and MATHEWS, M.V. (1969) 'Analysis of instrument tone', *Physics Today* 22 (2): 23–30.

RISSET, J.C. and WESSEL, D.L. (1982) 'Exploration of timbre by analysis and synthesis', in D. Deutsch (ed.) (1982) *The Psychology of Music*, New York: Academic Press, pp. 25–58.

ROADS, C (ed.) (1985) *Composers and the Computer*, Los Altos, Calif.: W. Kaufman.

——(1989) *The Music Machine*, Cambridge, Mass.: MIT Press.

ROADS, C. and STRAWN, J. (eds) (1985) *Foundations of Computer Music*, Cambridge, Mass.: MIT Press.

RODET, X. and COINTE, Y. (1984) 'FORMES: composition and scheduling processes', *Computer Music Journal* 8 (3): 32–50, reprinted in Roads (1989: 405–23).

RODET, X., POTARD, Y. and BARRIÈRE, J.B. (1984) 'The CHANT Project: from the synthesis of the singing voice to synthesis in general', *Computer Music Journal* 8 (3): 15–31.

SCHAEFFER, P. (1966) 'Traité des objets musicaux' (with sound examples), Paris: Edition du Seuil.

SCHOTTSTAEDT, W. (1977) 'The simulation of natural instrument tones using frequency modulation with a complex modulating wave', *Computer Music Journal* 1 (4): 46–50, reprinted in Roads and Strawn (1985).

——(1983) 'Pla: a composer's idea of a language', *Computer Music Journal* 7 (1), reprinted in Roads (1989: 285–94).

SCHRADER, B. (1982) *Introduction to Electroacoustic Music*, Englewood Cliffs, NJ: Prentice-Hall.

STRAWN, J. (ed.) (1985) *Digital Audio Signal Processing*, Los Altos, Calif.: W. Kaufman.

WESSEL, D. (1979) 'Timbre space as a musical control structure', *Computer Music Journal* 3 (2): 45–52.

WESSEL, D.L. and RISSET, J.C. (1979) 'Les illusions auditives', in *Universalia (Encyclopedia Universalis)*, pp. 167–71.

DISCOGRAPHY

Music from mathematics. Decca DL79103

Voice of computer: MATHEWS, PIERCE, RISSET, SLAWSON, TENNEY. Decca DL710180.

J. APPLETON, Mussems sang, Zoetrope, In deserto. Folkways FTS 3345.

J. RANDALL, Mudgett, Nonesuch H71245.

M. SUBOTNICK, Silver apples of the moon. Nonesuch H71174.

W. USSACHEVSKY, Computer piece. CRI 2D 268.

B. TRUAX, Sonic landscapes. IRC, Vancouver, SMLP 403.

HILLER, ISAACSON, BAKER, Computer Music from the University of Illinois. Heliodor H/HS 25053.

I. XENAKIS, ST10. EMIVSM C061–1011.

G.M. KOENIG, Function Blau. Philips 6740 002.

J. CAGE with L.J. HILLER. HPSCHD. Nonesuch H71224.

C. DODGE, Speech Song, The story of our lives, In celebration. CRISD 348.

AUSTIN, CELONA, DODGE, HAYNES, PENNYCOOK, International Computer Music Conference Recording. CRI SD 348.

L'IRCAM: un portrait. IRCAM 0001, Paris.

The Digital Domain: A Demonstration (MATTOX, MOORER, RUSH, etc.) Compact Computer Music Journal and WERGO.

KORDE, LIPPE, MABRY, RISSET, RUBIN, SCELSI, XENAKIS. Compact NEUMA, New Music Series Vol. 1.

LANSKY, ROADS, DASHOW, WAISVISZ, BARLOW, KASKE, New Computer Music. Compact Computer Music Journal and WERGO.

CHAFE, JAFFE, SCHOTTSTAEDT, Computer Music. Compact CCRMA.

ALBRIDGE, BALABAN, BRODY, CHILDS, DASHOW, DODGE, LUNN, ROADS, VERCOE, Music for instruments and computer. Compact MIT.

J. CHOWNING, Turenas, Stria, Phoné, Sabelithe. Compact WERGO 2012.

J.C. RISSET, Sud, Mutations, Dialogues, Inharmonique. Compact INA C003.

J.C. RISSET, Songes, Passages, Little Boy, Sud, Compact WERGO 2013.

J.C. RISSET, Moment newtonien No. 3. In Mille et un poèmes. Compact Planète No. 1.

Computer Music Currents: a joint venture of WERGO, Stanford's CCRMA and the Systems Development Foundation. This is a forthcoming series of compact discs featuring computer music by Albright, Arfib, Barrière, Bayle, Bennett, Bodin, Boesch, Chafe, Davidovsky, Decoust, DeLio, Dodge, Fulton, Goebel, Ghent, Harvey, Haynes, Jones, Karpen, Kessler, Koenig, Krupowicz, Lancino, Lansky, Lindwall, Lorrain, Loy, Maiguaschca, Motz, Nelson, Oppenheim, Petersen, Rai, Reynolds, Risset, Rush, Saariaho, Savouret, Schottstaedt, Smalley, Stroppa, Teitelbaum, Teruggi, Vaggione, Wessel, White, Wolman, Wishart, Yuasa.